KT-382-506

LEONARDO DA VINCI

'Witty, penetrating . . . this is a wise and moving book'
David Gelernter, *The New York Times*

'Quick. Put down *The Da Vinci Code* and pick up this
treasure-trove of material about the Renaissance sage. You'll feel
smarter in the morning . . . Charles Nicholl's gloriously rendered
portrait is rich in detail and a warm piece of storytelling'
Lisa Jennifer Selzman, *Houston Chronicle*

'Part of the beguiling thrill of Charles Nicholl's biography is the
manner in which he meticulously salvages the fragmentary
evidence, the missing half-lines . . . This gripping, beautifully
designed biography is scholarship at its most accessible, and
demotic' Jasper Rees, *Daily Telegraph*

'It is no small part of Charles Nicholl's achievement that his
Leonardo, though a genius, is thoroughly and convincingly
human, likeable and, in many important respects, an exemplary
person' Aidan Dunne, *Irish Times*

'Nicholl conjures up a fresh image of the artist . . . a book that no
student or scholar of Leonardo should be without'
Art Newspaper

'Clearly written by someone who is as fascinated by Leonardo as
by the Italy he once inhabited, this book takes us into the mind
of a man who never stopped asking why'
Royal Academy Magazine

Charles Nicholl has spent many years studying Leonardo's note-books and manuscripts to create this portrait of the artist. He is the author of nine books of history, biography and travel, including the celebrated *The Reckoning: The Murder of Christopher Marlow* (winner of the James Tait Black Prize for Biography, and the Crime Writers' Association 'Gold Dagger' Award for non-fiction), *Somebody Else: Arthur Rimbaud in Africa* (winner of the Hawthornden Prize), *The Fruit Palace* and *The Creature in the Map*. He has presented two documentaries for British television, and has lectured in Britain, Italy and the United States. He lives in Italy with his wife and children.

CHARLES NICHOLL

Leonardo da Vinci
The Flights of the Mind

PENGUIN BOOKS

PENGUIN BOOKS

Published by the Penguin Group
Penguin Books Ltd, 80 Strand, London WC2R ORL, England
Penguin Group (USA) Inc., 375 Hudson Street, New York, New York 10014, USA
Penguin Group (Canada), 10 Alcorn Avenue, Toronto, Ontario, Canada M4V 3B2
(a division of Pearson Penguin Canada Inc.)
Penguin Ireland, 25 St Stephen's Green, Dublin 2, Ireland
(a division of Penguin Books Ltd)
Penguin Group (Australia), 250 Camberwell Road, Camberwell, Victoria 3124, Australia
(a division of Pearson Australia Group Pty Ltd)
Penguin Books India Pvt Ltd, 11 Community Centre, Panchsheel Park, New Delhi – 110 017, India
Penguin Group (NZ), cnr Airborne and Rosedale Roads, Albany, Auckland 1310, New Zealand
(a division of Pearson New Zealand Ltd)
Penguin Books (South Africa) (Pty) Ltd, 24 Sturdee Avenue, Rosebank 2196, South Africa

Penguin Books Ltd, Registered Offices: 80 Strand, London WC2R ORL, England

www.penguin.com

Published by Allen Lane 2004
Published in Penguin Books 2005
13

Copyright © Charles Nicholl, 2004

Typeset by Rowland Phototypesetting Ltd, Bury St Edmunds, Suffolk
Printed in England by Clays Ltd, St Ives plc

For Kit –
'L'inglesino'

How could you describe this heart in words
without filling a whole book?

Note written by Leonardo da Vinci beside
an anatomical drawing of the heart, *c.* 1513

Contents

PART THREE

Independence: 1477–1482

PART FOUR

New Horizons: 1482–1490

PART FIVE

At Court: 1490–1499

PART EIGHT
Last Years: 1513–1519

Author's Note

A note on currencies and measurements. The reader will find a confusing range of Renaissance currencies here. The imperial lira, divided into 20 soldi of 12 denari each (like the £.s.d. of pre-decimal Britain), was a benchmark of sorts, but throughout Italy regional coinage was minted: florins, ducats, scudi, giuli, etc. For much of the period covered in this book, the Florentine florin and the Venetian ducat were worth around 4 lire. These are the three currencies chiefly used by Leonardo da Vinci.

To give some broad guidelines of value, in late-fifteenth-century Milan 1 lira would buy a month's supply of bread for a family of four, or 12 pounds of veal, or 20 bottles of country-wine, or 2½ pounds of candle-wax, or just over a pound of that luxury item, sugar. In the 1490s Leonardo purchased a 600-page book on mathematics, in folio, for 6 lire, and a silver cloak with green velvet trim for 15 lire. A fine horse cost 40 ducats or 160 lire. In Florence a building worker earned 2 florins a month, and a senior civil servant in the Signoria 11 florins a month. The great mansions of the Medici and the Strozzi cost in the region of 30,000 florins to build. In a tax return, Cosimo de' Medici declared assets of over 100,000 florins, and one may imagine that this was an understatement.

A measurement of length frequently used by Leonardo is the braccio. The word means 'arm', and is thus equivalent to the old English ell (no longer in use as a measure but still heard in 'elbow', which is where your ell bows). According to one interpretation, a Florentine braccio was 55.1 cm (21.6 inches) and a Milanese braccio 59.4 cm (23.4 inches), but some calculations in one of Leonardo's notebooks work out at 61.2 cm (24.1 inches) per braccio. I have rounded these out to a general conversion rate of 1 braccio = 2 feet. In measurements of distance Leonardo uses the miglia (mile) of a thousand passi (paces).

A staio, or bushel, was a volumetric measure for crops, but is met here as a measurement of land-area. A staio of land was a plot capable of producing 1 staio of barley per annum. Judging from tenancy agreements of the period (rent being paid in the form of produce), this was reckoned as about half an acre.

Translations from Leonardo's Italian are in general my own, though I have of course consulted the admirable translations of Jean Paul Richter, Edward MacCurdy, A. P. McMahon, Martin Kemp, Margaret Walker and Carlo Pedretti. Large parts of Leonardo's text remain untranslated into English. George Bull's translation of Vasari's *Lives* has been extremely helpful, though I have diverged from it in small points of interpretation.

In giving brief quotations in Italian I tend to give Leonardo's phrasing as he spelt it, which seems to be part of its timbre. I make the customary modifications for readability: *i* for archaic *j*; contractions expanded; elisions separated, etc. Sometimes, however, his spelling is too opaque to make much sense in a brief extract. Quotations from Italian poems of the period are given in the original spelling. In most other cases I have modernized.

I have also modernized dates. The Florentine calendar was still reckoned from 25 March (the Feast of the Annunciation, or Lady Day), so an event dated 1 February 1480 in a Florentine document actually occurred two months *after* an event dated 1 December 1480; here this date would be given in modern reckoning, as 1 February 1481.

My research for this book has been greatly assisted by staff at the Biblioteca Leonardiana in Vinci, the British Institute and the Archivio di Stato in Florence, the Biblioteca Statale in Lucca, the British Library, the Royal Library at Windsor, and (by no means least) the London Library. My thanks also to Antonio Natali, Alfio del Serra, Gianni Masucci, the Hon. Jane Roberts, Lauro Martines, Gordon Wetherell, Christie Brown, Bernie Sahlins and Liz Donnelly. I am grateful to Mrs Drue Heinz for the provision of a Writer's Fellowship at Hawthornden Castle, to the staff there, and to my fellow Fellows, who heard the first of these pages newly minted. I owe the genesis of this book to David Godwin, and its eventual fruition to my editor Stuart Proffitt, picture-editor Cecilia Mackay and copy-editor Bob Davenport, and also Liz Friend-Smith and Richard Duguid. Other debts are too numerous to record except in the broadest of *ringraziamenti* – to the people of the Compitese, who welcomed us; to my children, who boldly shared this Italian adventure; and to Sally, who makes it all possible.

Charles Nicholl
Corte Briganti
August 2004

Introduction: The Cooling of the Soup

In the Department of Manuscripts at the British Library is a sheet of geometrical notes by Leonardo da Vinci. It is one of his last pieces of writing: it probably dates from 1518, the year before he died. The paper is a dingy grey but the ink remains clear. There are some diagrams, and beside them a neatly blocked text written in his habitual, right-to-left 'mirror-script'. It is not, on the face of it, one of Leonardo's most exciting manuscripts, unless you happen to be an aficionado of Renaissance geometry. But it repays attention: it has a little twist in its tail. Three-quarters of the way down the page the text breaks off with an abrupt 'etcetera'. The last line looks like part of the theorem – the handwriting has hardly wavered at all – but what it actually says is '*perche la minesstra si fredda*'. He has left off writing 'because the soup is getting cold'.[1]

There are other small nuggets of domestic detail in Leonardo's manuscripts, but this is the one I like best. It is not that it tells us a great deal: that Leonardo ate a bowl of lukewarm soup on a day in 1518 hardly qualifies as an important piece of biographical data. What seems to make it special is a quality of surprise, of casualness. Into the dry abstractions of his geometrical studies has intruded this moment of simple, daily humanity. One sees an old man at a table, intently writing. In another room one sees a bowl of soup, intently steaming. Probably it is vegetable soup, for in later life Leonardo was a vegetarian. Probably it has been cooked by his serving-woman, Mathurine, to whom he would soon bequeath a 'coat of fine black cloth lined with fur' in recognition of her 'good service'.[2] Is it she who calls to Leonardo da Vinci to tell him his soup is getting cold? He continues to write for a few moments longer – the time it takes to write '*perche la minesstra si fredda*' – and then he puts down his pen.

There is also a hint of foreboding. As far as one can tell he never did return to these notes, and so this minor interruption seems to foreshadow the more definitive one soon to come. We might call this undistinguished-looking page 'Leonardo's last theorem' – yet another unfinished project.

The great enterprise of inquiry and exposition to which he has devoted his life tails off with this throwaway joke, this one-liner about the imperatives of dinner-time.

For the biographer, such glimpses behind the scenes are heartening. Leonardo was an extraordinary man, but his life constantly intersected with ordinariness, and it is perhaps at those points of intersection that the biographer – that emissary sent out from the ordinary world – can make some kind of contact with him. There are all those complexities and profundities and world-famous paintings to grapple with, all those things that make Leonardo uniquely Leonardo, but here at least he is, for a moment, someone much like the rest of us.

It is the task of this book to try to recover something of Leonardo the man – that is, Leonardo the real man, who lived in real time and ate real bowls of soup, as opposed to Leonardo the superhuman, multi-disciplinary 'Universal Man' with whom we are more habitually presented. They are one and the same, of course, and the story of his life is only another way of approaching his formidable and ultimately mysterious greatness as an artist, scientist and philosopher, but I think it is important to get away from the hagiographic idea of the universal genius. I am encouraged in this by some words of Leonardo himself. In one of his *profezie*, or prophecies – which are essentially riddles cast in a prophetic mode – he writes, 'There will appear gigantic figures in human shape, but the nearer you get to them, the more their immense stature will diminish.'[3] The answer to the riddle is 'the shadow cast by a man at night with a lamp', but I like to think that the answer might also be Leonardo da Vinci, whom I approach through the darkness, nervously hoping that his immense stature will diminish to human dimensions.

To write a book about Leonardo without once using the word 'genius' would be a feat worthy of the French author Georges Perec, who contrived to write a book without using the letter *e*. I have not expunged it entirely – it can be a useful translation of the Italian *ingegno*, which is often used in the Renaissance to mean something more than mere 'talent' or 'intelligence' – but it is a word to be used very sparingly. It can so easily obscure the humanity of those thus described. It celebrates their achievements as a species of marvel or miracle, which is partly true but mostly unhelpful. What Leonardo did is indeed miraculous, but one wants to ask how and why he did it, and not to have some foggy, semi-mystical idea of 'inspiration' provided as the answer. Shakespeare's admirers liked to claim he 'never blotted' a line, to which Ben Jonson countered robustly, 'Would he had blotted a thousand'[4] – he was, in other words, a superb poet but not an infallible one; his genius lay in the extent to which he overcame his fallibilities. Jonson added, 'I do honour his memory, on this side idolatry,' which is surely the best location for the biographer to be based. Of course Leonardo was a genius, but the term tends towards the idolatrous, and runs counter to his own rigorous and sceptical turn of mind, and so I avoid it.

Somewhat connected with the stereotype of genius is that of the 'Renaissance man'. I am not one who argues that the Renaissance 'never happened': it is a perfectly useful overview term to describe the cultural changes which took place in Europe during the fifteenth and sixteenth centuries (or, in the Italian reckoning, the Quattrocento and the Cinquecento). But again there are clichés to beware of. We think of the Renaissance as a time of great intellectual optimism: a 'new dawn' of reason, a shaking-off of superstition, a broadening of horizons. Viewed from the vantage-point of the late nineteenth century, which is when this rather triumphalist reading took definitive shape, it was all of these things. But what was it like while it was happening? The old beliefs are crumbling; it is a time of rapid transition, of venal political strife, of economic boom and bust, of outlandish reports from hitherto unknown corners of the world. The experience of the Renaissance – not yet defined by that word, not yet accounted a 'rebirth' – is perhaps one of disruption as much as optimism. The palpable excitement of the period is laced with danger. All the rule-books are being rewritten. If everything is possible, nothing is certain: there is a kind of philosophical vertigo implicit in this.

That heroic, aspirational sense of the Renaissance man is not wrong – indeed the subtitle of my book is precisely a celebration of the marvellous upward reach of Leonardo's intellect, those soaring 'flights of the mind' which enabled him to see so far and so much, and which I link metaphorically and psychologically to his lifelong obsession with actual bodily flight. But with the dream of flying comes the fear of falling, and we understand this Renaissance man better if we see him also as a trader in doubts and questions, and with them self-doubts and self-questionings.

The Universal Genius and the Renaissance man are like those 'gigantic' shadows in Leonardo's riddle. They are not quite an illusion, but they are the product of a certain point of view, and as you move closer you start to see, much more interestingly, the man who casts those shadows.

To pursue the story of Leonardo's life we must get back to the sources closest to him: the primary sources – contemporary and near-contemporary. Chief among these are his own manuscripts; indeed, this book has become in part a study of Leonardo the writer – a curiously neglected subject, considering his enormously prolific output, though for the most part one must understand 'writer' in a non-literary sense. There are something over 7,000 pages of manuscript in Leonardo's hand which still survive, and thousands more can be deduced to have existed but are now lost. Some of the latter may surface one day – two entire notebooks were discovered by chance in Madrid in 1967, and there have been tantalizing but unconfirmed sightings of the lost treatise on light and shade known as Libro W.[5]

The manuscripts survive in three forms: in bound collections, compiled after Leonardo's death; in notebooks which are more or less intact from the time when he owned them; and in single sheets. The most famous of the great miscellaneous collections is the Codex Atlanticus, in the Biblioteca Ambrosiana in Milan. In its original form, put together in the late sixteenth century by the sculptor and bibliophile Pompeo Leoni, the Codex Atlanticus was a massive leather-bound volume over 2 feet tall. It contained 401 folios, some of them whole sheets of Leonardo manuscript, but most of them a montage of smaller items, up to five or six on a page, sometimes glued down and sometimes mounted in windows so that both sides of the paper could be seen. The name of the codex has nothing to do with the ocean, but refers precisely to its large format – it is 'atlas-sized'. The name was coined by a librarian at the Ambrosiana, Baldassare Oltrocchi, who listed it in 1780 as a 'codice in forma atlantica'. In the 1960s this sumptuous scrapbook was dismantled and reordered so that all its constituent pieces are now mounted separately.

There are two other major miscellanies, both in England. One is the collection of drawings and manuscripts in the Royal Library at Windsor Castle. This is also an inheritance from Pompeo Leoni; indeed, some of the smaller fragments at Windsor were demonstrably snipped by Leoni out of larger sheets now in the Codex Atlanticus. It was at some point purchased by that avid collector Charles I, though no documentation of this survives. It surfaced in Kensington Palace in the mid eighteenth century: according to a contemporary account, 'this great curiosity' had been deposited in a 'large and strong chest' during the Civil War, and there lay 'unobserved and forgotten about 120 years till Mr Dalton fortunately discovered it at the bottom of the same chest in the beginning of the reign of his present Majesty [George III]'.[6] Among this superb assemblage of drawings and manuscripts are the famous folios of anatomical drawings. The other major collection is the Codex Arundel in the British Library, a hotchpotch of 283 folios written over a span of nearly forty years, among them that interrupted page of geometrical notes discussed above. The codex is named after the Earl of Arundel who purchased it in Spain in the 1630s.

To these collections of actual Leonardo manuscripts should be added another kind of miscellany – the Codex Urbinas in the Vatican, a compilation of Leonardo's writings on the subject of painting, put together after his death by his secretary and literary executor, Francesco Melzi. An abbreviated version was published in Paris in 1651; this digest is generally known as the *Trattato della pittura* (*Treatise on Painting*). At the end of the Codex Urbinas, Melzi lists eighteen Leonardo notebooks, large and small (*libri* and *libricini*), which he had used as source material: ten of these are now lost. Another small trove of fugitive Leonardiana is the Codex Huygens, now in New York, which contains late-sixteenth-century copies of lost Leonardo figure studies.

The collections are magnificent, but the true whiff of Leonardo is to be found in his notebooks. About twenty-five individual notebooks survive – the exact number depends on how you reckon them, as some of the smaller books have been bound into composite volumes: for instance the three Forster codices (Victoria & Albert Museum, London) actually contain five notebooks. The largest concentration of notebooks is in the Institut de France in Paris; they arrived in France en masse in the 1790s, Napoleonic booty expropriated from the Biblioteca Ambrosiana. Others are in Milan, Turin, London, Madrid and Seattle. There have been some pages lost here and there – a light-fingered bibliophile, Count Guglielmo Libri, stole several in the mid nineteenth century – but these notebooks are essentially as Leonardo left them. Some still have their original bindings: he favoured a kind of wrap-around cover of vellum or leather, fastened with a small wooden toggle passed through a loop of cord (an arrangement oddly suggestive of a duffel coat).

In size the notebooks range from standard octavo format, looking much like what we call exercise-books, down to little pocket-books not much bigger than a pack of playing-cards. The latter, which Francesco Melzi called *libricini*, served as both notebooks and sketchbooks, and some show clear signs of having been on the road with Leonardo. An eyewitness account of him in Milan mentions 'a little book he had always hanging at his belt'.[7] He had one such with him when he passed though Cesena in 1502 and made a swift sketch captioned, 'This is how they carry grapes in Cesena.'[8] You would see him there in the street like a reporter with his notebook, intently recording. The painter, he says, should always be ready to make sketches 'as circumstance permits':

Observe people carefully in the streets, and in the piazza, and in the fields. Note them down with a brief indication of forms, thus for a head make an O, and for

One of Leonardo's notebooks (Paris MS B) in its original binding.

an arm a straight or bent line, and the same for the legs and the body, and when you get back home work up these notes into complete form.[9]

Sometimes the notations acquire the compressed potency of poetry:

> *onde del mare di Piombino*
> *tutta d'acqua sciumosa*
> *dell'acqua che risalta del sito*
> *dove chadano li gran pesi perchussori delle acque*

[Waves of the sea at Piombino; all the water spumy; water which rears up from the place where great percussive weights of water fall.][10]

Or this dangling almost illegible haiku:

> *la luna densa*
> *ogni densa e grave*
> *come sta la lu*
> *na*

[The moon is dense; anything dense is heavy: what is the nature of the moon?][11]

Some of the notebooks are self-contained treatises of some sort, or at least a purposeful gathering on a particular subject – Paris MS C on light and shade, the Codex Leicester on geophysics, the small Turin Codex on the flight of birds, etc. – but even these contain plenty of extraneous material.

The keynote of Leonardo's manuscripts is their diversity, their multiple miscellaneity: a jostling, often cramped, agglomeration of interests. Dating pages is sometimes hard, because Leonardo has a repetitive habit of mind, circling like a bird of prey around his many interests, revisiting ideas and observations to work away at them again years later. He is aware of this difficulty, and apologizes to the notional future reader: 'Do not blame me, reader, because the subjects are many, and the memory cannot retain them and say, "This I will not write because I have already written it."' [12]

The manuscripts are a map of Leonardo's mind. They contain everything from the briefest half-sentence or squiggled calculation to fully worked-out scientific treatises and literary exercises. Their subject-matter ranges from anatomy to zoology by way of aerodynamics, architecture, botany, costume-design, civil and military engineering, fossil studies, hydrography, mathematics, mechanics, music, optics, philosophy, robotics, star-gazing, stage-design and viticulture. The great lesson of the manuscripts is that everything is to be questioned, investigated, peered into, worried away at, brought back to first principles. He sets himself tasks both large and small:

Describe how the clouds are formed and how they dissolve, and what causes vapour to rise from the waters of the earth into the air, and the causes of mists, and of the air becoming thickened, and why it appears more or less blue at different times . . .

Describe . . . what sneezing is, what yawning is, the falling sickness, spasm, paralysis, shivering with cold, sweating, fatigue, hunger, sleep, thirst, lust . . .

Describe the tongue of the woodpecker . . . [13]

Leonardo was, as Kenneth Clark put it, 'the most relentlessly curious man in history'. The notebooks log his great quest of interestedness. They tend cumulatively towards some grand idea of universal knowledge, but at any given point or page they are focused on the particular and the precise: observations, experiments, questions, solutions. He is the empiricist par excellence, and signs himself with a flourish '*Leonardo Vinci disscepolo della sperientia*' (which can be translated as either 'disciple of experience' or 'disciple of experiment').[14] His habit of inquisitiveness is even expressed in a little scribal tic, found on scores of manuscript pages: when he wanted to try out a new pen-nib, he habitually doodled the word *dimmi* – 'Tell me.' It is the sound of Leonardo inquiring, seeking another bit of data. Tell me what, tell me how, tell me why – there were doubtless many in Florence and Milan and elsewhere who had heard the challenging tones of the Leonardian *dimmi*.

In the *Trattato della pittura* Leonardo writes that a painting should show

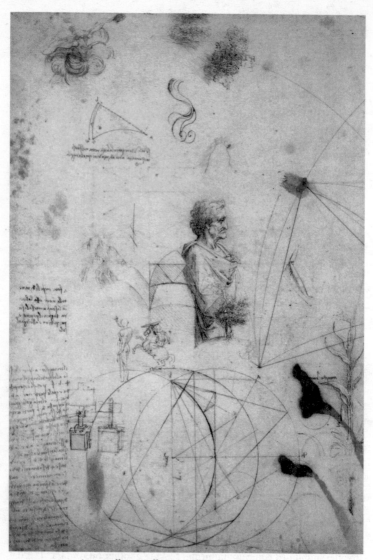

A typically miscellaneous sheet from about 1490.

'mental events' – *accidenti mentali* – through the physical gestures of the figures in it.[15] I think of this phrase when I read his notebooks, which are precisely filled with 'mental events', large and small, rigorously annotated, mingling curiously with the rich variety of ephemera – jokes, doodles, snatches of poetry, drafts of letters, household accounts, recipes, shopping-lists, cast-lists, bank statements, names and addresses of models, and so on – which is also to be found there.

The other major source of primary material is in the early biographies of Leonardo. The most famous is the account of him in Giorgio Vasari's *Le vite de' piu eccellenti pittori, scultori et architettori*, commonly known as *Lives of the Artists*. This famous book, first published in Florence in 1550, is fundamental to any biography of an early Italian artist, and generally justifies the puff it received from the aged Michelangelo:

> You, reilluming memories that died,
> In spite of time and nature have ensured
> For them [the artists] and yourself eternal fame.[16]

(The fact that Vasari worshipped Michelangelo, and devoted by far the longest of the *Lives* to him – about 40,000 words, compared with about 5,000 on Leonardo – may have had something to do with this.)

Despite Vasari's stature as a biographical source, and the charm of his style, we must recognize his shortcomings as a biographer: he is cavalier with dates, partial and subjective in his judgements, and tendentiously pro-Florentine (he was a protégé of the Medici). His worst failing, perhaps, is a weakness for narrative clichés. It may possibly be true that Leonardo's precocious brilliance led his master, Andrea del Verrocchio, to give up painting, but one cannot be sure, because other of Vasari's *Lives* feature this master-outshone-by-the-pupil trope. It is an old suit of rhetorical clothes which Vasari likes, and which he expects his readers to like, and it has no real value as historical evidence. But, for all the flannel, Vasari remains invaluable: he is an acute and extremely well-informed observer, and a sensitive critic, and though he had no first-hand knowledge of Leonardo – he was eleven years old when Leonardo died, and had never been outside the province of his native Arezzo – he undoubtedly knew people who did have such knowledge. He was actively gathering information for the *Lives* in the late 1540s.[17]

Vasari is the famous source, but he is not the only, or even the earliest, of Leonardo's early biographers, and it may be useful to say something about the other, less familiar, sources I will be using. The earliest is a brief biographical sketch written in the *zibaldone*, or commonplace-book, of a Florentine merchant, Antonio Billi, in the early 1520s – thus shortly after Leonardo's death. The original has disappeared, but the text is preserved in two sixteenth-century transcripts.[18] Almost nothing is known of Billi, but it has been conjectured that he had access to the lost memoirs of the Florentine painter Domenico Ghirlandaio. Billi's notes were later used, and much amplified, by another Florentine, who compiled an extensive account of various artists from Cimabue to Michelangelo. This unidentified author is generally known as the Anonimo Gaddiano, because his work survives in a manuscript formerly owned by the Gaddi family.[19] On internal evidence this 128-folio manuscript was compiled in about 1540. These are independent sources earlier than Vasari (though known to him), and the Anonimo in particular has some fascinating material. He includes some vivid anecdotes supplied by a Florentine artist whom he calls Il Gavina, who had first-hand knowledge of Leonardo.

Another concentration of contemporary interest in Leonardo was in Milan, where he lived and worked for many years (for more years, in fact, than he lived and worked in Florence), and there is important biographical material in a Latin manuscript by the Lombard historian, physician and emblem-maker Paolo Giovio, Bishop of Nocera, entitled *Dialogi de viris et foeminis aetate nostra florentibus* ('Dialogues concerning men and women famous in our time').[20] It was written on the island of Ischia in the late 1520s. Giovio probably knew Leonardo personally. They could have met in Milan, where Giovio was a practising physician from about 1508, or in Rome a few years later, when he was lecturing on philosophy at the Archiginnasio. His material on Leonardo was also known to the ubiquitous Vasari – indeed it was Giovio who first planted the seed of Vasari's *Lives*, during a lively discussion about the new art of biography, at a dinner-party in the apartments of Cardinal Farnese in Rome.[21]

Another Milanese source is the artist Giovanni Paolo Lomazzo, a very promising painter until he was blinded in an accident in 1571, at the age of thirty-three. Thereafter he devoted his considerable, somewhat chaotic energies to writing, and produced a series of books of which the most important is his *Trattato dell'arte della pittura* (*Treatise on the Art of Painting*), published in 1584.[22] He is a valuable commentator, because he was a total devotee of all things Leonardian: a specialist. He knew Leonardo's executor, Francesco Melzi, he studied the manuscripts of which Melzi had sole control, and he recorded some which are now lost. Lomazzo is sometimes a spanner in the works – he has ideas and information which run counter to the orthodoxies of Leonardo studies (such as his casual assertion that the *Mona Lisa* and the *Gioconda* are two separate paintings). He was also the first to state more or less openly that Leonardo was homosexual.

There are also the paintings, which are in some senses also documents. A Renaissance painting is not a personal statement in the way that a modern painting can be, but it can still tell us things about the man who painted it and about the circumstances in which he was working. It carries messages, both on the two-dimensional picture-plane (with the usual caveats about interpreting works of art biographically) and in the mysterious third dimension of the paint surface, with its micron-thick layers of suspended pigments (1 micron = 0.001 mm) which tell the story of a painting's composition just as the stratifications of a rock tell a geological story. Sometimes the touch of Leonardo's hand is recorded on the paint surface – smoothing or smudging – and occasionally a thumbprint. According to certain optimistic scientists, the paintings may carry the actual message of Leonardo's DNA, microscopically present in traces of blood and saliva, but at the time of writing this remains in the province of science fiction.

The most obviously documentary paintings and drawings are those which actually portray him. Anyone asked to visualize Leonardo da Vinci is likely to come up with that image of the bearded old sage in the famous self-portrait in the Biblioteca Reale at Turin. This drawing is controversial: the heavily faded inscription below it, in a contemporary hand, is tantalizingly illegible. Some claim it is not a self-portrait at all. I think it is, but I also think it has excessively suffused our visual sense of Leonardo. It is necessary to remind oneself that Leonardo was not *always* a druidic figure with a long white beard, any more than Shakespeare was always that bald chap with a goatee depicted in the engraving by Martin Droeshout. These images work their way into the collective unconscious, become a kind of shorthand. It is a moot point whether Leonardo had a beard at all before his late fifties: he is clean-shaven in the presumed self-portrait of *c.* 1481 in the *Adoration of the Magi* (Plate 1), and in the probable portrait in the Casa Panigarola fresco in Milan, of the mid-1490s (see page 312).

The Anonimo Gaddiano has a marvellous verbal snapshot of him: 'He was very attractive, well-proportioned, graceful and good-looking. He wore a short, rose-pink tunic, knee-length at a time when most people wore long gowns. He had beautiful curling hair, carefully styled, which came down to the middle of his chest.' There are nuances of fashion and sociology which are hard to catch, but the essential image is of someone very elegantly turned out, a bit of a dandy. This is one of the reminiscences of the shadowy painter called Il Gavina; other material supplied by him can be dated to around

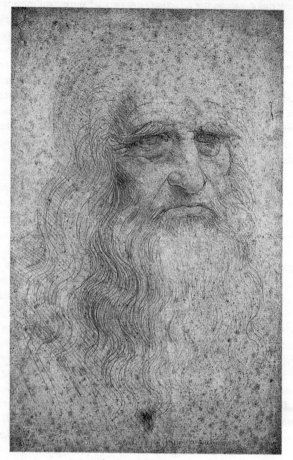

The Turin self-portrait.

1504–5, when Leonardo was in his early fifties. Once again, one notes, no beard is mentioned. The earliest certain portrait of him with a beard is the beautiful profile drawing in red chalk at Windsor (Plate 15). This is almost certainly the work of Francesco Melzi, perhaps with some retouchings by the master.[23] It is datable to *c.* 1510–12, and thus shows Leonardo nearing, or at, the age of sixty. This profile portrait became the model for posthumous depictions of Leonardo: it is echoed in various sixteenth-century portraits, including the woodcut which illustrates Vasari's biography of him in the 1568 edition of the *Lives*.

There are other portraits and self-portraits to be looked at, including what I believe to be a hitherto unidentified portrait of him by one of his most brilliant young pupils in Milan. The Turin self-portrait is our last glimpse of him: authentic and profound. It shows him much as he would have looked on that day in 1518 when he was called away from his studies because the soup was getting cold. The image is ultimately elusive, as Leonardo always is. You see that venerable, magus-like figure, Leonardo the genius; but then you look again and see an old man gazing out over distant memories.

PART ONE

Childhood
1452–1466

Things that happened many years ago often seem close and nearby to the present, and many things that happened recently seem as ancient as the bygone days of youth.

Codex Atlanticus, fol. 29v-a

➤➤ BIRTH ◂◂

Half a millennium ago the surroundings were not so very different. Standing on a hillside above the small Tuscan town of Vinci, one's eye would have travelled, as it does now, over a landscape shaped by centuries of agriculture – the reed-beds along the river, the narrow vineyards, the houses framed by shade-trees, and above them the olive-groves, with their particular kind of glitter when they catch the breeze, climbing up on terraces towards that variable, snaky tree line where the uplands of the Mont'Albano begin. The high slopes were thickly forested: wild pine and laurel, turkey oak, sweet chestnut. The hill-farmers milled chestnut flour, as some of them still do today; the chestnut-tree was called *albero di pane*, the bread-tree.

It was all probably a bit scruffier then. The ratio of wild to cultivated land was different; so too was the whole pattern of land ownership. But the picture was essentially the same: that patchwork composition one sees today. And in the middle of it, on a saddle of hill which seems both sheltered and strategic, stood Vinci itself, with its cluster of stone buildings around the twin towers of the castle and the church. Politically it was an outpost of the Florentine republic – it had been a possession of Florence since 1254, and for more than two centuries before that a possession of the Counts Guidi, who built the landmark castle. Florence was a long day's ride away via Empoli and Montelupo. Vinci was slow, provincial, agrarian; the countryside came right up to your windows.

Here Leonardo di Ser Piero da Vinci was born, on a spring evening in 1452. Exactly where – whether in the town or in the nearby countryside – remains unclear. The da Vinci, a respected local family with strong professional ties to Florence, certainly had a house in the town. In the *catasto*, or land-register, of 1451 it is described as '*una casa posta nel borgo di Vinci*'.[1] It was situated, in other words, in the area of town immediately outside the castle walls: Vinci's first, medieval suburb. It was probably

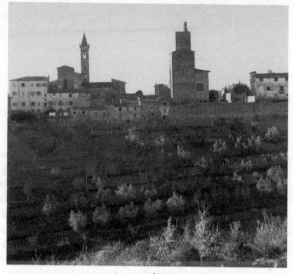

A view of Vinci.

located near the upper part of the sloping street now called Via Roma. It had a small garden about 3 staia in area. Among the family's immediate neighbours were the blacksmith, Giusto di Pietro, and the parish priest, Piero di Bartolomeo Cecci. It remains entirely possible that Leonardo was born in this house, but a strong mix of supposition and tradition insists that he was not. The supposition is that the birth of an illegitimate child, as he was, would have been accomplished more discreetly in one of the family's country proper-ties. The tradition is that he was born in a small stone house which is still to be seen in Anchiano, a hamlet in the hills 2 miles north of the town.

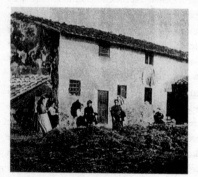

The house at Anchiano in a photo of c. 1900.

It is not known how old this tra-dition is: the most one can say is that it was current by the mid nineteenth century. It was first mentioned in print by Emanuele Repetti in 1845. He refers to the house in Anchiano as the place where Leonardo 'is reputed to have been born'. He stresses its modesty and typicality: a *casa colonica*, or tenant-farmer's house, of the kind found all over Tuscany.[2] Later in the century this identification was endorsed by the great Leonardo scholar Gustavo Uzielli, though he noted there was no 'sure confirmation' of it.

The house is a single-storey dwelling of local yellow-grey stone. The main building consists of three rooms, with a terracotta floor, a quantity of chestnut beams, and a large stone fireplace; at right angles to this is a smaller building with a bread-oven at the end of it. These two buildings correspond to the description of the house in old documents: a *casa di signore* for the owners to use when they wished, and a *casa di lavoratori* for the tenants who worked the land and paid their rent in the form of produce – oil, grain, wine, fruit, cheese, honey, timber, and so on. The L-shaped structure forms two sides of a courtyard open on the other two sides to the valley, though this area is now rather spoiled by municipal planting and paving. The exterior of the house seems in general over-restored, and one perhaps learns more from a hazy old photograph, dated around 1900, showing the place in its dilapidated, workaday state, with rough little windows punched through the façade, and a group of long-skirted women standing round a heap of harvested grapes.

Since the days of Repetti and Uzielli there has been a good deal of archival research on the house, which is documented back to the early fifteenth century. The tradition that connects it with Leonardo has some historical foundation, but the final step which makes it his birthplace is a leap of faith. The house certainly belonged to the da Vinci – the family crest, a winged lion, is carved on the façade – but the inconvenient fact of the matter is that it did not belong to them in 1452, when Leonardo was born. It was purchased by Leonardo's father, Ser Piero da Vinci, some thirty years later; it remained in the family until 1624, when it was sold to a Florentine convent by a descendant of Leonardo's half-brother Guglielmo. At the time of Leonardo's birth the house was owned by a notary, Ser Tomme di Marco. It was then described as a *frantoio*, or olive-mill. (According to Uzielli, writing in the late nineteenth century, an old millstone was still to be seen lying close by the house.) There are some faint links between the notary Ser Tomme and the da Vinci: there is a general professional connection – the da Vinci were a family of notaries – and there is a tantalizingly particular connection, for on 18 October 1449 Ser Tomme had a contract drawn up conveying a part-share in the property to two others, and the man who wrote up the contract, and signed it as a witness, was Antonio da Vinci, Leonardo's grandfather. Some notes relating to the contract show that

Antonio was there at Anchiano, in a certain 'farmer's house', when he was called on to draw up the contract. '*Si giocava a tavola*': he was playing a game of backgammon when this interruption came.[3]

This is piquant as to Antonio da Vinci's leisure pursuits, but his casual connection with the house cannot be counted as proof that his grandson was born there. It is certainly the *kind* of house the da Vinci would have had in the country. It expresses an important imagery of Leonardo's upbringing – that it was rural, close to the land, modest though by no means humble. It also answers to our desire for tangibility: to give a local habitation to the fact of his birth.

Though the place remains unproven, the date and even the hour of his birth are certain. The event was precisely recorded by this same grandfather Antonio, then about eighty years old, on the back page of an old notebook that had once belonged to *his* grandfather. On it he had already noted the births and baptisms of his own four children. There was just room at the bottom of the page to record this new arrival, this new generation – '1452. There was born to me a grandson, the son of Ser Piero my son, on the 15th day of April, a Saturday, at the 3rd hour of the night. He bears the name Lionardo.'[4] The clock was then reckoned from sunset (or more precisely from the ringing of the Ave Maria bell after vespers). The third hour of the night was about 10.30 p.m.

The baby was baptized, Antonio continues, by the parish priest, Piero di Bartolomeo: the family's next-door neighbour in town. This probably means the baptism took place in Vinci, in the parish church of Santa Croce. The rough stone baptismal font has been there continuously since Leonardo's time. The convention was to baptize the child the day after birth, in this case on Sunday 16 April, which in 1452 was the first Sunday after Easter, the *domenica in albis*. The baptism would have been entered in the Vinci baptismal register, but the earliest such register that survives dates from the 1550s.[5] No less than ten godparents were present at the baptism: a very generous number. (Compare the six who stood for Leonardo's father, Piero, and the average of two or four at christenings in Vinci in the sixteenth century.) Among Leonardo's godparents were two of the da Vinci's immediate neighbours in town: Papino di Nanni Banti, and Maria, daughter of Nanni di Venzo. Also present were Arrigo di Giovanni Tedesco, the German-born steward of the powerful Ridolfi family, which owned lands around Vinci, and a certain Monna Lisa di Domenico di Brettone, who reminds us that the name attached to Leonardo's most famous painting was a common one. ('Monna' or 'Mona' means simply 'Mistress' or 'Mrs'; it is a contraction of *Madonna*, 'My Lady', but is less aristocratic than that English equivalent.) If Leonardo's actual birth was somewhat sequestered – as the proponents of Anchiano suggest – the baptism seems to have been a full-blown affair, probably rounded off with a *festa* of some sort, with plenty of fine 'vermilion' wine from the da Vinci vineyards. Despite his illegitimacy, Leonardo was welcomed into the world and into the family. Nothing in Antonio's wording, or in the ceremony it records, suggests otherwise.

This precious record of Leonardo's birth and baptism was unearthed in the Florentine archives in the 1930s by a German scholar, Dr Emil Möller. (The fact that Möller's letter announcing the discovery has a postscript reading '*Viva il Führer! Viva il Duce!*' may not endear him to us, but does not alter the value of his discovery.) Leonardo is elusive, and his elusiveness seems often to extend into the historical record: documents prove ambiguous; facts turn into riddles. One is grateful for this matter-of-fact account, written in the firm, clear hand of his octogenarian grandfather, and for its placing of Leonardo's birth in the perennially tangible landscape of springtime in Vinci. The fig-trees are in bud, the terraces smell of wild marigold, and in sheltered spots the first olive-blossom is out: tiny yellow flowers foretelling the harvest to come.

⤜ THE DA VINCI ⤛

The da Vinci were a well-established family: not noble, not especially rich, not given much to magnificence, but a family of good stock and standing. They lived that enviable signorial double-life of the Quattrocento – *città e villa*: business in the city, farming in the country. They cultivated Florentine contacts and favourable marriages as assiduously as they managed their vineyards and orchards. They channelled profits into property. One does not want to romanticize their lifestyle, which doubtless had its discomforts and difficulties, but it seems to have suited them, and those of them whose life spans we know lived to a good age.

They were a family of notaries, a profession which had risen in importance with the mercantile boom of the previous century. It was the notary who drew up the contracts, attested the deals, lodged and protested the bills of exchange. They were the makers and keepers of record, and their work shaded into other roles – the attorney, the accountant, the investment-broker – which oiled the wheels of commerce. In Florence the notaries' guild, the Arte dei Giudici e Notai, was the most esteemed of the seven major guilds, or *arti maggiori*. The earliest da Vinci on record, Ser Michele, was a notary;

so was his son, Ser Guido. (The honorific 'Ser', loosely equivalent to the English 'Sir', was a prerogative of notaries and lawyers.) Ser Guido is recorded in a notarial act dated 1339: the first firm date in the family history. It was his old 'notarial book' which Antonio da Vinci used to record the family births, including that of Leonardo, who was Guido's great-great-grandson. The most celebrated of the da Vinci notaries was Guido's son, Ser Piero (whom I shall call Ser Piero the elder, to distinguish him from Leonardo's father). He was a high-flyer in late-fourteenth-century Florence, the last years before the rise of the Medici. In 1361, a year after his notarial investiture, he was a Florentine envoy at the court of Sassoferrato; later he was notary to the Signoria, the governing body of the Florentine republic. His brother Giovanni was also a notary; he appears to have died in Spain in about 1406 – a da Vinci who travelled: atypical in that.[6]

For these generations of fourteenth-century da Vinci, Florence was their day-to-day home, the political and commercial capital where they had to be; Vinci was the home of their forefathers and their inherited properties, and the place they escaped to from the summer city heat. Vinci was not always a good place to be. It stood close to the western border of Florentine influence, and was harried fairly frequently by Florence's enemies. In the 1320s the Lucchese strongman Castruccio Castracani ('The Castrator of Dogs') was camped below the walls for more than six years, and the town later received the unwelcome attentions of Sir John Hawkwood, the Essex-born *condottiere*, whose paramilitary army, the White Company, struck fear into the countryside. This was in 1364. Hawkwood – whose name was Italianized to Giovanni d'Acuto, thus becoming John Sharp – was then in the pay of Pisa, but in later years he was a staunch Florentine commander, and he is commemorated in the city's cathedral, astride a white charger, in a mural portrait by Uccello which Leonardo certainly knew. It has been argued that Hawkwood was the model for the Knight in Chaucer's *Canterbury Tales* – the 'parfit gentil knyght' being a heavily ironic portrait of a man who was actually a ruthless mercenary. Chaucer was himself in Florence in the early 1370s on a diplomatic mission. Ser Piero the elder, moving in a political ambit in these years, may have met both these redoubtable Englishmen. 'War' – in other words, beware – these 'questmongers and notaries', wrote Chaucer in 'The Parson's Tale', reminding us that the profession was not always reputed honest.[7]

The son of Ser Piero the elder – apparently his only son – was a man of a very different stamp. This was Leonardo's grandfather Antonio, of whom we have already heard: he who was glimpsed at a game of backgammon in Anchiano; he who punctiliously noted the family's births and baptisms.

Born in about 1372, he was probably apprenticed to his father, but he did not become a notary. As far as we know he chose to live exclusively in Vinci, cultivating what might be called the air of an early Renaissance country gent.

And it is in Antonio's time, in the year 1427, that Florence's first *catasto* was enacted, a new system of land-tax applied to all property-owners within the republic. It required them to declare the annual produce of their land, on which they were taxed at the rate of 1.5 per cent, and the members of their family, for whom they received an allowance of 200 florins each. These tax-deductible dependants were referred to simply as *bocche*, or mouths. The tax returns elicited by the *catasto*, now catalogued into a series of pungent bundles in the State Archive in Florence, provide a kind of Domesday Book of Quattrocento Tuscany, in the pages of which the da Vinci family – and thousands of others, both richer and poorer – swim into clearer historical focus. Thus in the first *catasto* of 1427, when Antonio was in his mid-fifties, we find him married and with an infant son.[8] His wife was Lucia, twenty years his junior, the daughter of yet another notary. Her family home, Toia di Bacchereto, was on the eastern flank of Mont'Albano, not far from Vinci; the family also produced ceramics, specializing in painted maiolica work that had a wide clientele. Antonio's child – a '*fanciullo*' of fourteen months – was named, after both his grandfathers, Piero. This was Leonardo's father, born 19 April 1426. The following year Lucia bore another son, Giuliano, but he is not mentioned in subsequent tax returns and must have died in infancy. This loss was partly repaired in 1432, with the birth of a daughter, Violante.

At this time Antonio owned a farm at Costereccia, near Vinci, and some other smaller country properties: their annual produce amounted to 50 bushels of wheat, 5 bushels of millet, 26 barrels of wine, and 2 pitchers of oil. He also owned two plots of building-land in Vinci, one within the walls and one without. In 1427 the family were actually living not in one of their properties, but in a 'little house in the country', owned by a man who owed Antonio money. This was a convenient arrangement: the debt was repaid in rent-free accommodation, and Antonio was able to claim that he was technically '*sanza casa*' ('without a house') – not surprisingly, these early Italian tax returns are full of the sound of people trying to sound poorer than they were. Six years later, in the *catasto* of 1433, he and his family are recorded as living in Vinci, in a 'little house' with 'a bit of garden'[9] – these diminutives are once again for the tax-man's benefit.

Antonio is an attractive character, and an important one in that he was the head of the family for most of Leonardo's childhood. He was an educated

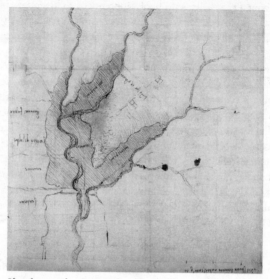

Sketch-map by Leonardo showing one of the family's properties near Vinci.

man – to judge from his handwriting – who chose the life of a country squire over the stresses and rewards of a professional career in Florence. He sounds not unlike his younger contemporary the Florentine lawyer Bernardo Machiavelli, father of the famous author, who similarly turned his back on the rat-race for the quieter pleasures of the *contado*. Bernardo was a scholarly man: there is an account of him taking a copy of Livy's *History of Rome* to the bookbinder's, and leaving as a deposit 'three flasks of vermilion wine and a flask of vinegar' from his vineyard.[10] He typifies a certain stratum of Tuscan intellectual life – the educated, book-loving countryman – and there may have been something of this in Antonio da Vinci. The choice of these men was one that embraced a certain hardship, or was perceived to do so. As Niccolò Machiavelli said of his childhood, in his usual tart way, 'I learned to do without before I learned to enjoy.'[11] Leonardo too would value a certain spareness and simplicity in his lifestyle, and this was a remnant of his country upbringing.

The family pendulum swung again, and Antonio's first-born son, Piero, took to the world of 'questmongers and notaries' with relish. The dynamic Ser Piero the younger was a reincarnation of his grandfather and namesake, and would rise to similar positions of eminence in Florentine financial affairs. By 1446 he had left Vinci: Antonio's *catasto* of that year does not include him among his dependants. He was probably invested as a notary in the following year, at the conventional age of twenty-one; the earliest legal document in his hand is from 1448. A couple of years later he was practising in Pistoia, perhaps living with his sister, Violante, now married and settled there. He also appears in Pisa, but soon he follows the well-trodden path to Florence and begins to establish his career there. His notarial insignia – a kind of trademark, not unlike a printer's device – can be seen on a contract dated November 1458. It is hand-drawn, and shows a cloud with the letter *P* in it, and something issuing from the cloud which looks partly like a sword and partly like a stylized tree.[12] The contract involves the Rucellai, one of Florence's premier merchant-families, with whom Leonardo would later have some dealings.

One might call Piero a typical da Vinci – ambitious, urbane, not entirely warm-hearted – but that more contemplative, country-loving strain in the family make-up was continued in Antonio's youngest son, Francesco, born in 1436. Like his father, Francesco had no notarial ambitions: a bit of speculative silk-farming was the nearest he got to the business world. Again like his father, he seems to have lived all his life in Vinci, looking after the family's farms and vineyards. In his tax return in 1498 he wrote simply, 'I am in the country without prospect of employment.'[13] Francesco was just fifteen when Leonardo was born: a very young uncle, and a vital figure in Leonardo's early development. It has been noted that in the first edition of the *Lives* Vasari erroneously describes Ser Piero da Vinci as Leonardo's uncle. It is possible that this curious mistake (which is duly corrected in the later edition) reflects some half-understood tradition about Leonardo being closer to his uncle than to his father.[14] It may well be true that Piero was an absent, busy and not very caring father. It is certainly true that he left nothing to Leonardo in his will: he had numerous legitimate children by then, but to leave him nothing is surely significant. Uncle Francesco, by contrast, died childless, and left his entire estate to Leonardo – an inheritance bitterly contested by Piero's legitimate children.

This was the family that Leonardo was born into, a collection of averagely complex individuals whose particular quirks are mostly irrecoverable, but also expressive in a more schematic sense of those twin aspects of Renaissance social identity – *città* and *villa*, urban and pastoral, active and contemplative – whose relative merits were addressed by so many writers and indeed painters of the time, as they had been at least since the time of the

Roman poet Horace. It is not hard to see these twin aspects reflected in Leonardo's life and work. He lived most of his adult life in cities, partly but not entirely out of professional necessity; yet his potent love of the countryside, of its forms and atmospheres, is evident throughout his paintings and writings.

The da Vinci genes are to some extent highly mappable. We perceive the broad outlines of Leonardo's family heritage; we grasp something of the social, cultural, financial, physical and even psychological milieu into which he was born. But this is, of course, only half of the genetic story. Of the other side – of his mother and her antecedents – we know next to nothing. In the story of Leonardo's formative years she is an area of deep shadow, though, as with his paintings, one's eye is drawn to those lustrous areas of darkness, as if they have some secret to impart.

↠ CATERINA ↞

The heart does not beat nor the lung breathe while the child is in the womb, which is filled with water, for if it were to draw a breath it would be instantly drowned. But the breathing of the mother, and the beating of her heart, work in the life of the child.　　　　　　　　　　　　　Anatomical MS C2, fol. 11r

Spring arrives in Vinci; a young woman prepares for the birth of her first child. What we know of Leonardo's mother at this point in early 1452 can be summed up very briefly. Her name was Caterina. She was about twenty-five years old. She was carrying the child of Ser Piero da Vinci, but he would not, or could not, marry her.

Caterina is generally described as a 'peasant girl' (*contadina*) or a 'serving-girl' (*servitore*). In one version she is the daughter of a woodcutter in the Cerreto Guidi, then an extensive area of oak forest south-west of Vinci. These are only assumptions: the last is more embroidered, but is of no great antiquity. They are all versions of the basic assumption, which is that Caterina was a poor, lower-class girl, and that this was why Piero could not marry her. This may be right, but it is not the only possible reason for Piero's rejection of her. Another, perhaps more pressing, is that he was already betrothed. He got married to a rich Florentine notary's daughter called Albiera in 1452 – eight months at the most after Leonardo's birth. His bride was sixteen years old. It is likely that the marriage, and the financial entailments that came with it, were planned in advance. The rejection of the pregnant Caterina may thus have been a matter of contract, in this notarial world of the da Vinci, as much as a matter of class. Early *catasti* have been combed for some sign of her and her family in Vinci, but no suitable Caterina has been found. (Her approximate birth-date of *c.* 1427 is known from a much later document.) Her apparent absence from the Vinci *catasto* has been thought to show the humbleness of her origins, though it could simply show that she came from somewhere else.

That Caterina was a poor young woman without land or status is certainly plausible, but it is a curious fact that the only early biography of Leonardo to mention her says more or less exactly the opposite: '*Era per madre nato di buon sangue*' – 'He was born, through his mother, of good blood.' The author of this comment is the Anonimo Gaddiano, writing sometime around 1540 – a good source, though not impeccable. He is also the earliest biographer to say that Leonardo was illegitimate.[15] None of the other early sources – Billi, Giovio, Vasari, etc. – mentions this. (In the case of Vasari, who certainly knew the Gaddian manuscript, he must have chosen not to mention it.) The Anonimo may conceivably be right about Caterina's 'good blood', though it may equally be an interpolation by him to counterpoise the slur of illegitimacy.

Whatever her origins, it must surely be true that Leonardo was conceived out of passion: a love-child. Whether the passion was fleeting and carnal, or whether Piero 'really loved' Caterina but had to marry another, we cannot say. On a sheet of anatomical drawings dated to about 1507 Leonardo wrote, 'The man who has intercourse aggressively and uneasily will produce children who are irritable and untrustworthy; but if the intercourse is done with great love and desire on both sides, then the child will be of great intellect, and witty, lively and lovable.'[16] The idea is traditional – the bastard Edmund in Shakespeare's *King Lear* says much the same – but perhaps Leonardo thought it had a particular relevance to his own conception. If so, the irritable children produced of a loveless union may refer to his legitimate and much younger half-brothers, with whom he was engaged in a bitter lawsuit in the year he wrote this note.

A year or so after Leonardo's birth, perhaps sooner, Caterina was married – one is tempted to say married off – to a local man. He went by the name of Accattabriga or Accattabrighe, a nickname meaning literally 'one who begs [*accatta*] a quarrel [*briga*]', thus 'Trouble-Seeker' or 'Mischief-Maker'.[17] This may be a personal description, or it may denote that he had been a soldier, as a brother of his had been and as his son would be. Accattabriga was a popular nickname among mercenaries – a famous

Florentine captain of the day, Jacopo da Castelfranco, was so-called. In this context it broadly means 'Tough Guy'.

Accattabriga is first named as Caterina's husband by the ever informative Antonio da Vinci. In his 1457 tax return Antonio lists the five-year-old Leonardo among his dependants, and describes him as 'Lionardo, son of the said Ser Piero, born illegitimate to him and Chaterina who is now the wife of Achattabriga'.[18] Her husband's full name was Antonio di Piero Buti del Vacca. At the time of his marriage to Caterina he was about twenty-four years old – a couple of years younger than her – and was described as a *fornaciaio*, or furnace-worker. He was a lime-burner, working the local stone to produce lime for mortar, pottery and manure. His kiln was at Mercatale, on the Empoli road a few miles south of Vinci; he rented it from the monks of a Florentine monastery, San Pier Martire. The monastic records show that he rented it between 1449 and 1453, the probable year of his marriage, and that in 1469 it was rented by Ser Piero da Vinci, possibly on Accattabriga's behalf. Today there is a small industrial estate at Mercatale, a rather down-at-heel place.

For generations Accattabriga's family, the Buti, had worked the land at Campo Zeppi, on a low rise above the Vincio river a short walk west of Vinci, in the parish of San Pantaleone. They owned their land, and were thus a cut above the tenant-farmers, but they lived close to subsistence, and in the *catasti* one sees the arc of the family fortunes moving downward throughout the fifteenth century. Here Caterina came to live with her husband, perhaps with a dowry paid by the da Vinci, and here she lived for many decades thereafter. That the infant Leonardo came with her is plausible but not certain. In the 1457 *catasto* he is listed as a member of the da Vinci household, but this has a fiscal element – he is worth 200 florins as a tax-deductible *bocca* – and may not reflect the practicalities of the situation. Probability, said Bishop Berkeley, is the great guide in life, and, though this is not always a good maxim for the biographer, I think probability tells us pretty forcibly that in his earliest years Leonardo spent much of his time at Campo Zeppi, in the care of his mother, and that this slightly ragged little settlement of houses set down along a ridge-top is as much the scene of his infancy as Vinci itself, or the more conventional but more tenuous Anchiano. Ser Piero's life was in Florence, with his new wife, the notary's daughter Albiera di Giovanni Amadori. She is Leonardo's city stepmother as Accattabriga is his country stepfather. The emotional lines of his childhood are already complicated.

Around 1454, when Leonardo was two, Caterina gave birth to a daughter. The child was christened Piera, which has caused unnecessary frissons. A lovelorn echo of Ser Piero? Probably not: the girl is named, conventionally enough, after Accattabriga's mother, who appears in the tax records as 'Monna Piera'.[19] In 1457 a second daughter, Maria, was born. The family is caught in the snapshot of their *catasto* declaration of 15 October 1459: Accattabriga and 'Monna Chaterina his wife'; Piera, aged five; and Maria, aged two. They are living at Campo Zeppi together with Accattabriga's father, Piero; his stepmother, Antonia; his elder brother, Jacopo; his sister-in-law, Fiore; and his nieces and nephews, Lisa, Simone and the baby Michele. The house is valued at 10 florins, their land at 60 florins. The land, part cultivated and part waste ground, furnishes 5 bushels of grain a year, and their vineyard produces 4 barrels of wine. These figures place them on an economic level much lower than the da Vinci.

There followed in quick succession three more children: Lisabetta, Francesco and Sandra. By 1463, the year of Sandra's birth, Caterina had produced six children in eleven years, the five legitimate ones doubtless christened at the tiny parish church of San Pantaleone, across the river from Campo Zeppi, today dilapidated and not much used except by the pigeons who scratch and fidget on the roof of the colonnaded portico. Caterina's only legitimate son, Francesco, born in 1461, did not prosper: he joined up as a soldier, and was killed at Pisa by a shot from a *spingarda* – a military catapult – at the age of about thirty.[20]

We glimpse Accattabriga, perhaps living up to his nickname, on a late summer's day in 1470. He is enjoying a day out at Massa Piscatoria, down in the *padule*, the marshlands stretching between Mont'Albano and the Pisan hills to the west. It is a religious holiday – for the birth of the Virgin Mary, 8 September – but the village celebrations are marred by a fight or riot (*tumulto* is the word used) and Accattabriga is among those called as a witness at a judicial inquiry a couple of weeks later. His companion that day was one Giovanni Gangalandi, described as a *frantoiano* – an owner or worker of an olive-press – at Anchiano. Again we are reminded of the smallness of the Vinci world.

Caterina's marriage to Antonio Buti, a.k.a. Accattabriga, began as a marriage of convenience – the signorial convenience of the da Vinci, for whom she was a social embarrassment; the more pressing convenience of Caterina herself, a fallen and discarded woman, in a situation which led some to destitution. There was probably some financial inducement for Accattabriga to accept her, and perhaps the vaguer inducement of a family link with the posher da Vinci. Accattabriga continues to feature in the minor business dealings of the family. In 1472, in Vinci, he witnesses a land-contract for Piero and Francesco da Vinci; a few years later he is in

Florence, witnessing a will notarized by Ser Piero. Francesco da Vinci in turn acted as a witness when, in August 1480, Accattabriga came to sell some land, a small plot called Caffaggio, abutting on to the church-lands of San Pantaleone; the purchasers were the Ridolfi family, who swallowed up much of the Buti land over the years. But if the marriage began as a convenience, an exercise in Vincian problem-solving, it was at least a long and fruitful one, and in the *catasto* of 1487 we find Accattabriga and Caterina still together, with four of their five children in residence (Maria either married and living elsewhere or possibly dead). 'Monna Catterina' is listed as sixty years old: the only documentary clue to her date of birth. The property at Campo Zeppi has been split up between Accattabriga and his brother; they are assessed on a 'half-house' worth 6 florins, and just over 5 staia of land.

We know little of Leonardo's stepfather, Accattabriga, a looming presence in the child's early life – perhaps more so than his real father and grandfather. What we do know brings in a note of rural poverty, of manual work, of tough-guy violence – a glimpse, perhaps, of the milieu awaiting this illegitimate child if he does not make it his business to escape from it.

Accattabriga died in about 1490, in his early sixties, after which there is one last adventure in Caterina's life – but this belongs to a later chapter.

⤖ 'MY FIRST MEMORY . . .' ⤚

Leonardo's earliest memory was not ostensibly of his mother, or his father, or anyone else. It was of a bird. Many decades later, in his early fifties, he was writing some notes on the flight of birds – his famous perennial theme – and in particular on the flight-patterns of the fork-tailed red kite, *Milvus vulgaris*, when something triggered in his memory, and at the top of the sheet he wrote the following brief note:

Writing like this so particularly about the kite seems to be my destiny, since the first memory of my childhood is that it seemed to me, when I was in my cradle, that a kite came to me, and opened my mouth with its tail, and struck me several times with its tail inside my lips.[21]

It has long been debated whether this strange little vignette is truly a memory, a *ricordazione* as Leonardo calls it, or whether it is a fantasy. And, if it is a fantasy, there is further debate – at least down in the psychiatric wing of Leonardo studies – as to where it properly belongs in his life. Is it truly from childhood: an early dream or nightmare so vivid that it now seems an actual memory? Or is it an adult fantasy which has been 'projected' back on to his childhood, but which is actually more pertinent to the writer of the note – the middle-aged Leonardo of *c.* 1505 – than to the infant in his cradle?

Kites were a common sight riding the updrafts of the Mont'Albano above Vinci. You can see one today if you are lucky. They are unmistakable – the long forked tail, the wide, elegantly cambered wing-span, the soft yet intense russet colouring through which, at the wing-ends and the tail-feathers, the light of the sky glows. The bird's outline and wheeling flight are transferred in English to the man-made kind of kite, though in Italy this is called an eagle (*aquilone*). Kites are of all the raptors the most adapted to human society: they are scavengers and camp-followers. Their presence in Elizabethan London is attested by Shakespeare, and they can be seen today in towns and villages all over the Third World. Among British troops in India they were known as 'shite hawks'. According to the British falconer Jemimah Parry-Jones, kites 'take advantage of easy pickings whenever possible', and are 'renowned for their habit of stooping down and stealing food from plates'.[22] As this last comment shows, it is entirely possible that there was an actual experience behind this memory of Leonardo's. A hungry kite had 'stooped' or swooped down in search of some morsel, and had frightened the baby in his cradle. However, the strange and memorable part of the account – that the bird pushed its tail into his mouth, and struck or drummed his lips with it (*percuotesse* in Leonardo's archaic spelling: the root idea is of percussion) – is much less likely to have happened, and is therefore a component of fantasy, an unconscious elaboration of the memory.

Leonardo's own wording encourages the idea that fantasy is present. Though he calls the incident a memory, it has a sort of blurred quality which expresses that uncertainty one has about early memories and the extent to which they are constructions rather than genuine recollections. His earliest memory was that 'it *seemed*' to him that a kite came down. There is a tentativeness. He is grasping back at something which is potent in his mind but not quite clear to his reason. He thinks it happened, but maybe it did not. He has already used the word 'seems' earlier in the sentence: it 'seems to be my destiny' to study kites. The word 'destiny' is also interesting, because in this context it suggests what we would call a compulsion or fixation. He is saying that something impels him to keep returning to this bird, to keep writing about it so 'particularly'. 'Destiny' conveys that this is something other than conscious volition, that some hidden process is at work.

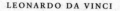

In one sense, Leonardo's thing about kites is precisely connected to his renewed interest in human flight in the years around 1505. The small codex 'On the Flight of Birds', now in Turin, was composed at this time. It includes a famous pronouncement: 'The big bird will take its first flight above the back of the Great Cecero, filling the universe with amazement, filling all the chronicles with its fame, and bringing eternal glory to the nest where it was born.'[23] This is generally taken to mean that Leonardo was planning a trial flight of his flying-machine or 'big bird' from the summit of Monte Ceceri, near Fiesole, just north of Florence. A jotting on the same folio of the codex shows his presence near Fiesole in March 1505.[24] Thus the memory of the kite comes to mind at a time when he is intensely preoccupied with the possibility of human flight, and becomes a kind of personalized source for that preoccupation. The kite flew down to him and showed him his 'destiny' while he was still in his cradle.

The first psychological study of Leonardo's kite fantasy was by Freud: *Eine Kindheitserinnerung des Leonardo da Vinci* ('A Childhood Memory of Leonardo da Vinci'), published in 1910. Freud essentially analyses the story as if it were a dream, with unconscious meanings and memories coded within it. The key to it, he thinks, is the infant Leonardo's relationship with his mother. Some of what he says on this score is untenable because he argues connections with the mother based on symbolic associations of the vulture (he was using a faulty German translation of Leonardo's note, which incorrectly rendered the bird as *Geier*, a vulture).[25] His learned excursus into Egyptian vulture-symbolism must be discarded, along with much else that seems to the biographer too specifically or elaborately 'Freudian'. But the basic perception – that this dream or fantasy of Leonardo's, specifically placed in his

Birds in flight, from the Turin Codex of c. 1505.

32

cradle, is connected with his feelings about his mother – seems a valuable psychoanalytical insight.

According to Freud, the kite putting its tail in the infant's mouth is a buried memory of being breast-fed: 'What the fantasy conceals is merely a reminiscence of sucking – or being suckled – at his mother's breast, a scene of human beauty that he, like so many artists, undertook to depict with his brush.' (Freud is referring here to the *Litta Madonna*, painted in Milan in the late 1480s.) Being breast-fed is 'the first source of pleasure in our life', and the impression of it remains 'indelibly printed on us'.[26] But this idea that the kite's tail represents the mother's nipple can take us only so far, because the fantasy is not just, or even primarily, an image of infantile security. The feel of it is quite different. The bird's action seems to become threatening, intrusive, percussive. This might be taken to mean that Leonardo's feelings about his mother were themselves ambivalent, that a fear of her rejection or hostility is expressed in this more oppressive overtone. One recalls the birth of Caterina's first daughter in 1454, when Leonardo was two: an age at which a child is prone to feel the advent of a new baby as a disaster of removed maternal affection. Alternatively – and this is more Freud's line – the disturbing aspect of the kite's tail is phallic, representing the threatening competition of the father.

Freud applied these perceptions to what he knew of Leonardo's upbringing, which in 1910 was not as much as we know today, though the outline of it was clear enough from Antonio da Vinci's informative *catasto* declarations, which had been published a few years earlier. The fantasy 'seems to tell us', Freud says, that Leonardo 'spent the critical first years of his life not by the side of his father and stepmother but with his poor, forsaken, real mother'. In this critical phase of infancy, 'certain impressions become fixed and ways of reacting to the outside world are established,' and what here became established was precisely the father's extraneousness. Ser Piero was absent from the home, outside the intense circle of the mother–child relationship, but was also a threat to it, a potential disruption. Thus the kite fantasy suggests an early tension between the comfort of the mother and the threat of the father, setting the scene for later tensions: 'No one who as a child desires his mother can escape wanting to put himself in his father's place, can fail to identify himself with him in his imagination, and later to make it his task in life to gain ascendancy over him.'[27] That Leonardo's father had died in 1504 – close enough to the approximate date of the note about the kite – may be significant. Critics of Freud's analysis say that this is piling highly speculative psychology on top of highly speculative history, and they are right, but it has a coherence to it. In the matter of Leonardo's childhood we have only nuances of knowledge, and the speculations of Dr Freud seem to me to be worth listening to.

There is another piece of writing by Leonardo about kites, not apparently known to Freud, which leads into the same sort of terrain. In this, Leonardo cites a folkloric association of the kite with *invidia* – envy or jealousy: 'One reads of the kite that when it sees its offspring in the nest becoming too fat, out of envy it pecks at their ribs and refuses to feed them.'[28] This is from his 'bestiary', a collection of emblematic sayings and stories about animals, inscribed in a small notebook he was using in Milan in the mid-1490s. It is therefore some years earlier than the writing down of the kite 'memory'. It echoes a passage from a popular miscellany, the *Fiore di virtù*, by the thirteenth-century friar Tommaso Gozzadini – a book Leonardo is known to have owned. While it does not have the weight of personal association which freights the more famous memory, it seems to link interestingly with it. Here too we have a relationship between a kite and a baby (in this case its own chicks). The keynote of the vignette is the withdrawal of parental love. What should be a comforting and sustaining figure – the bird on the nest feeding its young – becomes an image of disturbing hostility: the kite 'pecks' the child with its beak, as in the memory it 'strikes' the child with its tail. Again one could take this either as a fear of the mother turning from feeder to destroyer ('*quod me nutrit me destruit*' in the old emblematic tag) or as a fear of the father as a hostile rival for his mother's affections. Again the kite leads to an area of childhood fears and tensions.[29]

Another passage that would certainly have interested Freud occurs in one of Leonardo's collections of *profezie* – those riddles and word-games humorously cast into prophetic mode. One of the fascinations of these is their tendency to communicate unexpected meanings beyond the answer to the riddle. An example is the prophecy which says, 'Feathers will raise men, as they do birds, towards heaven.' The stated answer is 'quills', which write uplifting words; but the covert answer would seem to be 'human flight'. Similarly, 'Flying creatures will support men with their very feathers' (answer: 'feather beds').[30] The most compelling of these is the *profezia* whose answer is simply 'dreaming', and which is surely nothing less than an account of Leonardo's own troubled dreams:

It will seem to men that they see unknown destructions in the sky. It will seem that they are flying up into the sky, and then they are fleeing in terror from the flames that pour down from there. They will hear all kinds of animals speaking in human language. Their bodies will glide in an instant to various parts of the world without moving. In the midst of darkness they will see the most wonderful splendours. O marvel of the human species, what frenzy has led you thus? You will speak with animals of every species and they will speak with you in human language. You will see yourself fall from great heights without harming yourself. Torrents will sweep you along and mingle in their rapid course . . .

The next line is rendered illegible by a tear in the paper. Visible is '*Usera[i] car[. . .]n madre e sorell [. . .]*'. Carlo Pedretti conjectures that the sentence read, '*Userai carnalmente con madre e sorelle*' – 'You will have sex with your mother and sisters.' He compares a phrase in the bestiary, on the lustfulness of the camel: '*Se usasse continuo con la madre e sorelle mai le tocca . . .*'[31] Thus these dreams of 'flying up into the sky' and 'speaking with animals' mingle strangely with a fantasy of incestuous relations with the mother. Once again we are in the kind of terrain mapped out by Freud in his analysis of the kite fantasy.

These psychological undertones are also discernible in one of Leonardo's most mysterious paintings – his *Leda and the Swan* (Plate 29). The painting is lost, but can be partly reconstructed from preliminary sketches by Leonardo and from full-size copies by his pupils or followers. The earliest known sketches are dated to 1504–5 – precisely contemporary with the note about the kite. The theme is from classical mythology. Jupiter or Zeus, in love with the Spartan princess Leda, transforms himself into a swan and impregnates her, and from their union are born – or, in the paintings, quite literally hatched – two pairs of twins: Castor and Pollux and Helen and Clytemnestra. This – the bird, the mother, the half-bird children hatching strangely from their shells in the foreground – seems to revisit once more the ambit of the kite fantasy. Like that fantasy, the painting is clearly connected with Leonardo's preoccupation with flight at this time. '*Cecero*' – as in Monte Ceceri, from which Leonardo planned to launch his 'big bird' or flying-machine in *c.* 1505 – means 'swan' in Florentine dialect.

Another painting, the Louvre *Virgin and Child with St Anne*, adds a curious footnote to this kite story. The painting is late, *c.* 1510, but a version was in existence – in the form of a full-scale preparatory cartoon – by 1501, so it too belongs broadly to this period of Leonardo's early fifties. The painting is patently on a theme of motherhood. St Anne is the mother of Mary, though it is often noted that Leonardo's depiction of her makes her look much the same age as Mary, and thus seems another reflection of the tangled relations of Leonardo's childhood, with its trinity of Caterina,

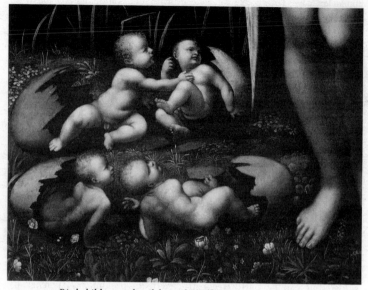

Bird children: a detail from the Uffizi Leda and the Swan.

Albiera and Lucia – mother, stepmother and grandmother. There the matter might have rested but for the curious discovery by a Freudian follower, Oskar Pfister, of a 'hidden bird' lurking in the folds of the Virgin's gown or mantle. This was in 1913, and Pfister – following the original Freudian slip – calls the bird a vulture, but this is not critical. The 'bird' is best obtained by turning the composition on its side. Once pointed out, it certainly seems to be there, but (like those implanted memories of childhood) is it *really* there? This is what Pfister saw: 'In the length of blue cloth which is visible around the hip of the woman in front [i.e. Mary], and which extends in the direction of her lap and her right knee, one can see the vulture's extremely characteristic head, its neck, and the sharp curve where its body begins.' He discerned the bird's wing as following the length of the cloth where it runs down to Mary's foot. Another part of the cloth 'extends in an upward direction and rests on her shoulder and on the child', and here Pfister saw the bird's 'outspread tail', complete with 'radiating lines which resemble the outlines of feathers'. And, strangest of all – 'exactly as in Leonardo's fanciful childhood dream' – the tail 'leads to the mouth of the child, i.e. to Leonardo himself'.[32]

There are three possible explanations of this 'picture puzzle', as Pfister

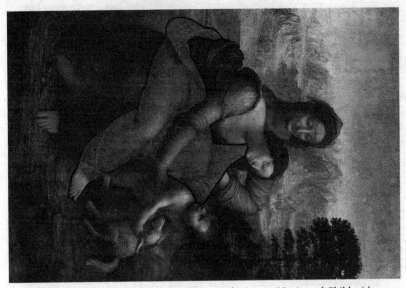

The hidden bird discerned by Oskar Pfister in the Louvre Virgin and Child with
St Anne.

called it. The first is that Leonardo deliberately put a bird there. The second
is that he has involuntarily projected the bird's shape into this meditation
on motherhood. The third is that the bird is no more than a chance alignment
of lines and shadows, and has no significance other than as a rendition of
drapery – a virtuoso painterly skill which Leonardo had been honing for
thirty years. The safest answer is the last one – if safety is what one wants.

In these ways this first memory – of a bird which 'came to' him in his
cradle – echoes to him across the years, intertwined with feelings of maternal
love and loss, and with the vaunting ambition of mechanical flight, as if he
might thereby meet again that half-remembered, half-imagined visitor from
the sky.

➤➤ AT THE MILL ◄◄

Just out of Vinci, on the right-hand side of the road leading north towards
Pistoia, is a large stone house called Il Molino della Doccia. It is now a private
house, but within living memory it was still a working olive-mill or *frantoio*,

and it was certainly known as such to Leonardo, who captioned a swift but precise sketch of an olive-press with the words 'Molino della Doccia di Vinci'. He drew this in about 1504 or 1505, presumably on a visit back home.[33] It belongs to the same period as his note about the kite, and perhaps it too contains an element of reminiscence. Standing there in the Molino della Doccia he is surrounded by the sights and smells of his childhood.

Leonardo was a country boy. He grew up, broadly speaking, on the farm – whether at his stepfather's smallholding at Campo Zeppi or his grandfather's modest estates around Vinci – and he was immersed from his earliest years in the world of agricultural production: of ploughing and ditching, of planting and harvesting, of orchards and grain-fields and vineyards and olive-groves. Even more than wine, olive-oil was the typical, identifying product of the Tuscan hill-country. Besides its culinary virtues, the oil was used as fuel for lamps, as a lubricant, as a medicine or ointment, and for various other practical purposes. In Vinci and a thousand places like it the olive-harvest was an affair which involved the whole community; it still has a special place in Tuscan village life. An old country jingle announces that the olives are ready by early October – '*Per Santa Reparata* [8 October] *l'oliva è oliata*' – but in fact the harvest is an event straggling over several weeks between October and early December. The fruit was beaten down with long sticks, typically a stem of the cane-grass *Phragmites communis*, which grows in profusion along the rivers. One of Leonardo's 'prophecies' contains an image of the olive-harvest: 'There will pour down from the direction of the sky that which gives us food and light.' The answer to this riddle is 'olives falling from the olive-trees'.[34] Gathered up in baskets, the fruit was taken to olive-mills like the Molino della Doccia to be ground and pressed. Today's olive-mills tend to be powered by electricity rather than by water or animals, but some still use the basic system of stone-milling and torque-pressing employed in Leonardo's day. The *frantoio*'s humid aromatic air, the slithery floor, the pitchers of cloudy greenish oil, the prized *olio nuovo* – all these are unchanged.

Next to Leonardo's sketch of the olive-press at the Molino della Doccia, and clearly inspired by it, is a more complicated mechanism which he captions, '*Da macinare colori ad acqua*' – 'For grinding colours by means of water'. This reminds us that the painter too worked with the fruits and products of the land. The colours he used came from plants, barks, earths and minerals, which needed to be milled and ground to turn them into usable powdered pigment. There are frequent references to studio apprentices having the job of 'grinding colours', usually with a pestle and mortar. The device sketched out on this sheet is designed to mechanize this task.[35]

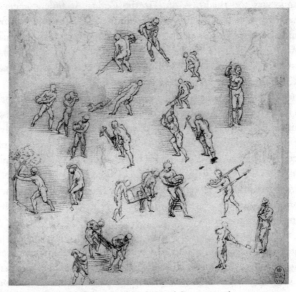

Agricultural labour, from a sheet of drawings of c. 1506–8.

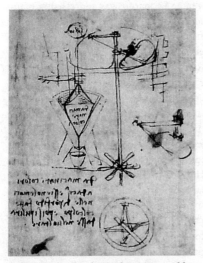

Machine for grinding colours inspired by the Vinci olive-press.

There is a connection here between the processing of olives in the olive-mill and the processing of paints in the artist's workshop. The connection is even closer when one remembers that Leonardo was pre-eminently a painter in oils. The oils most frequently used for painting were linseed and walnut: Leonardo experimented throughout his life with different mixes – adding various kinds of turpentine, crushed mustard seed, and so on – but these were the staples. Both were produced in the same way, and using the same kind of machinery, as olive-oil (which was not generally used for painting because it was too thick). A note in the Codex Atlanticus suggests his personal involvement in the pressing of walnut oil: 'Walnuts are surrounded by a thick rind like a skin, and if you do not remove it when you make oil from them, this skin tinges the oil, and when you work with it the skin separates and comes to the surface of a picture, and this is what makes it change [i.e. discolour].'[36]

There are other drawings of olive-presses in his notebooks, and they may well belong within this context of producing oil for painting. A horse-drawn mechanism described as a 'press for olives and nuts' is closely analysed in one of the Madrid notebooks. The specifications for this are very precise: 'The iron piece marked a is one finger wide,' and 'The bag which holds the nuts or olives is of thick wool, woven like the saddle-girth of a mule.'[37]

There is a continuity here from childhood. The olive-mills of Vinci are a kind of prototype of the artist's workshop: the grinding and pressing, the pungent smell of fresh oils.

Another rural activity that Leonardo would undoubtedly have seen as a child was the weaving of wickerwork baskets out of shoots of osier. This was a speciality of the region, in which the osier willow (*Salix viminalis*) abounds. It is in fact connected with the very name of Vinci, and so had a special appeal for Leonardo.

In the days and afterdays of his fame Leonardo was addressed in many epigrams and epigraphs, and almost without fail they throw in a pun on Vinci and *vincere*, to conquer. In fact the origin of the name has nothing to do with conquest: it comes precisely from an old Italian word for the osier, *vinco* (Latin *vincus*). And the Vincio river which flows past Vinci is obviously 'the river where osiers grow'. The word derives from the Latin *vinculus*, a bond (the osier shoot being much used for binding), and is found in Italian literature describing metaphorical types of bonds and bindings, as in Dante's 'sweet bonds' (*dolci vinci*) of love.[38] To pursue the etymology for a moment, the Latin *vincus* is connected to the old Norse word for an osier, *viker*, from which comes the English 'wicker', as in wickerwork, and also 'weak', which has a root-meaning of pliability. Thus, curiously, the Vinci word-game that begins with the idea of vanquishing arrives at weakness and pliability.

Leonardo took this local craft of wickerwork and made it his personal emblem, one might almost say his 'logo'. There exists a series of engravings based on his designs, probably done in Venice shortly after 1500, which feature complex interwoven patterns, and in the middle the words '*Academia Leonardi Vinci*'. The play on *vinci* = osiers is undoubtedly intentional. The courtier and poet Niccolò da Correggio is known to have devised

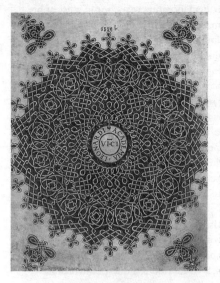

a '*fantasia dei vinci*' – presumably a knot-design of some sort – for the Marchioness of Mantua, Isabella d'Este, in 1492.[39] Leonardo doubtless found the pun on his own name irresistible, and perhaps part of its appeal was that it also contained a memory of the osier-weavers he had seen in his childhood around Vinci. The weaving was accounted woman's work, and it is not unlikely that Caterina practised it, and so Leonardo's knot-patterns would retrace on paper the mesmeric movements of his mother's hands as she plaited the soaked shoots of osier into baskets. He was already

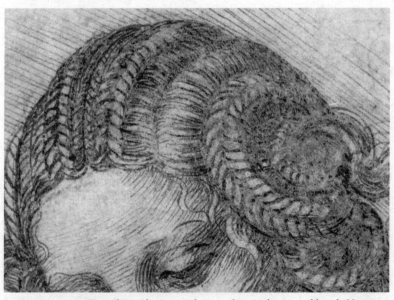

Interweavings. Knot-design for Leonardo's 'academy' (above), and braided hair in a study for the head of Leda.

producing this sort of design during his Florentine years, for in a list of his drawings written in about 1482 he mentions '*molti disegni di groppi*' ('many drawings of knots'). These were doubtless knot-patterns of the sort later exemplified by the Venice engravings: Vasari specifically uses the word *groppo* when talking about those engravings.[40] These elaborate entwinings and intricacies are also found in decorative patterns on the dresses of the *Mona Lisa* and the *Lady with an Ermine*, in braidings of hair and purlings of water, and in the interwoven foliage of his frescos in the Sala delle Asse in Milan. Giovanni Paolo Lomazzo refers to the latter when he writes, 'In the trees we find a beautiful invention by Leonardo, who makes all the branches form into various bizarre knot-patterns.'[41] Lomazzo seems to have understood the basic connection when he uses the verb *canestrare* to describe the creation of these knot-patterns: this means precisely 'to weave like a basket [*canestra*]'.

Thus etymologically 'Vinci' leads, in a characteristic Leonardian way, away from the military machismo of *vincere*, as symbolized by the town's fortress of Castello Guidi, to the ambivalent, circuitous, non-achieving form of the interwoven *vinci* – a fantasia, a visual riddle, a question which never reaches an answer.

⤙ SPEAKING WITH ANIMALS ⤚

> *Man has great power of speech, but what he says is mostly vain and false; animals have little, but what they say is useful and true.*   Paris MS F, fol. 96v

A dog lying asleep on an old sheepskin; a spider's web in the vineyard; a blackbird among the thorn-bushes; an ant carrying a grain of millet; a rat 'besieged in his little home' by a weasel; a crow flying up to the top of a tall bell-tower with a nut in its beak – all these beautifully specific images of country life are to be found in Leonardo's *favole*, or fables, written in Milan in the early 1490s. These fables embody a rich vein of country lore. They are Aesopian in character – and we know from one of his book-lists that Leonardo owned a copy of Aesop's fables – but they seem to be original to him in their particularities and their phrasing. They are brisk narratives, some only a few lines long, in which animals and birds and insects are given a voice, and a story to tell.[42] They have a connection, perhaps, with Leonardo's dream-life, as glimpsed in that 'prophecy' I quoted in relation to his kite fantasy – 'You will speak with animals of every species and they will speak with you in human language.' The kite fantasy itself seems to belong within the animistic world of the fables – it could almost *be* one of the fables, except that it would have been turned the other way around and told from the kite's point of view: 'One day a kite looked down from the sky and spied an infant asleep in his cradle . . .' One would like to know how that version of the story might have continued.

It is not unusual for a somewhat solitary child growing up in the country to form a strong affinity with animals, and once they are part of his life he is never quite happy out of their company for long. That Leonardo 'loved' animals is almost a truism. Vasari says:

He took an especial delight in animals of all sorts, which he treated with wonderful love and patience. For instance, when he was passing the places where they sold birds, he would often take them out of their cages with his hand, and having paid whatever price was asked by the vendor, he would let them fly away into the air, giving them back their lost liberty.

His famous vegetarianism seems part of this relationship. (There is no evidence that he was a life-long vegetarian, but he certainly was in later years.) A letter of 1516 from an Italian traveller in India, Andrea Corsali, describes the Gujarati as a 'gentle people . . . who do not feed on anything that has blood, nor will they allow anyone to hurt any living thing, like our Leonardo da Vinci'.[43] One of Leonardo's closest associates, the eccentric Tommaso Masini, held similar views: 'He would not kill a flea for any reason whatever; he preferred to dress in linen so as not to wear something dead.'[44]

Leonardo's fables and prophecies show him acutely sensitive to animal suffering, but his respect for creatures does not merge into sentimentality. The anatomical manuscripts contain many animal studies, ranging from a bear's foot to a bovine womb: these were undoubtedly based on his own dissections. And there was that 'odd-looking' lizard, brought to him one day by the Pope's gardener, which he kept in a box to 'frighten the life out of his friends', having first fitted it up with wings, horns and a beard 'attached with a mixture of quicksilver'. How much the lizard enjoyed this *jeu d'esprit* is not recorded. This Vasarian anecdote has a touch of the childish prank about it, but is placed in Leonardo's Roman years, when he was in his early sixties. It may or may not be apocryphal.

Leonardo 'always kept' horses, Vasari says. In itself this would be unremarkable – all but the poorest in Renaissance Italy 'kept' a horse – so one assumes that Vasari means something more: that Leonardo was a particular connoisseur of horses. This could anyway be inferred from the many beautiful studies of horses in his sketchbooks. The earliest of these belong to the late 1470s. They are preparatory sketches for an Adoration of the Shepherds which is either lost or (more likely) never got past the planning stage. In keeping with the homely imagery of this subject, they show familiar worka-day horses of the kind he would have known from the farm. The horse shown from behind, cropping grass, is bony and a bit ungainly. The same mood of unromanticized reality is in a companion sketch (the paper-type is identical) showing the ox and ass.[45] A little later are the studies for the unfinished Adoration of the Magi (1481–2), which features a number of horses and horsemen in the background. These are more dynamic and roman-tic. One of these early studies – the horse and bareback rider, formerly in the Brown Collection in Newport, Rhode Island – is currently the world's most expensive drawing. It was sold at Christie's in July 2001 for $12 million, equalling the world record for a drawing set by Michelangelo's study for a Risen Christ the previous year: the Leonardo sketch, postcard-sized, works out at a little less than $1 million per square inch.[46] There are many later studies of horses – for the equestrian statue of Francesco Sforza (c. 1488–94), for the Battle of Anghiari mural (c. 1503–6), for the funeral monument of the condottiere Giangiacomo Trivulzio (c. 1508–11) – but the early Florentine sketches are among the loveliest. These are the cart-horses and punches of his agricultural childhood, rather than the martial coursers and chargers required for those later, more militaristic, commissions.

Drawing horses was something that Leonardo couldn't stop himself doing – witness the drawing at Windsor of a military chariot. The point of the drawing is the fearsome machine itself, with its toothed wheels and cannon-ball flails, but he cannot resist individuating the two horses which draw the vehicle, one of which turns with ears pricked and eyes alert, as if startled by an unexpected presence. Again these are farm-horses rather than war-horses: if you cover up the chariot, this is just a team of two pulling a cart or plough.[47]

In the British Museum is a wonderfully fresh and natural sketch of a dog, and I am tempted to say that it – or she, for it is demonstrably a bitch – was Leonardo's dog. It is a small, low-built, smooth-haired terrier type still to be seen all over Italy. Its character is beautifully caught. The dog sits more from obedience than volition – the ears flattened down in an ingratiating way, the mouth almost smiling, but the eyes alert to the more interesting world beyond the temporary imperatives of its master. Other Leonardo drawings show a very similar dog, but it does not follow that they are all the same animal. A red-chalk sketch of a dog in profile is found in a pocket-book dating from the late 1490s. This is some twenty years after the

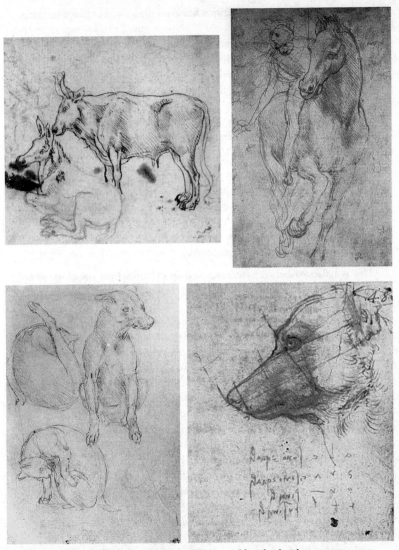

Animal studies. Above: ox and ass, and horse and bareback rider, preparatory studies for Florentine paintings. Below: study of a sitting dog and a cat, and proportional profile study of a dog.

obediently sitting dog in the British Museum drawing, so almost certainly shows a different individual.[48]

One of my favourite moments of Leonardian light relief concerns dogs. On a page of Paris MS F, a mid-sized notebook he was using in about 1508, occurs a short text which has the look of one of his scientific 'demonstrations' or 'conclusions', but the title of the text actually reads, '*Perche li cani oderan volentieri il culo l'uno all'altro*' – 'Why dogs willingly sniff one another's bottoms'. (I like that 'willingly'.) The explanation he gives is that they are establishing how much 'essence of meat' (*virtù di carne*) can be discerned there:

The excrement of animals always retains some essence of its origin . . . and dogs have such a keen sense of smell that they can discern with their nose the essence remaining in the faeces. If by means of the smell they know a dog to be well-fed, they respect him, because they judge that he has a powerful and rich master; and if they discern no such smell of that essence [i.e. of meat] they judge the dog to be of small account, and to have a poor and humble master, and therefore they bite him.[49]

This is balanced between accuracy – dogs do indeed get olfactory information in this way – and humorous exaggeration of the sociological niceties involved.

Cats feature both in early and in late drawings, and again there seems good reason to take them as cats belonging to Leonardo, or at least attached to his studio in their time-honoured capacity as rat-catchers. If his wonderful sketches for a *Madonna and Child with a Cat* (another lost or abandoned work of the late 1470s)[50] were done from life, as they certainly seem to have been, we might deduce that the cat who features in them is not only a real and particular cat, but also a trusted cat. The child is shown hugging, squeezing and generally mauling it around; at some stages the animal looks pretty reluctant, but it is trusted not to harm the child. Another studio cat is discernible in a brief note of *c.* 1494: 'If at night you place your eye between the light and the eye of a cat, you will see that its eye seems to be on fire.'[51] The famous page of cats at Windsor – or of a single cat in various positions – is one of his late drawings, probably done during his years in Rome, 1513–16. On closer inspection one of the cats turns out to be a diminutive dragon.[52]

I hazard an addendum to Vasari: that Leonardo 'always kept' dogs and cats as well as horses; that animals were a part of his life.

⇥ THE 'MADONNA OF THE SNOW' ⇤

The country boy learns the shapes and contours of the land. He knows the trails that lead in and up and around: the hilly paths and the disregarded corners. He knows 'a certain spot, somewhat steep, where a beautiful bit of woodland ends above a rocky track' – a location found in one of Leonardo's fables, in which a 'rolling stone' laments the restlessness that caused it to leave that charming spot.[53] The moral of the fable is that those who 'leave a life of solitary contemplation to come and live in the city' will regret it. As Leonardo sits in Milan writing these words, that image of a rocky track winding through the woods carries a touch of personal nostalgia. It sums up for him the country life which he too has left behind.

Leonardo's love of the countryside can be seen throughout his work – in the luminous, mysterious landscapes of his paintings; in his superbly detailed drawings of plants and trees and woodlands. It is found also in his note-books, which display a deep knowledge – botanical, agricultural, folkloric – of the natural world. They contain references to over 100 species of plant and 40 different trees. They have something to say about puff-balls and truffles, mulberries and nutmegs, nettles and thistles, wolfbane and wormwood.[54] This detailed botanical knowledge adds a dimension of scientific exactitude to the poetic depiction of nature in his paintings.

In the *Trattato della pittura* he stresses the importance of the painter getting out into the country, experiencing it at first hand (by no means a universal practice among Renaissance artists). It is presented like a pilgrim-age: you must 'quit your home in town, and leave your family and friends, and go over the mountains and valleys into the country'. You must 'expose yourself to the fierce heat of the sun'. It would be easier, he says, to get everything second-hand, from other artists' paintings or from some poetic description in a book – 'Wouldn't that be more convenient, and less tiring, since you can stay in a cool place without moving about and exposing yourself to illness?' But, if you did only that, your soul could not experience, through the 'window' of the eye, the inspiring beauties of the countryside: 'It could not receive the reflections of bright places; it could not see the shady valleys.'[55] The proper way to experience nature, he insists, is alone. 'While you are alone you are entirely your own; and if you have but one companion you are but half your own.' The painter should 'withdraw apart, the better to study the forms of natural objects'. He should 'remain solitary, especially when he is intent on studying and considering those things which

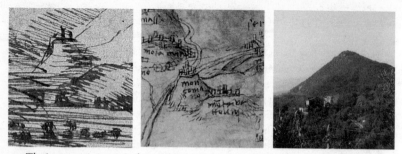

The 'mnemonic icon'. Left to right: detail from Leonardo's landscape drawing, 1473; detail from his map of Tuscany, c. 1503; Monsummano viewed from near Montevettolini.

continually appear before his eyes, and which furnish material to be carefully stored up in the memory'. This desire for solitude, Leonardo warns, will not be understood by others: 'I tell you, you will be thought crazy.'[56]

These words were written in about 1490; they are reprised on a page of the Codex Atlanticus written twenty-five years later, in a short text headed '*Vita del pictore filosofo ne paesi*' – 'The life of the painter-philosopher in the country'. Again he stresses that the painter should 'deprive himself of companions'. And he gives this beautiful synopsis of the receptiveness that the artist must cultivate: 'His brain must be changeable according to the variations of the objects that present themselves in front of it, and it must be free from all cares ... Above all his mind should be like the surface of a mirror, which takes on all the diverse colours of the objects placed before it.'[57]

As with his deep attachment to animals, I see Leonardo's habit of solitary rambling as something embedded in his country childhood. The mind free of cares, the senses alert, the brain as receptive to impressions as the surface of a mirror – it is almost explicitly a childlike state of mental openness that the painter is striving to recreate.

It has been argued that part of the power of Leonardo's painted landscapes is precisely that they contain a poetic memory of the landscapes of his childhood. According to his French biographer Serge Bramly, what we see in the backgrounds of his paintings is 'Leonardo's private landscape': a recreation of the rougher, upland topography of Vinci, 'the rocks, mountain streams and escarpments of his childhood ... magnified by the double lens of art and memory'.[58] Leonardo himself seems to touch on this idea in the

Trattato della pittura, where he says that looking at a painted landscape can trigger off memories of other, real landscapes 'in which you once took pleasure'. In that fictive landscape 'you can see yourself again, a lover with your beloved, in the flowering meadows or under the soft shadows of the green trees.' The lover and his (female) sweetheart add a decorative touch, but the core idea is of landscape encoding and evoking a memory: '*tu possi rivedere tu*'.[59]

This link between landscape and memory is to be found most precisely in Leonardo's earliest dated work, which is indeed a landscape, drawn in pen and ink, now in the Uffizi (Plate 2). It is a physically small drawing – it measures $7\frac{1}{2} \times 11$ inches, just a little less than a sheet of A4 paper – but as a composition it is wonderfully dramatic and spacious. It shows a panoramic view of precipitous craggy hills and wide waterlogged flatlands stretching away to further hills on the horizon. The drawing has the look of a sketch done *in situ*: the penwork is rapid, suggestive, impressionistic, sometimes almost abstract – the trees on the right-hand side of the drawing, for instance – yet for all its sweep and swirl the landscape is punctuated with arresting detail: a castle bristling on a promontory, tiny boats in the wetlands, a waterfall. These in turn lead the eye on through the landscape, to what seems to be the focal point of the vista – a distant, conical, tower-topped hill rising suddenly from the haze of the plain. This feature also serves to identify the landscape: the conical hill is quite unmistakably that of Monsummano (or Monsomano, as Leonardo writes it on one of his maps).[60] This lies north-west of Vinci, about 8 miles away as the crow flies, a couple of hours' walk via the road that winds down through Lamporecchio and Larciano. We are, quite specifically, in the landscape of Leonardo's childhood.

If the tump is Monsummano other features of the landscape are deducible: the flatlands are the Padule di Fucecchio lying south-west of Monsummano; the mountains beyond are those of the Val di Nievole; the lower rounded hills to their left suggest Montecarlo; and so on. These are ingredients in the landscape, but as soon as one tries to relate them to a map of the area – or to actual views from actual hills – the drawing promptly recedes back into mystery. The distinctive form of Monsummano is visible from many vantage-points in the Mont'Albano, but no one has yet found the particular spot which provides this particular vista.[61] My own belief, having tracked the area in search of it, is that no such spot exists. The castle or fortified village in the left foreground is a particular problem: none of the candidates suggested – Montevettolini, Larciano, Papiano – can be found in that sort of spatial relationship with Monsummano. Another difficulty is that to look across the *padule* to Monsummano you would have to be somewhere up in the Pisan hills, but if you were, Monsummano itself would not have the shape it has in the drawing. In short, the drawing is an imagined or idealized view of the landscape around Vinci. It incorporates real places, vividly and beautifully sketched, but is not a real view. What it shows cannot be found and photographed, though it could perhaps be re-created, loosely, by a cunning collage of photos. Or perhaps it could be re-created by flying above the land in a hang-glider (I confess I have not tried this), for the viewpoint most powerfully suggested is an aerial one. It is a bird's-eye view: the imagination soars above the land, and this is what it sees. One recalls a phrase in the Turin Codex on the flight of birds: 'The movement of the bird' – in other words the 'big bird' or flying-machine – 'must always be higher than the clouds, so that the wings don't get wet, and so that one can see more of the land.' '*Per iscoprire più paese*': precisely what is achieved, thirty years earlier, in the high-gliding viewpoint of the Uffizi drawing.[62]

In the upper left-hand corner of the drawing, in the earliest known example of his handwriting, Leonardo wrote, '*Di di santa Maria della neve addi 5 daghossto 1473*' ('On the day of the Madonna of the Snow, 5 August 1473'). This tells us that he made the drawing at the age of twenty-one, after he had been living and working in Florence for some years. The drawing may be connected with the landscape background of Verrocchio's *Baptism of Christ*, which was commissioned in about 1473 and which is known to contain additions by Leonardo. The precise date of the drawing also has some bearing on the landscape itself, for the Madonna of the Snow was particularly venerated at a little chapel outside the fortified village of Montevettolini. This chapel, now called the Oratorio della Madonna della Neve, stands just a mile or so from the southern foot of Monsummano. The foundations of the chapel date from the late thirteenth century: it was a modest 'tabernacle' or shrine, smaller than it is today, but important enough to house a rather fine fresco of the Madonna and Child flanked by four saints, whose style has been compared to the Quaranesi altarpiece (1425) by Gentile da Fabriano.

The story of the Madonna of the Snow began as a legend about the founding of the church of Santa Maria Maggiore, on the Esquiline Hill in Rome. According to the story, the site of the church was dictated by a miraculous fall of summer snow on the hill. The church was founded in the fourth century, but the legend does not appear until the medieval period. The Madonna of the Snow was one of various cultish images of the Virgin Mary which spread through Italy at this time. They were associated with special powers, and their shrines were often, as at Montevettolini, built outside the confines of a town or village. A fifteenth-century diarist, Luca Landucci, refers to the healing powers of another image of the Madonna 'in a tabernacle about a bow-shot from Bibbona'.[63]

The *festa* of the Madonna of the Snow on 5 August has been celebrated at the Montevettolini chapel for centuries, and it is celebrated there still, though the old ladies sitting out in the evening sun will tell you in chorus that it is no longer what it was, when the village was thronged with visitors (*invitati* – guests – was their word). This diminution is blamed on the youth of today, who are *sempre in giro*, always out and about, and have no time for such traditions. Nothing seems to be happening at all until around sunset, when the little piazza outside the chapel suddenly begins to fill. A group of men in white short-sleeved shirts assembles: the village marching-band. An old red van extrudes an awning and becomes a snack-bar. The priest arrives with his vestments folded over his arm. The image of the Madonna – neither very old nor noticeably snow-related – is carried out into the porch of the chapel, shrouded in a curtain of pale-blue taffeta. A mass is held, and then the procession begins, winding up from the chapel on a circling route around the base of the village walls – the tump of Monsummano looming huge to the north – then in through the old Porta Barbacci. The priest intones prayers through a push-button megaphone; the image of the Madonna sways aloft, borne on her sedan chair by four thickset men. This twilight walk on a warm August evening is wonderful and slightly surreal. The lights twinkle in the lowlands below, and the *andante* accompaniment of the band seems, even at its most solemn, to betray traces of jauntiness.

The landscape, the date, the once-thronged local *festa* to which both seem to lead: how do these all fit together?

To arrive at some kind of answer we must first pose another question: where was Leonardo da Vinci on 5 August 1473? Taking this piece of paper at face value, the implication is that he was sitting with his sketchbook on a hillside somewhere near Vinci making this marvellous drawing. Some would argue there is further evidence of this on the reverse of the drawing. Here one sees another sketch of a landscape – unfinished, minimal – and a cryptic scribbled phrase which reads, '*Io morando dant sono chontento.*' The word *dant* can be taken as a contraction of *d'Antonio*, but the overall meaning of the phrase is elusive. Bramly translates it to mean, 'I, staying with Antonio, am happy.' He further reasons that as the Antonio cannot be Leonardo's grandfather, who had died some years previously, it must be his stepfather, Antonio Buti, a.k.a. Accattabriga. This suggests that the drawing

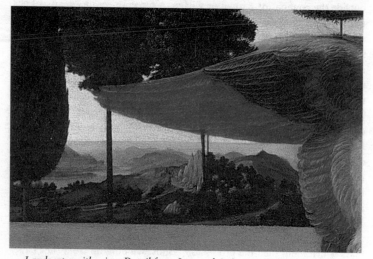

Landscape with wing. Detail from Leonardo's Annunciation, *c. 1470–72.*

was done during a visit to Vinci, while staying with his mother and her family at Campo Zeppi and feeling 'happy'. The escape from the city in August – where else would he be but back in Vinci? But this interpretation is speculative. Carlo Pedretti interprets the phrase as merely a detached doodle reproducing or rehearsing the opening words of some contract: 'I, Morando d'Antonio, agree to . . .' If this is right, the words contain no personal meaning, and offer no evidence of Leonardo's presence at Vinci.[64] He might as easily have been in Florence, in which case the keynotes of the drawing are imagination and memory: it is a Vincian vista conjured up in the mind's eye, a memory of walking over the hills to the summer fair at Montevettolini. This is how Pedretti characterizes the drawing: as a *'rapporto scenico'* – a visual drama, a piece of theatre – centred on the 'mnemonic icon' of Monsummano.[65]

My search for the 'real' landscape of this drawing proved fruitless, but I did find one view which I think might be significant. That 'mnemonic' sight of Monsummano is visible not only from high points around Vinci. It can also be seen looming up straight ahead of you (though several miles distant) on the road that runs between Vinci and San Pantaleone – the road, in other words, which Leonardo would have known so well as a child walking to and from his mother's house at Campo Zeppi. Its 'mnemonic' power may thus have been imprinted on Leonardo's eye and mind very early on, perhaps in association with his mother. I also note that the iconic features of the Uffizi drawing are echoed in the landscape of Leonardo's *Annunciation*, a work dating from the early 1470s and thus broadly contemporary with the drawing. The same conical hill with nipple-like protuberance can be discerned (more clearly since the restoration of 1999). It is on the horizon immediately to the left of the announcing angel; on the picture surface it lies within the crook of the angel's wing. Closer to us, again echoing the drawing, is a tall cluster of rocks whose sheer verticals counterpoint the feminine curves of the tump; and beyond stretch those long hazy expanses of commingled land and water suggestive of the marshy *padule* below Vinci. The repetition of this motif adds to one's sense of its rootedness in Leonardo's psyche, and the apposition of the breast-shaped hill and the bird-like wing takes us back once more to that 'first memory' of the kite, which Freud interprets as a memory of feeding at his mother's breast.

→→ EDUCATION ←←

All our knowledge has its foundation in our senses . . .
Trivulzio Codex, fol. 20v

I have tried to piece together some fragments of Leonardo's experience as a boy growing up in and around Vinci. There are the emotional currents whose patterns one can only guess at – the broken family, the absent father, the troubling dreams, the mother on whose love everything is staked – and there is the daily reality of the Tuscan countryside with which these emotions become somehow entwined, so that years later some hard-to-grasp meaning remains encoded in the flight-patterns of a kite, in the smell of freshly pressed oil, in the weave of a wicker basket, in the shapes of the landscape. These are the few recoverable parts of Leonardo's sentimental education: things which 'seem to be his destiny', and which echo on through his adult life as a 'painter-philosopher'.

Of his more formal education – or lack of it – we know very little. Vasari is the only early biographer to touch on the subject, and his comments are brief and circumstantial. He describes Leonardo as a brilliant but unpredictable pupil:

He would have been very proficient at his early lessons if he had not been so volatile and unstable. He set himself to learn many things only to abandon them almost immediately. When he began to learn arithmetic, in a few months he made such progress that he bombarded the master who was teaching him with questions and problems, and very often outwitted him.

Vasari also mentions that Leonardo studied music, and that, whatever else he was doing, 'he never left off drawing and sculpting, which suited his imagination better than anything.' Nothing in this suggests any specific knowledge on Vasari's part: it conforms to a general idea of Leonardo's personality and accomplishments. Vasari assumes that Leonardo had a teacher, but the word *maestro* does not convey whether this was a schoolmaster or a private tutor. There was probably a *scuola dell'abaco* (an 'abacus school') in Vinci; the conventional age to attend was around ten or eleven.

Leonardo famously described himself as '*omo sanza lettere*', an 'unlettered man'.[66] He means, of course, not that he was illiterate, but that he had not been educated in the scholarly language of Latin. He had not received the kind of schooling or tuition which led to university, and so to the study of the seven 'liberal arts' (so-called precisely because they were not tied to the necessity of learning a trade) – grammar, logic, rhetoric, arithmetic, geometry, music and astronomy. He had followed instead the course of practical apprenticeship. This was certainly an education, though it took place in a workshop rather than an ancient university, it taught skills rather than intellectual accomplishments, and it was conducted in Italian rather than Latin.[67] Leonardo later embarked on a crash course in Latin – a notebook filled with Latin vocabulary dates from the late 1480s – but he remained wedded to the vernacular as a means of discourse no matter what the subject. Late in life he wrote, 'I have so many words in my mother tongue that I should rather complain of not understanding things well than of lacking words with which to express the ideas of my mind.'[68] Though he makes some excursions into consciously literary modes, the overall tone of his style, as preserved in his notebooks, is spare, practical, colloquial, laconic. In his paintings he is a master of nuance, but as a writer he tends towards the flat and colourless. He is (to borrow a phrase of Ben Jonson's) a 'carpenter of words'.

This distinction between university education and artisan training should not be taken too rigidly. The whole trend of Renaissance art was to narrow the gap, to stress that the artist could and should belong to the ranks of scholars, philosophers and scientists. An early advocate of this was Lorenzo Ghiberti, the master of the Florentine Baptistery doors, who writes in his *Commentaries* (1450), 'It is fitting that the sculptor and painter have a solid knowledge of the following liberal arts – grammar, geometry, philosophy, medicine, astronomy, perspective, history, anatomy, theory, design, and arithmetic.' Leon Battista Alberti draws up a similar list of desirable accomplishments in his *De re aedificatoria*. Both writers are echoing the precepts of the great Roman architect Vitruvius.[69] All these subjects, and more, became Leonardo's province – he is the epitome of the multi-disciplinary 'Renaissance man'.

When Leonardo styles himself an *omo sanza lettere* he is being sardonic about his lack of formal education, but he is not devaluing himself. On the contrary, he is stating his independence. He is proud of his unletteredness: he has achieved his knowledge by observation and experience rather than receiving it from others as a pre-existent opinion. Leonardo is a 'disciple of experience', a collector of evidence – 'better a small certainty than a big lie'.[70] He cannot quote the learned experts, the retailers of *ipse dixit* wisdom, 'but I will quote something far greater and more worthy: experience, the mistress of their masters'. Those who merely 'quote' – in the sense of follow or imitate as well as cite – are '*gente gonfiata*': they are, literally, puffed or pumped up by second-hand information; they are 'trumpeters and reciters of the works of others'.[71]

Against the second-hand he opposes 'Nature', which in this context means both the physical phenomena of the material world and the innate powers and principles which lie behind them: all that is studied in 'natural philosophy'. 'Those who take for their standard anything but Nature, the mistress of all masters, weary themselves in vain.' The trope of Nature as female mistress, or *maestra*, is conventional but seems to have had a particular allure for Leonardo, who repeats it throughout the notebooks. 'She' has a power greater than the masculine greatness of reasoning and learning. In painting too, he says, the painter should never imitate another's manner, because if he does he will be 'a grandson rather than a son of Nature'.[72] He commends Giotto as the classic self-taught artist: 'Giotto the Florentine . . . was not content with imitating the works of Cimabue, his master. Born in mountain solitudes inhabited only by goats and such beasts, and being guided by Nature to his art, he began by drawing on the rocks the movements of the goats which he was tending.'[73] This passage – one of the few in which Leonardo refers admiringly to an earlier artist – has resonances with his own lack of formal education.

Thus 'unlettered', for Leonardo, means also 'uncluttered': the mind is not filled with the lumber of precepts. It belongs with a crucial Leonardian idea of clarity: of seeing the visual evidence of the world before him with an accuracy and insight that lead into the heart of things. For Leonardo the key organ in understanding the world is not the brain but the eye: 'The eye, which is called the window of the soul, is the chief means whereby the understanding may most fully and abundantly appreciate the infinite works of Nature,'[74] he writes in one of his many *paragoni*, or comparisons, designed to show the superiority of painting over those supposedly more gentlemanly arts like poetry. His thousands of pages of manuscript are written in despite of his distrust of language as something that interposes and equivocates, something that can often obscure the messages which Nature imparts. A telling comment is found in the Codex Atlanticus, discussing the design of machinery: 'When you want to achieve a certain purpose in a mechanism, do not involve yourself in the confusion of many different parts, but search for the most concise method: do not behave like those who, not knowing how to express something in the appropriate vocabulary, approach it by a roundabout route of confused long-windedness.'[75] Here language itself is associated with confusion and lack of clarity: words tangle things up, they are an over-elaborate mechanism. It is possible that this carries a social overtone of Leonardo as a man who lacks conversational facility, a man prone to gnomic utterances and discomfiting, abstracted silences. This would run counter to the early biographers, who make him a charming conversationalist, but I wonder if that was more a performance than a natural proclivity.

Vasari gives us a picture of a boy whose deep interest in art underlay his more fitful studies in subjects like mathematics: 'He never left off drawing and sculpting, which suited his imagination.' Again one wants to resist the idea of the genius in a vacuum, and ask what kind of artistic education he had. We have no idea of any tuition he had before his apprenticeship in Florence, though there is an interesting speculation that his grandmother Lucia may have contributed. As mentioned, her family owned a pottery at Toia di Bacchereto, near Carmignano, a few miles east of Vinci: the kiln was later inherited by Leonardo's father. The maiolica ceramics they produced were well known in Florence; one presumes a high quality of workmanship. Some geometric patterns of Leonardo's recall the tracery designs used in ceramics, and may hint at an early interest awoken by visits to his grandmother's family.[76]

We can say something of the artistic influences that percolated into the provincial world of Vinci. In the church of Santa Croce, where Leonardo was christened, stood a fine polychrome wood sculpture of Mary Magdalene. It probably dates from the late 1450s: during Leonardo's childhood years it would have been a recent and probably costly purchase. It is visibly influenced by Donatello's famous Magdalene sculpture (*c.* 1456), and may be the work of a pupil of Donatello's such as Neri di Bicci or Romualdo de

Candeli. This powerful piece might be cited as Leonardo's first discernible contact with High Renaissance art. Another very Donatellesque work is the *Madonna of the Welcome*, a marble bas-relief in the church of Santa Maria del Pruno in nearby Orbignano.[77] Via these provincial imitations comes the formative influence of Donatello: an ageing figure from the heyday of the early Renaissance, a former colleague of Ghiberti and Brunelleschi. His sculptures – expressive, tense, saturated in the spirit of classical antiquity – influenced all who followed, including Leonardo's teacher, Verrocchio, who was primarily a sculptor. Donatello died in Florence in 1466, around the time of Leonardo's arrival in the city.

Further afield Leonardo might also have seen the magnificent early-fourteenth-century bas-reliefs by Giovanni Pisano on the pulpit of Sant'Andrea in Pistoia – a city where his aunt Violante lived and where his father had business interests. It is also very likely he visited the river-port of Empoli, the nearest town of any size to Vinci, and a transit point to Florence. We know that Accattabriga's father went there, as his debt to the town for unpaid tolls is mentioned in one of the family's tax returns. At Empoli the young Leonardo could have seen paintings by artists of the stature of Masolino and Agnolo Gaddi.

Here too he would see the great sweep of the Arno river – an educational experience, one might say, in view of his deep interest in the principles and patterns of water-flow – and on a sandbank not far from the town the remains of the ill-fated *Badalone*, the enormous paddle-wheeled barge built by Filippo Brunelleschi to transport marble up to Florence.[78] It ran aground on its maiden voyage, depositing 100 tons of finest white marble into the Arno silt. This occurred in 1428, thus within living memory: a resounding failure, but a heroic one. Brunelleschi was a giant of the early Renaissance, a visionary architect and engineer, and the rotting hulk on the river-bend brings a whisper of grandeur from a world far different from Vinci.

Consideration of Leonardo's education tends away from any idea of formal schooling – he was certainly not taught Latin; he had a lifelong preference for first-hand experience over book-learning; and his first awareness of art is likely to have been gained more from looking at sculptures and carvings in local churches than from any specific training in artistic principles.

One other feature of Leonardo argues strongly for his education as informal and largely autodidactic – his handwriting. The reasons for Leonardo's 'mirror-writing' have been much debated. (It is correctly mirror-script, rather than just writing backwards. Not only does the whole line of script move from right to left, but each letter is formed in reverse; for

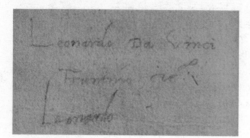

Two signatures. 'Leon-
ardo Vinci disscepolo
della sperientia', *written
in his mirror-script; and*
'Leonardo da Vinci Fior-
entino', *written effortfully
from left to right.*

instance, a Leonardo *d* looks like a normal *b*.) There is certainly a strong
psychological element of secrecy in this – it is not exactly a code, but it is a
kind of veiling which makes the reading of his manuscripts an intrinsically
taxing experience. We know that he was continually on guard against the
pilfering of his ideas and designs.

But the root of his mirror-writing is probably very simple. Leonardo was
left-handed. Writing from right to left comes naturally to the left-hander.
Educational pressure normally prevails against this; in Leonardo's case,
without such pressure, it established itself as the habit of a lifetime.[79] His
handwriting would develop over the years, from the florid, looped style of
the 1470s to the dense, minimal script of forty years later – these changes
are an important tool for the dating of his manuscripts – but its direction
remains the same. It moves defiantly from right to left; it is difficult, and
different (and, in the typical association, 'sinister'). This strange script
is another aspect of the 'unlettered' Leonardo, of the profound mental
independence which was perhaps the greatest legacy of his rural childhood.

PART TWO

Apprenticeship
1466–1477

Florence is a place of transit through which many outsiders pass.

Codex Atlanticus, fol. 323r-b

Sometime in the mid-1460s the teenage Leonardo left Vinci for Florence, where he was apprenticed to the sculptor Andrea del Verrocchio. It is a decisive point of transition, and we know very little about it. According to Vasari, who is our only source on the subject, the apprenticeship was arranged by Leonardo's father:

One day Ser Piero took some of Leonardo's drawings along to Andrea del Verrocchio, who was a good friend of his, and asked if he thought it would be profitable for the boy to study drawing. Andrea was amazed to see what extraordinary beginnings Leonardo had made, and urged Piero to make him study the subject. So Piero arranged for Leonardo to enter Andrea's workshop. The boy was delighted with this decision.

Vasari does not say how old Leonardo was, but his use of the word 'boy' (*fanciullo*) shows his picturing of the scene. The matter is 'arranged' between the father and the master – this would include a financial arrangement – and the boy is informed of their 'decision'. The conventional age to begin apprenticeship was around thirteen or fourteen: in Leonardo's case this would mean he entered Verrocchio's studio in about 1466. This is only a vague guideline: many started younger, and some older – Fra Bartolomeo seems to have been apprenticed at the age of ten, Mantegna and Caravaggio at eleven, Michelangelo and Francesco Botticini at thirteen, Benvenuto Cellini at fifteen.[1]

We know something, at least, of Ser Piero's circumstances at this time: he was fast approaching forty, his notarial career was flourishing, but it was also a time of change. His wife, Albiera, having finally conceived after nearly twelve years of childless marriage, died in childbirth. She was buried in June 1464, aged about twenty-eight.[2] This was no doubt a personal loss for Leonardo too: many years later he was still in touch with Albiera's brother,

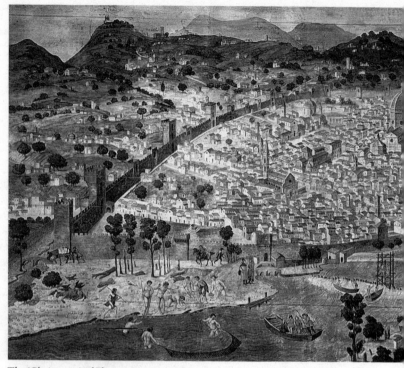

The 'Chain map' of Florence, c. 1470–72.

Alessandro Amadori. The following year Ser Piero married again: another notarial match, no doubt advantageous. His bride was Francesca, the daughter of Ser Giuliano Lanfredini; she was fifteen years old. They set up home in a house on Via delle Prestanze, at the northern corner of the Palazzo della Signoria: a prestigious address. The house (no longer extant) belonged to the powerful merchants' guild, the Arte dei Mercanti; it was sub-let to Ser Piero for the sum of 24 florins a year.[3]

The death of Leonardo's grandfather, the aged patriarch of his Vinci childhood, may also have been a precipitating factor in his move to Florence. Antonio was certainly dead by 1465, when Ser Piero refers to him as '*olim Antonius*', 'the late Antonio'.[4] Ser Piero was now the head of the family. It was time to discharge some responsibilities concerning the future of his son – his only child, indeed, as the months pass and his new wife proves as unproductive as her predecessor in the marriage bed.

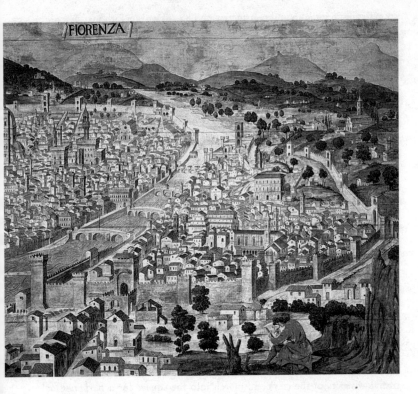

FIORENZA

Thus family circumstances tend to confirm a speculative date of *c.* 1466 for the beginning of Leonardo's apprenticeship. His childhood – that landscape of memory and loss to which so much of his later work seems to refer – is over. He moves from it into the adult, urban, competitive world of his father: the world of guilds and contracts and deadlines, into which he would never quite fit.

Florence in the mid-1460s was a city of some 50,000 people. The punctilious Benedetto Dei – diplomat, traveller and later an acquaintance of Leonardo's – reels off the following statistics. The city walls stretch for 7 miles and are fortified with 80 watch-towers. Within the walls there are 108 churches, 50 piazzas, 33 banks, and 23 large *palazzi* or mansions 'where live the lords, officials, chancellors, stewards, suppliers, notaries, functionaries, and their families'. There are 270 woolworkers' shops, and 84 woodworkers' studios specializing in intaglio and marquetry, and 83 silkworkers' shops.[5] We are in a pre-eminent city of craftsmanship, a city with more woodcarvers than butchers. Also a city of fashion, a centre of the garment industry: weavers, dyers, tanners, furriers – and clothes shops galore to tempt a teenager keen to slough off the dowdier mien of the countryside.

The walls and watch-towers have mostly gone, but the central landmarks of Leonardo's Florence are all still there – the cathedral or Duomo of Santa Maria del Fiore, with its stupendous brick cupola by Brunelleschi; Giotto's slender, elegant bell-tower next to it; the Baptistery with Ghiberti's bronze-relief doors; the tall-towered Palazzo della Signoria (not yet called the Palazzo Vecchio); the Bargello or Palazzo del Podestà; the guildhall and grain-store of Orsanmichele; and the Ponte Vecchio, the oldest of the four stone bridges spanning the Arno river. All these can be seen in the panoramic 'Chain map' of c. 1470–72, with its vignette of a young draughtsman in the corner, sketching the view from a hill to the south, and looking curiously like how one imagines the young Leonardo.[6] There are a few differences in today's view. The bell-tower beside Santa Croce is no longer there – it was destroyed by lightning in 1529 – nor is the teeming, odoriferous city market, the Mercato Vecchio, which was demolished in the late nineteenth century. The Piazza della Signoria, the political hub of the city, was even larger than it is today: in theory it could accommodate the entire adult male population of the city, for in times of crisis the bell of the Signoria would toll – it was known from its low booming tone as La Vacca (The Cow) – and citizens would assemble under the banners of their *gonfaloni* (the sixteen adminis-trative districts of the city) and march into the square for a *parlamento*. When Charles VIII of France briefly occupied the city in 1494 he threatened to 'sound the trumpets' as a sign for his soldiers to sack the city: he received the famous Florentine retort – 'And we will ring our bells.'[7]

Florence was a beautiful city, but not a gay or extravagant one. The mercantile virtues of thrift, industry and public-mindedness were constantly pronounced, if not always pursued. These were also deemed to be republican virtues, for Florence was proud of its independence of despotic dukes and kings. Around the base of Donatello's statue of *Judith and Holofernes*, then in the courtyard of the Palazzo Medici, were carved the words '*Regna cadunt luxu surgunt virtutibus urbes*' – 'Kingdoms fall through luxury, cities rise through virtues.'[8] A certain opulence was a sign of these 'virtues', and the great art-works of the Florentine Renaissance convey messages of prestige and spending-power as much as of truth and beauty; but the line between civic pride and decadent lavishness was a fine one. Greed, said the acerbic wit Poggio Bracciolini, is 'the emotion which makes civilization possible'. The rich merchant who commissioned a religious work for a church, often with his own image inserted into the picture, was in part atoning to God for the size of his profit-margins. 'The faith of my Florentines is like wax,' said the preacher Savonarola: 'a little heat is enough to melt it.'[9]

Florence in Quattrocento paintings has a sombre, muted look. It was a city built of sandstone: the honey-brown *pietra forte*, the softer grey *pietra serena*. There was little of the coloured plaster which we now think of as typically Italian, and less of the multicoloured marble on the exterior of the churches. (The Duomo's marble façade was not completed until 1887.) The town-houses were built of large rectangular blocks of stone, with that characteristic roughened or 'rusticated' surface which gives the façade of a large *palazzo* the look of a squared-off cliff. There was a building-boom. According to Benedetto Dei, thirty new *palazzi* had sprung up in the last twenty years (he was writing in about 1470). Each of the prominent families had its grand *palazzo* – the Rucellai, the Tornabuoni, the Spini, the Pazzi, the Benci: some of these families have a part to play in Leonardo's story – but none was grander than the Palazzo Medici on Via Larga, begun in the late 1450s to a design by Michelozzo Michelozzi. There were Donatello statues in the courtyard; in the master bedroom hung Uccello's *Battle of San Romano*; in the chapel a glittering fresco by Benozzo Gozzoli depicted members of the family in the procession of the Magi. Here also was the great library created by Cosimo de' Medici. These *palazzi* were company headquarters as much as private homes: they had chamberlains and counting-houses. They were also something like clan headquarters: they signified that a certain part of town was the patch of a certain great family.

This building-boom was seen as a sign of civic health and was actively encouraged by the authorities. A law would soon be passed offering a forty-year exemption from local taxes to anyone building a new *palazzo*. The diarist Luca Landucci watched the construction of the Strozzi palace from the doorway of his apothecary shop opposite. He grumbled, 'The streets round about were full of mules and donkeys carrying away the rubbish and bringing gravel, which made it difficult for people to pass. All the dust and the crowds of onlookers were most inconvenient for us shopkeepers.' None the less, he watched and recorded as the building took shape: the digging of the foundations, the pouring in of chalk and gravel, the first cornices, the laying of the rough projecting stones called *bozzi* above them. People threw medals and coins into the trenches for good luck. Another small trader, Tribaldo de' Rossi, recalls visiting the site with his four-year-old son, Guarnieri: 'I held Guarnieri up in my arms, so he could look down into the foundations. He had a little bunch of Damascus roses with him, and I made him throw them in. I said: You will remember this, won't you? And he replied: Yes.'[10]

For many, these new *palazzi* seemed to represent a new and heartless monumentality – they were the mansion-blocks and high-rises of the day, sweeping away the more crowded, intimate feel of medieval Florence. More than twenty houses were demolished to make way for the Palazzo Medici, just as Ser Piero's house on Via delle Prestanze, probably Leonardo's first home in the city, would later be demolished to make way for the grandiose Palazzo Gondi. The *palazzi* were the visible face of Florentine political and social power. This was a world which Ser Piero touched, as a provider of professional services to the Medici and others. There are doors through which he passes, but for his adolescent son – illegitimate, provincial, sketchily educated – those massive rusticated walls are a gesture of exclusion. For all its meritocratic propaganda, the city had its inner sanctums of power and influence. 'In Florence', says a character in Machiavelli's play *The Mandrake*, 'if you don't have power even the dogs won't bark in your face.'[11]

In the 1460s, power meant the Medici family and its huge network of allies and cronies. When Cosimo de' Medici died in 1464, an official decree of the Signoria accorded him the title 'Pater Patriae' – a suitably vague term which recognized the family as a kind of presidential dynasty without actually stating it. The Medici were the *de facto* rulers of Florence: they governed by stacking the city's executive offices with supporters, and by sheer supremacy of wealth from their banking and business interests.[12] Cosimo's son Piero (known as Il Gottoso – 'the Gouty') succeeded him: already nearing fifty, bookish and unhealthy, he had neither the political skills nor the popular touch of his father. His plan to call in massive sums lent by the Medici bank caused alarm. Factions arose, topographically described as the Poggio and the Piano: the Hill and the Plain. The anti-Medici faction, centred on the rich and irascible Luca Pitti, were *del poggio*, referring to the high ground south of the Arno where the Palazzo Pitti was built; the Medici loyalists were *del piano*. After an attempted coup in 1466, the chief agitators of the Poggio were exiled; they enlisted military support from Venice, always ready to cause Florence trouble, and in July 1467 there was a clash of troops near Imola. These emergencies are the backdrop of Leonardo's first years in the city. Piero's charismatic son, Lorenzo, was waiting in the wings, and would take power, at the age of twenty, in 1469.

Amid these vicissitudes it was canny of Ser Piero da Vinci to specialize in providing notarial services to the city's religious foundations, which were less vulnerable to the winds of political change. He had connections with various monastic orders, among them the Servites of Santissima Annunziata and the Augustinians of San Donato, both of which would later commission works from his son.[13]

It is conventional to depict Leonardo's arrival in Florence as a moment of wide-eyed revelation – the young country bumpkin dazzled by the energy and splendour of the great city – but it is possible that he had visited Florence before he went to live and work there. Nor do we know (as is often assumed) that Leonardo immediately entered Verrocchio's studio on his arrival in Florence. It has been suggested that the mathematics teacher mentioned by Vasari – he whom Leonardo bamboozled with questions – may have been a Florentine tutor hired by Ser Piero to train up his son as a notarial assistant.[14] In theory Leonardo's illegitimacy barred him from entering the profession, but there was no reason why he shouldn't make himself useful in the office for a while. Leonardo's early handwriting, with its rather effortful flourishes and curlicues, has been thought of as 'notarial'.

Ser Piero's office was a few minutes' walk from his home. It was a former draper's shop, and was furnished – as the rental agreement brightly explained – with 'a counter suitable for the practice of notary'. It is described as being 'opposite the door of the Palagio del Podestà', in other words the Bargello.[15] It was probably in the range of semi-subterranean shops, set into the old Roman walls below the church of La Badia, where today one sees Snack Bar La Badia and Fantini's gold-shop. This street, which is now part of Via del Proconsolo, was then called Via de' Librai (Booksellers' Street). Next to it was Canto de' Cartolai (Paper-Merchants' Corner). These provided the raw materials of Ser Piero's *métier* as the maker and keeper of records, the inscriber of transactions, the official noter-down. There is, perhaps, an echo of his father's trade – and of his father's mentality – in Leonardo's almost obsessive production of written material, the reams of paper which record his own multifarious transactions with the world.

We may, at any rate, imagine a period of uncongenial clerking in that little office opposite the Bargello. But if this was the course that Ser Piero had envisaged for his son, he wisely changed his mind.

→→ RENAISSANCE MEN ←←

Politics, commerce, fashion, noise, building-dust, dogs in the street – but to these perennial ingredients of big-city life must be added something less definable, for fifteenth-century Florence was also, as the guidebooks never fail to tell us, the 'cradle of the Renaissance', or anyway one of the cradles. What the Renaissance was, and when and why it happened, are not precisely definable. The schoolroom version is that it began with the Fall of Constantinople in 1453, in which case we might take a Hungarian arms-manufacturer named Urban to be the man responsible for it, his new siege-cannon being a crucial factor in the breaching of Byzantium's triple-walled defences by the armies of the Ottoman sultan Mehmet II.[16] This was certainly a decisive moment, as a stream of refugee scholars fanned up through Italy with their bundles of rescued manuscripts containing the stored-up wisdom of Greek science and philosophy: Euclid, Ptolemy, Plato, Aristotle – names already known in Italy, of course, but only partially studied. These Byzantine immigrants were still quite recent arrivals when Leonardo came to Florence. One such was the great Aristotelian scholar Joannes Argyropoulos, whose name occurs in a list written by Leonardo in the late 1470s: someone he knew, or wished to know.[17]

But this influx of Byzantine Greek scholarship only accelerated a flow of ideas which had been going on for centuries. Arabic science, much of it based on the Greek tradition, had been percolating into Europe since at least the twelfth century; the humanist revival of classical Roman culture was already in full swing. These too are part of the Rinascimento or Renaissance in its primary sense: a 'rebirth' of classical learning. The doctrine of the sudden break between the Middle Ages and the Renaissance is largely a construction by nineteenth-century commentators like Jacob Burckhardt and Jules Michelet. Their purpose, according to the Marxist historian Arnold Hauser, was 'to provide a genealogy for liberalism': in other words, the Renaissance was moulded into a model for later ideas of rationalist political enlightenment.[18] Nowadays the pendulum of interpretation has swung away from this 'new dawn' rhetoric, and the sources of the Renaissance are sought in less glamorous socio-economic factors – not the fall of Constantinople but the rise of double-entry accounting and the international bill of exchange, which created an economic climate in which ideas and art flourished.

None the less, Michelet's stirring slogan for the Renaissance agenda – '*la découverte de l'homme et de la nature*': 'the discovery of man and nature'

– expresses pretty well the mood abroad in the Florence of the 1460s, a city brimming with new ideas and forms which were often old ideas and forms re-examined in a new and modern light.

The intellectual luminaries of the Medici circle were men like the philosopher Marsilio Ficino and the scholarly poets and translators Agnolo Poliziano and Cristoforo Landino, but this refined coterie held no lasting attraction for Leonardo, though he had some interesting contacts with it. For Leonardo, the man who symbolized the new Renaissance mood more than any other was Leon Battista Alberti, whose books he later owned and whose ideas reverberate through his notebooks. Alberti is often called the 'first Renaissance man' – a loose term, but one that conveys his importance as a role-model. The same epithet is often applied to Brunelleschi, but Brunelleschi had been dead for twenty years when Leonardo arrived, whereas Alberti was still a living presence. Then in his sixties, he summed up those qualities of versatility and intellectual rigour which we now think of as Leonardian. He was an architect, author, classical scholar, art-theorist, musician, stage-designer, town-planner – the list could go on. After his death in 1472, Cristoforo Landino wondered, 'Where shall I put Alberti? In what class of learned men shall I set him? Among the natural scientists [fisici], I think. Certainly he was born to investigate the secrets of Nature.'[19] That last sentence echoes in the mind as a potential synopsis for Leonardo.

Alberti was also famed for his style and elegance: 'the avatar of grace', someone called him. The cultivated man, Alberti said, 'must apply the greatest artistry in three things: walking in the city, riding a horse, and speaking', but to these must also be added another art, 'namely that none of these seems to be done in an artful way'. He was a remarkable athlete – it was said he could jump right over a man from a standing start, and could throw a coin up inside the Duomo so that it hit the roof of the cupola[20] – and from the look of his self-portrait, in a bronze medallion of c. 1450, he was handsome and fine-featured, with a powerful Ciceronian profile. Physical beauty, stylish clothes, good manners, fine horses – these were always important to Leonardo, part of his contemporary image, despite the contradictory pull towards the rough-and-ready ways of the countryside.

As Leonardo might also have noted, Alberti was an illegitimate son. His father was a prosperous Florentine merchant forced to leave the city for political reasons; he settled in Genoa, where Alberti was born in 1404. As with Leonardo, Alberti's illegitimacy is an important paradox: it was a disadvantage of status, but it gave him a certain marginality, an exemption from family expectations and traditions, which proved in the long run beneficial. He was driven, as his biographer Anthony Grafton puts it, 'to avenge in the realm of intellect his initial defeats in the counting-house'.[21] He created a career for himself which hadn't really existed before: a kind of freelance consultant in matters architectural, scientific, artistic and philosophical. In this role he served the papal Curia and the courts at Urbino and Mantua, as well as the Medici and Rucellai in Florence. It was this kind of role that Leonardo later aspired to when he looked beyond the Florentine horizon to the Sforza of Milan.

For Burckhardt, Alberti was the shining new light of Italian humanism, but there were also in him those strata of doubt, and self-doubt, which I have already suggested are part of the Renaissance psyche. He struggled with the demons of depression; he was, says Grafton, 'a tightrope performer of self-creation'. Spring and autumn made him melancholy, he said, because all those flowers and fruits made him feel how little he had produced in his life – 'Battista,' he would tell himself, 'now it's your turn to promise some sort of fruits to the human race.' Leonardo too would have this haunting sense of non-achievement which is the downside of the expansionist Renaissance mood. If the possibilities are endless, the realization of them can only ever be partial.[22]

Another aged guru whose name occurs in Leonardo's notebooks is Paolo dal Pozzo Toscanelli, born in 1387, renowned as an astronomer, astrologer, mathematician, geographer, physician and linguist – the grand old man of Florentine science. Back in the 1420s he was a friend of Brunelleschi's, and was said by Vasari to have assisted the architect in designing the cathedral dome. He was also close to Alberti, who dedicated his witty *Intercenales* (*Dinner Pieces*) to him, 'mindful of our long friendship'. Much of Toscanelli's work is lost, but a long manuscript survives, largely autograph, in the same Florentine collection which contains the Anonimo Gaddiano's biographical sketches. Its Latin title translates as 'The immense labours and long vigils of Paolo Toscanelli concerning the measurement of comets'; it contains remarkably accurate measurements of the paths of various comets, including the appearance of Halley's Comet in 1456.[23] These labours and vigils are the currency of the new empiricism: the insistence on direct observation, the accumulation of raw data, the testing and questioning of ancient wisdom – Toscanelli is an early role-model for Leonardo as 'disciple of experience'. He is best known today as the geographer and cartographer who questioned the old Ptolemaic world-map and thereby contributed to Columbus's discovery of America. In around 1474 he wrote a letter to a Portuguese churchman, Fernão Martines, in which he demonstrated, with the support of a map, that the shortest way to Asia was to sail west across the Atlantic (or the 'Ocean Sea', as it was then called) at the latitude of Iberia. It is plausible that Columbus knew of this via his connections with the King of Portugal.

Poliziano wrote of Toscanelli, 'Paolo traverses the earth with his feet, and the starry sky with his mind, and is at once mortal and immortal'[24] – an elegant metaphorical synopsis of the aspirations of the Renaissance scientist.

Alberti and Toscanelli sum up an idea of the 'Renaissance man' as it might have been perceived, if not so called, in the Florence of the mid-1460s: men, in Landino's phrase, 'born to investigate the secrets of Nature'. How much their names impinged on the fourteen-year-old trainee painter Leonardo da Vinci we cannot say – his references to them are of course later – but they are part of the air he breathes, this wonderful cerebral oxygen of the Renaissance, and they provide a blueprint for his own multi-disciplinary career, a tradition that he follows. He would certainly have studied Alberti's *De pittura* as part of his training under Verrocchio, and have stood in admiration before the cool classical façades of Santa Maria Novella and the Palazzo Rucellai.

The painters and sculptors of Florence felt themselves to be part of the new spirit of discovery, though artistically this was a time of transition rather than high achievement. The great *maestri* who had dominated the mid-century were ageing or dead. Among the painters, Fra Angelico had died in 1455, Andrea del Castagno in 1457, and Domenico Veneziano in 1461. (The latter, for reasons implicit in this list, was not murdered by Castagno, as was colourfully rumoured by Vasari.) The pre-eminent sculptor of the day, Donatello, whose influence we have seen percolating into Vinci, died in 1466. The troublesome friar Fra Filippo Lippi had left Florence for the last time, to work on the cathedral frescos at Spoleto, and to die there in 1469. Paolo Uccello, the great practitioner of pictorial perspective, was a spent force, declaring mournfully in his tax return of 1469, 'I am old, infirm and unemployed, and my wife is ill.'[25]

The new generation of artists flourishing in the mid-1460s were brilliant professionals, though not the towering figures of yesteryear. The important studios were those of Verrocchio (who was at this stage still primarily a sculptor); the Pollaiuolo brothers, Antonio and Piero; Neri di Bicci, the pupil of Donatello; Benozzo Gozzoli, the pupil of Fra Angelico; and Cosimo Rosselli. There was also the hugely successful workshop of Luca and Andrea della Robbia, which specialized in glazed terracotta works. Up-and-coming young artists to watch were Sandro Filipepi, better known as Botticelli (born *c.* 1444), and the fresco specialist Domenico Ghirlandaio (born 1449), who becomes the great visual journalist of Florentine life. Many, if not all, of these artists would soon be personally known to Leonardo in the intimate studio world of rivalries and collaborations. Michelangelo and Raphael had not yet been born. Nor had the great chronicler of Florentine art, Giorgio Vasari.

⤜ ANDREA'S *BOTTEGA* ⤛

When we speak of Leonardo 'entering the studio' of Andrea del Verrocchio we should avoid extraneous notions of what an artist's studio was and what it looked like. The word generally used in Leonardo's day was *bottega*, which means simply a shop or a workshop. This conveys well enough the daily reality of Verrocchio's studio. It was a workshop or indeed a small factory devoted to the production of works of art. Some studios were specialist, but Verrocchio's was decidedly not. Over the years it produced paintings of various types and sizes; sculptures in marble, bronze, wood and terracotta; goldwork, silverwork and ironwork; tombstones, marriage-chests, jousting-pennants, heraldic devices, suits of armour, and theatrical sets and costumes. It was a commercial operation – Kenneth Clark has dubbed the studio 'Verrocchio & Co.' – and from Vasari onward there has been a tendency to think of Verrocchio as more a master-craftsman than a 'great artist'. 'The style of his sculpture and painting tended to be hard and crude,' opined Vasari, 'since it came from unremitting study rather than any inborn gift.'[26]

Though best known as a sculptor, Verrocchio had actually trained as a goldsmith, and was a member of the goldsmiths' guild. In this he followed Brunelleschi, Donatello, Ghiberti, Antonio del Pollaiuolo and Ghirlandaio, who all trained first as goldsmiths. One of his masters was a certain Francesco di Luca Verrocchio, from whom he took his professional name (his real name was Andrea di Cione). It was not unusual for an apprentice to adopt his master's name: to become, within the ambit of trade secrets, his 'son' – a trope of initiation. The name of Piero di Cosimo, for instance, signifies that he is the 'son' of his master, Cosimo Rosselli. In one of the earliest references to Verrocchio as an independent artist he is styled Verrocchino or 'Little Verrocchio'. He in turn became one of the foremost teachers of his generation. As well as Leonardo, his pupils and assistants included the painters Pietro Vanucci (known as Perugino) and Lorenzo di Credi, and the sculptor Agnolo di Polo, and he seems to have had good relations with other independent artists like Botticelli, Ghirlandaio,

Francesco Botticini, Biagio d'Antonio and Francesco di Simone Ferrucci, all of whom were associated with his workshop at one time or another.

Verrocchio's *bottega* was in the parish of Sant'Ambrogio, towards the eastern flank of the city walls. He was a local boy – he was born and raised here, and though he died in Venice his body was brought back to be buried, next to his father, in the parish church. He was born sometime between 1434 and 1437, and was thus about thirty when he became Leonardo's master. His father, Michele, is documented as a *fornaciaio* or kiln-worker, as Leonardo's stepfather Accattabriga had been; his elder brother, Simone, entered the church. The family home still stands, deduced from documents to be the tall house on the north-western corner of Via del Agnolo and Via de' Macci. Verrocchio's *bottega* was close by, on Via Ghibellina, close to the forbidding, windowless walls of the city's prison, Le Stinche, which stood on the present-day site of the Teatro Verdi.[27]

The studio where Leonardo began his apprenticeship was just a short walk from Ser Piero da Vinci's offices opposite the Bargello. This suggests the intimacy of the city – the physical closeness of family and work, everyone in walking and talking distance of each other – but in these crowded cities there are invisible social boundaries, and you would have crossed one as you walked out from the well-appointed city centre into the crowded, artisan neighbourhood of Sant'Ambrogio. The names of the streets give a flavour of the area – on Via della Salvia, where sage and other herbs were once sold, we get a smell of the area. A speciality of the neighbourhood was earthenware: you went to Via dei Pentolini for the small two-handled cooking-pots of that name, and to Via delle Conche for larger washing-pots. North of the church was Via della Mattonaia, or Brickworks Street, perhaps the site of Michele di Cione's business as a *fornaciaio*. Moving on east towards the walls you arrived at a pair of rather grim-looking convents for *murate* – immured nuns or anchoresses. At the Monasterio delle Murate were 150 nuns; they passed their time making silver and gold embroidery, for which Savonarola reproved them. Next to it was the convent of Santa Verdiana, named after the anchoress par excellence, St Verdiana of Castelfiorentina, a thirteenth-century *murata* who is said to have lived for thirty-four years in a walled-up cell with only two snakes for company. Beyond the city gate – the Porta alla Croce – was greenery and space: how often Leonardo must have walked there to clear his head.[28]

Andrea's studio cannot be tied to a precise building on Via Ghibellina, but we know broadly what it looked like. The typical *bottega* was a large, open space on the ground floor, opening on to the street, usually with living-quarters at the back or upstairs. Walking between Sant'Ambrogio and Santa Croce you can still see vestiges of *botteghe*. Old arched entrance-ways are visible in the brickwork, and sometimes there is a pizzeria or laundromat or car-repair shop where the interior shape has been preserved: the low, vaulted ceiling; the workspace stretching back the whole width of the building to a glimpse of the yard out back. From a doorway on Via delle Casine comes the sound of hammering, the flare of a welding-torch. Thus Leonardo's first experiences of artistic life in *c.* 1466: physical, dusty, noisy; the penetrating smells of varnishes and solvents; more like a kind of garage than a studio.

At this time Andrea del Verrocchio was in the first flush of success. In 1467, a busy year, he was completing work on Cosimo de' Medici's tomb in the Medici church of San Lorenzo, and beginning work on one of his sculptural masterpieces, the large bronze group of *Christ and St Thomas* for one of the exterior niches of Orsanmichele. Both these were plum commissions. The sculpture was commissioned by the powerful Tribunale della Mercanzia, the law-court for cases involving guildsmen and traders – an organization with which his 'good friend' Ser Piero da Vinci had connections. At the convent of San Marco, he was also involved in the casting and mounting of an enormous bronze bell, later known as La Piagnona after the followers of Savonarola, the *piagnoni* or weepers.

Another famous Verrocchio bronze has recently been dated back to this period, and is of particular interest because it is possible that Leonardo was the model for it. This is Verrocchio's *David*. It is just over 4 feet tall, and shows David as a wiry, curly-haired youth with the profusely bearded head of Goliath at his feet. Traces remain of what was probably extensive gilding on the figure's boots, armour and hair. The sculpture is now in the Bargello, just a few hundred yards from where it was created. It is sometimes dated to the mid-1470s, because in 1476 it was sold by Lorenzo de' Medici to the Signoria, but the Verrocchio expert Andrew Butterfield has shown that on stylistic grounds it is much earlier. He dates it to *c.* 1466: it was perhaps a commission by Lorenzo's father, Piero, for the garden of the Medici villa at Careggi.[29] If this date is right, the statue belongs to Leonardo's earliest days at the *bottega*. What could be more natural than that this handsome new assistant should be the model for the boy-warrior David? That Leonardo was a beautiful youth is stated by all the early biographers. A visual compari-son of the David with the probable self-portrait in the *Adoration, c.* 1481, adds some conviction to this. There is no early documentation to support the idea, but it is persuasively possible that Verrocchio's graceful, skinny, wavy-haired *ragazzo* is the fourteen-year-old Leonardo.

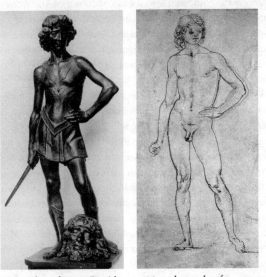

Verrocchio's bronze David, c. 1466, *and a study of a young man in the pose of David from the Ferrucci sketchbook.*

If it is, we have another likeness of him (though a second-hand one) in a pen-and-ink drawing of a naked young man in the exact pose of Verrocchio's *David*. This drawing is now in the Louvre. It was formerly part of a sketchbook, now dispersed, belonging to the Florentine sculptor Francesco di Simone Ferrucci. On another page of the sketchbook Ferrucci notes that Lorenzo di Credi – another pupil of Verrocchio's – has furnished him with some of Verrocchio's 'models' (clay figures, drawings, templates) to copy. On yet another page, among some sketches of an angel, is a line of right-to-left handwriting that looks remarkably like Leonardo's. The precise date of the sketchbook is uncertain: the mention of Credi cannot be much earlier than the late 1470s, and some of the pages have written material dated 1487–8.[30] The drawing is unlikely to be a direct study of the young model who stood for David, but is plausibly a later copy by Ferrucci of one of Verrocchio's own preparatory sketches for the sculpture. Thus filtered and approximated, and with some guesswork thrown in, it shows us the young Leonardo da Vinci standing naked in the studio on Via Ghibellina.

Nothing expresses more pungently, or more poignantly, the reality of the Florentine artist's studio than the inventory of Verrocchio's possessions left at his *bottega* after his death in 1488. This is not the *bottega* on Via Ghibellina – he had moved to a more central location near the Duomo sometime before 1480 – but the address does not really matter. I transcribe the list exactly, with its modulations intact. There was a feather bed, a white bed-cover, a mattress, a pair of sheets, a painted bed-frame, a dining-table, a bench for the table, a well-bucket, a chest to keep grain in, a jar of oil, three casks containing 14 barrels of wine, a large cask of vinegar wine (*agresto*), a model of the cupola (of the cathedral), a fine lute, a Bible in the vernacular, a copy of the *Cento novelle*, a printed *Moscino*, Petrarch's *Trionfi*, the *Pistole* of Ovid, a picture of the head of Andrea, a terracotta of a baby, a large painting, a sphere, two old chests, a figure of St John, two pairs of bellows worth 15 florins, two pairs of small bellows, two heads in half-relief, an anvil, a sculpture of Our Lady, a head in profile, two porphyry pestles, a pair of pincers, a funeral monument for the Cardinal of Pistoia, a large sculpted figure, three rough-cast putti and their clay models, various hammers of various sizes, a kiln with various iron tools, a quantity of firewood of pine and other sorts, and five moulds for making cannon-balls both large and small.[31]

Amid the domestic lumber and artistic equipment, a couple of items catch the eye. The 'fine lute' confirms Vasari's statement that Verrocchio was a musician; it is possible that Leonardo's musical skills developed under Verrocchio's aegis. The books also give us a sense of the mental texture of the *bottega*. Three of them are well-known works of a cultivated but popular sort: leisure reading. There is the *Cento novelle*, a collection of stories by the fourteenth-century Florentine novelist Franco Sacchetti, closely modelled on Boccaccio. There is Petrarch's *Trionfi* (*Triumphs*): moralistic poems in *terzine*. And there is an edition of the *Pistole*, or *Epistles*, of Ovid, also known as the *Eroides*, probably in the Italian translation by Luca Pulci published in Florence in 1481. Leonardo himself later owned a copy of this, as well as a copy of Ovid's *Metamorphoses*.[32] The other book mentioned among Verrocchio's effects – the 'printed *Moscino*' – may be Leon Battista Alberti's *Mosca* (*The Fly*), a humorous work based on Lucian's *Laus muscae* (*In Praise of the Fly*).

The mention of a portrait or self-portrait ('a picture of the head of Andrea') in the inventory is tantalizing. It is unlikely to be the half-length oil-portrait in the Uffizi, showing a dark, thin-lipped man with a rather dour expression. This is often said to be a portrait of Verrocchio, but it more probably depicts Verrocchio's sometime pupil Perugino – its similarity to the signed self-portrait of Perugino in the Collegio di Cambio in Perugia is striking.[33] There is a woodcut portrait of Verrocchio in Vasari's *Lives*, apparently showing him in middle age. Some of these woodcuts, produced en masse in the late 1560s, are pure guesswork as portraits, but in this case the image leads us to another. The face has strong similarities to a powerful pen-and-ink portrait in the Uffizi which is certainly of the Verrocchio school (see page 86). This may well be a portrait of Verrocchio: it would show him around the age of forty. It is not a handsome face – broad, double-chinned, faintly epicene – but the intensity of the gaze is startling. This drawing is not itself the item listed in the inventory (which is described as a *quadro*, and was therefore a painted portrait), but it may be connected with it. It is as near as we get to a likeness of Leonardo's teacher.

→→ LEARNING THE TRADE ←←

Many wish to learn how to draw, and enjoy drawing, but do not have a true aptitude for it. This is shown by their lack of perseverance, like boys who draw everything in a hurry, never finishing or shadowing ...   Paris MS G, fol. 25r

While serving as a junior worker or dogsbody in the studio, and perhaps as a model, Leonardo was also a pupil or *discepolo*, receiving specific instruction from Maestro Andrea. A contract drawn up in 1467 gives us an idea of what the apprentice expected to be taught. In it the Paduan painter Francesco Squarcione undertakes to teach his pupil 'the principle of a plane, with lines drawn according to my method', and how to 'put figures on the said plane' and 'place objects there, as namely a chair or a bench or a house', and how to represent a man's head in foreshortening in isometric rendering', and the 'system of a naked body'.[34] Thus broadly the pupil would learn the techniques of perspective and of figure-drawing. Squarcione also promises to 'keep him with paper in his hand' and to 'provide him with models'. These 'models' would be Squarcione's own drawings, as well as real objects and people. The pupil spent much time copying from the master's 'model book'.

Paper was expensive, and pupils also practised with a coated wood panel and a metalpoint stylus. In his famous handbook, the *Libro dell'arte*, Cennino Cennini recommends 'a little boxwood panel, nine inches square'. This should be smoothed down 'with cuttle such as goldsmiths use', and then coated with bone-ash moistened with saliva: for the bone-ash use chicken bones, he advises, 'just as you find them under the dining-table'.[35] Leonardo's earliest drawings on paper show him habitually using a leadpoint or silverpoint stylus before filling the lines in with pen and ink.

Draughtsmanship – *disegno* – was the foundation of this artistic education. This is stressed by Vasari, who specifies that Ser Piero arranged
for Leonardo to 'study drawing' with Verrocchio, and it was stressed by
Leonardo himself when he became a *maestro* with pupils of his own.
According to Paolo Giovio, 'Leonardo would not permit youngsters under
the age of twenty to touch brushes and colours, and would only let them
practise with a lead stylus, diligently following the best examples of the
ancients, and imitating the force of nature and the lineaments of the body
with the simplest lines.'[36] That this reflects the practice in Verrocchio's busy
commercial studio is unlikely – Leonardo was certainly painting before he
was twenty – but it echoes the strict grounding in metalpoint draughtsmanship that he learned from Verrocchio. He had as good a master as he
could get: Verrocchio was probably the finest draughtsman of his generation
in Florence. Vasari's famous collection included some of Verrocchio's
works, 'done with the greatest patience and judgement', among them 'several
female heads with lovely expressions and hair, which Leonardo was always
imitating for their beauty'. Various examples of these survive. Vasari's
'always' is not merely rhetorical: a black-chalk portrait by Verrocchio in
the British Museum is closely echoed in Leonardo's sketches for *Leda*, done
more than thirty years later.[37]

Vasari also owned some Leonardo drawings, including early studies of
drapery, done on linen, which he describes as among Leonardo's exercises
as a studio-pupil: 'He made clay models, draping the figures with rags
dipped in plaster, and drew them painstakingly on fine Rheims cloth or
prepared linen. These drawings were done in black and white, with the
point of the brush, and the results were marvellous, as one can see from the
examples I have in my book of drawings.' Several of these early drapery
studies survive. Some can be related to drapery in the Uffizi *Annunciation*,
which is probably Leonardo's earliest complete painting (*c.* 1470–72).[38] A
drawing at Christ Church College, Oxford, is a study for the angel's sleeve
in the *Annunciation*; it is a fragment from a larger folio which probably
once contained a sketch of a head (perhaps the angel's head), some traces
of long curly hair being visible at the right margin. The sleeve can also be
compared to that of the San Gennaro angel, a small terracotta statue recently
attributed to Leonardo (plate 8).

Leonardo's brilliance in this respect prefigured the Mannerists, who make
so much of drapery. 'He took it beyond mere academic exercise,' says
Alessandro Vezzosi: he 'brought out all its latent abstraction and force'.[39]
Enlargements of these drapery studies look like versions of the rocks and
mountains of his later landscapes. The subject continued to exercise him:

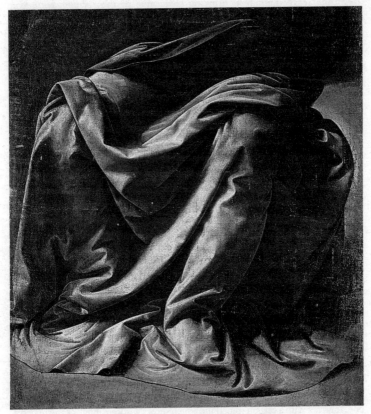

One of Leonardo's drapery studies on linen.

there is a chapter in the *Trattato della pittura* entitled 'On Dresses, Draperies and Folds'. A drapery 'must fit the body and not appear like an empty bundle of clothes' – thus 'inhabited drapery'. And he continued to refine the visual distinctions:

Thin cloths, thick cloths, new and old cloths; with pleats broken up and with pleats entire; soft ruffles, shaded and less shaded, reflected and not reflected, expeditious and confused, according to their placing and their colours; garments according to rank, long and short, flying and stiff according to the movements, such as fit the figure and such as flutter upward or downward.[40]

79

Another early Leonardo drawing suggestive of the *Annunciation* is a study of a lily (Plate 3). It is crisply done in black chalk gone over with pen and ink, and given a sepia wash heightened here and there with white. It resembles the lily in the *Annunciation*, but is not an actual study for it as it slants the other way. It looks closer to the lily in Verrocchio's *Madonna and Child with Two Angels* (National Gallery, London), but the painting has been cropped and only part of the flower is visible. The drawing has some faint lines in the lower third of the paper, hard to see in reproduction: these seem to be geometric studies of perspective, reinforcing the context of apprenticeship in which the drawing was done.

Also part of the apprentice's curriculum was modelling in clay and terracotta. Vasari says that 'in his youth' Leonardo 'made in clay several heads of laughing women, of which plaster casts are still being made, as well as some children's heads executed as if by a mature artist'. No trace remains of any 'laughing women', and, though there are plenty of putti in Verrocchio's monumental sculptures, there is nothing to suggest that any are by Leonardo.

Leonardo's early career as a sculptor is mysterious. There is a beautiful terracotta head, a *Cristo giovanotto* or *Youthful Christ* (see page 122), which is thought to be his work, though opinions differ about whether it is an early work or from the mid-1490s (it has affinities with some studies for the disciples of the *Last Supper*). It may be the 'little head' later owned by Giovanni Paolo Lomazzo:

I have also a little terracotta head of Christ when he was a boy [*fanciullo*], sculpted by Leonardo Vinci's own hand, in which one sees the simplicity and purity of the boy, together with a certain something which shows wisdom, intellect and majesty. He has an air which may be the tenderness of youth but which seems also old and wise.[41]

Lomazzo has interesting things to say about Leonardo's activities as a sculptor because he had seen a manuscript, now lost, in which Leonardo speaks of sculpture as the 'sister of painting', and says, 'I have delighted in her, and I delight in her still,' instancing as 'witness' of this his various efforts as a sculptor – 'horses, and legs, and heads, and also human [i.e. lifelike] heads of Our Lady, and youthful Christs both full length and in part, and numerous heads of old men'.[42] This passage (assuming Lomazzo is reporting the lost manuscript faithfully) makes one look in turn at the famous list in the Codex Atlanticus, dated *c.* 1482, in which Leonardo catalogues various works he had completed before his departure to Milan.

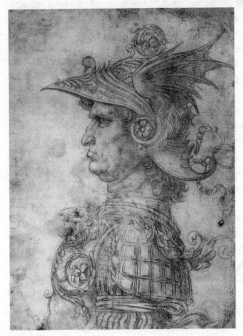

Metalpoint drawing of a warrior in profile, probably based on a bas-relief by Verrocchio.

Some of these – 'many heads of old men', 'many full-figure nudes', 'many legs, feet, and gestures [*attitudini*]' – may be sculptures or clay models rather than drawings.[43]

He would also have learned the techniques of moulding and carving in relief (*rilievo*). There is a pair of terracotta angels in bas-relief in the Louvre which are certainly products of the Verrocchio workshop, and are sometimes attributed to Leonardo because of their similarity to the painted angel in the *Baptism of Christ*. Vasari mentions a bas-relief in bronze by Verrocchio showing the bellicose Persian emperor Darius; it is now lost, but is almost certainly recorded in Leonardo's expressive metalpoint portrait of a warrior in profile, now in the British Museum.[44]

From life-drawing and perspective studies and clay-modelling, the pupil moves finally to the profession of painting. It is not certain when Verrocchio himself began painting, nor is it known who trained him. The first documentation of him as a painter is from 1468, when he submitted designs for a series of paintings of the Seven Virtues for the Palazzo della Mercanzia, though he was probably active before that.[45] The studio's chief output was small to medium-size Madonna and Child paintings. There are many of these in the style now called Verrocchiesco; their chief antecedent is the sweet and lustrous Madonnas of Fra Filippo Lippi, and through him the Netherlandish influence. They tend towards prettiness, but have also a robust sense of volume and movement derived from Verrocchio's work as a sculptor. On stylistic grounds the small half-length *Madonna and Child* in Berlin is probably one of the earliest, *c.* 1468. Other examples are the *Ruskin Madonna* in Edinburgh; the *Madonna and Child with Two Angels* in the National Gallery, London; the *Madonna of the Sea* in the Accademia, Florence; the *Dreyfus Madonna* in Washington, DC; and the *Madonna of the Carnation* in Munich. Most of these are dated to the early to mid-1470s. They are all panel paintings, done on wood; canvas was not yet in use as a support, and there is no evidence that Verrocchio & Co. ever undertook fresco work, which was a speciality of the Ghirlandaio shop.

But long before Leonardo put brush to panel he would have toiled away at the basic mechanics of painting. He must learn the suitability of various different woods for the panel – poplar, walnut, pear, service-tree. Of these, poplar was the staple of the studios – especially the white poplar known as *gattice*, a cheap, serviceable wood much used by carpenters and joiners. He must learn to prepare the different types of gesso, the gypsum-based white distemper which was coated on to the panel, forming the 'ground' on to which the paint was applied: the final layers of silky *gesso sottile* arrived at a smooth, brilliant-white surface with low absorbency. Over the years Leonardo would experiment with ever more sophisticated custom-made gessoes:

Coat it [the panel] with mastic and white turpentine of the second distillation . . . then give it two or three coats of *aqua vitae* in which you have dissolved arsenic, or some other corrosive sublimate. Then apply boiled linseed oil in such a way that it penetrates every part, and before it cools rub it well with a cloth to dry it. Over this apply a liquid white varnish with a stick, then wash with urine.[46]

Thus prepared the panel was ready for the next step of the process: the transfer of preparatory drawings on to the virgin white surface. A full-scale drawing for the whole composition was often used: the 'cartoon', from the Italian *cartone*, a large sheet of paper. The outlines of the drawing were 'pricked' with little holes; one sees these perforations on many drawings. The cartoon was fixed flat against the panel and dusted with finely powdered charcoal or pumice. This is the process known as 'pouncing' (in Italian *spolveratura*); 'pounce' is a corruption of 'pumice'. The dust passes through the perforations of the drawing and leaves a tracing on the panel, which is now ready for painting.

The tradition within which Leonardo first worked was that of tempera painting, though oil painting was soon to become the dominant new medium. A tempera is any kind of binding agent which will 'temper' powdered colours and make them workable, but in the Quattrocento the term invariably refers to egg tempera: colours mixed with fresh egg-yolk (or, for manuscript illumination, egg-white) and thinned with water. Egg tempera dries almost instantly, though several tones lighter than when wet, and is tough and long-lasting. The lustrous fresco cycles of Florence – Masaccio's in the Carmine, Gozzoli's in the Palazzo Medici, Ghirlandaio's in Santa Maria Novella – were all painted *a fresco* (on fresh wet plaster) with tempera. To the sounds and smells of the *bottega* we must add those of the chickens that produced the eggs required for the pictorial output of a busy studio.

Oil painting was already established – a technique imported from the Netherlands – but was still mainly used as a finish, modifying the opaque tempera layer with a rich transparent film or glaze. It was a decorative adjunct to tempera work.[47] Leonardo is on a technical cusp: he begins within the tempera tradition, but is soon enthused by the richness of oils, of which he became a master. He recognized the subtleties of modelling and shading which oils offered. The quick drying of tempera meant that you had to depict shadow by lines ('hatching' and 'cross-hatching'), but with oils there was a new dimension of layered brushwork with which to achieve depth of tone and optical complexity – that 'smoky' look, or *sfumato*, which is one of his trademarks. And, crucial for Leonardo's perfectionist style, there was no need to hurry.

The *discepolo* must also be versed in the arcana of colours – the materials which yielded them, the manner of preparing them, the effects of blending them. Some colours were from local earths (ochres, umbers, sienas), some were from plants (vegetable black), and some were products of noxious but fairly simple chemistry (lead white, lead–tin yellow). These provided a working basis for the painter's palette. A traditional mix for flesh tones was yellow ochre, vegetable black and lead white; Cennino calls this *verdaccio*.

But for the brilliant hues sought by the painter and his customers more exotic materials were needed. The pre-eminent pigment of early Italian painting was the vivid poetic blue called *oltremare*, or ultramarine, made by grinding lapis lazuli ('stone of azure': the Latin *lazulus* derives from the Persian *lazhward*). This 'stone' is a naturally occurring silicate rich in sulphur. The word 'ultramarine' sounds as if it refers to a blue more intense than sea-blue, but simply means that it came from 'beyond the seas'. It was imported stuff, and fearfully expensive, and so became a byword for the value, and hence prestige, of a painting. The contract for Ghirlandaio's *Adoration of the Magi* (1485) stipulates that 'the blue must be ultramarine of the value of about 4 florins an ounce' – though this sort of approach was dying out and cheaper substitutes like Prussian blue and azurite were becoming common.[48]

Other important mineral-based pigments were green malachite, widely used for landscape and foliage,[49] and the brilliant red *vermiglio*, or vermilion, obtained from grinding cinnabar (red mercuric sulphide). The word comes from the Latin *vermiculus*, a little worm, because the red of cinnabar was compared to the red dye extracted from an insect, the kermes. Another insect was the source of 'lac' or 'lake', which was added to powdered pigments to produce a sheeny glaze.

Recipes for producing particular colour-effects fill the popular manuals like Cennino's *Libro dell'arte* and Ghiberti's *Commentarii*, and there are many in Leonardo's manuscripts. In the Codex Atlanticus, written with the ornamental flourishes associated with Leonardo's earlier writing, we find:

Take green [i.e. malachite] and mix it with bitumen, and this will make the shadows darker. And for lighter shades mix green with yellow ochre, and for even lighter green with yellow, and for the highlights pure yellow. Then take green and turmeric together and glaze everything with it . . . To make a beautiful red take cinnabar or red chalk or burnt ochre for the dark shadows, and for the lighter ones red chalk and vermilion, and for the highlights pure vermilion, and then glaze with fine lake.[50]

These raw materials explain why the painter was a member of the Arte dei Medici, Speziali e Mercai, the Guild of Physicians, Apothecaries and Mercers. The apothecary dealt in exotic stuffs of all sorts: you went to him for spices, drugs, herbs, potions and pharmaceuticals. Old-fashioned Italian pharmacies still refer to themselves as *spezierie*, spice-shops. From these pungent premises the painter purchased his visual spices. Also specializing in the supply of pigments in Florence were the Ingesuati friars of San Giusto alle Mura. Filippo Lippi, Botticelli, Ghirlandaio and Michelangelo are documented as customers, and so is Leonardo, who in the summer of 1481 paid 4 lire for 'one ounce of *azzuro* [azurite] bought from the Ingesuati'.[51]

All this was required technical knowledge for the prentice painter, but there were other, less palpable, forms of knowledge he must learn. As well as a workshop or art factory, the *bottega* was a haunt of artists, a forum of discussion and gossip, a hotbed of new techniques and ideas. This was the university of the unlettered Leonardo.

A painter closely associated with the emergence of the Verrocchio style is Sandro Botticelli. He was an independent painter, but his earliest works are Madonna and Child panels much in the Verrocchio mould – or perhaps Verrocchio's are in the Botticelli mould: we have no knowledge of Verrocchio's training as a painter, and he was probably ready to learn from the younger artist, who had been trained by the great Filippo Lippi, and who became, after Lippi's death in 1469, the master of his illegitimate son Filippino. Botticelli must be an important influence on Leonardo's fledging as a painter in the late 1460s and early 1470s – an influence one could argue from the angel of the *Annunciation*, which has something of the stylized balletic look one associates with Botticelli. He was seven or eight years older than Leonardo. He was a rather highly strung man, and became a devotee of Savonarola, though Vasari also paints him as a habitual practical joker.

Leonardo left few comments on his artistic contemporaries, but he does comment on Botticelli. The tone is surprisingly critical. He speaks dismissively of Botticelli's 'dull landscapes', and he is doubtless thinking of Botticelli's unrealistic, mythological forests when he says, 'Do not, as many do, paint all kinds of trees, even when equally distant, the same kind of green.' Another tilt is found in Leonardo's humorous complaint about lack of 'decorum' in an Annunciation: 'I saw some days ago a picture of an angel making the Annunciation, who seemed to be chasing Our Lady out of the room, with movements which displayed the kind of offensiveness one might show to a hated enemy, and Our Lady seemed as if she was going to throw herself in despair out of the window.' This probably refers to the Annunciation that Botticelli painted for the Guardi family chapel in about 1490, where the angel could be interpreted as crouching aggressively, though the interpretation is mischievous. A similar wilful criticism is found in a note about perspective which begins, 'Sandro! You do not say why these second things seem lower than the third.' This refers to Botticelli's *Mystic Nativity* of 1500, where hierarchical ranks of angels are placed in defiance of the laws of perspective.[52] All this carping seems uncharacteristic. It may have a psychological element: a desire to outshine an early influence, to define himself by his difference. Imitation for Leonardo was a form of weakness.

Another painter in the purlieus of the *bottega* was Pietro Vanucci, known as Il Perugino – 'the Perugian'. Born near Perugia in the late 1440s, he had studied under an Umbrian master – probably Piero della Francesca – before coming to Florence, so he was not a junior apprentice like Leonardo. He is

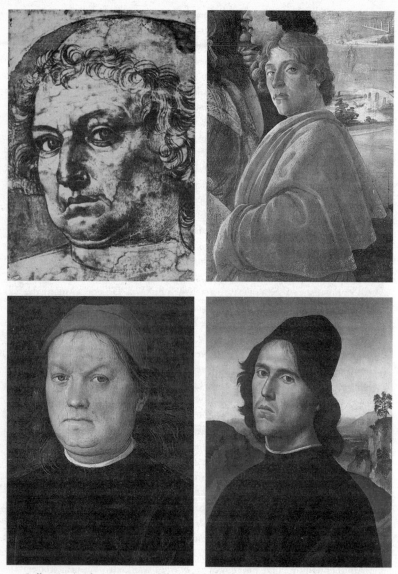

Colleagues in Florence. Upper left: probable portrait of Andrea del Verrocchio by one of his pupils. Upper right: Sandro Botticelli, probable self-portrait from his Adoration of the Magi, *c. 1478. Lower left: Pietro Perugino, self-portrait, 1500. Lower right: Lorenzo di Credi, self-portrait, 1488*

accorded the prefix 'Mag' (i.e. *magister* or *maestro*) in a Florentine document of 1472. Like Leonardo, he swiftly made the transition to oil painting. Perugino's name is coupled with Leonardo's in a rhyming chronicle by Giovanni de Santis, the father of the painter Rafaello, or Raphael:

> *Due giovin par d'etade e par d'amori*
> *Leonardo da Vinci e 'l Perugino,*
> *Pier della Pieve, ch'e un divin pittor ...*

This describes Leonardo and Perugino as 'two young men, equal in age and equal in love', though of the two it is Perugino who is singled out as the 'divine painter'.[53]

The other well-known pupil of Verrocchio was a handsome young goldsmith's son, Lorenzo di Credi. Born in about 1457, he was younger than Leonardo and junior at the studio. The earliest of his accepted works, the *Madonna and Child with St John the Baptist and St Donatus* in Pistoia, was begun in about 1476. One of the predellas of this altarpiece was a small *Annunciation* which is obviously based on Leonardo's painting of the subject, and was possibly a collaboration between them.[54] In 1480 Credi's widowed mother stated in her tax return that Lorenzo earned a wage of 12 florins a year at the studio. This would be a basic wage, augmented by payments for specific work on specific commissions. After Verrocchio's departure for Venice in the early 1480s, Credi was in effective charge of the workshop, and he was named by Verrocchio as his heir and executor.[55] According to Vasari, Verrocchio 'loved' Lorenzo more than any of his other pupils – perhaps an idea of homosexuality is being trailed here: how justly we do not know. The frequent claim that Leonardo was 'introduced' to homosexuality at Verrocchio's studio is unsubstantiated.

We know nothing of Leonardo's relations with Perugino or Credi. Neither is mentioned in his manuscripts – nor for that matter is his teacher, Verrocchio. Carping criticism or lofty silence: we do not get much sense of gratitude to the artists from whom and with whom Leonardo first learned his craft.

Finally the apprentice is ready to paint, which in practice means he is ready to paint some *part* of a painting. It is a truism of the Renaissance workshop that paintings were collaborative, and that a work 'by' a certain artist was often only partly painted by him, the rest being done by assistants and apprentices working under his supervision. Sometimes there were contracts that restricted the amount of delegation. One of Piero della Francesca's contracts stipulated that 'no painter may put his hand to the brush' except Piero himself, and Filippino Lippi had to agree that his fresco in the Strozzi chapel in Santa Maria Novella would be 'all by his own hand, especially the figures'.[56] But in general it was accepted that a studio painting was not exclusively the work of the *maestro*.

One of the most charming products of Verrocchio's studio is the small panel painting of *Tobias and the Angel* in the National Gallery, London. It was painted around 1468–70. The story of Tobias (or, in Italian, Tobiolo) is found in the apocryphal Book of Tobit: it tells of a boy's quest to heal his father's blindness, and of the guardianship of the angel Raphael during his adventures. It has the lineaments of a legend or fairy tale, and a comforting undertone of family values, and it had become a popular pictorial theme. Verrocchio's *Tobias* is one of several from this time: there are very similar versions by the Pollaiuolo brothers and by Francesco Botticini, all featuring the fish and the dog which are part of the story. The Pollaiuolo painting, in oils, is the earliest of the three; Verrocchio follows its composition.[57] He has given the two figures more energy and movement – the wind catches at their cloaks; the tassel of Tobias's belt mingles wittily with a tiny tree in the distance. But the angel's wings are not as good as the Pollaiuolos', and the background is perfunctory – Verrocchio had no real feeling for landscape.

According to art historian David A. Brown, it is precisely this technical limitation which provides the clue to the painting's combined authorship: 'Verrocchio's way of representing nature was inexpert, but contrary to expectation the creatures in the London panel, like the human figures in it, outclass those in the Pollaiuolo painting.'[58] The animals, in other words, are too good for Verrocchio. The fish's scales shimmer in tones of grey and white; though done in traditional tempera technique, a sense of light and surface is brilliantly caught. And the little white dog that skips along beside the angel: it is the same breed in both paintings – a Bolognese terrier – but in the Verrocchio painting it is alive, alert, trotting. Its long silky fur straggles and flows, painted with such finesse that the dog is diaphanous. You can see the line of the previously painted landscape beneath it. The animal seems to hover like a hologram just above the picture surface: a fairy-tale dog (Plate 4).

The dog and the fish are palpably not the work of Verrocchio himself, whose robust, sculptural style is seen in the two principal figures. They are the work of an assistant, and that assistant is surely Leonardo da Vinci. A comparison of the dog's fur with the hair of Leonardo's angels of the early 1470s shows close similarities. There is probably also a contribution by Leonardo in the curls of Tobias's hair, which has the same unruly quiff as the angel of Leonardo's *Annunciation*. Microscopic analysis shows left-handed brush-strokes in the curls above Tobias's ear. Other Verrocchio paintings

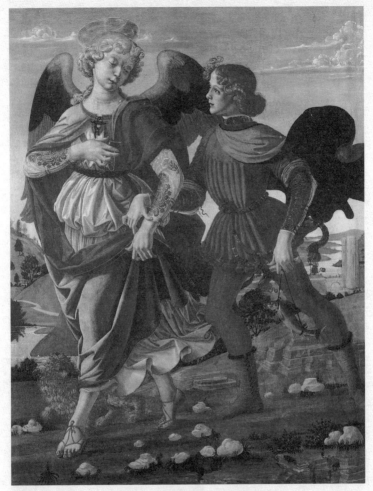

Verrocchio's Tobias and the Angel.

may contain early Leonardo brush-strokes in some fold of drapery or some corner of the landscape, but these are the first discernible contributions – a little dog, a fish, a cascade of curly hair, all done with that delicate, shimmery touch which would be perfected over the years, but which seems already to be the trademark of this remarkable apprentice.

➤➤ SPECTACULARS ◄◄

On 7 February 1469 a *giostra*, or joust, was held in Florence in honour of the twenty-year-old Lorenzo de' Medici: his rite of passage into public life and a celebration of his forthcoming marriage to Clarice Orsini (a Roman bride, and at this stage an unpopular choice). He rode through the streets with his troupe of cavaliers, from the Palazzo Medici to the tourney-lists in Piazza Santa Croce. The splendour of his accoutrements goes without saying – the silks and velvets and pearls, the chased armour, the white charger given him by the King of Naples – but let us look for a moment at the banner which flutters above him, specially designed for the occasion: a 'standard of white taffeta'. The poet Luigi Pulci describes the design on it. It was 'decorated with a sun above and a rainbow below, and in the middle a lady standing in a meadow, wearing a robe in the antique style [*drappo alessandrino*] embroidered with gold and silver flowers'. In the background was 'the trunk of a bay-tree with several withered branches and in the middle a single green branch'.[59] The bay-tree (*lauro*) puns on 'Lorenzo'. His father was ailing – he would be dead by the end of the year – but Lorenzo was the puissant new growth on the family tree.

Lorenzo's standard was the work of Andrea del Verrocchio. It has long since disappeared, and was hardly one of his major works, but it speaks volumes about the *bottega*'s prestige at this moment of semi-princely succession. Lorenzo's standard, we can be sure, was the best that money could buy. It also reminds us of the artists' involvement in every visual aspect of Florentine civic life – not just in paintings and sculptures and architecture, but in the sumptuous ephemera of public pageants like the *giostra*. The Florentine calendar was awash with spectaculars of all sorts. There was carnival in the weeks

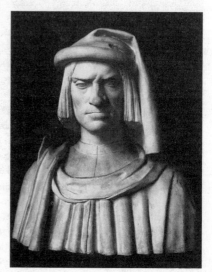

Portrait bust of Lorenzo de' Medici by Verrocchio.

before Lent, and the holy processions of Easter, and then the celebrations of Calendimaggio or May Day, which carried on intermittently until 24 June, the feast-day of the city's patron saint, St John the Baptist. There were 'lion-hunts' in the Piazza della Signoria, and football matches in Piazza Santa Croce – *calcio storico*, as the game is now called: twenty-seven a side, and 'played less with the feet than the fists' – and there was the annual horse-race, the Palio, intensely contested between the city's *gonfaloni*. The race-track crossed the city from the Porta a Prato to the Porta alla Croce; the Vacca tolled three times for the start; the winner's trophy was the eponymous *palio*, a talismanic piece of crimson silk trimmed with fur and gold tassels. A famous jockey of the day was Gostanzo Landucci, brother of the diarist Luca.[60]

The Medici understood the therapy of public festivities, and under Lorenzo these spectacles were much encouraged. It might be muttered up on 'the Hill' that this was to distract the people while their liberties were being eroded by Medici cronyism and vote-rigging, but if there was a politic element of 'bread and circuses', there was also Lorenzo's genuine relish for festivity. Carnival was becoming an ever more elaborate spectacle. There were torchlit parades of decorated wagons, the ancestors of the modern carnival-float. It was traditional for these to represent the various guilds, and many of the carnival songs were profession-related – 'The Song of the Tailors', 'The Song of the Oil-Makers' and so on – but now the fashion was for more courtly classical or mythological themes. Increasingly lavish and ingenious, these festive juggernauts became a kind of triumphalist political rhetoric: they were indeed called *trionfi* (triumphs), recalling the victory pageants of imperial Rome, but now emphasizing the power and glory of the Medici. And, as of old, bawdy songs and catches were sung – only now the smart set was requesting such numbers as the 'Song of the Sweetmeat-Sellers' and the 'Triumph of Ariadne and Bacchus', both written by Lorenzo himself, and others by his literary friends Agnolo Poliziano and Luigi Pulci. Lorenzo's herald, Battista del Ottonaio, was a particular expert in this genre.

The supercharged pageantry of Medici jousts and carnivals was the popular theatre of the day, and all the festive hardware that went into it – the standards, banners, costumes, masks, armours, caparisons and triumphal wagons – came out of the workshops of Verrocchio and his ilk. One does not see Leonardo as the kind of jovial extrovert who revels in the mayhem of carnival, but as theatre it transfixes him. We would surely find his face among the crowd at Lorenzo's *giostra* – he had perhaps worked on the standard; he was a connoisseur of horses and horsemanship; he would later be involved in *giostra* entertainments in Milan. I fancy we would also find him among the crowd outside the Duomo on Easter Sunday, watching the famous *scioppio del carro*, an incendiary rendition of the descent of the Holy Spirit in which a cartload of fireworks, hauled up from the Porta al Prato by a team of white oxen, was set off by an artificial dove propelled along a wire strung between the Duomo and the Baptistery. There is a memory of this, perhaps, in the sketch of a mechanical bird on a wire in the Codex Atlanticus, captioned 'bird for the comedy'. The early biographers agree that Leonardo created flying-machines of this more illusionist, theatrical sort: 'Out of a certain material he made birds which can fly.'[61]

Another form of public theatre was the *sacra rappresentazione*, or sacred show, the Florentine equivalent of the medieval English miracle plays. These shows were performed on holy days in churches and cloisters by young boys belonging to religious foundations. They were big productions, conspicuously financed by the Medici and others. There were special effects – huge revolving discs to change the scenery; wires and pulleys to make actors fly through the air. According to Vasari, Brunelleschi invented many of the cunning devices or *ingegni* that made such special effects possible. At San Felice there was a performance of the Annunciation every 25 March (the Feast of the Annunciation, or Lady Day). Heaven was up among the roof-trusses, and Mary's house was on a stage in the nave; the angel Gabriel was perilously winched down on a wooden cloud to make his announcement. Another popular *rappresentazione* was performed on Ascension Day at the Carmine monastery. These shows enacted the same religious scenes that the painter depicted; their groupings and gestures and *tableaux vivants* fed into the more subtle narrative conventions of the paintings. A visiting bishop made this connection, commenting after a performance of the Annunciation that 'the angel Gabriel was a beautiful youth, dressed in a gown as white as snow decorated with gold, exactly as one sees heavenly angels in paintings.' As Leonardo prepared to paint his own version of the Annunciation, these witnessed scenes were part of what he had to work with.[62]

Leonardo's love of theatre takes wing later in Milan, but is grounded here in the jousts and processions and *sacre rappresentazioni* of Medici Florence. He is the handsome, slightly quizzical young man standing at the edge of the crowd – rapt but alert, observing and calculating, working out how it's done.

In 1471 Verrocchio and his assistants were involved in preparations for another kind of spectacular: the state visit of the Duke of Milan. Verrocchio was commissioned by Lorenzo de' Medici to make a helmet and suit of armour 'in the Roman style' as a gift for the Duke, and the studio was also called on to redecorate the guest apartments of the Palazzo Medici. This marks the first definite presence of Leonardo in the Medici ambit – as an interior decorator, no more – as well as his first contact with the Milanese court, which would become his habitat in years to come.

The visit was controversial. The old duke, Francesco Sforza, had been one of the Medici's principal allies, but his son Galeazzo Maria Sforza, who succeeded him in 1466 in his early twenties, was a sinister and profligate young man with a reputation for appalling cruelty. According to the Milanese chronicler Bernardino Corio, 'he did things too shameful to write down.' Some things which did get written down (though this does not guarantee their truth) were that he 'violated virgins and seized the wives of other men', that he cut the hands off a man whose wife he fancied, and that he ordered a poacher to be executed by forcing him to swallow a whole hare, fur and all.[63] The Medici's enemies argued that this undesirable young duke should be ditched, and that Florence should return to its old alliance with Venice, but Lorenzo maintained that good relations with Milan were essential to Florentine prosperity. The fact that Galeazzo's wife, Bona of Savoy, was a daughter of the King of France added a further diplomatic dimension.

The Duke's magnificent cavalcade entered Florence on 15 March 1471. A document in the Milanese court archives entitled '*Le liste dell'andata in Fiorenza*' gives us an idea of its size – about 800 horses in all, carrying a retinue of courtiers, chaplains, butlers, barbers, cooks, trumpeters, pipers, dog-handlers, falconers, ushers, pages, wardrobe-mistresses and footmen (among the latter one called Johanne Grande, or Big John).[64] A portrait of Galeazzo by Piero del Pollaiuolo, probably painted during this visit, shows a hooked nose, a sardonic curve of the eyebrow, a small mouth, a glove held in a fastidious hand. Among the troupe was Galeazzo's younger brother Ludovico, known for his swarthy looks as Il Moro – 'the Moor'. Still a teenager, and still on the periphery of Milanese power-politics, he was a young man to watch. Ten years after this first glimpse of him, Leonardo would be heading north to seek his patronage.

In view of this later allegiance, the Florentine reaction to the Duke's visit is interesting, for it suggests something that, perhaps unconsciously at this stage, attracted the young Leonardo. Machiavelli criticized the hedonism – as we would say, the 'consumer culture' – of young Florentines at this time, and particularly associated it with the pernicious influence of this Milanese visit:

There now appeared disorders commonly witnessed in times of peace. The young people of the city, being more independent, spent excessive sums on clothing, feasting and debauchery. Living in idleness, they wasted their time and money on gaming and women; their only interest was trying to outshine others by luxury in costume, fine speaking and wit . . . These unfortunate habits became even worse with the arrival of the courtiers of the Duke of Milan . . . If the Duke found the city already corrupted by effeminate manners worthy of courts and quite contrary to those of a republic, he left it in an even more deplorable state of corruption.[65]

We do not know the precise motives of Leonardo's move to Milan in the early 1480s, but it may be that some of these 'courtly' qualities given such a negative spin by Machiavelli – snazzy clothes, witty banter, effeminate manners – were more congenial to him than the robustly bourgeois ethos of republican Florence.

There were *sacre rappresentazioni* put on in the Duke's honour, among them a Descent of the Holy Ghost to the Apostles, performed at San Spirito, the Brunelleschi church on the Oltr'Arno. On the night of 21 March a fire broke out during the show, causing panic and considerable damage. For the preachers of Florence it was divine retribution for the decadence and opulence of the Milanese, and their feasting during Lent, but a spark of that fire glows on in Leonardo's memory.

⤞ ON THE LANTERN ⤝

In 1470 or early 1471 a minor Florentine painter called Biagio d'Antonio Tucci produced a painting of *Tobias with Three Archangels*, a variation on the popular Tobias theme which Verrocchio and Leonardo had also tackled.[66] Behind the figures is the familiar view of Florence – walls, towers, hills and, in the middle, the great dome of the cathedral. It is conventional enough, but Biagio painted what he actually saw, and what he saw was a tall and rather complicated wooden scaffolding around the marble lantern on top of the dome. The painting thus becomes a unique visual record of the finishing touch being applied to the dome. The main structure of the cupola had been completed nearly fifty years previously by Brunelleschi – 'challenging the sky itself', as Vasari memorably phrased it – but it had never been crowned with the orb and cross specified in Brunelleschi's original design. This project was now entrusted to Verrocchio & Co., and if one could apply some kind of magical magnifying-glass to Utili's painting one might discern certain figures perched aloft on the scaffolding, and one of those figures might be Verrocchio's assistant Leonardo da Vinci.

This prestigious contract had been awarded to Verrocchio by the cathedral's *fabbriceria*, or works department, in September 1468. The following spring he travelled to Venice and Treviso to purchase high-quality copper for the orb. The finished orb – or, as it is invariably called, the *palla* or ball – was 8 feet in diameter and weighed more than 2 tons.[67] According to Vasari, the casting 'required much care and ingenuity, to make it possible to enter the ball from below, and make it proof against damage from the wind'. The mould for it is probably the 'sphere' mentioned in the post-mortem inventory of Verrocchio's possessions.

On Monday 27 May 1471 the ball was hoisted to the top of the marble lantern which tops the dome, 350 feet above the ground. The ledgers of the Opera del Duomo record the payment of 2 lire 'to buy bread and wine for the workmen when they put up the ball'. The work of installing it and securing it to its plinth took three days, then on 30 May the cross was placed on top of it. Among the crowd watching below was the apothecary Luca Landucci: 'They placed the cross on the said ball, and the canons and many other people went up, and sang the *Te Deum* there.' The accounts note that 3 lire was paid 'to the trumpeters of the Palagio [i.e. the Signoria] ... for their trouble when they played on the lantern when the cross was put up'.[68]

Leonardo certainly had first-hand knowledge of the project, and of the engineering problems involved. A memorandum in one of his notebooks contains a specific recollection: 'Remember the solders used for soldering the ball on Santa Maria del Fiore.'[69] This note is datable to *c*. 1515, when he was involved in a scheme to manufacture parabolic mirrors, made of a number of facets soldered together. He is looking back more than forty years to that vertiginous Florentine project in which he had assisted as a young man.

It cannot, of course, be proved that Leonardo was perched up on that scaffolding high above the rooftops of Florence, 'challenging the sky itself'. But where else would we expect to find him?

The project drew Leonardo close to the work of the already legendary figure of Filippo (or Pippo) Brunelleschi, the master architect of the dome, who had done so much to give a new status to the Renaissance architect-engineer. He was a small, ugly, combative man: he was 'insignificant to look at', says Vasari, 'but his genius was so commanding that we can surely say he was sent by heaven'. The famous anecdote of the egg summed up the man's provocative flair. In the competition to build the cupola, we learn, Brunelleschi refused to divulge his plans, but won the competition with a kind of wager or dare. He said 'that whoever could make an egg stand on end on a flat piece of marble should build the cupola, since it would show how intelligent each man was'. An egg was duly brought, and the competing experts tried in vain to make it stand on end. Then Filippo stepped up and 'graciously taking the egg he cracked its bottom on the marble and made it stand upright.' The others complained that they 'could have done as much', but Filippo laughed and said 'they could also have vaulted the cupola if they had seen his models.'[70] This incident is probably apocryphal, but its mix of showmanship and originality (what we would call 'lateral thinking') is right, as is the strong motive of professional secrecy. He was plagued by fears, often justified, of piracy and plagiarism – another Brunelleschian feature inherited by Leonardo.

The dome remains one of the wonders of European architecture – it is still, nearly 600 years later, the largest masonry dome in the world. According to modern estimates it contains some 4 million bricks and weighs about 36,000 tons, and it was built without a 'centring' (a wooden framework to support the masonry). It is in fact two domes, one nestling inside the other: the larger one measures 180 feet between its opposite edges. Each dome is formed of eight self-supporting arching segments, built simultaneously and reinforced by circular hoops.[71] One of Brunelleschi's innovations was the introduction of safety harnesses: only one mason fell to his death during the building of the dome – a remarkable record by the standards of the day.

The placing of a 2 ton copper orb or 'ball' on top of the dome posed engineering problems not dissimilar to those originally confronted by Brunelleschi – primarily how to get it up there. Leonardo's involvement in the project would have provided him with direct access to the cathedral workshop, and to Brunelleschi's famed designs for hoists and cranes. Studies recording the overall forms and some of the details of Brunelleschi's devices are found in a clutch of Leonardo drawings in the Codex Atlanticus; these are generally dated to the late 1470s, but probably reflect this earlier involvement in cathedral engineering. The same machines are found in the notebooks of other Renaissance engineers, but the way Leonardo isolates and analyses particular components strongly suggests he was working directly from the original machines.[72] One drawing shows the *collo grande* ('big neck'), a machine built by Brunelleschi in 1421, which served as the main hoist for lifting worked stone and other heavy materials to the top of the cathedral. Its particular feature was a gearing mechanism which meant that the hoist could either raise or lower materials without the animals turning the windlass at its base having to change direction. Another drawing shows Brunelleschi's revolving crane, designed to provide a stable and precise way of placing worked stones during the construction of the dome. Another gives detailed sketches of a crane running on circular rails. All these

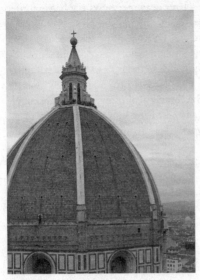

Florence cathedral, showing dome, lantern and orb.

devices would have been directly relevant to the hoisting and placing of the copper sphere.[73]

On a folio of the late 1480s, thinking about a naval attack system, Leonardo notes that he must 'make a cast of one of the 3 screws at the Opera di Santa Liberata'.[74] This is another name for Florence's cathedral, and he is referring to yet another Brunelleschi mechanism – for keeping cables at high tension – to be found in the cathedral workshop. At around this time Leonardo was himself thinking about domes and cupolas, in connection with a project at Milan cathedral. Close reflections of Brunelleschian architecture are

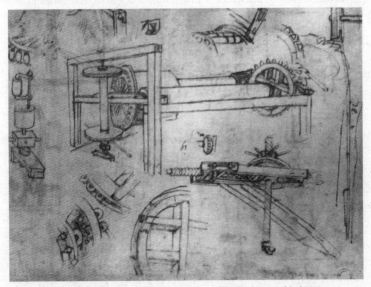

Technical study by Leonardo of Brunelleschi's reversible hoist.

found in his studies for this, and a later drawing shows the herring-bone arrangement of bricks in a dome, again echoing the great prototype in Florence.[75]

One can today make a vertical pilgrimage to the base of the lantern of the Duomo. A stairway of 463 stone steps leads up from an entrance on the south side of the transept, debouches briefly at the lower rim of the cupola – where one walks past the huge sandalled feet and flapping hems of the Vasari fresco of the *Last Judgement* – and then twists up behind the wainscots of the cupola to emerge on top of the city, with the rooftops of the old centre spread below, and the streets radiating through them like the spokes of a slightly squashed bicycle wheel. One can see the line of Via Ghibellina where the *bottega* was, and the tall spire of the Badia marking the site of Ser Piero's office, and then looking north there is the huge sandstone cube of the Palazzo Medici, still looking as if it has just been rolled into place.

Here Leonardo stood on an early summer's day in 1471. One senses the grandeur of the occasion for him – in part a euphoria from the bird-like altitude, and in part a sense of the powers of Brunelleschian technology, the precisely calibrated magic which could throw up this gravity-defying structure halfway to heaven. It is an inspirational Renaissance moment.

✢ FIRST PAINTINGS ✢

In the summer of 1472, at the age of twenty, Leonardo was registered as a member of the Florentine painters' confraternity, the Compagnia di San Luca. The company's ledgers record that 'Lyonardo di Ser Piero da Vinci *dipintore*' was charged 32 soldi for the privilege of membership. This included 16 soldi for his annual subscription, to be paid in monthly instalments from 1 July 1472, and 10 soldi as a contribution to the company's observances on the feast-day of St Luke, 18 October.[76] St Luke, who was supposed to have painted a portrait of the Virgin Mary, is the patron saint of painters. Also registered as new members in this year were Verrocchio, Botticelli, Perugino, Domenico Ghirlandaio, the Pollaiuolo brothers, and Filippino Lippi: the cream of Florentine painting in the early 1470s.

Founded in the mid fourteenth century, the Compagnia di San Luca was a loose grouping or sodality of painters of all sorts. Others were established in Siena and Milan, and later there were versions in Paris, Rome and London. (The last of these, St Luke's Club, also called the Virtuosi, was founded in 1638 by Anthony Van Dyck, and met at the Rose Tavern in Fleet Street.) The original Florentine Compagnia had a religious overtone, but it was essentially an artists' 'club', and no doubt a convivial one. It was distinct from the painters' guild, the Arte dei Medici e Speziali, though it shared some of the guild's functions. Many of its members were also members of the guild, but this was not obligatory (as is shown by the appearance of Filippino Lippi in the 1472 register, aged about fifteen and too young to be a guild member). In practice the guild's control over artistic affairs was much in decline, and many artists preferred not to join. This decline was largely due to the increasing mobility of artists in search of patronage: the guilds had a strictly local axis of influence, and art was becoming a national and international market. We don't know if Leonardo ever became a member of the Arte dei Medici e Speziali – the guild records are fragmentary – but there is no evidence that he did.

The records of the Compagnia di San Luca are also very patchy, and it is not clear why all these painters are recorded as joining in the same year; possibly there had been an earlier hiatus in the company's activities. None the less, Leonardo's appearance in the company's *libro rosso* is a tangible marker in the otherwise shadowy chronology of his artistic development. By mid-1472 he is a *dipintore*: a practising painter.

What whole paintings had Leonardo done by this time? There are various possibilities (leaving aside his contributions to Verrocchio's *Tobias*, which are charming but limited), and the most obvious is the *Annunciation*, now in the Uffizi (Plate 5). It was probably painted for the monastery of San Bartolomeo at Monte Oliveto, in the hills south-west of Florence. It was certainly there by the late eighteenth century, when it is first documented.[77] In 1867 it was bought by the Uffizi; according to a label on the back of the panel, it was then hanging in the sacristy at San Bartolomeo. Its oblong format suggests it may have been designed to be placed above the furniture of the sacristy: there is a similarly shaped intarsia *Annunciation* by Giuliano da Maiano in the north sacristy of Florence cathedral. It is known that San Bartolomeo was partly rebuilt in 1472 – the portal, attributed to Michelozzi, bears this date – and the painting may have been commissioned as part of the refurbishment. Today the monastery is a military hospital.

Before its transfer to the Uffizi, the painting was believed to be by Domenico Ghirlandaio. It was first attributed to Leonardo in the Uffizi catalogue of 1869. This attribution is now almost universally accepted, though there remain one or two revisionist doubters. What the doubts correctly convey is that the style of the work is hard to differentiate: this is the young

Leonardo, still visibly associated with Verrocchio's shop and its prevalent forms and techniques. David A. Brown sums it up well: 'Combining innovative and lyrical passages with borrowings and mistakes, the *Annunciation* is the work of an immensely gifted artist who was still immature.'[78] The borrowings are evident in the face and colouring of the Virgin, in the raised little finger of her hand – a typical Verrocchio mannerism – and in the ornate decoration of the lectern, which echoes Verrocchio's work on the Medici sarcophagus in San Lorenzo, completed in 1472.[79] The mistakes are essentially of perspective. The right-hand cypress-tree, for instance, appears to be in the same plane as the other cypresses, but to read it as such would make the receding wall next to it impossibly long. More critically, the spatial relationship between the Virgin and the lectern is illogical. Read from the pedestal upward, the lectern is nearer to us than she is, but read from her right hand downward it should be further away from us. Her awkwardly elongated right arm is a result of this irresolution. Both these compositional errors occur on the right-hand side of the painting. The other side – the angel, the garden, the wonderful melting vistas – seems richer and more accomplished. It has been thought they may have been done at different times. Overall the painting has a certain stylized stiffness, and gains its effect from the ephebic beauty of the angel and from what Martin Kemp calls its 'myopic focus' on individual detail.[80]

The subject was one of the most popular in Renaissance art, and almost every painter of note has one or more versions of it. It dramatizes the moment when the young Mary is visited by the angel Gabriel and is told that she will become the mother of the Messiah (Luke 1:26–38). The text was the subject of much exegesis by commentators and preachers, who expounded the five 'attributes' of the Virgin during the colloquy narrated by Luke – *conturbatio*, or disquiet ('she was troubled'); *cogitatio*, or reflection (she 'cast in her mind what manner of salutation this should be'); *interrogatio*, or enquiry ('How shall this be, seeing I know not a man?'); *humiliatio*, or submission ('Behold the handmaid of the Lord'); and *meritatio*, or worth, which describes her beatified status after the angel has departed. It can be shown that different Annunciation paintings focus on different 'attributes'. Thus Filippo Lippi's in San Lorenzo clearly expresses Mary's disquiet, as does Botticelli's in the Uffizi (the one criticized by Leonardo for its overdone gestures – too much *conturbatio*, in other words), while Fra Angelico's in San Marco focuses on her humility.[81] These show an interesting interrelation between the theology of the pulpit and the visual vocabulary of the studio, but Leonardo's *Annunciation* seems less easy to pin down: the raised left hand suggests a remnant of *conturbatio*, while the expressionless smoothness of the Virgin's face suggests the onset of *humiliatio*. There is thus a glimmering of a psychological dynamic, of those *accidenti mentali* or mental events which Leonardo sought to express in mature works like the *Last Supper* and the *Virgin and Child with St Anne*. We sense an unfolding story, an implied before and after, within the depicted moment. This is also conveyed by that problematic right hand: it holds open the book that the Virgin was reading before the angel arrived. This gives a suddenness to this archetypal event: the angel's visit is still a momentary interruption.

This book is itself a traditional part of Annunciation iconography: Mary is reading an Old Testament prophet on the coming of the Messiah. The look of the page is meant to suggest Hebrew, but the text is in fact visual rhubarb – meaningless combinations of letters. If you look closely you can see that one of the lines simply reads 'm n o p q'. The riotous spring flowers and grasses of the foreground are also conventional. The Feast of the Annunciation was on 25 March, and was associated with springtime (the biblical location of the episode, Nazareth, means in Hebrew 'flower'). The lily in the angel's hand reflects this, and was particularly emphasized in Florentine art because the city's coat of arms featured lilies. In one aspect Leonardo's treatment was apparently not standard, however. The preacher Fra Roberto Caracciolo spoke of painters having 'licence to give angels wings to signify their swift progress in all things',[82] but it appears there were conventions on this. Leonardo gave his angel short, strong wings – real birds' wings – but these were later lengthened by an unknown and not very sympathetic hand. The extension, in a dull chestnut-coloured paint, stabs into the deeper plane of the landscape, which is vestigially visible through the paint surface of the addition.

Among the various Madonna and Child compositions emanating from the Verrocchio workshop in the early 1470s, one has a particular claim to be by the hand of Leonardo. This is the *Madonna of the Carnation*, now in the Alte Pinakothek in Munich. The Madonna is generically in the Verrocchio mould – the pale, rather Nordic, look; the blonde ringlets; the downturned eyes – but she has particular affinities with the Virgin of Leonardo's *Annunciation*. They wear the same dusky blue dress set off by red sleeves, and the same golden mantle. The brooch, with its suggestive topazy gleam, is a Leonardo trademark of the future, as in the *Benois Madonna* and the *Virgin of the Rocks*. Perhaps most characteristic is the drama of the landscape glimpsed through the loggia behind her – a range of rugged, serrated, rocky peaks quite unlike the more staid Tuscan

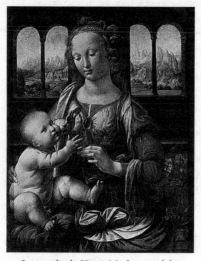

Leonardo da Vinci, Madonna of the
Carnation.

backgrounds found in other
workshop productions, but such
a feature of Leonardo's later
paintings like the *Madonna of
the Yarnwinder*, the *St Anne*, and
the *Mona Lisa*.

In the foreground, almost
brushed by the mother's elbow,
is a vase of flowers. This serves
to identify the Munich panel as
the one that Vasari describes in
his life of Leonardo as a 'very
fine' Madonna with 'a carafe
of water with some flowers in
it'. The word *caraffa* precisely
describes the kind of wide-
bellied glass bottle depicted in
the painting. Vasari goes on to
praise the 'dewdrops of water'
on the flowers, which are 'more
convincing than the real thing', but the painting is in poor condition and
this detail is no longer apparent. Vasari unquestioningly attributes the
painting to Leonardo, and places it within the ambit of his years with
Verrocchio. He also says that it was later in the possession of Pope Clement
VII. Clement was the illegitimate son of Giuliano de' Medici, Lorenzo's
younger brother; Giuliano was one of Verrocchio's patrons, and it is possible
that the painting was commissioned by him. Kenneth Clark thought the
painting 'charmless', but had no doubt it was by Leonardo – it 'has the
unpleasant vitality of immature genius'.[83]

The intrinsically Leonardian details, the correspondences with the *Annunciation*, the early attribution by Vasari: these make a strong case for the
Madonna of the Carnation as a genuine Leonardo of the early 1470s.
Another Verrocchiesque Madonna and Child which is sometimes claimed as
his is the *Madonna of the Pomegranate* in the National Gallery at Washington, DC, also called the *Dreyfus Madonna* after a previous owner. It is a very
sweet painting, but there is nothing to relate it specifically to Leonardo. Clark
thought it an early work by Lorenzo di Credi. The softness and roundness
of the modelling are very reminiscent of Lippi, and suggest once again the
influence of Botticelli in the formation of the Verrocchiesque style.

*

Also from this period is the famous collaboration between Verrocchio and Leonardo, the dramatic *Baptism of Christ*, now in the Uffizi (Plate 7). It was painted for the church of San Salvi – Verrocchio's elder brother, Simone di Cione, was the abbot there, and was probably instrumental in the commission.[84] Vasari makes it out to be Verrocchio's last painting:

Andrea was working on a panel-picture showing the baptism of Christ by St John, for which Leonardo painted an angel holding some garments, and despite his youth he did it so well that the angel was far better than the figures painted by Andrea. This was the reason why Andrea would never touch colours again – he was ashamed that a boy understood their use better than he did.

This is a portable sort of anecdote, and should not be taken at face value. Leonardo was probably about twenty-one when the painting was done, and not therefore a 'boy'. It is pretty certain he also painted the misty distant landscape in the background: the left-hand side of the landscape echoes the topography of the 'Madonna of the Snow' drawing in the Uffizi, the date of which – 5 August 1473 – ties in well enough with the *Baptism*.

I am never very happy with the conventional idea, launched by Vasari and spun more or less continuously since, that Leonardo's kneeling angel is the best thing about the painting and knocks his teacher's work into a cocked hat. This seems pure 'Leonardolatry'. The two central figures, which are exclusively Verrocchio's, are very powerful – the features of the Baptist gaunt and hard-bitten; Christ with a humble, half-ugly ordinariness (the face-type an import from the Netherlands, like the blonde Madonnas). I am also struck by the beauty of Christ's feet, as seen through the prism of the baptismal river, or really a stream, that runs over a bed of reddish-brown rock. The Leonardo angel is certainly exquisite, with his tightly curled golden hair and his alert turning movement. It shows already a subtlety of moulding and movement far beyond that of his master, who remained wedded to sculptural modes. (The figure of the Baptist is closely related to Verrocchio's bronze Christ at Orsanmichele.) But the human drama, the tragic foretelling, the sense of great strengths greatly tested – these are all Verrocchio's. If his painted figures lack something in technique, they lack nothing in the raw power of the scene. Beside them Leonardo's angel seems brilliant but perhaps slightly facile: a prize-winning essay by a young virtuoso.

→→ **THE DRAGON** ←←

The *Annunciation*, the *Madonna of the Carnation*, the *Baptism of Christ*: just three devotional works among many that emanated from Verrocchio's studio, but each of them touched with the lustrous brush of the young Leonardo da Vinci. Other works belonging to this first Florentine period are mentioned by the early biographers but are now lost. Particularly to be regretted is the loss of the work described by the Anonimo Gaddiano as 'a painting of Adam and Eve in watercolours'. According to Vasari, Leonardo was commissioned to do this after painting the angel in the *Baptism*. He says it was 'a cartoon for a tapestry to be woven of gold and silk in Flanders and sent to the King of Portugal, showing Adam and Eve when they sinned in the earthly paradise'. Both biographers state that Leonardo's cartoon was now – i.e. in the 1540s – in the house of Ottaviano de' Medici. Vasari's description of it seems to be first hand, and what entranced him was the depiction of the Garden of Eden:

For this he drew with the brush in chiaroscuro, with the highlights in lead white, a luxuriant meadow of grass with animals in it, done with such care and such fidelity to nature that nothing in the world could be more inspired or perfect. There is a fig-tree, shown foreshortened, with its leaves and its branches depicted with such loving care that the mind reels at the thought that a man could have such patience. And there is a palm-tree, where the radiating shapes of the palms are caught with such marvellous skill that no one without Leonardo's understanding and patience could have done it.

Vasari adds an interesting note that the painting had been given to Ottaviano de' Medici by Leonardo's uncle. This cannot be Uncle Francesco (who had died in 1507, and who was anyway unlikely to have been hobnobbing with any Medici), but it could be Alessandro Amadori, canon of Fiesole, who was the brother of Leonardo's first stepmother, Albiera. Leonardo continued to know him long after Albiera's death in 1464, and late in life was wondering 'whether the priest Alessandro Amadori is still living or not'.[85] It is possible that Leonardo gave his *Adam and Eve* cartoon to Amadori when he left Florence in 1482, just as he gave the unfinished *Adoration of the Magi* to his friend Giovanni de' Benci. The technique of the cartoon – drawn with a brush in chiaroscuro and highlighted with lead white – is similar to that of the *Adoration*, which also features a beautifully drawn palm-tree.

Also at this time Leonardo did 'a painting in oils showing the head of a

Medusa attired with a coil of serpents': apparently his first work on a classical theme. It is mentioned by the Anonimo and by Vasari (though only in the second edition of the *Lives*), and is perhaps the work listed in the Medici collection in about 1553 as 'a picture on wood of an infernal fury, by the hand of Leonardo da Vinci, without ornament'.[86] No trace remains of it, though it was for a long while confused with the Medusa tondo by Caravaggio.

Another lost early work of Leonardo's survives only in a long anecdote told by Vasari. The passage reads like an episode from an Italian *novella*, and it is quite possible the painting it refers to is pure fiction, but the story is told at length, and with a good deal of circumstantial detail, and one cannot help feeling that there may be something in it. It begins convincingly enough: 'The story goes that when Ser Piero da Vinci was at his house in the country, one of his farmworkers paid him a visit . . .' The peasant had made a 'buckler' or circular shield (*rotello*) from a fig-tree he had cut down, and he asked if Ser Piero could take it to Florence to have it painted. Ser Piero was glad to oblige the man, 'who was very adept at snaring birds and catching fish, and was much used by Ser Piero in these pursuits'. He duly brought the buckler to Florence, and asked Leonardo to paint something on it. Leonardo examined it with an air of disdain – it was 'warped and crudely made' – but a few days later he set to work:

He straightened it in the fire, and handed it over to a wood-turner who worked it up from the rough and clumsy thing it was into something smooth and even. Then, having given it a coat of gesso, and prepared it according to his own methods, he began to consider what he could paint on it, so as to terrify anyone who encountered it, like the head of the Medusa once did. To this purpose Leonardo collected lizards, geckos, crickets, butterflies, locusts, bats and other strange creatures of this sort, and brought them to a room of his own to which no one but himself was admitted, and taking and adapting different parts of these creatures, he made a most fearsome and horrible monster . . . and this he painted, showing it emerging from the dark cleft of a rock, belching forth venom from its mouth and fire from its eyes and smoke from its nostrils.

He took so long over this work that the stench of dead animals in his room was unbearable, but 'Leonardo did not notice this because of his great devotion to his art.' By the time he had finished it, both his father and the *contadino* had forgotten all about it. Leonardo sent to his father to tell him it was ready:

And so, one morning, Ser Piero went along to that room of Leonardo's to get the buckler, and knocked at the door. Leonardo came to the door and told him to wait a moment, and then he went back into the room, and arranged the buckler on an easel, and shaded the window so the light was dim, and then he invited him in to see it. On first sight of it, taken completely by surprise, Ser Piero gave a sudden start, not thinking it was the buckler and that what he saw was painted on it. He began to back away, but Leonardo stopped him, and said, 'The work has served the purpose it was made for, so now you can pick it up and take it away, because it has done what was expected of it.' And Ser Piero thought the whole thing quite marvellous, and loudly praised Leonardo's capricious imagination.

This marvellous anecdote is unprovable but in its essentials quite plausible. It is a Florentine story – within Vasari's narrative it is placed together with the painting of the *Baptism of Christ*, the lost *Adam and Eve*, and the *Madonna of the Carnation*: thus in the early 1470s *chez* Verrocchio. The setting is interesting. We are in the workshop – Leonardo straightens the ill-made buckler 'in the fire', and prepares it with gesso 'according to his own methods' – but Leonardo has also his private studio: 'a room of his own to which no one but himself was admitted'. This probably reflects accurately enough the arrangements at the *bottega* – anyway by the mid-1470s, when Leonardo would have had the status of chief assistant. The story also has a strong sense of Leonardo as fantasist, hatching up this gothic creature – this *animalaccio*, as Vasari calls it – in the privacy of his room. One recalls a comment in the *Trattato della pittura*: 'If the painter wishes to depict creatures or devils in hell, with what an abundance of invention he teems.'[87]

The story is further shored up by some dragon studies at Windsor, and a drawing of a dragon fight in the Louvre, both belonging to the 1470s, and by a passage in the *Trattato* where Leonardo recommends precisely the kind of combinatory technique that we hear of in the Vasarian anecdote: 'You cannot fabricate any animal that does not have parts that are recognizable as belonging to other animals. If therefore you wish to make . . . a dragon, take for its head that of a mastiff or a setter, for its eyes those of a cat [etc.].'[88] Lomazzo speaks of a painting by Leonardo of a dragon fighting a lion, 'done with such art that no one who looks at it can tell which of them will be the victor'. He adds, 'I once had a drawing taken from this picture which was very dear to me.' There is a dramatic drawing of just this subject in the Uffizi, thought by some to be a copy of an original Leonardo drawing.[89] These dragon studies – some actual, some rumoured – cannot be taken as evidence that the painted shield of Vasari's story ever existed, but they show that Leonardo was no stranger to the theory and practice of painting dragons.

The story is also suggestive of the prickly, competitive relationship between the painter and his father. Leonardo enjoys playing a trick on Ser Piero: he makes him jump with his revelation of the dragon. The father in turn plays an underhand trick, for the story ends with him surreptitiously selling the shield: 'He bought another buckler from a pedlar, painted with a heart pierced by an arrow, and gave it to the peasant, who was grateful for the rest of his days. Later, secretly, he sold Leonardo's buckler to some merchants in Florence for a hundred ducats.' Ser Piero profits financially, as usual, but is somehow the loser in another sense: he comes out of the story like Wilde's cynic, 'who knows the price of everything and the value of nothing'.

The real underhand trick that Ser Piero played on Leonardo at this time was to become a father again. In 1475 he married for the third time, and the following year, a few weeks short of his fiftieth birthday, the long shadow of marital barrenness was lifted with the birth of a son. The child was duly baptized Antonio, in memory of Ser Piero's father and in confirmation of his status as Ser Piero's son and heir – his first-born in legal if not biological terms.[90] For Leonardo this was surely a blow. It cemented his illegitimacy. Up till then he had enjoyed the protection and encouragement of his father, however gruffly expressed; he perhaps hoped that, if no other child was born to Ser Piero, he might in the fullness of time become his heir. With the birth of Antonio di Ser Piero da Vinci in 1476 Leonardo is disinherited. He is once again the bastard son, the second-class citizen. Somehow, without really meaning to, Vasari's story partakes of this – the cheating father, the secretly spurned gift, the lost legacy of the hundred ducats. Ser Piero walks off down the street, with the painting under his arm, glad to be out of that strange shady room smelling of dead lizards.

⤜ GINEVRA ⤛

L'aer d'intorno si fa tutto ameno,
Ovunque gira le luci amorose . . .
Agnolo Poliziano, *Stanze per la giostra*

Leonardo's portrait of Ginevra de' Benci (Plate 6) was first mentioned in the early sixteenth century by Antonio Billi, and then by the Anonimo and

Vasari, but for a long while the painting was thought to be lost. It was only at the beginning of the last century that it was identified with a small half-length panel portrait then obscurely housed in the Prince of Liechtenstein's collection in Vaduz castle.[91] The sitter, it was noticed, was posed in front of a juniper-tree – in Italian *ginepro*, and hence a typical pun on 'Ginevra'. Other findings have followed, confirming that this is indeed Leonardo's *Ginevra*. The painting is now in the National Gallery of Art in Washington, DC – the only major Leonardo work outside Europe. It was his first portrait. I would also call it his first masterpiece.

It is a small painting – little more than 15 inches tall, though it used to be rather larger – but it has an extraordinary intensity of atmosphere. The face is pale, round, melancholic; it glows against the juniper's dark foliage like the moon coming out of cloud, and indeed the light which falls on the more distant background, glinting on water and hovering over thin, ghostly trees, could as well be moonlight as the more conventionally supposed twilight. The sitter's eyelids are heavy, her gaze abstracted; whatever those feline eyes are looking at, they do not seem to see. She is looking into a distance not physically measurable. She is, as we would say, miles away. Her hair, fair or auburn, is smooth and glossy where it has been combed down against her head – a hint of perfumed macassar hovers about her – but where it frames her face it forms a little cascade of ringlets. Amid the hermetic stillness of the picture these twirling, twisting, highlit curls give a sudden sense of release, of constraints thrown off. They are a force of vitality amid the painting's almost oppressively serene atmosphere. They are also, already, a kind of Leonardo trademark (see his Tobias; see his angels): they are what the discerning customer wants from him.

I call this Leonardo's first masterpiece: a subjective and ultimately unhelpful term, but the one that best expresses the frisson of beauty and mystery which the painting provokes. It was certainly painted within the Verrocchio ambit. It has a close affinity with Verrocchio's marble *Woman with a Bunch of Flowers* (Bargello, Florence), which may well be a portrait of Ginevra as well. But the poetry of the picture is not something learned from Verrocchio: it is the product of the painter's own particular sensibility. It is the first Leonardo painting where one has a sense of looking *through* the picture-plane, as through a window, into some charmed space. It shows the world seen in a kind of trance. The alabaster smoothness of Ginevra's face contributes to this dream-like quality: she is not quite human. This was a desired effect – the paint surface of the face was smoothed by Leonardo's own hand.

*

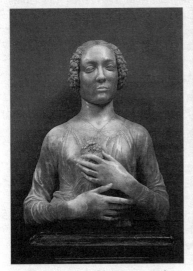

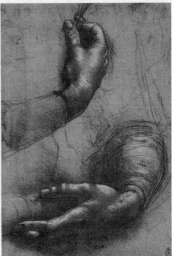

Verrocchio's marble Woman with a Bunch of Flowers, *c. 1476.*

Probable study for the hands of Ginevra de' Benci in the lost portion of her portrait.

Ginevra de' Benci – or 'La Bencina', as Poliziano calls her – was young, witty, beautiful and rich.[92] The poet Alessandro Braccesi wrote of her, '*Pulchrior hac tota non cernitur urbe puella / Altera nec maior ulla pudicitia*' – 'In all the city you will not find a more beautiful girl, nor any more modest.' She was born in the summer of 1457, probably on the Benci estates at Antello, south of Florence. The family had risen to eminence on the coat-tails of the Medici, whom they served as bankers and advisers. Ginevra's grandfather Giovanni, of lower-middle-class origins, had been a close business associate of Cosimo de' Medici; her father, Amerigo de' Benci, was director of the Medici bank in Geneva. The family had a handsome city *palazzo* in the Santa Croce quarter, on what is now Via de' Benci. In the *catasto* of 1457, the year Ginevra was born, Amerigo was estimated as worth over 26,000 florins, making the Benci the wealthiest family in Florence after the Medici (who were worth four times as much). Amerigo was also a noted art-collector and patron. He was not the commissioner of Leonardo's portrait – he died in 1468, still in his thirties – but it will be of interest that he was an early patron of the Florentine philosopher Marsilio Ficino, to whom he gave a rare Greek manuscript of Plato.

In January 1474, at the age of sixteen, Ginevra was married to a cloth-trader, Luigi di Bernardo Niccolini. It used to be thought that Leonardo's picture was a wedding-portrait, commissioned by her husband, but Ginevra was more famously associated with the brilliant but rackety Venetian diplomat Bernardo Bembo, and recent evidence strongly suggests that it was he who commissioned it. Bembo arrived in Florence, as Venetian ambassador, in January 1475; he was in his early forties, with a wife and a son in tow, and a mistress and a love-child somewhere else in his life, but he swiftly threw himself into a highly public 'Platonic' affair with Ginevra. Such an affair was permissible: he was, within the conventions of the day, her *cavaliere servente*, though there are suggestions that their relationship strained against the boundaries of chastity. Cristoforo Landino wrote a poem about it, joking that only two letters of her name need to be changed for her to become one with her lover, 'and though she was once Bencia, her name will be Bembia'. The poet Braccesi soothed the pains of separation by 'gathering the violets that Ginevra deliberately let fall from her bosom so that he could secretly carry them to Bernardo'. (The flowers in Verrocchio's sculpture may allude to this amorous game, though they are usually identified as primroses.) A note in Bembo's own hand describes her as 'the most beautiful of women, and famous for her virtue and her manners'. Ginevra was herself a poet, and doubtless responded in verse to Bembo's chivalric attentions. Only a single line of her poetry has survived: '*Chieggo merzede e sono alpestro tygre*' – 'I beg for mercy; I am a wild tiger.'

On the reverse of the panel Leonardo painted an emblematic device which features again the identifying visual pun of the juniper. A juniper-branch is surrounded by a wreath composed of branches of laurel and palm. On a scroll is the motto '*Virtutem forma decorat*' ('The form adorns virtue'), expressing the Platonic–Petrarchan commonplace that outward physical beauty embodies inner spiritual virtue.[93]

This device is unexpectedly informative. To begin with, it is off-centre, both vertically and laterally; part of it is actually missing off the side-edge of the panel. This clearly shows that the panel has been cut down at some point. Assuming the device was placed centrally on the reverse, the panel must have been a few inches wider on the right-hand side (in other words, on the left-hand side of the portrait itself), and longer by about a third, the lost portion being at the bottom of the panel. This has fascinating implications for the portrait itself, which must originally have shown Ginevra almost down to her waist. In the Windsor collection is a beautiful study of hands – or actually a pair of studies, each concentrating on a different hand.

The right hand is holding something, though quite what is not clear. The lines may suggest the stalks of a posy of flowers, for once again there is a close visual connection with the hands of Verrocchio's *Woman with a Bunch of Flowers*. This drawing may well be a study for the hands of Ginevra de' Benci as they appeared in the lost lower portion of the portrait.[94] The real Ginevra's beautiful hands and her 'fingers white as ivory' are mentioned by both Landino and Braccesi.

The device on the reverse also confirms the portrait's particular connection with Bernardo Bembo, for Bembo used precisely the emblem of the laurel and palm which is here shown enclosing the sprig of juniper. It has been found in two Bembo-related manuscripts now in England. One version of it, in Bembo's own hand, is in his autograph copy of Marsilio Ficino's *De amore* (a commentary on Plato's *Symposium*, written in the early 1460s and published in 1469); it was in the margin of this manuscript that Bembo wrote the words about Ginevra which I quoted earlier. Another version of the wreath is in Eton College library, in a manuscript copy of *Bembicae Peregrinae* ('The Travels of Bembo'), a poem describing his journey to Spain in 1468–9.[95] Leonardo's device thus shows Ginevra emblematically entwined with Bembo. This confirms that the portrait was commissioned not, as was hitherto assumed, by her husband on the occasion of their marriage in 1474, but by her Platonic lover a year or two later. Bembo was ambassador in Florence for two spells – between January 1475 and April 1476, and between July 1478 and May 1480. On stylistic evidence the earlier sojourn gives a more likely date for the commissioning of the picture.

The first notice of Bembo in Florence records his presence at the *giostra* of Giuliano de' Medici on 28 January 1475. It was probably here that he met Ginevra for the first time, and was swept up in the ethos of courtly love which was very much the theme of Giuliano's *giostra*, as can be gauged from Poliziano's elegant, sweet-toothed poem, *Stanze per la giostra*, which commemorated it. The couplet I quote at the opening of this chapter gives the typical tone – 'Sweet the air all around, the lights of love flickering everywhere'.[96] It is quite likely that the Verrocchio studio designed standards for Giuliano's *giostra*, just as they had done earlier for Lorenzo's. There is a Verrocchio sketch of Venus and Cupid in the Uffizi: its elongated triangular shape strongly suggests that it is a study for a standard. The Venus is a typically elegant and mellow Verrocchio female. The Cupid, with his quick, darting movements – one hand reaching an arrow from his quiver, the other saucily reaching to bare the goddess's breast – has been attributed to Leonardo.[97]

The icon of the *giostra* was Giuliano's own mistress, the young Genoese beauty Simonetta Cattanei, wife of Matteo di Vespucci. (She was Giuliano's mistress in the same playfully 'Platonic' sense that Ginevra was Bembo's mistress, but Vespucci did not enjoy his role as Platonic cuckold and there arose tensions between the Vespucci and the Medici as a result.) Within the iconography of the *giostra* Simonetta was associated with Venus, the goddess of love: there is a great deal of decorative verse from Poliziano about this. This in turn ties in with an old tradition that Simonetta was the model for Venus in Botticelli's *Birth of Venus*, and for the equally Venusian figure on the left-hand side of his *Primavera*. In the latter she stares intently at a dark young man reaching up for an apple – this is plausibly a portrait of Giuliano. These paintings were commissioned in the early 1480s by Giuliano's cousin Lorenzo di Pierfrancesco de' Medici for his villa at Castello.[98] By the time they were painted both Simonetta and Giuliano were dead – she from consumption in 1476, and he from an assassin's dagger in 1478. Her image is nostalgically evoked, a memory of the enchanted moment of the *giostra*.

Is it possible, I wonder, that the poetic Venusian theme which emanates from the *giostra* of 1475, and which is later evoked in these famous Botticelli paintings, may also be a clue to the particular ambience of Leonardo's *Ginevra*? A brief passage from the work of Marsilio Ficino suggests that it is. In his *De vita coelitus comparanda* (*Of Drawing down the Life of Heaven*), written in the early 1470s, Ficino discourses on what can be summed up as Neoplatonic magic, and one of the sections of his treatise deals with the designing of talismans. One of these talismans, which gives 'health and strength', is described as 'an image of Venus as a young woman [*puella*], holding apples and flowers, and dressed in white and gold'.[99] I think Leonardo's portrait may have been conceived, at Bembo's request, as a kind of talismanic, Venusian image of Ginevra. She is not holding an apple (as far as we know), but she is probably holding flowers; her dress is golden and her bodice is white; her hair and her face echo this colour-scheme. In this reading, Leonardo's picture shows us Ginevra as Venus, just as Botticelli's pictures – later, and hence perhaps derivatively – show us Simonetta Cattanei as Venus. For Ficino, of course, Venus symbolized spiritual rather than sexual love – as in the *De amore*, which we know Bembo owned, where the 'ecstasy [*furor*] of Venus' is said to 'transmute the spirit of man into a god, by the ardour of love'.[100] In Bembo's eyes and in Leonardo's, this sort of meaning would attach to the painting: a talisman of philosophical love.

Bembo's involvement with the philosopher Ficino in these years is well documented. He attended Ficino's Platonic 'academy' at Careggi, he corresponded with him, he wrote his praise of Ginevra in his own copy of Ficino's *De amore*. His whole courtship of Ginevra is done within an ambience of dilettante Neoplatonism. The Benci were also part of the Ficino circle. We know that Ginevra's father gave Ficino a rare Greek manuscript of Plato; we know also that two of her cousins, Tommaso and Giovanni di Lorenzo de' Benci, were scholarly assistants of Ficino's.

In these ways the Ginevra portrait brings Leonardo close to Ficino's academy of philosophers and poets. The commissioner and the subject of the portrait both belong in that circle, and the painting itself has a Ficinian shimmer of love and magic. Leonardo is perhaps on the sidelines – a mere studio hand, a hired craftsman, but one whose brilliant intelligence would be recognized. Leonardo was not a Platonist: the 'disciple of experience' has a different agenda, and the 'first causes' he seeks are not the emanations of the Platonic 'World Mind'. In the broad philosophical divide of the day he is an Aristotelian, absorbed in the workings of the material world rather than the numina of the spirit. But to the aspiring young artist of the mid-1470s, Ficino must have been a charismatic figure, and his desire to communicate complex ideas in a clean, simple prose – and in Italian, too: the *De amore* was translated into Italian in 1474, 'so that this health-giving manna should be within the reach of all' – would have impressed Leonardo. And how could he resist Ficino's stirring synopsis of Plato's philosophical aspirations: that the minds of those who practise philosophy have 'recovered their wings through wisdom', and so can 'fly back to the heavenly kingdom'?[101]

There is some fragmentary evidence of Leonardo's connection with the Ficino circle on a page of the Codex Atlanticus. This has a list of names in Leonardo's hand, at the head of which is a certain Bernardo di Simone; on the verso of the sheet the name appears again in a series of doodles or pen-trials, in mirror-script: '*bernardo di sim / di di disimon / ber bern berna*'.[102] A plausible candidate for this man on Leonardo's mind is Bernardo di Simone Canigiani, who was one of Ficino's pupils. The date of the sheet, judging from the script and the early technological drawings on the verso, is around 1478–80. Snatches of text are found on the page. Leonardo is in melancholy or indeed philosophical mood: '*Chi tempo ha e tempo aspetta perde l'amico*' ('He who has time and waits for time will lose his friend'); and '*Come io vi disse ne di passati, voi sapete che io sono sanza alcuni degli amici*' ('As I told you in days gone by, you know that I am without any friends'); and this haunting little memo:

Essendomi sollecitato
S'amor non è che dunque

[Now I am fired up, if there is no love, then what?]

There is something of this melancholy, love-lorn tone in the Ginevra portrait itself. The young woman's expression is ethereal, but one glimpses in it also a more human truth, which is that behind these amusing Platonic posturings lie real hearts that get broken. In the *catasto* of 1480, Ginevra's husband, Luigi – I am tempted to call him her long-suffering husband – spoke of the costs he had incurred because of her 'sickness'. This cannot be taken as gospel (because of the motive of tax relief), but it coincides well enough with Bembo's last departure from Florence, in May 1480, and with the tradition that Ginevra retired thereafter to the country. Two sonnets addressed to her by Lorenzo de' Medici suggest this. He praises her decision to 'leave the passion and evil of the city' and never 'gaze back on it'. We do not know if she really devoted herself to a life of prayer in rustic seclusion, as implied by these poems, but it is true that little is heard of her after her brief and brilliant courtship with Bembo, and what little there is seems retrospective: a noted beauty of a bygone age. She died, a childless widow, in about 1520.

→→ THE SALTARELLI AFFAIR ←←

Platonic love-games or real emotions? The question which hovers over the Ginevra portrait now enters more closely into the story of Leonardo's life.

In early April 1476 an anonymous denunciation was posted in one of the receptacles placed around the city for that purpose, known as *tamburi* (drums) or, more picturesquely, *buchi della verità* (holes of truth). A notarized copy of this document survives among the archives of the Ufficiali di Notte – the Officers of the Night and Conservers of the Morality of Monasteries, who were essentially the Florentine night-watch, though they could as well be described as the vice squad. It reads as follows:

To the officers of the Signoria: I hereby testify that Jacopo Saltarelli, the brother of Giovanni Saltarelli, lives with him at the goldsmith's shop in Vacchereccia, directly opposite the *buco*; he dresses in black, and is seventeen years old or thereabouts. This Jacopo pursues many immoral activities and consents to satisfy those persons who request such sinful things from him. And in this manner he has performed many things, that is, he has provided such services to many dozens of persons of whom I have good information, and at the present time I name some of them. These men have sodomized the said Jacopo and so I will swear.

The informer provides the names of four of Jacopo's alleged consorts or customers. They are:

- Bartolomeo di Pasquino, goldsmith, living on Vacchereccia
- Lionardo di Ser Piero da Vinci, living with Andrea del Verrocchio
- Baccino the doublet-maker, living near Orsanmichele, in that street with the two large wool-shearers' shops leading down to the loggia of the Cierchi; he has opened a new doublet shop
- Lionardo Tornabuoni, alias 'Il Teri', dressed in black

Against these four names is written, '*absoluti cum conditione ut retamburentur*'. This indicates that they were at liberty pending further inquiries, and that they were obliged to attend the court when summoned. They did so two months later, on 7 June. It seems the case against them was formally dropped.[103]

This rather lurid document was first published in 1896, but had certainly been known about before that. In the fourth volume of his edition of Vasari, published in 1879, Gaetano Milanesi refers to 'certain charges' against Leonardo but declines to say what they were. Jean-Paul Richter and Gustavo Uzielli similarly refer to an unspecified crime: Uzielli calls it a 'malicious rumour'. When the *denuncia* was finally published by Nino Smiraglia Scognamiglio, he was at pains to say that Leonardo was 'above suspicion' in the matter, and was 'a stranger to any form of love that was against the laws of nature'.[104]

Since Freud, and subsequent studies like Giuseppina Fumagalli's *Eros e Leonardo*, this initial period of denial seems quaint. It is now widely accepted that Leonardo was homosexual. At least one of his early biographers, Giovanni Paolo Lomazzo, is explicit on the subject: in his *Sogni e raggionamenti* of *c.* 1564 he imagines the following dialogue between Leonardo and Phidias, the great sculptor of antiquity. Phidias asks Leonardo about one of his 'favourite pupils':

PHIDIAS: Did you ever play with him that 'backside game' which Florentines love so much?

LEONARDO: Many times! You should know that he was a very fair young man, especially around the age of fifteen.

PHIDIAS: And are you not ashamed to say so?

LEONARDO: No! Why should I be ashamed? Among men of worth there is scarcely greater cause for pride . . .[105]

Lomazzo is particularly referring to Leonardo's relationship with his Milanese pupil Giacomo Caprotti, known as 'Salai'. Vasari is more discreet, but his description of Salai probably trails the same idea: 'He was extraordinarily beautiful and comely, with lovely curling hair which Leonardo adored.' The adjective Vasari uses – *vago*: comely, pretty, charming – probably contains an overtone of effeminacy. Other young men flit into view in contexts suggestive of homosexuality – an apprentice called Paolo; a young man called Fioravanti: we shall meet these later. And while the preponderance of male nudes in Leonardo's sketchbooks is conventional, some of his drawings are frankly homoerotic. The obvious instance is the so-called *Angelo incarnato*, with its full-frontal erection (see page 468). This drawing is in turn related to the Louvre *St John*, probably his last painting: a meltingly poetic study of an androgynous-looking young man, with the cascading curls which he 'adored' in Salai, and which are a constant in his work from the first studio paintings of the early 1470s.

There are some who would like to keep Leonardo's sexuality in this poetic, Pateresque mode of shimmery young angels and androgynes, but they have to contend with such documents as folio 44 of the Codex Arundel, which has a kind of vocabulary list consisting of punning variants of the word *cazzo*, an impolite term for the penis; or the drawing in one of the Forster notebooks which Carlo Pedretti has nicknamed *Il cazzo in corso* (The Running Cock); or the recently recovered verso of a fragment in the Codex Atlanticus which features two phalluses, with legs attached so they look like cartoon animals, one of which is nudging with its 'nose' a circle, or hole, with the name 'Salai' scribbled above it. The latter graffito is not by Leonardo, but suggests what passed for humorous comment among his pupils and apprentices.[106]

It is all, in the end, a matter of interpretation. Like most students of Leonardo today, I interpret him as homosexual – though there is some piquant evidence, which I will look at later, that he was not exclusively so. The allegation laid against him in 1476 is plausible enough, though this is not the same as saying it was true.

What did it mean to be gay in Quattrocento Florence?[107] Predictably, the answer is complex and ambiguous. On the one hand, homosexuality was widespread, as is suggested by Lomazzo's dialogue, where the 'backside game' of sodomy is particularly associated with Florence; the Germans went as far as to use the word *Florenzer* (Florentine) to mean a sodomite. In Medici circles, homosexuality was openly tolerated: the sculptor Donatello, the poet Poliziano, the banker Filippo Strozzi were all known to be gay.

Botticelli was reputed to be, and like Leonardo he was the subject of an anonymous *denuncia*; and among later gay artists there were Michelangelo and Benvenuto Cellini. The latter was apparently omnivorous: he recounts his heterosexual conquests with gusto in his autobiography, but it is a fact that in 1523 he was fined by the Florentine magistrates for 'obscene acts' with one Giovanni Rigogli. Accused by the sculptor Bandinelli of being a 'filthy sodomite', Cellini replied with a flourish, 'I wish to God that I knew how to exercise such a noble art, for we read that Jupiter practised it with Ganymede in paradise, while here on earth it is practised by the greatest emperors and kings.'[108] This catches, if ironically, the same idea which Lomazzo gives to Leonardo in his dialogue: that homosexuality is a 'cause for pride' among 'men of worth'.

Another factor is the Florentine craze for Platonism. Plato's ideal of love between men and boys was well known; there is much about this in Ficino's *De amore*, and though Ficino stressed it as chaste and asexual, it is clear that ideas of 'Platonic' or 'Socratic' love served as a fashionable disguise for homosexuality. We have found Leonardo close to the Ficino circle: a congenial tone of refined male eroticism may have been one of its attractions.

All this gave a new gloss to homosexuality in 1470s Florence, but not one that was recognized by the vice-hunting Officers of the Night. Sodomy was nominally a capital crime, punishable (in theory but almost never in practice) by burning at the stake. A statistical survey of Office of the Night prosecutions shows that over a 75-year period (1430–1505) more than 10,000 men were charged with sodomy – a rough average of 130 a year. Of these, about one in five was found guilty. A few were executed; others were exiled, branded, fined or publicly humiliated.[109] Thus the charges levelled against Leonardo in 1476 were by no means uncommon, and by no means trifling. He was almost certainly arrested; he was in danger of savage punishment. Between the philosophical languors of Platonic love and the holding-cells of the Office of the Night is a long drop.

Prosecution, moreover, was the sharp end of a more general disapproval among the God-fearing majority. Homosexuality was routinely denounced from the pulpits, though not all went as far as the preacher Bernardino da Siena, who exhorted the faithful to spit on the floor of Santa Croce and shout, '*Al fuoco! Bruciate tutti i sodomiti!*' ('To the fire! Burn all sodomites!') Things got worse in 1484, when a papal bull effectively stigmatized homosexuals as diabolical: their 'heretical perversions' were on a par with having 'carnal knowledge with demons', as witches were said to do. Those of a literary turn could read of the eternal punishment meted out to homosexuals in Dante's *Inferno*. In the seventh circle of hell are found the 'violent against God, Nature and Art' – respectively blasphemers, sodomites and usurers. The sodomites, a 'wretched crew' (*turba grana*) or 'filthy scum' (*tigna brama*), are condemned to wander round in an endless circle across a 'burning desert'. Both the desert and the self-completing circle (*'fenno una rota di se'*: 'they made of themselves a wheel') are an image of sterility: sodomy is a taboo – a 'violence against nature' – because non-generative.[110] In this more subtle Dantesque reading – more so than in the homophobic rantings of the preachers – lies real disquiet. Leonardo knew the work of Dante, and quotes from him in the notebooks. He would also know Botticelli's illustrations for the *Divine Comedy* – the earliest drawings probably date from the 1470s; some engravings based on them were included in Landino's edition of Dante, published in Florence in 1481. We have only the later series, done in the mid-1490s for Lorenzo di Pierfrancesco de' Medici,[111] but its image of naked homosexuals tormented with firebrands and shuffling around in a circle like an eternal chain-gang tells us something of the guilt and foreboding that might haunt a sensitive young man under arrest for sodomy.

This is the backdrop of the denunciation handed in to the authorities in April 1476. We know nothing for certain of its motives except this: it was intended to cause trouble for Jacopo Saltarelli, and for the four men accused of consorting with him. It was an act – or anyway the first stage of an act – of criminalization.

Who was Jacopo Saltarelli? His accuser tells us that he was about seventeen, and had a brother called Giovanni, with whom he lived and worked at a goldsmith's shop on the Vacchereccia. In the Florentine *catasti* we find the Saltarelli to be a numerous clan clustered within a precise area, the Gonfalone Carro, of the Santa Croce quarter: of the seven Saltarelli families listed in the 1427 register, six are from this *gonfalone*. The wealthiest of these is Giovanni di Renzo Saltarelli, assessed at 2,918 florins; his occupation is given as *vaiaio o pellicaio*, a dealer in furs, and especially in the grey-blue squirrel fur called *vaio*. In 1427 Giovanni had seven dependants, and a generation later, in the *catasto* of 1457, we find three of his sons, Bartolomeo, Antonio and Bernardo, still living in the same neighbourhood.[112] It seems likely that Jacopo Saltarelli was of this clan; if so, he too probably grew up in the neighbourhood of Santa Croce, where Leonardo also lived and worked.

One notes how intensely parochial are this *denuncia* and its references. Two of the accused, Saltarelli and Pasquino, live and work on the Vacchereccia. (It is not quite clear from the phrasing whether they live and work

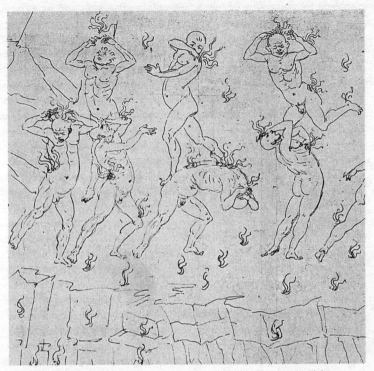

The torments of homosexuality. Detail from Botticelli's illustration of the seventh circle of hell in Dante's Inferno.

in the same goldsmith's shop or in neighbouring ones.) The informer is a local man too, for the shop where Jacopo works is described as standing opposite the *buco* or *tamburo*, presumably meaning the one into which the report was posted. The Vaccereccia is the short, wide street leading out of the south-western corner of the Piazza della Signoria. A couple of blocks to the north is Via dei Cimatori, where another of the accused, Baccino the doublet-maker, lives. The *denuncia* is at the level of a nosy neighbour scandalized by certain comings and goings. Or perhaps the neighbour is a competitor. Another goldsmith's shop on the Vaccereccia was owned by the artist Antonio del Pollaiuolo; he declares it among various 'small possessions' in his tax return of 1480. It was run by Paolo di Giovanni Sogliani, who is described as Pollaiuolo's 'painter and assistant'.[113] Is it possible the accusation was posted by Sogliani, thus conveniently causing problems for two rival goldsmiths, Saltarelli and Pasquino, and for a rival painter, Leonardo? The use of the anonymous *denuncia* against business rivals remains a feature of Italian life to this day.

The odd man out is the last-named on the list of sinners: Leonardo Tornabuoni, or 'Il Teri'. No address is given for him, probably because everyone in Florence knew that you found a Tornabuoni at the Palazzo Tornabuoni, on the wide and well-appointed street running up from the Ponte Santa Trinità. The Tornabuoni were one of the leading families in the city. Their long alliance with the Medici was cemented in the early 1440s by the marriage of Piero de' Medici to Lucrezia Tornabuoni. She was much loved by the chroniclers and commentators: affectionate, witty, a poet and a businesswoman – the kind of new Florentine woman who paved the way for women like Ginevra de' Benci of the next generation. Lucrezia's brother Giovanni was the manager of the Rome branch of the Medici bank, but was also linked to the Medici's old antagonists the Pitti through his marriage to Luca Pitti's daughter Francesca. It was Giovanni who commissioned the wonderful Ghirlandaio frescos in Santa Maria Novella. Various Tornabuoni can be seen there, caught by Ghirlandaio's camera; perhaps Leonardo Tornabuoni is among them.

The Tornabuoni were a large family, and this Leonardo has not been precisely identified, but the fact that he is some kind of relative of Lorenzo de' Medici's mother seems to add another dimension to the proceedings. Some have wondered if there are political cross-currents at work. Has Leonardo da Vinci got caught up in some kind of smear campaign against Leonardo Tornabuoni, and through him the Medici? Like my own slur against Pollaiuolo's shop-manager, this remains uncorroborated. What perhaps seems more likely is that the Tornabuoni–Medici connection adds a dimension of influence *after* the event: that certain words would have been whispered in certain ears to ensure that the affair was dealt with swiftly and discreetly. The word 'absolved' next to Leonardo's name tells us that the charges against him were dropped. It does not tell us that he was innocent of them, and the presence of a Medici protégé on the charge-sheet makes it quite probable that it was influence rather than innocence that got him off.

According to the informer, Jacopo Saltarelli 'consents to' sex and has 'provided such services to many dozens of persons'. It is not quite clear whether Jacopo is being presented as a promiscuous young homosexual or as a male prostitute. This distinction is imprecise, but seems important: is Leonardo consorting with a lover or visiting a rent-boy? On the whole the tone seems quite upmarket: the Vacchereccia is a good address, where

Saltarelli is gainfully employed as a goldsmith's apprentice or assistant. There is also that sleight of hand so common in informers' reports – there are supposedly 'many dozens' of visitors, but only four of them have names and faces. Four lovers do not exactly make a boy a prostitute, even if he receives certain gifts from them afterwards.

When Smiraglia Scognamiglio first published the *denuncia*, in 1896, he conjectured that Leonardo had been unjustly accused because he had used Saltarelli – innocently – as a model. This is certainly plausible, though now we accept the truth of Leonardo's homosexuality we might think of the artist–model relationship as a context rather than an exculpation. The possibility that Jacopo served Leonardo as an artist's model is strengthened by a cryptic note which Leonardo wrote, and then crossed out, on a sheet in the Codex Atlanticus. The sheet is datable to around 1505, and the words that Leonardo wrote are these: '*Quando io feci domeneddio putto voi mi metteste in prigione, ora s'io lo fo grande voi mi farete pegio*' – 'When I made a Christ-child you put me in prison, and now if I show Him grown up you will do worse to me.'[114] This is very hard to interpret, but one reading would be that the Christ-child was a work for which Jacopo had posed as a model; that this had caused problems with the Church authorities when Jacopo was denounced as a homosexual; and that similar problems were now brewing over a painting or sculpture showing the 'grown-up' Christ. The only extant work of Leonardo's that could be described as a 'Christ-child' is the terracotta head of the *Youthful Christ*, which is plausibly dated to the 1470s. Is this Jacopo, with the long hair and the downturned eyes, and that 'air' – in the words of Giovanni Paolo Lomazzo – 'which may be the tenderness of youth, but which seems also old'?

Another young man who strikes me as a possible image of Jacopo is seen in a drawing in the Pierpont Morgan Library in New York (page 123). This certainly emanates from the Verrocchio circle, and has been attributed to both Verrocchio and Leonardo. It shows a very pretty, round-faced youth with thick ringletted hair; his full lips are in a slight pout which, together with the languidly hooded eyes, gives him a smouldering look and a general air of arrogant self-esteem. The drawing, in three-quarter profile, has an odd affinity with the Virgin of Leonardo's *Annunciation*, raising the same kind of disturbing crossover between homoeroticism and sacred subjects as the *Youthful Christ*. A Verrocchio drawing in Berlin probably shows the same model. This too was once attributed to Leonardo, whose name is written in a curatorial hand in the bottom right-hand corner. It is pricked for transfer, and may be an early study for one of the angels in the Fortaguerri monument, commissioned in 1476. He is, at any rate, the kind of pretty

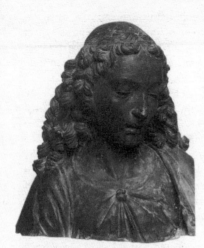

Terracotta head of the Youthful
Christ, *attributed to Leonardo.*

young model who sits for the artists of Via Ghibellina, and if certain 'sinful things' were suggested he looks like he might consent to them.

The idea that Leonardo's riddling comment about the Christ-child refers back to the Saltarelli affair would suggest that the *denuncia* of 1476 led to a period of imprisonment. It was probably brief – perhaps only arrest and detention by the Officers of the Night – but it would have left its mark. It adds a certain edge to some curious contraptions which Leonardo drew and described for releasing men from prison. They are found in the Codex Atlanticus – a machine for ripping the bars off a window, and another captioned 'To open a prison from the inside'.[115] (p. 147) They date from around 1480. They are among Leonardo's earliest inventions, and they perhaps relate to this captivity experienced in 1476, and still on his mind thirty years later: 'you put me in prison.' Freedom, Leonardo once wrote, is 'the chiefest gift of Nature',[116] and everything we know about him suggests that confinement of any kind – physical, professional, intellectual and indeed emotional – was irksome to him.

The Saltarelli affair is the first but not the only suggestion of Leonardo's homosexuality during his early years in Florence. There is another cryptic memorandum to consider – cryptic because partly illegible – which is found on a sheet of drawings and diagrams in the Uffizi.[117] Among the drawings is a pair of heads, one of which may be an early self-portrait (see page 175). The writing is typical of Leonardo's earlier 'notarial' hand, full of scrolly decorative curlicues; in some parts it looks as if he is doodling or trying out a new pen. At the top of the sheet Leonardo has written something about a young man called Fioravanti di Domenico living in Florence. It is difficult to read, and where the paper is smudged at the top left-hand corner quite impossible. This is how J.-P. Richter transcribed the lines in the 1880s:

> *Fioravanti di domenicho j[n] Firenze e co[m]pere*
> *Amantissimo quant'e mio . . .*

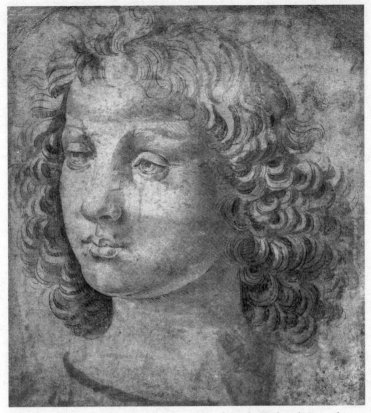

Pen and ink portrait of a young man, c. 1475, from the studio of Verrocchio.

He translates this as 'Fioravanti di Domenico in Florence is my most beloved friend, as though he were my [brother],' the last word being a conjecture for the illegible scribble at the end of the second line. In his 1913 study of Leonardo, Jens Thiis provided a rather different reading:

> *Fioravanti di domenicho j[n] Firenze e che aparve*
> *Amantissimo quanto mi e una vergine che io ami*

This would give us, 'Fioravanti di Domenico in Florence is one who seems very loving towards me, and is a virgin whom I might love.'

Carlo Pedretti prefers Richter's reading, but sees in the second line subsequent to '*mio*' only 'calligraphic squiggles which make nonsense'. It is certainly hard to muster all the minims that Thiis claimed to see there, so one cannot say that the note goes into overt homosexuality, but clearly Leonardo had very warm feelings towards his 'beloved' Fioravanti. The standard patronymic form of the name makes it unlikely he will ever be identified.[118] It is possible his features are preserved on some page of Leonardo's Florentine sketchbooks, but like Jacopo Saltarelli he remains elusive – not a face but a certain tone, or frisson.

→→ 'COMPANIONS IN PISTOIA' ←←

It was perhaps convenient, in the wake of the Saltarelli affair, that Verrocchio should have important works afoot in the city of Pistoia. On 15 May 1476 – precisely during that edgy period between accusation and acquittal – he won the commission to produce an enormous marble cenotaph in Pistoia cathedral in memory of Cardinal Niccolò Fortaguerri. There were disputes – the Consiglio of Pistoia had voted 300 florins for the work; Verrocchio wanted 350. In early 1477 Piero del Pollaiuolo submitted a model which the Consiglio was disposed to accept, but the dispute was arbitrated by Lorenzo de' Medici, who decided in favour of Verrocchio.[119]

Around the same time, Verrocchio was commissioned to produce an altarpiece in memory of a former Bishop of Pistoia, Donato de' Medici, a distant relative of Lorenzo's. This altarpiece, with a Verrocchiesque Madonna and Child flanked by St Donatus and St John the Baptist, was painted by Lorenzo di Credi – it is his first securely dated work. It was substantially under way by 1478, but once again there were financial disagreements and it was not finished until about 1485. There are strong signs that Leonardo was involved in the original conception of this altarpiece. A small preparatory study in tempera for the figure of St Donatus (the namesake of the Medici bishop whom the altarpiece commemorates) has recently been proposed as his. There is a silverpoint drawing of St John the Baptist at Windsor which has strong similarities with the St John in Credi's altarpiece.[120] And there is that small *Annunciation* in the Louvre, which was originally one of the predellas (the narrow painted panels at the bottom) of the Pistoia altarpiece, and which is demonstrably based on the composition of Leonardo's *Annunciation*. It is sometimes said that the predella version is also by Leonardo, but it is more likely to be by Credi working under Leonardo's supervision.

These pictorial links suggest Leonardo's involvement in the early stages of the Pistoia altarpiece. He was by now the most accomplished painter in

Verrocchio's studio, and it is natural to find his junior colleague Credi working under his supervision. Leonardo would also have been involved in the early stages of the Fortaguerri cenotaph, and there is a terracotta model for the monument in the Victoria & Albert Museum which some believe to be partly his work. These Pistoia projects of *c.* 1476-7 would have offered Leonardo a welcome change of scene in the aftermath of the Saltarelli affair. Pistoia was a town he knew: in fact he had family there – his aunt Violante had married a Pistoiese. It was just the kind of pleasant provincial backwater to which a young man might retreat – to which he might be dispatched by his employer – while the storm of scandal blew over back in Florence.

Some confirmation of this is found on the same sheet of notes and drawings which contains that amorous reference to Fioravanti di Domenico. At the bottom of the page is a fragmentary sentence. The beginning of it is torn away; what remains is the phrase '*e chompa in pisstoja*' – 'and companions in Pistoia'. (*Chompa* is a contraction of *compare*, an affectionate word meaning a comrade or buddy.) Another fragment on the page bears the date 1478. Sometime before this, we infer, Leonardo had made some friends in Pistoia. It is possible that Fioravanti was himself one of them; another may have been the Pistoiese poet Antonio Cammelli, who can be discerned in Leonardo's company a couple of years after this. This hard-to-read scribble is further evidence that Leonardo took the opportunity to put some space between him and Florence in the period after the Saltarelli scandal.

A few miles west of Pistoia stands the little hilltop village of San Gennaro, with its Romanesque *pieve*, or parish church, founded by Neapolitan refugees fleeing an eruption of Vesuvius in the early sixth century. Leonardo certainly knew the village, for he marks it on one of his maps of central Tuscany, connected with a project to canalize the Arno river via Pistoia and Serravalle.[121]

Inside this church, on a low pedestal by the west door, is a small terracotta statue of an angel. Ignored for centuries, it was recognized about fifty years ago as being 'of the school of' Verrocchio, and is now accepted as being entirely by the hand of Leonardo da Vinci (Plate 8). It is a beautiful piece, alert and full of movement. Some parts are modelled with precision, others with a note of carelessness and speed which is more typical of a *bozzo*, a rough model, than of a finished sculpture. The angel's right arm is an unmistakable echo of the *Annunciation* angel, and the long curling hair is a Leonardo trademark. I am struck by the wonderful realism of the right foot, extending slightly over the pediment – the bossed knuckles, the well-worn sandal, the downward curl of the little toe. The pose of the angel is echoed in some figures on a page of Francesco Ferrucci's sketchbook – the same sketchbook which has that drawing of the model for Verrocchio's *David*; the figures are not by Leonardo, but there is a line of writing on the page which seems to be his.

Nothing is known of the provenance of this piece. It was certainly at San Gennaro by the eighteenth century: its first appearance in the records is on 31 July 1773, when a workman's ladder fell on it and broke the upper part into several pieces. It was painstakingly restored by a local man named Barsotti. A thin crack like an accident-scar is still discernible on the angel's forehead. The traces of paint – yellow, green and red – which can be seen on the sculpture are probably the restorer's, but may indicate an original colouring from which he was working: in other words it was originally a polychrome sculpture, as was conventional in church statuary when the material was terracotta or wood.[122] It remains a mystery how a sculpture by Leonardo da Vinci comes to be standing in an unregarded corner of a small country church near Pistoia. One answer might be that it has been here from the beginning – that is, from the time it was created, in about 1477, by a young Florentine artist temporarily holed up in the area and glad for a small local commission, glad for the respite of the green Tuscan hills.

On an April day in 1477 Leonardo turns twenty-five. I imagine him staring at his face in the mirror – an action whose complex optometrics he will later puzzle over under a rubric beginning, 'Let *a–b* be a face which sends its simulacrum to the mirror *c–d*.'[123] He wonders how much he likes what he sees. He is no longer, by the standards of life expectancy in Quattrocento Florence, quite a young man. He has in some measure become what he will always be.

To others that face in the mirror was one of great beauty and translucent intelligence. The early biographers are unanimous on this. Paolo Giovio, who had known him personally, said, 'He was by nature very courteous, cultivated and generous, and his face was extraordinarily beautiful.' A French writer at the court of Louis XII, Jean Lemaire, speaks of Leonardo's 'supernatural grace' – this is in a poem published in 1509, and is probably also a first-hand impression.[124] The Anonimo Gaddiano says, 'He was very attractive, well-proportioned, graceful and good-looking,' with beautiful hair, arranged in ringlets, 'down to the middle of his chest'. None of these sources refers to the long beard which is such a feature of the mythos, and which is probably a late addition to the Leonardo look.

Vasari is insistent to the point of hyperbole. Leonardo was a man of 'outstanding beauty' and 'infinite grace' – 'He was striking and handsome, and his great presence brought comfort to the most troubled soul . . . He owned nothing, one might say, and he worked very little, yet he always kept servants and horses.' If Vasari were writing today he might have summed up that 'great presence' which could lift people's spirits, that effortless grace with which 'he commanded everyone's affection', as 'charisma'. Vasari also presents Leonardo as a man of great physical strength and dexterity: he was 'so strong he could withstand any violence; with his right hand he could bend the iron ring of a doorbell, or a horseshoe, as if they were lead'. One has to put some of this down to Vasari's heroizing tendency; there are echoes here of Leon Battista Alberti's alleged athletic prowess, which should also be taken with a pinch of salt. It is a trope, a rhetorical expression of Leonardo as all-round superhero. It perhaps suggests Vasari's desire to rectify an overtone of effeminacy in the earlier biographers' descriptions of Leonardo's beauty.

Whether or not he could bend horseshoes with his bare hands, the consensus is that Leonardo was a handsome, tall and imposing figure, a fine horseman, a tireless walker. He was also, we know, a snappy dresser – something of a dandy. His hair is carefully coiffed. He wears rose-pink tunics, fur-lined coats, jasper rings, boots of Cordova leather. There is about him a touch of fastidiousness: 'Take fresh rosewater and moisten your hands with it, then take flower of lavender and rub it between your hands, and it will be good.'[125] In one of his comparisons between the painter and the sculptor he pictures the latter sweating and dirty with labour, 'his face smeared with marble dust so he looks like a baker'. The painter, by contrast, works 'at ease'; he is 'well dressed'; he 'moves a light brush dipped in delicate colours' and 'adorns himself with the clothes he fancies'.[126]

But we cannot understand this rather showy young man without seeing also the strains of uncertainty and loneliness and dissatisfaction in the face that looks out from the mirror, the sense of himself as an outsider: illegitimate, unlettered, sexually illicit. These moods will be concealed more and more hermetically in an aura of aloofness. They are glimpsed in scattered fragmentary phrases of his manuscripts – little chinks of darkness: 'If freedom is dear to you, do not reveal that my face is the prison of love . . .'[127]

PART THREE

Independence
1477–1482

He is a poor pupil who does not go beyond his master.

Forster MS 3, fol. 66v

In about 1477 Leonardo set up his own studio in Florence. This was a natural progression: he had been ten years with Verrocchio as pupil, apprentice and assistant. The portrait of Ginevra shows him already breaking the envelope – it is visibly linked to the Verrocchio ambit, but its poetic tone is something entirely new. He now enters into the first, difficult period of independence: a young *maestro* in a crowded, competitive market.

The first clear sign of his new independence is a contract he signed on 10 January 1478, but there is another document, recently discovered, which gives us a curious hint of the ambience of Leonardo's *bottega*. It is a letter from Giovanni Bentivoglio, Lord of Bologna, to Lorenzo de' Medici, and it concerns a young man whose name is given in the letter as 'Paulo de Leonardo de Vinci da Firenze'.[1] There was a flutter of excitement in the Italian press when this came to light in the 1990s, since the formation of his name could suggest that this Paolo was a hitherto unsuspected son of Leonardo da Vinci. A moment's reflection makes this unlikely: for reasons implicit in the letter, Paolo cannot have been born much after 1462, when Leonardo was ten. Far more likely is that he was an apprentice of Leonardo's. As noted, it was conventional for an apprentice to take on the name of his master, as Verrocchio had done.

So it seems we have here the name of one of Leonardo's first apprentices, and with the name comes a story. From Bentivoglio's letter, which is dated 4 February 1479, we learn that Paolo had been sent away from Florence 'some time ago', because of the 'wicked life he had followed there'. This exile was to 'reform' him and to 'remove him from the bad company he kept'. It seems that Lorenzo de' Medici was personally involved in this, for when Paolo arrived in Bologna he was promptly imprisoned, and Bentivoglio specifically says that this was at Lorenzo's request: 'In compliance with letters from Your Magnificence he was put in prison.' Paolo spent six months in jail, but after his release, 'having purged himself of his sins', he 'devoted himself to the art of marquetry, which he had already begun to learn there [i.e. in Florence], so that he has become a skilled craftsman, and pursues it as his trade'. He is now anxious to return to Florence, and his brothers have written to Bentivoglio asking for this. This is the motive of Bentivoglio's letter – to seek Lorenzo's 'benevolent permission and good pardon' so that Paolo can return. He is a reformed character, says Bentivoglio; he promises henceforth 'to be an honest man, and live in an orderly manner'.

It is a spicy story, and it leads back to Leonardo, who is identified patronymically as Paolo's master. Given that he was in jail in Bologna for six months, and had thereafter established and supported himself as an *intarsiatore* or marquetry artist, we can say that the date of Paolo's scandalous exit from Florence must have been at least a year, if not more, before the date of the letter – thus late 1477 or early 1478. We can reconstruct the situation retrospectively, as follows. In 1477 Leonardo had a Florentine apprentice or servant named Paolo. He was probably a teenager. He had brothers whose social status was not negligible: Bentivoglio twice mentions them in his letter. He perhaps did not have a father, whose role the brothers seem to be taking in the affair – this would tie in with his status as Leonardo's adoptive 'son' in the studio sense. He already had some training in marquetry, the highly skilled and much demanded craft of inlaying wood. He lived, however, a 'wicked life', and was involved in 'bad company' (*mala conversatione*), and by early 1478 he had been hustled out of the city. The nature of this wickedness is not actually stated, but it is very likely that it was homosexuality. A further imputation – only an imputation, but hard to avoid – is that among the bad company from which young Paolo needed rescuing was his master, Leonardo da Vinci. And so to the names of Jacopo Saltarelli and Fioravanti di Domenico we add another of Leonardo's boyfriends. That he is also, within the workshop convention, Leonardo's 'son' is a detail that Freud would have enjoyed getting to grips with.

Thus a whiff of scandal hangs over Leonardo's fledgling studio. Little more than a year after his brush with the Officers of the Night, he is once again touched by charges of homosexuality. Lorenzo de' Medici perhaps had notice of that first scandal, since it also touched a member of his mother's family, and he is certainly involved in the expulsion of Paolo di Leonardo.

Despite this inauspicious overtone, Leonardo received his first recorded commission as an independent painter on 10 January 1478.[2] It was a commission from the Signoria for a large altarpiece to hang in the chapel of the Palazzo Vecchio, the Capella di San Bernardo. He was not actually the Signoria's first choice for the job – the commission had been turned down by Piero del Pollaiuolo the previous month. It seems a highly prestigious offer, and it was backed up with a cash advance of 25 florins, paid in mid-March, so it is curious that Leonardo never delivered the work. It is his first abandoned project, the first of the renegings which will dog his professional career.

The new altarpiece was to replace an earlier painting by Bernardo Daddi which showed the apparition of the Virgin to St Bernard, and the agreement indicates that Leonardo was to produce a painting on the same theme. No trace of any sketch or study for a *Vision of St Bernard* can be found among his drawings, but it is just possible that an echo of this ghostly work is discernible in a painting by Filippino Lippi. According to the Anonimo Gaddiano, Leonardo had actually started work on the painting, and it was later finished from his preparatory drawings by Filippino. There is indeed an altarpiece by Filippino showing the Vision of St Bernard: a fine work, now in the Badia Fiorentina. It was painted in the mid-1480s for the Pugliese family chapel at Marignolle, near Florence; the donor, Piero del Pugliese, appears bottom right. Is the Anonimo right? Is that cluster of Madonna and angels on the left – which can certainly be called 'Leonardesco' – an actual rendition of a lost Leonardo cartoon of *c.* 1478? It is possible, though one of the angels has a strong affinity with Leonardo's *Annunciation*, and does not therefore need a putative lost drawing to explain its Leonardesque look.[3]

A partially obliterated sentence on that page of notes and drawings which mentions Fioravanti di Domenico reads: '[. . .]*mbre 1478 inchomincai le 2 vergini Marie*'. The date may be September, November or December 1478. Which are the 'two Virgin Marys' or Madonnas that Leonardo began at that time? And are they the same as the two Madonnas that appear in his list of *c.* 1482, which itemizes various works he had done in Florence and was taking with him to Milan? They are described on the list as 'a Madonna finished' and 'another almost, which is in profile'.

Kenneth Clark believed that the Madonna in profile was the *Litta Madonna*, now in St Petersburg. The finished painting is certainly later: it is a product of Leonardo's Milanese studio, probably from the end of the 1480s. But Clark argues that it was begun in Florence, and was brought to Milan in precisely the unfinished state mentioned in the list of 1482. In its finished form it has manifestly non-Leonardian aspects, such as the strange changeling head of the child: these are the work of one of his Milanese pupils, Giovanni Antonio Boltraffio or Marco d'Oggiono. But there is a silverpoint studio drawing for the head of the Madonna, done on greenish paper, which is certainly by Leonardo.[4]

The Florentine genesis of the *Litta Madonna* remains unproved. We are on much surer ground with another Leonardo painting in the Hermitage – the *Benois Madonna* (Plate 9). Stylistically it belongs to Leonardo's first Florentine period. It is very probably one of the '2 *vergini*' he began in 1478, though whether it is also the 'finished' Madonna of the 1482 list is less certain: some aspects of the painting seem to lack finish.

This small (19 × 12 inches) oil painting, somewhat inexpertly transferred to canvas in the nineteenth century, is one of Leonardo's most underrated works. It has, for all its imperfections of detail, a sweetness and freshness and movement which immediately lift it beyond the posed, hieratic elegance of the Verrocchio Madonnas with their blonde hair and lifted little fingers. This Madonna is demonstrably a girl, not even a very beautiful girl. Her long, braided, auburn hair cascading down her left shoulder suggests for a moment the Simonetta Cattanei look – but only for a moment: again one has a sense of the role-models which Leonardo is conspicuously rejecting. She is the antithesis of Botticelli's languid, pretty, almond-eyed Madonnas. The great Bernard Berenson – who always preferred Leonardo's drawings to his paintings – found her frankly ugly: 'a woman with a bald forehead and puffed cheek, a toothless smile, blear eyes and furrowed throat'.

Also quite foreign to Verrocchio is the new dark, velvety tonality of the painting. The figures are lit dramatically amid the suggestive greys and russets of the background. The tone is muted, modest, domestic. Technical examination shows an underlying preparation of dark umber, with the colours spread over it 'in sediments, like a dew'.[5]

There are enigmas about the detail. There has been some retouching: the Madonna's neck and the child's right hand show signs of a later, flattening brush; the lower part of the drapery has also lost something. But it is the mouth which usually causes the viewer problems. The Madonna seems, as Berenson unkindly stresses, to be toothless. According to de Liphart, who examined the work in 1909, her half-open mouth revealed 'the presence of her teeth almost imperceptibly drawn on the black preparation beneath', but these vestiges seem now to have disappeared completely due to oxidization of the varnish.[6] The empty window is also problematic. Has something been unaccountably covered over here, or is it an original Leonardian trick? Deprived of the view it expected, the eye turns back with a renewed sense of the interiority of the scene. The high placing of the window gives the couple a sense of sequesteredness. They are not on view to the world: our glimpse of them is privileged. This is reinforced by the absence of eye-contact – neither mother nor child is looking at the spectator; the scene is enacted between the two of them, and is centred on the flower which the child contemplates. This small white flower is not, as is sometimes said, a sprig of jasmine, which is a five-petalled flower (and is represented as such in the Uffizi *Leda*), but is a member of the four-petalled family known as Cruciferae. According to the botanist William Embolden, it is probably the bitter cress, *Eruca sativa*, which traditionally symbolized Christ's passion, both in its cruciform shape and in its bitterness.[7] As in the later *Madonna of the Yarnwinder*, the Christ-child contemplates a symbol of his own future agony. The mother who smilingly proffers the flower does so unknowingly; she is shielded from her tragic future as the child is from his.

The panel (as it originally was) has a story of romantic vicissitudes. Its whereabouts until the early nineteenth century are uncertain, though it may be the Madonna and Child described in 1591 as a 'small panel in oils from the hand of Leonardo', which was then in the house of the Botti family in Florence. In the 1820s it unexpectedly surfaced in the Crimean province of Astrakhan. According to one account, it arrived there in the baggage of an itinerant Italian musician. By 1824 it was in the possession of the Sapojnikov family of Astrakhan; it was on this date, according to family records, that it was transferred to canvas by a restorer named Korotkov. The painting was later in France, in the collection of the artist Léon Benois, whose wife was a Sapojnikov. After his death she returned to St Petersburg. The *Benois Madonna*, as it was now called, was exhibited there for the first time in 1908, and was purchased for the Hermitage by Tsar Nicholas II in 1914.

There are three drawings closely tied to the *Benois Madonna* – a head of a child in the Uffizi, which catches the infant's intentness as he inspects the flower; a Madonna and child with a bowl of fruit in the Louvre; and a sheet of studies in the British Museum.[8] These in turn lead to other sketches relating to the Madonna and Child (or anyway the mother and child) which belong to this period. A charming and little-known drawing in the Escola de Belas Artes in Oporto has something of the Benois touch; it shows the child sitting on the mother's lap while she washes his feet in a basin. Until recently this was attributed to Raffaellino da Reggio, a mid-sixteenth-century follower of Taddeo Zuccaro. In 1965 it was identified as a Leonardo by Philip Pouncey, who spotted some traces of Leonardo's handwriting showing through from the back. As the drawing has been laid down, and cannot be removed from its mount without risk, only part of the Leonardo text on the verso has been deciphered. (In Leonardo's mirror-world, of course, the words that show through can be read in regular left-to-right form.) It is a vocabulary list. Seven words can be made out, all beginning with *a – affabile, armonia*, etc. This relates the Oporto drawing to one in Windsor, which shows a plump baby sitting in the crook of his mother's arms and which also has alphabetical word lists on the verso.[9]

Also part of this nexus of drawings of the late 1470s is a sketch of the Madonna and child with the infant St John, also at Windsor. This may have been worked up into a full cartoon, or possibly even a finished painting, since the Madonna and child are reproduced almost exactly in a painting by Andrea da Salerno in Naples. In the drawing the three figures are compressed into a pyramid, a compositional device that Leonardo returned to in the *St Anne* ensemble twenty years later. There is the hint of a landscape behind the figures, which shows his characteristic love of craggy hills already developed. This drawing is the first version of a grouping which resonates through Leonardo's work – the meeting of Christ and St John the Baptist as children (an episode found only in the Apocrypha). It recurs in the *Virgin of the Rocks*, and later in the National Gallery cartoon of the *Virgin and Child with St Anne and St John the Baptist*. This grouping is rare in Italian art at this time: Leonardo is innovating, or to put it another way, the grouping comes to him from somewhere other than pictorial convention. Recalling the circumstances of his childhood, one might wonder if this recurrent 'other' child, this outsider who looks in at the self-completing duo of the Madonna and Christ, has a particular resonance for Leonardo, whose relationship with his mother seems fraught with a fear of rejection.

But the mood of these Florentine mother-and-child studies is not rejection but celebration: the mother dandling, feeding, washing and – if the *Litta Madonna* is truly a part of this group – suckling her child. And most joyous of all is the series of the Madonna and child with a cat. As in the *Benois Madonna*, there is that emphasis on the youth of the Virgin Mother – the young woman almost still a girl. (One thinks of the teenage peasant Mary in Pasolini's *Gospel According to St Matthew*.) These sketches are among the most vibrant of Leonardo's Florentine works. Their rapidity and compassion make them jump off the page: they belong, in the way that a finished painting does not, to the reality of the moment in which they were sketched. These people are actual presences, in the studio or in a room. There are four pages of very rapid sketches: mixtures of pen, charcoal and metalpoint. The figures intertwine – a ballet of movements – as the intent young man scribbles away, the pen hurrying to capture the momentary truth of their bodies and gestures, of their lives. Then come four more finished studies, one of which is traced through on to its verso, where

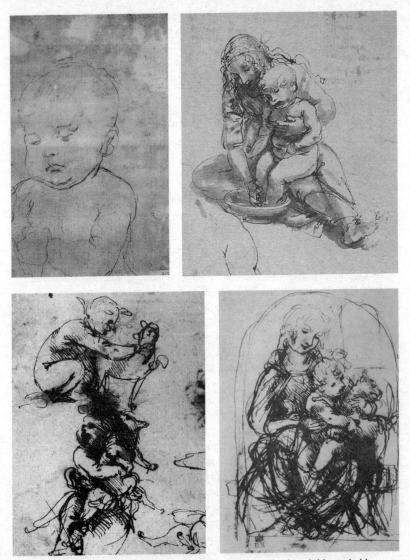

Mothers and children, c. 1478–80. Upper left: head of a child, probably a preparatory sketch for the Christ-child of the Benois Madonna. Upper right: the Oporto drawing known as Il Bagnetto. Lower left: sketches of a child with a cat. Lower right: study for a Madonna and child with a cat.

Leonardo experiments with a different position for the head of the mother. The most finished of all, precise and serene, is the lightly washed pen-and-ink drawing in the Uffizi.[10]

There is no evidence that these marvellous drawings ever resulted in a painting, except in so far as they are stages towards the greatest of his early Florentine paintings, the *Adoration of the Magi*, where the child reaching out from his mother's lap is very similar. But the cat has vanished, and with it goes the vibrant, jocular note of the drawings.

➤➤ THE HANGED MAN ◂◂

Shortly before midday on Sunday 26 April 1478, a sudden commotion disturbed the celebration of mass in Florence cathedral. As the priest raised the host, and the sanctuary bell tolled, a man named Bernardo di Bandino Baroncelli pulled a knife out from under his cloak and plunged it into the body of Giuliano de' Medici, younger brother of Lorenzo de' Medici. As he reeled back, Giuliano was stabbed ferociously and repeatedly by another man, Francesco de' Pazzi: there were found to be nineteen separate wounds on the body. Lorenzo was himself the target of two other assassins in the congregation – malcontent priests – but they bungled the job. Bleeding profusely from a wound in his neck, he was hustled into the safety of the north sacristy. The great bronze doors were locked behind him, though in the scuffle one of his friends, Francesco Nori, was fatally stabbed, also by the knife of Bernardo di Bandino.

This was the day of the Pazzi Conspiracy,[11] also called the April Plot, a desperate attempted *coup d'état* against the rule of the Medici, fomented by the rich Florentine merchant-family the Pazzi, discreetly backed by Pope Sixtus IV, and involving various anti-Medici interests including the Archbishop of Pisa. There are contemporary accounts of the plot by the poet Agnolo Poliziano, who was actually in the cathedral when the attacks happened; by the diarist Luca Landucci, who witnessed the grisly reprisals that followed; and by Florentine historians like Machiavelli and Francesco Guicciardini. The construction of the event which is found in these sources, and which has been handed down to our own day, is either overtly or implicitly pro-Medici, but a recent book by Lauro Martines has opened up other angles. The plotters' motives were tangled, but there were genuine grievances at the cynicism of Medici power-politics – what Martines calls Lorenzo's 'piecemeal usurpation' of Florence's much-trumpeted political freedoms by bribery, vote-rigging and pilfering of public funds.[12] The assassination of the Duke of Milan a year or so previously was a precedent – the death-blows similarly struck during high mass in the city's cathedral – and the barbarous execution of his assassins was a portent.

In the confusion at the cathedral the assassins escaped, but the other half of the plan – the taking of the Palazzo della Signoria by a contingent of Perugian mercenaries – had failed, and when Jacopo de' Pazzi galloped into the piazza shouting '*Popolo e libertà!*' ('For the people and freedom!') he found the doors of the Palazzo barred. The warning bell known as La Vacca was booming from its tower; armed citizens were pouring into the streets; the uprising had failed. Jacopo, the head of the family in Florence, had initially been sceptical about the putsch, which was promoted by his nephew Francesco, head of the Pazzi bank in Rome. 'You will break your necks,' he warned the conspirators. He was eventually persuaded, though his prediction proved accurate, and his own neck was among those that got broken.

Now began the bloody reprisal. The grim etiquettes of Florentine public execution were suspended: the first night was nothing less than a mass lynching. According to Landucci, there were more than twenty conspirators hanging out of the windows of the Signoria and the Bargello. A further sixty, at least, died over the next few days. On that first day, as the revenge squads roamed the streets, Lorenzo appeared at a window of the Palazzo Medici, a scarf bandaged around his wounded neck: the vanquisher. According to Vasari, Verrocchio was commissioned to produce three life-sized wax figures of him, dressed exactly as he was at that moment of bitter triumph. No trace of these remains, nor of Botticelli's portraits of the hanged traitors, for which the painter received 40 florins in mid-July.[13] Thus the studios served their political masters.

On 28 April Lorenzo received a discreet visit from Ludovico Sforza, Leonardo's future patron – the younger brother of the assassinated duke, Galeazzo Maria. Though the latter's ten-year-old son, Gian Galeazzo, was duke apparent, Ludovico was now the strongman of Milan. It was he who controlled the puppet-strings, and he would retain them, remarkably, for more than twenty years. He brought condolences and promises of support to Lorenzo.

Of the four assassins in the cathedral, three were captured. Francesco de' Pazzi was hanged on the first night of the conspiracy, and the two priests who had bungled the assault on Lorenzo perished on 5 May – it is said they were castrated before being hanged. The fourth man, the double-murderer Bernardo di Bandino, was cleverer or luckier, or both. In the first confusion after the killing of Giuliano he had hidden, just a few yards from the murder scene, in the bell-tower of the cathedral. Somehow, despite the watch set for him, he got out of Florence; he made it to the Adriatic coast at Senigallia and thence took ship out of Italy. He disappeared. But the eyes and ears of the Medici were everywhere, and in the following year came news that Bandino was in Constantinople. Diplomatic representations were made by the Florentine consul, Lorenzo Carducci; envoys were loaded with gifts; and Bandino was seized by the officers of the Sultan. He was brought back to Florence in chains, was interrogated and doubtless tortured, and on 28 December 1479 was hanged from the windows of the Bargello.[14]

Leonardo was there, for the sketch by him showing Bandino's hanging body was undoubtedly done *in situ*. The punctilious notes in the top left-corner of the paper record exactly what Bandino was wearing for the occasion: 'Small tan-coloured berretta; doublet of black serge; a black jerkin lined; a blue coat lined with fox fur [literally 'throats of foxes'] and the collar of the jerkin covered with stippled velvet, red and black; black hose.' These notes give an air of reportage to the drawing: a small moment of history is being witnessed. They also suggest that Leonardo intended to work the drawing up into a painting of the sort that Botticelli had produced the previous year. Perhaps he had been commissioned to do so, or perhaps he was just struck by this scene taking place virtually on the doorstep of Ser Piero's house.[15]

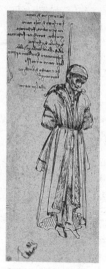

Bernardo di Bandino Baroncelli hanging.

As the body dangles in its final indignity, with bound hands and unshod feet, Leonardo captures a strange sense of repose. Bandino's thin face with the downturned mouth has almost a wistful look about it, as if contemplating from this new and drastic vantage-point the errors he had committed. In the bottom left-hand corner Leonardo does another drawing of the head, adjusting its angle slightly, giving to it that tilt of exhausted resignation so often seen in depictions of the crucified Christ.

→→ ZOROASTRO ←←

It is time now to rescue from obscurity one of the most curious and engaging figures in Leonardo's retinue: Tommaso di Giovanni Masini, generally known by the imposing alias of 'Zoroastro'. He is mentioned by the Anonimo Gaddiano as one of Leonardo's assistants during the painting of the *Battle of Anghiari* fresco in the Palazzo Vecchio, and this is confirmed by documents recording payments to him in April and August 1505; these describe him as Leonardo's *garzone*, whose job was 'to grind the colours'.[16] This precise mention of him, and the rather lowly status he is accorded, have led most biographers to assume that he was a young apprentice of Leonardo's in 1505. But in fact he was already part of Leonardo's circle in Milan in the 1490s – he is mentioned (as 'Geroastro') in an anonymous Milanese poem dedicated to Leonardo in about 1498 – and there is other evidence suggesting that their association goes back to this first Florentine period.

Tommaso was born in about 1462, in the village of Peretola, in the flatlands between Florence and Prato. He died in Rome in 1520, at the age of fifty-eight, and was buried in the church of Sant'Agata dei Goti.[17] A brief and colourful sketch of his life is found in Scipione Ammirato's *Opusculi*, published in Florence in 1637.

Zoroastro's name was Tommaso Masini; he was from Peretola, a mile out of Florence. He was the son of a gardener, but claimed to be the illegitimate son of Bernardo Rucellai, the brother in law of Lorenzo the Magnificent. Then he joined up with [*si mise con*: literally, 'he placed himself with'] Leonardo Vinci, who made him an outfit of gall-nuts, and for this reason he was for a long time known as Il Gallozzolo ['the Gall-Nut']. Then Leonardo went to Milan and with him went Zoroastro, and there he was known as Indovino ['the Fortune-Teller'], since he professed the arts of magic. Later he was in Rome, where he lived with Giovanni Rucellai, castellan of Sant'Agnolo, and then with Viseo, the Portuguese ambassador, and finally with Ridolfi. He was a great expert on mining techniques ... When he died he was buried in Santa Agata, between the tombs of Tressino and Giovanni Lascari. On his tomb there is an angel with a pair of tongs and a hammer, striking at the skeleton of a dead man, representing the faith he had in the resurrection. He would not kill a flea for any reason whatever. He preferred to dress in linen so as not to wear something dead.[18]

This has its obscurities, but gives us an attractive idea of Zoroastro as something between a jester, a magician and an engineer – and also a vegetarian, as Leonardo was reputed to be. The outfit of gall-nuts is curious, but has a parallel in some notes about masquerade costumes, where Leonardo describes an outfit made by sticking grains of black and white millet on to cloth varnished with turpentine and glue.[19] However, Ammirato does not suggest a theatrical context: he seems to mean that Leonardo made this unusual appliqué outfit, perhaps a cloak, and that Tommaso, being an eccentric young man, wore it, and so earned the nickname.

Zoroastro is probably the 'Maestro Tommaso' referred to by Leonardo in some accounting notes of 1492–3:

Thursday 27 September: Maestro Tommaso returned [to Milan]. He worked on his own account until the penultimate day of February . . .

On the penultimate day of November we reckoned up accounts . . . Maestro Tommaso had nine months to pay. He then made 6 candlesticks.[20]

This would place him as an independent craftsman working under the aegis of Leonardo's Milanese studio. He is a metalworker, which ties in with Ammirato's mention of his interest in mining. In another near-contemporary source – a Venetian manuscript which has some copies of Leonardo machinery – he is described as a 'blacksmith'.[21] In 1492–3 Leonardo was involved in a very ambitious project – the casting of the gigantic equestrian statue known as the Sforza Horse – and doubtless the expert metallurgist Masini was involved in that too, and in many other projects: military, architectural and indeed aviational.

Zoroastro has a mercurial quality: his status is hard to define. He is 'Maestro Tommaso' to Leonardo, but to the accountant reckoning up the costs of the *Anghiari* fresco he is only a *garzone* or shop-assistant mixing the colours. He is also probably 'Tommaso my servant' – '*mio famiglio*' – who makes household purchases for Leonardo in 1504. If so, we have some samples of his handwriting preserved among Leonardo's papers in the Codex Arundel: a rounded, well-formed script.[22]

Another first-hand account of Zoroastro has recently surfaced. It is in a letter from Dom Miguel da Silva, Bishop of Viseo – a courtly and well-connected Portuguese who is one of the interlocutors in Castiglione's book *The Courtier*. The letter, dated 21 February 1520, is addressed to Giovanni Rucellai, the son of Bernardo. (This tends to validate Ammirato's account of Zoroastro, which mentions his connection with both da Silva and the Rucellai.) At some point before the letter, we learn, Zoroastro had been living at the Rucellai country villa, Quaracci, outside Florence. Da Silva writes of visiting the house, where he was pleased to find 'everything arranged just as if Zoroastro was still there – a great many cooking-pots with dried-up paste, and other pieces of pots that had already been in the fire, were to be seen all over the place'. These 'cooking-pots' are to be understood as chemical vessels – retorts, alembics, etc. – as the continuation of da Silva's letter makes clear:

Zoroastro is now in my house [in Rome] and governs me completely. We have some secret special rooms, and in the corner of a nice square room, in a place that once served as a little chapel, we have set up an excellent kitchen [i.e. laboratory], where I do nothing but puff with the bellows and pour out tremendous torrents of melted lead. We make spheres which shine brilliantly and in which appear strange human figures with horns on their heads and crabs' legs and a nose like a prawn. In an old fireplace we have made a furnace, built up with bricks, and here we distil and separate the elements of everything; and with these we extract the fire from a marine monster [*dactilo marino*] which forever burns and shines. In the middle of the room there is a large table cluttered with pots and flasks of all sorts, and paste and clay and Greek pitch and cinnabar, and the teeth of hanged men, and roots. There is a plinth made of sulphur polished up on a lathe, and on this stands a vessel of yellow amber, empty except for a serpent with four legs, which we take for a miracle. Zoroastro believes that some gryphon carried it through the air from Libya and dropped it at the Mamolo bridge, where it was found and tamed by him. The walls of this room are all daubed with weird faces and drawings on paper, among which is one of a monkey who is telling stories to a crowd of rats who are attentively listening, and a thousand other things full of mystery.[23]

This vivid account gives us Zoroastro the alchemist, distilling and decocting strange brews; Zoroastro the keeper of strange reptiles; and indeed Zoroastro the artist, daubing the walls of his Roman laboratory with grotesque faces and talking animals. He is almost like a comic, folkloric version of Leonardo da Vinci. His interest in alchemy or chemistry (broadly the same activity at this time, but with different ends in view) is cognate with his work as a metallurgist. I cannot resist attributing to him the recipe written out by Leonardo, probably in the late 1480s. Headed 'Deadly smoke' (*Fumo mortale*), and appearing on a sheet related to naval warfare, its constituents are:

Arsenic mixed with sulphur and realgar
Medicinal rosewater
Venom of toad – that is, land-toad
Slaver of mad dog
Decoction of dogwood berries
Tarantula from Taranto[24]

This seems to me pure Zoroastro; it is almost a little poem.

A few months after Miguel da Silva wrote his letter Zoroastro was dead. His epitaph, inscribed on his tomb in Sant'Agata, commemorated him as 'Zoroastro Masino, a man outstanding for his probity, his innocence and his liberality, and a true Philosopher who looked into the darkness of Nature to the admirable benefit of Nature herself'. Leonardo would not have minded this for his own epitaph: *'ad naturae obscuritatem spectat . . .'*

The memory of Zoroastro lingered on. The comic novelist Anton Francesco Grazzini (known by the fishy pen-name of Il Lasca – 'the Roach') includes a 'crazy' magician called Zoroastro in his collection *Le Cene (Suppers)*. Grazzini was born in Florence in 1503, and was writing the *Cene* in mid-century. It is possible the character is loosely based on the real Zoroastro, though too loosely to be biographically useful. Grazzini's Zoroastro is a comic-book magician, a stereotype, and there is no way of knowing if his physical appearance – a 'tall, well-built, sallow-complexioned man, with a surly face and a proud manner, and a bushy black beard which he never combed' – agrees with that of Tommaso Masini.[25]

Tommaso has been undervalued by Leonardo scholars: he always seems just a picturesque footnote – an eccentric hanger-on with a strong line in hocus-pocus. There is a folkloric element in all the early descriptions of him – in Ammirato's sketch as much as in Grazzini's fictionalized version, even in da Silva's letter, which is an actual report of him, though doubtless pepped up for the amusement of Giovanni Rucellai. Leonardo's version of him, as far as he gives us one, is rather different: Tommaso the maker of candlesticks, the grinder of colours, the purchaser of provisions – filling eminently practical roles. One notes also the enduring of his relationship with Leonardo. According to Ammirato he had already 'joined up' with Leonardo before the latter's departure from Florence in *c.* 1482; he goes with Leonardo to Milan, and is glimpsed there, in Leonardo's studio, in the early 1490s; back in Florence, in 1505, he is mixing colours for the *Anghiari* fresco. This already covers twenty-five years of acquaintance (though not necessarily continuous employment); it is also possible they were in Rome together in 1513–16. Tommaso may have been something of a joker, but he was clearly no fool. The range of his protectors and hosts in Rome is also impressive: Giovanni Rucellai, da Silva, Giovan Battista Ridolfi.

When Ammirato says that Tommaso 'joined up' with Leonardo, he means that he entered Leonardo's studio as an apprentice or assistant. He perhaps replaced young Paolo di Leonardo in 1478, when the latter had been chased out of Florence for 'wicked' behaviour. Tommaso would then have been sixteen: a gardener's son from Peretola, but already a young man of some promise. According to Ammirato, he claimed to be Bernardo Rucellai's natural son: this is either a Zoroastrian joke or more likely a misunderstanding by Ammirato, who is the only source for it. (Rucellai was thirteen when Tommaso was born, making the paternity improbable though I suppose not impossible.) More likely is that he was a protégé or prodigy of Bernardo Rucellai, as he later was of Rucellai's son Giovanni. Bernardo was an assiduous member of Ficino's academy, and in later years would found his own Platonic academy at the Orti Oricellari, or Rucellai Gardens, round the corner from Santa Maria Novella. The 'Zoroastrian' side of Tommaso Masini may have its beginnings precisely in the ambit of Ficinian magic, with which we find Leonardo associated through his connection with Bernardo Bembo and the Benci.

One does not want to lose the colourful Zoroastro of legend: magic and alchemy and their attendant showmanships were doubtless part of his act, and part of his attraction to those upmarket Roman hosts. (Alchemy, of course, had an added attraction – the remote but tempting possibility of infinite wealth.) But there is a real man behind the showmanship, and he was valued by Leonardo. A man of probity, says his epitaph: an innocent, a philosopher.

THE TECHNOLOGIST

If Tommaso Masini the future metalworker and alchemist was already an apprentice or assistant of Leonardo's in the late 1470s, he would be associated with Leonardo's early efforts as an engineer. It is from this period that we find the first concerted signs of Leonardo the technologist. They are found in the Codex Atlanticus and in the pages of Vasari, who describes various technological interests pursued by Leonardo while 'still a young man [*giovanetto*]', which is vague but certainly means while he was still in Florence. Whether any of these ideas were translated into actual projects is doubtful.

As we saw, Leonardo had gained first-hand knowledge of Brunelleschi's ingenious hoists and cranes in 1471, when he was involved in the placing of the *palla* on top of the Duomo. He seems to have returned to this interest in around 1478–80, which is the probable date of those drawings of Brunelleschian lifting-devices in the Codex Atlanticus. Vasari mentions

Leonardo's interest in heavy lifting-gear: 'He demonstrated how to lift and draw great weights by means of levers, hoists and winches.' These would be particularly appropriate for an ambitious project described by Vasari:

Among his models and plans was one he proposed several times to the ingenious citizens then governing Florence, which showed how to raise the temple of San Giovanni [i.e. the Baptistery] in order to place steps under it, without any damage. His arguments were so powerful that many people were persuaded it could be done, until they left his company and thought it over, and realized it was impossible.

The idea is not as outrageous as Vasari implies. A similar feat – the moving of a church tower – had been achieved twenty-five years before, in Bologna, by the engineer Aristotele Fioravanti. Raising the Baptistery would have had advantages both aesthetic (to bring it up to the level of the Duomo opposite) and practical (to protect it from the periodic flooding of the Arno). The idea of placing it on steps was still current a century later, when Vasari's friend Vincenzo Borghini published two engravings of an imagined reconstruction of the Baptistery 'classicized' and placed on a plinth with steps.[26]

That curious device I mentioned earlier 'for opening up a prison from the inside' is a further application of Brunelleschian engineering. The drawing in the Codex Atlanticus shows a stout three-legged winch with a screwed bolt at right angles; the bolt has a gripping mechanism on the end which Leonardo refers to as its 'tongs' ('*tanagli*'). In one of the drawings it is shown ripping out the iron bars of a window. This machine might come under the heading of military hardware, but it might equally be referred back to Leonardo's memories of imprisonment – '*voi mi metteste in prigione*' – after the accusation concerning Jacopo Saltarelli. It is conceivable that this device is mentioned in an obscure corner of Vasari's *Lives* concerning a Florentine blacksmith named Caparra: 'Some young citizens brought him a drawing of a machine which could break and tear iron bars by means of a screw, and they asked him to make it for them.' The blacksmith angrily refused, thinking it a 'thief's device' for 'robbing people or disgracing young girls'. He thought the young men were of good sort ('*uomini de bene*'), but wanted nothing to do with this 'villainy'.[27] Could this drawing be the one now found in the Codex Atlanticus, and could Leonardo be one of those dubious but basically decent young citizens who approached Caparra to make it?

Vasari also says that Leonardo 'designed mills, fulling machines, and engines that could be powered by water', and this is echoed in an early sheet showing millstones, grinders and ovens. Other early drawings feature

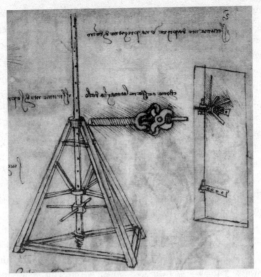

Early technology. Leonardo's devices for 'opening up a prison' and (below) for raising water.

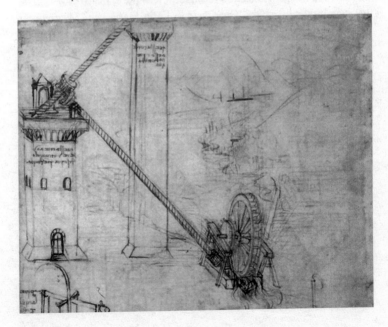

hygrometers for measuring moisture in the air, and hydraulic devices for raising water. The latter show Leonardo's early interest in the Archimedean
screw, a device which raises water through a helix rotating inside a cylinder.[28]
These drawings, or ones very like them, occur in his list of works written in
c. 1482: 'some machines for waterworks' and 'some machines for ships'. The
list also mentions 'drawings of furnaces', but these seem to have been lost.

These are some of Leonardo's earliest technical drawings; they belong
still to the somewhat two-dimensional style of the Quattrocento engineer,
which one sees in the drawings of contemporaries like Buonaccorso Ghiberti,
Francesco di Giorgio Martini and Giuliano da Sangallo. Only later, following his studies of the 'human machine', does the true Leonardian technical
drawing develop: multifaceted, sumptuously detailed, fully modelled and
shaded without losing its analytical function – a visual language with which
to explain mechanical processes and structures.

On another sheet of the Codex Atlanticus belonging to this time there is a
list of eight names: a circle of acquaintances, or perhaps acquaintances to
which Leonardo aspired.[29] Of the five whose names can be identified, one,
Domenico di Michelino, is a painter; the remaining four are scientists and
scholars. This is again Leonardo the nascent scientist of the late 1470s. The
first item on the list reads, 'Quadrante di Carlo Marmocchi'. Marmocchi
was an engineer and mathematician in the service of the Signoria: the
'quadrante' referred to may be either a treatise written by him or an actual
quadrant – an instrument for measuring the altitude of stars – owned
by him. 'Benedetto de l'Abaco' refers to another well-known Florentine
mathematician, also known as Benedetto Arithmeticus.

The best-known person on the list is the one whom Leonardo simply calls
'Maestro Paolo the physician' – almost certainly a reference to the great
Paolo dal Pozzo Toscanelli, whose position as the grand old man of Florentine science I have already mentioned. One of his disciplines which would
have interested Leonardo was optics. Toscanelli is thought to be the author
of a treatise on perspective, a copy of which survives in the Biblioteca
Riccardiana in Florence. It includes discussions of aerial perspective, optical
illusion, and the observation of celestial phenomena. This work was well
known in the Quattrocento, and was used as a kind of artist's handbook on
perspective; Leonardo seems to be citing it in some notes headed 'Reasons
for the increased size of the sun in the west'.[30] An interesting drawing in the
Codex Atlanticus belongs to this period. It shows a man looking through a
'perspectograph' (p. 175) – an optical device which helped the artist to
reproduce an object in correctly scaled proportions. Under a caption reading

'Put your eye to the tube' (in other words the sight-hole) it shows a young man in a long loose gown, with curly hair topped off with a *berretta*.[31] This may well be a self-portrait: the figure has some similarity to the probable self-portrait in the *Adoration of the Magi*, painted in 1481–2.

The last name on Leonardo's list is 'Messer Giovanni Argiropolo'. This is the Greek scholar Joannes Argyropoulos, probably the most famous Aristotelian in Italy.[32] He was born in Constantinople in about 1415 and, like so many Byzantine scholars, sought asylum in Italy after the fall of the city in 1453. For fifteen years (1456–71) he was public lecturer at Florence's university, the Studio, where he discoursed on the Aristotelian texts – the Ethics, Physics, Metaphysics, Analytics, etc., all of which he translated into Latin. He was a vital figure in the Renaissance re-evaluation of Aristotle, which stressed the analytic, scientific side of his philosophy, as opposed to the metaphysics which had been grist to the mill of medieval scholarship. Argyropoulos influenced a whole generation of Florentine intellectuals – Ficino, Landino and Poliziano were all his students and admirers, as was Lorenzo de' Medici. In 1477, after a spell in Rome, he resumed his post at the Studio, but his star was fading and he was ousted; he left Florence in 1481. Leonardo's note belongs to this last declining phase of his influence. Like Toscanelli, another ageing guru, Argyropoulos was a pioneer of clear-sighted empiricism. All 'researchers of immortal wisdom' were grateful to him, wrote Poliziano, for chasing the 'mists and glooms' from their eyes.

On the same sheet as these names appear, Leonardo drew a sketch of a clock using compressed air, and this in turn evoked some morose-seeming thoughts about the passage of time and the fear of 'this miserable life' passing 'without leaving some memory of ourselves in the minds of mortals'. This gives his list of scholars and scientists an air of resolution, a determination to seek out and cultivate these important men, to try to do something memorable so that his 'course should not be sped in vain'.

Lifting huge weights, ripping out the iron bars from windows, raising and channelling water – these are the first aspirations of Leonardo the young technologist: a pitting of human and mechanical ingenuity against the brute forces of gravity; a harnessing of natural energies. In the hydraulic devices and Archimedean screws we find the genesis of one of the great energy principles of Leonardian physics – the spiral, or, as Leonardo calls it, the *coclea* (snail-shell), in which resides the force of screws, drills, propellers and turbines, and, in nature, tornadoes and whirlpools. The vortical power of water is eloquently described in Alberti's treatise on civil engineering, *De re aedificatoria* (which Leonardo certainly knew): 'The rotation of waters

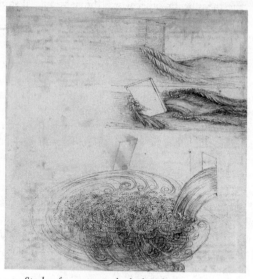

Study of currents and whirlpools, c. 1508–10.

or whirlpools is like a liquid drill, which nothing is hard enough to resist.'[33] The force of the vortex fascinated Leonardo – a fascination expressed most powerfully in the late drawings known as the 'Deluge' series, but already present, in miniature, in the cascading ringlets of the *Ginevra*.

And there is something else in these rudimentary technical folios: the ultimate defiance of gravity. There is a scruffy-looking page among the Leonardo drawings in the Uffizi, dated *c.* 1478–80.[34] On the verso of it is the earliest extant drawing of a Leonardo flying-machine. It is no more than a doodle, but quite unmistakable. It is seen from directly above or directly below; it has reticulated wings like a bat's, a fanned-out tail like a bird's, and a cockpit or framework shaped rather like a kayak. To the side of it is a more detailed drawing of a mechanism which would manoeuvre the wing by means of a handle operated by the pilot. The restricted movement of the handle suggests that this is essentially a hang-glider (as opposed to later designs that have mechanisms to make the wings actually flap up and down). This is confirmed on the other side of the sheet, in the upper left-hand corner, by a single zigzag line with the note '*Questo è il modo del chalare degli uccelli*' – 'This is the method by which birds descend.' The line shows a bird's descent as an angled fall punctuated with short upthrusts to break the momentum.

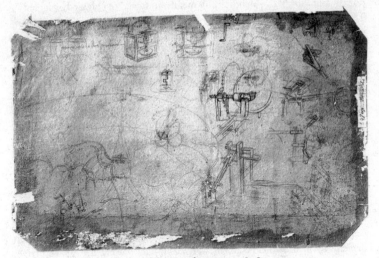

The first flying-machine, c. 1478–80.

This brief sentence and the scarcely perceptible line which illustrates it constitute Leonardo's first known pronouncement on the mechanics of avian flight, already linked – as the machine on the verso clearly shows – to the dream of human flight: his 'destiny', as he would later put it, remembering or inventing that kite which flew down to him in his cradle.

→→ 'POETS IN A HURRY' ←←

On another list written around this time we find the name Antonio da Pistoia. This refers to the rough-diamond poet Antonio Cammelli, known as 'Il Pistoia' or 'Il Pistoiese', who opens up another aspect of Leonardo's Florentine circle in the late 1470s.[35] They may have met when Leonardo was in Pistoia in 1477: Cammelli is plausibly one of those 'companions in Pistoia' to whom Leonardo refers. Some poems found among Leonardo's papers are probably in Cammelli's hand; one of them can be dated quite precisely to around November 1479.

Now in his mid-forties, Cammelli was one of the finest vernacular poets of his generation. He typifies the slangy, ribald, satirical style often called *burchiellesco*, after an early exponent of the genre, the Florentine barber Domenico di Giovanni, called Il Burchiello. The name derives from the phrase *alla burchia*, which literally means 'in haste' or 'higgledy-piggledy'. These 'poets in a hurry', dashing off poems with a feel of improvisation, and with a deliberate roughness and slanginess, were the jazz poets or rap artists of the Quattrocento – a very different breed from humanist poets like Poliziano and Landino with their classical allusions and Petrarchan conceits. Others who belong within this vein of *anti-classicismo* are the Florentines Luigi Pulci and Bernardo Bellincioni, and somewhat later Francesco Berni, born down the road from Vinci, in Lamporecchio, in 1498. Berni paid tribute to Cammelli – '*O spirito bizarro del Pistoia!*' – and the great satirist Pietro Aretino praised the 'sharpness and speed' of his pen.[36]

Cammelli wrote 'sonnets', but not in the fourteen-line form later adopted in Elizabethan England. The term was more generic: *sonetto* simply means 'a little song', and is scarcely distinguishable from other lyric forms – *frottole, rispetti, strambotti*, etc. – which these poets used. Their verses were often performed to music, and some poets, like Serafino Aquilino, were noted musicians as well. Cammelli is occasionally romantic but more often cynical, as in the spirited poem '*Orsu che fia?*' ('What are you up to?'), much of it spoken by the poet's frustrated wife:

> *Io starei meglio moglie d'un sartore,*
> *che mi mettria tre punti in uno occhiello.*
> *Ognor tu scrivi e canzone e rispetti,*
> *vivo a marito a guisa di donzella:*
> *che'l diavol te ne porti e tua sonnetti ...*

[I'd be better off married to a tailor: he'd put a few stitches in my button-hole. You spend every hour writing songs and catches, I'm living with a husband who's like a girl: the devil take you and your sonnets ...]

The poet's reluctance, it turns out, is not just because he's composing his 'songs and catches', but because he fears she will get pregnant again:

> *Quel che a te piace a me non par bel gioco,*
> *ch'io non vo' piu cagnoli intorno al foco ...*

[That game you like I'm not so fond of, because I don't want any more pups round the fireside ...][37]

Poverty, hunger, disappointment and imprisonment are common themes, delivered in a defiantly humorous tone. A typical sonnet plays variations on Cammelli's ugliness – he is 'thin and scrawny', he looks like a 'screech-owl without a beak', and so on – and then delivers the punchline:

Dunque chi vol veder guardi mi tutto:
Un uom senza dinar quanto par brutto.

[So take a good look at me all who wish: how ugly a man looks when he
has no money.]

Some of the satirical poems are just a catalogue of ingenious insults – the
railing which Cammelli calls 'talking pepper' (*dire pepe*) – but his typical
tone is charming and nonchalant:

Cantava il concubin della gallina;
La rugiada sul giorno era nei prati . . .

[The hen's lover-boy was singing; the dew of the day was on the
meadows . . .][38]

The elegant Cardinal Bibbiena summed up Cammelli's style well: '*le facezie,
il sale e il miele*' – 'jokes, salt and honey'.

It is very likely that Cammelli wrote the short, humorous poem in Latin
distichs found on a sheet in the Codex Atlanticus.[39] The occasion of the
poem was the siege of Colle Val d'Elsa by the troops of the Papal League in
November 1479 – this was part of the war that followed the Pazzi Conspiracy. The town capitulated on 14 November, its walls having been
reduced to rubble by an enormous piece of siege-artillery nicknamed La
Ghibellina. This gun is the subject – indeed the imagined speaker – of the
poem found in Leonardo's papers, which begins:

Pandite iam portas, miseri, et subducite pontes
Nam Federigus adest quem Gebellina sequor . . .

[Now throw open your gates, you miserable creatures, and let down your
drawbridges, for Federico is here whom I, Ghibellina, follow . . .]

'Federico' is Federico da Montefeltro, Duke of Urbino, one of the generals
of the anti-Florentine league. On the same sheet are various drawings
of artillery by Leonardo: the poem and the drawings belong together –
companion pieces.

Cammelli is the likely author *per se*, and there are other circumstantial
pointers. His patron at this time, the Ferrarese courtier Niccolò da Correggio, was a senior military figure in the Florentine alliance, and Cammelli
may have done some soldiering under his banner. We know Cammelli was

in Florence in the summer of 1479 – on 20 August he answered a court summons for debt – so it is not improbable he was there in late November or December, the presumed date of the poem.

If this eccentric little *braggadoccio* is from the pen of Il Pistoiese, so too are some other passages in the Codex Atlanticus written in the same hand. One is a quite personal poem addressed to Leonardo, or perhaps rather a draft of a poem. Unfortunately it is obscured by a large ink-blot, but infra-red imaging has made at least part of it legible. The title of the poem can be partially read as 'S [. . .] 4' – probably '*Sonetto* 4'. It begins:

> *Lionardo mio non avete d[. . .]*
> *Lionardo perche tanto penato[?]*

[My Leonardo you don't have any [. . .] Leonardo, why so troubled?]

The rest is hard to interpret, but seems to harp on a note of reconciliation or apology: the last word of the poem is *perdonato*, pardoned. Also written on this page are fragments of poetry in Leonardo's mirror-script. There are two quotes from Ovid – 'Things done without any witnesses, things known only to the dark night' and 'O Time, the consumer of all things' – and one from Petrarch. And there is a lovely little couplet – very Cammellesco, but actually a quotation from Luca Pulci (brother of Luigi):

> *Deh non m'avete a vil ch'io son povero*
> *Povero e quel che assai cose desidera*

[Don't despise me because I'm poor: a man is poor when he desires many things.][40]

This page gives us a sense of Leonardo opening up to the possibilities of poetry, perhaps under the capricious influence of Cammelli.

Another poem in the same handwriting appears to be a satirical sally against Bernardo Bellincioni, a Florentine poet in much the same *burchiellesco* vein as Cammelli, but younger. Bellincioni was a favourite of Lorenzo de' Medici, with whom he exchanged scurrilous sonnets, and of Lorenzo's mother, Lucrezia Tornabuoni, and hence a suitable target for the irascible Cammelli.[41] Leonardo probably knew him too – they certainly knew one another later, in Milan, and collaborated together. They were the same age, and Bernardo was a poor boy raised up by his wit – a type Leonardo liked. He was a sparky, difficult young man: an *enfant terrible*. The Medici poet and priest Matteo Franco was an enemy – Bellincioni wrote a sonnet against him, beginning, '*Taci, non ciarlar piu che tu schimazzi*' ('Be quiet, stop chattering, or you'll turn into a monkey'). The acerbic Luigi Pulci liked him, and praised his wit in his own great work, the burlesque epic *Morgante maggiore*, published in 1481 – a book which Leonardo later owned, and from which he quoted. Thus the Florentine literary currents flow in and around Leonardo's studio.

If one were looking for a literary influence on Leonardo, the rough and laconic Cammelli would seem more congenial to him than the more mannered style of Poliziano, whose influence we felt hovering over the Ginevra portrait. Leonardo was never an exponent of belles-lettres; there are some forays into literary modes, but his writing style is terse, vernacular and tending to roughness of finish, and if it achieves poetry at times it does so through lucidity and density of expression, not through verbal tricks and pretty assonances.

There is something heartening about the friendship with the hard-bitten poet from Pistoia – that '*Lionardo mio*' certainly suggests friendship – though we also learn from that poem that Leonardo is *penato*: literally 'pained', therefore troubled, stressed, downcast (though it can also mean 'hard-working', as in one who 'takes pains' over something). And he is 'poor', but philosophical about being so. Business at the *bottega* was not booming, we might infer, but the evenings were convivial.

✦ THE MUSICIAN ✦

Leonardo's connection with rimesters like Cammelli and Bellincioni leads us to another of his accomplishments – one that is often forgotten. The early biographers are unanimously agreed that he was a brilliant musician, and that he was particularly good at playing the 'lyre'. He must already have excelled during these years in Florence, since both the Anonimo and Vasari insist that when he went to Milan, probably in early 1482, he was presented to the Milanese court not as a painter or technologist, but as a musician. This is such a singular idea that one can only believe it is true.

The *lira* which Leonardo played was not the harp-shaped lyre of classical antiquity, such as is plucked in comic scenarios of Elysium. It was a more recently evolved instrument known as the *lira da braccio*, literally the 'arm lyre'. It was essentially a variation on the *viola da braccio*, which in turn was the forerunner of the violin. Typically the *lira da braccio* had seven strings. Five were melody strings, tuned by pegs set in a heart-shaped peg-box. They were played with a bow, and were stopped with the fingers against a fingerboard to produce different notes. In addition it had two open strings

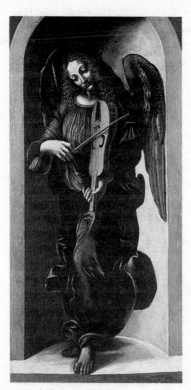

Angel playing a lira da braccio *in the panel attributed to Ambrogio de Predis.*

(*corde di bordone*) running outside the fingerboard: these were 'drones' producing only one tone, and were plucked with the thumb of the left hand (or perhaps in Leonardo's case the right) to produce a beat. These open strings, being comparable in sound and technique to those of a lyre, gave the instrument its name. A sixteenth-century Venetian *lira da braccio* is in the National Music Museum in South Dakota. It has a sentence in Latin painted round its carved ribs: 'While the horse goes over the sheep, back and forth, the wood returns a mellifluous sound.' This punning pastoral motto – referring to the horsehair of the bow, the sheep-gut of the strings, and the wood of the *lira* – sounds like one of Leonardo's riddling prophecies.[42]

In paintings of the period, the *lira* or *viola da braccio* (it is often hard to tell which) is frequently shown being played by an angel. It features in pictures by Giovanni Bellini, Carpaccio, Raphael and Mantegna, and in a page-border illumination in the Sforza Book of Hours. It is definitely a *lira da braccio* being played by the angel in the panel by Ambrogio de Predis in the National Gallery in London – you can clearly see the drone-strings passing outside the angel's left thumb. This painting was originally a side-panel for Leonardo's *Virgin of the Rocks*; it was painted by one of his chief colleagues in Milan, and may reflect something of the experience of watching – and listening to – Leonardo play.

Thus Leonardo's instrument is essentially a prototypical fiddle, a violin *avant la lettre*. When and from whom he learned to play it is not known. Vasari makes music one of the accomplishments of the boy Leonardo, but this may be biographer's hindsight. We know that Verrocchio had a lute

Musical games. A sketch for a fantastical stringed instrument, and a riddle using musical notation, both from the late 1480s.

among his possessions: this suggests that music was played in the *bottega*, and perhaps it was taught there, informally at least. Benvenuto Cellini, writing of his father Giovanni's apprenticeship in Florence in the 1480s, says, 'According to Vitruvius, if you want to do well in architecture, you must have some knowledge of both music and drawing. So Giovanni, having achieved skill at drawing, began to study music, and at the same time he learned to play excellently on the viola and the flute.' Cellini also says that the Florentine *pifferi* (pipers) and other musicians who played on civic occasions – his father among them – were all very respectable artisans, and 'some of them were of the *arti maggiori*, such as silkworkers and woolworkers, and for this reason my father did not think it unworthy to pursue this profession'.[43] Both these comments seem relevant to Leonardo – that a proficiency in music went with the study of art and architecture; and that there was a strong tradition of music-making among the Florentine guilds.

What kind of music did Leonardo da Vinci play? No compositions by him survive, and the soundtrack of late Quattrocento Florence is loud and various – the fifes and drums of the *pifferi*, the sing-along 'catches' of carnival, the instrumental preludes and interludes that accompanied the *sacre rappresentazioni*, the fashionable dance tunes of Guglielmo Ebreo, the virtuoso organ music of Francesco Squarcialupi. Vasari gives us a clue (or at least an assumption) when he adds apropos Leonardo's musical talents, 'He was also the most skilled improviser in verse of his time.' This pictures Leonardo accompanying himself on the *lira* while reciting or singing poems extempore. Viola-type instruments were particularly associated with this. The Flemish musician Johannes Tinctoris, at this time resident composer at the Neapolitan court, recommended the viola for 'the accompaniment and ornamentation of vocal music and the recitation of epics'. The tradition of the *improvvisatore* lasted into modern times. The Scottish novelist Tobias Smollett described a performance by one in 1765: 'When the subject is given, his brother tunes his violin to accompany him, and he begins to rehearse in recitative, with wonderful fluency and precision. Thus he will, at a minute's warning, recite two or three hundred verses, well-turned and well-adapted.'[44] Such skills shade into those of the *frottolista* – the singer of love-songs. *Frottole* ('Trifles') were essentially sung poems: the term is used generically to cover a variety of lyric forms – sonnets, odes, *strambotti*, etc. – set to music. These compositions have been described as 'half-popular, half-aristocratic' – they used popular tunes, but in a manner designed to please the cultivated listener. The heyday of the *frottola* was a little later than Leonardo's arrival in Milan – around the turn of the century – and is particularly associated with the Mantuan court of Isabella d'Este, where accomplished poet-musicians like Serafino Aquilino held sway.

We can say broadly that if Leonardo were a typical *lira da braccio* player in Florence in *c.* 1480 he would probably be playing the kind of light, amorous, chordal music typified by the Medici carnival-song and the Mantuan *frotella*. He would be singing or reciting the love-poems of Petrarch and Poliziano and Lorenzo de' Medici, or indeed the more abrasive ditties of Cammelli and Bellincioni, many of which were certainly intended to be performed in this way. His association with Cammelli evokes evenings of rough-and-ready entertainment – spectral one-off performances of '*Orsu che fia?*' and other numbers, with Il Pistoiese on vocals and Leonardo da Vinci on fiddle. Leonardo was not typical, however, and one looks also for other moods. There was another well-known Florentine who played the *lira da braccio* – the philosopher Marsilio Ficino, who composed 'Orphic hymns' (as he called them), and performed them on the *lira*. Thus another kind of influence on Leonardo emanates from the rarefied philosophical soirées at Careggi. It is possible his involvement with the Ficino circle awakened a new sophistication in Leonardo the musician. He later called music a 'representation of invisible things' – a phrase with a strong whiff of Platonism.[45] And so to the pleasant sawings and strummings of the *frottolista* is added something a little other-worldly and ethereal which makes you stop and close your eyes as the music steals over you.

I said that no compositions by Leonardo remain, but there are little ghosts of musical phrasing which emerge from some of the riddles he invented.

There are half a dozen riddles using musical notation in the Windsor collection. They are usually a combination of pictorial, musical and verbal symbols. The example illustrated here can be read easily enough (once one knows that the Italian for a fish-hook is *amo*), as follows:

amo [drawing of a fish-hook]; *re sol la mi fa re mi* [musical notes]; *rare* [written]; *la sol mi fa sol* [musical notes]; *lecita* [written].

This produces the following romantic ditty: '*Amore sola mi fa remirare, la sol mi fa sollecita*' – 'Only love makes me remember, it alone fires me up.' The two passages of musical notation can be picked out on a keyboard – DGAEFDE AGEFG. This is a melody by Leonardo da Vinci.[46]

According to Vasari, Leonardo constructed a special *lira da braccio* to impress his Milanese hosts: 'He took with him a lyre that he had made himself, mostly of silver, in the shape of a horse's skull, a very strange and novel design which made the sound fuller and more resonant.' There do not seem to be any designs for this in the notebooks, though according to the eighteenth-century scholar Carlo Amoretti, who was familiar with Leonardo's manuscripts in the Biblioteca Ambrosiana before they were carted off to France, there once existed a drawing of a *lira* which may have been the 'skull-lyre' referred to by Vasari. This bizarre instrument has been conjecturally reconstructed by a team of musical scholars and instrument-makers in Cremona.[47] There are various other strange instruments in the notebooks – ingenious versions of hurdy-gurdies, zithers, harpsichords, mechanical drums, a '*viola organista*', and so on. And in around 1490 Leonardo conducted a little experiment in harmony: 'The plucked string of a lute will produce a corresponding movement in a similar string of the same pitch on another lute, and this can be seen by placing a piece of straw on the string similar to the one that is played.'[48]

Another fragment of information comes from the Anonimo Gaddiano, who tells us that Leonardo taught music to a young man called Atalante Migliorotti, and that Migliorotti accompanied him to Milan – and so another of Leonardo's motley Florentine circle swims into focus. Atalante di Manetto Migliorotti was born, probably illegitimate, in about 1466, and was thus sixteen when he travelled to Milan with Leonardo. One of the drawings which Leonardo took to Milan, as listed in *c*. 1482, may be a portrait of him: '*una testa ritratta d'Atalante che alzava il volto*' ('a portrait of Atalante raising his face').[49] A beautiful drawing of a naked young man playing a stringed instrument may also show him. (The instrument, drawn in metalpoint, has not been inked in and is almost invisible in reproduction.)[50] We don't know how long Atalante stayed in Milan with Leonardo: he is next heard of in Mantua in 1491, singing the title role in Poliziano's opera *Orfeo* for the delectation of Isabella d'Este. He seems to have established himself as an instrument-maker, for in 1493 he was commissioned by Isabella to make her a guitar, 'with as many strings as he liked', and in 1505 he wrote to the Marquis of Mantua (Isabella's husband) to tell him he had constructed a new twelve-stringed *lira* 'of unusual shape', perhaps recalling that bizarre silver lyre his *maestro* had made so many years before.

⤙ ST JEROME AND THE LION ⤚

'Leonardo, why so troubled?' wrote the poet Cammelli, and something of this mood can be seen in Leonardo's powerful and anguished *St Jerome*, begun in about 1480. The painting, now in the Vatican, is unfinished; it is in the same state of monochrome underpainting as the *Adoration of the Magi*, which was commissioned in early 1481 and abandoned when Leonardo left for Milan the following year. Preparatory studies – 'many figures of St Jerome' – are mentioned in the list of c. 1482, but do not survive. The only drawings that can be specifically related to the painting are a pair of lion's heads seen at the bottom of one of his Madonna and Child sheets of the late 1470s.[51]

St Jerome in the wilderness was a very popular subject. There are versions by Masaccio, Piero della Francesca, Mantegna, Bellini and Lorenzo Lotto; the saint was also portrayed writing in his study, as in Ghirlandaio's fresco in Ognissanti, which was painted around the same time as Leonardo's picture. A Greek scholar of the fourth century, St Jerome (or Girolamo or Hieronymus) was the most learned and eloquent of the early Church fathers, famous for his Latin version of the Bible (the Vulgate). He symbolized a conjunction of religion and intellectual humanism, and was attractive to painters for the dramatic potential of his spell as a hermit in the Syrian desert. Historical sources suggest this was a sojourn of about five years, c. 374–8, when Jerome was in his thirties, but he is almost always depicted as an old man. So he is in Leonardo's version, though unusually he is beardless. His features are reminiscent of a famous classical bust of the Stoic philosopher and dramatist Seneca, further stressing him as a classical as well as Christian figure.[52]

The painting shows the emaciated saint striking himself with a stone: the iconography of Jerome penitent. Every tendon is visible in the tautness of

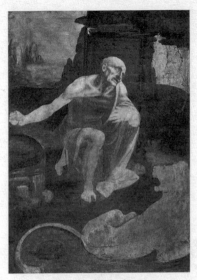

Leonardo's unfinished St Jerome,
c. 1480.

the neck and shoulders: this is in a sense the first of Leonardo's anatomical drawings. Other conventional features of the Jerome iconography have been roughed in – the cardinal's hat, which is the red blob immediately beside the drapery; the crucifix, just visible in the squiggled drawing at the upper right edge of the picture; the skull, bottom left, in the arc of the lion's tail; and, of course, the lion itself. Among the painting's dynamics is one of sightlines: the lion looks at the saint; the saint looks at the crucified body of Christ.

There is no early documentation of the painting, but in a curious little window in the rock in the upper right corner can be discerned the roughed-out sketch of a church. This is a typical allusion to St Jerome as a founding father of the Church, but it has also a more specific allusion. To a Florentine viewer, the church's classical façade with two curved architraves would be instantly recognizable as that of Santa Maria Novella, designed by Leon Battista Alberti, and completed in 1472. This was a monument to the Rucellai family, whose name is carved on the front, and whose emblem of a sail (signifying good fortune) is mimicked in those distinctive curves. Its presence here may refer to the patron of Leonardo's *St Jerome* – not Alberti's great benefactor Giovanni Rucellai, who was now dead, but his son Bernardo. We have met him fleetingly in earlier chapters: an enthusiastic follower of Ficino, and a probable protector (or reputed 'father') of the eccentric young Tommaso Masini, a.k.a. Zoroastro. Generous, scholarly and deeply versed in classical antiquities – see his learned tract *De urbe Roma*, written in 1471 – Bernardo Rucellai seems a good candidate for the commissioner of the painting.[53]

As in all the paintings, Jerome is accompanied by a lion. This is actually a long-running Renaissance confusion: the saint who won the friendship of a lion by pulling a thorn out of its paw was San Gerasimo rather than San

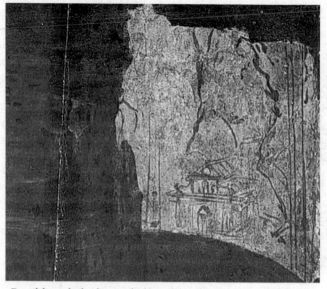

Detail from the background of St Jerome, *showing a church similar to Santa Maria Novella (below).*

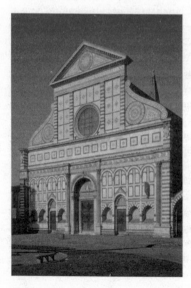

Girolamo, but the lion was by now ingrained in the latter's iconography.

Leonardo's lion is brilliant: a few deft lines are all there is, but they give the creature a sleek, feline curve. It was almost certainly drawn from life. There was a famous 'lion-house' in Florence, round the back of the Signoria. On special occasions lions were brought out into the Piazza della Signoria for a 'lion-hunt': the young Luca Landucci witnessed one such, put on for a visit by the Duke of Milan in the early 1450s – the lion 'threw himself upon a terrified horse, which dragged him from the Mercanzia to the middle of the piazza'. Landucci also records visiting the lion-house in 1487: 'There was a keeper with whom they were quite tame, so that he could go into their cages and touch them – especially one of them.'[54]

Leonardo undoubtedly saw these lions, for in one of the anatomical manuscripts at Windsor he recalls, 'I once saw how a lamb was licked by a lion in our city of Florence, where there are always twenty-five or thirty of them, which breed there. With a few licks that lion took off most of the fleece which covered the lamb, and having thus stripped it he ate it.' The passage is datable to the 1500s, but may record a much earlier experience. It is an interesting counterpoint to a more literary passage in Leonardo's 'bestiary': 'When lambs are given as food to caged lions they submit to them as if to their own mother, so that it is often seen that the lions do not wish to kill them.'[55] This is the emblematic and rather sentimental view of the lamb lying down with the lion. The actual reminiscence is by contrast precise, clipped, realistic, unflinching. We see him there, watching intently, grimly, the destructive efficiency of the beast.

In the *St Jerome*, by a perspectival twist, the lion in the foreground is the spectator of the saint's mortification. It is watching him. Its mouth registers something between a leonine growl and a look of open-mouthed surprise: this gives the painting that quality of momentary drama which Leonardo seeks. In a sense – via a pun on *leone* and Leonardo – the lion stands for the artist himself. This verbal connection is found in one of Leonardo's rebuses or picture-puzzles, drawn in the late 1480s for the delectation of the Milanese court. It shows a lion engulfed in flames next to a table. It is captioned '*leonardesco*' (i.e. *leone*, lion + *ardere*, to burn + *desco*, a table or desk). *Leonardesco* is, of course, the adjective formed from Leonardo: the rebus is thus a punning self-portrait or logo. Leon Battista Alberti had used a similar pun (Leon/*leone*) in his *Fables*, comparing himself to the lion 'burning with the desire for glory': Leonardo probably knew this work.[56]

And so the presence of the painted lion also suggests the presence of the painter Leonardo, both of them witnesses of the saint's suffering.

The topography of the painting is curious. Conventionally St Jerome is depicted sitting outside a hermit's cave. That squarish space in the upper right of the painting might have suggested the entrance to his cave, but as it opens up to the distant view of a church it becomes a kind of window instead. Are we therefore *in* the cave, looking outwards? The painting, in its unfinished state at least, does not resolve this question. The haunting *Virgin of the Rocks*, begun a couple of years later, is also set in a fantastical kind of cave or grotto, with vistas glimpsed through rocky apertures.

These settings seem to link with an interesting text in the Codex Arundel, which describes Leonardo's feelings as he looks in at the mouth of a dark cave.[57] Its rather florid handwriting is typical of the first Florentine period: it probably dates from around 1480, and is broadly contemporary with these paintings. The page begins with four fragmentary drafts describing a volcanic eruption, rather hyperbolic and effortful – 'the vomited-forth flames', etc. – but then the writing changes gear, and a little story or episode emerges, a single paragraph set down simply and without any orthographic sign of hesitation:

Having wandered some way among sombre rocks I came upon the mouth of a huge cavern, in front of which I stood some while, astounded by this place I had not known about before. I stooped down with my back arched, and my left hand resting on one knee; and with my right hand I shaded my lowered and frowning brows; and continually bending this way and that I looked in and tried to make out if there was anything inside, but the deep darkness prevented me from doing so. I had been there for some time, when there suddenly arose in me two things, fear and desire – fear of that threatening dark cave; desire to see if there was some marvellous thing within.

This is a consciously literary piece – the earliest of Leonardo's efforts in this direction – but it has a vividness which suggests that it may contain a stored-up memory, possibly from childhood. This would place it alongside the kite fantasy: a rare piece of personal narrative, expressing a similar kind of psychological ambiguity – 'fear and desire'.

One could say that the *Virgin of the Rocks* precisely shows 'some marvellous thing' within the darkness of the cave: in that iconic grouping, the redemptive message of Christianity is foretold in the meeting of the infants Christ and St John. Part of the impact of the painting is this sweetness amid the gloomy, rocky setting. It reverses an opposite expectation, for in the medieval imagination such cavern-mouths suggested the entrance to the underworld or hell. This too is found in Leonardo's work – not in a painting but in a stage-set, for a performance of Poliziano's musical drama *Orfeo*, about the descent of Orpheus to the underworld to rescue Eurydice. Sketches show a range of rocky mountains which opens by cunning machinery to reveal a circular chamber within. This theatrical cavern is specifically an image of hell: it is the 'residence', as Leonardo puts it, of Pluto, the god of the underworld. In his notes he envisages the dramatic moment of disclosure: 'When Pluto's paradise opens up, there appear devils playing on twelve drums shaped like infernal mouths, and there is Death, and the Furies, and Cerberus, and many naked children weeping, and there are fireworks of various colours.'[58]

In these ways Leonardo revisits the 'dark cave' of the Arundel text, and the fears and desires it evokes. In his *St Jerome* it is a place of desolation and rigorous self-denial; in the *Virgin of the Rocks* it is a scene of serene benediction; and on a stage in Milan it is a vision of hellfire. What is revealed there remains ambiguous, as it is in the original text, and perhaps if the cave has a meaning it is precisely that: the ambiguity of the unknown. If one looks into the dark secrets of Nature, what will be revealed there – something terrible or something marvellous?[59] Thus Leonardo, glimpsed in this rare little fragment of self-reflection: the hesitant explorer, loitering at the cave's mouth. We sense again the edginess that accompanies the great Renaissance quest for knowledge: those moments when he wondered if the darkness were better left unilluminated.

⤞ THE GARDENS OF THE MEDICI ⤝

We have some fragmentary knowledge of Leonardo's 'circle' in Florence – his pupils Tommaso and Atalante; his literary chums Cammelli and Bellincioni; his philosophical gurus Toscanelli and Argyropoulos; his boyfriends Jacopo and Fioravanti. We assume his continued acquaintance with fellow artists on the Florentine scene – Botticelli, Pollaiuolo, Ghirlandaio, Perugino, Credi, Filippino Lippi and others – though none is mentioned in his writings except Botticelli, and he slightingly. (Verrocchio left Florence for Venice in 1480, and as far as we know did not return before his death eight years later.) We know also of certain more elevated contacts, who might be called his patrons – the Benci family, Bernardo Rucellai, and perhaps others of that upmarket Platonic set centred on Ficino's academy at Careggi. But of his relations with the city's premier family, and particularly with Lorenzo de' Medici, we know almost nothing.

If the Anonimo Gaddiano is to be believed, Leonardo was a favoured protégé of Lorenzo's: 'As a young man he was with the Magnificent Lorenzo de' Medici, who provided for him, and employed him in the gardens in the Piazza di San Marco in Florence.' Lorenzo purchased these gardens in 1480, as a present for his wife, Clarice; they belonged to the Dominican convent of San Marco, where the Medici had their well-appointed cells, decorated by Fra Angelico, to which they retired for devotional interludes. He created a kind of sculpture-park there, under the management of Bertoldo di Giovanni, a former pupil of Donatello, and artists were invited to study this inspirational collection of classical statues and to do restoration work on them.[60]

The Anonimo's statement is often repeated as historical fact, but I think it should be treated with caution. The idea that Lorenzo provided lodging for Leonardo (the Anonimo uses the phrase *stare con*, which generally means 'to live with') and paid for his upkeep (*provisione*) is not mentioned at all by Vasari. There is a similar disparity on the matter of Leonardo's visit to Milan in 1482. According to the Anonimo, Leonardo was 'sent' there by Lorenzo, but Vasari says he was 'invited' there by Ludovico Sforza. Vasari was himself a protégé of Duke Cosimo de' Medici, and would surely have given his patron's illustrious ancestor any credit that was due for fostering the talent of the young Leonardo. The Anonimo's biography, which Vasari knew and used, gives him two opportunities for doing so, but in each case he rejects them. He omits any reference to Leonardo being supported by Lorenzo, and he contradicts the idea that Leonardo was an emissary of Lorenzo's in 1482. I suspect Vasari's removal of Lorenzo from the story is based on some knowledge of the case. His silence almost amounts to a statement – that Leonardo was *not* supported and encouraged by Lorenzo.

Another reason for suspecting the Anonimo's statement about Lorenzo and Leonardo is that the phrasing would correctly describe Lorenzo's patronage of the young Michelangelo some ten years later. Thus Vasari: 'Michelangelo always had the keys to the garden [of San Marco] . . . He lived in the Medici household for four years . . . He was given a room, and ate at Lorenzo's table, and received an allowance of 5 ducats a month.'[61] All this is backed up by other sources: the four years would be *c.* 1489–92. It may well be that the Anonimo, writing half a century after the event, mixed things up, and believed it was Leonardo who was the recipient of these benefits. I do not want to remove Leonardo completely from the inspiring ambience of Lorenzo's sculpture-garden. He may well have had access to it – the sculptural overtones of the portrayal of St Jerome may be a direct result of it, as is argued by Pietro Marani and others. But the broader idea that Leonardo was a favoured protégé of Lorenzo's is not borne out.[62]

Leonardo's career with Verrocchio certainly brought him into contact with the Medici – the preparations for the Milanese visit of 1471; the painting of standards and banners for the *giostre*; the portrait of Ginevra de' Benci, whom Lorenzo much admired; the Pistoia altarpiece in memory of a Medici bishop. But once he steps out of the circle of Verrocchio's *bottega* the nature of the record seems to change. In 1476 he is involved in a homosexuality case with embarrassing overtones for the Tornabuoni family – the family of Lorenzo's mother. The following year another scandal results in the exile, personally approved by Lorenzo, of Leonardo's pupil or servant Paolo. In 1478 Leonardo undertakes but fails to complete an important commission for the Signoria (the San Bernardo altarpiece). In 1479 he sketches the hanging body of Giuliano de' Medici's assassin, but is not apparently commissioned – as Verrocchio and Botticelli had been – to produce a full-scale piece of Medici propaganda. None of these on their own would count as evidence of Lorenzo's negative view of Leonardo, but taken together they seem to add up to that.

Further indication emerges in 1481, when Lorenzo dispatches various artists to Rome, as part of the new mood of amity between Florence and the papacy. The artists chosen to assist in the decoration of the newly built Sistine Chapel are Perugino, Botticelli, Ghirlandaio and Cosimo Rosselli. Their joint contract to paint ten *storie* or scenes from the Bible is dated 27 October 1481. This was an immensely prestigious commission, as well as a very valuable one: Ghirlandaio received 250 ducats for his *Calling of St Peter and St Andrew*.[63] Leonardo may have been passed over for purely practical reasons (he was not a fresco painter; he was busy with another commission), but it adds to my feeling that he was not among Lorenzo's favourite painters: that he was considered too unreliable, too difficult, and perhaps too openly homosexual to represent Florence in this role of cultural ambassador. So at least it may have seemed to him in October 1481, as those other – in his eyes inferior – artists packed their bags and headed off for Rome.

Late in his life – probably in Rome in about 1515 – Leonardo wrote, '*Li medici mi crearono e distrussono*.'[64] This can be translated either as 'The Medici created me and destroyed me' or as 'Physicians created me and destroyed me.' The first interpretation could indeed imply that Leonardo was supported by Lorenzo at the beginning of his career, and thus 'created' by the Medici, but to say he was also 'destroyed' by the family would be a curious statement to make in 1515, when he was living in Rome at the expense of Lorenzo's son Giuliano, with whom he was on very good terms. The line has a perfectly valid meaning without invoking the Medici at all. Leonardo elsewhere describes physicians as the 'destroyers of lives' (*destruttori di vite*), and he was in general critical of the profession. He was by then in his early sixties, and his health was failing. A pun on *medici* and Medici may be somewhere in his mind as he writes this, but the line cannot be taken as evidence of Lorenzo's active patronage.

This chapter is a tissue of negative evidence, which is never very readable, but I think it worth questioning the customary casual assertion that Leonardo in Florence was a protégé of the Medici. His brilliance must have been noticed but one senses a note of exclusion: a young man who doesn't quite fit.

There is a tiny profile drawing by Leonardo which looks very like a portrait of Lorenzo. It is one of those 'Windsor fragments' taken from sheets in the Codex Atlanticus.[65] On stylistic grounds it is dated to *c.* 1485 or later: in other words, it was drawn in Milan. It may therefore be a recollection of the man, but is not a sketch done *dal vivo*.

⇥ THE *ADORATION* ⇤

In early 1481 Leonardo was commissioned to paint a large altarpiece for the Augustinian monastery of San Donato at Scopeto, a village outside the city walls not far from the Prato Gate. It was a rich monastery, which also purchased works by Botticelli and by Filippino Lippi. From 1479 its business affairs had been handled by Ser Piero da Vinci, who is likely to have been involved in the commission, and perhaps in the rather tricky details of the contract. In so far as the contract seems unsatisfactory from Leonardo's point of view, one discerns an element of exasperated difficulty – something has to be done to get Leonardo on his feet, and this is the best that Ser Piero can manage.

The initial agreement was made in March 1481; it stipulated that Leonardo should deliver the painting 'within twenty-four months, or at the most within thirty months; and in case of not finishing it he forfeits whatever he has done of it, and it is our right to do what we want with it'. These terms are not unusual, but suggest that Leonardo already has a reputation for unreliability. The form of payment, however, is unusual. He does not apparently get any cash in advance. Rather, he receives 'one-third of a property in the Val d'Elsa' which had been bequeathed to the monastery by 'Simone, father of Brother Francesco'. The property is inalienable ('he can make no other contract on it'), but he has the option, after three years, of selling it back to the friars, 'if they so wish', for the sum of 300 florins. With this property comes a complication: Leonardo is obliged to pay 'whatever is necessary to furnish a dowry of 150 florins for the daughter of Salvestro di Giovanni'. This entailment was probably part of the original bequest by Simone father of Francesco – paying a dowry for some poor family of one's acquaintance is a form of charity found often in wills of the period. Leonardo also undertakes to provide 'the colours, the gold and all other costs arising' at his own expense.[66]

The upshot of this curious contract is that the monastery offers to pay Leonardo 150 florins (the agreed value of the property minus the debt entailed with it). This payment is in arrears (he cannot sell the property for three years), and does not include any provision for expenses. The final sum is not bad, but the circumstances are inconvenient. The property in the Val d'Elsa – a rustic region to the south of Florence – is the only thing he receives up front: perhaps he went to live in it.

By June, three months after the initial agreement, the difficulties of the situation are becoming apparent. He has had to ask the monastery to 'pay the above-mentioned dowry, because he said he does not have the means to pay it, and time was passing, and it was becoming prejudicial to us'. For this service his account with the friars has been debited 28 florins. It is further docked for sums advanced by the monastery to purchase colours for the work. Also in June, we learn, 'Maestro Leonardo the painter' has received 'one load of faggots and one load of large logs' as payment for decorating the monastery clock. In August he 'owes us for one *moggia* [about 5 bushels] of grain which our carter carried to him at his own house'. (This house is presumably the property in Val d'Elsa.) And on 28 September – the date of the last document in the series – he 'owes us for one barrel of vermilion wine'.[67]

These are the realities of Leonardo's circumstances in 1481: he cannot afford to buy his paints; he buys grain and wine on credit; he does odd jobs for the monastery and is paid in firewood. And, as the nights draw in, the first lineaments of the altarpiece begin to take shape on a panel of poplar wood.

The product of this contract, and of these straitened circumstances, is the *Adoration of the Magi*, the last and greatest of his early Florentine works (Plate 10). It is the largest of all his easel paintings: 8 feet tall and nearly as wide (2.46 × 2.43 m). The dimensions, and the unusually square format, presumably reflect the space available above the altar of San Donato.

The painting was never delivered (which is perhaps just as well, as the monastery was completely demolished in the early sixteenth century). It was left unfinished when Leonardo departed for Milan in early 1482. According to Vasari, he left it for safe-keeping at the house of his friend Giovanni de' Benci, the brother of Ginevra. It passed into the Medici collection sometime before 1621, when it was listed among the paintings at the Palazzo Medici. It is now one of the most famous paintings in the Uffizi, though it is more accurately an underpainting. The complex composition has been blocked in, but much of the detail is perfunctory: it is a work still in draft. The paint media are lamp-black mixed with diluted glue, and lead white. There is some over-painting in brown, though it has recently been questioned if these marks are Leonardo's. The painting's overall tawny-brown tonality is due to discoloration of later layers of varnish.

The subject-matter is one of the most popular in Renaissance painting – the arrival of the three kings or magi to pay homage to the infant Christ at Bethlehem. Leonardo would undoubtedly have known Benozzo Gozzoli's fresco in the Palazzo Medici and Botticelli's version of the subject in Santa Maria Novella, commissioned by Giovanni Lami of the Guild of Money-changers in about 1476. (This, now in the Uffizi, is the second of four surviving Adorations by Botticelli: the earliest, perhaps before 1470, is in the National Gallery in London.) Leonardo has used all the conventional ingredients, but the painting is revolutionary in its handling of the large group. This is not a procession but a stormy swirl of figures and faces – over sixty figures altogether: people and animals. In its cloudy unfinished form there is something ambiguous about this populousness: this crowd in attitudes of worship and wonder seems almost a mob. The mother and child are enclosed in space, a still point at the centre of the picture, but the press of the crowd around this space suggests also their vulnerability. Something is about to engulf them. This vortex of menace foretells the child's story as surely as the symbolic gifts proffered by the kings.

There are some subtleties of religious interpretation.[68] The roots of the central tree snake down to touch the head of Christ – an allusion to the prophecy of Isaiah: 'There shall come forth a rod out of the stem of Jesse, and a branch shall grow out of his roots.' The broken architecture, with shrubbery growing out of the masonry, is a conventional allusion to the ruined 'house of David', which the birth of Christ will re-establish – workmen are just visible, on the stairs, busily rebuilding – but the shape of the building is specifically Florentine. Its columns and arches echo the presbytery of San Miniato del Monte, the oldest church in Florence after the Baptistery, reputedly built on the burial-site of the city's most famous Christian martyr, Minias or Miniato. Like the façade of Santa Maria Novella in *St Jerome*, this visual reference anchors formative religious beliefs in a Florentine landscape.

These various components of epiphany iconography are there, but one very basic ingredient is missing. Where is Joseph? Invariably featuring in other Adorations, he is here indistinct. Is he the bearded man in the right-hand group with his hand raised to his brow in amazement? Or is he the pensive figure watching from the sidelines on the extreme left of the painting? Probably the former, but the ambiguity is paramount: the father is unidentified, submerged into the periphery. One might resist a psychoanalytical interpretation of this, but it is a motif too recurrent to ignore – Leonardo *always* excises Joseph from the Holy Family. He is missing from the *Virgin of the Rocks* (which narratively takes place during the flight from Egypt, and so ought to include him), and he is missing from the various versions of the *Virgin and Child with St Anne*, where the third member of the family is not the child's father but his grandmother. One does not have to be a Freudian to feel that there are deep psychological currents here.

In early 2001 the Uffizi announced its intention to clean and restore the *Adoration*. This aroused an immediate hue and cry, led by the doyen of anti-restorers, Professor James Beck of Columbia University, New York.[69] The painting was too delicate, its shadows and nuances too complex, its patina too intrinsic to be restored. When I spoke about this to Antonio Natali, Director of Renaissance Art at the Uffizi, he used the favourite word of the pro-restoration lobby – 'legibility'. He spoke eloquently of the painting as a 'buried poem'. 'If you were studying Petrarch, would you read a few words here, a few words there? No. It is the same with a painting – you want to be able to read *all* of it.'

That the painting is in poor condition is not in doubt. The paint surface is covered by a dirty 'skin' of later varnishings: heavy mixes of glue, oil and resins. In the darker areas of the panel these have formed a thick brown patina. They also have the *imbianchimento* or whitening caused by oxidization: those tiny reticulations which glaze the surface – the shattered-windscreen effect. But the opponents of restoration query the idea of legibility, seeing it as a desire to 'clarify' something that (in the case of the *Adoration*, at least) the artist himself deliberately left ambiguous. The current spate of restorations, it is argued, panders to a modern taste for brightness and crispness – for photographic or electronic types of clarity. Restoration is thus a commercial decision by the galleries: a matter of marketing as much as conservation. 'The real issue is philosophical,' says Professor Beck. 'Do we really want the paintings of the past to be modernized? Cleaning this picture is like a seventy-year-old person having a face-lift.'

The technical departments of the Uffizi are in a nondescript courtyard across the street from the gallery. In a small room on the second floor, laid across three trestles so it resembles a large picnic table, is Leonardo's *Adoration*. The room is small and white-tiled; there is cream-coloured paper over the windows, admitting the *luce velata* which is wholesome for paintings. From a hook hang a feather-duster and a supermarket carrier-bag. The vaguely chemical smell makes one think of a medical laboratory or a vet's operating-theatre. The imagery of medicine, of the painting as a great and aged patient, is frequently evoked by restorers. The situation is somehow intimate: the painting stripped of its gallery grandeur, horizontal, awaiting intervention.

The famous restorer Alfio del Serra prowls around it, sizing it up – these are the early weeks of the process, and the controversy has caused a hiatus. Del Serra is a stocky Pistoiese in his early sixties, with cropped white hair and a short-sleeved shirt. He has the look of an artisan, which is how he likes to be considered. His list of restorations includes works by Martini, Duccio, Cimabue, Giotto, Mantegna, Perugino, Raphael and Titian. Among his recent projects have been Botticelli's *Birth of Venus* and Leonardo's *Annunciation*. He shrugs about the controversy: it has at least given him time with the painting, time to get to know it. 'Every restoration', he says, 'is a work of interpretation. There are no automatic or universal rules which can be applied in every situation. You need sensitivity, respect, knowledge – to continually ask yourself questions: that is what's needed.'[70]

We crouch down and peer beneath at the back of the picture. The panel is formed of ten vertical planks or boards glued together; the transverse supports were added later, perhaps in the seventeenth century. The planks are of a fairly uniform width (about 9 inches across) but a narrower one is stuck on the left-hand edge, presumably to increase the painting to the commissioned size. Del Serra points out the problem of *convessità*, or bowing, in the middle boards, which threatens to crack the paint surface. This stems partly from the casual attrition of time and humidity, but also reflects Leonardo's choice of wood 500 years ago. Del Serra explains with diagrams the importance of the original wood. To create the boards, a section of a tree trunk – in this case of the serviceable white poplar called *gattice* – is cut vertically. The cut nearest the centre, the *radiale*, is the best, because the tree rings are symmetrically balanced; the outer cut, or *peripherale*, is not so good. Del Serra has recently restored the *Annunciation*, and is familiar also with the *Baptism of Christ*: in both cases the actual panels are in excellent condition. Those were paintings done within the Verrocchio workshop: quality materials were used. For the *Adoration* – an independent work, done when he was buying grain and wine on tick from his employers – Leonardo made do with the cheaper cuts. In this, adds del Serra, he was foreshadowed by Cimabue, the *maestro* of Giotto, who used 'very thin pieces of wood, of the kind that the carpenter would throw away' – in short, offcuts.

Del Serra is relaxed and unceremonious with the painting: he does not quite lean his elbow on it as we talk, but one feels that he might. He wets a plug of cotton-wool and briefly polishes a small area of the picture: the faintly sketched heads of an ox and an ass on the right-hand side, so easily missed, suddenly emerge from the gloom.

In the months to come the story of the restoration would become yet more tangled. Late in 2001 the Uffizi decided to commission a technical examination of the painting by the art-diagnostician Maurizio Seracini. After months of painstaking analysis Seracini dropped a bombshell: the reddish-brown over-painting seen on various parts of the *Adoration* was not done by Leonardo. The clue lay in microscopic analysis of cross-sections of tiny paint samples – that mysterious, micron-thick dimension of the paint surface. In almost every cross-section he took, he found that the top layer of brown paint had penetrated into the lower, earlier, monochrome stratum. By the time the colour was brushed on to it, the surface had cracks and fissures deep enough for the wet brown paint to seep down into them. Seracini says – and this is the crux – that this cracking could have occurred only over a significant period of time, perhaps fifty to a hundred years. The top layer was thus painted after Leonardo's death, by an unknown artist following the cavalier tenets of his day about how to improve a painting.[71]

Seracini's interpretation of the evidence has since been challenged, but in the face of this new dimension of controversy, the restoration project was quietly and wisely shelved, and the *Adoration* now hangs once more in the Leonardo Room of the Uffizi, its dirt and mystery intact while the arguments continue.

This unfinished masterwork of Leonardo's Florentine years provides deep but elusive insights into his mentality, his manner of working, his handling of various threads of Christian symbolism and Florentine-heritage imagery, his extraordinary sense of dynamism and vortical flow. But it has something else to tell us, for at the far right-hand edge of the painting stands a tall young man in a long cloak who is almost certainly a self-portrait of Leonardo at the age of about twenty-nine (Plate 1).

The issue of Renaissance self-portraiture is a thorny one, because the visual evidence is often circular, but we know that Italian artists of the Quattrocento often included a self-portrait in group-paintings, and that the convention was to show the artist looking outward from the picture, defining himself as a mediator between the fictive scene he has created and the real world of the spectator. In some cases the self-portrait is certain, as in Gozzoli's *Procession of the Magi*, where the artist helpfully identifies the face looking out of the crowd by painting his name on his hat. More often one is making deductions, or attending to contemporary deductions. The woodcut portraits of artists that adorn the second edition of Vasari's *Lives*

(cut by the German engraver Christopher Coriolano to Vasari's instructions)
are a useful indicator. For instance, it is clear from the woodcut of Masaccio
that Vasari considered the dark, rather sullen face in the *Tribute Money* –
one of Masaccio's frescos in the Brancacci chapel – to be a self-portrait.
This is generally accepted, but Vasari is never foolproof: he modelled the
portrait of Cimabue on a figure in Andrea da Firenze's *Church Triumphant*
in Santa Maria Novella, but the figure in question wears the insignia of the
Order of the Garter and is almost certainly a visiting Englishman.[72]

The first habitual self-portraitist was Fra Filippo Lippi, who peers at us
from the crowd in the Barbadori altarpiece (formerly in San Spirito and
now in the Louvre). Commissioned in 1437, this work shows Lippi in his
early thirties; he gets progressively older in the *Coronation of the Virgin*
(Uffizi), completed in 1447, and in the *Martyrdom of St Stephen* in Prato
cathedral, done in the 1450s. In all these he appears as a swarthy, round-
faced friar with faintly comic sticking-out ears. These ears become a kind
of shorthand, a distinguishing feature. They are prominently displayed on
the sculpted head on his tomb in Spoleto cathedral. This was added in about
1490, twenty years after Lippi's death, but his big ears were remembered.

Andrea Mantegna is another mid-century painter whose work was full of
self-portraits. His puffy, worried-looking face in monochrome is seen in one
of the *trompe l'œil* pilasters of the Camera degli Sposi (Wedding Bedroom)
in the Gonzaga castle in Mantua. It conveys a witty sense of the artist
imprisoned in his own fantasia. The young man peering out of the darkness
in his *Presentation at the Temple* (Berlin) is also a self-portrait. The painting
is connected to his marriage in 1454 to Nicolosia Bellini, sister of the
Venetian painter Giovanni Bellini. (Bellini's own version of the *Presentation*
is almost identical in composition, except that there are now two figures
looking on from the right, one of whom is Mantegna again and the other
Bellini. The model for the Madonna in both paintings is probably Nicolosia
herself.) Again these images have a particular unifying feature – the downward curve of the mouth – and again this is echoed in the woodcut portrait
of Mantegna in Vasari's *Lives*.[73]

By the early 1480s, when Leonardo was working on the *Adoration*, this
self-portraiture had become a convention. The unlovely features of Perugino
look from a row of faces in his fresco *St Peter Receiving the Keys*, identifiable
by comparison with the certain self-portrait of *c.* 1500 in the Collegio di
Cambio in Perugia. And it is surely the handsome, dark-eyed face of Domenico Ghirlandaio looking out from so many of his frescos.

This inclusion of the artist is in part a confident statement of personal
identity, and indeed status: he includes himself just as he includes the

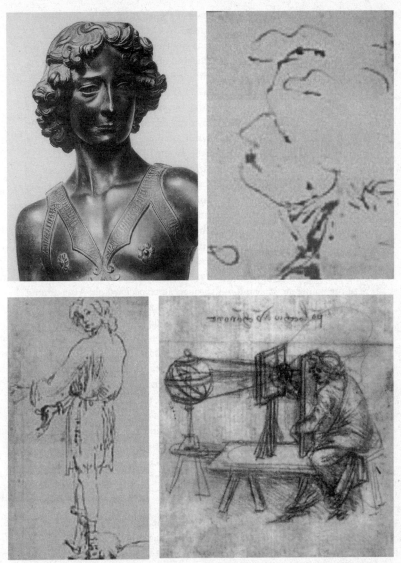

Images of the young Leonardo? Upper left: detail from Verrocchio's David, c. 1466. Upper right: doodle from the 'Fioravanti folio', 1478. Lower left: study for the commentatore *of the Adoration, c. 1481. Lower right: artist using a perspectograph, c. 1478–80.*

features of the 'donor' or commissioner of the painting. In his 'mediating', outward-looking position the artist fulfils the role of what Leon Battista Alberti called the *commentatore* or commentator. Alberti describes this figure as an essential component of the kind of painting he calls a *storia* – a history or story – which essentially means a painting of a scene or episode with a number of figures in it. 'In the *storia* there should be one who alerts and informs us as to what is happening, or who beckons us with his hand to look.'[74] The highly populated depictions of the Adoration are a classic example of the painting as *storia*, a rendition of an archetypically dramatic scene or story. The young man on the edge of the crowd in Leonardo's *Adoration* fulfils exactly the role of the *commentatore* as laid down by Alberti, and he occupies exactly the same position as the young man turning outward in Botticelli's *Adoration* (p. 86), who is also believed to be a self-portrait. Leonardo would certainly have known this work, completed a couple of years previously for the church of Santa Maria Novella.

Visual comparisons seem to confirm that this is Leonardo on the edge of the painting. The face has similarities with the face of Verrocchio's *David*, and with the face of the young man on the Fioravanti folio, and with the face of the young artist who looks through a perspectograph. Also, among the pen-and-ink studies for the *Adoration* at the Louvre there is a tall, long-haired young man who does not correspond to any figure in the actual painting, but whose turning gesture suggests he may be an early study for the *commentatore*; this can also be thought of as a self-portrait.

A dab of wet cotton-wool in the Uffizi restoration labs, and the handsome, broad-faced young man glowers briefly. What is his mood? He turns away from the central figures of the mother and child, though his right arm seems to extend back, inviting us to look at them. He is the commentator: detached, cool, marginal, quizzical, perhaps even sceptical. He brings us this momentous scene, but is not part of it.

⊱ LEAVING ⊰

The young man looks out and away, beyond the frame which contains and constrains him. Sometime after September 1481 – the date of the last reference to him in the San Donato accounts – Leonardo left Florence for Milan. He would not return (as far as we know) for more than eighteen years, though this is a hindsight he did not have at the point of his departure, so we cannot say whether he was definitively and defiantly *leaving* – turning his back on his home city, his father, his stalled and uncertain career – or whether he was simply going away for a while: a trip up north, a taste of something new.

As I have already mentioned, the rather surprising circumstance of Leonardo's departure for Milan is that he went there as a musician. As also noted, there is a discrepancy in the early accounts as to whether he was 'sent' by Lorenzo de' Medici or 'invited' by Ludovico Sforza. Behind this small crux lies a larger question: in what kind of mood did Leonardo leave Florence? Was he sent as a cultural ambassador, someone appreciated as an example of Florentine talent and ingenuity? Or did he leave under a cloud, with a sense of failure and frustration – his paintings unfinished, his lifestyle controversial, his reputation a mix of brilliance and difficulty? This is not really an either/or question: both moods can be accommodated. Leonardo was ready to go, and Lorenzo was ready to let him go. Restlessness and expedience – two powerful motivations which here coalesce into a single curious fantasy: a violin with a silver sounding-box in the shape of a horse's skull.

The date of Leonardo's removal is uncertain. The last record of him in Florence (that delivery of 'vermilion wine' from the San Donato vineyards) is dated 28 September 1481; the earliest record of him in Milan (the contract for the *Virgin of the Rocks*) is dated 25 April 1483. The Anonimo says he was thirty years old when he left: if we take this literally, the date of his departure was sometime after 15 April 1482.

One interesting possibility is that Leonardo went as part of the retinue of Bernardo Rucellai and Pier Francesco da San Miniato, who were dispatched to Milan as Florentine *oratori* or envoys in early 1482.[75] There is certainly no difficulty in associating Leonardo with the popular and scholarly Bernardo Rucellai, the fashionable Platonist, patron of Tommaso Masini, and plausible commissioner of Leonardo's *St Jerome*. He was now in his late thirties. He was one of the richest men in the city, and brother-in-law of Lorenzo de' Medici; he would remain in Milan for four years, the last two (1484–6) as resident Florentine ambassador. A sonnet by the gossipy poet Bernardo Bellincioni may pinpoint Leonardo's connection with Rucellai and his fellow envoy to Milan, Pier Francesco da San Miniato. It is headed '*S a Madonna Lucretia essendo l'auctore a Fiesole*' – it is, in other words, a sonnet written at Fiesole and addressed to Lucrezia Tornabuoni, mother of Lorenzo de' Medici. It refers to a 'Messer Bernardo' and a 'Piero' who are plausibly identified as Rucellai and San Miniato, and it contains the lines:

A Fiesole con Piero é Leonardo
E fanno insieme una conclusione

[At Fiesole with Piero is Leonardo, and together they reach an
agreement.][76]

Bernardo and Pier Francesco were nominated *oratori* on 10 December 1481,
and they left Florence for Milan on 7 February 1482. This may give us the
date of Leonardo's departure.

Shortly before he left, Leonardo drew up that list of his Florentine works
from which I have frequently quoted. These are the paintings, drawings and
models he is taking with him to Milan: his portfolio. It includes 'two
Madonnas', one of which is probably the *Benois Madonna*; and 'certain
figures of St Jerome'; and a portrait of Atalante Migliorotti 'raising his face';
and 'some machines for ships' and 'some machines for water'; and 'many
flowers drawn from nature'; and 'many designs of knots' or *vinci*. These are
identifiable with known Leonardo works of the late 1470s, but this document is also melancholy in that many of the items cannot now be identified
and have almost certainly been lost. Where are the '8 St Sebastians', or the
'head of a gypsy', or the 'head of the Duke' (probably, for reasons that will
soon become apparent, the late Duke of Milan, Francesco Sforza)? In some
cases the description is not even intelligible – were the '*4 disegni della tavola
da santo angiolo*' drawings done for a painting featuring a holy angel or for
a painting in the church of Sant'Angelo? And for that matter are the
'*componimenti d'angioli*' compositions of angels or angles? His fascination
with hair is already apparent – five separate entries identify the drawing by
referring to the hair ('a head in profile with fine hair', 'a full face, with curly
hair', 'a head of a girl with tresses gathered in a knot', etc.). In among the
art-works one spots a *calcedonio*, or chalcedony – a precious stone of the
quartz kind, of which agates and cornelians are the best-known varieties.

The folio on which the list appears has some other surprises. The first
item on the list (or what is given as the first item in modern transcriptions)
– 'a head, full face, of a young man with a fine head of hair' – was written
by someone other than Leonardo, and possibly at a different time. It is
upside down in respect of the rest of the list, and is written from left to right.
The hand is almost identical with the one which wrote the Latin distichs
about the gun called La Ghibellina and the blotted sonnet beginning '*Leonardo mio*' – the hand, in other words, of the Pistoiese poet Antonio Cammelli.
In the bottom left-hand corner of the folio is a rather unskilful caricature,

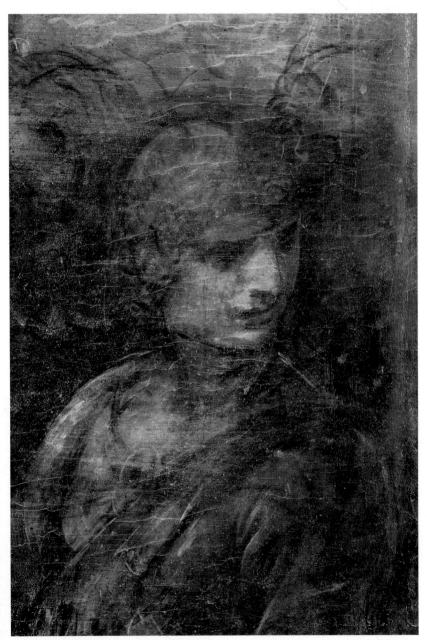

1. Leonardo at twenty-nine. Probable self-portrait from the *Adoration of the Magi*.

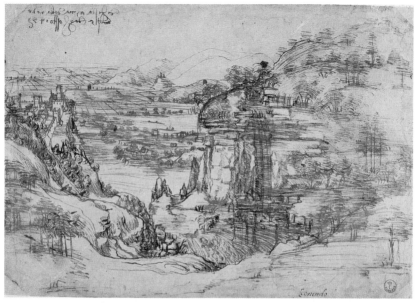

2. Landscape near Vinci, in Leonardo's earliest dated drawing.

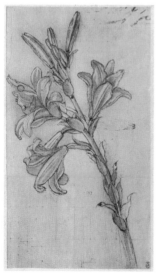

3. Study of a lily.

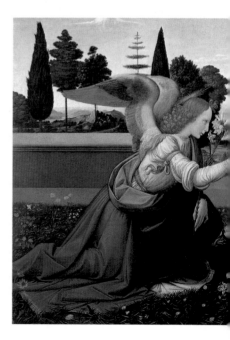

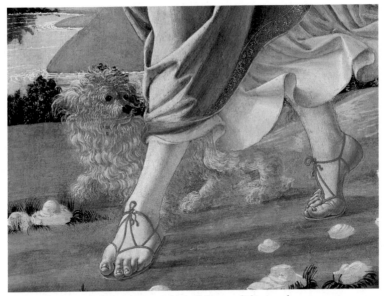

4. The dog from Andrea del Verrocchio's *Tobias and the Angel*, probably contributed by Leonardo.

5. *The Annunciation*.

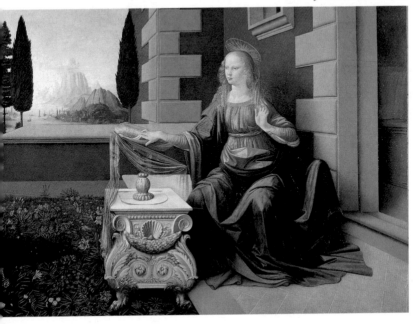

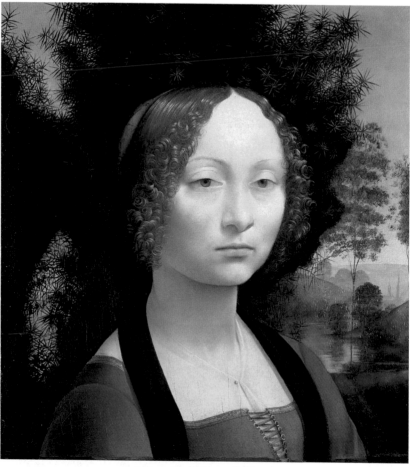

6. Portrait of Ginevra de' Benci.

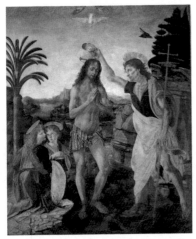

7. Verrocchio's *Baptism of Christ*, with kneeling angel and landscape by Leonardo.

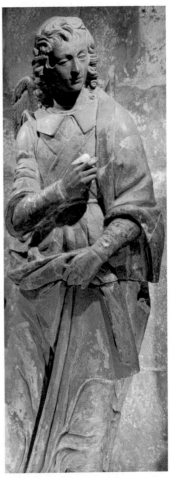

8. Terracotta angel at San Gennaro, attributed to Leonardo.

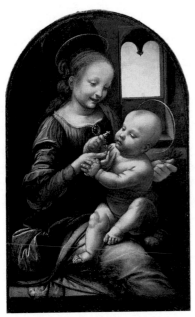

9. The *Benois Madonna*.

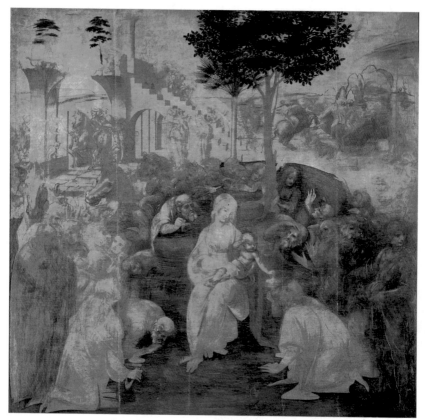

10. The *Adoration of the Magi*, left unfinished in 1482.

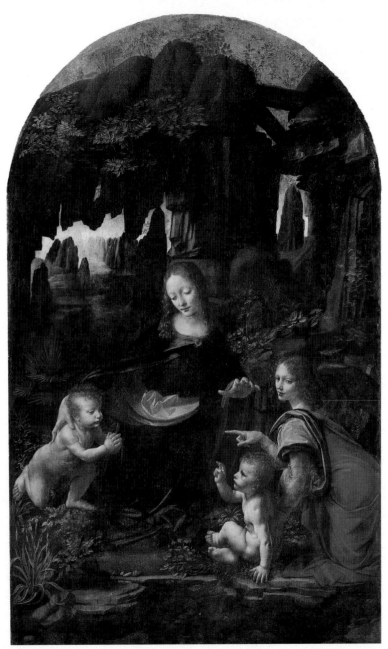

11. The Louvre *Virgin of the Rocks*.

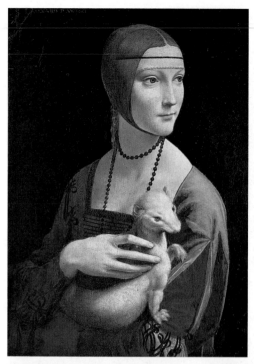

(Left)
12. *The Lady with an Ermine*, a portrait of Cecilia Gallerani.

(Below left)
13. *The Musician*.

(Below right)
14. Portrait called *La Belle Ferronnière*, probably of Lucrezia Crivelli.

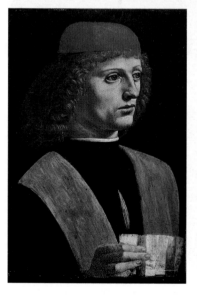

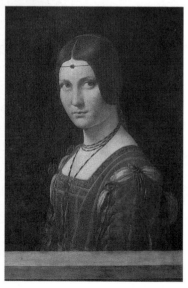

List of works by Leonardo, c. 1482, on a much doodled sheet of the Codex Atlanticus.

in profile, of a glum-looking young man with long hair and a *berretta*. I wonder if this is a last image of Leonardo in Florence – '*Lionardo mio . . . perche tanto penato?*' – 'My Leonardo, why so troubled?' Perhaps this drawing is the handiwork of Il Pistoiese himself, or perhaps of Zoroastro, whose laboratory-walls in Rome were 'daubed with weird faces'.

If the list of works is a retrospective document, the famous 'letter of introduction' to Ludovico Sforza looks ambitiously forward to Leonardo's future in Milan. It was probably written up in Florence, ready to be presented to Ludovico at the earliest opportunity. The copy that survives is in a handsome scribal hand, perhaps a professional scrivener's, though as there are some minor changes and insertions it cannot be the presentation copy.[77] It is an elaborate prospectus of the skills that Leonardo can offer, very confidently phrased, though pretty surprising in that the skills are mainly those of military engineering, in which he has at this point no known expertise or experience. This is the new role he dreams of as he prepares to leave Florence: engineer to the Duke of Milan.

He begins with a wordy flourish:

My most illustrious Lord,

I have sufficiently seen and examined the inventions of all those who count themselves makers and masters of instruments of war, and I have found that in design and operation their machines are in no way different from those in common use. I therefore make bold, without ill-will to any, to offer my skills to Your Excellency, and to acquaint Your Lordship with my secrets, and will be glad to demonstrate effectively all these things, at whatever time may be convenient to you . . .

Then follows a numbered list of the 'instruments' whose secrets he will offer Ludovico – a brochure of military hardware:

1. I have methods for making very light and strong bridges, easily portable, and useful whether pursuing or evading the enemy; and others more solid, which cannot be destroyed by fire or assault . . .
2. When a siege is under way I know how to remove water from the trenches, and to make all manner of bridges, covered ways, scaling-ladders and other devices suitable for this sort of operation.
3. If the place under siege cannot be reduced by bombardment, because of the height of its banks or the strength of its position, I have methods for destroying any fortress or redoubt even if it is founded upon solid rock . . .
4. I have certain types of cannon, extremely easy to carry, which fire

out small stones, almost as if it were a hailstorm, and the smoke from these will cause great terror to the enemy, and they will bring great loss and confusion . . .

5. I have ways of silently making underground tunnels and secret winding passages to arrive at a desired point, even if it is necessary to pass underneath trenches or a river.

6. I will make armoured cars, totally unassailable, which will penetrate the ranks of the enemy with their artillery, and there is no company of soldiers so great that it can withstand them. And behind these the infantry can follow, quite unharmed and encountering no opposition.

7. In case of need I will make cannon and mortar and light artillery, beautifully and usefully constructed, quite different from those in common use.

8. Where bombardment turns out to be impractical I will devise catapults, mangonels, caltrops,[78] and other wonderfully effective machines not in common use . . .

9. And when the fight is at sea I have many kinds of highly efficient machines for attack and defence, and vessels which will resist the attack of heavy bombardment, and powder and fumes.

'In short,' he sums up, 'I can contrive an infinite variety of machines for attack or defence.' The question that immediately occurs, and would soon be occurring to Ludovico Sforza, is: Could he? It is possible – Leonardo had a base of engineering skills; he had a capacity to learn fast; he had the metalworker Tommaso Masini working with him – but there is no evidence that any of these machines ever existed except on paper.[79] The document has a sci-fi air about it, as if his imagination is running ahead of him. It is the pitch of a multi-talented dreamer who will fill in the details later.

At the end of the letter Leonardo remembers that he is also an artist – 'in painting I can do everything that it is possible to do' – and he adds a last specific offer to Ludovico which some believe to be the true motivation of his trip to Milan: 'I would be able to begin work on the bronze horse which will be to the immortal glory and eternal honour of the Prince your father's happy memory and of the famous house of Sforza.' Here is the first mention of the great equestrian statue of Francesco Sforza which would occupy Leonardo, ultimately fruitlessly, for years to come. In 1480 his former master Verrocchio had gone to Venice to create a similar work: the equestrian statue of the *condottiere* Bartolomeo Colleoni. News of a Sforza commission had been buzzing round Florence for a couple of years: the Pollaiuolo studio had already produced some designs.[80] These monuments were grand, expensive, highly public productions: Leonardo is thinking big.

He wraps these documents up carefully, with that secretive air he has: an inventory of the past and a prospectus of the future. They go into the travelling-chest or the saddle-bag, along with the drawings and half-finished paintings, and the clay figurines, and the lustrous chalcedony, and the silver lyre in its case.

PART FOUR

New Horizons
1482–1490

. . . Seggendo in piuma
In fama non si vien, ne sotto coltre,
Sanza la qual chi sua vita consuma
Cotal vestigio in terra di se lascia
Qual fummo in aere ed in acqua la schiuma.

*[Lying in a featherbed will not bring you fame, nor
staying beneath the quilt, and he who uses up his
life without achieving fame leaves no more vestige
of himself on earth than smoke in the air or foam
upon the water.]*

Lines from Dante's *Inferno* copied out by Leonardo,
Windsor fol. 12349v

Leonardo estimated the journey from Florence to Milan as 180 miles – he always used the pre-metric *miglia* in computations of distance.[1] A modern road-atlas gives it as 188 miles. Taking some broad guidelines from contemporary journeys, an average day's coverage on horseback was between 20 and 30 miles (two to three stages a day, if you were using post-horses), so we might be talking of a journey of about a week. The typical route lay north over the Apennine mountains to Bologna, the road running parallel to today's A1 autostrada, and then across the lower reaches of the Po valley to the little city of Modena, part of the Este fiefdom.

For the zealous student of Leonardo manuscripts Modena has one singular association: it is the subject of a Leonardo dirty joke. There are ribaldries scattered among the notebooks, but this one is particularly frankly delivered. It is a joke, or rather a sarcastic comment, about the high entrance toll charged by the Modenese authorities:

A man going to Modena had to pay a toll of 5 soldi to enter the city. He made such a fuss and commotion that he attracted various bystanders who asked why he was so astonished. And Maso replied, 'Of course I'm astonished to find that a whole man can get in here for a mere 5 soldi, when in Florence I have to pay 10 gold ducats just to get my cock in, and here I can get my cock and balls and all the rest of me in for such a trifling amount. God save and protect this fine city and all who govern her!'[2]

My translation approximates to the rudeness in the original – thus 'cock' for *cazzo* and 'balls' for *coghone* (i.e. *coglioni*). The reference is, of course, to paying for sex with a Florentine prostitute. The introduction of the name Maso ('Tom') halfway through the story may just be a joke convention of the 'Right-said-Fred' sort, or it may indicate that this pungent bit of badinage was spoken by a man known to Leonardo, in his hearing. It could even have been spoken by Tommaso Masini, a.k.a. Zoroastro, on a day in early 1482 as they passed through Modena en route for Milan.

They travel on through the lowlands of the Po – Reggio Emilia, Parma, Piacenza, and finally Milan, its Gothic spires emerging from the wintry Lombard plain. The Romans called the town Mediolanum (*in medio plano*, in the middle of the plain). The conquering Lombards garbled this to Mayland, whence Milano. It was a crossroads town that just kept on growing: its site was not strategic, not healthy, not usefully close to any of the rivers – the Po, the Adda, the Ticino – which bound the plain. In winter the climate is wet and misty, and so one imagines Leonardo's arrival: everything tinged with that muted northerly light which will seep into his paintings.

Milan in 1482 was a city on the make. The population was around 80,000, somewhat larger than Florence's, though the city lacked the political and commercial structures which gave Florence its cohesive identity. Milan was an old-style feudal city-state, controlled by a ruling dynasty whose power was muscular and military more than legislative. The Sforza were very recent nobility. A generation earlier, in 1450, Ludovico's father, Francesco Sforza, had succeeded the city's previous rulers, the Visconti, and proclaimed himself Duke of Milan. The family name went back only to Ludovico's grandfather, a farmer turned mercenary, Muzzo Attendolo, who used Sforza as his fighting name (from *sforzare*, to force or compel). To Romantic historians like Jules Michelet, the Sforza were 'heroes of patience and cunning who built themselves up from nothing', but to their contemporaries these *soi-disant* dukes were 'uncouth soldiers'.[3] This was to the advantage of the now itinerant artist Leonardo da Vinci, since the *arriviste* was always a hungry patron. Ostentation and display were Sforza bywords: substitute pedigrees. The city had already a gloss of northern sophistication, imbued with Burgundian fashions and German technology. Leonardo had glimpsed this glamour ten years earlier when the Sforza cavalcade had dazzled and scandalized the citizenry of Florence.

The shape of medieval Milan – the Milan that Leonardo knew in the 1480s – can still be discerned on a modern map, the ellipse of the long-vanished city walls traceable along a series of wide streets which now serve as the city's inner ring-road. The original walls – built in the late twelfth century, after the destruction of the city by the Holy Roman Emperor Frederick I, known as Barbarossa, or Redbeard – are to be distinguished from the outer ring of bastioned walls, some portions of which are still remaining (e.g. the Bastione Porta Venezia at the top end of the public gardens). These latter walls were built by the Spanish in the mid sixteenth century, and did not exist in Leonardo's time. The circumference of the medieval walls was a little over 3 miles – about the same as the extant walls of Lucca – and thus walkable in some three-quarters of an hour. Considering that the population of 'Lucca *dentro*' is today less than 10,000, one sees how jam-packed were the 80,000 of Quattrocento Milan. Ten gates punctuated the walls. Eight of them are specified on a rough sketch-map of the city in the Codex Atlanticus; below it is a rapid bird's-eye view of the city from the west, showing the castle, the cathedral and the tall pointed tower of San Gottardo.[4]

Arriving from the south, the Florentine delegation of Rucellai and San Miniato – with its presumed retinue including Leonardo da Vinci, Tommaso Masini and Atalante Migliorotti – would probably have entered by the Porta Romana. Its marbled frontage was carved with fierce reliefs of 'St Ambrose driving the Arians out of Milan with a Whip', and a 'Man with a Dragon' (traditionally believed to be a portrait of Barbarossa). The names of the twelfth-century masons who carved the reliefs are signed in the stone: Girardi and Anselmo.[5]

Pressing on through the city, passing the massive Gothic accumulations of the cathedral, the delegation would arrive at the forbidding bulk of the Castello Sforzesco dominating the northern flank of the city. Formerly known as the Castello San Giovio, it had been enlarged and fortified by Ludovico's brother Galeazzo Maria in the late 1460s, moving the power-centre away from the old Castello Visconti next to the cathedral. An anonymous Florentine who saw it in 1480, two years before Leonardo, sums it up as a 'beautiful and very strong castle surrounded by ditches, covering half a square mile or more, with a walled garden about 3 miles in perimeter'.[6]

From the outside the castle is a grim redoubt of darkened red-brick walls. Through the hugely tall entrance-tower, designed by the Florentine architect Filarete, you enter into the hugely wide outer courtyard – size clearly mattered to the Sforza – and thence into the moated-off inner courtyards to the north: on the right the Corte Ducale, used for court functions, on the left the smaller Cortile della Rocchetta, where the Duke's private apartments were – an inner sanctum, ringed by walls and soldiers. The elegant colonnades added by Ludovico do not lessen the sense that this is a heavily guarded enclave in an era of justifiable paranoia.

Leonardo, arriving, could not know how much of his life he would spend in this fortress-court, as his relationship with the generous but unpredictable Ludovico ebbed and flowed. He has left his mark, faintly, in the decorated walls and ceiling of the Sala delle Asse, in the north-eastern corner of the

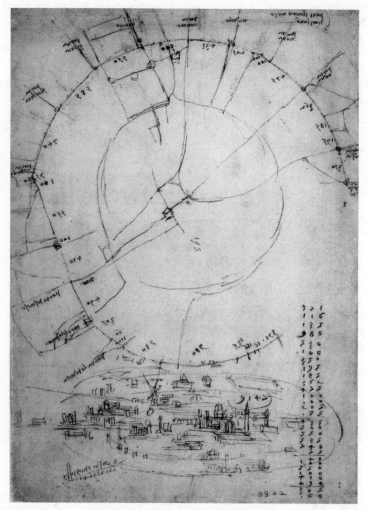

Leonardo's sketch-map of Milan, c. 1508.

castle. Faintly, because the restoration done a hundred years ago involved extensive repainting – you are aware of this inside the room but by chance my first view of it was from outside, round the back of the castle, where the walls are choked with ivy, and hooded crows nest noisily in the ventilation-slits, and through an upstairs window you catch a glimpse of that lush

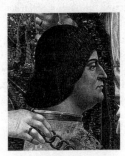

Ludovico Sforza by an unknown Lombard artist, from an altarpiece of the early 1490s.

bower of interwoven branches which Leonardo painted there in 1498, and which now conspires with the crows to remind us of the vanity of political power in the face of Nature, 'the mistress of all masters'.

Arriving in Milan in mid to late February 1482, the Florentines found the city in the throes of the 'Ambrosian carnival', a celebration which combined the pre-Lenten carnival with the feast-day of St Ambrose or Ambrogio, the city's patron saint, on 23 February. This is a context which makes sense of Leonardo's musical entrée into Milanese court society, as stated by the Anonimo and elaborated by Vasari: 'Leonardo was invited to Milan by the Duke, who was a great lover of *lira* music . . . and he outplayed all the musicians who had gathered together there to play.' We can perhaps imagine some kind of *concorso* – a contest or competition – as part of the court's carnival festivities. The likely setting for this would be the state apartments in the Corte Ducale. A later note by Leonardo may refer to a similar occasion: 'Tadeo, son of Nicholaio del Turco, was nine years old on Michaelmas Eve in the year 1497; he went that day to Milan, and played the lute, and was judged one of the best players in Italy.'[7]

Thus, as an entertainer, Leonardo da Vinci enters the world of Ludovico Sforza, Il Moro, the strongman (though not yet, as Vasari calls him, the

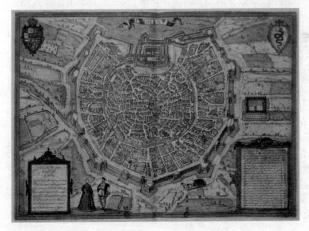

Engraved map of Milan by Josef Hoefnagel, c. 1572.

Duke) of Milan. This is probably their first meeting, though Leonardo would certainly have seen him ten years ago in Florence, when Ludovico accompanied his brother Galeazzo Maria on that sumptuous state visit. They were exact contemporaries: Ludovico – the fourth legitimate son of Francesco Sforza – was born at Vigevano in early 1452. The nickname Il Moro, 'the Moor', is partly a pun on one of his given names, Mauro, and partly because of his dark complexion. He used a Moor's head on his coat of arms; on a painted wedding-chest he is depicted on horseback escorted by a Moorish halbardier. Another of his emblems, in this pun-mad world, was a mulberry tree (also *moro*), a reference to Milanese silk-production, which he enthusiastically promoted. When Galeazzo Maria was assassinated, in 1476, Ludovico moved swiftly to isolate the widowed Duchess, Bona of Savoy, and the legitimate Duke, the ten-year-old Gian Galeazzo. As regent he ruled as Duke in all but name. He was ruthless, ambitious and avaricious, of course, but he was also pragmatic and intelligent (at least until his weakness for astrology and augury began to get the better of him), and he was genuinely keen to create a Milanese Renaissance. In the many stereotyped portraits of him, all in profile, he is burly, fleshy, big-chinned. The portrait of him in the Pala Sforzesca or Sforza altarpiece (now in the Brera Gallery) is a study in self-esteem. He might be humming to himself the chorus of a popular propagandist song:

> There is one God in heaven,
> And on earth there is one Moor.[8]

On 6 March Bernardo Rucellai dispatched a report back to Lorenzo de' Medici. He has discussed with Ludovico 'the project and design of the fortress at Casalmaggiore'; Ludovico has expressed his satisfaction. Perhaps Leonardo's presence in the Rucellai retinue relates also to this fortification project on the Po. He is here as part of what would today be called 'technical cooperation' between Florence and Milan, as well as for his skills as a maker and player of novelty musical instruments.

For a moment Leonardo is himself a novelty. His music has charmed the Moor's ear, and his engineering expertise seems useful. It would now be expeditious for him to present to Ludovico that famous 'letter of introduction' or 'prospectus' he has brought with him, with its tempting list of military hardware – cannons and armoured cars, siege-machines and tunnel-borers and Bailey bridges – which he 'knows how' to produce. There are drawings done in Milan which visualize some of these machines, so perhaps Ludovico was interested. The portable cannon or mortar which 'fires out small stones, almost as if it were a hailstorm', is found in a drawing of

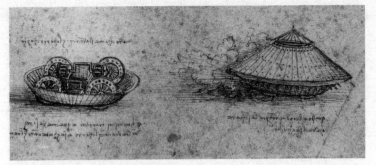

Leonardo's armoured car, c. 1487–8.

about 1484 at Windsor; on its verso are sketches of a fortified town under bombardment. The armoured car is seen in a drawing in the British Museum of *c*. 1487–8, and discussed in a note of the same date in Paris MS B, which states that such vehicles 'take the place of elephants' – a curiously archaic observation. In these military projects, says Martin Kemp, 'practical invention, antique precedent and imaginative implausibility are seamlessly mingled'.[9]

The appeal of the weaponry outlined in the prospectus, and worked over in later drawings, is perhaps as much psychological as practical. It is a pitch at the ambition, vanity and vulnerabilities of the Quattrocento despot; it is a rhetoric of omnipotence. The superb drawing of an artillery-yard or foundry, with naked dwarfed workers manhandling giant levers and gun-carriages – Fritz Lang's *Metropolis* springs to mind – conveys the sense of technological drama and grandeur which is also implicit in these promises: that Brunelleschian frisson. Will the Moor, Leonardo wonders, be the patron who can measure up to his dreams and aspirations? A certain disillusion on this point is evident, for above his drawing of the scattershot cannon he writes a half-sentence: 'If the men of Milan would for once do something out of the ordinary . . .'[10]

Almost as an afterthought, it seems, Leonardo's prospectus ends with some reference to his skills outside the theatre of war:

In time of peace I believe I can give complete satisfaction, equal to any other man, in architecture, in the design of buildings both public and private, and in guiding water from one place to another. Also I can undertake sculpture in marble, bronze or clay, and in painting I can do everything that it is possible to do, as well as any other man whoever he may be.

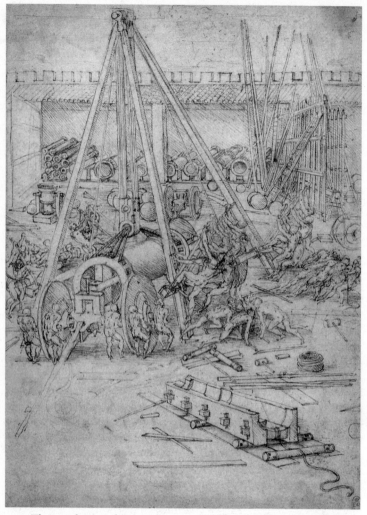

Theatre of war. A dramatic drawing of a Milanese ordnance foundry.

To us it is strange to find Leonardo the painter, sculptor and architect bringing up the rear behind Leonardo the manufacturer of tanks, mortars and bombards. But that is his construction of the situation: a perception of the priorities of Sforzesco Milan, and perhaps also – as Vasari so often says – a mistaken perception of his own gifts.

⇥ EXPATRIATES AND ARTISTS ⇤

Lombardy was a foreign country: they did things differently there. The climate, the landscape, the lifestyle, the language – a German-influenced dialect, heavy on the zs, in which a Giovanni was Zoane and a Giorgio was Zorzo – were new and strange. The musical soirée and the military promises are not enough to suggest (as is often implied) that Leonardo was swept instantly into Milanese court life. He was more than ever an outsider, an expatriate, a beginner-again. This is both an isolating experience and a self-defining one: he will seldom appear in Milanese records without the epithet 'Fiorentino' appended to his name. He becomes a Florentine in a way he never was, and never would be, in Florence.

There was a strong Florentine presence in Milan, and this was probably Leonardo's milieu in his first months here. The commercial arm of Florentine influence was present in the customary form of the Medici bank. Its head-quarters was a large *palazzo* on what is now Via Bossi, given to Cosimo de' Medici by Ludovico's father; you entered through an ornately carved Corinthian arch in which Lombard and Tuscan motifs were diplomatically combined. It was a meeting-place as much as a counting-house – a kind of consulate for itinerant Florentines. The chief Medici agents in Milan were the Portinari family, whom Leonardo certainly came to know. In a memorandum of the early 1490s he reminds himself to 'ask Benedetto Portinari how the people go on the ice in Flanders'.[11]

A well-known Florentine living in Milan in 1482 was the veteran traveller, author and diplomat Benedetto Dei, now in his mid-sixties. He had first visited the city in the late 1440s, and was there when, as he put it, 'Francesco Sforza took it with his sword in hand.' He too knew the Portinari, and in 1476 he travelled to France and the Netherlands as their agent. (The same business links presumably account for Benedetto Portinari's knowledge of Flemish ice-skaters.) Leonardo may have already met Dei in Florence, where he was a friend of the scientist Toscanelli and the poet Luigi Pulci. The latter addressed a sonnet to him, '*In principio era buio, e buio fia*' ('In the beginning was the dark, and the dark will always be' – a provocative parody of Genesis), which caused some scandal. One gathers from it that Dei was of a sceptical turn of mind on matters religious:

> *Hai tu veduto, Benedetto Dei,*
> *Come sel beccon questi gabbadei*
> *Che dicon ginocchion l'ave Maria!*

Tu riderai in capo della via
Che tu vedrai le squadre de' Romei . . .

[Have you seen, Benedetto Dei, how foolish are those hypocrites who
kneel and mumble their Ave Marias! You would laugh from the top of the
street if you could see the hordes of pilgrims bound for Rome . . .]

Pulci was denounced by the philosopher Ficino for these infamies he had
'spewed out against God'. All this was in early 1476, around the time of
Leonardo's portrait of Ginevra, with its Ficinian overtones. Pulci and Dei –
like Antonio Cammelli – represent a spikier, more sceptical mood which
seems to have been congenial to Leonardo. Between 1480 and 1487 Dei
was more or less continuously in Milan, in the service of Ludovico Sforza.
He was now at the apex of his career as a diplomat and reporter: the man
who knew everyone and everything, *'la tromba della verità'* ('the trumpet
of truth'). He collected and distributed news via a network of correspondents
that ranged from his family and friends in Florence, whom he encouraged
to write weekly, to the powerful dynasties of the Gonzaga, the Este, the
Bentivoglio.[12]

Leonardo certainly knew this busy, gregarious Florentine, well placed
though not always well paid as a political adviser to the Moor. (Dei speaks
rather bitterly of having to 'brave the plague' in order to obtain his 'tip'
from Ludovico.) He would have listened with interest to Dei's tales of his
travels in Turkey, Greece, the Balkans and North Africa: there were not
many men who could give you, as Dei could, a first-hand account of life in
Timbuktu. This interest is evident in a curious text of Leonardo's, a kind of
spoof travelogue or newsletter which begins 'Dear Benedetto Dei'. It is
datable to *c.* 1487, which was about the time of Dei's departure from Milan.
Its obviously fictive nature suggests an element of parody – Dei was regarded
as a teller of tall tales. Its story of giants perhaps recalls the famous *Morgante
maggiore* of Dei's old friend Luigi Pulci, a book Leonardo is known to have
owned.[13]

Another Florentine in the Moor's service was Piero di Vespucci. He had
been clapped up in the Stinche after the Pazzi Conspiracy, charged with abet-
ting the flight of the conspirators, though more probably because he was
an old enemy of Giuliano de' Medici. The enmity stemmed from Giuliano's
courtship of Simonetta Cattanei, who was married to Piero's son Matteo. In
1480 Vespucci was 'restituted in all his rights', but chose rather the dignity
of exile.[14] Ludovico welcomed him, and made him a ducal councillor, but
in 1485 he was killed in a skirmish in the neighbouring town of Alessandria.

Bankers, diplomats and exiles: these men constitute an inner circle of Florentine influence at the court of the Moor, and would have been useful contacts for Leonardo. Another was Bartolomeo Calco, a distinguished Florentine Hellenist scholar, whom Ludovico appointed as his secretary, as part of his drive to 'purify the coarse speech of the Milanese'. There are implications of intellectual snobbery in this phrase, and perhaps the Florentines' presence was resented by the home-grown courtiers. A later Florentine protégé was the gossipy rimester Bernardo Bellincioni, whom Leonardo had known in Florence, though he was probably not in Milan until about 1485.

Artistically Milan was an eclectic mix. As a crossroads city, it sucked down influences from the north – German, French, Burgundian, Flemish – as well as those of neighbouring artistic centres like Venice and Padua. The city was full of Franco-German masons and sculptors, whose Gothic-influenced work adorned the cathedral. The chief engineer in charge of the cathedral works in the early 1480s was a German, Johann Nexemperger, from Graz. This mix of influences impeded the development of an identifiable local style, but in the new Sforzesco era of ostentation and aspiration there was plenty of artistic business. In 1481 the Milanese painters' confraternity, the Scuola di San Luca, had some sixty members.

The greatest artist working in Milan in 1482 was another immigrant, though he came from the rougher country of Le Marche east of the Apennines. This was the painter and architect Donato Bramante. He became a good friend of Leonardo, who refers to him in a note as 'Donnino', and it seems likely that this friendship was formed early on. Bramante was born near Urbino in 1444: he was eight years older than Leonardo. As a youth he perhaps met the great Alberti at the Urbinese court of Federico da Montefeltro. He lived an itinerant life as a painter before settling in Milan in the 1470s. In 1482 he was working on his first major architectural commission, the oratory of Santa Maria. He was esteemed by the Milanese court poets, and himself wrote spirited satirical squibs. Vasari describes Bramante as a kind and genial figure, and also mentions his fondness for playing the lute. He is portrayed by Raphael in the *School of Athens* fresco and in a chalk drawing now in the Louvre: these much later images show a strong, round-faced man with scanty, dishevelled hair.[15]

Among the local artists prominent at this time were the Brescia-born Vincenzo Foppa, who had absorbed the influences of Mantegna and Giovanni Bellini, and whose mastery of a certain shimmery, silvery light seems to anticipate Leonardesco light-effects, and younger artists like Ambrogio da Fossano (known as Il Bergognone – 'the Burgundian'), Bernardino Butinone, and Bernardo Zenale. But the local artists most closely associated with Leonardo's first years in Milan were the de Predis family, two of whom are documented as his colleagues or partners in early 1483.

The de Predis studio was a thriving family concern: four brothers were active. The eldest, Cristoforo (who is described in documents as *mutus*, a mute), worked chiefly as an illuminator, producing wonderfully detailed miniatures in the manner of the Flemish masters. Leonardo's particular relationship – one that lasted many years – was with Cristoforo's younger half-brother Ambrogio, born in about 1455. He began his career in Cristoforo's studio; his earliest documented works, *c.* 1472–4, are miniature illuminations in a book of hours for the Borromeo family. He later worked with another brother, Bernardino, at the Milanese mint. By 1482 he had begun to make his mark as a portrait painter; in that year the Duchess of Ferrara gave 10 braccia of satin to '*Zoane Ambrosio di Predi da Milano dipintore de lo Ill. Sig. Ludovico Sforza*'. He was thus already 'painter to Ludovico' at the time of Leonardo's arrival, probably specializing in por-traits, at which he excelled.[16]

Leonardo soon came to know this well-connected family of artists, and in the contract of April 1483 for the *Virgin of the Rocks* he is a partner of Ambrogio and Evangelista de Predis. It is a mutually useful partnership – Leonardo is the older and artistically senior, but the de Predis have the contacts and the clientele. In the contract, Leonardo is styled 'master', while Evangelista and Ambrogio appear without title. He appears to be lodging with them, or anyway near them, for all three have the same address: 'the parish of San Vincenzo in Prato *intus*'. The early Romanesque church of San Vincenzo in Prato lay just outside the south-western stretch of the walls, near the Porta Ticinese. The part of the parish designated '*intus*' – within the walls – would be the area now bounded by the Piazza della Resistenza and the Circo Torcio. Here Leonardo was lodging in the early months of 1483, with Zoroastro and Atalante Migliorotti in attendance and the de Predis workshop at his disposal.

➤➤ THE *VIRGIN OF THE ROCKS* ◄◄

The tangible product of Leonardo's association with the de Predis brothers is the beautiful and mysterious painting known as the *Vergine delle Rocce*, or *Virgin of the Rocks* (Plate 11). Part of the mystery is intrinsic – the mood elusive, the tone crepuscular, the iconography hermetic – but the painting is also historically mysterious. It is extensively documented, but the story the documents tell is tangled and contradictory. The painting exists in two distinct versions, similar but not identical, whose exact relationship is debated. The consensus view is that the version in the Louvre is the earlier, *c.* 1483–5, and is essentially pure Leonardo, while the version in the National Gallery, London, was painted later, by Ambrogio de Predis and Leonardo, though how much later depends on one's interpretation of the documents.

The beginning, at any rate, seems clear enough. The painting was commissioned by a contract dated 25 April 1483, drawn up by a notary named Antonio de' Capitani.[17] This document, recovered from the archives a century ago, is the earliest record of Leonardo's presence in Milan. The contract is between Leonardo – '*magister Leonardus de Vinciis florentinus*' – and Evangelista and Ambrogio de Predis on the one hand and a religious group called the Confraternity of the Immaculate Conception on the other. The commission is for an *ancona* (an altarpiece with a curved top) to adorn the Confraternity's chapel in the church of San Francesco Grande. This was a prestigious contract: San Francesco Grande, founded by the Visconti in the early fourteenth century, was the biggest church in Milan after the Duomo. (It was destroyed in 1576; the site is now filled by the Garibaldi Barracks.) The Confraternity, for all its holy trappings, was a tight-knit club of rich Milanese families: the Corio, the Casati, the Pozzobonelli, et al.

The artists were to produce three painted panels – a central panel 6 feet tall and 4 feet broad, and two smaller side-panels. The dimensions were specified because the paintings were to fit into an existing wooden frame, an elaborate piece by the *intagliatore* Giacomo del Maino, carved with figures in bas-relief. The painters also undertook to colour and gild the frame, and to do any repairs to it that might be needed. We can guess the likely division of labour: Evangelista, whose known career is confined to miniaturist work, would decorate the frame; the court painter Ambrogio would do the two side-panels; and the centrepiece would be entrusted to the Florentine *maestro*.

The deadline was the following 8 December, the feast-day of the Immaculate Conception: a tight delivery time, less than eight months away. The fee offered was 800 lire, though the schedule of payments seems unfavourably leisurely. The painters were to receive a down payment of 100 lire on 1 May 1483, then 40 lire a month from July 1483. As the painting was due for delivery in December 1483, over half their payment would be in arrears. This contract has the same grudging sound to it as Leonardo's contract with the friars of San Donato for the *Adoration*.

*

This is the beginning of the story, but from this moment of absolute clarity – a dated document, a comprehensible agreement – the matter swiftly goes off into more familiar Leonardian mists of uncertainty.

The *Virgin of the Rocks* is undoubtedly the painting that resulted from this commission, but it is oddly divergent from the client's specifications. According to the contract, the central panel was to show the Madonna and Child surrounded by a troupe of angels and two prophets, while the side-panels were to feature four angels each, singing or playing musical instruments. Apart from the Madonna and Child, none of these requirements is met by the *Virgin of the Rocks*, which has one angel, no prophets, and an unstipulated infant St John; the side-panels are also deficient, having only one angel each.

One possible reason that has been advanced is that Leonardo was already working on the painting, or some version of it, and that he carried on with this composition regardless of the details of the contract. Kenneth Clark believed that the Louvre *Virgin of the Rocks* was actually begun in Florence, as he also proposed for the *Litta Madonna*.[18] It is true that the painting has a Florentine feel: in the prettiness of the face, the movement of the head, and the long ringletted hair, the Madonna and the angel are still Verrocchi-esque. But this is to be expected anyway – indeed it would be expected by the Milanese clients, who were choosing Leonardo precisely because they wanted something in the sophisticated Florentine manner. The later, London version of the painting has a very different mood. It is more austere; the faces have a pale, waxy sheen; it has a flatter, sadder, more reclusive beauty. If the Paris version is crepuscular in tone, this one has the harder edge of moonlight. The addition of haloes – rigorously absent from the first version, as from almost all Leonardo's Florentine Madonnas – looks like a doctrinal requirement from the Confraternity.

The relationship between these two works is still mysterious, and the mystery is not much illuminated by a series of later legal documents on the subject, mostly disputatious, the latest of which dates from 1508, twenty-five years after the original commission. These show that the painters had indeed delivered the work, in about 1485, but that there were disagreements over the payment. These remained unresolved, and in about 1492 Leonardo and Ambrogio de Predis addressed a *supplica* to Ludovico Sforza, seeking his help in getting payment from the Confraternity.[19] The painting is described, with that marvellous reductiveness of the legal document, as '*la Nostra Donna facta da dicto fiorentino*' – 'the Madonna done by the said Florentine'. We learn that they had asked for a *conguaglio*, or adjusted payment, of 1,200 lire, claiming that the 800 lire they had received, as per the contract, had barely paid for the work on the frame alone. The Confraternity had responded by offering them a paltry 100 lire. They now ask for a fairer payment, or instead for permission to take back the painting, for which they have been offered payment elsewhere. This mention of another potential purchaser for the painting may hold a clue. Was the interested party none other than Ludovico himself, and was the *Virgin of the Rocks* the unnamed *pala* or altarpiece which he sent as a wedding-present to Emperor Maximilian in 1493, on the occasion of his marriage to Ludovico's niece Bianca Maria? A comment in the earliest Leonardo biography of all, the brief sketch in the notebook of Antonio Billi, may suggest that it was: 'He did an altarpiece for Lord Lodovico of Milan, which is said to be the loveliest painting you could possibly see; it was sent by this Lord into Germany, to the Emperor.' The *Virgin of the Rocks* is the only altarpiece he is known to have painted in Milan. It was not actually 'done for' Ludovico, as Billi has it, but it may well have been purchased by him from the Confraternity in 1492 or 1493, and sent as a gift to Maximilian. The presence of Ambrogio himself at the imperial court in Innsbruck at this time lends further credence to this.[20]

The removal of the painting to Germany might also explain how it ended up in the Louvre. Some of the Louvre's Leonardos arrived in France with Leonardo himself, in 1516, but there is no indication that the *Virgin of the Rocks* was one of them. It could plausibly have migrated from the Habsburg collection to France in or after 1528, when Maximilian's granddaughter Eleonora married François I, and thence to the Louvre. The painting was certainly in France by 1625, when it was seen at Fontainebleau by Cassiano dal Pozzo.

The concomitant of this theory is that it furnishes a specific reason for the second version of the painting: the London version. It is a substitute, a copy painted for the Confraternity to replace the painting sent off to the Emperor. In this scenario, the London version would have been begun sometime between 1493 and 1499, the date of Leonardo's departure from Milan, and it would be this painting, rather than the Paris version, which is referred to in the later litigations of 1503–8. This sort of date would be supported by the beautiful red-chalk drawing of an infant in profile in Windsor, which is exactly in the position of the Christ-child in the London version, and has a drawing-style typical of the mid-1490s.[21]

The *Virgin of the Rocks* is one of Leonardo's most enigmatic paintings. The eye is immediately drawn to that extraordinary ballet of hands in the foreground – the hand of the mother which shelters, the hand of the angel which points, the hand of the child which blesses.

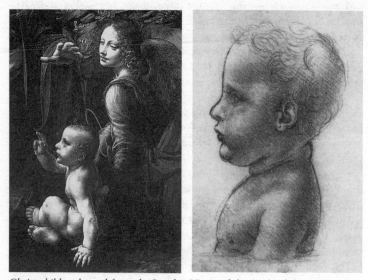

Christk-child and angel from the London *Virgin of the Rocks (left), and study in red chalk for the head and shoulders of the child.*

For the rocky landscape which gives the painting its name there are possible antecedents in Filippo Lippi's *Nativity*, now in Berlin, and Mantegna's *Adoration of the Magi*, painted in the early 1460s for the Gonzaga of Mantua. These both imagine the site of the Nativity as a little cave in the rocks. However, Leonardo's painting shows the meeting of the infant Christ and St John, which traditionally took place during the Holy Family's flight from Egypt. (The meeting is not in the Bible, but is found in the apocryphal gospel of St James.) The rocks are an image of wilderness and desert (the latter in the Renaissance sense: an uninhabited or deserted place).[22] There is the hint of a narrative in this stillest of paintings: the family have been travelling, they are resting, dusk is falling; they will sleep here in this tough but sheltering recess. I have already mentioned the motif of the cave or *caverna*, found in that compelling text of *c.* 1480 now in the Codex Arundel: the painting shows precisely 'some marvellous thing' within the gloom of the cave. We have a sense, as we look at it, of revelation. We are positioned somewhat like the narrator in that text, who has 'wandered some way among sombre rocks', and now stops short: 'I came upon the mouth of a huge cavern, in front of which I stood some while, astounded . . .'

This interplay of the natural setting and the devotional image disclosed within it is underscored by a range of beautifully realized wild flowers with symbolic religious attributes. To the right of the Virgin's head is the columbine (*Aquilegia vulgaris*), whose popular name suggests the dove (*colomba*) of the Holy Ghost, and just above her right hand is a species of galium known in English as Our Lady's Bedstraw and traditionally associated with the manger. Below the foot of the infant Christ are cyclamen, whose heart-shaped leaves make it an emblem of love and devotion, and by his knee is a basal rosette of primrose, an emblem of virtue (as in Verrocchio's sculpture of the *Woman with a Bunch of Flowers*). Another familiar plant, seen below the kneeling St John, is the acanthus (*Acanthus mollis*), traditionally planted over graves, and considered a symbol of the resurrection because of its rapid growth of brilliant glossy green leaves in spring. Also in the painting, in the cornices of the rock, is the hypericum, or St John's wort, its small dots of red on yellow petals representing the blood of the martyred St John.[23] These symbolic associations were part of a visual vocabulary shared by the painter and the more cultivated of his spectators, but here the exactitude and empathy of the painting insist also that these are real plants, and that what we are seeing is material Nature – rocks and stones and vegetation – spiritually transmuted. The central figure of the scene is the Madonna to whom the Confraternity of the Immaculate Conception make their obeisances, but she is also in some measure that female personification of Nature – 'the mistress of all masters' – to whom Leonardo was more particularly devoted.

⤖ WAYS OF ESCAPE ⤙

In 1485 Milan was in the midst of a three-year epidemic of bubonic plague. Leonardo had had some experience of the plague in Florence: there was an outbreak there in 1479, but it had subsided after a few weeks. This was far worse. According to some estimates, possibly exaggerated, it killed nearly a third of the urban population. We know the imagery: the ravaged neighbourhoods, the foggy air, the corpses carted off to mass burials. Hysterical rhetoric from the pulpits. Fraught self-examination in search of the glandular swellings or 'buboes' which are the tokens of infection. On 16 March 1485 there was a total eclipse of the sun, ominously interpreted. Leonardo viewed it through a large sheet of perforated paper, as recommended in a brief note headed, 'How to watch the eclipsed sun without damage to the eyes'.[24]

All through this epidemic Leonardo was working on the *Virgin of the Rocks*: there is no reason to assume he was anywhere else than Milan, in the de Predis studio near the Porta Ticinese. We know Leonardo's fastidiousness: a man with the scent of rosewater on his fingers. The foul smells assail him, as do the teeming crowds and the infections they carry – in his own words, 'this congregation of people herded together like goats, one behind the other, filling every corner with stench and spreading pestilence and death'.[25] The painting is a charmed space from which all this is excluded: a cool stony grotto miles away from anything, conferring the benedictions of the wilderness.

Around this time he wrote down a recipe for a medicine – it is perhaps a plague nostrum:

> Take seed of medicinal darnel . . .
> spirits of wine in cotton
> some white henbane
> some teasel
> seed and root of aconite.
> Dry it all. Mix this powder with camphor and it is made.[26]

Out of this cauldron of the plague, and given urgency by it, come the earliest of Leonardo's concerted thoughts about the shape and practice of the 'ideal city'. This was a topic much in vogue in the Renaissance. Alberti and Filarete had discoursed on it, and the great Roman architect Vitruvius before them; we can imagine Leonardo conversing on the subject with his learned friend Donato Bramante. His notes and drawings, dated about 1487, show an airy, geometric, futuristic city of piazzas and loggias and tunnels and canals ('futuristic' in that curious cul-de-sac sense: the future as it was envisaged in the past). The city would be built on two levels – the upper level for pedestrians, social, aesthetic, akin to the 'pedestrian areas' in modern cities, while the lower level, giving directly on to a network of canals, would be for the movement of goods and animals, for traders and warehouses, and for the dwellings of what he calls 'ordinary' people. The streets are wide, the height of the façades regulated, the chimneys tall to disperse smoke high above the roofs. He recommends spiral staircases in the public buildings, because square staircases have dark corners which people use as urinals. Improved sanitation was much on his mind, no doubt in response to the plague. He has some thoughts on the ideal lavatory as well – not quite a flushing toilet, as invented by Sir John Harington a century later, but well appointed: 'The seat of the latrine should be able to swivel like the turnstile in a convent and return to its initial position by the use of a counterweight. The ceiling should have many holes in it so that one can breathe.'[27]

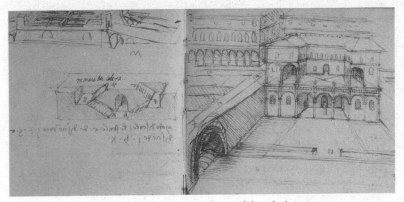

Notes and drawings on a theme of the 'ideal city'.

It is also at this time that his thoughts turn again to the compelling motif of human flight:

See how the beating of its wings against the air supports a heavy eagle in the highly rarefied air . . . Observe also how the air in motion over the sea fills the swelling sails and drives heavily laden ships . . . So a man with wings large enough, and duly attached, might learn to overcome the resistance of the air, and conquer and subjugate it, and raise himself upon it.[28]

The passage continues with his description and sketch of a parachute: 'If a man has a canopy of coated linen 12 braccia [24 feet] wide and 12 long, he can throw himself down from any great height and not hurt himself.' This suggests he was now seriously considering the possibility of manned flight: why else would he be thinking about a parachute?

Leonardo's pyramid-shaped parachute remained on the drawing-board until 26 June 2000, when an English skydiver, Adrian Nicholas, test-jumped it from 10,000 feet over the Kruger National Park in southern Africa. The parachute was made almost exactly to Leonardo's specifications, except that cotton canvas was used instead of linen. The canopy, lashed to pine-wood poles, weighed nearly 200 pounds – about forty times heavier than conventional modern parachutes – but despite this weight the drop went perfectly. Nicholas fell 7,000 feet in five minutes: a slow descent. He cut himself loose for the final descent by conventional parachute – the one flaw in the Leonardo model being that it was not collapsible, so there was a danger of the whole contraption landing on top of him. 'I had a feeling of gentle elation and celebration,' said Nicholas afterwards. 'I could

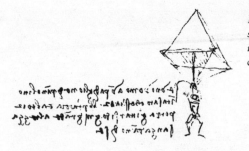

Leonardo's parachute: sketch and specifications in the Codex Atlanticus, c. 1485.

not resist saying, "Mr Da Vinci, you kept your promise, I thank you very much." '[29]

These are ways of mental escape from the plague-ridden city – the benevolent wilderness of the *Virgin of the Rocks*, the airy boulevards of the utopian city, the wide open spaces of the skyway. But there are things a man cannot escape, things within himself, and another product of this same period is a curious and revealing series of allegorical drawings now at Christ Church College, Oxford.[30] They have two themes – the inevitability of pain after pleasure, and the assaults of envy on virtue – but these themes tend to blur into one another, and one feels that the drawings are really about the same thing: the fundamental dualism of experience, the negative that every positive must have, the inevitable 'other' which lurks and destroys. They are rather crudely drawn: there seems to be a sense of urgency in them.

Pleasure and Pain are represented as a hybrid male creature with a single body sprouting two heads and two pairs of arms. The caption says, 'Pleasure and Pain show themselves as twins, because the one is never without the other, as if they were stuck together [*appiccati*].' Pain is an old man with a beard; Pleasure is young and long-haired. The drawing thus provides a commentary on the many sketches and drawings Leonardo made, at different times and in different styles, of an old man (often the so-called 'nutcracker-man', with the jutting chin and imploded lips suggesting toothlessness) facing a young, pretty, curly-haired man. Two captions beneath the figure tell us that one foot of this hybrid body stands on gold, the other in mud.

Another part of the text reads, 'If you take pleasure know that he has behind him one who will bring you tribulation and repentance.' Leonardo can never resist a pun, and this tribulation (*tribolatione*) is represented by the mysterious little spiked objects that fall from the old man's right hand,

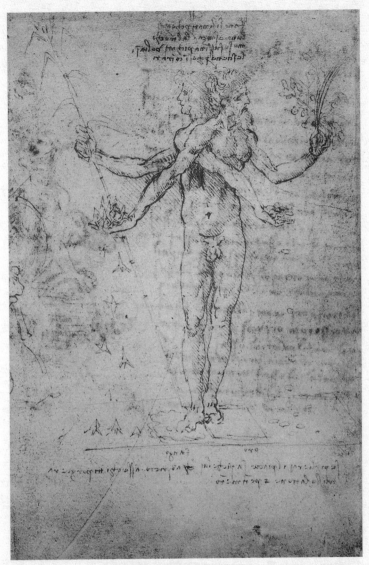

Allegory of Pleasure and Pain.

which are a weapon known in Italian as *tribolo*. In English it is called a 'caltrop', i.e. a heel-trap (Latin *calx* = heel). They feature in a drawing of the later 1480s, captioned '*triboli di ferro*', with a text explaining how they are to be scattered on the ground at the bottom of ditches to impede the advance of the enemy. Commenting on this passage, Count Giulio Perro recalled that 'Some years ago [he was writing in 1881], when they were building the new riding school at the castle of Milan, they found two of them, which I saw myself, and they were precisely the same as those described and drawn by Leonardo.'[31] This pun relates the drawing to Leonardo's activities (or wished-for activities) as a military engineer.

Pain lets fall the little spikes of tribulation in one hand, and in the other he brandishes a branch which presumably represents the flagellum of repentance. Pleasure's action mimics him: he drops a trail of coins out of one hand, for pleasure is expensive (remember the Modena joke: 'I have to pay 10 gold ducats just to get my cock in'), and he holds a reed in the other. Leonardo's explanation of the reed is fascinating, because it is one of those rather rare double-layered texts – not unlike the note about the kite – where an ostensible subject-matter suddenly parts to reveal another, more personal subject entirely. He explains that Pleasure is shown 'with a reed in his right hand, which is useless and has no strength, and the wounds it inflicts are poisonous'. This is the overt emblematic meaning, but it shades into a kind of reminiscence or reverie as follows:

In Tuscany they use reeds as a support for beds, to signify that it is here that one has vain dreams, and here that a great part of one's life is consumed, and here that so much useful time is wasted, that is in the morning, when the mind is composed and rested, and the body is fit to begin new labours, and then so many vain pleasures are taken, both by the mind, imagining to itself impossible things, and by the body taking those pleasures which are often the cause of the failing of life [*mancamento di vita*]: and this is why they use the reed for this purpose.

One can assume that the use of woven reeds in Tuscan beds was for practical rather than symbolic reasons, and that the moral he draws and elaborates in this rather breathless syntax is more personal. This is a moment of confession: he has 'vain dreams', i.e. sexual fantasies, when he lies in bed in the mornings; he feels bad about it because he should be up and about doing things, and perhaps because the nature of the fantasies is homosexual. That the phallic stem in Pleasure's hand is only a weak and 'useless' reed is pretty clearly a symbol of detumescence, which the tenor of the text might suggest is post-masturbatory rather than post-coital. The note of infection – 'the wounds it inflicts are poisonous' – completes the sense of self-disgust which has welled up around this image, and seems to connect it once more to the poisonous infections of the Milan plague.

The 'Virtue and Envy' drawings lead in the same direction: they express the same idea that these opposite qualities are intrinsic to one another, and they do so with an imagery that tends towards the erotic. 'Virtue', one remembers, does not just mean moral goodness: it means that strength (literally 'manliness', since 'virtue' derives from the Latin *vir*) of spirit and intellect which tends towards excellence. Virtue, broadly, is one's higher or better self, in all its manifestations; Envy is what attacks and degrades and compromises it. Like Pain and Pleasure, Virtue and Envy are shown as two entwined bodies. The text beneath them reads, 'The moment Virtue is born, she gives birth to Envy against herself, for you will sooner find a body without a shadow than virtue without envy.' In the drawing, Envy is being stabbed in the eye with an olive-branch and in her ear with a branch of laurel or myrtle. This, Leonardo explains, is 'to signify that victory and truth offend her'. Though the text describes Virtue as female ('she gives birth to Envy'), this is not at all clear in the drawing – the figure has no visible breasts – and the choreography of the figures suggests coition as much as parturition: indeed, it is similar to a famous anatomical drawing at Windsor showing a hemisected couple in coitus.[32]

In another drawing two female figures are shown riding a giant toad: a caption identifies them as Envy and Ingratitude; behind them hurries the skeletal figure of Death with a scythe – again one senses the plague ethos. Envy is shooting an arrow on the point of which is fixed a human tongue: a recognized image of 'false report'. Another drawing has Envy riding on a skeleton. In both these drawings she is depicted as an old woman with hanging breasts ('lean and wizened'), but she wears 'a mask upon her face of fair appearance'. This imagery of the riding woman has sexual overtones. It echoes a curious early sketch of Leonardo's, in which a young woman with painted cheeks is riding on the back of an old man. This drawing is generally called *Aristotle and Phyllis*.[33] It is known that the philosopher Aristotle married a much younger woman, the niece of a friend, and though he was only about forty at the time, the story was elaborated into an idea of the aged philosopher besotted by the nubile young beauty. 'Phyllis riding on the back of Aristotle', says A. E. Popham, is 'one of those subjects dear to medieval cynicism, typifying the subjugation of intellect by love. It belongs to the same cycle of stories as that of Virgil in the basket and Samson and Delilah.'[34] On the back of the sketch Leonardo writes a string of words: 'mistresses pleasure pain love jealousy happiness envy fortune penitence'.

This sketch of Aristotle and Phyllis may be a few years earlier than the

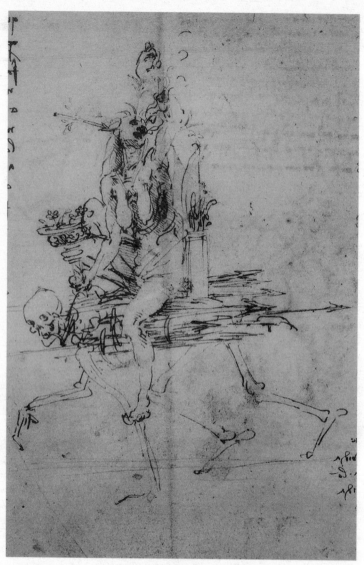

Allegory of Envy riding on Death.

Oxford allegories, but we are in the same mental terrain. The subject-matter of the sketch is intrinsically erotic; the allegories are more tortuously eroticized. In these drawings there is a sense of entrapment or entropy – all momentum will be nullified by its opposite; everything put together will fall apart; the gold will return back to mud. A man strives upward, but he is always dragged back by the contrary pull, which may be the envy and malice of others, but which is more critically something inside himself: the fatal, guilty, energy-sapping weakness or 'infection' of his sexuality.

➤➤ THE FIRST NOTEBOOKS ◄◄

The earliest intact Leonardo notebooks that we know of date from the mid-1480s. Most of the documents and sketches we have looked at so far are loose sheets bound into one or other of the great miscellanies, or preserved in collections like that at Christ Church College, Oxford. Some of them may have originally been part of a notebook or sketchbook, but on the evidence that remains Leonardo started 'keeping' notebooks around the middle of the 1480s. There is a sense of a rapprochement with the written word, a resolution of difficulties and resentments about the nature of his education, of his being an '*omo sanza lettere*'. This seems in part a technical proficiency, for now Leonardo's handwriting becomes speedier and more succinct; it loses what Augusto Marinoni calls the 'superfluousness and floweriness' of his earlier hand.[35]

The oldest surviving notebook is probably Paris MS B, in the Institut de France. It is conventionally dated *c.* 1487–90, though one or two pages may be a little earlier.[36] It is a standard *quaderno* or exercise-book: the pages measure 9 × 6½ inches, roughly the size of letter-paper today. It survives in its original vellum cover, with a flap closed by means of a toggle and loop. Textually it is almost intact, but physically it is split in two. The original notebook contained 100 folios, but in the 1840s it was one of the targets of the piratical Count Libri, who excised the last gathering (folios 91–100) and sold it, with other thefts, to the English bibliophile Lord Ashburnham. The pages were returned to Paris, but they are still bound separately from the rest of the notebook.

The subject-matter of MS B is amazingly various. The bound notebook is precisely a format which accommodates diversity, which ranges one interest frictively against another – an ongoing compendium of Leonardian enthusiasms. It has material on architecture, including that utopian city of the future, and some designs for churches. It has a good deal of military technology, both practical and 'futuristic'. There are submarines and sinister-looking stealth-attack craft, 'good for firing bridges at night; the sails must be black'.[37] There is the Architronito, a steam-powered cannon made of copper, which Leonardo claims to have adapted from Archimedes: when water is poured into the heated breach the steam-pressure shoots out the cannon-ball – 'The sight of its fury and the sound of its roar will seem like a miracle.'[38] There is always a sense of drama in his military machines: the 'theatre of war'. Elsewhere there are muscular toiling workmen, and a soldier grappling up the side of a wall. All this connects with Leonardo's continuing aspiration towards the role of architect and engineer to the Sforza.

And flying is still much on his mind. MS B has the first detailed designs for the classic Leonardo flying-machine, correctly called an ornithopter – a machine using the principles of a bird's flight, as distinct from the helicopter, which uses the principle of the helix or screw. (The second element of these words is from Greek *pteron*, wing.) A thrilling series of drawings, running from folios 73 to 79, is thought by some to be the most coherent of all his flying-machine designs.[39] They include two versions of the 'horizontal ornithopter', in which the pilot lies prone with the wing-apparatus on his back, using pedals and handles to work the wings up and down, and operating directional controls by means of cords and levers. In the drawing on folio 75, Leonardo adds the innovation of 'the rudder mounted on the neck' – a long, finned tail with a rope or connecting-bar running the length of the craft to a brace round the pilot's neck. On folio 79 he sketches out a different horizontal ornithopter, but this is more complicated and less plausible than the previous version, and then over the page we come to the more fantastical-looking 'vertical ornithopter', in which the pilot stands upright within a nacelle or cockpit, operating four giant wings that give the craft the look of a dragonfly. The two pairs of wings 'beat criss-cross, the way a horse moves'. The pilot uses his head, as well as his hands and feet, to move the sliding wing-mechanisms: the head, Leonardo estimates, 'will have a strength equal to 200 pounds'. The cockpit would be 20 braccia (about 40 feet) long; the wing-span 40 braccia. A later folio shows the launch-pad: a platform on retractable ladders, 20 braccia high. (This number and its multiples recur throughout the flying-machine experiments.) The bird analogy is at work here too: 'See the swift, which put on the ground cannot take off because it has short legs . . . These ladders serve as legs.'[40]

As with the military machinery, the word 'sci-fi' springs to mind – not to mention 'Heath Robinson'. Were these machines ever built, or are they elaborate pipe-dreams? None of these drawings, notes Martin Kemp, 'is

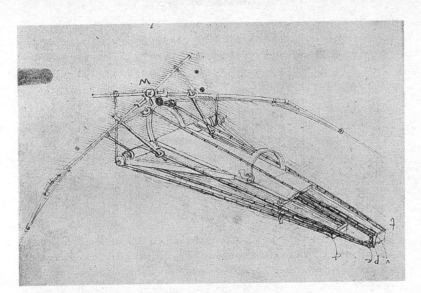

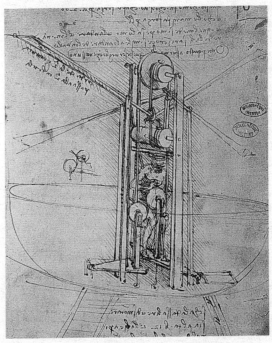

The ornithopter.
Flying-machine
designs from Paris
MS B, showing hori-
zontal and vertical
versions.

wholly resolved, complete and unambiguous'; they 'constitute an unfinished debate about ways and means'.[41] But it was not all theory – a dramatic drawing on the verso of folio 88 shows a huge artificial wing undergoing trials. A man struggles to work a wooden lever which causes the wing to flap. The instructions read:

If you want to test the wings properly make a wing from paper, mounted on a structure of net and cane, 20 braccia long and the same length broad. Attach it to a plank weighing 200 pounds, and apply a sudden force, as shown above, and if the 200 pound plank is lifted before the wing comes back down you can count the trial a success. Be sure that the force is rapid.

He concludes laconically, 'If the desired effect is not achieved, do not waste any more time on it.'[42]

Elsewhere Leonardo contemplates a prototypical helicopter: if 'this screwed instrument' is turned rapidly, he writes, 'the screw will find its female in the air and will climb upward'. Like the parachute, the blades of this primitive helicopter should be covered with 'linen starched to stop up its pores'.[43]

Flying-machines and weaponry, cities and churches, cogs and wheels, geometric figures – and much else: MS B also contains that drawing of a stringed instrument with a monster's head which has been loosely associated with the *lira da braccio* which Leonardo brought to Milan a few years earlier. This is on the first of the pages stolen by Libri, folio 91; a related series of knives and scimitars with fantastically carved handles follows on folio 92.

The last page, folio 100 verso, was also the outer cover – when the book was out of its vellum carrying-case – and was thus the receptacle, over the years, of scribbles and lists and doodles: a miscellany of moments in the *studiolo* or study of Leonardo da Vinci. In the top left-hand corner is a numerical calculation, probably of money; to the right of it is a list of words, of which one (*sorbire*) is destined for a Latin word-list in another notebook, the Trivulzio Codex. Then comes a memorandum list of mostly cryptic import ending, 'Ask Maestro Lodovicho for the water pipes, the small oven, the tinderbox, the perpetual motion [machine?], the small bellows, the forge-bellows.'[44] Below this are three rows of hieroglyphs of vaguely Hebraic aspect and then, further down, four rapid sketches showing a moth, a bat, a dragonfly and a butterfly. Beneath the bat, before the long tear in the lower left-hand corner begins, are the words *'animale che fuge dell'uno elemento nell'altro'* – a beautiful and typically Leonardian synopsis of flight: 'animal that flees from one element into another'. In the lower right-hand corner is a sketched figure which Marinoni describes as 'a cloaked man in an act of reverence', but the face is comically drawn, and he seems less to be kneeling in reverence than crouching. His hand reaches out to grasp the lower part of the bat's wing, which has itself been doodled and cross-hatched, giving it a certain fleshiness, so the grasping or groping figure takes on a faintly lecherous aspect, and is certainly a potential impediment to the winged creature so keen to 'flee' to another element. He seems to belong with the Virtue–Envy, Pleasure–Pain conflict of the Oxford allegories: he is what drags you back down. Such are the unconscious patterns caught in the nap of this old notebook-cover.

There are two other notebooks which belong to this first period, conventionally dated *c.* 1487–90. One is a small pocket-book which is part of the Forster codices in the Victoria & Albert Museum.[45] It deals with Archimedean screws or *cocleae* (literally snail-shells) to raise water, and other hydraulic machines. It has a number of chemical recipes, which perhaps reflect the presence of Zoroastro, or 'Maestro Tommaso' as Leonardo calls him in 1492. It investigates the enigma of perpetual motion, a subject he later dismissed as an illusion, the fruit of '*superstizione*', on a par with the chimerical gold-making dreams of the alchemist.

The other early notebook is the Codex Trivulzianus or Trivulzio Codex. It is named after the Milanese family which owned it in the eighteenth century; there is no specific connection with Giangiacomo Trivulzio, the Renaissance *condottiere* whom Leonardo knew. It shares with its contemporary MS B an interest in architecture, and it contains some witty caricatures – among the earliest of the grotesques which become a fascinating sub-genre of Leonardo's drawings – but what fills most of its pages is a painstaking series of Latin vocabulary lists. Hundreds of words are listed and when necessary translated into Italian: this is a crash-course in what was still the international language of learning and philosophy. We have a sense of labour, of homework, of punishing schedules.

On an early page of the Trivulzio Codex[46] is a column of five words, as follows:

donato
lapidario
plinio
dabacho
morgante

At first glance this looks like another vocab list, but it is not. The words are abbreviated book-titles. There is no heading, so we don't know for sure that these are books that Leonardo owns, but as all of them occur in later book-lists, which are certainly inventories of his library, it seems that this is indeed the earliest known account of the books on Leonardo's shelf. Are these his only books at this time? It is not unlikely: printed books were expensive, still something of an innovation. They were not always welcomed by the bibliophiles of the day: the Florentine bookseller Vespasiano da Bisticci praised the Duke of Urbino's library of manuscripts, 'beautifully illuminated and bound in silver and scarlet', then added, 'Had there been one printed volume there, it would have been ashamed in such company!'[47] Leonardo's later lists suggest a rapid acquisition of books – a list in the Codex Atlanticus, which belongs to the early 1490s, enumerates forty books, while the famous Madrid inventory of 1504 contains 116 volumes.

The five books of the Trivulzian list are a snapshot of his interests in the late 1480s. *Donato* refers to a popular book of Latin grammar and syntax, *De octo partibus orationis*, by Aelius Donatus; there were numerous editions in the fifteenth century, and in fact the term *donato* became a standard shorthand for any Latin grammar-book (and *donatello*, a little Donato, for an elementary grammar-book). Its presence here ties in with the Latin vocabulary lists.

The term *lapidario* is too vague to identify with certainty: it is some kind of manual about precious stones and minerals. The nineteenth-century bibliophile Count Girolamo d'Adda – the first to study Leonardo's reading systematically – thought it might be an Italian translation of the *Liber lapidum* (*Book of Stones*) written by a twelfth-century French bishop, Marbodeus. This book, also called *De gemmis* (*Concerning Gems*), particularly treats of the medicinal properties of precious stones.[48]

Plinio undoubtedly refers to the *Historia naturalis* of Pliny the Elder, the observant, scholarly, credulous author who was killed in the eruption of Vesuvius in AD 79. His *Natural History* was an immensely popular repository of classical knowledge and lore, covering geography, natural science, inventions and the arts. He was a native of Como, and was considered a local hero in Lombardy. The edition Leonardo owned was probably the Italian translation by Cristoforo Landino, published in Venice in 1476. Leonardo had probably known Landino in Florence.

Dabacho (i.e. *d'abaco*) is again too broad a term: the word 'abacus' in this context could mean any book of arithmetic. There was a well-known *Trattato d'abaco* by Paolo Dagomari, but this was aged. A more up-to-date work was the *Nobel opera de arithmetica* by Piero Borgi da Venezia, published in 1484; Leonardo refers elsewhere to 'Maestro Piero dal Borgo'.

Morgante takes us back again to Florence, to the popular romantic epic by Luigi Pulci, the scurrilously irreligious friend of Lorenzo de' Medici and Benedetto Dei. This burlesque, slangy work – in a style not unlike that of Antonio Cammelli, though more sustained and subtle in form – appeared in two stages. The longer, 28-canto, version, known as the *Morgante maggiore*, was published in Florence in 1482. Leonardo quotes from it more than once; it is also likely he took from it the nickname Salai – meaning 'Little Devil' – which he gave to his wayward young Milanese apprentice Giacomo Caprotti.

Grammar, natural science, mathematics, poetry: a small row of books on the autodidact's shelf, but as we have seen, this is only the beginning of Leonardo's bibliophilia. The book-list written in red chalk on a sheet in the Codex Atlanticus seems to belong to about 1492: on the verso of it are some notes which are transcribed almost verbatim in Paris MS A, which is of this date.[49] By this time, perhaps five years after the minimal Trivulzian list, Leonardo's library has increased to thirty-seven books. (There are forty items listed, but the three volumes of the *Decades* of Livy are given as three separate works, and the *Epistles* of Filelfo is mentioned twice.)

Broadly speaking, of these thirty-seven books six are philosophical and religious in nature, fifteen are scientific and technical texts, and sixteen are literary works. The first category includes the Bible, the Psalms, a *Lives of the Philosophers* and a work identified as '*de immortalita d'anima*', which is almost certainly an Italian version of Ficino's *Theologia platonica*, published in Latin in 1481 with the sub-title '*De animarum immortalitate*'. The scientific works are predictably various – works on mathematics, military science, agriculture, surgery, law, music, chiromancy and precious stones, and three separate books on health. (Does one discern a note of hypochondria?) It is the abundance of the literary category which is perhaps the surprise. Admittedly the category is broad: I have included among the literary texts three books on grammar and rhetoric, which are about how to write, and one travel book (an edition of 'Giovan di Mandivilla' or John de Mandeville) which is certainly more fiction than fact. The rest are an impressive collection of prose and poetry, including classical works by Aesop, Livy and Ovid, an edition of Petrarch, the sub-Dantesque *Quadrire-gio* by the Dominican friar Federigo Frezzi, the prose collection called the *Fiore di virtù*, the bawdy doggerel *Il Manganello*, the burlesque poems of 'Il Burchiello', the *Facetiae* of Poggio Bracciolini, the *Epistles* of Filelfo, the *Driadeo* by Luca Pulci, and the *Morgante* by his brother Luigi Pulci – the latter presumably the copy listed in the Trivulzio notebook. These are books read for pleasure, for much-needed relaxation.

⤜⤜ TALL TALES, SMALL PUZZLES ⤜⤜

It was probably on a day in 1487 that Leonardo availed himself of some spare paper from a discarded cathedral ledger and, on a pair of blank versos, drafted a picturesque story about a giant in Africa.[50] He addressed it to the traveller and epistler Benedetto Dei, one of the Florentines about the Milanese court. Dei left Milan in 1487, which is the sort of date suggested by the handwriting of the draft: the piece may have been intended as a gift or presentation to him. Perhaps it was recited at some farewell do, with Zoroastro suitably accoutred in the role of the giant; or perhaps, like so many of Leonardo's *ghiribizzi*, or caprices, it never got any further than this fragmentary draft. It begins:

Dear Benedetto Dei – To give you news of things here in the East, you should know that in the month of June there appeared a giant who comes from the deserts of Libya. This giant was born on Mount Atlas, and was black, and fought against Artaxerxes, and against Egyptians and Arabs, Medes and Persians. He lived in the sea and fed on whales, sea-serpents and ships.

It goes on to describe an earth-shaking battle between the giant and the human inhabitants of the region, involving much Gulliverish description of the tininess of the people, 'scurrying furiously over his body like ants over the trunk of a fallen oak'. Awakened by the 'smarting' of their stabs, the giant utters a 'growl like a terrifying clap of thunder' and 'lifting one of his hands to his face finds it to be full of men, clinging to its hairs'.

Richter glosses it as a 'piece of railery'; we would perhaps call it a 'spoof' – an obviously fantastical account dressed up as a traveller's newsletter. Most travel narratives at this time were written in the epistolary form. It is thus a joke about the dubious veracity of such accounts, and perhaps a particular jibe – a good-natured one – at Benedetto Dei as a purveyor of such tall tales. The setting ties in with Benedetto's own African travels, accounts of which he doubtless seasoned with the traditional dash of pepper and salt.

Leonardo may have had in mind the legend of Antaeus, the giant killed by Hercules, who was also said to come from Libya. More particularly, the giant is a fearsome caricature of the African Negro – his 'black face most horrible', his 'bloodshot eyes', his 'wide nostrils', his 'thick lips'. There is no doubt that Leonardo is cheerfully indulging racial stereotypes here. Whether he is parodying hyperbolic travel-writers or expressing some unresolved feelings of his own is hard to tell. Black Africans were exotic but by no means unknown in Italy; they were painted by many Renaissance artists – especially in Adoration scenes, where they accompany the stranger-kings or magi – though not by Leonardo. They were associated with sexual prowess, as in the bawdy *Il Manganello*, listed among Leonardo's books in *c.* 1492, in which a rich merchant's wife admires her 'Ethiopian' servant's *gran manganello* (large tool).[51] The name 'Moor' attached to Ludovico probably included an overtone of sexual power; the word then meant black African rather than (or as well as) Maghribi Arab-African – Shakespeare's Othello, undoubtedly black, is the 'Moor of Venice'.

This Negroid monster ends up eating everyone, and trampling down their houses, and so Leonardo's little spoof links to that theme of cataclysmic destruction which is one of his recurrent obsessions, most famously expressed in the 'Deluge' drawings. The story ends with this rather haunting sentence: 'I do not know what to say or what to do, for everywhere I seem to find myself swimming head downwards through that huge throat and remaining buried in that great belly, in the confusion of death.' This evokes the old short-story trick of the narrator getting finally swept up in the events he describes – in this case being devoured by the giant – but it has also a dream-like quality expressed in the floating syntax ('everywhere I seem to find myself swimming'), and one has a sense that this is more than just a narrative device, that Leonardo is accessing something interior to him: a nightmare of being swallowed and submerged whose meaning may well be found in the last word of the sentence. One remembers that 'prophecy' of Leonardo's which turns out to be a kind of dream-notebook: flying and falling, speaking with animals, incestuous desires.

There is another picturesque black giant in a later notebook. This is less interesting, because the passage was transcribed from another book, Antonio Pucci's *Queen of the Orient*, though Leonardo's desire to copy this particular passage is itself noteworthy. His transcription is not exact. I particularly like the change in the first line: where Pucci describes the giant as 'blacker than coal [*carbone*]' Leonardo alters this to 'blacker than a *calabrone*'.[52] A *calabrone* is a big black flying beetle, still common in Tuscany: within the insect kingdom it is indeed a giant. He has added a single syllable and transformed a cliché into a precise, concrete and poetically apt simile worthy of his old friend Il Pistoiese.

We have an idea of Leonardo's growing assurance with language, with literary effects, with the nuts and bolts of narrative. The story of the giant, though a bagatelle in itself, shows these skills. It belongs to the period in the later 1480s when he begins to acquire a basic library of prose and poetry, and when he becomes a habitual keeper of notebooks. The latter are certainly not literary. The language in them is work-related – descriptions, observations, problems, solutions, lists – but has none the less an ideal of lucidity and concision, a consciousness of writing as a vital supplement to the visual language of which he was already a master. Those books of grammar and rhetoric on his shelf perhaps relate more to his scientific studies, his role as explainer, than to his altogether vaguer literary aspirations.

For Leonardo, writing in the literary sense remains peripheral. (Somewhat paradoxically, one of his favourite literary exercises was the *paragone*, or comparison, between painting and poetry, in which painting was always argued to be superior; this debate forms part of the introduction to the *Trattato della pittura*.) He cultivates literature, it seems, principally as a social or courtly skill. In Florence he keeps the company of poets like Cammelli and Bellincioni, but his own achievements in that area are confined – as far as we know – to his skills as an *improvvisatore*, a song-and-dance man with his *lira da braccio*. The letter to Dei belongs within the same sort of sphere – an entertainment, a *jeu d'esprit*, probably written for a specific occasion. Its beautiful last sentence is an unexpected gem: a little *coup de théâtre* which ends the performance on a haunting, unsettling note. I see this as the typical mode of Leonardo as writer – lowbrow formats, plain-speaking style, moments of unexpected poetry.

Leonardo's taste for puns and word-games is part of his interestingly limited view of the writer, and there is a fascinating page of the late 1480s which belongs precisely to this stratum of literary trickery, and which again affords certain oblique glimpses into his mental processes. It is a large sheet in the Windsor collection, crammed with what Kenneth Clark rather quaintly calls 'puzzle writing' – what are more generally called rebuses or cryptograms.[53]

A rebus is a word or name or sentence expressed pictorially: a visual code. Though the game is to avoid words, it is of course a thoroughly verbal game, since the solution of the puzzle depends entirely on linguistic connections and often on double meanings. The word 'rebus' may be derived from carnival newsletters headed '*De rebus quae geruntur*' ('concerning things that have been happening', i.e. current events), which avoided libel by using pictorial and hieroglyphic symbols in place of names; or more soberly from the explanatory formula '*non verbis sed rebus*' ('not with words but with things'). There had long existed in Italy a fondness for these punning cryptograms – the heraldic rebus representing the name of a family was particularly popular – though the more sophisticated rule-book for composing emblems and *imprese* had not yet been formulated.

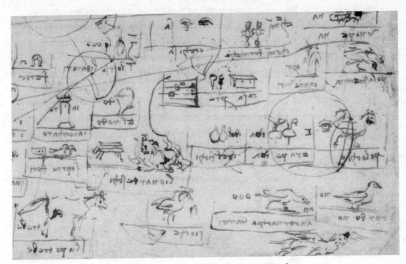

Part of the large sheet of rebuses at Windsor.

Leonardo manages to squeeze a total of 154 rebuses on to the two sides of the Windsor sheet. (Some other fragments of picture-writing, of the same period, bring the total to something like 200.)[54] The pictographs themselves are hurriedly drawn: the finesse is in the mental ingenuity. Sometimes a picture alone is used, but often there is a combination of pictures and words or letters (not a 'pure' rebus, therefore). The sheet seems to be a working draft, in which ideas are tried out; some of the ropier ones were doubtless discarded. Beneath each rebus is written the key, the punning solution to the visual riddle. Thus the solution to the rebus showing a stook of corn and a rock is *gran calamità*, a great calamity, via puns on *grano* = grain and *calamita* = a magnetic stone. An *o* and a pear (*pera*) = *opera*, works. A face (*faccia*) and a donkey (*asino*) = *fa casino*, a slang phrase meaning someone is making a total hash of things. Some of the puns recur as he moves into whole sentences – thus 'if the' (*se la*) is always represented by a saddle (*sella*), and 'happy' (*felice*) by a fern (*felce*). These have become part of a reusable picture vocabulary.

There is a sense here of Leonardo as intellectual court-jester – these are party pieces, pen-and-ink entertainments. One imagines him hovering, the enigmatic quizmaster, as the courtiers struggle to guess the answer. There would also be a practical spin-off, since pictographs were popular as architectural decoration. According to the Milanese architect Cesare Cesariano, the Sforza castle was decorated with such allegorical hieroglyphs, though these are no longer to be seen. Leonardo's friend Bramante later designed an inscription in honour of Pope Julius II for the Vatican Belvedere, in which 'Julio II Pont Maximo' is spelt out in carved pictographs. Thus the rebus-skill Leonardo is practising here has also a practical application for the aspiring architect of the mid-1480s.

Practical or not, there is a touch of the psychiatrist's 'free association' games in the rebus. His mind is roving between different levels of meaning, between pictures and letters, enjoying the semiotic frissons out of which come strange hybrid meanings. Some of the phrases he comes up with have a certain psychological piquancy: '*siamo scarico di vergogna*' – 'we have got rid of all shame'; '*ora sono fritto*' – 'now I am done for [literally fried]'. And the psychiatrist might raise a momentary eyebrow at that tiny scribbled self-portrait I mentioned earlier, apropos the lion in *St Jerome* – the lion in flames = *leone* + *ardere* = Leonardo. As a self-identifying pun or hieroglyph it seems rather bleak: the lion, axiomatically noble and powerful, is consumed and destroyed. We seem to be once more in the agitated sphere of the Oxford allegories. Even here, in these courtly quiz-games, we find that words open up chinks of Leonardo's inner life.

Also designed for courtly entertainment were Leonardo's riddling 'prophecies', some of which I have already quoted. One of them has what amounts to a stage-direction added to it: 'Say it in a form of frenzy or craziness, as if from a madness in the brain.'[55] They were delivered, in other words, in a kind of mock-oracular ecstasy or *furor*. An obvious candidate for this performance would be Zoroastro, one of whose nicknames was Indovino, 'the Prophet' or 'Soothsayer'; the word has an overtone of mystic hocus-pocus (cf. *indovinello*, a riddle) which fits these joke predictions.

The humour of the prophecies lies in their ingeniously anti-climactic explanations. Mostly they turn on simple little twists of meaning, not unlike the visual puns of the rebuses – those who will 'walk on top of the trees' are men wearing wooden clogs, and those who will 'walk on the skins of great beasts' are men wearing shoes of ox-leather, and those who will 'go as fast as the quickest of creatures by means of the stars' are men using spurs, which are star-shaped. The 'bodies' which will 'grow when the head is taken from them, and diminish when the head is put back' are pillows. The animal which will be 'seen with its tongue up another's arse' refers to the butcher's custom of wrapping up pigs' and calves' tongues in entrails.[56] These are the meanings which the audience has to guess.

But there is also an element of double-bluff: the prophecies are often pungently expressive little texts, which linger in the mind after they have been explained and deflated. Like the spoof newsletter to Dei, they stray into an imagery of cataclysm and violence. They also express an idea of Nature as the wounded, exploited victim of man's rapacity:

There will be many who will flay their mother and turn her skin inside out. [Those who till the land]

Men will severely beat what gives them life. [Those who thresh grain]

The times of Herod will return, when innocent children shall be taken from their nurses, and will die with great wounds at the hands of cruel men. [Kids]

With merciless blows many little children will be taken from the arms of their mothers and thrown to the ground and then torn to pieces. [Walnuts, olives etc.][57]

This ecologically compassionate view of nature is also found in Leonardo's fables, which were probably also written for recital at court. As far as can be established, the thirty or so fables that survive are original compositions.[58] They emulate Aesop, but are not borrowed from him. Leonardo may also have known Alberti's collection, the *Apologhi* (not published till 1568, but doubtless available in manuscript). The fables are full of an animistic sense of the landscape as a living thing. It is not only animals that are given a voice, but also trees and plants and stones. They become sentient creatures, capable of feeling pain – a pain constantly inflicted on them by man. A chestnut-tree is envisaged as a protective parent whose 'sweet children' – the nuts – are torn from her. The 'hapless willow' is 'maimed and lopped and ruined'. Harvest is wounding. Here is a very short fable about a walnut-tree, almost a gnomic little prose-poem: '*Il noce mostrando sopra una strada ai viandante la richezza de sua frutta, ogni omo lapidava.*' (The nut-tree by the roadside showed off to travellers the richness of its fruit; everyone stoned it.)[59]

Leonardo liked jokes, and he wrote down a number of them – a conventional activity to which no special significance should be attached: the *zibaldoni*, or commonplace-books, of the day are full of jokes. The written-down joke must be considered a pale reflection of the told joke. One imagines Leonardo's delivery of them to be rather deadpan, false-solemn. The pleasantness of his conversation, as enthused over by Vasari, suggests a man who could be verbally entertaining. I have suggested there is also an opposite impression, of a certain taciturnity and aloofness, but for all that, being funny and making people laugh – and laughing himself – was a part of

Leonardo's life. It is perhaps no accident that his most famous painting is known in Italy as *La Gioconda* – *The Jocund* [or indeed *Joking*] *Woman*.

Leonardo's jokes are of variable quality: some of them turn rather tediously on puns, and one or two of them seem to have lost whatever point they had down some lexical cul-de-sac. Some are satirical – particularly anti-clerical – and some are dirty, in what we would think of as a robust, Chaucerian vein. Both the satire and the bawdy have antecedents in the tales of Boccaccio and his imitators, and more immediately in the Renaissance collections of *facetiae* – pleasantries – pre-eminently those of Poggio Bracciolini, some of which are quite salty.

Jokes appear scattered throughout Leonardo's notebooks and manuscripts. Here are a few.

A man was trying to prove on the authority of Pythagoras that he had lived in this world before, and another man would not accept his argument. So the first man said, 'As a sign that I have been here before, I remember that you were a miller.' And the other, thinking this was said to mock him, replied, 'You are right, for now I remember you were the ass which carried the flour for me.'

A painter was asked why he produced such beautiful figures, though they were dead things, and yet produced such ugly children. To which he replied that he made his paintings by day and his children by night.

A woman was washing clothes, and her feet were very red with cold. A priest who was passing by was amazed by this, and asked her where the redness came from, to which the woman immediately replied that it was caused by a fire she had underneath her. Then the priest took in hand that part of him which made him more priest than nun, and drawing near to her, asked her very politely if she would be kind enough to light his candle.

If Petrarch was so madly in love with bay-leaves it's because they taste so good with sausage and thrush.[60]

This last joke puns on *lauro*, the bay-tree, and Laura, to whom Petrarch's love-poems are addressed.

⤳ ARCHITECTURAL PROJECTS ⤲

In 1487 the *fabbriceria* or works department of Milan cathedral was considering the crowning of the central part of the cathedral with a *tiburio*, or domed crossing-tower, and Leonardo was among those who submitted designs for this. He constructed a wooden model, with the help of a carpenter called Bernardo, and received small subventions from the *fabbriceria* to cover the expenses of making the model: there are seven payments listed between July 1487 and January 1488.[61] (This circumstance may explain why he used discarded cathedral paper to write his 'newsletter' to Benedetto Dei.) Other architects tendering for the job included his friend Donato Bramante.

A drawing in Paris MS B shows a system of buttresses designed to give a broader base to the drum of the *tiburio*; the accompanying text describes an experiment to demonstrate the distribution of weight on an arch:

Let a man be placed on a weighing-device in the middle of a well-shaft, then have him push out his hands and feet against the walls of the well. You will find that he weighs much less on the scales. If you put weights on his shoulders you will see for yourselves that the more weight you put on him, the greater will be the force with which he spreads his arms and legs and presses against the wall, and the less will be his weight on the scales.[62]

This elegant if rather dangerous experiment illustrates the property of arches to distribute weight transversely rather than placing it all on the supporting columns. The spreadeagled figure in the well-shaft makes me think of Leonardo's famous 'Vitruvian Man' – also of Zoroastro, whom I always imagine as the man who steps up to perform this sort of 'demonstration'; I also imagine him as the test-pilot strapped in to the ornithopter.

Among Leonardo's papers is a draft of a presentation speech connected with the *tiburio* project. It begins with a flourish, '*Signori padri diputati*' – 'My lords, fathers, deputies'. Its theme is an analogy between the visual and structural harmonies of architecture and the harmonious balance of the body. In buildings, as in bodies, 'health is maintained by a balance or concord of elements, and is ruined and undone by a discord in them'. Thus the architect is like a kind of physician:

You know that medicines, when they are properly used, restore health to invalids, and that he who knows them thoroughly will make the right use of them if he understands the nature of man, of life and its constitution, and of health. He who knows these things thoroughly will know also what opposes them, and will be a more effective healer than any other. This too is what the sick cathedral needs – it needs a doctor-architect, who understands the nature of the building, and the laws on which correct construction is based . . .

This analogy is not original to Leonardo: it is found in the writings of Renaissance architects like Alberti and Filarete, and before them in

Vitruvius.[63] Leonardo develops the theme quite exhaustively in this draft, of which I have only quoted a fraction. Imagined as an actual speech it sounds flannelly, pedagogic, repetitive. One feels this sort of thing is not his forte. Then suddenly he is tired of the performance, and the draft ends with what is almost a linguistic shrug: 'Choose me or choose another who demonstrates the case better than I do; set aside all sentiments.'

It is doubtful that the speech was ever delivered. The *tiburio* project entered the usual limbo of delay, and it was three years before the contract was awarded. Leonardo seems by then to have lost interest: he was not even on the final shortlist.[64] The 'consultation' was held at the castle on 27 June 1490, with Ludovico and the Archbishop of Milan in attendance. The winning design was by the Lombard architects Amadeo and Dolcebuono.

Also from this time is a series of designs for 'temples' – churches based on a central altar.[65] Leonardo could have found examples of these in the architectural tracts of Vitruvius and Alberti, though as this type of church design is particularly associated with Bramante's later work, there may already have been an exchange of ideas between them. Bramante's remodelling of Santa Maria delle Grazie (where Leonardo painted the *Last Supper*) employed a semi-centralized design.

The temple illustrated here (from one of the pages of MS B stolen by Libri, and now bound separately) is beautifully realized. It has been shown that the ground plan is based on a complex geometrical system called the theta progression. Again there is the influence of Alberti, who recommended 'natural proportions' in architecture 'which are not borrowed from numbers but from the roots and powers of squares', but again one suspects the personal influence of Bramante, who was undoubtedly more proficient in mathematics and geometry than Leonardo at this stage.[66] A note at the lower left of this page shows Leonardo thinking about real churches as well as geometrical progressions. He wonders whether the campanile, or bell-tower, should be separate, as in the cathedrals at Florence and Pisa, where the bell-towers 'show their perfection on their own', or whether it should be incorporated into the church, 'making the lantern serve as the bell-tower as at the church of Chiaravalle'. The medieval abbey of Chiaravalle was a few miles from Milan; Leonardo elsewhere mentions an astrological clock there, which 'shows the moon, the sun, hours and minutes'.[67]

On a folio datable to early 1489 are drawings showing an elevation and ground-plan of a small domed edifice, but this is not a temple or church. The captions identify it as the 'pavilion of the Duchess of Milan's garden'.[68]

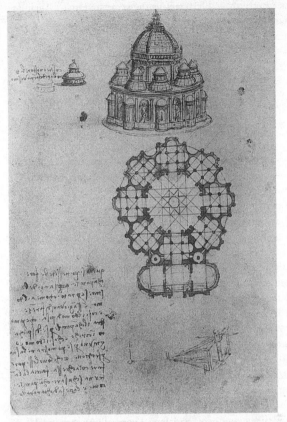

Design for a 'temple' based on a central altar.

This refers to the already existing pavilion in the park of the Sforza castle, described in an account of 1480 as a brick building 'surrounded by running water and hedges in the form of a labyrinth'; it was probably used as a *bagno* or bath-house during the steamy Milanese summer. Perhaps the plan to remodel the pavilion was connected with the marriage of the young Duke of Milan to Isabella of Aragon, granddaughter of the King of Naples, in February 1489. A lost folio of Paris MS B may have had another design for the pavilion, and notes for the decor: walls of pink marble, white baths, mosaics with a representation of the goddess Diana, and 'spouts in the form of eels' heads for hot and cold water' – all this on the testimony of the nineteenth-century French biographer Arsène Houssaye, who saw the notebook before its mutilation by Count Libri. A later note about the plumbing of 'the Duchess's *bagno*' probably refers to the same building.[69] I include this among Leonardo's early architectural projects, but the latter note shades towards Leonardo the odd-job man.

⇥ THE MOOR'S MISTRESS ⇤

> ... *Con sua pictura*
> *La fa che par che ascolti e non favella.*
> Bernardo Bellincioni – *Sonnet*

The early notebooks buzz with plans and projects which are impressively diverse – diversity is already Leonardo's trademark – but which are also part of a single plan or project: employment at the court of Ludovico Sforza. The military hardware, the urban planning, the flying-machines, the architectural designs, even the courtly word-puzzles – all these, which today survive fossilized on paper, were part of Leonardo's bid to become the Moor's multi-talented *tecnico* or expert, the ingenious 'engineer' in the broadest post-Brunelleschian sense of the word. How far Ludovico responded to all this we don't know: he was doubtless impressed by the brilliance of the Florentine, but was this translated into specific patronage? Perhaps, like his fellow Florentine Benedetto Dei, Leonardo drew a small *mancia* – a tip, a dole, an irregular stipend – from the Sforza coffers; perhaps he was given money to develop his ideas for assault-submarines and steam-powered cannon; perhaps he was paid for redesigning the Duchess's 'pavilion' in the castle gardens. It does not add up to much – a reminder of the sour proverb voiced by a Milanese courtier of the day, Tommaso Tebaldi: '*Chi vive al corte muore al spedale*' – 'He who lives at court dies in the poorhouse.'[70] So the notebooks tell us more, at this stage, about Leonardo's aspirations and ambitions than about what he lived off. In fact Leonardo's first identifiable commission from Ludovico himself is not in the realm of engineering or architecture. It is a painting of the Moor's beautiful young mistress, Cecilia Gallerani.[71]

Ludovico Sforza was not a model of depravity like the Duke his brother, but he enjoyed the sexual perks of despotism. He tended to regard his female subjects much as he regarded the harts and hinds of his private hunting-grounds – his for the taking – and, whatever her personal feelings in the matter, any young woman on whom his eye alighted knew this favour to be a passport to a world of comfort and privilege for herself and her family. Cecilia Gallerani was born in early 1473; her father, Fazio, was a public official who had served as ambassador to both Florence and Lucca; her mother, Margherita Busti, was the daughter of a noted doctor of law. Cecilia was a girl of a good but not spectacularly rich family, and as her father died when she was seven years old, and as she had six brothers who took precedence over her, she was only comparatively a child of luxury. She was bright and well educated, and was later a patroness of writers, among them the novelist Matteo Bandello. That she was alluringly pretty could be deduced from many poems and letters written about her, but the deduction is unnecessary because she lives – to borrow the cliché of the time – in Leonardo's portrait of her, otherwise known as *The Lady with an Ermine* (Plate 12).

When she became Il Moro's mistress is not recorded but can be fairly closely guessed. A document of June 1487 formally releases her from a childhood marriage-contract to Giovanni Stefano Visconti; the likelihood is that Ludovico's amorous interests lie behind this. She was then just fourteen years old: young, but not unusually so. By the early summer of 1489 Cecilia was no longer living with her family, but in an unspecified property in the parish of Nuovo Monasterio; it is hard to resist interpreting this as a love-nest. In this same year her brother Sigerio killed a man during a dispute, and escaped justice through the personal intervention of Ludovico. On this circumstantial evidence it seems that Cecilia became Ludovico's paramour in about 1487, though it is not until 1490 that we have incontrovertible evidence of the liaison in the time-honoured form of a pregnancy.

Though Cecilia's marriage-plans had proved expendable, Ludovico's were a weightier matter. Since 1480 he had been pledged, for sound political reasons, to the daughter of the Duke of Ferrara, Beatrice d'Este, and the time was now fast approaching for the marriage to be solemnized: a major dynastic alliance to be celebrated by a major public display of Milanese power-pageantry. On 8 November 1490 the Duke of Ferrara received a rather disconcerting dispatch from his ambassador in Milan, Jacopo Trotti, who reported that Ludovico's intentions towards '*la madonna Duchessa nostra*' (i.e. Beatrice) were uncertain, because he was still besotted with '*quella sua innamorata*' (i.e. Cecilia). 'He keeps her with him at the castle, and wherever he goes, and wants to give her everything. She is pregnant, and as beautiful as a flower, and often he brings me with him to visit her.' Perhaps feeling he has warmed a little too much to his theme, Trotti concludes diplomatically, 'But time, which cannot be forced, makes all things ready' – even here he cannot resist a slightly overheated pun on Sforza and *sforzare*, which means also to force sexually.

The wedding of Ludovico and Beatrice went ahead as planned, and was celebrated in sumptuous style on 16 January 1491, but Cecilia continued to exert her spell, and a month after the wedding Ambassador Trotti reported that Il Moro had spoken to him 'in his ear', and told him 'he wished he could go to La Rocca [his private apartments at the castle] and make love to Cecilia, and be with her in peace, and this was what his wife wanted too, because she did not want to submit to him'. Apparently Beatrice was refusing to sleep with Ludovico while he persisted in his dalliance with Cecilia. On 21 March, however, Trotti reports that Ludovico has ordered Cecilia away from the castle: 'He no longer wants to touch her or have relations with her, now she is so big, and will not do so until she has delivered him a son.' In April she is reported to be living in an apartment in the city provided by Il Moro, perhaps again that property in Nuovo Monasterio.

On 3 May she gave birth to a son. He was christened Cesare Sforza Visconti. The poet Bellincioni rushed out a trio of sonnets celebrating the birth, calling her 'Isola' ('Island', a pun on Cecilia/Sicilia), and congratulating her on being the vessel which had brought the 'seed of the Moor to fruition'. The poet's friendly relations with Cecilia are shown in a later letter, of February 1492, in which he tells Ludovico:

I dined yesterday morning with My Lady Cecilia, and stayed there till evening, and am her favourite, and I swear to God we had such fun with Signor Cesare, who is nice and fat, I mean fat. And because I guessed he was going to be a boy I know I will ever be in his Lordship's [Cesare's] good graces.[72]

Alas not so: the plausible rimester was dead by the end of the summer.

To Bellincioni also we owe the earliest reference to Leonardo's portrait, in a sonnet addressed, in his usual cavalier tone, to Nature:

> O Nature how envious you are
> of Vinci who has painted one of your stars,
> The beautiful Cecilia, whose lovely eyes
> Make the sunlight seem dark shadow
>
> .   .   .   .
>
> Think this: the more lively and lovely she is,
> The more glory you'll get in ages to come.
> Give thanks therefore to Ludovico
> And to the genius and the hand of Leonardo,
> Who both wish to share her with posterity.[73]

As far as I know, this is the earliest literary description of a Leonardo painting. It contains the rather acute observation I quote at the top of this chapter: 'Con sua pictura / La fa che par che ascolti e non favella' – 'By his art he makes her look as if she's listening, and not talking.' This catches something of the poise of the portrait: her air of attentiveness to something beyond the picture-space. Does it also contain a personal reminiscence of Cecilia – 'e non favella': for once she isn't chattering?

This is the painting's backdrop: sex and gossip and poetry at the Sforza court. Like Leonardo's earlier portrait of Ginevra de' Benci, it is an image of a woman created for the delectation of her lover. But up here in Milan the action is rawer: this is no Platonic crush like Bembo's for Ginevra, and the portrait of Cecilia has an erotic frisson quite absent from the serene, lunar depiction of Ginevra. The hand caressing the furry animal is a sexual allusion; the fashion accessories – the gold frontlet, the black band, the tied veil, the necklace – suggest the restrained, captive status of the concubine. I am reminded of a passage in the Trattato della pittura, where Leonardo argues that the painter has the same kind of power as a poet to 'inflame men with love' – he can make them 'fall in love with a painting'. He tells this story:

It once happened that I made a picture representing a divine subject, and it was bought by a man who fell in love with her. He wished to remove the emblems of divinity in order to be able to kiss the picture without scruples. But finally conscience overcame his sighs and desires, and he was obliged to remove the painting from his house.[74]

This cannot be the portrait of Cecilia, of course, but the idea of a painting as a kind of love-object, an erotic inducement, is suggestive of it.

The ermine cradled in the girl's arms brings a train of symbolic and folkloric associations into the painting. The ermine, Mustela erminea, is the northern variety of stoat whose winter-fur is white (though in the painting the creature's coat is discoloured by varnish, and appears yellow-brown). The animal was associated with purity and cleanliness, as in Leonardo's own 'bestiary' compiled in the early 1490s: 'The ermine, because of its temperance . . . will rather let itself be taken by hunters than take refuge in a muddy den, in order not to stain its purity.'[75] This claim is not original to Leonardo – it is among the many items in his bestiary drawn from his well-thumbed copy of the Fiore di virtù. The ermine also appears as a symbol of purity in Vittore Carpaccio's portrait of a knight (c. 1510), where a cartouche above the animal reads, 'Malo mori quam foedari' – 'Better to die than to be besmirched.' This association of purity adds a partly ironic refinement to the portrait: the symbolic in contrapposto with the erotic. Another connection of the ermine is a learned linguistic pun. The Greek word for a weasel or stoat is *galé*, which puns on Cecilia's family name of Gallerani: this is parallel to the juniper or *ginepro* in Ginevra's portrait. This is the sort of stuff Leonardo liked – or knew that his customers liked – though it seems unlikely that he would have known this rather obscure bit of Greek vocabulary; perhaps he had a bit of help from Ludovico's secretary, the Hellenic scholar Bartolomeo Calco.

These meanings play over the ermine, but the creature has a more particular significance. It is an emblematic allusion to Ludovico himself, who in 1488 was invested with the title of the Ermine ('L'Ermellino') by Ferrante di Aragona, King of Naples (grandfather of Isabella of Aragon, who was soon to marry young Duke Gian Galeazzo). A sonnet of Bellincioni's styles Ludovico *'l'italico morel, bianco ermellino'* (the Italian moor, the white ermine).[76] The animal cradled in Cecilia's arms is thus an emblem of the man to whom she is bound, socially and sexually, and indeed one notes its vigilant eye, and powerfully muscular foreleg, and the claws splayed out against the girl's red sleeve. As so often, Leonardo renders the emblematic so powerfully that it doubles back into the actual, and one has a sense of the ermine as predator, as it is in nature, and as Ludovico was. It is very likely Leonardo drew the creature from life – ermines were imported to Milan by furriers; there is a letter from a traveller in Moscow promising to send Ludovico's brother 'beautiful sables, ermines, bears, and white hares, alive or dead'.[77] Stoats and their relatives (weasels, martens, ferrets, etc.) make decorative pets, so the portrait as a whole is not fantastical: it achieves its resonances within an image of almost photographic realism, beautifully lit against a black backdrop.

Though discarded, Cecilia remained in the Moor's affections, and as the mother of one of his natural sons she was favoured. She was awarded lands at Saranno, north of Milan, and in 1492 she was married off to a Cremonese, Count Lodovico Bergamini. She created a little salon at the Palazzo Carmagnola in Milan; among those who paid court there was the author Matteo Bandello, who dedicated two of his *novelle* to her, and praised her wit and learning, and her Latin verses.

The portrait remained in her possession, and on 26 April 1498 the avid *collectionneuse* Isabella d'Este wrote to her with a typically peremptory request (though the tone is not unfriendly considering that Isabella was Beatrice's sister):

We happened today to be looking at certain beautiful portraits done by Zoanne Bellino [i.e. Giovanni Bellini]; and we began to discuss the works of Leonardo, and wished we could see some of them to compare with the paintings we have here. Recalling that L. V. did your portrait from the life, would you be so good as to send it to me, by this present bearer whom we send for this purpose. As well as serving the purpose of comparison, it will give us the pleasure of seeing your face. As soon as we have studied it we will return it to you.

On 29 April Cecilia replied that she was sending the portrait,

though I would send it more willingly if it looked more like me. Your Ladyship should not think this is due to any failings on the part of the *maestro*, whom I truly believe to be without equal. It is solely because the portrait was done when I was at an imperfect age, and my face has since changed completely, so that if you put the portrait and me side by side, no one would think it was me represented there.[78]

This was by no means the last of the picture's peregrinations. After Cecilia's death, in 1536, it remained in Milan. In the eighteenth century, according to Carlo Amoretti, librarian of the Biblioteca Ambrosiana, 'it was still to be seen in Milan, in the collection of the Marquises of Bonasana'. He also implied that there were other paintings based on it: a St Cecilia holding a zither, and another in which 'this renowned lady is painted as she was in the first portrait, done by Leonardo himself in the flower of her youth, but instead of the zither she seems to hold in her hand a fold of her gown'.[79] Then, in about 1800, the portrait was bought by the Polish prince Adam Jerzy Czartoryski, and given to his mother, Isabella. She hung it in her picture gallery, called the Gothic House, in the family estate at Puławy, near Cracow. It was at this time that the erroneous inscription was added to the top left-hand corner:

LA BELE FERONIERE
LEONARD D'AWINCI

A note by Isabella Czartoryski explains that the picture 'is supposed to be the portrait of the mistress of François I, King of France. She was called La Belle Ferronnière as she was believed to be the wife of an ironmonger.' (The idea that Leonardo painted this semi-legendary Frenchwoman has proved tenacious, and the same title is now given – equally erroneously – to another of his Milanese portraits.)

In 1842 the Czartoryski family were living in exile in Paris, and had the painting with them; it was in Paris for three decades, in their apartments at the Hôtel Lambert, but the French art establishment seems to have known nothing of it. Arsène Houssaye's exhaustive catalogue of 1869 lists the painting as lost. After the Franco-Prussian War the family returned to Poland, and in 1876 the *Lady with an Ermine* was exhibited in public for the first time, in the Czartoryski Museum at Cracow. By the early twentieth century it had been accepted and celebrated as an authentic Leonardo, and identified as the portrait of Cecilia Gallerani documented by Bellincioni and others.

It had a last adventure during the Second World War. Just before the Nazi invasion of Poland in 1939 it was hidden at Sieniawa, with other treasures of the Czartoryski collection – a Rembrandt landscape, a Raphael portrait – but the hiding-place was discovered. The *Lady* was briefly exhibited at the Kaiser Friedrich Musum in Berlin, and was reserved for Hitler's private museum (the '*Führerauftrag*') at Linz, but instead it wound up in the private collection of the Nazi governor of Poland, Hans Frank, at whose villa in Bavaria it was discovered in 1945 by the Polish-American Committee. Thus the fortunes of love and war are etched on this small painted panel of walnut-wood which issued from the studio of Leonardo da Vinci in *c.* 1489.

→→ THE MILANESE STUDIO ←←

By the late 1480s Leonardo had established his own studio in Milan. This was essentially a version of the Florentine studio in which he had himself trained – a *bottega* or workshop turning out commissioned work under the guiding influence of the *maestro*. Some of its products, like the portrait of Cecilia, were almost entirely his own work. Others would be mostly painted by assistants working under his supervision, with occasional masterly interventions and corrections from him. This is the sort of set-up described by a visitor to Leonardo's later studio in Florence, where '*Dui suoi garzoni fano retrati, e lui a le volte in alcuno mette mano*' – 'Two of his assistants make copies, and he from time to time puts his own hand to them.'[80] Sometimes the assistants were working from an original template by Leonardo, whether a painting or cartoon, and sometimes they were working more freely within an overall style or 'look' which was the studio's trademark. As we have seen, some contracts made a financial distinction between the work of the master and that of his assistants. In a note written in about 1492, and thus referable to the Milanese studio, Leonardo criticizes 'foolish painters' who complain that they 'cannot work up to their best standard because they have not been paid enough': they should have the sense to 'keep by them' a range of paintings, 'so they can say: this is at a high price, and that is more moderately priced, and that is quite cheap'.[81] Presumably the work that was 'quite cheap' had a lesser contribution from the *maestro*.

In that imagined dialogue between Leonardo and Phidias in Giovanni Paolo Lomazzo's *Sogni* (which also discusses Leonardo's fondness for the 'backside game' of homosexuality), Leonardo says, 'My compositions were admired even when they were later painted by my followers' – the word used is *creati*, servants: literally those he has 'created'. This again refers to studio practice: the use of the master's work as the prototype for later copies – in some cases, as in the *Leda*, only the copies survive.

Another first-hand account comes from Paolo Giovio. He notes how strict Leonardo was about his pupils learning their craft slowly and thoroughly: he 'would not permit youngsters under the age of twenty to touch brushes and colours, and would only let them practise with a lead stylus'. Giovio also speaks tellingly of the 'crowd of young men [*adolescentium turba*] who contributed so much to the success of his studio'. This sounds like a precise evocation – Leonardo's unruly young entourage: a gang of adolescents.

We can reconstruct some of the personnel of Leonardo's first Milanese studio. It would certainly have included Ambrogio de Predis, and perhaps also his brother Evangelista until his early death in 1491. These were his partners on the *Virgin of the Rocks*, and Ambrogio continues to be linked with Leonardo as collaborator, partner and occasional disputant for another twenty years or so. Two other early assistants were Giovanni Antonio Boltraffio and Marco d'Oggiono, both named by Vasari as Leonardo's 'pupils'.[82]

Boltraffio was born in about 1467, the illegitimate offspring of a wealthy, patrician family. His illegitimacy, which gives him an emotional link to Leonardo, did not mar his fortunes: there hangs over him (rightly or wrongly) a reputation of the rich amateur, one of what Shakespeare called the 'wealthy curlèd darlings'. On his tombstone in San Paolo in Compito it was claimed that he pursued a lifelong dedication to painting '*inter seria*', again suggesting amateurism, though what his other more 'serious' activities were is unrecorded. Vasari calls him a 'skilful and discerning artist', which is faint praise. At his best he is a painter of great poetry and subtlety: see his *Madonna and Child* in the Poldi Pezzoli museum in Milan, and his *Narcissus* in the Uffizi. The poet Girolamo Casio, whose portrait Boltraffio painted, described him as the '*unico allievo*' ('only pupil') of Leonardo: not literally, of course, but in the sense of 'the only true disciple'.[83] Marco d'Oggiono was the son of a prosperous goldsmith; the family came from Oggiono in the Brianza region north of Milan, but his father, Cristofero, was established in the city by the mid-1460s, and Marco was probably born there. By 1487 he had his own apprentice, Protasio Crivelli (possibly a relative of Lucrezia Crivelli, whose portrait Leonardo later painted). Like Boltraffio, he enters the aegis of Leonardo's studio as a trained painter of independent means: they are not apprentices but young associates. Both are mentioned in a memorandum of Leonardo's concerning the misdeeds of the ten-year-old Giacomo Caprotti, or Salai, who joined the household in the summer of 1490:

> On 7 September [1490] he stole a pen worth 22 soldi from Marco, who was living with me. This pen was silverpoint and he took it from Marco's study . . .
> On 2 April [1491], Gian Antonio left a silverpoint pen on top of one of his drawings, and Giacomo stole it from him.[84]

These are snapshots inside the walls of Leonardo's studio – the assistant's little work-room or *studiolo*; the silverpoint pen lying on top of a drawing; the kid who steals things whenever he can. Boltraffio's brilliance with silverpoint can be seen in some extant drawings like his Christ (interpreted by some as a Bacchus) in Turin; this was a drawing method little known in Lombardy, and was spread through Leonardo's influence.

Another early member of Leonardo's *bottega* was the enigmatic Francesco Napoletano. Until recently his only certain work was the striking *Madonna and Child with St John the Baptist and St Sebastian* in the Zurich Kunsthaus, which is signed along the base of the Madonna's throne. Both the saints show close acquaintance with Leonardo prototypes.[85] We now know a little more of Francesco thanks to the archival research of Janice Shell and Grazioso Sironi.[86] His name was Francesco Galli; he was born in Naples, at an unknown date, and he died in Venice in about 1501. At the time of his death he was living with a *cohabitrix* or partner named Andreina Rossini, and had two young children by her; one infers that he was not very old when he died. The date of his death shows that the strongly Leonardesco flavour of his output is not just a later imitation; he was active during the 1490s, imbibing the influence of Leonardo at first hand. He is almost certainly the Francesco Galli named as a designer of minting-dies for coinage in a ducal letter of 8 August 1494; another designer mentioned in the same letter is Leonardo's colleague Ambrogio de Predis. This places Francesco in the milieu of Milanese portraiture. There were close links between the designing of medals and coins and the painting of portraits: the Lombard portrait convention was the full profile known to art-historians as the 'numismatic model'.

To these names can be added Tommaso Masini or Zoroastro, who is probably the 'Maestro Tommaso' mentioned in a note of September 1492; he is described as having 'returned' to the studio at that date, and was therefore part of it sometime before. And there is the German called Giulio who was a new arrival in March 1493.[87] These two were not painters, however, but metalworkers.

In the draft of a huffy letter to Ludovico complaining about money owed to him ('It vexes me greatly that having to earn my living . . .'), Leonardo refers to the financial burden of having supported six dependants for three years: '*Ho tenuto 6 bocche 36 mesi*' – precisely the language of the *catasto*, as if this little group of apprentices and assistants were indeed his family.[88] The draft, undated, is probably from about 1495. These six *bocche*, or dependants, he was supporting in the early 1490s might be Boltraffio, Marco d'Oggiono, Francesco Napoletano, Salai, Zoroastro and Giulio the German. (Ambrogio de Predis was a collaborator but not an assistant receiving board and lodging.)

Later lists show a fairly continuous influx of new apprentices during the later 1490s – Galeazzo, Benedetto, Ioditti, Gianmaria, Girardo, Gianpietro, Bartolomeo.[89] Only the last two, who appear on a list of *c.* 1497, are identifiable. Gianpietro is probably Giovanni Pietro Rizzoli, known as Giampietrino, who became one of Leonardo's most brilliant assistants during the second Milanese period; and Bartolomeo may be Bartolomeo Suardi, the follower of Bramante known as Bramantino. There were also many younger Lombard painters who were profoundly influenced by Leonardo and who are called his 'disciples', among them Cesare da Sesto, Bernardino Luini, Andrea Solario and Giovanni Bazzi (a.k.a. Il Sodoma), though none of them can be shown to have actually studied under the *maestro*. These are the 'Leonardeschi', whom Kenneth Clark dubbed 'the smile without the Cheshire cat'. Giovanni Paolo Lomazzo has these later disciples in mind when he has Leonardo say, 'In the conception and design of religious subjects I was so perfect that many people tried to take the spirit of those figures which I had previously drawn.'[90]

From Leonardo's Milanese studio there emanated a series of courtly portraits and religious paintings of a high quality which doubtless commanded high prices. The portrait of Cecilia Gallerani is one. Three other paintings are also considered wholly or largely Leonardo's.

The Musician (Pinacoteca Ambrosiana, Milan) is one of the most vivid of the studio portraits (Plate 13). A small half-length panel-portrait in oils, it shows a handsome young man with long, curling, fairish hair under a bright red *berrettino*. It is Leonardo's only known portrait-painting of a man, though there are many portrait-drawings in his sketchbooks. The painting was not listed among the pictures of the Borromeo bequest of 1618 which forms the nucleus of the Ambrosian collection. It is first heard of in the catalogue of 1686, where it is described as a 'portrait of a Duke of Milan' and is attributed to Bernardino Luini. In 1905 the painting was cleaned, revealing a musical score in the sitter's right hand, and from this comes the portrait's customary title.[91]

It is often said that the musician portrayed by Leonardo is Franchino Gaffurio, who was choirmaster of Milan cathedral from 1484 until his death nearly forty years later. Compositions by him, for three, four and five voices, are extant in the cathedral archives. He was also a prolific author, one of the first to expound musical theory in vernacular Italian. A note of Leonardo's about a 'book of musical instruments' may refer to Gaffurio's *De harmonia musicorum instrumentorum* (1508).[92] The musical score in the portrait has mostly disappeared, but a stave can faintly be seen, and the letters 'Cant. Ang.'. According to Serge Bramly, this refers to a composition by Gaffurio called the *Canticum angelicum*, but this seems to be a misreading. There was a book of music theory by Gaffurio, *Angelicum ac divinum opus musicae*, but it was not published until 1508, some twenty years after the probable date of the portrait, and is too tenuous a link to explain the phrase.

Gaffurio was known to Leonardo, and was the kind of high-ranking Milanese figure who might be expected to sit for a studio portrait, but doubts remain. There are other portraits of him – a painting at Lodi, his birthplace, and a woodcut on the title-page of his *De harmonia* – and neither of them particularly resembles the man in the Leonardo portrait. There is also the question of his age. The portrait is conventionally dated to the same period as the portrait of Cecilia, *c*. 1488–90: Gaffurio was then in his late thirties, which seems too old for the musician in the Ambrosiana.

Another possibility is that the portrait shows a young musician and singer whom Leonardo knew well – his former pupil Atalante Migliorotti.[93] In 1490 Atalante performed the title-role of Poliziano's operetta *Orfeo* in a performance at Marmirolo, near Mantua, commissioned by Isabella d'Este. It is possible that Leonardo was involved in the production (he later staged a production of *Orfeo* at Milan), and plausible that he was commissioned to portray the handsome, alert face of its young star. We know he had done so before – that 'portrait of Atalante raising his face', probably a drawing, in the list of works of *c*. 1482. Atalante was about twenty-four in 1490, and seems to me a more likely candidate for Leonardo's *Musician* than the cathedral choirmaster and musicologist Gaffurio.

Parts of the *Musician* – the paintwork of the tunic, for instance – seem perfunctory. The painting is sometimes described as 'unfinished', but this may be the result of an artistic decision of Leonardo's – a deliberate casualness at the periphery which frames the intensely finished face at the centre. There is a similar question about the portrait of Cecilia Gallerani: is the poor formation of her left hand due to later botching (perhaps in the early nineteenth century, when the inscription was added), or was it purposely left like that by Leonardo? Scarcely delineated, the hand merges into the darkness which surrounds the lit central group of the woman and her four-legged friend; more precisely figured it would have altered the shape and emphasis of the composition. Such blurred or squiggled peripheries were extremely common in drawings, but not in painting, where a uniform finish was conventional. X-ray examination reveals a window in the background, similar to the one in the *Benois Madonna*; this was later covered with the dark paint of the background, perhaps with the same motive of minimizing distractions. This is a feature of the Milan portraits – soothing, velvety backgrounds against which the foreground figures seem spotlit, as if performing in some subtle metaphorical cabaret or show.

The sultry full-face portrait called the *Belle Ferronnière* (Plate 14), now in the Louvre, probably dates from the mid-1490s. It is less engaging and subtle than the *Lady with an Ermine*, but may belong with it in a particular sub-group of Leonardo's output – portraits of Sforza concubines. This beautiful lady with her sensual mouth and her direct challenging gaze – unusually focused on the viewer rather than some patch of ether beyond – is almost certainly a portrait of Lucrezia Crivelli, the successor to Cecilia Gallerani in the Moor's extramarital affections. There is independent evidence that Leonardo painted her portrait, and of his extant works this is the most likely to be the result.[94] As with Cecilia, the young lady's pregnancy signalled a change in her status and provides an approximate *terminus ad quem* for the painting. Lucrezia gave birth to a son, Giovanni Paolo, acknowledged as Ludovico's, in March 1497. In the same year Ludovico's wife Beatrice died suddenly, and he entered a period of melancholy retreat: she was sparky and popular, and was loved if not always well treated by the Moor. The painting of Lucrezia, and the poet's casual reference to her as the Moor's 'lover', are more likely to be before these events, perhaps *c.* 1495–6.

The breast-feeding Madonna, known after its nineteenth-century owner

Duke Antonio Litta as the *Litta Madonna*, is a mysterious painting but in many ways a typical studio production. Her head is closely based on a famous drawing in the Louvre, which is certainly authentic Leonardo, but the painting is generally attributed to a Milanese assistant, perhaps Marco d'Oggiono rather than the more idiosyncratic Boltraffio, though it is possible that both had a hand in it.[95] How much of the finished painting is Leonardo's can only be guessed at. There is a certain cloying sweetness in the big-eyed, full-lipped child which seems inauthentic. Sentiment in Leonardo can hover on the brink of sentimentality – the *Madonna of the Yarnwinder* is another instance – and this tendency easily becomes a sickliness in Leonardesco works by second-rate followers like Marco d'Oggiono. (His kissing *Holy Children* at Hampton Court is a glaring example of Leonardesco chocolate-box; one of the children is similar to the child of the *Litta Madonna*.) The landscape is perfunctory. The goldfinch revealed in the child's left hand lacks the sprightliness and telling detail which Leonardo would give to it. Only the soft, subtle moulding of the Madonna's face and neck, and the trademark shimmering of the *bambino*'s curls, suggests his intervention with the paintbrush. This is a studio piece precisely as observed in that description of Leonardo's later Florentine studio: 'Two of his assistants make copies, and he from time to time puts his own hand to them.'

This sequence of paintings represents the lesser peaks of Leonardo's output as a painter: a series of commercial productions lit with the *maestro*'s particular touch or aura. Many other paintings can be plausibly described as the products of his studio if not of his brush. There is Ambrogio de Predis's beautiful profile portrait the *Lady with a Pearl Necklace*, sometimes identified as Beatrice d'Este, and his equally striking portrait in the National Gallery, London, showing a young man with gingery hair in the Milanese 'page-boy' bob and a coat with a leopard-skin collar, and dated 1494.[96] There is Boltraffio's beautiful *Madonna and Child* (Poldi Pezzoli, Milan), so Leonardesque in its dynamic dramatic pose, and his glittering, effeminate portrait of Girolamo Casio (so effeminate, in fact, that the seventeenth-century connoisseur Inigo Jones thought it was Leonardo's portrait of Ginevra de' Benci: Jones read the letters woven on the sitter's jacket as 'G.B.', but in fact they are 'C.B.' – probably a reference to Casio's *innamorata*, Costanza Bentivoglio).[97] There is Marco d'Oggiono's bland but faithful copy of the *Virgin of the Rocks*. There are the various Milanese versions of a Salvator Mundi (or Christ the Saviour) which probably refer back to an original Leonardo composition.

In one case we have a documented contract. On 14 June 1491 Boltraffio

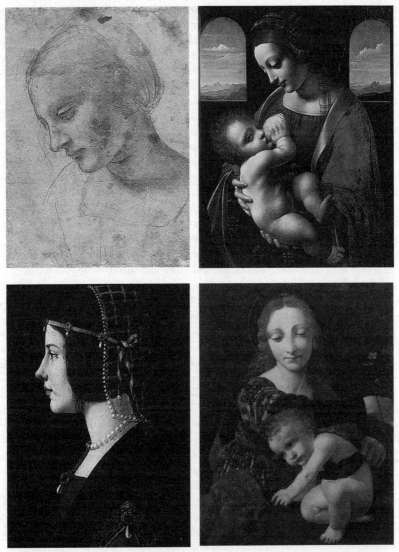

The Milanese studio. *Upper left: Leonardo's silverpoint study for the* Litta Madonna. *Upper right: the* Litta Madonna, *a collaborative studio production of c. 1490. Lower left: Ambrogio de Predis,* Lady with a Pearl Necklace, *perhaps a portrait of Beatrice d'Este. Lower right: Giovanni Antonio Boltraffio,* Madonna and Child.

and Marco d'Oggiono were commissioned to paint an altarpiece for the Milanese church of San Giovanni sul Muro. The clients were the Grifi brothers, who had endowed a chapel there in memory of their father, Leonardo Grifi, Archbishop of Benevento. The painters were contracted to deliver the altarpiece by the November following (in time for the feast-day of St Leonard, to whom the chapel was dedicated), but failed to do so; it was not finished till 1494. The painting is the *Resurrection of Christ with Saints Leonard and Lucy*, now in Berlin.[98] The upper half is attributed to Marco, and the kneeling saints to Boltraffio. The whole work is shot through with Leonardo influences: the pyramidic composition, the spiralling *contrapposto* of the risen Christ, the rocky striations of the landscape. The contract describes the two painters as *compagni* or partners. There is no mention of Leonardo in the document, but we know from the Salai memorandum that both artists were part of the Leonardo *bottega* in 1491. It is an independent commission within the aegis of the studio, much as Leonardo's portrait of Ginevra was an independent commission within the aegis of Verrocchio's studio. The agreed fee for the Grifi altarpiece was 50 ducats – not a huge sum (compare the 200 ducats offered to Leonardo and the de Predis brothers for the *Virgin of the Rocks* in 1483).[99] This reflects its status: a workshop production entrusted to the secondary rank of artists within the studio. It is, as Leonardo puts it, 'quite cheap'.

THE ANATOMIST

The earliest datable signs of Leonardo's interest in anatomy – the first drawings, the first purposeful notes – belong to the late 1480s. These are the outset of one of his most profound achievements. In terms of what he actually contributed – of the difference he made – his work as an anatomist is far more significant than his work as an engineer, or inventor, or architect. He mapped and documented the human body more rigorously and specifically than had been done before; his anatomical drawings constituted a new visual language for describing body-parts, as his mechanical drawings did for machines. There is a certain dogged courage in these investigations, which were beset by taboos and doctrinal doubts, and which depended on the stressful and repulsive procedures of post-mortem examination in pre-refrigeration circumstances. Leonardo's anatomy exemplifies his belief in practical, empirical, hands-on investigation: a probing and revaluing of the received wisdom of the ancients – Galen, Hippocrates, Aristotle – who were still the mainstay of the 'medical schools'.

The orthodox felt that anatomy was a curiosity too far: man was made in God's image, and should not be stripped down like a piece of machinery. Anatomy reveals what 'Nature has carefully concealed', wrote the early humanist Colluccio Salutati, 'and I do not see how the caverns of the body can be viewed without effusion of tears.' At least once Leonardo's activities brought him into confrontation with the Church: in Rome in 1515 an ill-wisher 'hindered me in anatomy, denouncing it before the Pope and also at the hospital'.[100]

Leonardo's anatomical studies belong under the heading 'Leonardo the scientist', but are also vitally connected with Leonardo the artist: they bridge the gap between those roles, or show that it is not really a gap at all. Anatomy was one of the building-blocks of painting, like geometry and mathematics. Beneath an anatomical drawing showing the nerves of the neck and shoulders Leonardo writes, 'This demonstration is as necessary to good draughtsmen as is the origin of words from Latin to good grammarians.'[101] One thinks of the *Last Supper* with its taut, twisting, tensing neck-muscles expressing the drama of the moment. His interest in anatomy thus arises – like the slightly later interest in optics – as a corollary to his work as a painter, and perhaps more particularly to his role as a teacher of painting to the pupils and apprentices of his Milanese studio. Here dawns the ideal of the 'painter-philosopher', whose art is based on a profound scientific knowledge of everything he depicts; here begin the painstaking tracts and treatises later incorporated into his great posthumous handbook, the *Trattato della pittura*. For the early biographers this programme was a mixed blessing: Giovio had no doubt that Leonardo's small output as an artist was due to his time-consuming study of the 'subordinate branches of his art', chief among them anatomy and optics. Vasari too regarded these investigations as tangential and ultimately debilitating.

Leonardo would probably have studied anatomy under Verrocchio. The Florentine figurative style of the 1470s – Antonio del Pollaiuolo's paintings, Verrocchio's sculptures – was strong on anatomical detail and drama. Pollaiuolo made detailed studies of human musculature, apparently from dissections, before producing the famous *Battle of the Nude Men*.[102] Leonardo would have known of, and perhaps known, the Florentine anatomist Antonio Benivieni, a friend of Lorenzo de' Medici. Benivieni studied the functions of the heart and other internal organs, but his chief interest was dissecting corpses after execution, looking for anatomical indices of criminal behaviour. His treatise *De abditis causis* (*Of Hidden Causes*) reports his findings after twenty such dissections.

There may be other Florentine sources to consider, but it is here in Milan that the interest in anatomy surfaces powerfully. In 1489, in fact, Leonardo was planning a 'book' – a manuscript treatise – on the subject. There is written evidence of this: vestigial drafts and contents-lists, one of them dated 2 April 1489. Leonardo later gave this projected book or treatise the title *De figura umana* (*Of the Human Figure*), again suggesting the link between anatomy and painting.[103]

In 1489 the thirty-six-year-old Leonardo contemplated that universal symbol of mortality, a human skull. On three sheets now at Windsor he drew eight studies of the skull – profiles, cross-sections, views at oblique angles from above.[104] The drawings are delicate, beautifully shaded and rather eerie. Different studies select different details – one shows the blood-vessels of the face; another shows the relation between the orbit and the maxillary antrum (eye-socket and jawbone); another peers down into the empty cranium and traces the intercranial nerves and vessels. But the chief interest, as shown in the accompanying notes, is less scientific than metaphysical. One of the studies shows the skull squared for proportion, and beside it Leonardo writes, 'Where the line $a–m$ is intersected by the line $c–b$, there will be the confluence of all the senses.'

This 'confluence of the senses' he is trying to pinpoint is the *sensus communis* postulated by Aristotle. It was the part of the brain where sensory impressions were coordinated and interpreted. It was described as the most important of the brain's three 'ventricles', the others being the *imprensiva*, where raw sensory data were gathered, and the *memoria*, where the processed information was stored. 'Ventricle' suggests merely a place or cavity, but the *sensus communis* was active as well. In a computer analogy it was the CPU or central processing unit: both a physical entity and a metaphysical system. In some notes contemporary with the skull studies, Leonardo defines the classical theory thus:

The common sense is what judges the things given to it by the other senses. The ancient speculators concluded that man's capacity to interpret is caused by an organ to which the other five senses refer everything . . . They say that this common sense is situated in the centre of the head between the zones of impression and memory.

The *sensus communis* was thus the home of reason, imagination, intellect – even the soul. Leonardo again:

It seems that the soul resides in this organ . . . called the Common Sense. It is not spread throughout the body as many have thought, but is entirely in one part,

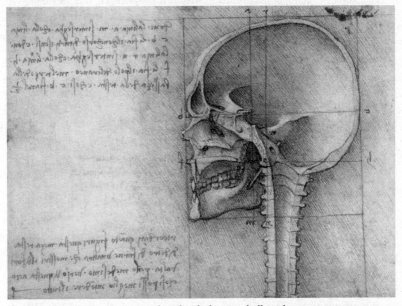

'The seat of the soul'. Sectional study of a human skull, with measurements to locate the sensus communis.

because if it were all-pervading and the same in every part, there would have been no need to make the organs of the senses converge . . . The Common Sense is the seat of the soul.[105]

Taking this at face value, one arrives at the extraordinary notion that in the proportional skull study at Windsor, illustrated above, Leonardo furnishes an actual grid-reference for the site of a man's soul. This would of course be over-literal. Leonardo is inquiring rather than assuming; he refers the theory to 'ancient speculators', mainly Aristotle, and he notes the implications it has for other ancient speculations – Platonic, Hermetic – which held the soul to be infused everywhere. None the less this is a typical Leonardian leap – a measure of thrilling investigative potential. It will surely be possible – by the kind of lucid, dispassionate study these drawings exemplify – to find the inner secrets of a man's mind. *If* there is a 'common sense' we can surely locate it; *if* there is a soul it surely resides there. One hears him in these notes: at once the magician and the sceptic. He peers fastidiously into the nooks and chambers of the skull, his eye burning with that fierce but ambiguous curiosity in which are commingled 'fear and desire – fear of that threatening dark cave; desire to see if there was some marvellous thing within'.

On the verso of one of the skull studies he writes the date, 2 April 1489, and then the following list of subjects to be investigated. It begins with questions specific to the head and face, and thus connected to the skull series:

> Which tendon causes the motion of the eye, so that the motion of one eye moves the other.
> Of frowning.
> Of raising and lowering the eyebrows.
> Of closing and opening the eyes.
> Of flaring the nostrils.
> Of opening the lips with the teeth shut.
> Of pouting with the lips.
> Of laughing.
> Of astonishment . . .

Then suddenly, and typically, the scope of the inquiry broadens, and from the muscular mechanics of laughter and astonishment he turns, with hardly a pause, to

> Describe the beginning of man, and what causes it within the womb, and why a child of eight months cannot survive.
> What sneezing is.
> What yawning is.
> Falling sickness
> spasm
> paralysis
> shivering with cold
> sweating
> hunger
> sleep
> thirst
> lust

He then moves on to the body's systems of tendons and muscles – 'Of the tendon which causes movement from the shoulder to the elbow', and 'Of the tendon which causes movement of the thigh', etc. This subject-matter may be related to another early anatomical study, showing the tendons of the arm and leg.[106] Its technical deficiencies suggest a drawing done at a dissection, hence rougher and more hurried.

Already in this programme of anatomical studies we sense that urge towards comprehensiveness which becomes a debilitating feature of Leonardo's scientific investigations: *everything* must be explained anew, each topic opening up to reveal scores of other topics in need of examination.

Also part of this course of study 'of the human figure' is a series of drawings which tabulate the proportions of the human body and establish mathematical ratios between its different parts.[107] Here again we find the influence of Vitruvius, the great Roman architect and military engineer of the first century AD, whose writings constitute a unique record of classical theory and practice on the subject of harmonious proportions. There are a number of drawings on this subject at Windsor, dated around 1490, and there are others now lost which are known through copies in the Codex Huygens, a manuscript treatise compiled in the latter half of the sixteenth century, probably by the Milanese artist Girolamo Figino, who was a pupil of Leonardo's former assistant Francesco Melzi and had access to Melzi's enormous collection of Leonardo papers.

The most famous of these proportional studies – indeed one of the most famous drawings in the world – is the so-called 'Vitruvian Man', or the '*Homo ad circulum*', which has become a kind of logo for Leonardo and his aspiring mind. Like most very famous works, it is more often looked at in the isolating spotlight of fame than in the context in which it was created.

The Vitruvian Man is a drawing in pen and ink on a large sheet of paper (13½ × 9½ inches) now in the Accademia in Venice.[108] Its presence in Venice is probably connected to the printing of Fra Giocondo's folio edition of the works of Vitruvius, published in Venice in 1511, which contains an engraving based on the drawing. Above and below the drawing are handwritten texts. The upper text begins:

Vitruvius the architect says in his work on architecture that the measurements of man are distributed by Nature as follows: that 4 fingers make one palm, and 4 palms make one foot; 6 palms make a cubit [a forearm, from the Latin *cubitus*, elbow]; 4 cubits make a man's height . . .

These ratios – quoted from the opening of Book 3 of Vitruvius's *De architectura* – continue down to the punctilious: 'from the elbow to the tip of the hand will be the fifth part of a man; from the elbow to the armpit will be the eighth part of a man', etc. Beneath the drawing is a scale given in units of fingers and palms.

The Vitruvian Man.

The drawing shows a single man in two distinct positions: these correspond to two sentences in the text. The man who stands with his legs together and his arms out horizontally illustrates the sentence written directly below the drawing: '*Tanto apre l'omo nelle braccia quanto è la sua altezza*' – in other words, the width of a man's outspread arms is equal to his height. The man is therefore shown enclosed in a square, each of whose sides measures 96 fingers (or 24 palms). The other figure, with his legs astride and his arms raised higher, expresses a more specialist Vitruvian rule:

If you open your legs so much as to decrease your height by $1/14$th, and raise your outspread arms till the tips of your middle fingers are level with the top of your head, you will find that the centre of your outspread limbs will be the navel, and the space between the legs will be an equilateral triangle.

This man is shown enclosed in a circle of which his navel is the centre.

Part of the drawing's power is its interplay of abstract geometry and observed physical reality. The body of the man is synoptic but beautifully contoured and muscled. The feet actually seem to be standing on the lower line of the square, or pushing against the hoop of the circle. The double figure introduces a sense of movement which might be a gymnast's or, indeed, that of a man moving his arms up and down like the wings of a bird. The body is delineated with clean, spare, diagrammatic lines, but the face has been treated rather differently. It is more intensely worked, more dramatically shadowed: it glowers.

I have sometimes wondered if the Vitruvian Man is actually a self-portrait. In a literal sense perhaps not – the drawing is dated *c.* 1490, and the man looks older than thirty-eight. It is also the case that the face exemplifies proportions listed in the accompanying text – for instance that the distance from the roots of the hair to the eyebrows is equal to the distance from the tip of the chin to the mouth. The features are in this sense ideal or prototypical. And yet the whole idea of the drawing seems to be a physically realistic rendering of these abstract bio-geometrical symmetries, and so the stern-looking man in the circle seems to be *someone*, rather than a cipher – someone with penetrating, deeply shadowed eyes, and a thick mane of curly hair parted in the middle. At the least I would say that there are elements of self-portraiture in the Vitruvian Man: that this figure which represents natural harmonies also represents the man uniquely capable of understanding them – the artist-anatomist-architect Leonardo da Vinci.

⤕ THE SFORZA HORSE ⤔

On 22 July 1489 the Florentine ambassador in Milan, Pietro Alamanni, dispatched one of his regular newsletters to Lorenzo de' Medici in Florence. It included the following:

Prince Ludovico is planning to erect a worthy monument to his father, and in accordance with his orders Leonardo has been asked to make a model for a large horse in bronze, ridden by the Duke Francesco in full armour. As His Excellence has in mind something wonderful, the like of which has never been seen, he has directed me to write to you, to ask if you would kindly send him one or two Florentine artists who specialize in this kind of work. It seems to me that although he has given the commission to Leonardo, he is not confident that he will succeed.[109]

Though there are some uncertainties about Leonardo's fitness for his task, at least in the mind of Ambassador Alamanni, this letter is a crucial document. By mid-1489 Ludovico has commissioned Leonardo, at last, to create the great Sforza Horse so long spoken of. Despite the doubts, the commitment is a serious one: the 'model' which Ludovico has ordered from him is not a scaled-down miniature but a full-size version of the statue in clay, which would then be used to create the mould for the bronze itself. Ludovico has the later stages in mind when he requests two Florentine specialists 'in this kind of work' – i.e. large-scale metallurgy and furnace-work – though in the event Lorenzo wrote back saying no such *maestro* was available.[110]

Over the last seven years we have seen Leonardo striving to establish himself at the court of the Sforza, and with this major public commission we can at last say he has arrived. It links with other signs of preferment – the portrait of Cecilia Gallerani, undoubtedly commissioned by the Moor, and the remodelling of the Duchess's 'pavilion' in the castle garden, which also probably bears Ludovico's personal imprimatur. These too can be dated to around 1489.

Leonardo had certainly done something on the Horse before 23 April 1490, for on that day he noted in a new notebook, now Paris MS C, '*Chomincai questo libro e richomincai il cavallo*' – 'I began this book and I began again on the horse.' Elsewhere there is a note of payment: 'On 28 April I received from the Marchesino [Ludovico's treasurer Marchesino Stanga] 103 lire.' The missing year is probably 1490, thus five days after the note in MS C, and plausibly referring to an official payment connected with the Sforza Horse, on which he was now setting to work in earnest.[111]

*

The antecedents of this great but ultimately fruitless venture go back to the late 1460s, when the idea of a giant equestrian statue to honour Francesco Sforza was first mooted. News of the project had buzzed around the Florentine studios: there is a design for the statue by Antonio del Pollaiuolo, now in Munich. Leonardo himself first voiced his interest in the Horse in his 'prospectus' addressed to Ludovico in 1482. By then he had a smattering of experience, as he had probably assisted in the planning stages of Verrocchio's equestrian statue of Bartolomeo Colleoni: a sheet at Windsor has a proportional analysis of a horse which is certainly connected with the Colleoni project.[112] Verrocchio's last years were devoted to this great work, erected in Venice. The question of its influence on Leonardo is complicated: he had probably not seen the sculpture itself (there is no evidence that he had visited Venice by this stage) but it must have been there in his mind, the yardstick by which his own efforts must be measured – all the more so, perhaps, after the death of his old master in 1488, with the statue unfinished, leaving the field open to the pupil who had always sought to 'go beyond' him.

How does Leonardo envisage the Horse as he begins drawing up plans and designs in the last months of 1489? The short answer is that, typically, he envisages it as different from anything that has gone before. There were four famous equestrian statues in Italy – the Marcus Aurelius in Rome, dating from the second century AD; the slightly later classical sculpture called *Il Regisole* in Pavia; Donatello's statue of the *condottiere* Gattamelata in Padua, done in the mid-1450s; and Verrocchio's Colleoni monument in Venice, still unfinished. Without exception they showed the horse walking or trotting. In each case the horse had its left foreleg raised, to suggest its forward motion, and the other hoofs rested on the plinth. In contrast to this norm, the earliest drawings for the Sforza Horse show that Leonardo envisaged it dramatically rearing up. The finest of these is the study in metalpoint on blue prepared paper at Windsor, elegant and full of energy, though Clark – a particular expert on Leonardo's horse studies – finds the modelling less 'full and learned' than later studies.[113]

The chief problem with this design is technical – how to support the enormous weight of a large bronze horse with only its rear legs grounded on the base. The drawing attempts a solution: a fallen enemy beneath the horse's front hoofs. On another page is a more perfunctory sketch, with a tree-stump beneath the rearing horse.[114] But the problem of stability remains: the concept is dramatic but impractical, and perhaps this is the reason for Ludovico's misgivings about Leonardo, as reported by Ambassador Alamanni: 'He is not confident that he will succeed.'

Leonardo soon abandoned this idea, and the next phase of drawings shows the horse in the more conventional trotting pose. This rethink seems to have been inspired by his viewing of the *Regisole* in Pavia in June 1490. The train of thoughts set off by this sculpture is preserved on a sheet in the Codex Atlanticus. At the top of this page he writes five sentences, each beginning with a new line, so they have the look of maxims or *sententiae*. They sound like them too, but one feels they are maxims he has just made up, as he stands in awe before the *Regisole* and ideas fizz in his head in connection with his own horse, which he had 'begun again' a couple of months earlier. The page is cropped at the top, so the first line has been lost (one can see the remnant of it). It perhaps mentioned another equestrian monument, which would explain the abrupt beginning of the next line, which is now the first:

The one in Pavia is to be praised most of all for its movement.
It is more praiseworthy to imitate antiquities than modern things.
Beauty and utility cannot go together, as is shown in castles and in men.
The trot has almost the quality of a free horse.
Where natural vivacity is missing we must supply it artificially.

On the same folio he did a small sketch of a trotting horse, doubtless inspired by the *Regisole*: this is perhaps the first drawing in this new phase in the design of the Sforza Horse.[115]

It was not, of course, only sculptural models that Leonardo consulted. From this period comes a series of vibrant studies of horses quite obviously done from life – sleek, ponderous animals, rippling with vitality (Plate 16). We are reminded of a personal source for the Sforza Horse: Leonardo's lifelong love of horses, Leonardo the rider. The horses he drew were from the stables of the young Milanese courtier and soldier Galeazzo Sanseverino, who was soon to improve his fortunes by marrying one of Ludovico's illegitimate daughters. Leonardo refers particularly to 'Messer Galeazzo's big jennet', called Siciliano.[116]

The trotting horse as exemplified by the *Regisole* in Pavia was almost certainly the pose adopted for the clay model of the Sforza Horse which was eventually made in about 1493. We don't know for sure because the model was destroyed, and the sculpture itself was never cast: it is another of Leonardo's unfinished projects. Even his failures have a kind of magic about them, however, and half a century later the writer Pietro Aretino will say of a sculptor's plans to make an equestrian statue, 'He would have made a cast of the horse in such a way that Leonardo's at Milan would no longer be talked of' – implying that Leonardo's model was still being 'talked of' long after its destruction.[117] But these later phases – the creation and destruction of the Horse – belong to a later chapter.

➺ AT THE CORTE VECCHIA ➻

With the official commission to create the Sforza Horse comes the tangible benefit of official accommodation, and it was probably at this time that Leonardo took up residence at the Corte Vecchia. This spacious new housing is a sign of his status, though in truth it was the colossal Horse itself which needed the space.

The Corte Vecchia had once been the *palazzo* and power-centre of the Visconti, the first great Milanese dynasty; during the Sforza era it was superseded by the Castello Sforzesco, and became known as the Old Court. It stood close to the Duomo, on the south side of the piazza, a grand but dilapidated symbol of former times. It was heavily fortified with towers and moats; inside the walls the buildings ranged around two large courtyards surrounded by porticos.[118] One part of the palace was used for the melancholy young Duke Gian Galeazzo's apartments, though increasingly Ludovico preferred him safely sequestered at the forbidding Certosa fortress in Pavia. No trace of the Corte Vecchia remains today: it was demolished in the eighteenth century to make way for the grandiose Palazzo Reale.

On one of those sheets of picture-puzzles or rebuses at Windsor there is a ground-plan of a palace which is probably the Corte Vecchia. The plan clearly predates the rebuses, for they are cunningly worked into its empty spaces, as if inserted into the rooms of the palace as notional miniature frescos. A later note gives some dimensions: 'The hall of the Corte is 128 paces long and 27 braccia wide.'[119] A pace (*passo*) is broadly reckoned as 30 inches, and a braccio as 24 inches, so we are talking about a vast space over 300 feet long and over 50 feet wide. This faded old Visconti ballroom was perhaps Leonardo's workshop for the Sforza Horse.

It was certainly the Horse which was associated in people's minds with Leonardo's tenancy of the Corte. The Milanese court poet Baldassare Taccone writes stirringly:

> *Vedi che in Corte fa far di metallo*
> *Per la memoria di padre un gran colosso*

[See in the Corte how he [Ludovico] is having a great colossus made out of metal in memory of his father.][120]

And in his famous eyewitness account of Leonardo at work on the *Last Supper* Matteo Bandello speaks of seeing Leonardo 'leaving the Corte Vecchia, where he was working on his marvellous clay horse'.[121]

But it was not only the horse that required such space – there was also the ornithopter or flying-machine. A tantalizing page of the Codex Atlanticus has rough sketches showing a wide-spanned flying-machine, and a ladder leading up to it, and a note which reads, 'Close up the large room above with boards, and make the model large and high. It could be placed up on the roof above, which would be in all respects the most suitable place in Italy. And if you stand on the roof, on the side where the tower is, the people on the *tiburio* won't see you.'[122] This is clearly the roof of the Corte Vecchia – close enough to the *tiburio* of the Duomo to be seen by the men at work up there. The tower which serves to conceal his activities from them would be either a tower of the Corte itself or the bell-tower of the adjacent church of San Gottardo, which had served as the Visconti's chapel when the Corte was their *palazzo*. The presence of workmen on the *tiburio* would be more probable after 1490, when the building of it began.

Leonardo may have actually tested a flying-machine in Milan. The mathematician and philosopher Girolamo Cardano, who thought Leonardo an 'extraordinary man', states unequivocally that he 'tried to fly, and failed'. Cardano was born in nearby Pavia in 1501; he was twelve when Leonardo left Milan for the last time. He may be recording some personal knowledge.[123]

It would also be the Corte Vecchia referred to in a note about fossils in the Codex Leicester: 'In the mountains of Parma and Piacenza are to be found a multitude of shells and corals. When I was making the great horse in Milan, a large sackful of them was brought to me in my factory by some peasants.'[124] The word Leonardo uses is *fabbrica*, which gives a sense of size and activity: a factory, or indeed a complex organization of specialist workers like the *fabbriceria* or works department of the cathedral nearby.

So this was now Leonardo's home in Milan – a grand but rather aged *palazzo*, with colonnaded courtyards and draughty corridors, situated on the edge of the Piazza del Duomo. Here were his hangar-like workshops for the Horse and the flying-machine, his studio turning out court portraits and comely Madonnas, his study full of notebooks and manuscripts, the little rooms or *studioli* of his assistants, his laboratory for Zoroastran experiments, his shelves and chests and curios, his larders and stables, his cupboards full of pewterware – the 11 small bowls, 11 larger bowls, 7 dishes, 3 trays and 5 candlesticks carefully inventoried in a notebook of the early 1490s.[125]

There is a makeshift element to his accommodation – a disused Italian *palazzo* is not a homely place – but one knows also of Leonardo's desire for cleanliness and order, his domestic fastidiousness. On a folio dated 23 April 1490, and therefore quite possibly written at the Corte, he says, 'If you want to see how a person's soul inhabits his body, look at how his body treats its daily abode; if the latter is disordered, so the body will be kept in a disordered and confused way by the soul.' In another text written around this time he envisages the painter at work in 'his dwelling full of charming pictures, and well-kept, and often accompanied by music or readings of various fine works'.[126] One hears for a moment the tune of a *lira da braccio* floating out into the courtyard. This is an idealized picture, of course. It omits the carpenter who wants paying, the courtier inconveniently dropping by, the missing silverpoint pens, the dog scratching its fleas in the corner – the daily life of this busy, flourishing studio which is his creation and his livelihood.

PART FIVE

At Court
1490–1499

When Fortune comes grasp her with a firm hand –
in front, I tell you, for behind she is bald . . .

Codex Atlanticus, fol. 289v

⇢ THEATRICALS ⇠

The new decade dawned auspiciously with a theatrical entertainment to celebrate the recent wedding of Duke Gian Galeazzo to Isabella of Aragon.[1] It was a masque or operetta entitled *Il Paradiso* – words by Bernardo Bellincioni, set and costumes by Leonardo da Vinci. It was performed in the Sala Verde of the castle on the evening of 13 January 1490 – the earliest documented piece of theatre in which Leonardo was involved.

Gian Galeazzo was now twenty years old, a pale, studious, melancholy young man: his relationship to his overbearing uncle Ludovico can be seen graphically in a document bearing both their signatures. Isabella of Aragon, a year younger, was his beautiful royal cousin: her father, Alfonso, was heir to the kingdom of Naples; her mother was Ludovico's sister Ippolita Maria. Isabella's beauty was much commented on: she was 'so beautiful and radiant that she seemed like a sun' said the Ferrarese ambassador Jacopo Trotti (whose appreciation of such matters we hear also in his comments about Cecilia Gallerani). An exquisite red-chalk drawing by Leonardo's assistant Boltraffio is traditionally said to portray her.

In the first edition of Bellincioni's poems, published posthumously in Milan in 1493, the text of *Il Paradiso* is introduced as follows:

The following operetta was composed by Messer Bernardo Belinzon for a festivity or rather representation called *Paradiso*, which was done at the request of Lord Ludovico in praise of the Duchess of Milan, and it was called Paradiso because there was made for it, with the great genius and skill of Maestro Leonardo Vinci the Florentine, a Paradise with all the seven planets orbiting round. The planets were represented by men having the appearance and costume described by the poets, and these planets all speak in praise of the said duchess Isabella, as you will see when you read it.[2]

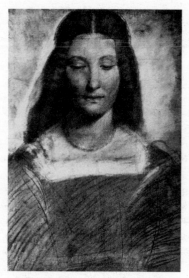

Red-chalk portrait by Boltraffio,
believed to show Isabella of Aragon.

Reading between the lines of this blurb it seems that Leonardo's visuals were the memorable thing about the show, rather than the perishable poetics of Master Belinzon or Bellincioni, and fortunately we have an eyewitness account from the observant Ambassador Trotti.

The hall was draped with festoons of evergreen foliage; the walls covered with silk. On one side was a sloping stage, 40 feet long, covered in carpets, and below it a lower stage for the musicians. On the other side was the 'Paradise' itself, veiled behind a silk curtain until the moment of revelation. The evening began at eight; the musicians – pipes, trombones, tambourines – struck up a Neapolitan tune in honour of the radiant young Duchess, who danced beautifully. There followed a series of pretended 'embassies' to her, each a pretext for dances and masques: Spanish and Turkish, Polish and Hungarian, German and French. It was nearing midnight when the actual *rappresentazione* began. The lights went down, the silk curtain was drawn back and there was the Paradise:

Il Paradiso was made in the shape of a half egg, which on the inner part was all covered with gold, with a very great number of lights, as many as stars, and with certain niches [*fessi*] where stood all the seven planets according to their degree, high and low. Around the top edge of this hemisphere were the twelve signs [of the Zodiac], with certain lights behind glass, which made a gallant and beautiful spectacle. In this Paradiso were heard many songs and many sweet and graceful sounds.[3]

A collective gasp at this shimmering apparition, and then the *annunziatore* steps forward – a boy dressed up as an angel, as in the Florentine *sacre rappresentazioni* familiar to both Bellincioni and Leonardo – to begin the show.

Il Paradiso shows us Leonardo the courtly spectaculist, the special-effects man. It was the multimedia extravaganza of its day – physically constructed out of wood and cloth, transformed and animated into something ethereal by a combination of colour, lighting, music, ballet and poetry. The show was reprised later in the year for another high-society wedding. In the notebooks a few brief snatches are all that remain – a sketch showing 'white and blue cloths woven in chequers' to 'make a heaven in a stage set', and a list of expenses including 'gold and the glue to affix the gold', and 25 pounds of wax 'to make the stars'.[4]

Almost exactly a year later Leonardo was involved in the joint nuptial celebrations of Ludovico's wedding with Beatrice d'Este and that of his niece Anna Sforza with Alfonso d'Este (Beatrice's brother). As part of the festivities a joust was organized by Galeazzo Sanseverino, the dashing young captain who was now the Moor's son-in-law (he had married Ludovico's illegitimate daughter Bianca on 10 January 1490; they were doubtless among the guests of honour at the performance of Il Paradiso three days later). His prowess at riding, jousting, wrestling, vaulting and the 'handling of various weapons' is recorded in Castiglione's The Courtier in a passage beginning, 'Consider the physical grace and agility of Signor Galeazzo Sanseverino.'[5] On 26 January 1491, Leonardo notes, 'I was at the house of Messer Galeazzo da San Severino to organize the pageant for his joust.' He mentions some of Sanseverino's footmen putting on their costumes as 'omini salvatichi', or wild men.[6] The uomo selvatico was a popular folklore figure, cognate with the Green Man of medieval England – an image of the irreducible power of Nature, and of man in a state of primitive innocence. He wore caveman garments – animal skins, or leaf and bark – and flourished a knotty club: these would be the traditional template for Leonardo's costume-design. (One recalls Zoroastro's 'outfit of gall-nuts'.) Contemporary accounts of the joust describe 'a great company of men on horses, accoutred like wild men, with huge drums and raucous trumpets'. Sanseverino himself carried a golden shield painted with an image of a bearded man, thus a 'barbarian', and presented himself at the ducal dais announcing he was 'the son of the King of the Indians'. In 1491 this must refer to India itself rather than the New World – Columbus and his caravel Santa Maria had not yet left Spain – but it is prophetic of how the imagery of the wild man would become associated with native Americans. Onlookers particularly noted his splendid golden helmet with spiralled horns, and on top of it the figure of a winged serpent, with a long tail stretching right down to the back of his horse – a Leonardo 'dragon', in short. The whole ensemble 'demonstrated ferocity'.[7]

Like his dragons, Leonardo's wild men were designed to be bizarre and scary. Leonardo's theatrical work gives him access – in the way that paintings did not – to the purely fantastical, the exotic, the grotesque. In the *Trattato della pittura* he writes:

If the painter wishes to see beauties that charm him it lies in his power to create them, and if he wishes to see monstrous things which are frightening, or buffoonish, or ridiculous or really pitiable, he can be lord and creator thereof . . . If a painter wishes to depict creatures or devils in hell, with what an abundance of invention he teems.[8]

He uses the word 'painter' generically, but in fact none of his paintings contains this grotesque or hellish sort of material with which – so he says – his imagination 'teems'. (The nearest one gets are the *Adoration*, where the swirl of faces tends to the sinister, and the lost *Leda*, whose subject-matter is erotically grotesque.) It is in his drawings that his fantasy is given free rein, and most of his 'monstrous' creations on paper can be related to his role as a creator of masques and pageants. A typical example is the black-chalk sketch at Windsor showing a masquerader wearing an elephant's head with a trumpet coming out of the top of it, and playing a pipe or flute which is fashioned as the elephant's trunk. Possibly the whole apparatus is a kind of bagpipe, with the bag contained in the pot-belly of the costume and the overhead trumpet as the drone.[9]

The elephant-musician is witty, but other drawings are harder to fathom: they shift meanings as you look at them. A pair of animal masks seem to be nightmare versions of dogs: one a shaggy, demented-looking pug or Pekinese, the other an idiotic hound with coiffed hair, dead eyes, and a distended lower lip lolling open to reveal ovine teeth.[10] We are in horror-story terrain: strange laboratory hybrids. If you turn the 'pug' upside down the face becomes a bat. This creature has some kind of bit and bridle attached: this may indicate a mask to be worn by a costumed servant pulling a chariot or float. The drawing style suggests the early 1490s, so this was probably for a Sforza festivity also.

Leonardo's theatrical skills were remembered by his Milanese biographer Paolo Giovio, who describes him as 'the inventor and arbiter of all refinement and delights, especially theatrical ones'. This stresses the elegance of his creations – as no doubt seen in *Il Paradiso* – but there is this other, more bizarre side to them: these wild men and monsters which give vent to the darker fantasies of their creator. At the least these courtly ephemera offered Leonardo an excuse for a tonic bit of melodrama, so different from the cool, reined-in style of the Milan studio works.

These theatrical monsters and hybrids are closely akin to another genre in which he was particularly active in the late 1480s and early 1490s – his

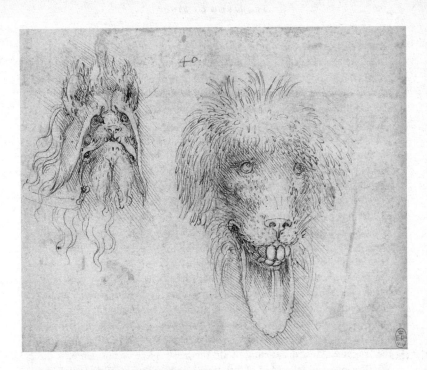

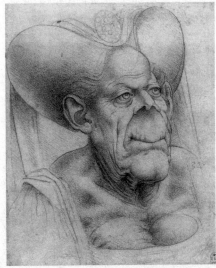

*Monsters. Two festive masks of
the 1490s (above), and a
grotesque portrait of an old
woman, in a later copy by
Francesco Melzi.*

grotesques, showing hideously exaggerated and caricatured features, particularly of old men and women, mostly in profile, mostly in pen and ink. There is an element of satire in them: a private revenge, perhaps, on the snobberies and pomposities of court life. But while some may be caricatures of specific individuals, more often they seem to be pure meditations on ugliness and deformity, suggesting a slightly obsessive fascination with, in his own words, the 'buffoonish, ridiculous and really pitiable'. These swollen, elongated, imploded faces are the flip side of his Vitruvian studies of ideal human proportions: paradigms of physiological discord. They are scattered through the Windsor collection, some original and some by a copyist, probably Francesco Melzi. The copies, which catch the humour but not the nuances, could appear without demur in a children's comic like the *Beano*. Engravings of Leonardo's grotesques by Wencelaus Hollar circulated in England in the seventeenth century; one of these – a corpulent, frog-like dame – has passed into English visual folklore as the Ugly Duchess in Tenniel's illustrations for *Alice in Wonderland*.[11]

The *cartone*, or cartoon, has a Quattrocento meaning, but these grotesques of Leonardo's are essentially cartoons in the modern sense. They are antecedents of the merciless physiological exaggeration found in cartoonists from Gillray to Robert Crumb, and they have the capacity of great cartoons to be funny and then something more: there is a stratum of disquiet amid the laughter. Most disquieting of all, the masterpiece of this genre, is the Windsor pen-and-ink group of five grotesque heads, generally dated to the early 1490s (Plate 18). The drawing is intrinsically dramatic, but the narrative of the scene is unclear, and this elusiveness of meaning compounds the air of threat which emanates from the drawing. Something is happening here, but you don't know what it is: it is like a scene from a nightmare or hallucination, or indeed a lunatic asylum – one thinks of the mad courtroom scene in *King Lear*, or of Peter Weiss's *Marat/Sade*. The central character is crowned with a wreath of oak leaves, as if a victorious Roman emperor, but you know from looking at him that he is not an emperor, just a deluded old man who somehow thinks he is. Around him press four figures in a mode collectively menacing: two full-face figures, one manically laughing or yelling, the other fixedly or inanely curious, and two figures either side of him, one hideous, hook-nosed and blubbery, the other a thin malevolent crone with gap-teeth and a headscarf. Both are usually described as women, though this seems to me ambiguous. The old man is the centre of their attention: there is a sense of malevolent encouragement – the hand of the crone on the left seems to push and hold him there in the centre of the group. Comedy, derision, cruelty, pathos: the viewer is left to choose his reaction.

The old man with his toothless 'nutcracker' profile is a recurrent character in Leonardo's sketchbooks, and here (as elsewhere) one feels it to be a kind of cipher of Leonardo himself: the impotent, paltry, self-deluding figure who is the dark twin of the great Renaissance achiever.

The drawing was famous, and the figures are closely echoed in two paintings by the contemporary Flemish master Quentin Massys, and later in engravings by Hollar.[12] In the eighteenth century the four figures surrounding the old man were seen as 'illustrations of the passions', or of the four 'temperaments' or 'humours'. Jean-Paul Richter gave this a more modern, psychiatric twist, claiming they represented (from right to left) dementia, obstinacy, lunacy and imbecility, with the crowned central figure a 'personification of megalomania'.[13] These interpretations seem too schematic. Martin Clayton, the current librarian at Windsor, has recently titled the drawing, *A Man Tricked by Gypsies*. He interprets the creature to the right as reading the old man's palm. There has probably been some loss of paper along the right-hand edge, but what remains of the man's arm and the woman's hand could certainly suggest this. The woman on the left, whom Kenneth Clark interpreted as 'putting her arm round the central figure', is in Clayton's view reaching round under his sleeve to steal his purse. He relates this to various contemporary accounts of gypsy trickery, and particularly to an edict of April 1493 ordering the banishment of gypsies from Milan, 'on pain of the gallows', because of their criminal behaviour as 'bandits, ruffians and charlatans'.[14] It is possible that the drawing belongs in this context of official hostility to the gypsies – indeed, it is possible that Leonardo himself had some experience of their wiles. In a list of household expenses in the Codex Atlanticus occurs the surprising notation 'for telling a fortune . . . 6 soldi', and in the Madrid book-list are two works on chiromancy or palmistry ('*de chiromantia*' and '*de chiromantia da Milano*').[15]

This is a convincing interpretation, but one still feels there is more to the drawing – a surreal or psychotic aura which makes it more than a simple scene of street-trickery. A painting of about 1520 by Quentin Massys incorporates three of the figures from the drawing, but the scene he displays is a 'mock' or 'grotesque' betrothal: the figures based on the two 'gypsy women' are now decidedly more male than female, while the actual 'bride' of the painting is an androgynous figure with long wavy hair suggestive of another Leonardo type, so it is possible that the betrothal is homosexual. Coins are spilling out of the elderly bridegroom's money-bag: there is trickery afoot, but this is not a pickpocketing scene *per se*. I wonder if Massys knew something we don't about the references of Leonardo's drawing.

Giovanni Paolo Lomazzo, who assiduously collected memories of Leonardo in the decades after his death, recounts the following:

There is a story told by men of his time, who were his servants, that he once wished to make a picture of some laughing peasants (though in the event he did not paint it, but only did a drawing). He picked out certain men whom he thought fitted the bill, and having become acquainted with them he arranged a party for them, with the help of some friends, and sitting down opposite them, he started to tell them the craziest and most ridiculous things in the world, in such a way that he made them fall about laughing. And so without them knowing he observed all their gestures and their reactions to his ridiculous talk, and impressed them on his mind, and after they had left he retired to his room, and there made a perfect drawing which moved people to laughter when they looked at it, just as much as if they were listening to Leonardo's stories at the party.

One cannot quite discern the 'Five heads' in this – only two of the heads are laughing, and anyway the mood is different – but the story encapsulates the idea of Leonardo's belief in first-hand observation, the underpinning of visual reportage which makes even these surreal drawings so vivid and tactile. Cristoforo Giraldi, a Ferrarese at the court in Milan, a contemporary of Leonardo's, says much the same:

When Leonardo wished to depict some figure . . . he went to the places where he knew people of that kind gathered, and he observed their faces and manners, and their clothing, and the way they moved their bodies. And when he found something which seemed to be what he was after, he recorded it in metalpoint pen in a little book which he always had hanging at his belt.[16]

⇥ 'OF SHADOW AND LIGHT' ⇤

'On 23 April 1490 I began this book' – the 'book' being the manuscript now known as Paris MS C. It is composed of fourteen sheets, folded to form twenty-eight folios; the paper is large-format, quite thin, and bears a curious watermark consisting of a small circle with two wavy lines – it looks like a tadpole with two tails, but the reference is doubtless to the Visconti serpent, a traditional Milanese emblem. This is the first of Leonardo's manuscripts which can be described as a concerted treatise: its subject is the behaviour of light. It is summed up by Francesco Melzi as 'a book of shadow and light'.[17] But though it has a lot of detailed material on this subject, Leonardo cannot stay on one track for long, and there are plenty of notes and drawings on other topics – physics, acoustics, games and jokes, water, and so on. Some pages contain small, highly specific drawings of objects (hammers, bells, knives, a wine-barrel, an axe splitting a log, etc.) which are a relief from the austere diagrams of the main text. It is a highly scientific work: a rigorous blend of optics and geometry. The writing is neat; the diagrams are painstaking, with subtle gradations of light and shade suggested by meticulous parallel hatching in pen and ink. It comes to us direct from Leonardo's desk at the Corte Vecchia in 1490–91, broadly contemporary with his portrait of the musician, with its bold *chiaroscuro* ('bright and dark') effects.

Like the anatomical treatise planned in 1489, Leonardo's 'book of shadow and light' is part of his complete-science-for-the-painter project, and belongs within the studio ethos of these years: the *maestro* imparts his wisdom. And, as with the early anatomy studies, there is a dangerous blossoming of the subject, a Hydra-like proliferation of the tasks in hand. It soon appears that the current text is only a beginning. On a closely written folio in the Codex Atlanticus is set down an ambitious programme for seven 'books' on the subject:

In my first proposition concerning shadows I state that every opaque body is surrounded, and its surface clothed, in shadow and light; and on this I build the first book. Then also, these shadows are in themselves composed of varying qualities of darkness, because they are caused by the absence of varying quantities of light rays; and these I call primary shadows [*ombre originale*], because they are the first shadows, which cover an object and are fastened on to it, and on this I will build my second book.

The third book will be on *ombre derivate*, or secondary shadows, and so on, through to the seventh.[18]

In another manuscript of this period Leonardo defines different kinds of light-source ('secondary light', 'luminous reverberation', etc.) and different qualities of light, such as the 'constrained air' (*aria restretta*) of light entering through a window, and the 'free light' (*lume libero*) out in the countryside.[19] He uses the word *perchussione* – percussion – for the falling or striking of light on an object. This conveys a sense of light as something dynamic. Elsewhere he defines light as one of the 'spiritual powers', in which 'spiritual' has the Aristotelian meaning of 'immaterial' or 'imperceptible': energy without mass.[20]

Thus drily and rather doggedly Leonardo sets out the rules for depicting shadow and light, which 'are the most certain means by which the shape of any body comes to be known' and are therefore essential to 'excellence in the science of painting'.[21] We find here the scientific basis of the most subtle and elusive effects of Leonardo's *sfumato* or 'smoky' style, in which (in his own definition) 'shadows and highlights fuse without hatching or strokes, as does smoke'.[22] This nuanced style of *sfumatura* is exemplified in the *Mona Lisa*, in which it becomes something more than a depiction of light and shade – it is a mood or atmosphere, an autumnal suffusion of transience and regret. The gradations of *sfumatura* are also a mode of depicting distance, and thus an adjunct to perspective. In the *Trattato* Leonardo considers the depiction of things as they are 'lost because of distance' – nearer objects are 'bounded by evident and sharp boundaries', while those more distant have 'smoky, blurred boundaries'.[23] He calls this the '*prospettivo de' perdimenti*' – 'the perspective of loss' (as distinct from the perspective of size). This resonant phrase again suggests a mental atmosphere as much as a visual phenomenon: the distances that stretch behind the figure of Mona Lisa are a poetic distillation of this 'perspective of loss'.

Also on his desk at this time was a smaller, thicker notebook, in standard octavo format, now Paris MS A. It originally had 114 folios, consecutively numbered by Leonardo, but it later suffered from the attentions of Count Libri, who tore out a section of fifty folios, of which seventeen have never been seen since.[24] MS A is essentially a painter's manual, though very different from the traditional Florentine manuals like Cennino Cennini's. It deals directly with painting techniques, and treats various subjects – optics, perspective, proportion, movement, mechanics, etc. – from a painter's point of view. It also has more on the subject of light and shade, including this, which makes one think once again of the *Mona Lisa*:

When you wish to make a portrait of someone do it in dull weather, or as evening falls . . . See in the street towards evening, or when the weather is bad, how much grace and sweetness can be seen in the faces of the men and women. Therefore, O painter, use a courtyard where the walls are coloured black, with some kind of overlapping roof . . . and when it is sunny it should be covered with an awning. Alternatively work on the painting towards evening, or when it is cloudy or misty, and this will be the perfect atmosphere.[25]

These are the practicalities of Leonardo's more subtle and sombre tonality, so different from the sharp-edged, sunlit aesthetic of his Florentine training.

Among the technical details to which the notebook is mainly devoted there is an unexpected glimpse of Leonardo's imaginative processes, the 'arousing' as he puts it, 'of the mind to inventions':

Look at any wall marked with various stains, or at a stone with variegated patterns, and you will see therein a resemblance to various landscapes . . . or to battles with figures darting about, or strange-looking faces and costumes: an endless variety of things which you can distil into finely rendered forms. And the same thing that happens with walls and stones can happen with the sound of bells, in whose peal you will find any name or word you care to imagine.[26]

The same idea surfaces, in different wording, in the *Trattato*, where it is part of one of his disputes with Botticelli: 'Merely throwing a sponge soaked in various colours at a wall will leave a stain in which a beautiful landscape can be seen . . . I say that a man may seek out in such a stain the heads of men, animals, battles, rocks, seas, clouds, woods and other similar things.' This kind of visual fantasy or free association channels into productivity that side of Leonardo which is the dreamer and the drifter: 'confused things kindle the mind to great inventions'.[27]

In MS A we find the first blueprint for the *Trattato della pittura*, and it was used by Melzi more extensively than any other source when compiling material for the *Trattato*. Leonardo himself may have elaborated the note-book into a more formal text. In 1498, in the dedicatory epistle of *Divina proportione*, the mathematician Luca Pacioli states that Leonardo has 'already finished' a 'worthy book on painting and human motion' (*degno libro de pictura e movimenti humani*). This may be the same as the 'book' referred to later by Lomazzo, who speaks of Leonardo discussing the relative merits of painting and sculpture 'in a book of his which I read a few years ago, which he wrote with his left hand, at the request of Ludovico Sforza, Duke of Milan'. This comparison between painting and sculpture, which features at the beginning of the *Trattato*, is found in draft form in MS A. These comments suggest that sometime before 1498 Leonardo copied material from MS A into a 'book' – i.e. a bound manuscript – for the delectation of the Moor.[28]

On the first page of MS A is a small drawing showing the 'shadow made by a man', illustrating a point about the penumbra of shadows. Beneath it the explanatory text begins, 'If the window *a–b* lets sunlight into a room, the sun will make the window appear bigger and will also diminish the shadow of a man, in such a way that when the man compares this reduced shadow of himself with . . .' I omit the rest, which gets complicated, because an incidental point is altogether more arresting. This tiny perfunctory sketch is a kind of self-portrait: the man whose shadow will be shaped 'exactly as shown above' must also be the man who is making the drawing, and that man is certainly Leonardo da Vinci. It does not show his features, only his

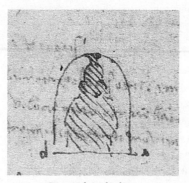

Leonardo's shadow.

silhouette, 'clothed' in shadow, as he stands in front of an arched window, perhaps at the Corte Vecchia, on a sunny day in the early 1490s.

The carefully laid-out pages of the Paris notebooks C and A, with blocks of text and illustrations, suggest that Leonardo had in mind something similar to the technical manuscripts of Francesco di Giorgio Martini, the Sienese architect and engineer. Leonardo certainly knew these – one which he actually owned is now in the Biblioteca Laurenziana in Florence, with his notes and doodles in the margin[29] – and the fact that Martini was in Milan at this time makes me think the influence is specific. He was certainly there by 1489, when he was preparing a model for the *tiburio* of the cathedral, and in the summer of 1490 he and Leonardo travelled together to Pavia. Martini was now in his early fifties, a man of immense experience. We have some interesting details of the trip, and a strong sense that Leonardo enjoyed it – a break from the easel and the desk.

In early June 1490 Martini was invited by the works department of Pavia cathedral to advise about rebuilding works there, and at Ludovico's suggestion Leonardo went with him. On about 18 June they set off from Milan, on horseback, with a retinue of 'engineers, associates and servants', among which we may perhaps include Zoroastro, the resident engineer and special-effects man of Leonardo's entourage. It is no great distance to Pavia: about 20 miles. On arrival they put up at an inn called Il Saracino (The Saracen). Their bill, amounting to 20 lire, was settled by the *fabbriceria* on 21 June: the document describes them as having been 'invited for a consultation' – they are consultants.[30]

Politically a satellite of Milan, Pavia was a small, proud city which called itself *civitas centum turrium*, the city of a hundred towers. Its famous university, founded in the fourteenth century, included Petrarch and Christopher Columbus among its alumni. The place seems to have invigorated Leonardo. I have already mentioned his elated reaction to the equestrian statue, *Il Regisole*, which set in train new thoughts for the Sforza Horse, but there are many other small traces of the visit in his notebook, and these in turn reflect back to us an image of Leonardo himself, on this pleasant-seeming summer jaunt, observing and inquiring, penetratingly interested in everything. Here he is down on the riverside, watching some excavation-works:

I was watching them strengthening the foundations of a stretch of the old walls of Pavia, which are on the banks of the Ticino. Of the old piles which were there, those of oak were as black as charcoal, while the ones made of alder were as red as brazil-wood [*verzino*], and were still quite heavy, and hard as iron, and not stained at all.[31]

And here he is outside the old Visconti castle, observing that 'The chimneys have six rows of openings, each distant from the next by one braccio.' We follow him into the castle's famous library, assembled by Galeazzo Visconti II, where he finds a manuscript by the Polish mathematician Witelo, and notes, 'In Vitolone there are 805 conclusions in perspective.' Later, back in Milan, he will write, 'Try to get Vitolone, which is in the library at Pavia, and which treats of mathematics.'[32] The manuscript coveted by Leonardo cannot be identified, as the contents of Pavia library were dispersed during the French occupation of 1500.

Among these Pavian notes is an unexpected little sketch: a swift ground-plan marked *lupinario* – a brothel. Is this from Pavia too? Did he visit it? Perhaps. If not for the traditional reason, then because a brothel was as worthy of interest as a cathedral or a riverside building-site or a manuscript by the learned Witelo. Also because brothels were a likely, indeed traditional, source of artist's models – I will look later at the possibility that the model for Leonardo's lost *Leda* was a prostitute.

⤜ LITTLE DEVIL ⤛

I fed you with milk like my own son.
Codex Atlanticus, fol. 220v–c

Leonardo was back in Milan by mid-July, as is shown by a note, written in an offhand style which conceals its emotional significance: '*Jachomo vene a stare cho mecho il dí della madalena nel mille 490*' – 'Giacomo came to live with me on St Mary Magdalen's day [22 July] 1490.'[33]

'Giacomo' was a ten-year-old boy from Oreno, near Monza, a few miles north of Milan. His full name was Giovanni Giacomo (or Giangiacomo) di Pietro Caprotti, but he is better known to the world by his nickname, Salai. Not much is known of his father, Pietro: he was certainly not well-off, and we know of no connection with a trade, but he may not have been quite the humble peasant – nor Giacomo quite the *enfant sauvage* – that is usually depicted. In a legal document Pietro is described as '*filius quondam domini Joannis*' – 'son of the late Master Giovanni'. The honorific '*dominus*' is loose, but suggests that Salai's grandfather Giovanni, after whom he was named, owned some land and had some status. At any rate, Pietro was prepared to pay for Giacomo's upkeep at the studio of the great Leonardo da Vinci – perhaps because the boy showed talent; perhaps because he wanted to be rid of him; perhaps because Leonardo had spotted him and wanted him. Giacomo seems to have been an only son, though there is a pair of greedy sisters who appear later in the story.[34]

The boy was taken on, presumably, as a *famiglio* – servant, errand-boy, dogsbody and, frequently, studio model – but also with a view to training him up as a painter, and indeed he became a very competent painter in the 'Leonardesco' mould. He was also, in the meantime, what we would now-adays call a handful, or indeed a right little tearaway, and it was not long before he had acquired his lifelong nickname, Salai. It first appears in a note of payment written by Leonardo in January 1494. The name means 'Little Devil' or 'Demon', or perhaps 'Imp' – linguistically it appears to be an import from Arabic; more immediately it occurs in Luigi Pulci's evergreen comic epic *Morgante maggiore*, a work which appears in every book-list Leonardo compiled. The diminutive, Salaino, was also used, causing later confusion with the Leonardesco painter Andrea Solario: a mythical 'Andrea Salaino' flits through nineteenth-century accounts of Leonardo's circle in Milan.[35]

The list of Giacomo's misdemeanours during his first year of service or pupillage at the Corte Vecchia is probably the longest continuous account of another person's activities to be found in all Leonardo's writings. (I exclude his attempts at literary narrative.) Its intention is precisely an account, since it itemizes the expenses arising from the boy's misdeeds; it also includes a list of his clothing expenses. The last date in it is September 1491, and it seems to have been written at a single sitting – the ink colour is a uniform dark brown – so the whole passage was actually written down about fourteen months after Giacomo's arrival. It was no doubt intended for the father, who was to foot the bill, but it acquires *in extenso* a curiously personal coloration, a tone of exasperated fondness, so that what is intended as a rather crotchety list of complaints achieves a quality almost of reverie.

The narrative begins 'on the second day', i.e. Monday 23 July:

On the second day I had 2 shirts cut for him, a pair of stockings and a jerkin, and when I put aside the money to pay for these things he stole the money out of my purse, and I could never make him confess, though I was quite certain of it.   *4 lire*

The day after this I went to supper with Giacomo Andrea, and the aforesaid Giacomo ate for 2, and did mischief for 4, in so far as he broke three table-flasks, and knocked over the wine, and after this he came to supper where I . . . [sentence unfinished]

Item. On 7 September he stole a pen worth 22 soldi from Marco who was living with me. It was a silverpoint pen, and he took it from his [Marco's] studio, and after Marco had searched all over for it, he found it hidden in the said Giacomo's chest.   *1 lira*

Item. On 26 January following, I was at the house of Messer Galeazzo da San Severino, arranging the pageant for his joust, and certain footmen had undressed to try on costumes for the wild men in the pageant. One of them left his purse lying on a bed, among some clothes, and Giacomo got to it and took all the money he could find in it.   *2 lire 4 soldi*

Item. At that same house Maestro Agostino da Pavia gave me a Turkish hide to have a pair of short boots made, and within a month this Giacomo had stolen it from me, and sold it to a shoemaker for 20 soldi, and with the money, as he himself confessed to me, he bought aniseed sweets.   *2 lire*

Item. Again, on 2 April, Giovan Antonio [Boltraffio] having left a silver-point on top of one of his drawings, this Giacomo stole it. And this was of the value of 24 soldi.   *1 lira 4 soldi*

In the margin, summing it all up, Leonardo writes four words: *ladro bugiardo ostinato ghiotto* – thief, liar, obstinate, greedy. Thus Giacomo's very bad report. But is there not a twinkle in the *maestro*'s eye as he delivers it?

The account finishes with a list of clothing expenses, from which it appears that Salai was furnished with one cloak, six shirts, three jerkins, four pairs of stockings, one lined doublet, twenty-four pairs of shoes, a cap and some laces, at a total cost of 32 lire. This list of clothing expenses is headed 'The First Year', and like the rest of the document, seems balanced between accountancy and romance.

This picaresque narration of mischief and thievery has almost an air of silent-movie comedy: the artful dodger in action, with suitable tiptoeing music from the piano accompaniment. It is full also of wonderful detail – the aniseed gobstoppers, the Turkish leather, the purse on the bed, the little flasks of oil broken on the floor. But perhaps the most telling entry is the second: 'I went to supper with Giacomo Andrea, and the aforesaid Giacomo ate for 2 . . .' This supper was probably at the house of the architect Giacomo

Andrea da Ferrara: Leonardo is a guest, and little Giacomo accompanies him. This is two days after his arrival in the studio. What is his status on this summer evening? Leonardo's diminutive attendant? His amusing mascot? His new little pretty-boy? Despite his unruly behaviour, he is brought along again, on another evening – 'after this he came to supper where I . . .' – but Leonardo lets the sentence trail away. Perhaps best, in this document to be read by Salai's father, not to dwell on these extramural jaunts. The keynote here is companionship: Giacomo is with him, at his side. Leonardo enters here on the longest relationship of his adult life, for Salai will remain a continuous presence in his inner circle for twenty-eight years. However, it is not quite clear when they last saw one another: Salai was not a witness of Leonardo's will in 1519. Their last parting may have been a break-up, though if so it did not alter Leonardo's generous provision in his will.

For Leonardo this rough diamond, this *gamin*, seems to answer a need. He is 'Salaino', his 'Little Devil', a sprite of misrule. There is almost a sense of projection: that this part of Leonardo's own make-up – the practical joker, the wayward idler – is incarnated in the form of impish young Giacomo, and he himself is thus freed of it, that he may devote himself to the more rigorous and ill-humoured business of work, study and experimentation. Bad Giacomo is Leonardo's scapegrace.

That it was also a homosexual relationship cannot really be doubted, though proponents of an improbably saintly Leonardo have argued that his life was celibate. Vasari comments on Salai's beauty: 'In Milan Leonardo took for his servant [*creato*] a Milanese named Salai, who was extraordinarily graceful and attractive. He had beautiful hair, curled and ringletted, in which Leonardo delighted.' This says a lot without actually saying it. Lomazzo is blunter, albeit through the literary veil of an imagined 'dialogue' between Leonardo and the antique sculptor Phidias. Phidias refers to Salai as one of Leonardo's 'favourite pupils', and asks, 'Did you ever play with him that "backside game" which Florentines love so much?' To which Leonardo replies: 'Many times! You should know that he was a very fair young man, especially around the age of fifteen.' Lomazzo is a tricky but well-informed source: he seems to be saying that on reaching adolescence Salai became Leonardo's sexual partner. The Freudian view is that the homosexual's love of young boys (or boyishly pretty young men) is an unconscious recreation of his own childhood, and thus of the lost emotional climate of maternal love. Again we arrive at an idea of identification: that when he looks at the face of Salai Leonardo half-consciously sees himself as he was when he was a boy. Salai's mother was also called Caterina: another link in this psychological chain.

And we can surely look at Salai's face as well. Caution is required, because some drawings have been described as portraits of Salai when they cannot possibly be. The earliest of these, on a Windsor sheet with a Florentine Madonna and Child, were drawn around the time he was born. An epicene young man in profile, also in Windsor, is dated on stylistic grounds to the late 1480s and cannot be him either.[36] The portraits which have a real claim to be of Salai are similar to these but have individualizing characteristics. In other words he had a certain look which resembled Leonardo's often-doodled ideal of male beauty, which is precisely what attracted Leonardo to him.

The most plausible portraits are the twinned profiles in Windsor, the one to the right in a mixture of red and black chalk on pinkish prepared paper, the other to the left (illustrated here) in black chalk on white paper. He differs from what Clark calls 'the Verrocchiesque boys of Leonardo's early work' in the rounder, more sensual chin, and in the hairstyle, which is shorter and more tightly curled – precisely the feature Vasari singles out: 'He had beautiful hair, curled and ringletted, in which Leonardo delighted.' Particularly idiosyncratic is the smooth line of his brow – that undented flow between the forehead and the bridge of the nose. On stylistic grounds, such as the subtle handling of the chalk, the drawings are dated around 1508, the beginning of Leonardo's second sojourn in Milan. They would show Salai in his late twenties – a languorous, rather exquisite young man who retains a deceptively boyish look. He has heavy-lidded eyes, registering halfway between amusement and boredom. You can see him today lounging in the piazza or nipping through narrow streets on a *motorino*.

Earlier versions of this distinctive profile are found in a drawing attributed to Boltraffio, showing a young man crowned with a garland of oak leaves, and in an engraving of an androgynous figure in profile in the British Museum.[37] The latter bears the logo 'ACHA. LE. VI.' (i.e. Achademia Leonardi Vinci), which points to the late 1490s: I will look at this elusive Milanese 'academy' in a later chapter. These works emanate from Leonardo's studio, and may possibly be versions of a lost Leonardo drawing of Salai done at this time. Boltraffio's moody *Narcissus*, known in two versions (Uffizi and National Gallery, London), has the same browless profile and ringletted hair.

If these are based on Salai, so too is the young man in the double portrait in red chalk by Leonardo at the Uffizi: the characteristic line of the brow is just visible beneath a fringe of thick curls. He is gazed on intently by an old bald man with the characteristic toothless profile. The old man's right hand

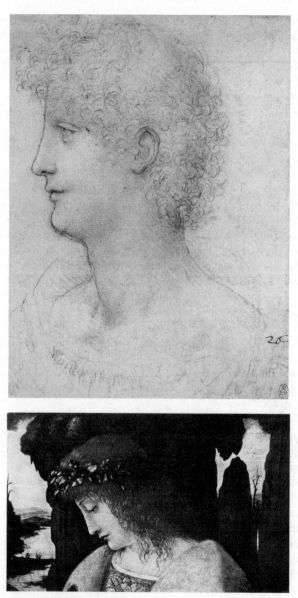

The Salai look. Profile portrait in black chalk at Windsor (above), and the Narcissus *by Boltraffio.*

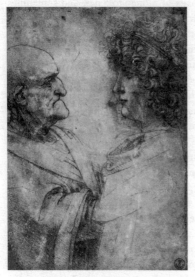

Old man gazing on beautiful youth,
c. 1497–1500.

seems to rest on the youth's shoulder, but the forearm has not been drawn, so the two bodies merge into a single torso, recalling the allegorical drawings of Pleasure and Pain. This drawing is also dated to the late 1490s, showing Salai in his late teens. There is an overtone of rueful comedy, as in that first memorandum of misdeeds, but now the humour has self-deprecation and pathos in it. The old man gazes across a gulf of time at this boy whom he loves, this boy who is a mirror of his own lost boyhood. Leonardo was at this point in his mid-forties, a man still in his prime, but here (as elsewhere) he cartoons himself as this geriatric 'nutcracker man'. This may be an imagery of sexual uncertainty: the man who wishes to be a lover finds himself instead a superannuated father-figure. The tone of the drawing suggests the wistful fondness of a sugar-daddy for his arrogant toyboy.

Salai grew up from the artful dodger of 1490 to become the stylish and not entirely trustworthy young man whom one sees in these portraits. The documents support the sugar-daddy notion, as the usually frugal Leonardo splashes out on finery for his spoiled young protégé. A note headed 'Salaino expenses', dated 4 April 1497, records the gift of a particularly snazzy cloak:

4 braccia of silver cloth	15 lire 4 soldi
green velvet for the trim	9 lire
ribbons	9 soldi
small rings	12 soldi
for the making	1 lira 5 soldi
ribbon for the front stitching	5 soldi

After totting these up, Leonardo adds, 'Salai stole the soldi,' presumably meaning he kept the change. Later Salai gets three gold ducats 'which he said he needed in order to buy a pair of rose-coloured stockings with their trimmings'. Leonardo also notes loans of money to Salai, and sometimes there are smaller sums lent by Salai to Leonardo. In October 1508 'I lent thirteen crowns to Salai to complete his sister's dowry.'[38] And then there was the saga of the house outside the Porta Vercellina, given to Leonardo by the Moor in about 1497, leased to Salai's father after Leonardo's departure from Milan, and by degrees seeming to become Salai's own property or usufruct, which he rents out and refurbishes, and which is formally bequeathed to him and his successors 'in all perpetuity' in Leonardo's will.[39]

Gifts are the currency of this relationship. One can see Salai as a rather avaricious young man: he milks the generosity and fondness of his master. There are quarrels, too, and reconciliations. On a sheet of the Codex Atlanticus we read the following: 'Salai, I want to rest, so no wars, no more war, because I surrender.' (The words are not in Leonardo's hand; they are oddly appended to a shopping-list, as if the person writing the list had at that moment heard or overheard them.)[40] But other qualities shine through their long relationship. Salai is pupil, servant, copyist, catamite, companion, factotum, favourite, confidant – providing the 'good and kind services' for which he is remembered in Leonardo's will. From the moment of his arrival in the summer of 1490 this bad boy with the face of an angel is an inseparable part of Leonardo's retinue: his shadow.

→→ HUNTING BEARS ←←

On Sunday 15 April 1492 Leonardo celebrated his fortieth birthday. What he felt about this, if anything, is unrecorded. On 12 October 1492 Columbus sighted land – probably Watling's Island in the Bahamas – on his westward journey across the 'Ocean Sea', and thereafter landed at Haiti and Cuba. No trace either of this momentous news, which buzzed through Europe after Columbus's return in March 1493.

That Leonardo left no comment on the discovery and exploration of the New World is curious in one so committed to other kinds of discovery.[41] His interest in exotic travel was remarkably slight, and his own ambit was small – he did not travel much further south than Rome, and he left Italy for the first and only time when he was sixty-four. (It used to be thought he had visited Constantinople in c. 1502–3, but the evidence does not add up.) One could counter this by saying he was a voyager of the mind; or, less rhetorically, by saying he was an intensive traveller of relatively short journeys, each of them for a man of his curiosity a *lungissima via* of impressions and experiences – raw empirical data to be noted and pondered.

Leonardo loved to be physically on the move, on foot or on horseback. One recalls his clarion-call to the painter: you must 'quit your home in town, and leave your family and friends, and go over the mountains and valleys into the country' – words written down around this time, and preserved in Melzi's transcription in the *Trattato*.

Looking north from the roof of Milan's cathedral, or from the towers of the Corte Vecchia, his eye would trace the dramatic peaks of the Alpine mountain-range called Le Grigne. On at least three occasions, and probably more, Leonardo journeyed up into the Alps: the earliest of these treks can be dated to the early 1490s. There are probably engineering contexts for these trips – the study of water-courses for canalization projects; the surveying of mineral deposits; the perennial search for timber – but a fascination with mountains was evident in the *Madonna of the Carnation* of the early 1470s, and is so much a feature of his late work, so we can guess that these treks were experiences he valued for their own sake: an adventure, an escape from the city, an immersion in pure natural forms.

The transit point was the lakeside town of Lecco. The old road between Lecco and Milan is known as the Carraia del Ferro, the Iron Road, because it brought down ore from the quarries of the Valsassina. Views from this road looking north-east to the Grigne compare closely with drawings of a mountain range in the Windsor collection, and Lecco itself may be depicted in a dramatic, stormy drawing which is a kind of Alpine equivalent of the sweeping Tuscan landscape of the 'Madonna of the Snow' sheet. A town is seen in the middle distance, framed by forbidding peaks; a lake – perhaps the Lago di Lecco – is glimpsed beyond, half-hidden in the cloudburst. In the *Trattato della pittura*, among the subtle effects which the painter can represent and the sculptor cannot, is listed 'rains behind which can be discerned cloudy mountains and valleys'.[42]

These drawings belong to later trips, but from Lecco northward we have the remnants of Leonardo's own travel-notes from a journey or journeys made in the early 1490s.[43] They were probably written up afterwards – the paper shows no sign of having been carried through the mountains. This is a brisk topographical report on the Alpine region around Lake Como, but just beneath the surface of the text we sense Leonardo da Vinci on the trail: a tall figure, punctiliously kitted out, part of an expedition, probably, but somehow solitary within it. He walks with an easy rhythm, pausing often to note and to sketch in one of those little books he had always 'at his belt'. The terseness of the text in part reflects its status as a report, but catches also the highly focused acuity of his observations.

Above Lecco looms the southern range of the Grigne, dominated by

Mount Mandello: 'The largest bare rocks that are to be found in this part of the country are on Mount Mandello ... It has at its base an opening towards the lake, which goes down 200 steps. Here at all times there is ice and wind.' The 200-step descent he describes is a mule-trail which can still be seen.[44] It snakes along the side of the mountain above Rongio, following the course of the Meria river. Where the river forks it goes up steeply, on steps, to a grotto which is probably the 'opening towards the lake' described by Leonardo.

North and east of the Grigne massif, the party enters the Valsassina:

In Val Sasina, between Vimognio and Introbbio, on the right-hand side as you go in by the road from Lecco, you find the Troggia river, which falls from a very tall rock, and where it falls it goes underground and the river ends there. Three miles further on there are mines of copper and silver near a place called Prato Santo Pietro, and mines of iron, and fantastical things ... Here *mapello* grows abundantly, and there are great rock-falls and waterfalls.

This *mapello* is a variety of aconite, *Aconitum napellus*, still common in the area, and known locally as *mapel*.[45] The plant appears in the *Virgin of the Rocks*, at the left shoulder of the Virgin, and *mapello* also occurs in Leonardo's recipe for 'deadly smoke'.

Higher and deeper he goes, into the Valtellina, north-east of Lake Como.

The Valtellina, as it is called, is a valley enclosed in high and terrible mountains ... This is the valley through which the Adda flows, having first run more than 40 miles through Germany. In this river the fish called *temolo* breed; they live on silver, of which there is plenty be found in its sands ...

At the head of the Valtellina are the mountains of Bormio, terrible and always covered with snow. Here there are ermines [*ermellini*, but more probably, at this altitude, marmots] ...

At Bormio are hot springs, and about 8 miles above Como there is the Pliniana, which swells and ebbs every six hours, and its swell provides power for two mills, and its ebb makes the water dry up.

He later recalls this Fonte Pliniana (whose strange behaviour was first noted by Pliny the Elder, a native of Como) in the Codex Leicester. 'I have seen it myself,' he writes: 'when the water ebbs it falls so low that it's like looking at water down in a deep well.'[46]

Leonardo's notes touch on something other than the prodigious natural phenomena of the region. He is struck by the austere but well-adapted lifestyle of the upland people: the land is tough but fertile, and things taste good. In the Valtellina 'they make strong wine, in good quantities, but there are so many cattle that the locals will tell you they make more milk than wine.' And there are 'good inns' where you can dine well for a few soldi – 'The wine costs no more than one soldo a bottle, and a pound of veal one soldo, and salt ten denari, and butter the same, and you can get a basketful of eggs for one soldo.' Add some bread (which 'everyone here may sell', not just licensed bakers) and we have the ingredients of a delicious and recuperative Alpine dinner after a hard day's hiking. Good portions too: 'The pound up here has thirty ounces.'

The wildest area he describes in these notes is the 'Chiavenna valley' – in other words the valley of the Mera river, which flows down from Mount Chiavenna to debouch into Lake Como. The mountain is right up against the border with Switzerland: not far across the border is St Moritz.

In the Chiavenna valley . . . are very high barren mountains with huge rocks. Among these mountains you see the water-birds called *marangoni* [cormorants, but this seems unlikely; perhaps wild geese]. Here grow firs, larches and pines. There are deer, wild goats, chamois and terrible bears. It is impossible to climb up without going on hands and feet. The peasants go there at the time of the snows with huge devices to make the bears tumble down the slopes.

This is very vivid – scrabbling up the precipitous slopes; birds flying up from the pine woods. And those 'terrible bears' trapped by the locals with devices that make them '*traboccare giù*' – a dynamic verb: literally, 'to overflow' or 'spill over'; thus to fall face downward, as for instance into a hunter's pit or *trabocchetto*. The device is perhaps a system of trip-wires.

There is a drawing by Leonardo of a head of a bear, and another that is usually said to show a bear walking, though in neither case can one say for sure that the bear is alive.[47] The 'walking' animal could as easily be a dead bear suitably propped up, as in countless 'big-game hunter' photos; the extruded tongue and the turned-up eye in fact suggest this. A series of anatomical studies at Windsor, once unhelpfully catalogued as showing 'the foot of a monster' but since 1919 identified as the hind-leg of a bear, also belongs to this time.[48] Leonardo did not need to go into the Alps in order to see a bear – there were plenty brought into the city: live bears for perform-ance; dead bears for fur – but it seems likely that these drawings are connected with his experience of bear-hunting in the Chiavenna valley in the early 1490s.

Another Alpine expedition took him even higher, for in a note which argues that 'the blue we see in the air is not an intrinsic colour' but is caused by atmospheric effects, he writes, 'This may be seen, as I myself have seen it, by anyone who goes to the top of Monboso.' Opinions differ as to which mountain 'Monboso' is. The probable location is Monte Rosa, which seems also to have been known as Monte Boso (from the Latin *buscus*, wooded), particularly on its southern side, which is the side Leonardo would have climbed.[49] The highest peaks of Monte Rosa (15,200 ft) were not conquered till 1801, but Leonardo is probably not claiming to have been at the very top. He was there in July, he tells us, but the year is not specified. Even in July, he notes laconically, the ice was 'considerable'.

The all-important phrase in this note – the phrase implicit in all these notes concerning his Alpine excursions – is this: 'I myself have seen it.' He would understand the words of the great German physician Paracelsus, written in the 1530s: 'He who wishes to explore Nature must tread her books with his feet. Writing is learned from letters but Nature from land to land. One land, one page. Thus is the Codex Naturae, thus must its pages be turned.'[50]

↦ CASTING THE HORSE ↤

Here is a story to gladden every library-mole's heart. In February 1967 a specialist in early Spanish literature, Dr Jules Piccus of the University of Massachusetts, was in the Biblioteca Nacional in Madrid, looking for manuscripts of medieval ballads or *cancioneros*, when he came upon two stout volumes bound in red morocco leather, measuring about 9 by 5 inches. He was astonished to find that they contained a collection of drawings and writings described on the title-page, in a Spanish hand of the eighteenth century, as '*Tractados de fortificación, mecanica y geometra*' by '*Leonardo da Vinci pintor famoso*'. That the library had once contained these volumes was known to a handful of scholars – they are mentioned in a couple of early inventories – but they were thought to have been lost or stolen. As it now turned out they had merely been mislaid, as can happen in great and aged libraries: they had disappeared into the miasma of the stacks.[51]

The earliest of the various *tractados*, or treatises, bound together in the two volumes is a small notebook of seventeen folios which forms the last section of Madrid Codex II. It contains detailed notes and instructions for the casting of the Sforza Horse. Two dated pages give its approximate chronology. Leonardo began it on 17 May 1491, on which date he wrote, 'Here a record shall be kept of everything relating to the bronze horse now under construction.' On another page is the date 20 December 1493, recording his decision to cast the horse on its side rather than upside down.[52]

The practical construction of the Sforza Horse consisted of three distinct phases: the making of the full-scale model in clay; the creation of the mould or form, a wax impression of the model sandwiched between two refractory layers pinned together by an iron framework; and the final casting of the statue in bronze, using the 'lost-wax' process in which the wax impression is melted away and molten bronze is poured into the emptied cavity between the refractory layers.[53] As we have seen, Leonardo's conception of the statue had evolved from the grandiose but impractical idea of the rearing horse to the more conventional trotting or prancing horse. His enthusiastic response to the *Regisole* in June 1490 may mark the transition, though it seems that the earlier idea lingered in his mind, for in one of his drawings of a mould the horse is shown rearing. But most of the casting diagrams, including those in the Madrid notebook, show it trotting, and it is pretty certain this was the final form of the sculpture in Leonardo's mind. A sketch of a trotting horse *à la Regisole* has notes which sound almost like a sculptor's mantra:

> Simple and composed movement.
> Simple and composed force.[54]

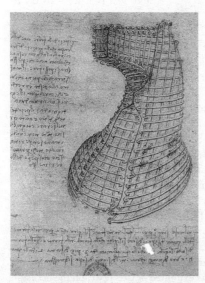

Armatured piece-mould of the head of the Sforza Horse, c. 1492.

He was working intensively on the construction of the mould in 1492. A sheet at Windsor has a sketch of the mould in two parts, and designs for the construction of pulleys and cogwheeled mechanisms, presumably for hoisting the mould.[55] The Madrid notebook has technical recipes:

Composition of the inside of the mould
Mix coarse river sand, ashes, ground brick, egg-white and vinegar together with your earth – but test it first.

Soaking the inside of the mould
As soon as you have re-baked the mould, soak it while still warm

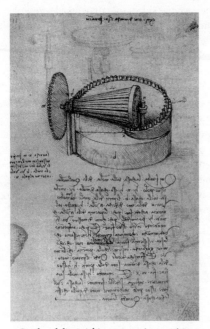

Study of diminishing power in a spring, from Madrid Codex I.

with Greek pitch, or linseed oil, or turpentine or tallow. Try each of them out and use whichever is best.

A meticulous red-chalk drawing shows the outer mould for the head and neck of the horse, held in place by the interlocking framework or 'armature' of wood and iron.[56]

In his *Life* of the Florentine architect Giuliano da Sangallo, Vasari says that Sangallo discussed the casting of the Horse with Leonardo, 'disputing the impossibility'. Documents show that Sangallo was indeed in Milan in October 1492.[57] The 'impossibility' would refer to Leonardo's decision – against traditional practice – to try to cast the horse as a single piece. Vasari thought (wrongly) that this was the reason for the non-completion of the statue: 'He carried the work forward on such a scale that it was impossible to finish it . . . It was so large that it proved an insoluble problem to cast it in one piece.'

Behind these technical notes and scribbled diagrams lie scenes of titanic industrial activity – the Corte Vecchia as a Vulcan's smithy: furnaces, kiln-pits, hoists and derricks, a scene reminiscent of that drawing of an artillery-foundry. One has to bear in mind the mountainous scale of the statue: it was 'colossal', in the words of Paolo Giovio, who probably saw the clay model as a boy. A measurement in the Madrid notebook shows that the Horse measured 12 braccia from hoof to head – that is, about 24 feet: the height of four tall men. The length between the hind fetlock and the raised foreleg would be about the same. Leonardo's Horse was thus something like three times lifesize. The quantity of bronze set aside for the final casting was 100 meira – about 75 tons.[58]

The clay model of the Horse was exhibited in late 1493, on the occasion of the marriage of Ludovico's niece Bianca to the Holy Roman Emperor,

Maximilian of Habsburg. The wedding was celebrated in Milan, by proxy, on 30 November. A clutch of celebratory poems was issued, all of them mentioning the Horse as part of their lauding of Ludovico. Baldassare Taccone writes:

> Vedi che in Corte fa far di metallo
> Per memoria del padre un gran colosso:
> I' credo fermamente e senza fallo
> Che Gretia e Roma mai vide el piu grosso.
> Guarde pur come è bello quel cavallo:
> Leonardo Vinci a farlo sol s'è mosso . . .

[See in the Corte how he [Ludovico] is having a great colossus made out of metal in memory of his father. I am certain that neither Greece nor Rome ever saw anything bigger. See how beautiful this horse is: Leonardo da Vinci alone has created it.]

As the bronze horse was never actually cast, Taccone must be referring to the model. Another rimester, Lancino Curzio, finds the horse so lifelike that he imagines it addressing some lines to an astonished observer.[59] Vasari: 'Those who saw the great clay model that Leonardo made considered that they had never seen a finer or more magnificent piece of work.'

By then Leonardo was already thinking about the casting process, for on 20 December 1493 he writes, 'I have decided that the horse should be cast without its tail, on its side, because if I were to cast it upside down the water would be only one braccio away, and . . . as the mould must stay underground for several hours, the head one braccio from the water would be affected by damp, and the cast would not take.'[60] These considerations refer to the pit in which the casting was to be done. To cast the horse upside down would require a pit 12 braccia deep, which would bring the head too close to the shallow water-table of the Lombard plain.

The creation of the great clay horse in 1492–3 is only a part of Leonardo's work as an engineer and mechanician, as is shown by the magnificent drawings in Madrid Codex I, begun on 1 January 1493 and worked at over a period of seven or eight years. On the cover-sheet Leonardo gives the notebook the title Libro di quantita e potentia (Book of Quantity and Force). It may also be the 'book on mechanical elements' and the 'technical book on physics' which he refers to elsewhere and which are otherwise unknown.[61] It is a marvellous manual of ingegni, a cornucopia of custom-made industrial devices – there are textile-machines and grain-mills and protypical windmills, and a spinning-wheel incorporating an automatic yarn-twisting mechanism, and various lifting-devices, including crane-hooks designed to disengage when the load touches the ground. But it is not primarily a book of inventions. Rather than showing complete working machines, it concentrates on the basic mechanical principles and move-ments involved. The remit is systematic and practical, geared towards the actuality of the assembly-line. Leonardo is quite literally getting down to nuts and bolts, not to mention chain-drives and belt-drives, universal joints and knuckle-joints, roller-bearings and disc-bearings, bi-directional screw-threads and epicycloidal gear-wheels. It is a boffin's paradise, as is conveyed infectiously by the first editor of the codices, Ladislaus Reti.

Leonardo's assistants are of interest here. The German Giulio (or Julius), who entered Leonardo's service in 1493, is mentioned in a note about disc-bearings supporting a horizontal axle: 'Giulio says he has seen two such wheels in Germany and they became worn around the spindle.'[62] And the metallurgist Tommaso Masini, or Zoroastro, was also an important assistant in these researches, as he no doubt was in the casting of the Horse. A note in one of the Forster notebooks tells us that 'Maestro Tommaso came back' in September 1492; he may have travelled up from Florence with Giuliano da Sangallo, with whom Leonardo was conversing the following month, 'disputing the impossibility' of the Horse. To Tommaso we might attribute the particular alloy of metals specified by Leonardo for the moving parts of a two-piece bearing-block. The material is essentially an 'anti-friction alloy', predating by centuries the substance patented by the American inventor Isaac Babbitt in 1839.[63]

Among the diagrams of Madrid I are drawings showing the moving parts of one of Leonardo's most fascinating creations – an automaton or robot in the form of a knight in armour. Mechanisms featuring gears with alterable teeth, and ingeniously compact motors regulated by a spindle, have been interpreted as part of the robot's 'programmable carriage'. This automatic knight was capable of bending its legs, moving its arms and hands, and turning its head. Its mouth opened, and an automatic drum-roll within the mechanism enabled it to 'talk'. There are sketches of the head and neck of this *cavaliere meccanica* in the Forster notebooks. It was exhibited in Milan in about 1495.[64] These automata become fairly common in popular and courtly *feste* in the sixteenth century, but Leonardo's seems to be one of the earliest. In fact his interest in automated movement goes back to his Floren-tine years. There is a sheet of technical drawings dating from the late 1470s which shows a wheeled platform powered by springs and controlled by a pinion-wheel. This was probably for use in Florentine pageants: it could carry some statue or carnivalesque effigy short distances. A reconstruction of it – dubbed in the press 'Leonardo's car' – was unveiled at Florence's History of Science Museum in April 2004. This earlier interest can be connected to one of Verrocchio's most popular creations – the putto which struck the hour on the clock at the Mercato Vecchio.[65] The principles of horology are an important background for Leonardo's automata, though according to Mark Rosheim, a NASA scientist who has reconstructed a working model of the robot-knight, Leonardo was moving far beyond the limitations of clockwork: his programmed carriage for automata is nothing less than 'the first known example in the story of civilization of the programmable analogue computer'.[66]

The knight is a wonderful blend of Leonardian enthusiasms – mechanics, anatomy, sculpture, theatre. He would create other such marvels, among them the mechanical lion which, in 1515, astonished King François I when it opened up to reveal a bunch of French lilies. Lomazzo says of this creature, 'it moved along by the power of its wheels', which for a moment gives an impression that he is explaining how it worked.[67]

⇢ 'CATERINA CAME . . .' ⇠

In the summer of 1493 a woman called Caterina arrived at the Corte Vecchia. She was still there early the following year, when she is mentioned in the household accounts. Then, probably in 1495, come the expenses of her funeral, also recorded by Leonardo.[68] We don't know who she was, but it is hard to resist the possibility that she was his mother, who in 1493 would have been in her mid-sixties, and since about 1490 a widow.

Leonardo records her arrival as follows:

On the 16th day of July.
Caterina came on the 16th day
Of July 1493.

One notes immediately the tic of repetition which is also found in the memorandum of his father's death a decade later. In the latter case it was interpreted by Freud as the psychological mechanism he calls 'perseveration', where deep emotions are sublimated or diverted into fussy repetitive action and 'indifferent detail'. 'The psychoanalyst', he writes, apropos Leonardo's note on his father's death, 'has learned long ago that such cases of forgetting or repetition are significant, and that it is the "distraction" which allows impulses that are otherwise hidden to be revealed.' This 'perseveration' is thus kin to the more famous 'Freudian slip', in which linguistic errors reveal a suppressed text.[69]

The account of Caterina's funeral is precisely a bland piece of accountancy. Here again one might discern that diversionary focus on 'indifferent detail':

Funeral expenses for Caterina

3 pounds of wax	27 soldi
For the bier	8 s
A pall over the bier	12 s
For carrying and placing the cross	4 s
For carrying the coffin	8 s
For 4 priests and 4 clerks	20 s
Bell, book and sponge	2 s
For the gravediggers	16 s
To the elder [*antiano*]	8 s
For the licence from the authorities	1 s
[Subtotal]	106 s
The doctor	5 s
Sugar and candles	12 s
[Total]	123 s

This is not an extravagant funeral. The costs amount to a little over 6 lire – he would spend four times that amount on a fancy silver cloak for Salai in 1497. The quantity of wax for tapers is 3 pounds; for his own funeral he would stipulate 40 pounds (10 pounds of wax 'in thick tapers' to be placed in each of four churches).

We cannot be certain that 'Caterina' was his mother, but if she wasn't who was she? Elsewhere in the notebooks those who come into his household to stay or live with him are all male: assistants, apprentices, servants. It was legally impossible for Caterina to have been an apprentice, and unlikely that she was a skilled assistant of some sort. The only plausible interpretation would be that she was a servant: a cook and housekeeper, let us say – much like the Mathurine or Maturina who later served him in France. These are the alternatives: that the Caterina of the Milanese notebooks was an otherwise unknown woman who served as his housekeeper for a couple of years or that she was his widowed mother, reunited with him in her last years, accommodated amid the trappings of his success, comforted by him on her deathbed in 1495, at the age of about sixty-eight. Either is intrinsically possible: one must make or refuse the leap of faith. Some have thought that the modesty of the funeral argues against her being his mother. But Caterina was essentially, in style and manner, a Tuscan *contadina*, and what one guesses of her character does not lead us to think she would wish to pretend otherwise. She is lined by the tough years of work on the little farm at Campo Zeppi. These exequies, simply but properly done, would be right for her.

Looking through the pocket-book Forster III, in which he recorded the arrival of Caterina, one finds Leonardo in philosophical mood. Among the brief maxims and musings which he jots down in its pages are these:

Wisdom is the daughter of experience . . .

This is the supreme folly of man – that he stints himself now so he will not have to stint later, and his life flies away before he can enjoy the good things he has laboured so much to acquire . . .

In some animals Nature seems a cruel stepmother rather than a mother; and in others not a stepmother but a tender mother . . .

Necessity is mistress and governess of nature . . .

The mirror vaunts itself when it has within it the reflection of a queen, but when she is gone the mirror is base once more . . .

The plant complains about the old dry stick placed beside it, and the old brambles which surround it. But the one makes it grow straight, and the other protects it from bad company.[70]

Also in use during the years 1493–4 were the three pocket-books now bound together as Paris MS H, in which are similar gnomic utterances:

Do not be a liar about the past . . .

All hurts leave a pain in the memory except for the greatest hurt of all, which is death, which kills the memory along with the life.[71]

Such *pensées* are scattered through his manuscripts, but this is a particular concentration of them. They belong to the time when the mysterious Caterina was living with him at the Corte Vecchia. Their imagery (mother, stepmother, governess, queen) and their themes of memory, transience and death add strength to the notion that this Caterina was indeed his mother. They reflect, with characteristic brusqueness, this autumnal reunion and the feelings which it brings to the surface.

→→ ECHOES OF WAR ←←

In 1494, amid the preparations for casting the Horse, and the disputes over the *Virgin of the Rocks*, and the revived emotions of his relationship with his mother, and the intricate mechanical studies of the Madrid codices, Leonardo pursued a round of daily life in which can be discerned some aspects of business and some of pleasure, and of which a few fragments remain in his pocket-books:

29 January 1494 – cloth for stockings	4 lire 3 soldi
lining	16 soldi
for making them	8 soldi
a jasper ring	13 soldi
a crystal [*pietra stellata*]	11 soldi

2 February 1494 – At the Sforzesca [Ludovico's summer palace at Vigevano] I drew 25 steps each of ⅔ of a braccia and eight braccia wide.

14 March 1494 – Galeazzo came to live with me, agreeing to pay 5 lire a month for his expenses . . . His father gave me 2 Rhenish florins.

20 March 1494 – Vineyards of Vigevano . . . In the winter they are covered with earth.

6 May [?1494] – If at night you place your eye between the light and the eye of a cat, you will see that its eye seems to be on fire.

[1494 – Estimate for decoration work, probably at Vigevano:]	
item: for each small vault	7 lire
outlay for azure and gold	3½ lire
time	4 days
for the windows	1½ lire
the cornice below the windows	6 soldi per braccio
item: for 24 pictures of Roman history	14 lire each
the philosophers	10 lire
for the pilasters, one ounce of azure	10 soldi
for gold	15 soldi[72]

Leonardo is glimpsed at Vigevano as the Sforza's interior designer, and he is also called upon to produce a different kind of design: propagandist political emblems – work that brings him into the realm of the Moor's image-maker. Ludovico's popularity was declining. In the clannish milieu of Quattrocento politics there were always those who felt themselves excluded and who formed a nucleus of resentment, and increasingly they had a focus. Ludovico's hunger for absolute power was by now quite blatant. He kept Gian Galeazzo and Isabella isolated in the gloomy fastness of the Certosa at Pavia, where the young Duke's health was failing. He severed relations with the King of Naples, who had protested against this treatment of his granddaughter. He courted the Emperor, who had the power to proclaim him the rightful Duke – the half a million ducats of dowry brought by his niece Bianca when she married the Emperor was widely seen as a bribe, at the taxpayer's expense, to obtain the dukedom.

Various sketches can be interpreted as ideas for political emblems, designed to express the official line that Ludovico was the only viable ruler of the dukedom and should therefore be recognized as such. One shows a dog warily confronting an aggressive-looking snake; the motto reads '*Per non disobbedire*' – 'Not to disobey'.[73] The snake or serpent (the heraldic device of the Visconti) is Milan; the dog traditionally represents fidelity or loyalty. The emblem seems to convey the message that Milan should not 'disobey' its faithful guardian Ludovico; the scroll carried round the dog's neck perhaps signifies that his leadership is sanctioned by the writ of law. Another sketched emblem shows a sieve with the motto '*Non cado per essere unito*' – 'I do not fall because I am united': a similar message of political unity.[74]

There is also an allegorical composition (as distinct from an emblem) – 'Il Moro with the spectacles, and Envy depicted together with False Report, and Justice black for Il Moro',[75] on a loose sheet now in the Bonnat Collection in Bayonne. The black-faced Moor holds spectacles, a symbol of truth, out towards Envy, who holds a banner depicting a bird pierced by an arrow. This is probably an idea for a piece of propagandist pageantry – a costumed, three-dimensional allegory. A similar description is found in a later notebook of *c*. 1497: 'Il Moro in the form of Fortune' with 'Messer Gualtieri [Gualtiero Bascapé, the Duke's treasurer] reverently holding up his robes behind him'. The 'terrifying form of Poverty' – female, like the depictions of Envy, Slander, etc. – is shown running towards a 'young lad'; the Moor 'protects him with his robe, and menaces this monster with a golden sceptre'.[76] Leonardo mentions Bascapé in a fragmentary draft of a letter of *c*. 1495 complaining of unpaid money: 'Perhaps Your Excellency did not give further orders to Messer Gualtieri, believing that I had money enough . . .'[77]

These political emblems and allegories seem trivial as drawings and unsubtle in the meanings they convey. One suspects that being part of the

Moor's propaganda-machine was not particularly congenial to Leonardo. He has a vested interest in the continued ascendancy of his patron, and is ready to lend his skills to that end. He collaborates, as he later did with the ruthless warlord Cesare Borgia. His livelihood depended on such collaborations, of course, but one should register the element of acquiescence, the shrug of political indifference. He is a man without illusions: he knows the harsh realities of power, and he learns to live with them. Opportunism is all: Fortune must be grasped by the hair as she passes – not a moment too late, 'for behind she is bald'. Perhaps his ambivalent feelings are in the emblem he sketches showing a blackberry-bush, with the motto '*Dolce e agro e pungente*' – 'Sweet and bitter and thorny'. Above it is written the word *more*, blackberries, punning on *amore*, love, but a further pun on Il Moro is hard to ignore, and with it perhaps an idea of the private bitterness of the artist in the pay of a despot.[78]

15 September 1494 – 'Giulio began the lock for my studio.'[79]

The locksmiths were busy in Milan at this time. Foreign troops were in the land – the French, en route for the Kingdom of Naples, to assert with force of arms their claim to that territory. Ludovico had welcomed them in: allies against the hostile Neapolitans. He and Beatrice entertained the French king, Charles VIII, with pomp and revelry at Pavia. The bravados of one of his generals, the Duc d'Orléans – whose grandmother was a Visconti, and who claimed therefore a right to the duchy of Milan – were ignored; Orléans was currently occupied in occupying Genoa. In Pavia Duke Gian Galeazzo lay dying. King Charles visited him, and pitied him, but was embarrassed by the Duchess Isabella, who tearfully pleaded with him to have mercy on her father, Alfonso, now King of Naples after the death of Ferrante a few months before. 'She had better have prayed for herself, who was still a young and fair lady,' observed the historian Philippe de Commines, who was in Charles's retinue. In these last days Gian Galeazzo seemed pathetically in Ludovico's thrall – 'longing on his deathbed for the uncle, who is far away, riding in splendour beside the French king'; asking one of Ludovico's gentlemen 'whether he thought his Excellency the Moor wished him well and whether he seemed sorry that he was ill'.[80]

21 October 1494 – Gian Galeazzo, aged twenty-five, dies at the Certosa di Pavia. Suspicions are rife that he has been poisoned by Ludovico.

22 October 1494 – Ludovico is proclaimed Duke at the Castello Sforzesco.

1 November 1494 – Ercole d'Este, Duke of Ferrara, father-in-law of Ludovico, arrives in Milan. He is alarmed, as many are, by Ludovico's

rapprochement with the French. He is keen to bolster his defences against the possibility of French incursion (or against the aggression of Venice, also mobilizing in response to the French presence). The Duke is also a powerful creditor – Ludovico is in debt to him to the tune of 3,000 ducats. Under pressure, Ludovico offers him a 'gift': a large quantity of bronze suitable for casting into cannon.

17 November 1494 – A diplomat in Milan writes:

The Duke of Ferrara . . . has ordered Maestro Zanin di Albergeto, to make him three small cannon, one in the French style and two in another style. He has received from the Duke [i.e. Ludovico] a gift of 100 meira of metal, which had been purchased to make the Horse in memory of Duke Francesco. The metal has been transported to Pavia, and thence down the Po to Ferrara, and the said Maestro Zanin has accompanied the Duke back to Ferrara to make the artillery.[81]

Thus casually a diplomatic report announces the requisitioning of the bronze which had been set aside for the casting of the Horse – a tremendous blow for Leonardo and his studio, and an irony he could hardly fail to note: the great martial creation of the Horse rendered down into actual weaponry. How brittle and insubstantial the works of the imagination when confronted with the necessities of war!

Around the same time news was reaching Milan of events in Florence: the French were camped outside the city; Piero de' Medici – Lorenzo's son and successor – had signed a disgraceful treaty granting them control of Pisa and other possessions; the citizens had risen in fury. On 9 November Piero and his two brothers, Giovanni and Giuliano, slipped out of the San Gallo gate, on foot, heading for sanctuary in Bologna. The Medici had fallen. Resentful mobs swarmed into the Palazzo Medici, smashing and looting – a foretaste of the destruction to come, as the power-vacuum was filled by the charismatic theocracy of Girolamo Savonarola, the fiery Dominican friar who had been a figurehead for reform in Florence, and whose pulpit-rhetoric of moral purification now became the reality of the 'Bonfires of the Vanities', in which many paintings, books and manuscripts were destroyed.

Thus the year which had begun pleasantly enough for Leonardo, measuring the water-stairs at Vigevano, ends amid distant echoes of war from his homeland, and the great defining project of the Sforza years in ruins. Fuming in his studio at the Corte Vecchia, he drafted a letter to Ludovico, but the page on which he wrote it has been torn in half, vertically, and on the half that remains we read only truncated stuttering sentences:

And if any other commission is to be given me by some . . .
Of the reward of my service, because I am not in a position to . . .
Not my art which I wish to change . . .
My Lord, I know your Excellency's mind is much occupied . . .
to remind your Lordship of my small necessities, and the arts put to
silence . . .
that for me to remain silent would make your Lordship think worthless . . .
my life in your service, holding myself always in readiness to obey . . .
Of the horse I will say nothing because I know the times . . .

And so on, to the last plaintive lines:

Remember the commission to paint the rooms . . .
I brought your Lordship, only asking that you . . .[82]

But enough. In theory the mutilation of the manuscript may have occurred
at any time before the compilation of the Codex Atlanticus by Pompeo
Leoni in the 1580s, but let us allow Leonardo da Vinci his moment of
petulance, and the fleeting minor satisfaction of ripping the paper in half
and stalking off to pace upon the roof of the Corte Vecchia, where on this
day none will dare to disturb him.

⤞ THE MAKING OF THE *LAST SUPPER* ⤝

As a boy in the 1490s, the future novelist Matteo Bandello was a novice
monk at the Dominican monastery of Santa Maria delle Grazie in Milan,
where his uncle Vincenzo was the prior. There he would pass the time
watching Leonardo da Vinci at work on the north wall of the refectory,
painting the great masterpiece of the Sforza era, the *Cenacolo* or *Last Supper*.

He would arrive early, climb up on to the scaffolding, and set to work. Sometimes
he stayed there from dawn to sunset, never once laying down his brush, forgetting
to eat and drink, painting without pause. At other times he would go for two,
three or four days without touching his brush, but spending several hours a day
in front of the work, his arms folded, examining and criticizing the figures to
himself. I also saw him, driven by some sudden urge, at midday, when the sun was
at its height, leaving the Corte Vecchia, where he was working on his marvellous
clay horse, to come straight to Santa Maria delle Grazie, without seeking shade,
and clamber up on to the scaffolding, pick up a brush, put in one or two strokes,
and then go away again.[83]

Bandello was writing this decades after the event. There is some telescoping: Leonardo probably began painting the *Last Supper* in 1495, and was not therefore 'working on' the clay horse – exhibited in late 1493 – at the same time. But this is none the less an authentic glimpse of the *maestro* at work. It expresses his creative rhythm, the bursts of strenuousness interspersed by those puzzling spells of silent cogitation which others – particularly those who were paying him – tended to mistake for dreamy inactivity. And it gives us that marvellous image of Leonardo striding through the streets, under the noonday sun, not thinking of comfort or shelter or indeed anything else except a suddenly achieved solution to some tiny problem of compositional detail. Those 'one or two strokes' remind us of the painstakingly cumulative nature of his art. That massive sweep of visual narrative which one sees on the wall of the Grazie is made up of thousands of tiny brush-strokes, thousands of microscopic decisions. The familiarity of a world-famous painting makes it seem somehow inevitable – how could it be other than it is? – but every inch has been fought for.

The church of Santa Maria delle Grazie lay beyond the old Porta Vercellina to the west of the castle. For some years (you might have heard it muttered) it had been a virtual building-site. In 1492 the choir and apse were demolished to make way for a new tribune and cupola, designed by Bramante, and in tandem with this it was decided to enlarge the contiguous monastery buildings. The renovation of the refectory was certainly completed by 1495 – this is the date inscribed on Donato di Montorfano's *Crucifixion* fresco which adorns the south wall. The *Last Supper*, on the opposite wall, was probably begun in this year. This whole renovation programme was commissioned and paid for by Ludovico, who intended the new setting to serve as a future Sforza mausoleum, a fitting monument to the ducal dynasty. This motivation became more pressing with the sudden deaths of his wife, Beatrice, and his daughter Bianca in 1497. These losses weighed heavily on the Moor, and introduced a period of sombre religiosity: his investment in the Grazie became emotional as well as financial, and he often took his meals at the refectory. Leonardo's great mural – it is not technically a fresco, since it was painted in oils – was thus the pièce de résistance of a prestigious Sforza project: a thoroughly modern work to crown this elegant modernization.[84]

To trace the making of 'this restless masterpiece', as Burckhardt called it, one must first turn to a sheet at Windsor which has an early compositional study in pen and ink.[85] It is still rooted in traditional Last Supper iconography – Judas in the excluded position, seen from behind, on the near side of the

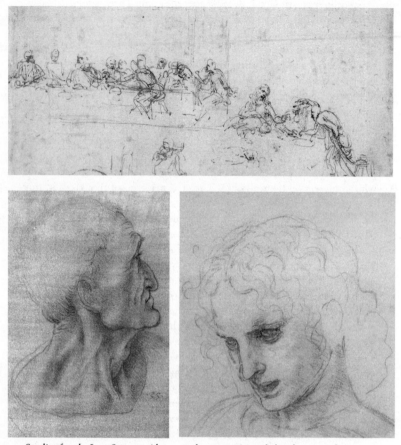

Studies for the Last Supper. *Above: early compositional sketches on a sheet at Windsor. Below: studies for the heads of Judas (left) and St James the Elder.*

table, and St John shown asleep next to Christ, a reference to his 'leaning on Jesus's bosom' when the announcement of betrayal was made. Both these figures would be jettisoned in the final version.

There are two separate drawings on the sheet. The left-hand sketch has ten figures: the sheet has probably been trimmed, losing the remaining three. There are arches lightly sketched behind the group – first thoughts for the background of the painting, the 'upper room' in which the supper took place. The right-hand sketch shows four figures, but is essentially a study of Christ and Judas. Here Leonardo is focusing on the dramatic moment of identification: 'He that dippeth his hand with me in the dish, the same shall betray me' (Matthew 26:23). Judas has climbed off his stool and is reaching forward with his hand to the dish. Christ's hand is tried out in two positions – raised as if about to reach forward; and having reached the dish and hovering in a moment of poignant contact with the hand of his betrayer. This smaller sketch has intensified the focus, found the dramatic fulcrum – that ghostly moment of contact. In focusing on this moment, Leonardo is already moving the story back a few frames from the more conventional Last Supper depiction showing the institution of the Eucharist.

The other constituent of this smaller sketch is the sleeping figure of St John with Jesus's arm resting on his back: a note of tenderness which is scriptural – John is the disciple 'whom Jesus loved' – but in sceptical irreligious circles John 'leaning on Jesus's bosom' was interpreted in terms of homosexuality. Among the blasphemies attributed to Christopher Marlowe a hundred years later was that Christ loved St John 'with an extraordinary love', and 'used him as the sinners of Sodoma'. One remembers the Saltarelli episode, with its subtext of official disapproval of effeminate young models being used to depict angels and boyish Christs. Leonardo separated the figures in the final painting, though of all the disciples John remains the youngest and most beautiful.

A little later, perhaps, is the sketch at the Accademia in Venice, its red chalk gone over in ink by another hand.[86] It seems cruder, largely because of the inking, but something of the compositional rhythm of the painting is emerging. The disciples are forming into groups; there is more emphasis on their individual features; they are identified in hurriedly written captions (Philip being mentioned twice). But Judas is still on our side of the table, and John is still slumped asleep.

These are glimpses into the early workings of Leonardo's conception of the painting: miniature blueprints, made with rapidity and concentration and a questioning temper – this way or this? But, as so often with Leonardo, the roots of the painting run deeper, and, though these are the first actual studies for the Grazie *Last Supper*, we find in the reservoir of his sketchbooks a much earlier sheet, datable to *c.* 1480, with a trio of linked sketches: a group sitting at a table, a figure apart with his head in his hands, and a figure who is undeniably Christ, pointing with his finger at the fatal dish.[87] These are not exactly studies for a Last Supper: the group is not the disciples, just five men at a table, passing the time in animated conversation – we might be at some village festivity, with men sitting round at trestle-tables.

But something has triggered in Leonardo's mind, which is realized in the swift poignant sketch of the Eucharistic Christ on the same sheet, and which grows to fruition in the great Milanese mural fifteen years later.

From the compositional studies in Windsor and Venice the focus moves in to the features of individual figures, and so we come to the famous series of heads in Windsor, mostly in red chalk, some highly finished. We see the characters emerging from a mist: Judas, Peter, St James the Elder, St Philip (the latter two almost certainly drawn from the same model, though in the painting they are individuated). There is a beautiful study for the hands of St John, and for the sleeve of St Peter.[88] These studies are complemented by brief comments in the Forster notebooks – that a certain Alessandro from Parma provided the model for Christ's hand; that 'Cristofano da Castiglione, who lives at the Pietà, has a good head'. There is a note headed simply '*crissto*', under which Leonardo writes, 'Giovanni Conte, the one with the Cardinal of Mortaro'; this may tell us the name of the model for Christ. According to the well-informed Luigi of Aragon, who saw the painting in 1517, some of the disciples were 'real portraits of Milanese courtiers and important citizens'.[89]

In a well-known passage, Leonardo lists some of the disciples' reactions:

One who was drinking and has left the glass in its position and turned his head towards the speaker.
Another twisting the fingers of his hand together, turns with stern brow to his companion, and he with his hands spread shows the palms and shrugs up his shoulders to his ears, and makes a mouth of astonishment . . .
Another who has turned, holding a knife in his hand, knocks over a glass on the table . . .
Another leans forward to see the speaker, shading his eyes with his hand.[90]

Some of these find their place in the finished painting – white-bearded St Andrew (third from left) shows his palms and shrugs up his shoulders. Others are transmuted, so that the man who turns with a knife in his hand (St Peter) is detached from the man who knocks over a glass, and the latter becomes a man (Judas) spilling a salt-cellar. At least one of these gestures is already enacted in that first compositional sketch in Windsor: in the smaller group, the figure between Christ and Judas 'shades his eyes with his hand'.

In these emotional dynamics, as much as in compositional planning, lies the radically new conception of Leonardo's *Last Supper*, breaking with the tradition inherited from the Middle Ages in which the disciples are a stiffly linear grouping ranged along the table. In Florence he would have seen versions by Taddeo Gaddi, Andrea del Castagno, Fra Angelico and Domenico Ghirlandaio.[91] The latter's elegant, almost languid fresco in the refectory of Ognissanti was completed shortly before Leonardo's departure for Milan. In Leonardo's version the line of diners is magically disrupted. We have instead a group whose outline is a kind of wave-formation, which Pietro Marani has compared to the optical diagrams of Paris MS C.[92] The waves are formed of four sub-groups, each of three disciples: knots and huddles of men suddenly in crisis. Leonardo has also found his dramatic moment: not the institution of the Eucharist, nor the identification of Judas, but the first shell-shock of Christ's announcement – 'Verily I say until you, that one of you shall betray me. And they were exceeding sorrowful' (Matthew 26:21-2). Thus the new fluency of the composition is in part the product of a narrative – almost a cinematic – decision: the moment that tells the story. This is well described by one of the first recorded commentators on the mural, Luca Pacioli. In the dedication of his *Divina proportione*, dated 14 December 1498, he writes:

One cannot imagine a keener attentiveness in the apostles at the sound of the voice of ineffable truth which says, '*Unus vestrum me traditurus est.*' Through their deeds and gestures, they seem to be speaking among themselves, one man to another and he to yet another, afflicted with keen sense of wonder. Thus worthily our Leonardo created it with his delicate hand.[93]

Pacioli's description is interesting because of his close connection with Leonardo at this time: it contains, perhaps, a refraction of Leonardo's own statements – on the quality of 'attentiveness' and 'wonder' which racks the dramatic intensity of the focus on Christ, and the sense of interplay among the apostles. This is how the painting works: the figures not in a row, but intertwined, speaking '*l'uno a l'altro e l'altro a l'uno*'.

And then there is Judas: the villain of the piece, and yet in the preparatory profile study at Windsor (page 294) a man more ugly than evil – almost a grotesque, but with hints of remorse and self-disgust which touch the profile with tragedy, or indeed with Christian forgiveness. (The recent restoration of the painting has recovered subtleties in the faces lost beneath later retouchings; Judas is an example of a face now nearer to the preparatory drawing than it was before the restoration.) He recoils from the words of Christ even as his hand moves irrevocably towards the piece of bread he will dip in the dish.

Of the face of Judas in Leonardo's *Last Supper* there is a well-known anecdote in Vasari: how the prior of the Grazie constantly badgered Leonardo 'to hurry up and finish the work', and complained of the artist's dilatoriness to the Duke. In response Leonardo told Ludovico he was still searching for a face evil enough to represent Judas, but that if he did not succeed 'he could always use the head of that tactless and impatient prior' as a model. At this the Duke roared with laughter, and 'the unfortunate prior retired in confusion to worry the labourers working in his garden.' This is one of those Vasarian anecdotes that proves to have a kernel of truth, or at least of contemporary witness. The story is lifted from the *Discorsi* of Giambattista Giraldi Cintio, published in 1554, and Cintio in turn had it from his father, Cristoforo Giraldi, a Ferrarese diplomat who knew Leonardo personally in Milan. The Giraldi version of the story purports to be a record of Leonardo's own words:

It remains for me to do the head of Judas, who was the great betrayer, as you all know, and so deserves to be painted with a face that expresses all his wickedness . . . And so for a year now, perhaps more, I have been going every day, morning and evening, down to the Borghetto, where all the base and ignoble characters live, most of them evil and wicked, in the hope that I will see a face which would be fit for this evil man. And to this day I have not found one . . . and if it turns out I cannot find one I will have to use the face of this reverend father, the prior.[94]

Whether or not the story is true, we are close here to an authentic recording of Leonardo. This is how Cristoforo Giraldi, who knew him, remembers or imagines him speaking: '*Ogni giorno, sera e mattina, mi sono ridotto in Borghetto . . .*'

The painting of the *Last Supper* began with the plastering of the refectory wall with an even layer of intonaco, which forms the structural base for the mural.[95] The intonaco of the middle section – where the main action was to be painted – is coarser, to provide better adhesion for the paint-layers on top: the join between the two sections is perceptible as a faint horizontal line near the middle of the foreshortened ceiling. One of the discoveries to emerge from the latest restoration is the vestige of a *sinopia*, or outline drawing, done directly on to the plaster – 'extremely concise red lines, executed freehand and with a fluid brush-stroke . . . to define the masses for his composition'. After this the gesso or ground was applied: modern analysis shows this to be 'a slightly granular mixture, 100–200 microns thick, composed of calcium carbonate and magnesium with a proteinaceous binding agent', and on top of that came a thin imprimatura of lead white. At this stage a number of incisions were made on the surface, mainly defining the form and perspective of the architectural setting, and – an eerie moment of precision – a small hole was punched in the centre of the pictorial area:

the vanishing-point. This hole can be seen in a magnified photograph: it is at a point on the right temple of Christ.

All these preparations remind us that this was a collective studio work (a point missing from Bandello's account, with its misleading sense of artistic solitude). Leonardo did not work alone on the painting, as Michelangelo reputedly did on the Sistine Chapel, but had a team of assistants – among them probably Marco d'Oggiono, who would produce one of the earliest copies of the mural; Salai, now about sixteen and working as a *garzone*; and Tommaso Masini, whose participation in a later large-scale mural (the *Anghiari* fresco in Florence) is documented. To these trusted assistants may be added the new intake of pupils and assistants whose names are found on two sheets of the Codex Atlanticus:[96]

Ioditti came on 8 September at 4 ducats a month.
Benedetto came on 17 October at 4 ducats a month.

The year referred to is either 1496 or 1497. Four ducats is the charge Leonardo exacts for their *retta*, or board and lodging; against this they can earn money for work they do as *garzoni*; thus by the end of the year Benedetto has earned nearly 39 lire – just under 10 ducats – which is approximately what he owed for his *retta* over that ten-week period. Benedetto's name appears also on an undated sheet, partly cut off at the margin, which records the studio personnel at around the same time:

[. . .]nco 4
[. . .]iberdo 4
Gianmaria 4
Benedetto 4
Gianpetro 4
Salai 3
Bartolomeo 3
Girardo 4

The first name is probably 'Franco', and may be a reference to Francesco Galli, known as Il Napoletano; the fifth may refer to Giampietrino Rizzoli; and the penultimate, who pays the lower *retta* of 3 ducats, may be Bartolomeo Suardi, known as Il Bramantino, the pupil of Leonardo's friend Bramante.

The painting itself probably began with the three heraldic lunettes above the depicted scene; they are now much damaged, but fragments of inscriptions and coats of arms, and a marvellous wreath of fruits and grasses, can still be seen. The painting of the central scene probably began on the left-hand side. We enter here the period described by Matteo Bandello – of intense work and arms-folded contemplation. Bandello's description is borne out by technical data: 'Leonardo's slow progress is confirmed by a few *pentimenti* [rethinks] and by the attentive refinement of important details . . . Each figure and each object on the table shows minor or significant revisions of outlines, which stray into the adjacent colours, testifying to the fact that Leonardo allowed himself great freedom in returning more than once to a given motif.'[97] Among the *pentimenti* identified by the restorers is a modification of the position of Christ's fingers, which were more extended in the original version.

In the summer of 1496, while he was at work on the *Last Supper*, Leonardo was also decorating certain rooms (*camerini*) – probably the apartments of Duchess Beatrice – in the Castello Sforzesco. This is the same job he mentions in the torn-up letter I quoted earlier: 'Remember the commission to paint the rooms . . .'

On 8 June 1496 there was some kind of scene, a rare losing of his cool. It is noted by one of the Duke's secretaries, who writes, 'The painter who is decorating the *camerini* caused something of a scandal today, and for this reason he has left.'[98] This tension is perhaps connected to another fragmentary draft letter to the Duke, in which Leonardo complains of financial strains: 'It vexes me greatly that you should have found me in need, and . . . that my having to earn my living has forced me to interrupt the work and to attend to lesser matters instead of following up the work which your Lordship entrusted to me.'[99] The important work is almost certainly the *Last Supper*, and the 'lesser' labours which have distracted him from it may be the decoration of the Duchess's chambers.

The tone of this letter is very tetchy: consider the scarcely veiled sarcasm of the phrase 'my having to earn a living' – an inconvenience with which the Duke was unfamiliar. He continues: 'Perhaps Your Excellency did not give further orders to Messer Gualtieri, believing that I had money enough . . . If your Lordship thought I had money, your Lordship was deceived.' The reference is to Gualtiero Bascapé, elsewhere described as *ducalis iudex dationum*, the Duke's judge of gifts, i.e. his dispenser of payments. It appears that some expected 'gift' had not been received: by 'gifts' are essentially meant payments provided in a form too irregular to be considered a salary. Accounts of Leonardo's payment for the *Last Supper* vary wildly. According to Bandello he was on an annual salary of 2,000 ducats, but another well-informed source (Girolamo Bugati, a friar at the Grazie in the mid sixteenth century) says the Moor paid him only 500 ducats per annum.[100] This would still compare well with the *Virgin of the Rocks*, for which Leonardo and Ambrogio de Predis had demanded 1,200 lire, or approximately 300 ducats.

In this griping letter, in this unexpected explosion of temper – 'something of a scandal' at the castle – we are privileged with a back-stage glimpse of Leonardo under the profound creative pressure of the *Last Supper*, which pressure is always exacerbated rather than relieved by diversions. It is the same Leonardo snapped by Bandello's camera, striding grimly up the hot silent street towards the Grazie.

Bandello has another story, which shows Leonardo in more relaxed mood – chatting with a distinguished visitor to the Grazie, Cardinal Raymond Peraud, Bishop of Gurck. Documents confirm the Cardinal's presence in Milan in late January 1497.[101] Leonardo climbs down off the scaffolding to greet him. 'They discoursed on many things,' recalls Bandello, 'and particularly on the excellence of painting, and some who were there said they wished they could see those paintings of antiquity that are so highly praised by great writers, so that they could judge whether the painters of our day could rank with the ancients.' Leonardo also entertains the company with the picaresque story of the young Filippo Lippi being seized by 'Saracens' and held as a slave, and eventually winning his freedom because of his skill at drawing. This story is familiar from Vasari's *Life* of Filippo Lippi.[102] Two questions arise: Did Vasari take the story from Bandello? And did Bandello really first hear it from the lips of Leonardo da Vinci? The most one can say in each case is: possibly. Bandello's *Novelle* were first published in Lucca in 1554 – four years after the first edition of the *Lives* – but they were certainly written earlier and were possibly available in manuscript. As for Leonardo, he could well have heard the story from Filippo's son Filippino, whom he knew in Florence in the 1470s, and with whom he had cordial relations. It is equally possible that the opportunist Bandello was making a good story even better by spuriously ascribing it to Leonardo.

Leonardo was still at work on the *Last Supper* in summer 1497. There is an entry in the monastery's ledger for that year, recording a payment of 37 lire to some workmen 'for work done on a window in the refectory where Leonardo is painting the Apostles'. And on 29 June 1497 Ludovico writes a letter to his secretary, Marchesino Stanga, in the course of which he says that he hopes that 'Leonardo the Florentine will soon finish the work he has begun in the refectory', so that he can 'attend to the other wall of the refectory'.[103] A note of ducal impatience is perhaps discernible here.

As is well known, Leonardo's great mural was innovative in less auspicious ways. He used a mix of oil and tempera for the painting, instead of the traditional *buon fresco* technique of painting on fresh plaster. This enabled him to work more slowly, and to repaint, but its disadvantages soon became apparent as the paint began to flake off. An inherent problem with damp exacerbated the situation. The deterioration of the paint surface was already visible during his lifetime. In 1517 the diarist Antonio de Beatis noted that the mural was 'beginning to spoil', and by the time Vasari saw it in the 1550s, there was 'nothing visible except a muddle of blots'.[104] This is doubtless a reason for the many early copies made of it, two of them – Marco d'Oggiono's and Giampietrino's – by painters who were probably involved in the creation of the original. It is also the reason for the extensive and intrusive restoration projects; the earliest which is documented was done in the early eighteenth century, but was probably not the first. In the 1930s, comparing the current state of the mural with these early copies, and with the preparatory studies in Windsor, Kenneth Clark lamented the loss of subtle nuances of expression beneath the deadening hand of the restorer: he thought 'the exaggerated grimacing types, with their flavour of Michelangelo's *Last Judgement*', suggested 'a feeble mannerist of the sixteenth century'.[105]

The painting's inherent, self-inflicted fragility seems now part of its magic. Reduced within a few decades to a 'muddle of blots', vandalized by Napoleonic soldiers in the early nineteenth century, and narrowly missed by Allied bombs in the summer of 1943, it is a miracle that it has survived at all.

The latest and most ambitious restoration, under Pinin Brambilla Barcelon, was unveiled in 1999, after more than twenty years' work at an estimated cost of 20 billion lire (approximately £6 million). Much of it was targeted at removing the superimpositions of previous restorations: an encrustation of varnishes and over-paintings which were teased away, scab by microscopic scab, in the hope that some original pigment remained beneath. In the words of Brambilla Barcelon, the painting was treated 'as if it were a great invalid'.[106] The restoration had its critics, as always – it had 'lost the soul' of the original – but what we now see is much closer to what Leonardo and his assistants painted on that wall, watched by the wide-eyed boy Bandello, just over 500 years ago. Closer, but of course partial – only about 20 per cent of the original picture surface survives. The painting hovers like a ghost on the wall, vestigial yet ravishingly restocked with expressions and gestures, and with the simple yet compelling details of that last meal: the half-filled beakers of wine, the filigree weave on the tablecloth, the knife which in the emotion of the moment St Peter grips like a murder-weapon.

⤞ THE 'ACADEMY' ⤝

Let no one read me who is not a mathematician . . .
Forster III, fol. 82v

The year 1496, shadowed with the great enterprise of the *Last Supper*, saw also the blossoming of a great friendship, with the arrival in Milan of the mathematician Fra Luca Pacioli – 'Maestro Luca' as Leonardo calls him.

Pacioli, from the small town of Borgo San Sepolcro on the southern edge of Tuscany, was in his early fifties. In his youth he had studied under Piero della Francesca, who had a studio there; he was deeply influenced by Piero's mathematical writings on perspective, and in Vasari's view he plagiarized them in his own later writings. In the mid-1470s he threw up a promising career as an accountant to become a friar of the Franciscan order, vowed to poverty, and for twelve years he was a wandering scholar, lecturing on philosophy and mathematics; he is glimpsed at Perugia, Naples, Rome, Urbino and Zadar in Venetian Croatia. In 1494 he published his first book, the encyclopedic *Summa de arithmetica, geometria e proportione*. Covering 600 close-printed pages in folio, it is written in Italian and is thus part of the modernizing drift away from Latin. A note in the Codex Atlanticus records Leonardo's purchase of a copy ('Aritmetrica di Maestro Luca') for 6 lire, and there are many extracts from it in his notebooks, some of them possibly related to the compositional geometry of the *Last Supper*.[107] As its title states, it is a summary rather than a work of great originality. It has sections on theoretical and practical arithmetic, and on algebra, geometry and trigonometry; it has a treatise of thirty-six chapters on double-entry bookkeeping, some interesting discussions on games of chance, and a conversion-table showing the currencies, weights and measures used in various Italian states. For all his contemporary status as a philosopher, there is a strong practical streak in Fra Luca; he is remembered for his adage that 'regular accounting preserves long friendships.'

The portrait of him by Jacopo de' Barbari is dated 1495. It shows him in the Franciscan habit and cowl, one hand resting on a book of geometry, the other pointing to a slate bearing a geometrical figure and the name 'Euclides' inscribed on the side. On the desk are the tools of the geometer's trade – chalk and sponge, set-squares, compass. A 3-D model of a polyhedron hangs like a giant crystal above his right shoulder. The large leather-bound book on the table, inscribed 'LI. RI. LUC. BUR.' (i.e. *Liber reverendi Luca Burgensis* – The book of the reverend Luca of the Borgo) refers to his

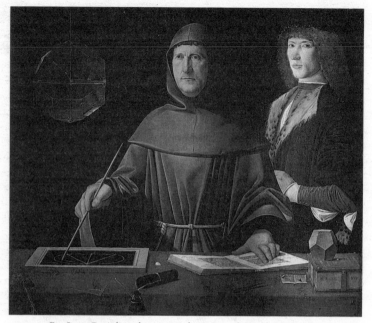

Fra Luca Pacioli in the portrait by Jacopo de' Barbari, c. 1495.

Summa, published the previous year. The handsome young man standing behind him is probably Guidobaldo da Montefeltro, Duke of Urbino, to whom the *Summa* was dedicated.

Pacioli arrived in Milan in late 1495 or 1496, so this fine portrait shows him much as he was when Leonardo first knew him. He was personally invited by the Moor, but it is possible that Leonardo was instrumental in recommending this new mathematical guru. They seem to have swiftly become friends, and by the following year they were collaborating. Pacioli was writing his masterwork, *Divina proportione*, and Leonardo was supplying the geometric illustrations. The first of its three books was completed by the end of 1498; two manuscript copies dated 14 December 1498 were presented to Ludovico and to Galeazzo Sanseverino. In the preface to the printed edition of 1509 Pacioli asserts that the diagrams illustrating 'all the regular and dependent bodies' (i.e. regular and semi-regular polygons) were 'done by that most worthy painter, perspectivist, architect, musician and master of all accomplishments [*de tutte le virtù doctato*] Leonardo da Vinci Fiorentino, in the city of Milan, where we worked together at the charge of

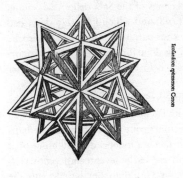

Dodecahedron designed by Leonardo,
in an engraving from Pacioli's Divina
proportione (1509).

the most excellent Duke of that city, Ludovico Maria Sforza Anglo, in the years of our health 1496 until 1499'.[108] In the presentation manuscripts these drawings are in ink and watercolour: they are probably copies by assistants. Engravings of them appear in the printed text of 1509; thus these obscure polygons and polyhedrons qualify as the first works of Leonardo to be published within the covers of a book: the first mass-production.

Mathematics, wrote Leonardo, offers 'the supreme certainty'.[109] It had been a part of his basic studio training, but now, under the wing of Luca Pacioli, he begins to plumb the more abstract world of geometry, the rule-book of harmony and proportion. His close study of Euclid can be found in two pocket-books of the late 1490s – Paris MSS M and I – though he was also conscious of lacunae in his knowledge of more elementary procedures, and issued one of his self-instructive memoranda: 'Learn from Messer Luca how to multiply square roots.'[110]

The collaboration between Leonardo and Luca Pacioli – evidenced in Leonardo's notebook and explicitly recalled in Pacioli's preface to the *Divina proportione* – is one of the historical foundations of Leonardo's elusive 'academy'. The existence of this academy is much disputed: the most one can say for certain is that it exists on paper, in that series of beautiful knot-designs which feature the words 'Academia Leonardi Vinci' (variously spelt, sometimes abbreviated). They seem to be intended as a device or emblem for this august-sounding body, but many believe this was just a Leonardo pipe-dream.

The designs are known exclusively from engravings (see page 41), almost certainly done in Venice in the first years of the 1500s: there is strong evidence that Albrecht Dürer saw prints of them on his visit to Venice in 1504–5.[111] The original drawings on which they are based do not survive, but a plausible account of them is that they were done in Milan in the late 1490s and that Leonardo brought them with him when he visited Venice – for the first time, as far as we know – in 1500. The originals would thus be contemporary with the complex interlacings of the Sala delle Asse ceiling, which Leonardo was working on in 1498, and which Lomazzo described as a 'beautiful invention' of 'bizarre knot-patterns'. They would also be contemporary with the polyhedric designs done for Pacioli's *Divina proportione*, which were drawn in Milan in or before 1498, and were also later engraved in Venice.

The original designs for the 'academy logo' seem to belong within the context of Leonardo's collaboration with Pacioli. The idea that the two men were the nucleus of a definable intellectual group or sodality has perhaps been dismissed too easily. There is in fact an independent sighting of it in an obscure little book published in the early seventeenth century: *Il supplimento della nobilita di Milano*, by Giralomo Borsieri. In this the author refers to 'the Sforza academy of art and architecture', and to Leonardo's role in it: 'I myself have already seen, in the hands of Guido Mazenta, several lectures [*lettioni*, literally 'lessons'] on perspective, on machines, and on buildings, written in a French script but in the Italian language, which had previously issued from this academy, and which were attributed to Leonardo himself.'[112] The bibliophile Mazenta, who certainly owned many Leonardo manuscripts, died in 1613. Sometime before this date he showed Borsieri a manuscript containing certain lectures or lessons attributed to Leonardo. The manuscript appears to be sixteenth-century – its 'French script' implies that it was produced during the period of French rule in Milan – but the lectures it contains were originally delivered, or 'issued', under the aegis of this 'Sforza academy', which can only have existed before the fall of Ludovico Sforza in 1499. All this is taking Borsieri's account at face value. The manuscript he describes has disappeared, and his description of its provenance cannot be verified. None the less, this is an independent account of Leonardo's 'academy' and of the subjects discussed there: perspective, mechanics, architecture.

Who else might be seen at a meeting of this high-level talking-shop? One obvious candidate is Leonardo's colleague Donato Bramante, architect of the Grazie, adept of Euclidian geometry, interpreter of Dante, and indeed another skilled creator of *groppi* or knot-patterns. (A manuscript note of Leonardo's refers precisely to certain '*groppi di Bramante*', and Lomazzo mentions his skill in this technique.)[113] Another possible luminary is the intellectual court poet Gasparé Visconti. He was a close friend of Bramante, of whom he wrote, 'You could more easily count the holy spirits in the heavens than reckon up all the knowledge Bramante has in him.'[114] Leonardo owned a copy of the 'Sonetti di Messer Guaspari Bisconti' (described thus in the Madrid book-list), probably referring to Visconti's *Rithmi*, published in Milan in 1493. We might also include the brightest of Leonardo's followers – Boltraffio or Bramantino perhaps – though whether there is room for the Zoroastrian showmanship of Tommaso Masini I am not sure. Other potential members can be found in Pacioli's mention of a debate – 'a notable scientific duel', as he puts it – which took place at the castle, in the presence of the Duke, on 8 February 1498.[115] Among the participants were the Franciscan theologians Domenico Ponzone and Francesco Busti da Lodi, the court astrologer Ambrogio Varese da Rosate, the doctors Andrea da Novara, Gabriele Pirovano, Niccolò Cusano and Alvise Marliano, and the Ferrarese architect Giacomo Andrea.

The last three on this list were certainly known to Leonardo. Niccolò Cusano, physician to the Sforza court, is briefly mentioned in a note ('*Cusano medico*'), as is his son Girolamo, to whom Leonardo sends his commendations via Melzi in *c.* 1508.[116] The Marliano family is mentioned frequently in his notes, mostly in connection with books –

An algebra, which the Marliani have, written by their father . . .
Concerning bones, by the Marliani . . .
Alchino on proportions, with notes by Marliano, from Messer Fazio . . .
Maestro Giuliano da Marliano has a beautiful herbal. He lives opposite the Strami, the carpenters . . .
Giuliano da Marliano the doctor . . . has a steward with one hand.[117]

Giuliano is the celebrated physician and author of *Algebra*; Alvise, who debated at the castle in 1498, is one of his sons. The architect Giacomo Andrea was Leonardo's host, in the summer of 1490, at that supper where the urchin Salai broke the oil-flasks.

Also present at this symposium at the castle is the Moor's son-in-law Galeazzo Sanseverino. Handsome, fashionable, intellectual, the famous champion of the tourney lists, and an accomplished singer, he was the 'prime favourite' of the Moor. Leonardo had known him at least since 1491, when he designed the 'wild-men' pageant for Galeazzo's joust, and when he was keenly interested in the horses in his stable as possible models for the Sforza Horse. Galeazzo was also a patron of Pacioli's, who was accommodated in his house when he arrived in Milan; one of the manuscripts of *Divina proportione* is dedicated to him. Pacioli also states that, among the sixty geometrical bodies designed by Leonardo for that treatise, a set of them was done for Galeazzo. If one is looking to give some reality to this fugitive little academy I would say that Sanseverino is a plausible patron or figurehead for it. Pacioli seems to say as much in his preface to the *Divina proportione*: 'In the circles of the Duke and of Galeazzo Sanseverino are philosophers and theologists, physicians and astrologists, architects and engineers and ingenious inventors of new things.'

A Leonardo manuscript now in the Metropolitan Museum in New York has a cast-list for a masque on the subject of Jupiter and Danae, with sketches. The play is almost certainly the *'commedia'* performed at the house of Sanseverino's elder brother Gianfrancesco, Count of Caiazzo, on 31 January 1496, with the Duke present.[118] It was written, in a mixture of *ottava* and *terza rima*, by Ludovico's chancellor, Baldassare Taccone (whose poem on the Sforza Horse I mentioned earlier). Leonardo's cast-list also names him – 'Tachon' – as one of the actors. A boy called Francesco Romano plays Danae; the priest Gianfrancesco Tanzi, former patron of the poet Bellincioni, plays Jupiter. This refined little cabaret on a classical theme, performed *chez* Sanseverino, is perhaps another emanation of the 'Sforza academy'.

The words 'Academia Leonardi Vinci' emblazoned on those labyrinthine knot-designs may not refer to a formally constituted 'club', but it seems to be something more than a pipe-dream. For Leonardo the word *accademia* would recall that Platonic academy of Ficino's, which he had known in Florence twenty years earlier – a nostalgia perhaps sharpened by the current fundamentalist climate of Savonarola's Florence. We might think of this Milanese 'academy' as a version of that Ficinian prototype: its scope perhaps broader, more multi-disciplinary, more 'scientific'. Pacioli's influence may be discerned here – the philosopher-mathematician reintroducing Leonardo to Platonic ideas which he had earlier rejected in favour of a more Aristotelian regime of experiment and inquiry. One sees the 'academy' as a loosely knit group of intellectuals who meet and discuss and give lectures and readings, sometimes at the castle and sometimes at the house of Galeazzo Sanseverino outside the Porta Vercellina, and sometimes no doubt at the Corte Vecchia, that great factory of marvels where there is always some curious new gadget to inspect, where there are drawings and sculptures to look at, and books to refer to, and music to call for. The rackety element of the retinue – that 'gang of adolescents' – is banished to the periphery; Zoroastro is under orders to behave himself. The shabby old ballroom looks good in the torchlight, though once these 'academics' get going sheer brain-power would serve to illuminate it.

Two curious works – a poem and a fresco – seem to belong within the ambit of this Milanese 'academy'.

The poem is an anonymous eight-page booklet called *Antiquarie prospetiche Romane* (*The Antiquities of Rome in Perspective*).[119] It is undated, but internal evidence suggests it was written in the late 1490s – it cannot be earlier than 1495, since it mentions an incident when Charles VIII's troops were in Rome (December 1494). The anonymous author styles himself '*Prospectivo Melanese depictore*', which one can either take as a comic alias ('Prospectivo Melanese the painter') or as a self-description ('the Milanese perspective painter'). The poem is written in what a recent editor calls 'semi-barbarous *terzine*', full of obscure Lombard colloquialisms, but among its obscurities one thing is certain: the poem is addressed, in very friendly terms, to Leonardo da Vinci – '*cordial caro ameno socio / Vinci mie caro*' ('dear cordial delightful colleague, my dear Vinci'). The author thus places himself as a member of Leonardo's circle, and he refers to at least one other member of that circle – 'Geroastro', who is presumably Zoroastro. There is also a cryptic allusion to the '*zingara del Verrocchio*' – 'Verrocchio's gypsy-woman'.

The poem is a sort of travelogue, describing the classical antiquities of Rome, and inviting Leonardo to meet the author there, to explore with him 'the vestiges of the Antique'. (Whether it was actually written in Rome is debatable: it is clearly addressed to a Milanese readership, and may have been written in Milan.) It contains much fulsome praise of Leonardo, including the usual puns on Vinci and *vincere*, to conquer. He is particularly praised as a sculptor who is 'inspired by antiquity': he can fashion 'a creature with a living heart and an aspect more divine than any other carving' – presumably referring to the Sforza Horse. He is also praised, interestingly, as a writer or speaker:

> *Vinci, tu victore*
> *Vinci colle parole un proprio Cato . . .*
> *Tal che dell arte tua ogni autore*
> *Resta dal vostro stil vinto e privato.*

[Vinci, you the victor conquer with words, like a true Cato . . . and through your skill all other authors find themselves defeated and outshone by your style.]

These lines perhaps refer to the debates and lectures of the 'academy'.

Some believe the author of the *Antiquarie* is Donato Bramante, who is known to have turned his hand to satirical sonneteering; but Bramante was not Milanese. Other attributions are to Ambrogio de Predis, Bramantino, Bernardo Zenale, and the up-and-coming young architect Cesare Cesariano, whose later writings on Vitruvius include an engraved version of Leonardo's Vitruvian Man with an erection. Of these only de Predis is likely to have called Leonardo his *socio* – partner or colleague; he is also known to have visited Rome at least once in the 1490s. The initials 'P.M.' which appear on the title-page presumably stand for 'Prospectivo Melanese', but could punningly stand for something like 'Predis Mediolanensis' as well.[120] The title-page has a curious engraving, featuring a naked man down on one knee in a position reminiscent of Leonardo's St Jerome. He holds a pair of compasses in his left hand and a sphere in his right hand, and he kneels inside a circle in which appear geometrical figures. In the background is part of a round colonnaded temple of the kind found in Paris MS B, and which is also associated with Bramante. The rocks in the background are perhaps a reminiscence of the *Virgin of the Rocks*. The accumulated references suggest the interests of the Milanese 'academy' – perspective, architecture, geometry, painting – and the whole tone suggests a coterie production for a private circle of intimates. It is possible that the *'libro danticaglie'* ('book of antiquities') which appears in the Madrid book-list is a record of Leonardo's own copy of it.

I would also relate to this sodality or academy Bramante's enigmatic *Men at Arms* frescos, now in the Brera Gallery but formerly in the Casa Panigarola on Via Lanzone. The cycle featured seven standing figures in fictive niches, and a half-length portrait of two Greek philosophers, Democritus and Heraclitus. Only two of the standing figures survive entire: one is a courtier carrying a mace, the other a warrior in armour flourishing a large sword. The others, who have lost their lower halves, are harder to individuate, but one wearing a laurel wreath is clearly a poet, and another seems to be a singer. According to Pietro Marani, the cycle expresses a Neoplatonic idea of the 'hero', whose *virtù* comes from a tempering of physical force (the warriors with weapons) and spiritual elevation (the singer and the poet).[121] The 'LX' monogram behind the philosophers may stand for *lex*, law, again with a Platonic overtone in which 'law' refers philosophically to the underlying harmonic order of things. The date of the frescos is uncertain, nor is it known who owned the house at the time they were painted there.[122] The figures are comparable to Bramante's fine panel painting *Christ at the Column* (also in the Brera), generally dated to the 1490s, and the philosophical tone seems to belong within the ambit of the 'academy'.

My interest centres on that double portrait of the philosophers Democritus and Heraclitus, seated at a table with a large terrestrial globe between them. Their identities are signalled by their traditional attributes of laughter and tears. Democritus was said to have laughed at the follies of mankind, and Heraclitus was known as the 'weeping philosopher' because of his pessimistic view of the human condition. This painting has an even more precise connection back to the Ficinian academy, for a picture on exactly the same subject hung in what Ficino called the *gymnasium*, i.e. lecture-room, of the academy at Careggi. Ficino writes, in his Latin edition of Plato, 'Have you seen, painted in my lecture-room, the sphere of the world with Democritus and Heraclitus either side of it? One of them is laughing and the other weeps.'[123] Historically earlier than Plato, the two philosophers represent fundamentally opposite responses to the human condition – another dualism which the Platonic adept sought to rise above, or to 'temper' into equilibrium.

By the time of the fresco's removal to the Brera, in 1901, the portrait of the two philosophers hung above a mantelpiece in the room containing the rest of the fresco, but an eighteenth-century description of the Casa Panigarola states that 'Heraclitus and Democritus were to be seen above the door in the next room', before being moved by the then owner into the frescoed room.[124] So the picture was originally a kind of introduction to the *Men at Arms* fresco: as you walked towards that sumptuously decorated room, the two philosophers greeted you at the doorway, invited you in, and generally set the tone of the experience – that tone including, for those who knew about such things, a direct allusion to the imagery of the Florentine academy of Ficino.

According to Lomazzo, some of the figures in the *Men at Arms* were portraits of Milanese contemporaries. Technical analysis tends to confirm this: each of the heads constitutes a whole *giornata* (a day's painting, measurable as a discrete area of plaster), which shows that Bramante was taking great care over their features. The philosophers certainly have a contemporary look. They do not have the usual attributes of ancient philosophers – no long beards or flowing antique robes. They are clean-shaven and, in the case of Heraclitus, in patently Renaissance costume. There is a good case for taking Democritus as a self-portrait. Comparison can be made with Raphael's portrait of Bramante in the *School of Athens* fresco in the Vatican, where he appears as Euclid, and in a related chalk portrait in the Louvre. These show him round-faced and very bald. The *School of Athens* was painted in about 1509, more than a decade after the Panigarola fresco, but the generic resemblance is strong: one notes particularly the incipient baldness of Democritus.

If Democritus is Bramante, who is Heraclitus? It is surely his friend and fellow philosopher Leonardo da Vinci, whose fascination with flux and movement could be seen as parallel to the philosophy of Heraclitus ('all things flow; nothing abides'), and whose general aura of mystery and wisdom might earn him the other epithet applied to Heraclitus, the 'Dark One'.[125]

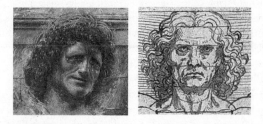

Two possible images of Leonardo in Milan. The philosopher Heraclitus, from a fresco by Donato Bramante (left), and the face of the Vitruvian Man.

There are further pointers to this identification. First, it has been noticed that the manuscript book on the desk in front of Heraclitus is written from right to left: the initial capital of the text is clearly shown at the top right-hand side of the page. Second, the depiction of the philosophers accords precisely with Leonardo's own instructions in the *Trattato della pittura*: 'He who sheds tears raises his eyebrows at their juncture and draws them together, producing wrinkles between and above them, and the corners of his mouth are turned down; but he who laughs has the corners of his mouth turned up, and his brows are open and relaxed.'[126] It is also notable that in a later Milanese painting of Heraclitus and Democritus, attributed to Lomazzo, Heraclitus is almost certainly an image of Leonardo according to the later template of the long-bearded sage, suggesting a connection in Lomazzo's mind which the Bramante fresco may have created.

Take away the tears and the wrinkled, sunken eyes – Heraclitan attributes of sorrow – and we see here a fresco portrait of Leonardo da Vinci painted by one of his closest friends (above). It shows him in his mid-forties, with long, dark curling hair, a fur-trimmed gown, and long-fingered hands elegantly laced together. It is one of only two images of Leonardo that remain from these years in Milan, the other being the 'Vitruvian Man' of *c.* 1490, whose face bears a strong similarity to Heraclitus.

✣ LEONARDO'S GARDEN ✣

In 1497 Leonardo became the owner of a plot of land with a vineyard. It was outside the Porta Vercellina, between the convent of the Grazie and the monastery of San Vittore. Strictly speaking this was not the first property that Leonardo owned – there was that heavily mortgaged house in the Val d'Elsa which features in the contract for the *Adoration* – but this was properly his, without strings attached, and it was still his when he drew up his will twenty-two years later. In the will it is described as 'a garden which he owns outside the walls of Milan'. That was how he remembered it, as the shadows lengthened around him in France: his garden.

It was a gift from Ludovico. No record survives of the actual transfer of the land to him, but the date is given in a later document concerning a neighbouring property. In this – a contract between the Moor's attorneys and a widow named Elisabetta Trovamala – reference is made to Leonardo's vineyard having been ceded to him by the Camera Ducale fourteen months previously; the contract is dated 2 October 1498, so Leonardo took possession of the vineyard in early August 1497.[127] This would have been around the time he completed the *Last Supper*.

The land covered an area of about 16 pertiche. The pertica (pole) is etymologically related to the English perch, but is a much larger unit. According to Leonardo it was equivalent to 1,936 square braccia. The value of the braccio is not precise – Milanese braccia were slightly longer than Florentine ones – but in rounded terms this makes the vineyard just over a hectare in area, or in English terms getting on for 3 acres, a good-sized country garden. According to Luca Beltrami's classic study *La vigna di Leonardo* (1920), its dimensions were approximately 200 m long by 50 m wide (220 × 55 yards) – long and thin, as vineyards often are.[128]

It is always described as Leonardo's vineyard or garden, but there was certainly a house of some sort on it. In a document of 1513 it is described as '*sedimine uno cum zardino et vinea*', which estate-agents today might translate as 'a detached residence with garden and vineyard'.[129] It was by then under the management of Salai: he rented part of it out, for 100 lire per annum, while reserving some of its rooms to accommodate his widowed mother. It was thus something more than a vineyard *casetta* or wine-shed, though not necessarily very grand. There is talk of building-works in the garden in 1515, but whether this was a new house or the original house being refurbished is not clear.

Leonardo's notes and sketch-maps minutely tabulate the lengths and breadths of his precious patch of land:

From the bridge to the centre of the gate is 31 braccia.
Begin the first braccia right there at the bridge.
And from that bridge to the corner of the road, 23½ braccia.

He disappears into a labyrinth of convertible units – parcels (*particelli*) and squares (*quadretti*) as well as perches and arms – and thence into related differentials of value. He calculates the value of the land at 4 soldi per quadretto, which works out at 371 lire per pertica, which gives an overall value of his land of '1931 and ¼' ducats.[130] These trailing sums – practical fruit of Paciolian arithmetic – convey Leonardo's sense of the land as a tangible asset, a conferring of substance and security, something one can understand as important to a 45-year-old man of no fixed abode and no steady income. We can also guess how much Leonardo loved it for itself, for its beauty and tranquillity and verdancy, its refuge from the pestered streets of summer in the city.

The site lies south of the Grazie, behind the row of buildings whose frontage runs along the south side of Corso Magenta. When Beltrami was researching the case eighty-five years ago there was still a vineyard here. Today you can still see a thin wedge of greenery, with that focused lushness of the town-garden, and you can celebrate this partial survival with a meal at the Orti di Leonardo restaurant, at a spot roughly corresponding with the eastern end of the vineyard. This part of town is now a residential area for the Milanese *haute bourgoisie*. The tall, ornate apartment-blocks have neoclassical balconies and an air of *Risorgimento* self-esteem. To the south lies the San Giuseppe hospital, and the old San Vittore monastery with its fine Renaissance cloisters. From there you cut back up towards the Grazie, along Via Zenale, with the ghostly vineyard on your right-hand side. This road, connecting the Grazie with San Vittore, was built or enlarged in 1498. Some plans in Leonardo's notebooks relate specifically to this project.[131] Perhaps the improvements to the road would enhance the value of his property: a kickback.

The area outside the Porta Vercellina was leafy and desirable, and there had been a good deal of development there in recent years, especially of houses and gardens for ducal functionaries. Among those who lived there was Galeazzo Sanseverino, the friend of Leonardo and Pacioli and probable patron of their 'academy'. The stables of this fine horseman were famous – some studies of stables by Leonardo, dating from the later 1490s, may be a project for renovating them.[132] According to a sixteenth-century chronicle, Arluno's *De bello gallico*, 'These stables were so beautiful and finely decorated that you would believe that the horses of Apollo and Mars yoked together were stabled there.' Vasari is perhaps referring to them when he writes of some frescos by Bramantino, 'Outside the Porta Vercellina, near the castle, he decorated certain stables, today ruined and destroyed. He painted some horses being groomed, and one of them was so lifelike that another horse thought it was real, and aimed several kicks at it.'[133]

Another prominent family, the Atellani family, were also given property here by the Moor. The front of their house was on the Vercelli road (present-day Corso Magenta); the garden at the back of it abutted on to

Leonardo's vineyard, forming its northern boundary. The house was later decorated with ceiling frescos by Bernardino Luini, full (like so much of Luini's work) with Leonardesque motifs; these belong to the early sixteenth century, when the Atellani house was the focus of one of the most distinguished intellectual circles in Milan.[134]

A note of Leonardo's refers to some other neighbours in this up-market suburb: 'Vangelista' and 'Messer Mariolo'.[135] It is tempting to think the former refers to his late colleague Evangelista de Predis, but it seems unlikely. 'Messer Mariolo' is Mariolo de' Guiscardi, a leading Milanese courtier, and it is probable that a series of architectural plans in the Codex Atlanticus refers to Leonardo's work on the Guiscardi mansion, which was described in 1499 as 'newly built and not yet finished'. One of these plans has some specifications in the hand of the client himself:

We want a parlour of 25 braccia, a guardroom for myself, and a room with two smaller rooms off for my wife and her maids, with a small courtyard.

Item, a double stable for 16 horses with a room for the grooms.

Item, a kitchen with attached larder.

Item, a dining room of 20 braccia for the staff.

Item, one room.

Item, a chancellery [i.e. an office].

Leonardo's own notes are revealing both of the requirements of rich, fussy clients and of his own fastidiousness:

The large room for the retainers should be away from the kitchen, so the master of the house may not hear their clatter. And let the kitchen be convenient for washing the pewter so it may not be seen being carried through the house . . .

The larder, wood-store, kitchen, chicken-coop, and servants' hall should be adjoining, for convenience. And the garden, stable, and manure-heaps should also be adjoining . . .

The lady of the house should have her own room and hall apart from the servants' hall . . . [with] two small rooms besides her own, one for the serving-maids and the other for the wet-nurses, and several small rooms for their utensils . . .

Food from the kitchen may be served through wide low windows, or on tables that turn on swivels . . .

The window of the kitchen should be in front of the buttery so firewood can be taken in.

I want one door to close the whole house.[136]

This last specification recalls a house-design in Paris MS B, within the ambit of the 'ideal city', with the note 'Lock up the exit marked *m* and you have locked up the whole house.'[137] This is eminently practical, but also suggestive of Leonardo's fierce tendencies to secrecy and privacy – the hermetic closure within an interior world.

Within his 'garden' Leonardo is his own man. He paces his boundaries, and inspects his vines, and sits under shady trees plotting improvements he will never get round to making. He potters. And in the castle, as if to celebrate this pastoral mood, he is also creating a kind of garden – the wonderful fictive bower of the Sala delle Asse.

In sombre mood after the death of his wife in childbirth in January 1497, Ludovico Sforza began to remodel the north wing of the castle for his private retreat. On the ground floor of the north tower was the Sala delle Asse, the Panel Room, so called because it had wooden panels featuring Sforza family crests round the walls. Leading off from this were two smaller rooms called the Salette Negre (the Little Black Rooms), which gave on to the charming but now dilapidated loggia spanning the castle moat.

Here Leonardo was at work in 1498, as we gather from reports by the Duke's treasurer Gualtiero Bascapé – the 'Messer Gualtieri' who is shown holding up the Moor's robes in an allegorical drawing by Leonardo:

20 April 1498 – The Saletta Negra is being done according to your commission . . . and there is agreement between Messer Ambrosio [i.e. the Duke's engineer Ambrogio Ferrari] and Magister Leonardo, so that all is well and no time will be wasted before finishing it.

21 April 1498 – on Monday the large Camera delle Asse in the tower will be cleared out. Maestro Leonardo promises to have everything finished by the end of September.[138]

Thus Leonardo was finishing decoration-work on the Salette Negre in April 1498, and the Sala delle Asse was being prepared for him to start work on it immediately. He undertook to 'have everything finished' by the end of September: five months away.

The frescoed ceiling of the Sala delle Asse is virtually all that is left to us of Leonardo's work as an interior decorator for the Sforza. Nothing remains of his work at the summer-palace of Vigevano in 1494, or in Beatrice Sforza's apartments – the *camerini* – in 1496, or indeed in the 'Little Black Rooms' which he was painting just before he set to work on the Sala delle Asse. In this large, long-windowed but intrinsically rather gloomy room he

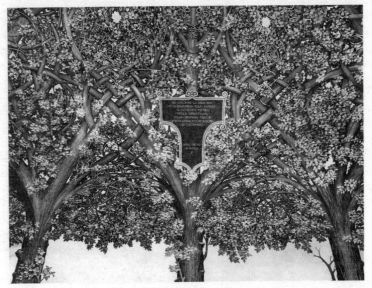

Part of the Sala delle Asse fresco.

created a wonderful fantasia, a rhapsody in green. A dense tracery of intertwined branches covers the walls and ceiling, creating a lush interior bower; through the glossy foliage meanders a golden rope, looped and knotted. G. P. Lomazzo is no doubt describing this room when he says, 'In the trees one finds a beautiful invention of Leonardo's, making all the branches form into bizarre knot-patterns, a technique also used by Bramante, weaving them all together' – a comment which links the Sala delle Asse with the intricate knot-patterns of the academy 'logo', the originals of which would have been created around the same time.

The pattern is created by eighteen trees, their trunks beginning at floor level. Some ramify horizontally; two pairs curve inward to form leafy arches over the room's two windows; and eight trunks ascend to the vaulted ceiling, there to converge on the central, gold-rimmed oculus bearing the jointed arms of Ludovico and Beatrice. The sturdy trees symbolize the strength and dynastic growth of the Sforza family (the rooted tree appears as a Sforza emblem in two roundels at Vigevano), while the golden thread running through the branches can be related to the d'Este *fantasia dei vinci*, and perhaps to the golden sleeve-patterns of the *Lady with a Pearl Necklace*, which may be a portrait of Beatrice by Ambrogio de Predis.[139]

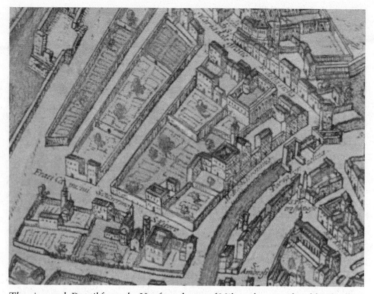

The vineyard. Detail from the Hoefnagel map of Milan, showing the old Vercellina Gate (the L-shaped structure to the right), and Santa Maria delle Grazie (top). The wide diagonal road at the centre is present-day Via Zenale; the vineyard lay within the walled area to the right of this.

This dazzling mural was rediscovered in 1893, when the heavy whitewash which then covered the entire room was removed from one of the walls. (Who whitewashed it in the first place, and for what discernible reason, is not known.) Under the direction of Luca Beltrami (then superintendent of works at the castle) the decor was restored, and the Sala was reopened to the public in 1902. The restoration has been roundly condemned ever since – 'in some ways almost an act of vandalism' – because of what seem to be excessive interpolations and additions.[140] The obvious interventions were removed in a later restoration (in 1954), but the relationship between what we now see and what Leonardo put there remains veiled.

One area that escaped the overzealous restorer is a patch of the north-eastern wall, near the window which looks out on to the back of the Salette Negre. It is a monochrome section of under-painting, apparently unfinished. Beltrami thought it a later addition, and had it covered up with a wooden panel, but it is now considered to be the work of an assistant executing a conception direct from the *maestro*. It shows the roots of a giant tree wrapped powerfully through strata of stone, which seem to be the foundations of an ancient ruined building. One is reminded of Leonardo's fable about the nut which lodges itself in the crannies of a wall, and germinates, 'and as the twisted roots grew thicker they began to thrust the walls apart, and force the ancient stones from their places. And then the wall, too late and in vain, bewailed the cause of its destruction.'[141]

If this was meant to suggest the rooted strength of the Sforza, events would swiftly give it another meaning. The dynasty celebrated so gorgeously in the spreading foliage of the Sala delle Asse was about to topple and fall, and with it the fortunes of many others, including Leonardo. There had been a note of contentment – the *Last Supper* completed and acclaimed, the camaraderie of the academy, the quiet pleasures of his garden. The features of that careworn philosopher in the Bramante fresco seem to have lightened a little. But this respite now proves to be brief, as in early 1499 news reaches Milan that the French are mustering an invasion-force under their new king, Louis XII – the former Duc d'Orléans, whose claim to the duchy of Milan Ludovico had unwisely laughed off five years previously.

⇥ 'SELL WHAT YOU CANNOT TAKE . . .' ⇤

As the French troops mass on the frontiers of Italy, Leonardo begins to wind up his affairs. On 1 April 1499 he disburses money:

Salai 20 lire
For Fazio 2 lire
Bartolomeo 4 lire
Arigo 15 lire[142]

Of these, Fazio is probably Fazio Cardano, father of the mathematician Girolamo Cardano: he perhaps appears here as a creditor. The others are assistants: Salai, now nineteen; Bartolomeo, who may be Bramantino; and a certain Arigo, a new name, probably a German like Giulio. ('Arrigo' is essentially Harry, from Heinrich; one remembers Leonardo's German godfather, Arrigo di Giovanni Tedesco.) The name appears again on a list of Leonardo's dated *c.* 1506–8.

On the same sheet, Leonardo grosses up the money in his cash-box, in various coinages – ducats, florins, grossoni, etc. It comes to a total of 1,280 lire. He then wraps the money up in paper packets, some white, some blue. He distributes them around the studio – one near the box where he keeps nails, others at either end of a 'long shelf', while in the cash-box itself he places only some 'handfuls of *ambrosini*', Milanese small change, wrapped in a cloth. This is vivid: the *maestro* arranging a little treasure-hunt; his placing of the coloured packages, just so. He is imagining the robbers or looters – they will be here soon enough. They will find the cash-box, of course, but not the packets casually concealed among the clutter. A cunning plan, though not without elements of that Freudian tic of 'perseveration', the disguising or deflecting of stress in fussy repetitive actions.

In May the French enter Italy; by late July, they have taken Asti and are at the fortress of Arazzo, menacing the edge of the dukedom. Then comes the surprise defection of Gianfrancesco Sanseverino, brother of Galeazzo, at whose house Leonardo's production of *Jupiter and Danae* had been performed. A note perhaps belongs to this time of military tension: 'In the park of the Duke of Milan I saw a 700 pound cannon-ball shot from a height of one braccio. It bounced 28 times, the length of each bounce having the same proportion to the previous one as the height of each bounce had to the next.'[143]

'On the first day of August 1499' – Leonardo calmly writes on a sheet in the Codex Atlanticus – 'I wrote here on movement and weight.' The page is indeed filled with notes on this subject: studies connected with the mechanical investigations of Madrid I and the physics ('*scientia de ponderibus*') of the Forster notebooks. On the same sheet are sketches and notes for the 'bath-house of the Duchess', and in a contemporary notebook, under the heading 'Bath-house', he notes, 'To heat the water for the stove of the Duchess add three parts of hot water to four parts of cold water.'[144] The Duchess must be Isabella of Aragon, widow of Gian Galeazzo. She was a neighbour, quartered in another part of the Corte Vecchia, together with her sick son, Francesco, the 'Duchino'. Perhaps Leonardo's helpfulness on the matter of her hot-water supply has an overtone of expediency. She was no friend of the Moor, who had kept her a virtual prisoner and whom she suspected of having poisoned her husband; her son would be among the first to be 'liberated' after the French occupation. Leonardo was thus close to one who looked forward to the arrival of the invader.

The French advance continued. Valenza fell on 19 August; next Alessandria. On 30 August Milan was in chaos, as a popular uprising was fomented by the anti-Sforza faction, led by Giangiacomo Trivulzio. The Duke's treasurer Antonio Landriani was killed. On 2 September, needing no astrologer now to read the signs, Ludovico Sforza fled Milan. He headed north, for Innsbruck, where he hoped to rally support from Emperor Maximilian. The keeper of the castle, Bernardino da Corte, surrendered his post, and on

6 September, with no resistance offered, Milan fell to the French. The following day, the chronicler Corio relates:

The mob gathered at the house of Ambrogio Curzio, and destroyed it completely, so that almost nothing of value could be found there; and the same was done to the garden of Bergonzio Botta, the Duke's master of payments, and to the *palazzo* and stables of Galeazzo Sanseverino, and to the house of Mariolo, Ludovico's chamberlain, recently built and not yet completed.[145]

Leonardo knew all these men and their families. He knew their houses – he was probably the architect of Mariolo's, just round the corner from his vineyard. He knew each and every one of the terrified horses in Galeazzo's stables.

On 6 October Louis XII entered the city in triumph. He remained there about six weeks – dangerous weeks of occupation, especially for those associated with the Moor. Did Leonardo deal with the French? Did he parlay? Almost certainly he did. There is the puzzling case of the 'Ligny memorandum', a sheet in the Codex Atlanticus on which he writes, 'Find Ingil and tell him that you will wait for him at Amor and that you will go to him to Ilopan.'[146] The first coded name – in so far as writing it backwards is a code – is 'Ligni', who is the French military leader Louis de Luxembourg, Comte de Ligny. It is possible that Leonardo had met him in 1494, when Ligny accompanied his cousin Charles VIII on that earlier, more diplomatic, French incursion into Milan. Now Leonardo wants to speak with him, and indeed to accompany him on some projected expedition to Naples ('Ilopan'). On the same sheet he determines to 'get from Jean de Paris the method of colouring *a secco*, and his method for making tinted paper'. Jean de Paris was the noted French painter Jean Perréal, who had accompanied the expedition. Elsewhere in the Atlanticus is a '*Memoria a M[aest]ro Leonardo*', in another hand, which exhorts him 'to produce as soon as possible the report [*nota*] on conditions in Florence, especially the manner and style in which the reverend father Friar Jeronimo [Savonarola] has organized the state of Florence'.[147] This request for political information may belong to the same rapprochement with the French.

Two years later, back in Florence, Leonardo was painting the *Madonna of the Yarnwinder* for the French King's favourite Florimond Robertet, and was turning down other commissions because of certain unspecified 'obligations' he had to the King himself. If these reflect personal contact with King Louis and with Robertet, that contact must have been made in Milan in 1499. He may also have met the charismatic Cesare Borgia, 'Il

Valentino', currently in command of a French squadron, and later his employer in the theatre of war.

Leonardo remained in Milan until December. The sheet with the Ligny memorandum also contains a list of things to do as he prepares for departure:

Have 2 boxes made.

Muleteer's blankets – or better, use the bedspreads. There are 3 of them, and you will leave one of them at Vinci.

Take the braziers from the Grazie.

Get the Theatre of Verona from Giovanni Lombardo.

Buy tablecloths and towels, caps and shoes, 4 pairs of hose, a chamois jerkin and skins to make others.

Alessandro's lathe.

Sell what you cannot take with you.

On 14 December he transferred the sum of 600 florins to an account in Florence at the Ospedale di Santa Maria Nuova. His Milanese bankers were the Dino family; the money was transferred by two bills of exchange for 300 florins each; some weeks would pass before the money was safely deposited in Florence.[148] His departure was probably precipitated by rumours of the Moor's imminent return to Milan. The French leaders had somewhat complacently decamped – Louis XII and Ligny to France; the army under Stuart d'Aubigny and Borgia to Ferrara – and loyalist factions were bruiting the Duke's return, boosted with Swiss mercenaries and imperial backing from Maximilian.

In the event the Moor's comeback was brief and inglorious, but Leonardo did not wait around for it. He was one who had stayed during the French occupation, one who could be said to have 'collaborated' with the occupiers. He could not expect much sympathy from a reascendant Moor. It was thus as a fugitive from his former patron, as much as a refugee from circumstances, that Leonardo left Milan in the last days of 1499. The transfer of his savings on 14 December was probably his last act in Milan: the final reckoning, nearly eighteen years after his ambitious arrival with his sheaf of drawings and his custom-built lyre and his retinue of louche young Florentines. It is a different Leonardo who leaves now: forty-seven years old, his chamois jerkin buttoned up against the cold, quitting the uncertain accomplishments of the Sforza years for an even more uncertain future.

PART SIX

On the Move
1500–1506

Motion is the cause of all life.

Paris MS H, fol. 141r

Leonardo's first port of call was Mantua, and the court of the young marchioness, Isabella d'Este. He had doubtless met her already in Milan: she was there in 1491, at the wedding of her sister Beatrice to Ludovico, and again in early 1495, when news came of the French victory over Naples – a matter that touched her more nearly because her husband, Francesco Gonzaga, was among those fighting the French. She knew of Leonardo's portrait of Cecilia Gallerani, which she had had sent to her so she could compare it with portraits by the Venetian *maestro* Giovanni Bellini; and she knew of Leonardo's musical protégé Atalante Migliorotti, whom she had summoned to Mantua in 1490 to sing the title role in a performance of Poliziano's *Orfeo*. In short, she and Leonardo were *au courant*, though whether there was much personal rapport between them is another matter.

Isabella d'Este was strong-willed, ferociously cultivated, and very rich. Though only in her mid-twenties, she ruled her court like an imperious *maîtresse* of a Parisian salon. The d'Este of Ferrara were one of the oldest and most illustrious families in Italy; their fiefdom included Modena, Ancona and Reggio. (There was also a German branch, founded in the late eleventh century, from which are descended the Este-Guelph houses of Brunswick and Hanover, and thence the British royal family.) Isabella was sixteen when, in January 1491, she married Francesco Gonzaga II, Marquis of Mantua, in a diplomatic triple-move of which the other parts were the marriages of her sister to Ludovico and of her brother to Ludovico's niece Anna. The Gonzaga had been sworn enemies of the Visconti of Milan, but through the marriages of these eligible sisters the Sforza and the Gonzaga were now allies to one another and to Ferrara.

Isabella arrived in Mantua in style, sailing in an aquatic fantasia down the Po and entering the small, elegant fortress-city in a triumphal carriage, her possessions spilling out of thirteen painted marriage-chests. She swiftly became an icon of this era of conspicuous consumption, an avid and some-times unscrupulous collector of precious and pretty things. She spoke petu-lantly of her sister's fortune – the Sforza were even richer than the Gonzaga, but Beatrice was not a collector. 'Would to God that we who spend willingly should have so much,' Isabella said. She built on the Gonzaga collection of gems, cameos and intaglios – small, portable assets which were popular collectables – but in the later 1490s her letters show a broadening of interest. 'You know how hungry we are for antiquities,' she writes to her agent in Rome in 1499. And 'We are now interested in owning some figurines and heads, in bronze and marble.'[1] These antiques and figurines were for the display-rooms she was creating in the Gonzaga castle – her famous *studiolo* and its companion room, the *grotta*. She began to commission paintings – her interest in Bellini and Leonardo, as evinced in her letter to Cecilia Gallerani, was part of this. Eventually the *studiolo* was decorated with nine large pictures: elaborate allegories specified by Isabella herself. Two were by the veteran Mantuan court artist Andrea Mantegna, two by Lorenzo Costa of Ferrara, and one by Leonardo's old stablemate Perugino; but none, despite her efforts, was by Leonardo.

Isabella was a woman of high intelligence and discernment. She was a patron of poets and musicians, and was an accomplished lutenist herself; the light amorous love-song known as the *frottola* was a speciality of her soirées. But she was above all a collector, her enthusiasm tending to obsessiveness. Among her possessions when she died in 1539 were 1,241 coins and medals; 72 vases, flasks and cups, of which 55 were of *pietre dure* (agate, jasper, etc.); some 70 statues and statuettes in bronze, marble and *pietre dure*, and 13 portrait busts; watches, inlaid boxes, pieces of coral, an astrolabe, a 'unicorn horn', and a fish's tooth 'three palms long'.[2]

Leonardo's half-length portrait drawing of Isabella, now in the Louvre, was almost certainly done in the winter of 1499–1500, while he was her guest at Mantua. One may call it his meal-ticket. It is a finished drawing done in black chalk, red chalk and yellow pastel. It has apparently been cropped at the bottom: an anonymous sixteenth-century copy (Christ Church, Oxford), which is close to the original in every other respect, shows that her hands are resting on a parapet, and that the extended index-finger of her right hand is pointing at a book which is also on the parapet. The drawing's large format suggests a preparatory cartoon for a painting, so do the perforations around the outline of the image, for transferring it on to the panel. Leonardo never delivered a painted portrait to her, though there is evidence that he started on one – of this lost work, more later.

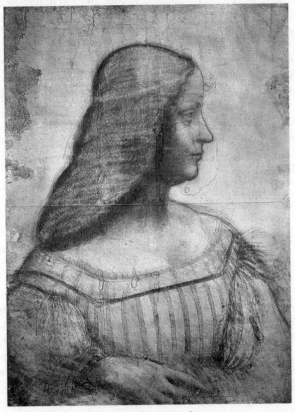

Isabella d'Este by Leonardo, 1500

The drawing presents a subtle contrast between the sweetness of the modelling and the intimated wilfulness in the profile. We see an aristocratic young woman complacent in the knowledge that her wishes will be satisfied by those – the portraitist, for instance – who are paid to satisfy them. The face is a little plump and a little 'spoilt': she might be given to pettishness; she might stamp her foot when vexed, or giggle when pleased. That Isabella was a princess of caprices we know from other sources. When her lapdog Aura died in 1512 she called for tributes – and got them, in both Latin and Italian. Machiavelli, a Florentine envoy in Mantua, noted testily that she got up late and received no official visitors before midday. The full profile – the 'numismatic' style of coins and medals – presents her in a noble, authoritative mode. The portrait shows both how she wanted to be seen and how Leonardo actually saw her, and so contains an ironic subtext about the expedient flatteries of the artist in need of protection in these difficult days.

Leonardo did not stay long in Mantua. He continued on to Venice, probably in February 1500. He was certainly there by mid-March, when he was visited by Lorenzo Guznago. A Ferrarese musician and instrument-maker now resident in Venice, Guznago had previously been at the Sforza court in Milan, and so probably knew Leonardo personally. On 13 March he wrote a letter to Isabella which included the following: 'Also here in Venice is Leonardo da Vinci, who has shown me the portrait of Your Ladyship, which is very true to nature and beautifully done. It couldn't possibly be better.' Behind the curtain of bland superlatives one discerns Leonardo in his lodgings in Venice; and beside him on the easel a portrait of Isabella d'Este. Guznago describes it as a *ritratto*, which almost certainly means a painting rather than a drawing. (*Ritratto* can also mean a copy, and in that sense can be a drawing, but this cannot be the meaning of the word here.) This painting may not be finished, but it is substantive enough to be praised as very lifelike and 'beautifully done'.[3]

This lost portrait of Isabella d'Este is of particular interest because it probably contained the first painted version of the hands of the *Mona Lisa*. The crossed hands of the cartoon – only partially present in the Louvre drawing, but reconstructable from the Christ Church copy (Plate 20) – are almost identical to those more famous hands: the fingers of the right hand and their light placing on the left forearm, which in turn rests flat on a solid surface (the parapet in the drawing, the arm of a chair in the *Mona Lisa*). Other anticipations of the *Mona Lisa* are discernible in the drawing. Isabella's hair is not quite distinct, but its shape – its lack of free fall – suggests that it is covered, as is Mona Lisa's, with a thin gauzy veil. And the bust is strongly suggestive of the *Mona Lisa* – the cut of the dress, the first faint indentation of cleavage, the position of the left shoulder – though of course in the *Mona Lisa* the sitter is turned slightly to her right (or to the left of the picture) while the bust of Isabella is turned to her left. This discrepancy can be removed by looking at the back of the Louvre drawing, where the figure of Isabella shows through in reverse (Plate 21). The image is extraordinary: a ghostly Mona Lisa hovers on the paper (though this is partly the result of staining, which obscures the profile of the face, so that the figure seems to have turned towards us).

There are many mysteries about the *Mona Lisa*, but here it seems we have something approaching a fact, which is that certain particulars of her pose and her appearance first appear in a portrait that Leonardo drew, and apparently began painting, in the first months of the year 1500.

Of Leonardo's brief sojourn in Venice – his first as far as we know – there are some small but interesting remains. On a much folded, much corrected sheet in the Codex Atlanticus is the draft of a report to the '*illustrissimi signori*' of the Venetian Senate concerning the possibilities of fortifying the Isonzo river (in the Friuli region north-east of Venice) against the threat of Turkish invasion. This appears to be an official commission. His visit to the area probably took place in early March, before a meeting of the Senate on 13 March at which they nominated certain 'engineers' to be sent to the Friuli.[4] The folds of the paper suggest that the sheet was carried in Leonardo's pocket, out in the field. A sketch in red chalk captioned 'Ponte de Goritia' and 'alta vilpagho' records his presence on the Wippach river near Gorizia. Another location is identified by a later note about the transport of artillery, which should be done 'in the way I suggested at Gradisca in the Friuli'.[5]

He affects a clipped, reportorial style: 'I have carefully examined the conditions of the Isonzo river . . .' He records the height of the floodwaters. He talks to the locals – 'from the country people I have learned that . . .' He comments dourly about the force of water being too powerful for man-made structures to resist. Some of his recommendations seem to have been put into practice, for in a late note in the Codex Arundel, referring to the French palace at Romorantin, he writes, 'Let the sluice be movable, like the one I set up in Friuli.'[6]

Another rather different technology interested him in Venice – printing. The city was at the forefront of the new technology of copper-plate engraving, in which the image was etched with corrosive acid (*aqua fortis*, or strong water) on a sheet of copper. The technique was still at an experimental stage, but Leonardo no doubt understood its potential for the reproduction of his technical drawings. The copper etching had a finesse of line not approachable by the traditional woodcut. It was probably during his stay in 1500 that the 'academy' designs were engraved and printed; six early exemplars survive in the Biblioteca Ambrosiana in Milan. Despite this interest, Leonardo remained snobbish about the superiority of the unique painting over the multiple reproductions of print: 'Painting does not produce endless children as printed books do; she alone is unique, and never gave birth to children who are exactly like her, and this singularity makes her more excellent than those that are published everywhere.'[7]

Of other artistic activities we know little. It is probable he met the new young *maestro* of Venetian painting, Giorgio da Castelfranco, known to the Venetians as Zorzi and to us today as Giorgione – 'Big George'. Leonardo deeply influenced his work. A painting like *The Tempest* (*c.* 1508) is a tribute to Leonardo's sense of colour and light, his *sfumato* technique, his dramatic momentary quality. Leonardo's brief stay in the city in 1500 is a particular moment of interchange within this more general influence.

In mid-April 1500 news reached Venice from Milan. There had been a brief resurgence of Sforza fortunes in early February, when loyalist troops under Ascanio Sforza and Galeazzo Sanseverino re-entered the city. But the Moor's bruited return was halted at Novara, and on 10 April his army of Swiss mercenaries was put to flight, and he himself was captured, ignominiously disguised as a servant. By 15 April Milan was back under French control.

On the inside cover of his pocket-book, Paris MS L, Leonardo jots down a brusque digest of this latest turn of events – the staccato sentences seeming to record this news almost as he hears it:

> The governor of the castle made prisoner.
> Bissconte [i.e. Visconti] dragged away and then his son killed.
> Gian della Rosa robbed of his money.
> Borgonzo began then changed his mind and so ran away from fortune.
> The Duke lost his state, and his goods, and his freedom, and none of his works was completed.

Some commentators have dated this to September 1499 – the first incursion of the French – but that the Duke has 'lost . . . his freedom' clearly refers to the capture of Ludovico at Novara. The imprisoned *castellano* is the French governor, who had surrendered the castle to the Milanese in February and was imprisoned when the French recaptured the city on 15 April. Gian della Rosa is probably the Moor's physician and astrologer Giovanni da Rosate, and Borgonzo is the courtier Bergonzio Botta. Leonardo does not mention the more dramatic fate of his friend the architect Giacomo Andrea. He was imprisoned by the French as a pro-Sforza conspirator, and despite influential pleas, was beheaded and quartered at the castle on 12 May. One infers that this had not yet happened when Leonardo wrote this note.

It was indeed true that the Moor had lost his freedom. He was taken to France and imprisoned at Loches, in the Touraine, and there he remained until his death, half-mad from captivity, eight years later. That 'none of his works was completed' is at once a reflection on the mutability of political fortunes and a more personal underlining of the abandonment of the Sforza Horse. Later he would learn of the vandalizing of the clay model of the

Horse by French archers, as recorded by the chronicler Sabba Castiglione. 'I remember,' wrote Castiglione nearly fifty years later, 'and with sadness and anger I say it now, this noble and ingenious work being used as a target by Gascon crossbowmen.'[8]

If Leonardo had been intending to return to Milan, these latest upheavals probably convinced him otherwise. Imprisonments, confiscations, murders. Sometime soon after 15 April he scribbles down these dire bits of news on a notebook cover. By 24 April he is in Florence.

⤜ BACK IN FLORENCE ⤛

On 24 April 1500 Leonardo withdrew 50 florins from his account at Santa Maria Nuova. He was back in Florence after an absence of eighteen years.[9] He found much that was familiar. His father, now in his mid-seventies, was still a practising notary, and still living in Via Ghibellina not far from the site of Verrocchio's old *bottega*. Perhaps the difficulties between the two were by now resolved: the boy had proved himself, and anyway the father had his legitimate children – eleven of them now, the youngest born just a couple of years earlier. The resentments between them had no particular focus any more, though they had perhaps become ingrained. Did Leonardo tell him of the last days of Caterina? Did Ser Piero wish to know?

In the artistic world some of the old faces had gone – the Pollaiuolo brothers were both dead, as was Domenico Ghirlandaio – but Leonardo's former colleague Lorenzo di Credi still ran the workshop he had inherited from Verrocchio, and down on Via della Porcellana Botticelli was still painting in his rarefied and now old-fashioned style. And in the offing – a name but not yet a face, for in 1500 he was down in Rome – was the arrogant new star, the magistrate's son from Caprese, Michelangelo di Ludovico Buonarroti, now twenty-five years old, and putting the finishing touches to his first sculptural masterpiece, the *Pietà*.

But something had gone from Florentine life with the eclipse – temporary though it would prove – of the Medici. These were the gloomy years after the Savonarolan theocracy, that 'Bonfire of the Vanities' which had eventually engulfed Savonarola himself, hanged and burned in the Piazza della Signoria on 23 May 1498. It was a time of financial crisis. Several of the guilds were on the verge of bankruptcy; taxes rose as a costly and ill-conducted war with Pisa – ceded to the French in 1494 – strained the resources of the treasury.

Gingerly Leonardo takes his place amid the familiar but altered landmarks of his youth. It is a time of uncertainty, a new beginning amid old haunts. To the Florentine eye he is strange and capricious. 'Leonardo's life', an observer reports in early 1501, 'is extremely irregular and haphazard [*varia et inderminata*], and he seems to live from day to day.'[10]

Though strange, Leonardo returned an acknowledged master, a famous man – the *Last Supper* his crowning achievement, the Sforza Horse his magnificent failure – and he did not lack offers of work. According to Vasari he was swiftly accommodated as a guest of the Servite friars of the church of Santissima Annunziata:

When Leonardo returned to Florence he found that the Servite friars had commissioned Filippino [Lippi] to paint an altarpiece for the high altar of the Annunziata. Leonardo remarked that he would gladly have undertaken this work himself, and when Filippino heard this, like the good-hearted person he was, he decided to withdraw. Then the friars, to secure Leonardo's services, took him into their house, and met all his expenses and those of his household.

The Santissima Annunziata, abutting on to the Medici sculpture-garden at San Marco, was one of the richest churches in Florence. The mother church of the Servite order, founded in Florence in the early thirteenth century, it had been remodelled by Michelozzo in the 1460s to accommodate the pilgrims who came to view a certain miraculous image of the Virgin. Lorenzo's father, Piero de' Medici, had financed these improvements: the tabernacle which contains the holy image bears the inappropriate-seeming inscription '*Costò fior. 4 mila el marmo solo*' ('The marble alone cost 4000 florins'). The monastery's notary was Ser Piero da Vinci, and this may have been a factor behind the hospitality offered to Leonardo and his 'household'.[11]

On 15 September 1500 the Servites commissioned a large gilded frame for the altarpiece from the architect and woodworker Baccio d'Agnolo. The specified measurements of the frame show that the painting was to be 5 braccia high by 3 wide (about 10 feet by 6 feet) – larger than any previous panel painting by Leonardo.[12]

Vasari continues:

He kept them waiting a long time without even starting anything, then he finally did the cartoon showing Our Lady with St Anne and the Infant Christ. This work not only won the astonished admiration of all the artists, but when it was finished for two days it attracted to the room where it was exhibited a crowd of men and women, young and old, who flocked there as if they were attending a great festival, to gaze in amazement at the marvels he had created.

This gives us a remarkable glimpse of Leonardo's prestige at this time. The completion of a Leonardo cartoon is something with the buzz of a theatrical 'first night'; crowds form in the normally quiet cloisters of the Santissima Annunziata.

The cartoon itself is lost. It is patently not the famous Burlington House cartoon in the National Gallery in London (p. 427), which was drawn some years later and which differs in composition. There is an eyewitness account of the Annunziata cartoon, written in April 1501 by Fra Pietro Novellara, vicar-general of the Carmelites. He describes the drawing as 'not yet finished', so his sight of it seems to pre-date the public viewing described by Vasari. Writing to Isabella d'Este about Leonardo's activities, Novellara says:

Since he has been in Florence he has only done one drawing, in a cartoon. It shows an infant Christ, of about one year old, almost escaping from the arms of his mother. He has got hold of a lamb and seems to be squeezing it. The mother, almost raising herself from the lap of St Anne, holds on to the child in order to draw him away from the lamb, which signifies the Passion. Saint Anne is rising somewhat from her seat; it seems that she wants to restrain her daughter from trying to separate the child from the lamb, which perhaps symbolizes the Church's desire that the Passion should not be impeded from running its course. These figures are life-size, but the cartoon is not so large because they are all seated or leaning over, and each figure is partly in front of another, towards the left-hand side. This drawing is not yet finished.[13]

This cartoon, unfinished in April 1501, is doubtless the one referred to by Vasari as drawing astonished crowds when it was completed. Annoyingly, however, Vasari's description of it is different: 'The virgin . . . is holding the infant Christ tenderly on her lap, and she lets her pure gaze fall on St John, who is depicted as a little boy playing with a lamb.' This tallies neither with Novellara's description (which features the lamb but no St John) nor with the extant London cartoon (which features St John but no lamb). The explanation is not hard to find, for Vasari adds that the Annunziata cartoon 'was subsequently taken to France', which is almost Vasarian shorthand for saying that he had not actually seen it. I suspect his description of the cartoon (like his description of the Mona Lisa which follows immediately after this passage) is cooked up from other accounts. Thus Novellara's is the only dependable record of the 1501 cartoon.

Though it differs in detail from the Burlington House cartoon, the cartoon described by Novellara is remarkably similar to the composition of the finished painting of the Virgin and Child with St Anne now in the Louvre.

The painting itself dates from the end of the decade, *c.* 1510, so it appears that the Annunziata cartoon is a lost prototype of the later painting, and the London cartoon an intermediate variation. There are various smaller pen-and-ink studies of this group. Two of these (in the Accademia, Venice, and in a private collection in Geneva) may be related to the Annunziata cartoon: indeed, the Geneva drawing has a very faded annotation on the verso, in a sixteenth-century hand, which has been read as '*Leonardo alla Nuntiata* [i.e. Annunziata]'.[14]

This is complicated, as Leonardo tends to be, but the upshot is that this subject of the Madonna and her mother, St Anne – this family group from which, the psychologist notes, the father is rigorously excluded – was one that Leonardo returned to repeatedly over a period of about ten years. The lost cartoon of 1501, the London cartoon of *c.* 1508, the Louvre painting of *c.* 1510, the smaller sketches of various periods – these are variations on a compositional theme, recurrent wheelings around a central image. This becomes a norm with Leonardo now – these long, slow evolutions, these masterpieces dense with recurrence: the *Mona Lisa*, the *Leda*, the *Baptist*.

Leonardo 'kept them waiting a long time' before producing the cartoon of the Virgin and St Anne, says Vasari, and we can fill in some of his other activities at this time.

In the summer of 1500 we glimpse him in the hills south of Florence, sketching the villa or country-house of the Florentine merchant Angelo del Tovaglia. This was probably in early August – a good time to be out of the city – for on 11 August a drawing he had done of the house was sent to the Marquis of Mantua, Leonardo's host a few months previously. Tovaglia was one of the Marquis's agents in Florence; the villa stood in the hills south of the city, with superb views over the Val d'Ema. As we gather from the letter that accompanied the drawing, the Marquis had been a guest there a couple of years previously, and had a whim to build a replica of it near Mantua.[15] A large folio at Windsor is probably a pupil's copy of this drawing. It shows an imposing house in 'rusticated' stone, a colonnaded loggia, a terrace and a garden. A drawing in the Codex Arundel, also not by Leonardo, seems to be a detail of the loggia, with some variation in the design of the columns.[16]

Looking at the loggia in the Windsor drawing, one notices that it is open at the back, enclosed only by a low wall on a level with the sills of the ground-floor windows. It looks rather like the sort of loggia on which Mona Lisa sits, which is discernible as a low balustrade behind her, with – just visible at either side of the painting – two rounded pediments suggestive of two columns outside the picture space (or possibly lost owing to a cutting-down of the picture). Raphael's sketch for his portrait of Maddalena Doni, which is generally believed to have been based on a drawing of the *Mona Lisa*, shows the loggia setting more clearly, though the line of the balustrade is higher in relation to the sitter than it is in the *Mona Lisa*. Part of the latter's complex and eerie charm is its slightly surreal double point-of-view, in which the landscape is seen from an implicitly aerial viewpoint but the woman herself is viewed as if you are standing in front of her. Like the cartoon of Isabella d'Este, those views over the Val d'Ema, framed by the columns of the loggia of Tovaglia's villa, may be another of the ghostly sources of the *Mona Lisa*.

Leonardo was also called on at this time as a consultant engineer. The church of San Salvatore dell'Osservanza overlooking Florence had suffered structural damage – 'breakings of the walls', in Leonardo's phrase – owing to slippage in the hillside beneath it. A summary of his recommendations is found in the Florentine state archives: 'Concerning S. Salvatore and the remedies required, Lionardo da Vinci said he has furnished a plan which shows the problem of the buildings in relation to the water-courses, which flow between the strata of rock to the point where the brick-factory is, and . . . where the strata have been cut is where the defect is.'[17] The decision to renovate the drainage-system and the water-channels – as recommended by Leonardo – was taken by the planners on 22 March 1501.

In the early months of 1501 Leonardo took a brief trip to Rome: as far as is known, his first visit – the disappointment of twenty years earlier, when he was passed over by the commissioners of the Sistine Chapel, not quite forgotten. All that is known of the visit is to be found on a folio of the Codex Atlanticus, which has a note: '*a roma attivoli vecchio casa dadriano*', and then lower down a note dated 10 March 1501 about changing money, written in a shaky hand suggestive of being in a cart or on horseback.[18] This suggests he was in Rome in early 1501, and that while there he visited the ruins of Hadrian's villa at Tivoli. The folio also contains a sketch of a circular fortress by a river with a four-pier bridge, which is probably the Castel Sant'Angelo. Several pieces of antique sculpture were excavated at Tivoli in March 1501 – the *Muses*, now in the Prado in Madrid – and Leonardo may have seen them. He no doubt met up with Bramante, who was beginning his great unfinished project of redesigning St Peter's. He also put together a series of designs of antique buildings and sculptures, in a 'book' which is now lost but which was seen by an anonymous Milanese artist who copied some of its drawings and annotated a view of the Teatro

Maritimo at Hadrian's villa, 'This is a temple which was in a book of Maestro Leonardo's, which was done at Rome.'[19]

Mantua, Venice, Florence, Rome – this is the restless, peripatetic tone of Leonardo's life in these first uncertain years of the new century.

⤞ THE INSISTENT MARCHIONESS ⤝

Back in Florence after that brief interlude in Rome, Leonardo returns to the Santissima Annunziata, and in early April 1501 he has a meeting with the well-connected churchman Fra Pietro Novellara, vicar-general of the Carmelites, who comes bearing somewhat peremptory requests from Isabella d'Este. Novellara's brief role as the Marchioness's message-bearer opens up a window on to Leonardo's circumstances and activities, and indeed his mentality, in Florence in 1501. The story, with its curious theme of pursuit and evasion, is told in three letters here translated in full for the first time.[20]

Isabella d'Este to Fra Pietro Novellara; Mantua, 29 March 1501

Most reverend,

If Leonardo Fiorentino the painter is to be found there in Florence, we beg you to discover what his situation is, and whether he has got under way with any work, as I hear that he has, and what work it is, and if you think he is likely to be staying there for some time. Thus Your Reverence could sound him out, as you know how, as to whether he intends to take up the commission to paint a picture for our study: if he is willing to do it, we will leave to his judgement both the theme of the picture and the date of delivery. And if you find him reluctant, you could at least try to persuade him to do me a little picture of the Madonna, in that devout and sweet style which is his natural gift. Would you also ask him to be so good as to send me another sketch of his portrait of us, since His Lordship our consort has given away the one he left here. If all this is done I will be very grateful to you, and to Leonardo himself for what he offers me . . .

Fra Pietro Novellara to Isabella d'Este; Florence, 3 April 1501

Most illustrious and excellent Lady,

I have just received Your Ladyship's letter, and will attend to your requests with all speed and diligence, but from what I understand Leonardo's life is extremely irregular and haphazard, and he seems to live from day to day. Since he has been in Florence he has only done one drawing, in a cartoon . . . [There follows the description of the *Virgin and Child with St Anne* cartoon quoted in the previous chapter.] He has not done anything else, though two of his assistants make copies, and he from time to time adds some touches to them. He devotes much of his time to geometry, and has no fondness at all for the paintbrush. I am writing this only so Your Ladyship should know that I have received your letter. I will do what you ask and advise Your Ladyship as soon as possible.

Fra Pietro Novellara to Isabella d'Este; Florence, 14 April 1501

Most illustrious and excellent Lady,
During this Holy Week I have learned of the intentions of Leonardo the painter, by means of his pupil Salai and some others who are close to him, and to make his intentions clear they brought him to me on Holy Wednesday [7 April]. In short, his mathematical experiments have distracted him so much from painting that he cannot abide the paintbrush. I apprised him of Your Ladyship's wishes and found him very willing to satisfy them, for the kindness you showed him at Mantua. We spoke freely, and arrived at this conclusion – that if he could free himself from his obligations to His Majesty the King of France without incurring disfavour, as he hoped to do within a month at the most, he would sooner serve Your Ladyship than anyone else in the world. In any event, once he has completed a little picture he is doing for a certain Robertet, a favourite of the King of France, he will immediately undertake the portrait, and send it to Your Excellency. I gave him two tokens to encourage him [*dui boni sollicitadori*]. The little picture he is working on is a Madonna who is seated as if she intended to spin yarn, and the Child has placed his foot in the basket of yarns, and has grasped the yarnwinder, and stares attentively at the four spokes, which are in the form of a cross, and as if he were longing for this cross he smiles and grips it tightly, not wishing to yield it to his mother, who appears to want to take it away from him. This is as much as I could get from him. Yesterday I delivered my sermon. May God grant that it bears fruits as plentiful as were its auditors.

These letters give us a glimpse of Leonardo the elusive celebrity. The meeting is fixed up through Salai, as if his personal secretary. The churchman is treated with politeness and evasion. Leonardo is 'brought' to him, they reach a 'conclusion', but when he comes to write to Her Ladyship he finds that the fruits of the meeting were not, after all, very plentiful: 'This is as much as I could get from him.'

We learn also about Leonardo's circumstances: that he is sick of painting, and 'cannot abide the paintbrush'; that he spends his time on mathematical and geometrical studies, continuing the influence of Luca Pacioli (who would himself be billeted in Florence shortly after this). And we find a confirmation of Leonardo's dealings with the French, presumably before

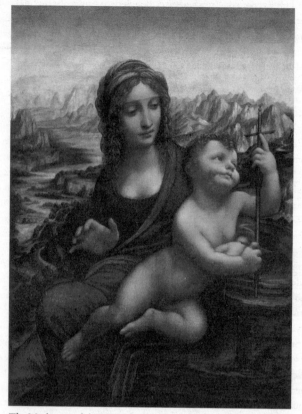

The Madonna of the Yarnwinder *(Reford version), by Leonardo and assistants, c. 1501–4.*

his departure from Milan, for he describes himself as under an 'obligation' to King Louis. It is hard to know what this obligation is: perhaps it is no more than the painting Novellara goes on to describe, which is for the King's 'favourite' Florimond Robertet.[21] Novellara may be exaggerating Leonardo's commitment a little: he is anxious not to give the impression that Leonardo is flatly rejecting the Marchioness's overtures.

This 'little picture' on which Leonardo was working in early 1501 was the *Madonna of the Yarnwinder*. The painting is known in various versions, of which two – both in private collections – have a claim to be partly in the hand of the *maestro*. These are conveniently known as the Reford and Buccleuch versions, though in fact the former is no longer in the Reford collection in Montreal, but in a private collection in New York, and the latter is – at the time of writing – no longer hanging on the staircase of the Duke of Buccleuch's country seat, Drumlanrig Castle, having been stolen in August 2003 by two men posing as tourists.[22] CCTV footage shows the painting being carried off under one of the men's coats as they walk towards a white car, an echo of the theft of the *Mona Lisa* from the Louvre in 1911 in which she left the gallery under the workman's 'smock' of Vincenzo Perugia. These thefts have an overtone of abduction – indeed, Perugia kept the *Mona Lisa* in his room for two years, hidden in a box under the stove, which is almost more a kidnapping than a theft.

Novellara's description of the painting is concise and accurate, but curious for its detail of the 'basket of yarns' at the child's foot, which is not found in any of the known versions. X-rays and infra-red reflectograms have revealed no trace of it, though the examination of the Reford painting did turn up an interesting *pentimento* – a curious flat-roofed building with a door or long window in the façade, placed in the middle distance to the left of the Madonna's head.[23] This was painted over, to become part of the gorgeous hazy landscape of river and rock that stretches off to the ice-blue mountains in the distance. In this landscape one discerns another antici-patory frisson of the *Mona Lisa*. There is in fact a precise echo: in both landscapes there is a long arched bridge spanning the lower reaches of the river (Plate 22). This is often identified with Ponte Buriano, near Arezzo, an area Leonardo travelled and indeed mapped in the summer of 1502.[24]

The iconography of the yarnwinder seems to be original to Leonardo, though it is part of a convention of the Christ-child contemplating symbols of his future Passion, as in Leonardo's early Florentine panels where the symbols are flowers – the blood-red carnation of the Munich *Madonna and Child*, the cruciform bitter cress of the *Benois Madonna*. Leonardo imbues the note of prophecy with his characteristic drama, the momentum of the moment – the flowing motion of the child towards the miniature cross, towards the picture-edge, towards the future; the protective motion of the mother's hand, seemingly arrested in a trance-like instant of tragic premonition. The modelling of the figures is faultless: this is the first figura-tive painting that we know of since the completion of the *Last Supper* four years previously, and it continues that painting's precise and learned depiction of significant gesture: the *moti mentali*. None of this alters one's feeling that the painting teeters on the edge of lushness: of all Leonardo's autograph works, this comes closest to the plumped-up sentimentality of

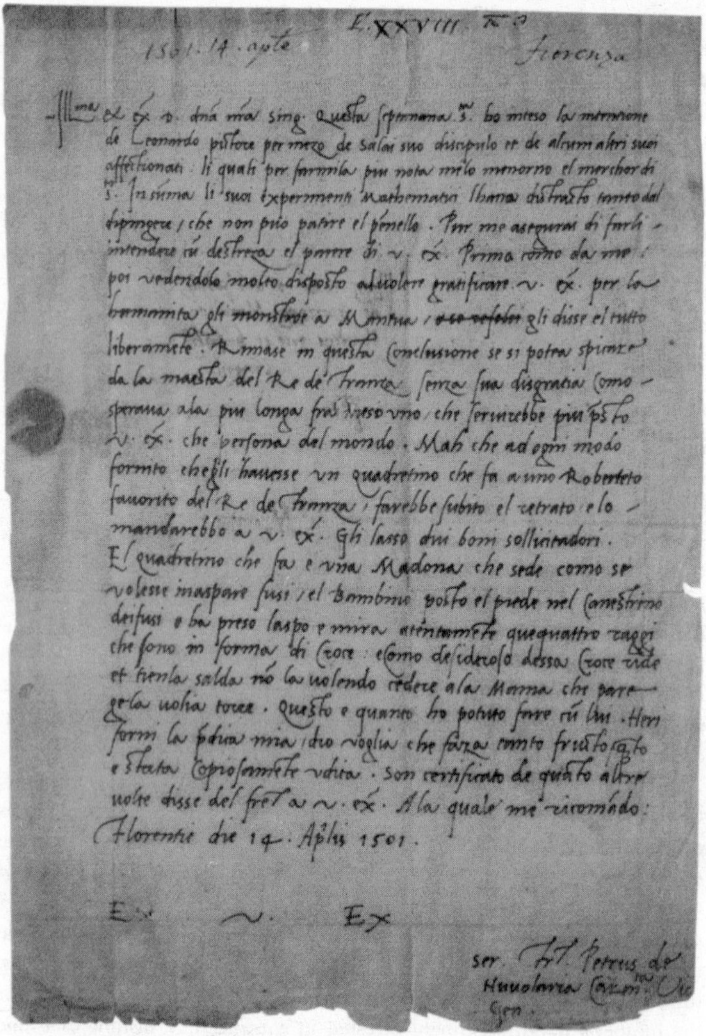

Fra Pietro Novellara to Isabella d'Este, 14 April 1501.

the 'Leonardesco'. The Madonna's extended hand echoes that of the *Virgin of the Rocks*, but is no longer a gesture of benediction. And the face has changed: the willowy girl in that enchanted grotto has become fleshier, broad-faced, more worldly. An innocence has gone.

In July the Marchioness was back on the offensive. She sent a personal letter to Leonardo, no longer extant. It was delivered to him by another of her go-betweens, one Manfredo de' Manfredi, as appears from the latter's report to Isabella, dated 31 July 1501:

I have delivered into his own hand the letter to Leonardo Fiorentino which Your Ladyship recently sent me. I gave him to understand that if he wished to reply I could forward his letters on to Your Ladyship and thus save his costs; he read your letter and said he would do so, but hearing nothing more from him I finally sent one of my men to him to learn what he wished to do. He sent back answer that for now he was not in a position to send another reply to Your Ladyship, but that I should advise you that he has already begun work on that which Your Ladyship wanted from him. In short, this is as much as I have been able to get from the said Leonardo.[25]

One sympathizes with Manfredo, caught between Isabella's irresistible acquisitiveness and Leonardo's immovable reluctance. The picture which Her Ladyship 'wanted from him' could be either her portrait or the painting for her *studiolo* which she speaks of in her letter to Novellara. Manfredo assures her that Leonardo has 'begun work' on it; if he is referring to the portrait, this will not much satisfy the Marchioness, who knows that Leonardo began work on it over a year ago. There is something heartening about Leonardo's aloofness, his refusal to dance to the tune of patronage. He was not in immediate need: he was comfortably billeted at the Annunziata, with his 'expenses met' out of the Servites' capacious coffers; he had a commission, and perhaps other promises, from the French court. He wanted head-space for all the other pursuits of his life: for the mathematics and geometry which promise him 'supreme certainty'; for the mechanical and technological interests which slowly fill the pages of the Madrid codices; and for the great dream of flight which is never far from his mind – the journey 'from one element to another', the journey away from all this chatter.

On 19 November 1501 he draws out another 50 florins from his savings at Santa Maria Nuova.[26] In May 1502, further to another request from Isabella, he views and values some antique vases formerly owned by the Medici. 'I showed them to Leonardo Vinci the painter,' writes yet another

LEONARDO DA VINCI

of her agents, Francesco Malatesta, on 12 May. 'He praised all of them, but
especially the crystal one, because it is all of one piece and very clear . . .
and Leonardo said that he had never seen a better piece.'[27] And between
these casually documented markers of the artist's day-to-day life, between
the visit to the bank and the viewing at the antique-dealer's showroom, there
fell a day of more personal and more ambiguous import: on 15 April 1502
Leonardo turned fifty.

⤏ BORGIA ⤎

Leonardo's opinion on the Medici vases, delivered to Francesco Malatesta
in May 1502, is the last we hear of him in Florence this year. In early
summer he is on the move again. He has a new employer: Cesare Borgia,
illegitimate son of Pope Alexander VI, a byword for ruthlessness and
cunning, the model for Machiavelli's 'prince'. Tales of murder, debauchery
and incest cluster round his family: his younger sister Lucrezia Borgia has a
particularly lethal reputation. Some of it is mythology; some of it is not.
Like the Moor, but even more so, Borgia was not a patron for the squeamish.
Freud believed that these strong men to whom Leonardo gravitated were
substitutes for the absent father of his childhood.

The Borgia family, originally Borja, was of Spanish origin (and bull-
fighting was one of Cesare's macho accomplishments). In 1492 Cardinal
Rodrigo Borja ascended the papal throne as Alexander VI. Sixty years old,
he was a notorious libertine and was fanatically devoted to the advancement
of his illegitimate children. A portrait of him by Pinturicchio shows a bald,
jowly man in a sumptuous robe kneeling unconvincingly before a holy
image. Guicciardini said of him, 'He was perhaps more evil, and more lucky,
than any other pope before him . . . He had in the fullest measure all the
vices of the flesh and of the spirit.'[28] The Florentine Guicciardini was hardly
neutral, but his judgement is echoed by others.

Cesare was Rodrigo's son by his Roman mistress, Giovanna or Vanozza
Cattanei. He was born in 1476; Lucrezia was born to the same mother four
years later. He was made a cardinal at the age of seventeen, though a visitor
to his *palazzo* at Trastevere found his style anything but churchy: 'He was
ready to go hunting, dressed in very secular silk and heavily armed . . . He
is intelligent and charming, and bears himself like a great prince. He is lively
and merry and loves society. This cardinal has never had any inclination for
priesthood, but his benefices bring him in more than 16,000 ducats a year.'[29]
In 1497 his younger brother Giovanni was found floating in the Tiber with

342

his throat cut: the first of many murders attributed to Cesare. It was said that Cesare envied his brother's secular powers (he was Duke of Gandia), whereas he had been given only church benefices. In 1498 he 'doffed the purple' in order to become captain-general of the Church, essentially commander of the papal troops. In France he negotiated an alliance between the Pope and the new king, Louis XII. In 1499 he married Louis's cousin, Charlotte d'Albret, and was created Duke of Valentinois; from this comes his Italian sobriquet Il Valentino, by which he was generally known to his contemporaries. In this year he was part of the French invasion force into Italy, and entered Milan alongside Louis XII. It was probably then that Leonardo first met him: twenty-three years old, tall and powerful, with blazing blue eyes; a brilliant soldier, a ruthless aspirer. His motto, recalling his imperial namesake, was '*Aut Caesar aut nullus*' – 'Caesar or nothing'.

Borgia's plan, for which Louis promised military support, was the conquest of the Romagna, a sprawling and lawless region north of Rome which was nominally under the suzerainty of the Pope but was in effect controlled by independent princelings and prelates. Over the next few months, with a large detachment of French troops, Borgia established a power-base in central Italy, brilliantly creating, as Machiavelli later saw it, a *de facto* 'principality' out of a hitherto formless region. By the end of 1500 he was master of Imola, Forlì, Pesaro, Rimini and Cesena. Faenza fell to him in spring 1501, giving him control of Florence's chief trade-route to the Adriatic. Swaggering under the new title of Duke of Romagna, Borgia now advanced threateningly on Florence itself. The republic parleyed nervously, with the upshot that Borgia was 'engaged' as a *condottiere* at the enormous salary of 30,000 ducats per annum – a Florentine spin on what was essentially the payment of protection-money. Borgia moved off, down to the Tyrrhenian coast, where he added the port-town of Piombino to his possessions.

For a while things were quiet, but in the early summer of 1502 came disquieting news. On 4 June the city of Arezzo rose unexpectedly against Florentine dominion, and declared for Borgia. A couple of weeks later, in one of his characteristic lightning-strikes, Borgia took Urbino, expelling his former ally Guidobaldo da Montefeltro. A Florentine envoy, Francesco Soderini, Bishop of Volterra, was swiftly sent to Borgia at Urbino, and with him went a high-flying civil servant in his early thirties, Niccolò Machiavelli.

In a dispatch of 26 June Machiavelli recounted their audience with Borgia.[30] Darkness had fallen; the doors of the palace were locked and guarded; the Duke was in peremptory mood, demanding 'clear sureties' of Florence's intentions. 'I know your city is not well-minded towards me but would abandon me like an assassin,' he said. 'If you refuse me for a friend you shall know me for an enemy.' The envoys murmured assurances and requested the withdrawal of the Duke's troops from Arezzo. The atmosphere was electric with tension, and Machiavelli's dispatch concludes in a tone of awestruck fascination:

This Duke is so enterprising that nothing is too great to be discounted by him. For the sake of glory and the enlarging of his dominions, he deprives himself of rest, yielding to no fatigue, no danger. He arrives in one place before anyone knows he has left the other, he gains the good will of his soldiers, he attracts to him the best men in Italy, and he has constant good luck. For all these reasons he is victorious and formidable.

Machiavelli was back in Florence by the end of the month. Not long after came the news that the 'formidable' Duke had taken Camerino and was setting his sights on Bologna.

It is in this context that Leonardo enters Cesare Borgia's service in the summer of 1502. Borgia was not nominally Florence's enemy, but he was a very dangerous and unpredictable new neighbour. Already stretched at Pisa, the Florentines could not expect to resist him if he chose to invade; the French, now alarmed by this voracious new baron they had in part created, were promising Florence money and soldiers, but could not be relied on. A game of rapprochement was Florence's only immediate tactic: it was imperative to maintain contact with him, to 'know him thoroughly' as the Renaissance saying went. We do not know how or exactly when Leonardo entered Borgia's employ, but it is plausible that his services were offered to Borgia by Soderini and Machiavelli – an offer of technical assistance which has also an overtone of intelligence-gathering. For Borgia, who attracts 'the best men in Italy', Leonardo is a skilled military engineer; for the Florentines he is a pair of eyes and ears – 'our man' at the court of Il Valentino.[31]

Leonardo's movements can be tracked with the aid of the pocket-book he carried with him through this summer, Paris MS L, though the chronology is not always clear. On the notebook's first page is a memorandum list which shows him putting together some of the necessary kit – compasses, a sword-belt, soles for boots, a light hat, a 'swimming-belt', and a leather jerkin. Also 'a book of white paper for drawing' and some charcoal. Another memo list, on a loose sheet now in the Codex Arundel, is probably contemporary. It begins, 'Where is Valentino?' (One recalls Machiavelli's comment about Borgia's lightning-fast progress: he is 'in one place before anyone knows he has left the other'.) This list includes an item, '*sostenacolo delli ochiali*', which might be either a frame for spectacles or a support for some optical device for mapping and surveying. (If the former, it is the first hint of the failing eyesight which becomes a problem in later years.) The list also mentions certain senior Florentines, including the diplomat Francesco Pandolfini, again suggesting a semi-official overtone to Leonardo's Borgia adventure.[32]

Leonardo was in Urbino by late July 1502, but his route there was circuitous – a rapid swing through various parts of the scattered Borgia dominion: a research trip. The first leg of the journey takes him down to the Mediterranean coast, to Piombino, then a recent Borgia conquest, now a small town through which tourists hurry to board the car-ferry to the island of Elba. His notes concern the town's fortifications and the capacity of the port. A note on the movement of waves is recorded as '*fatta al mare di Piombino*'. Some sketches show the coastline round Populonia, suggesting he travelled down the coast-road from Livorno.[33] From Piombino he cuts inland, eastward to rebel-held Arezzo, where he perhaps meets for the first time Borgia's confederate Vitellozzo Vitelli. Thence the road leads up into the highlands of the Apennines, where he gathers some of the topographical data that will later appear in his maps of the region. He perhaps saw at this time the graceful five-arched bridge spanning the Arno at Buriano, and the dramatic chimney-stack rocks, the Balze, which characterize the upper Arno valley from Laterina to Pian di Sco. It has been argued that this bridge and this landscape can be seen in the backgrounds of the *Madonna of the Yarnwinder* and the *Mona Lisa*.[34] The visual parallels are strong, and the dating is right, though the mountains of Leonardo's landscapes (first seen as early as the *Madonna of the Carnation* of *c*. 1474) are a synthesis of many viewpoints, both real and imaginary.

In Urbino, at the great honey-coloured *palazzo* of the Montefeltro, he meets again the charismatic Duke: it is nearly three years since they had met in Milan, and the years are marked on their faces. In his pocket-book Leonardo sketches the staircase of the palace and notes an interesting dovecote.[35] Maddening yet rather wonderful these tranquil, tangential observations: there is so much we want to know about his months at the court of the Borgia, and so little that he tells us. Apart from his query 'Where is Valentino?', Leonardo's only mention of Borgia (or 'Borges', as he writes it) concerns a manuscript: 'Borges will get me the Archimedes of the Bishop of Padua, and Vitellozzo the one at Borgo di San Sepolcro.'[36] These manuscripts are the spoils of war: intellectual plunder. A red-chalk drawing of a bearded, heavy-lidded man, shown from three angles, is probably a portrait of Borgia.

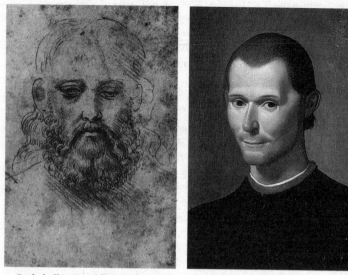

Red-chalk portrait by Leonardo believed to show Cesare Borgia.

Niccolò Machiavelli in the portrait by Santi di Tito at the Palazzo Vecchio.

They were not together long, for at the end of July Borgia travelled north to Milan to reassert his former friendship with Louis XII. Perhaps Leonardo hoped to go with him, but he did not. Instead, no doubt with specific instructions, he embarked on a brisk tour of Borgia's eastern territories. The itinerary can be reconstructed from a series of brief dated notes:

30 July – 'the dove-cote at Urbino'.
1 August – 'in the library at Pesaro'.
8 August – 'make harmonies out of the different falls of water as you saw in the fountain at Rimini on the 8th day of August'.
10 August – 'At the Feast of San Lorenzo at Cesena'.
15 August – 'On St Mary's day in the middle of August at Cesena'.[37]

At Cesena, the capital of the Romagna, his notebook is much in use. The place is picturesque, the customs particular. A drawing of a window is captioned, 'Window at Cesena: *a* for the frame made of linen, *b* for the window made of wood, the rounding at the top is a quarter of a circle.' Elsewhere he draws a hook with two bunches of grapes – 'This is how they carry grapes in Cesena' – and remarks, with his artist's eye, that the workmen digging moats group themselves into a pyramid.[38] He notes a rustic communication-system: 'The shepherds in the Romagna, at the foot of the Apennines, make large cavities in the mountains in the form of a horn, and in part of this they place a real horn, and this little horn combines with the cavity they have made, and produces a huge sound.'[39] The land is flat: he considers the possibility of windmills, still unknown in Italy. And he criticizes the local design of carts, which have two small wheels in the front and two high ones behind: this is 'very unfavourable to their momentum because there is too much weight on the front wheels'. This failing earns a sneer for this backward, broken-down region: the Romagna is 'capo d'ogni grossezza d'ingegno' – 'the chief realm of all idiocy'.[40] The tone is untypical; his mood is brittle.

On 18 August 1502 an impressively florid document was drawn up – Leonardo's passport. This was inscribed at Pavia, where Borgia was with the French court.

Caesar Borgia of France, by the grace of God Duke of Romagna and Valence, Prince of the Adriatic, Lord of Piombino etc., also Gonfalonier and Captain General of the Holy Roman Church: to all our lieutenants, castellans, captains, condottieri, officials, soldiers and subjects to whom this notice is presented. We order and command that the bearer hereof, our most excellent and well-beloved architect and general engineer Leonardo Vinci, who by our commission is to survey the places and fortresses of our states, should be provided with all such assistance as the occasion demands and his judgement deems fit.[41]

The document gives Leonardo freedom to travel within Borgia's dominions, with expenses paid 'for him and for his' – we perhaps discern Tommaso and Salai in this formula. He should be 'received with friendship and permitted to view, measure and carefully survey whatever he wants'. Other engineers 'are hereby constrained to confer with him and conform with his opinion'. It is a document to be flourished at roadblocks and checkpoints, at suspicious sentries and officious castellans – a reminder of the dangers out here on the frontiers of the new Borgia fiefdom.

Armed with these powers, Leonardo involves himself in various fortification works at Cesena and at Porto Cesenatico on the Adriatic. A sketch of the latter's harbour and canal is dated 6 September 1502 at nine o'clock in the morning.[42] Then Borgia returns from Milan and the campaigns begin again. A note in the Codex Atlanticus suggests that Leonardo was present at the taking of Fossombrone on 11 October. And a vivid anecdote in Luca Pacioli's De viribus quantitatis gives us a glimpse of Leonardo on the march with Borgia's troops:

One day Cesare Valentino, Duke of Romagna and present Lord of Piombino, found himself and his army at a river which was 24 paces wide, and could find no bridge, nor any material to make one except for a stack of wood all cut to a length of 16 paces. And from this wood, using neither iron nor rope nor any other construction, his noble engineer made a bridge sufficiently strong for the army to pass over.[43]

The measurements have been rounded out to make a mathematical point, but the story may well be authentic. Borgia's 'noble engineer' can only be Leonardo, who is presumably the source of the story: he and Pacioli were together in Florence in 1503.

There emerges from this period a sense of strenuousness. Leonardo tracks between these occupied towns and cities, these fortresses and castles, and all the long miles in between, the commandeered inns, and the dawn departures, and the middays sheltering from the sun. He has thrown himself into a world of physical technical work: pacing out measurements, recording currents, examining fortresses – the disciple of experience on the road, with his quadrant and his spectacles and his notebook. One senses an impatient putting-aside of the comfortable urban life of the last twenty years, in which – as it seemed to him – so much had been begun and so little completed. One senses again the Leonardo who advises the painter to 'quit your home in town', to 'leave your family and friends, and go over the mountains and valleys' and 'expose yourself to the fierce heat of the sun'. But we can also suspect that Leonardo's service of the Borgia was accompanied by a deep ambivalence about the nature of his employer and of the destruction and violence he was helping to spread as the Borgia's well-beloved military engineer. War is 'the most brutal kind of madness there is', Leonardo once wrote,[44] and during these months of 1502 he saw something of it at first hand. Hence those momentary notations in his notebook, in one sense fragments yet also complete in themselves – a dovecote, a fountain, a bunch of grapes, or those notes which simply say, 'I am here, on this day', and perhaps, given that tinge of danger that seeps into everything that Borgia touches, 'I am still alive.'

⤖ AUTUMN IN IMOLA ⤚

As the summer drew to a close, Il Valentino established his makeshift court at Imola, a small fortress-town on the old Roman road between Bologna and Rimini. It would be his headquarters for the winter; if the fortress could be made impregnable it might be his permanent headquarters. There are ground-plans of the fortress in Leonardo's papers, and some written measurements: the moat was 40 feet deep, the walls 15 feet thick – vital statistics in the Borgian world of shoot-outs and showdowns.[45]

Here, in the early afternoon of 7 October 1502, arrived Niccolò Machiavelli, sent once more to parley with the renegade Duke. A bony, cadaverous-looking man with a laconic smile, Machiavelli – Il Machia, as his friends called him, punning on *macchia*, a blot or stain – was not yet famous, hardly yet a writer, but the precision and perspicacity of his mind were already valued. He was thirty-three years old, well educated and well connected, but not rich. He had ridden out the stormy years of the Medici downfall and the Savonarolan theocracy, and from 1498 was Secretary of the Second Chancery, an influential if unglamorous post with a salary of 128 gold florins. Chancery officials were essentially civil servants, appointed by the Signoria to provide a continuum of political and diplomatic activity while the elected officials came and went. Machiavelli was the man behind the scenes, the speech-writer, the spin-doctor, and increasingly the political troubleshooter. He had acquitted himself well in negotiations with Louis XII in 1500, seeking continued French support in the draining Florentine war against Pisa; his reflections on that six-month diplomatic mission are found in *The Prince*.[46]

Machiavelli remained three months at the court of Il Valentino. His clipped dispatches from Imola are punctuated by pleas to be recalled to Florence. He had accepted the mission reluctantly, expecting it to be dangerous, uncomfortable and ultimately pointless. The Duke, as he always pointed out, was a pure man of action: it was one of his sayings that 'talk is cheap' – and talk was all Machiavelli had to offer him. He was Florence's *orator* or ambassador, but he had been given no commission to sign any treaty. His requests to be recalled were ignored. The Signoria wanted him there, reporting back about 'the hopes the Duke has'. His feisty young wife, Marietta, whom he had married the previous year, complained bitterly of his absence.

Even as he arrived in Imola, news was coming in of armed rebellion in Borgia's dominions by an alliance of malcontent captains – among them

Vitellozzo Vitelli, who had fomented the revolt in Arezzo – and ousted local potentates like the Duke of Urbino. Borgia laughed off their council of war at Magione: 'a congress of losers'. He said, with that raw eloquence which Machiavelli catches so well, 'The ground is burning under their feet, and it needs more water to put it out than they can throw.'[47] On 11 October he struck, sacking the fortress of Fossombrone which the rebels had captured a few days earlier. Leonardo, as the Duke's military engineer, was almost certainly present. In a note on fortresses in the Codex Atlanticus he writes, 'See that the escape passage does not lead straight into the inner fortress, otherwise the commander will be overpowered, as happened at Fossombrone.'[48]

At Imola is played out one of those piquant little cameos of history: three great names of the Renaissance holed up in a fortress on the windy plains of the Romagna, each seemingly watching the others with a vigilance that is part fascination and part nervy suspicion. It seems, at any rate, that Machiavelli and Leonardo struck up a cordial relationship: we will find them linked in certain Florentine projects over the next year – projects that suggest that Machiavelli valued Leonardo's skills as an engineer and an artist. Of their particular dealings in Imola we know nothing: Leonardo's name occurs nowhere in Machiavelli's dispatches. This silence may be diplomatic: Machiavelli knew his dispatches would be intercepted and read before they left Imola, and may have wished not to compromise Leonardo's somewhat delicate position as a Florentine in Cesare's service. But perhaps after all Leonardo is in there, incognito. Thus Machiavelli writes on 1 November that, having talked to a secretary of Borgia's, one Agobito, he then verified what he had gleaned by talking 'to another who is also acquainted with the Lord's secrets'. And on 8 November he speaks of an anonymous 'friend' whose analysis of Cesare's intentions is 'worthy of attention'. It is plausible that in both cases his unidentified source is Leonardo.[49]

Of Leonardo's presence in this heady atmosphere of power-politics we have the beautiful product of his map of Imola. Highly detailed and delicately coloured, it has been called 'the most accurate and beautiful map of its era'. A page of rough sketches for the map survives, much folded, with measurements written down *in situ* as he paced out the streets of Imola with this paper in hand.[50]

Leonardo's maps are the true fruits of these relentless travels of 1502. There is a beautiful bird's-eye map of the Val di Chiana (plate 17).[51] The central area, between Arezzo and Chiusi, can be correlated pretty closely with a

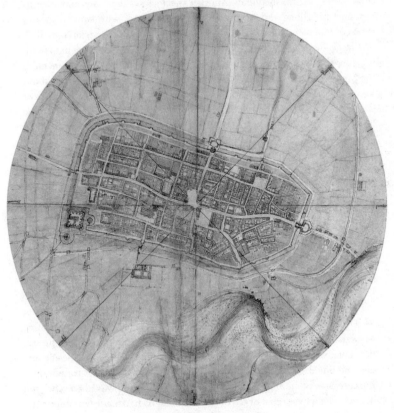

The map of Imola, c. 1502.

modern map; away from this area the measurements are more hypothetical. (The long lake at the centre of the map, the Lago di Chiana, has since been drained.) The verso of the map has the remains of sealing-wax round the edges: this would have been used to fix the map to a wall or board. The names of the villages and rivers are written in conventional left-to-right script, again suggesting the map was for presentation. It may well have been made for Borgia, though there is an alternative possibility that it was worked up a couple of years later in connection with plans for canalizing the Arno. A rough sheet at Windsor shows a bird's-eye view of the central area, listing the distances between various towns in the vicinity; these distances have been crossed through, suggesting that Leonardo referred to them when constructing the finished map. Another sheet shows the roads and streams around Castiglione and Montecchio in great detail, with some distances marked in braccia that were presumably paced out by Leonardo himself.[52]

A larger-scale map, oriented the same way as the Val di Chiana map (with north to the left), shows the whole river-system of central Italy. It includes the Mediterranean coast from Civitavecchia to La Spezia, a stretch of about 170 miles, and extends across to the Adriatic coast at Rimini. It has been shown that Leonardo's model was a manuscript map of c. 1470 then in the library at Urbino, but he has transformed it by using contour shading, abandoning the 'molehill' convention of Quattrocento mapping and giving a sense of objectively recorded terrain.[53] Leonardo would have been able to study the map in Urbino in late July 1502. This reinforces the idea that these maps were created in the context of his Borgia work, and some of them may have been actually done at Imola.

Machiavelli sickened. On 22 November he wrote from Imola, 'My body is in a bad way after a heavy fever two days ago.' On 6 December he asked once more to be recalled, 'to relieve the government of this expense, and me of this inconvenience, since for the last twelve days I have been feeling very ill and if I go on like this I fear they'll be bringing me back in a basket'.[54]

Borgia negotiated with the rebels: an illusory reconciliation. Then, on 26 December, Machiavelli reported grimly from Cesena, 'This morning Messer Rimino was found lying in the piazza cut into two pieces; he still lies there, so that everyone has had an opportunity to see him.' Beside him lay a bloodied knife and a wooden wedge, as used by butchers to split open the carcasses of animals. Rimino or Ramiro de Lorqua was not a rebel, but a loyal thug whose reign of terror in the Romagna had made him unpopular and hence expendable. 'The reason for his death is not yet clear,' Machiavelli added, 'except that such was the pleasure of the Prince, who shows us that he can make and unmake men according to their deserts.'

On the morning of 31 December Borgia entered Senigallia. There, under pretence of reconciliation, he met with the ringleaders of the rebellion: Vitellozzo Vitelli, Oliverotto da Fermo, the Orsini brothers. But the meeting was a trap. The rebels were seized and bound; their foot-soldiers camped outside the town-walls were disarmed. That evening Machiavelli scribbled a dramatic dispatch: 'The sack of the town continues although it is now the 23rd hour. I am much troubled in my mind. I do not know if I can send this letter having no one to carry it.' As for the rebels, 'It is my opinion they will not be alive tomorrow morning.' He was partly right: Vitellozzo and Oliverotto were strangled that night; the Orsini brothers lived a couple of weeks longer and were strangled at Castel del Pieve.[55] Was Leonardo also present at Cesena and Senigallia as his patron dispensed justice with the butcher's knife and the garrotte? It is not unlikely.

In the first weeks of 1503 Il Valentino took Perugia and Siena. Brief comments in Leonardo's notebook suggest he was with him in Siena. He admires an enormous church-bell, 10 braccia in diameter, and bids himself remember 'the way it moved and how its clapper was fastened'.[56] Again his notes are tangential, serene, escapist: he is looking the other way. On 20 January, during the siege of Siena, Machiavelli gratefully welcomed a new Florentine envoy, Jacopo Salviati, said his goodbyes to Valentino and Leonardo, and set off back to Florence, convinced that he had seen a new model of political leadership – decisive, lucid, ruthless, and quite divested of morality and religion. Ten years later, in *The Prince*, he wrote of Borgia:

If I summed up all the actions of the Duke I would not know how to reproach him. On the contrary it seems to me he should be put forward, as I have done, as a model for all those who have risen to empire by fortune and the arms of others. For with his great spirit and high intention he could not have conducted himself otherwise.[57]

Borgia proceeded to Rome in February 1503, to confer with his ailing father, Pope Alexander VI. Leonardo may have gone with him, but if so the visit was short, as he was back in Florence by the beginning of March.[58] The decision to quit Borgia's service – if it was his – was a wise one. Borgia's fortunes had reached their zenith, for with the death of his father on 18 August 1503 his true power-base of papal influence was shattered. The new pope, Julius II, refused to recognize his title of Duke of Romagna and demanded the restitution of his dominions. There followed a saga of arrest and escape, an anti-papal venture in Naples, and in 1507 an early death in Spain, in action as a mercenary, at the age of about thirty.

➤➤ A LETTER TO THE SULTAN ◄◄

In 1952 a remarkable document was discovered in the State Archives at the Topkapi Museum in Istanbul.[59] At the head of it, in elegant Turkish script, it is summarized as 'the copy of a letter that the infidel named Lionardo sent from Genoa'. If it is genuine, it is a contemporary Turkish translation of a letter in which Leonardo offered his engineering services to Sultan Bejazet (or Beyazid) II. At the bottom of the text the copyist notes, 'This letter was written on 3 July,' but he neglects to say which year. It was almost certainly

1503, in which case it was written in Florence, when Leonardo's mind was full of big technological projects after the Borgia adventure. (That the letter is described as 'sent from Genoa' need only mean that it arrived on a ship from Genoa.)

It begins, somewhat like the famous prospectus addressed to the Moor twenty years earlier, with offers of technological expertise: 'I your servant . . . will build a mill which does not require water, but is powered by wind alone' and 'God, may He be praised, has granted me a way of extracting water from ships without ropes or cables, but using a self-propelling hydraulic machine.' But these are only a warm-up before the main offer, which is to design and build a bridge over the Golden Horn:

I, your servant, have heard about your intention to build a bridge from Stamboul to Galata, and that you have not done it because no man can be found capable of it. I, your servant, know how. I would raise it to the height of a building, so that no one can pass over it because it is so high . . . I will make it so that a ship can pass under it even with its sails hoisted . . . I would have a drawbridge so that when one wants one can pass on to the Anatolian coast . . . May God make you believe these words, and consider this servant of yours always at your service.

The notebook Paris MS L, intensively in use during the Borgia adventure of 1502–3, contains what seem to be some working drawings connected with this project, though the design departs in some respects from the description in the letter. The drawing shows a beautifully streamlined structure with 'bird-tail' abutments. Leonardo captions it as follows: 'Bridge from Pera to Constantinople ['gostantinopoli'], 40 braccia wide, 70 braccia high above the water, 600 braccia long, that is 400 over the sea and 200 on the land, thus making its own abutments.'[60] The computation is well-informed: the width of the Golden Horn is about 800 feet so '400 braccia over the sea' is exactly right. The proposed length of the entire bridge (600 braccia = 1,200 feet) would have made it the longest bridge in the world at that time.

The probable source of this project is Leonardo's brief sojourn in Rome in February 1503. The previous year ambassadors from Sultan Bejazet had been in Rome conferring with Pope Alexander. It is likely that they mentioned the Sultan's desire for an Italian engineer to build a bridge over the Golden Horn – at the time there was only a temporary pontoon floating on barrels. Among those interested, according to Vasari, was the young Michelangelo: 'According to what I have been told, Michelangelo had a desire to go to Constantinople to serve the Turk, who had requested him, by means of certain Franciscan friars, to come and build a bridge from

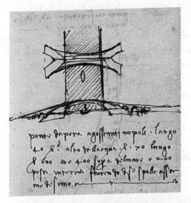

Sketch for the bridge at Constantinople (left), and Vebjørn Sand's realization at Aas (below).

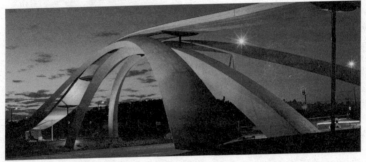

Constantinople to Pera.' Vasari places this during the period of Michelangelo's dispute with Pope Julius II in *c.* 1504. Much the same story is told in Ascanio Condivi's contemporary *Life of Michelangelo* (1553).[61]

Leonardo's visit to Rome in February 1503, in the suite of Cesare Borgia, thus provides the context: he learns of the Sultan's interest, he sketches a prototype in his notebook, and he pens his bombastic letter with suitable flourishes. It has been argued that the bridge's design was based on the Alidosi Bridge at Castel del Rio, on the road from Imola to Florence.[62] This was begun in 1499, and was probably still under construction when Leonardo could have seen it during his topographical researches around Imola in the autumn of 1502.

Like Leonardo's parachute, preserved in a small note of *c.* 1485 and tested in the air more than five centuries later, the bridge has recently been built according to Leonardo's specifications – albeit some 1,500 miles further north than its intended location on the Bosporus. On 31 October 2001 a scaled-down version of it (100 yards long) was unveiled at Aas, about 20 miles south of Oslo. Designed and built by Norwegian artist Vebjørn Sand, it was made out of pine, teak and stainless steel, and cost about £1 million. It serves as a pedestrian bridge over a motorway.

Leonardo never rests: he works on through the generations, through all the latter-day Leonardeschi – the artists and sculptors and robot-builders and sky-divers whose imaginations are touched by his brusquely captioned little drawings and the concentrated thinking-power that resides in them. 'It just had to be built,' Sand was reported as saying. 'It can be built in wood or stone, in any scale, because the principles work.' And so the spores of an idea dreamed up in 1503 eventually flower on Highway E18 south of Oslo.[63]

⤻ MOVING THE RIVER ⤺

Leonardo was back in Florence by the beginning of March 1503, hard-bitten from his months at the court of the brigand Duke. On 4 March he drew out 50 gold ducats from his account at Santa Maria Nuova. He records the transaction on a page which also has an enigmatic note: 'Get the Gonfalonier to cancel the book and the Ser [i.e. notary] to provide me with a written record of moneys received.'[64] The sense of 'cancel' is legalistic (Latin *cancellare*, to cancel a deed with criss-cross lines, from *cancellus*, a grating). The note is probably connected with the undelivered altarpiece for the Santissima Annunziata, a closing of the accounts, in which case the 'Ser' may be Ser Piero da Vinci, who was notary to the Servites of the Annunziata. Is this how Leonardo thinks of his father – 'il Ser', the sir or sire? The Gonfalonier is Piero Soderini, who in late 1502 had been elected Gonfalonier of the Florentine republic, in effect its prime minister: an upstanding but unimaginative man, whose dealings with Leonardo would not always be amicable.

On 8 April Leonardo lent 4 gold ducats to 'Vante *miniatore*' – the miniature painter Attavante di Gabriello, a man much the same age as Leonardo, and probably an acquaintance from younger days. 'Salai carried them to him and delivered them into his own hand: he said he will pay me back within the space of 40 days.' On the same day Leonardo gave Salai some money for 'rose-coloured stockings' – the same colour as his own 'tunic' (*pitocco*), as recorded by the Anonimo Gaddiano: 'He wore a short, rose-pink tunic, knee-length at a time when most people wore long gowns.'[65] One gets a hint of the dandified air of the Leonardo circle, somewhat at odds with the mood of republican Florence. This glimpse of Leonardo's garb was probably a memory of the Florentine painter whom the Anonimo calls Il Gavina or P. da Gavine.

On 14 June Leonardo withdrew another 50 gold florins from his account. He was perhaps in something of a parlous state: his future uncertain, his savings leaking away. We don't know where he was living at this time: the doors of the Annunziata were no longer open to him. It is perhaps around now that someone, probably a pupil, writes on a page in the Codex Atlanticus, 'Tra noi non ha a correre denari' – 'Round here the money's pretty tight . . .'[66]

But a new and exciting project beckoned, its purpose nothing less than changing the course of the Arno river. There were in fact two separate projects: the diversion of the lower Arno, which was a purely military tactic intended to cut Pisa off from the sea, and the more grandiose scheme of canalizing the entire river west of Florence to make it navigable. Machiavelli, now Soderini's right-hand man on military and political affairs, was closely involved in both of them. He had seen something of Leonardo's work as Borgia's engineer, and it may be that the Pisa diversion was first hatched up in conversations between them at Imola.

Pisa had been temporarily ceded to the French by Piero de' Medici in 1494, and had declared independence when the French withdrew from Italy the following year. Florentine efforts to retake the city had been embarrassingly ineffectual: the Pisans could hold out indefinitely while they had food and supplies coming in via their port at the mouth of the Arno. Hence this new stratagem – logical but technically ambitious – of rerouting the river and thereby, in the phrase of one of Machiavelli's assistants, 'depriving the Pisans of their source of life'.[67]

On 19 June 1503 Florentine troops took possession of the fortress of La Verruca, or Verrucola, a knoll which can still be seen on the southern slopes of the Pisan hills, overlooking the flatlands of the lower Arno. Two days later Leonardo was there. The officer in charge, Pierfrancesco Tosinghi, reported back to Florence: 'Leonardo da Vinci came in person, with some companions, and we showed him everything, and it seems to us that he found La Verrucola satisfactory, and that he liked what he saw, and afterwards he said he had thought of ways to make it impregnable.'[68] This brisk dispatch catches Leonardo in action on a summer day in the Pisan hills: his thoroughness ('we showed him everything'), his enthusiasm ('he liked what he saw').

A month later he was in the area again, as part of an official delegation led by Alessandro degli Albizzi. He was there by 22 July, when he dated a sketch of the lower Arno, and on the 23rd he took part in discussions at the Florentine battle-camp, probably at Riglione, as reported by a certain Captain Guiducci the following day:

Yesterday we received Alessandro degli Albizzi, bearing a letter from Your Lordship [Gonfalonier Soderini], together with Leonardo da Vinci and certain others. We studied the plan, and after many discussions and doubts it was concluded that the project was very much to the purpose, and if the Arno can really be turned or channelled at this point, this would at least prevent the hills from being attacked by the enemy.[69]

Also in the party was one Giovanni Piffero, whom the Signoria later reimbursed to the tune of 56 lire 'for a carriage with six horses, and the cost of meals, going with Leonardo da Vinci to level the Arno around Pisa'. He is elsewhere named as Giovanni di Andrea Piffero, and was in all probability Giovanni di Andrea Cellini, father of the famous sculptor Benvenuto Cellini, who was indeed a member of the *pifferi*, or pipers, of the Signoria.[70]

Captain Guiducci's dispatch of 24 July 1503 is the earliest specific mention of the Arno diversion, though the 'plan' which they studied and the authorizing letter from the Gonfalonier suggest that the project was well advanced on paper. The idea was to channel the river southward to an area of marshland near Livorno called the Stagno. The water would be diverted by weirs down a huge ditch, a mile long and 16 braccia (32 feet) deep, which would then fork into two smaller ditches. The distance between the river and the outflow at the Stagno diversion was about 12 miles, and Leonardo estimated that about a million tons of earth would have to be dug out for the ditches. In an early example of the time-and-motion study, he calculated how much earth a single worker could shift. Because the ditches would be so deep, he reckoned that a single bucket of earth from the bottom would be handled by fourteen workers before it reached the top. After some complex calculations he concluded that the entire project would require 54,000 man-days.[71] Alternatively, he says, 'various machines' could be used to speed things up. One such is the mechanical digger found in the Codex Atlanticus: measurements beside the drawing correspond exactly with those proposed for the Arno ditches, so it seems this machine was specifically designed for the job. Another computation reads, 'One shovel-load is twenty-five pounds; six shovel-loads made up one barrow-load; twenty barrow-loads made up a cart-load.'[72] These are the nuts and bolts of Leonardo's work as a civil and military engineer.

Digging on the Arno–Stagno canal did not begin for over a year. Leonardo was not actively involved at this later stage: another engineer or *maestro d'aqua*, one Colombino, was in charge, and some of what was done differed from Leonardo's plans. Work began on 20 August 1504 'at the tower of the Fagiano', which was demolished to provide building materials for the weir. The project was a total failure, and was abandoned after two months, amid growing unrest about unpaid wages. A report by Machiavelli's assistant Biagio Buonaccorsi sums up succinctly:

When the decision was finally made, a camp was established at Riglione, and *maestri d'aqua* were summoned. They said they required two thousand workers, and a quantity of wood to construct a weir to hold the river in, and divert it along two ditches to the Stagno, and they promised to complete the project within thirty or forty thousand man-days [significantly less than Leonardo's estimate] and in this hope the project was begun on 20 August [1504] with two thousand workmen hired at one carlino a day. In fact the project took much more time and money, and to no profit, for, in spite of these estimates, eighty thousand man-days were not enough to bring it even halfway . . . The waters never went through the ditches except when the river was in flood, and as soon as it subsided the water flowed back. The whole undertaking cost seven thousand ducats or more because as well as paying the workers it was necessary to maintain a thousand soldiers to protect the workers from attack by the Pisans.[73]

In early October 1504 disaster struck. There was a violent storm; several boats guarding the mouth of the ditches were wrecked, and eighty lives were lost. The walls of the ditches collapsed, and the whole plain was flooded, destroying many farms. By mid-October, less than two months after the work had begun, the project was abandoned. The Florentine army withdrew, the Pisans filled in the ditches, and the episode was quickly forgotten – another waste of time, money and lives in the long war with Pisa, which continued until 1509.

This abortive plan was part and parcel of Leonardo's more grandiose dream: the construction of a long canal which would obviate the navigational problems of the Arno and give Florence its own access to the sea. The river below Florence is not navigable because of the rapids between Signa and Montelupo 10 miles west of the city, and is shallow, silted and meandering for much of its course between there and Pisa: one recalls Brunelleschi's ill-fated *Badalone* beached on the sandbanks of Empoli. This grand canal is distinct from the military diversion project, but his involvement in the latter probably gave impetus to this larger canalization scheme, which he had been turning over in his mind for some time. The combined effect of them – had they worked – would have been to link Florence to the sea, thus enabling the city to participate in the great adventure of New World trade and exploration, excitement about which the Florentine navigator Amerigo di Vespucci did much to encourage in letters to his Italian patron Lorenzo di Pierfrancesco de' Medici, a digest of which was published in Florence in 1504.

This gives a topical impetus to an idea that had been around for a while: an Arno canal had been proposed as early as 1347, and Leonardo himself had been thinking about it for ten years or more. There is a sheet of notes on the subject in the Codex Atlanticus which, as it mentions Pisa as a beneficiary of the scheme, appears to have been written before the beginning of Florentine–Pisan hostilities in 1495. He wrote:

Sluices should be made in the valley of La Chiana at Arezzo so that when in the summer the Arno lacks water the canal will not dry up. The canal should be 20 braccia wide at the bottom and 30 at the top, and 2 braccia deep, or 4 so that 2 braccia of water can serve the mills and meadows, which will benefit the area, and Prato, Pistoia and Pisa will gain 200,000 ducats a year, and will contribute labour and money to this useful project, and the Lucchese the same, because the Lake of Sesto will become navigable. I shall make it go through Prato and Pistoia, and cut through Serravalle and debouch into the lake, so there will be no need of locks.[74]

He costs this out at a rate of 1 lire per 60 square braccia, though this does not include any estimate for the immense work of 'cutting through' the mountain at Serravalle.

There are maps and plans which date from 1503–4 and show the proposed route of the canal. In the corner of one is a note reading, 'They do not know why the Arno will never run in a straight channel: it is because the rivers which flow into it deposit earth where they enter, and take it from the opposite side, and so bend the river.'[75] One hears the touch of testiness, the magisterial note which some would have found trying. 'They' do not know this elementary fact which he must now for the umpteenth time explain.

The canal remained a dream – the failure of the military diversion was perhaps a discouragement, though the immense costs of the project were doubtless enough to discourage the Signoria anyway. No work was carried out, though the A11 autostrada between Florence and Pisa covers much the same route as the proposed canal, so one might say that Leonardo's vision was only wrong in so far as it failed to predict the demise of the waterway itself as a medium of transport. His imagination fell short of the internal-combustion engine.

These canalization projects, and others he later undertook in Milan, are another instance of Leonardo's lifelong fascination with water, its currents, pressures, vortices and refractions, which he noted, analysed, sketched and indeed painted so beautifully – the sullen gleam of the *padule* behind Ginevra, the marine vistas of the *Annunciation*, the rock-eroding rivers that meander implacably behind the *Madonna of the Yarnwinder* and the *Mona Lisa*.

⤜ MISTRESS LISA ⤛

Many dreams have been brought to your doorstep . . .
Nat King Cole, 'Mona Lisa' (lyrics by Jay
Livingstone and Ray Evans, 1949)

And what of the paintbrush, of which he had been so heartily sick, so *impaziente*, a couple of years previously? Was he painting again? It seems he was. In the summer of 1503, when he was not traipsing round the base-camps and excavation-sites of the Pisa campaign, when he was not computing the sluice-rates and shovel-hours needed to bring his cunning stratagem to pass, Leonardo was almost certainly at work on the picture that can justly be called – as it is in the subtitle of a recent book on the subject – 'the world's most famous painting'.[76]

'For Francesco del Giocondo Leonardo undertook to paint a portrait of his wife, Mona Lisa; he worked on it for four years and left it unfinished.' Thus briskly Giorgio Vasari begins his account of the *Mona Lisa*. It is the fullest contemporary account of the painting, and the only one to offer a name for the sitter – whether correctly or not is much debated. The painting is called the *Mona Lisa* on the basis of Vasari's identification, though as a title this was not much used before the nineteenth century. In Italy the painting is always known as *La Gioconda* (and in France as *La Joconde*). This seems also to refer to Lisa del Giocondo, but as *giocondo* is also an adjective, meaning jocund, it functions as a purely descriptive title: *The Jocund* [or *Playful*] *Woman*, *The Joker Lady* – perhaps even *The Tease*. Such a pun would be characteristic of the time, and of Leonardo, but those who disbelieve Vasari's identification say the title works perfectly well without any reference to Mrs Giocondo.[77]

After his informative first sentence, Vasari devotes a paragraph to praise of the painting's brilliantly lifelike qualities. Some of this is inaccurate, or at least off-key, because he had never actually seen the picture: it was, as he notes, 'now in the possession of King François of France at Fontainebleau'.[78] He lavishes particular praise on the sitter's eyebrows – 'completely natural, growing thickly in one place and lightly in another' – whereas the *Mona*

Lisa is notably eyebrow-less, and no trace of any previous eyebrows has been found beneath the paint surface. He concludes the passage with a little anecdotal coda: 'While he was painting her he employed singers and musicians and always had jesters to keep her merry and to chase away that melancholy which painters usually gave to portraits; and so in this picture by Leonardo there is a smile [*ghigno*] so pleasing that one seems to see something more divine than human.' This is nice, and chimes in with some of Leonardo's comments in the *Trattato* about the painter working in a refined atmosphere, but again it strikes one as off-key. Where, in the actual *Mona Lisa*, is the evidence of this merriment? There is the smile, or the ghost of one, but not the broad grin which is the usual meaning of *ghigno* (from which 'grin' comes). As he often does, Vasari is over-egging a second-hand account to make it sound richer. His description is often criticized because of its visual inaccuracy, though of course we have even less idea what the *Mona Lisa* looked like when Leonardo painted it. Its currently crepuscular appearance is the result of several centuries of protective varnish, tinged yellowish by oxidation. As early as 1625 a viewer complained of the picture being 'so damaged by a certain varnish that one cannot make it out very well'.[79] This is another aspect of the picture's obscurity – what the pro-restoration lobby would call its illegibility. She wears this veil of lacquer, with its thousands of tiny lesions or craquelures, and it will be a brave restorer who dares remove the veil to see what lies beneath.

Vasari does not actually give a date for the painting – dates are not his strong suit – but within the narrative of the *Life* he places it squarely in this second Florentine period, somewhere between the *St Anne* cartoon of 1501 and the *Battle of Anghiari* fresco of 1503–6. Given that Leonardo was painting very little in 1501, as we gather from Fra Pietro Novellara, and that he was in the service of the Borgia for much of 1502, this is generally interpreted to mean that he began work on the *Mona Lisa* sometime after his return to Florence in 1503. This is the date favoured by the Louvre, where its 500th birthday was celebrated in autumn 2003. It may also be the date favoured by a casual joke of Machiavelli's friend Luca Ugolini, who wrote to Niccolò on 11 November 1503 congratulating him on the birth of his first son – 'My very dear friend. Congratulations! Obviously Mistress Marietta did not deceive you, for he is your spitting image. Leonardo da Vinci would not have done a better portrait.' Perhaps Ugolini was thinking of the *Mona Lisa*, already taking shape in Leonardo's studio in November 1503, when he said this.[80]

I have noted over the last few chapters what seem to be anticipatory frissons of the *Mona Lisa* – the hands and bust of Isabella d'Este, the loggia of the Tovaglia villa, the bridge at Buriano, the landscape of the *Madonna of the Yarnwinder*. Some of these are debatable, though the first and the last are demonstrable parallels in works of 1500-1502. That unfinished portrait of Isabella d'Este, always just beyond our field of vision, is especially insistent – seen by Lorenzo Guznago in Venice in 1500; referred to by Isabella's agents in Florence in 1501-2 ('he will immediately undertake the portrait and send it' . . . 'he has already begun work on that which Your Ladyship wanted'), this lost work seems a kind of missing link between the extant drawing of Isabella and the *Mona Lisa*, a notional phase between the rigid full profile of the former and the nuanced, faintly skewed full face of the latter. A red-chalk drawing at Windsor, often described as a study for the *Madonna of the Yarnwinder*, might also be seen as a halfway stage on this arc of movement from the d'Este profile to the Gioconda gaze.[81] We know that this is how Leonardo worked, returning to images and ideas, circling round them, redefining them. Paintings evolve, metamorphose from one shape to another, like the pagan gods of the classical world. According to Vasari, Leonardo worked on the *Mona Lisa* for four years. This would make the date of composition *c*. 1503-7, its curtailment broadly coinciding with Leonardo's departure from Florence in early 1508. From around that time is a sheet of anatomical drawings containing nine studies of mouths and lips, with accompanying notes about the physiology of those 'muscles called lips'.[82] One of these studies, quite distinct from the others in its light, poetic tone, shows a mouth smiling – it is almost exactly the smile of the *Mona Lisa* (Plate 19).

Vasari's account of the painting is not ideal, but he is the only contemporary writer to give a name and a date to the portrait. Is he right? Increasingly it seems likely that he is. There are a great many alternative theories about who is portrayed in the painting, most of them proposed within the last hundred years. (André Coppier's 1914 article *La "Joconde" est-elle le portrait de Mona Lisa?* began the hunt.) I have been round the block, metaphorically speaking, with these contenders, and none of them has stood up to much inquiry. The alternative candidates – Isabella Gualanda, Pacifica Brandano, Costanza d'Avalos, Caterina Sforza et al. – are rather like the authors evoked to solve the Shakespeare 'authorship controversy'. Their proponents seek to solve a mystery, but one must first ask: is there really any mystery to solve?

Vasari's 'Mona Lisa' certainly existed.[83] She was Lisa di Antonmaria Gherardini, born on 15 June 1479. Her father was a respectable but not spectacularly wealthy Florentine; the family had a town-house near Santa

Trinità and a small estate in San Donato in Poggio, near Greve, where she was probably born. She married Francesco di Bartolomeo del Giocondo in March 1495, at the age of fifteen; he was a well-to-do businessman with interests in the silk and cloth trades, thirty-five years old, already twice widowed, and with an infant son, Bartolomeo. There is a family connection behind the marriage: Lisa's stepmother, Camilla, was the sister of Giocondo's first wife; Lisa would have been a child when Giocondo first knew her. By 1503, the presumed date for the portrait, she had borne Giocondo two sons, Piero and Andrea, and a daughter who had died in infancy. This loss is sometimes said to be a reason for the fine black veil that covers the Mona Lisa's hair, but this is unlikely: the baby had died four years earlier, in the summer of 1499. More probably the veil and the sombre-coloured dress are a fashion-statement: the 'Spanish' look, as worn by Lucrezia Borgia at her wedding with Alfonso d'Este in 1502, was all the rage. Francesco del Giocondo was in the garment-business: he knew all about the fashions. And so did the portraitist who, in Vasari's unexcited phrase, 'undertook to paint' the picture.

Giocondo was precisely the sort of client that Florentine artists sought – 'civis et mercator florentinus', as he is described in his marriage contract: citizen and merchant of Florence. He was the holder (on four separate occasions) of civic office, and among his business associates was Marcello Strozzi, whose sister Maddalena Doni was painted in Mona Lisa style by Raphael.[84] Another connection was with the Rucellai family: his first wife was a Rucellai, as was Lisa's stepmother. He was later linked with the Servites of the Annunziata, where he endowed a family chapel and commissioned for it an altarpiece of his patron saint, St Francis; this dates from the 1520s, but may reflect an earlier connection with the Annunziata. Giocondo's interest in art (or art-dealing) is also suggested by a post-mortem inventory of a small-time painter and sculptor, one Maestro Valerio, who died owing Giocondo money: Giocondo recouped the debt by taking the entire stock of Valerio's paintings, cartoons and sculptures.[85]

On 5 April 1503 Francesco del Giocondo completed the purchase of a house on Via della Stufa – a new home for him and Lisa and the three boys; the youngest, Andrea, was five months old, and was perhaps the reason for the move. A new home with walls to fill – what more natural than to fill one of them, as well-to-do home-owners did, with a portrait of your comely, desirable, fashionably dressed young wife: young but already, at the age of twenty-three, softened and broadened by motherhood.

*

Three scraps of documentation exist for the painting prior to Vasari's account. Do they support or contradict him?

The first known mention of the painting is by Antonio de Beatis, secretary to Cardinal Luigi of Aragon, whose diary records their visit to Leonardo's studio in France in 1517.[86] There the ageing *maestro* showed them three paintings. Two of these are readily identifiable from Beatis's descriptions as the *St John the Baptist* and the *Virgin and Child with St Anne*, both now in the Louvre; the third is almost certainly the *Mona Lisa*. It is described by Beatis (and, it is implied, by Leonardo himself) as the portrait of 'a certain Florentine lady, done from life at the instigation [*instantia*] of the late Magnifico Giuliano de' Medici'. The first part sounds like Lisa del Giocondo, who was certainly a Florentine lady, but the second part is more problematic. Giuliano was the third and youngest son of Lorenzo de' Medici; Leonardo's known relationship with him belongs to the years 1513–15, and to Rome rather than Florence.

For some this seems to offer an entirely different account of the painting from Vasari's, making it a late work (which the stylistic evidence would seem to confirm, and which the other two paintings shown to the visitors certainly were). This in turn has led to other candidates for the famous face. There is Giuliano's mistress, a young widow from Urbino named Pacifica Brandano, who bore him a child in 1511 – the funereal black veil which covers the Mona Lisa's hair might allude to her widowhood. And there is the beautiful and witty Isabella Gualanda, a Neapolitan who was in Rome at the right sort of time for Giuliano to be smitten by her, and who turns out to be a cousin of Cecilia Gallerani, whose portrait Leonardo had painted in Milan in the late 1480s.[87] Either of these women might plausibly have been painted at Giuliano's 'instigation', and the resulting portrait might have remained in Leonardo's hands when Giuliano became a married man, as he did in early 1515. However, neither of them was from Florence, which is required by Beatis's diary-entry. In fact Beatis's description of the painting seems to rule out the possibility that La Gualanda was portrayed in it. She was a famous Neapolitan beauty; it is likely that Luigi of Aragon and Beatis – themselves from Naples – would know what she looked like, and this likelihood is increased by the fact that Beatis mentions her, and her beauty, elsewhere in the diary.[88] If the portrait Leonardo showed them really was of her, Beatis would surely have said so; he certainly would not have described her as 'a certain Florentine lady'. These trails tend to double back on themselves, and the cases for the rival claimants start to look pretty thin.

It is generally held that Beatis scotches Vasari's identification of Lisa del Giocondo because she could not possibly have been a paramour of Giuliano de' Medici's: she was a respectably married woman, not a courtesan, and anyway Giuliano was in exile from Florence between 1494 and 1512. This *noli me tangere* argument seems to me questionable. Giuliano de' Medici and Lisa Gherardini were exact contemporaries, born in 1479. It is quite likely that they met, because their families were linked by intermarriage – Giuliano's aunt Nannina was married to Bernardo Rucellai, whose niece Camilla was married to Lisa's father: thus Lisa's young stepmother was Giuliano's cousin. It is therefore tenable that Giuliano and Lisa knew one another. They were fifteen years old in November 1494, when Giuliano fled the city with his family. A few months after this *bouleversement*, Lisa married the middle-aged widower Francesco del Giocondo, also known to her through her stepmother, Camilla.

If this were a novel or film-script I would stretch the evidence and say that there was a *tendresse* between Giuliano and Lisa: that they were teenage sweethearts separated by political misfortune. This 'star-crossed lover' scenario would have a sequel. In 1500 Giuliano de' Medici was in Venice. It would be natural for him to pay a call on his famous compatriot Leonardo da Vinci, who arrived in the city in February 1500; and if he did so he would probably have seen in Leonardo's studio – as Lorenzo Guznago did on 17 March – that unfinished portrait of Isabella d'Este which is a ghostly precursor of the pose and style, the 'look', of the *Mona Lisa*. In April Leonardo set off for Florence. Was it then that Giuliano de' Medici 'instigated' him to paint this portrait of a 'certain Florentine lady' whom he remembered as a beautiful girl, though now – he hears – married with children?

This is inadmissible, but serves to show that Leonardo's only known comment about the painting, as recorded by Antonio de Beatis in 1517, is not *per se* a disproof of Vasari's identification, as it is usually said to be. That Giuliano and Lisa were acquainted as teenagers is circumstantially probable; that there was a romance between them which the portrait in some way evokes or commemorates (much as the portrait of Ginevra evokes her affair with Bernardo Bembo) is unprovable but not incredible. This need not displace the more prosaic likelihood that her husband commissioned the portrait (as Vasari says he did): rather it deepens the emotional register of the picture, infuses it with nostalgia and melancholy and collusion – a hinted memory of those Florentine love-games of the old Medici days.

Another early document was found in the Milanese archives in the early 1990s.[89] It is an inventory of Salai's estate, drawn up after his sudden death in March 1524, in which are listed a number of paintings in his possession. Some of them have titles corresponding to known works by Leonardo. The high values assigned to them suggest that they were thought of as originals rather than copies. Whether they really were is another matter: Salai was a prolific and proficient copyist of the master's work. Among these is 'a painting called La Joconda', priced at 505 lire.[90] This has been thought to strengthen Vasari's case, since it shows that the painting was known as the *Gioconda* some years before his identification of its subject as Lisa del Giocondo.

A third document is usually passed over in silence because it is brief and erroneous, but I believe it has a bearing. In the Anonimo Gaddiano's biography of Leonardo occurs the following statement: '*Ritrasse dal naturale Piero Francesco del Giocondo.*' The usual interpretation of this is that the Anonimo is saying, in error, that Leonardo painted a portrait from life of Lisa's husband. In fact, as Frank Zöllner points out, the Anonimo is not saying that at all – Lisa's husband was Francesco; Piero di Francesco was her *son*.[91] This is even less likely, given that Piero was only eight when Leonardo left Florence in 1508. I suspect that the true error is one of copying. The Anonimo's manuscript is sometimes careless or fragmentary; there are omissions and insertions – for instance, the line immediately below the Giocondo notation reads, '*Dipinse a* [blank] *una testa di* [*Medusa* crossed out] *Megara.*' I believe the correct reading of the Giocondo sentence is similarly fragmentary. It is not '*Ritrasse dal naturale Piero Francesco del Giocondo*', but '*Ritrasse dal naturale per Francesco del Giocondo . . .*', where the omission marks represent a discontinued sentence: 'For Francesco del Giocondo he painted a portrait from life of . . .' Compare this to Vasari's opening, where the sentence is completed: '*Prese Leonardo a fare per Francesco del Giocondo il ritratto di Mona Lisa su moglie.*' If this is right, Vasari seems to be correctly using an original source that the Anonimo had in some way garbled.

The upshot of these fragments of evidence is that Vasari's account of the painting's genesis is probably right: it is a portrait of Lisa Gherardini, commissioned by her husband in about 1503, when she was in her early twenties. To some it seems unsatisfactorily prosaic that the world's most famous painting should depict an obscure Florentine housewife (the rival claimants are all more glamorous and aristocratic), but to me this kernel of ordinariness seems to add to the poetry. This is, at any rate, how the painting began. Vasari also says Leonardo 'left it unfinished', which presumably means it was unfinished when he left Florence in 1508. It was still in his possession nine years later, when Antonio de Beatis saw it, and it may well have evolved during this interim. This painting was a long-term companion, a continuous presence in a series of studios, the *maestro* alighting on it as occasion served, to retouch and rethink, to see in it things he had not seen before. In that long meditation the portrait is imbued with those subtle tonalities, those nuances of meaning one feels but can never quite define. The passage of time is written across the *Mona Lisa*: the evening light that falls on her face, the aeons of geological time in the mountain-forms behind her, and of course that almost-smile which is perpetually an instant away from becoming an actual smile: a future moment which will never arrive.

In another sense, as a cultural object, the painting had a long future ahead of it. Its axiomatic famousness is essentially a modern phenomenon. Early commentators enthused, but they did not seem to consider the painting particularly extraordinary or unique. The elevation of the *Mona Lisa* to iconic status happened in the mid nineteenth century; it was born out of northern Europe's fascination with the Italian Renaissance in general, and Leonardo in particular, and it was given a particular Gallic, or indeed Parisian, twist by the presence of the painting in the Louvre. Her image became bound up with the morbid Romantic fantasy of the femme fatale: that idea of an ensnaring, exotic *belle dame sans merci* which so exercised the male imagination at that time.

An important figure in the Gioconda's elevation to fatal status was the novelist, art-critic and hashish-smoker Théophile Gautier. For him she was 'this sphinx of beauty who smiles so mysteriously'; her 'divinely ironic' gaze intimates 'unknown pleasures'; she 'seems to pose a yet unsolved riddle to the admiring centuries'; and so on. In a telling aside during one of his rhapsodies, he remarks, 'She makes you feel like a schoolboy before a duchess.'[92] Another who quaked in her presence was the historian and Renaissance-enthusiast Jules Michelet. Looking at her, he wrote, 'you are fascinated and troubled as if by a strange magnetism'; she 'attracts me, revolts me, consumes me; I go to her in spite of myself, as the bird to the snake'. Similarly, in the Goncourt brothers' journal for 1860, a famous beauty of the day is described as 'like a sixteenth-century courtesan' who wears 'the smile full of night of the Gioconda'.[93] Thus the *Mona Lisa* was co-opted into a chorus-line of dangerous beauties alongside such luminaries as Zola's Nana, Wedekind's Lulu, and Baudelaire's Creole belle Jeanne Duval.

The famous description of the painting by the Victorian aesthete Walter Pater, first published in 1869, was certainly influenced by this extended bout of Gallic swooning. Yeats later paid Pater's flagrantly purple prose the compliment of chopping it up into free verse, in which form it sits more happily:

> She is older than the rocks among which she sits;
> Like the vampire,
> She has been dead many times,
> And learned the secrets of the grave;
> And has been a diver in deep seas,
> And keeps their fallen day about her . . .[94]

Oscar Wilde comments perceptively on this seductive Pateresque blarney, 'The picture becomes more wonderful to us than it really is, and reveals to us a secret of which, in truth, it knows nothing.'[95] But the idea of the *Mona Lisa*'s 'secret' continued to reverberate. In E. M. Forster's *A Room with a View* (1908), Lucy Honeychurch's sojourn in Tuscany gives her a touch of the Gioconda mystery – 'He detected in her a wonderful reticence. She was like a woman of Leonardo da Vinci's, whom we love not so much for herself as for the things she will not tell us.'[96]

Others reacted more sceptically, as in Somerset Maugham's novel *Christmas Holiday* (1939), where a quartet of art-lovers 'gazed at the insipid smile of that prim and sex-starved young woman'. Iconoclastic young critics like Roberto Longhi poured scorn on the painting, and even Bernard Berenson – though hardly daring to question 'a shaman so potent' as Pater – confessed to his covert dislike of this revered work: 'She had simply become an incubus.' When T. S. Eliot called *Hamlet* 'the *Mona Lisa* of literature' he meant it in a negative sense: that the play was no longer seen for what it was, but had become, like the painting, a receptacle for subjective interpretations and second-rate theories.[97]

The other life-changing event in the career of the *Mona Lisa* was her abduction from the Louvre on the morning of Monday 21 August 1911.[98] The thief was a thirty-year-old Italian painter-decorator and petty criminal, Vincenzo Perugia. Born in the village of Dumenza, near Lake Como, he had been in Paris since 1908, one of thousands of Italian immigrants in the city – the *macaroni*, as the French dubbed them. He had worked briefly at the Louvre, which was why he was able to get into the building unchallenged – and out again, carrying the *Mona Lisa* stuffed under his workman's smock. A police hunt ensued, but despite his criminal record, and despite his having left a large thumb-print on the frame, Perugia's name never came up. Among those suspected of involvement were Picasso and Apollinaire; the latter was imprisoned briefly, and wrote a poem about it. Perugia kept the painting in his lodgings, hidden under a stove, for more than two years. Then, in late November 1913, he sent a letter to an antique-dealer in Florence, Alfredo Geri, offering to 'return' the *Mona Lisa* to Italy. He demanded 500,000 lire.

The letter was signed 'Leonardo Vincenzo'. On 12 December, Perugia arrived in Florence, by train, with the *Mona Lisa* in a wooden trunk, 'a sort of seaman's locker'; he checked into a low-rent hotel, the Albergo Tripoli-Italia on Via Panzani (still in business, though now called – what else? – the Hotel La Gioconda). Here, in the presence of Alfredo Geri and Giovanni Poggi, the director of the Uffizi, Perugia opened the trunk, revealing some old shoes and woollen underclothes; then – as Geri relates – 'after taking out these not very appetizing objects [he] lifted up the false bottom of the trunk, under which we saw the picture ... We were filled with a strong emotion. Vincenzo looked at us with a kind of fixed stare, smiling complacently, as if he had painted it himself.'[99] He was arrested later that day. Efforts were made to turn Perugia into a cultural hero, but at his trial he proved a disappointment. He said he had first intended to steal Mantegna's *Mars and Venus*, but had decided on the *Mona Lisa* instead because it was smaller. He was imprisoned for twelve months; he died in 1947.

The theft and recovery of the *Mona Lisa* were the clinching of her international celebrity. Both unleashed a swarm of newspaper features, commemorative postcards, cartoons, ballads, cabaret-revues and comic silent films. These are the heralds of the painting's modern existence as global pop-icon. Marcel Duchamp's defaced Gioconda of 1919, saucily entitled *L.H.O.O.Q* (i.e. '*Elle a chaud au cul*', or 'She's hot in the arse') is the most famous of the send-ups, though it is pre-dated by more than twenty years by the pipe-smoking Mona Lisa drawn by the illustrator Sapeck (Eugene Battaile). And so the way was open for Warhol's multiple Gioconda (*Thirty are Better than One*); for Terry Gilliam's animated Gioconda in the *Monty Python* title sequence; for William Gibson's 'sprawl novel' *Mona Lisa Overdrive*; for the classic citations in Cole Porter's 'You're the Top', Nat King Cole's 'Mona Lisa' and Bob Dylan's 'Vision of Johanna'; for the joint-smoking poster and the novelty mouse-pad. Personally I suspect that I first became aware of the *Mona Lisa* through the Jimmy Clanton hit of 1962, which began:

> She's Venus in blue jeans,
> Mona Lisa with a pony tail ...

I'm not sure the ponytail would suit her, but the song's wonderful bubble-gum blandness illustrates well enough the fate that has befallen this mysterious and beautiful painting.

→→ THE *ANGHIARI* FRESCO (I) ←←

A summer spent dividing his time between excursions into the Pisan hills, conversations with Machiavelli, mathematical studies with Luca Pacioli, and portrait-sessions with Lisa del Giocondo (with or without musicians and comedians) sounds to me a pretty good summer for Leonardo da Vinci, but by the autumn he was considering a new commission, for a major public work equivalent in scale – and potential stress – to the *Last Supper*. The commission was for a fresco to decorate one of the walls of the enormous Council Hall (the Sala del Maggiore Consiglio, later the Sala del Cinquecento) on the first floor of the Palazzo Vecchio. The hall had been built in 1495, as part of the new republican dawn that followed the expulsion of the Medici.[100]

The original contract has not survived, but the commission can be dated around October 1503, for on the 24th of that month the Signoria issued instructions for Leonardo to be given the key to a large disused refectory known as the Sala del Papa (the Pope's Hall) in the monastery of Santa Maria Novella.[101] This official provision was doubtless to give him the space he needed for the huge cartoon which was to be the template of the fresco. A later contract, dated 4 May 1504, says that Leonardo had 'agreed some months previously to paint a picture in the hall of the Great Council', and had been paid an advance of 35 florins. The deadline for completing the work ('without any exception or cavil whatsoever') is given as the end of February 1505. Later documents show that he received a stipend of 15 florins a month while working on it.[102]

And so Leonardo takes up new quarters at Santa Maria Novella, with its magnificent Albertian façade which he had seen being built more than thirty years before, and its walls decorated with the luminous frescos of Domenico Ghirlandaio, with their portraits of Ficino and Luigi Pulci and Poliziano, and of the young Medici boys – faces from his youth, ghosts from another Florence. The Sala del Papa was in the ramble of buildings to the west of the church (now the Carabinieri headquarters, heavily sentried). The room was not in good condition – a further instruction from the Signoria orders that the roof should be repaired to make it rainproof. The windows were 'rough' and needed to be made secure. On 8 January 1504 a carpenter, Benedetto Buchi, was brought in with panels, runners, shutters and cross-bars to close them up.[103] These necessary building works perhaps pre-date Leonardo's definitive arrival. A fragmentary sheet in the Codex Atlanticus has an inventory of his household goods – forty-four items: chairs and tables, towels and napkins, brooms and candlesticks, a feather mattress, a copper basin, a soup-ladle, a frying-pan, 'lampstands, inkwell, ink, soap, colours', 'trivet, sphere, pen-holder, lectern, rod, sponge': the clutter of small necessities.[104]

Throughout February the scene resembles a building-site – the carpenter is making the platform and ladder, 'with all the necessary devices'. The main beam of the platform is a 5 braccia length of elm-wood; it is secured by a hawser or cable of hemp – in other words the platform is hanging rather than scaffolded, its height and position being adjustable by pulleys. A paper-merchant, Giandomenico di Filippo, arrives with a ream of paper which will be glued together for the cartoon. Another brings rougher, cheaper paper to cover the windows. Wax, turpentine and white lead are delivered from the apothecary's. A consignment of sponges arrives. Also at work is a builder, Maestro Antonio di Giovanni. He is making a doorway from Leonardo's private rooms which will 'go directly to the said cartoon' – we glimpse in this specification the punishing artistic labours to come: the blinkering, the solitude. Soon the work will take him over: soon he will be pacing from his room to the drawing and back again, wrapped up in concentration. One recalls Bandello's reminiscence of work on the *Last Supper* – the bursts of galvanic activity, the *longueurs* of arms-folded contemplation.

On 27 April Leonardo drew out another 50 florins from his bank-account. It seems the advance he had received from the Signoria was already spent.

War has been Leonardo's milieu over the past couple of years – as servant to the ruthless ambitions of the Borgia, as engineer to the Florentine war-effort against Pisa – and even here in his new studio in Santa Maria Novella he cannot quite shake off the connection, for war was precisely the subject of the work on which he was now embarking. The Signoria wished to decorate their great Council Hall with an emblematic scene from a famous Florentine victory. In 1440 – and thus still just about in living memory – an attack of Milanese troops under the *condottiere* Niccolò Piccinino had been beaten off by Florentine troops in an engagement outside the Tuscan village of Anghiari, in the hills not far from Arezzo. Leonardo may well have known the place: he would have passed that way en route to Urbino the previous year; it is marked on his map of the Val di Chiana.

Again Machiavelli is involved. Among Leonardo's papers is a long description of the battle, translated from a Latin account by Leonardo Dati.[105] The handwriting is that of Machiavelli's assistant Agostino di Vespucci; it was no doubt written at Machiavelli's suggestion, to give Leonardo information and ideas about the subject. It seems that a narrative fresco was envisaged, showing various scenes over a period of time. 'Begin with the address of Niccolò Piccinino to the soldiers ... Then let it be shown how he first mounted on horseback in armour and the whole army came after him, 40 squadrons of cavalry and 2,000 foot-soldiers', and so on. Dati's account of the battle includes a visionary scene where St Peter appears 'in a cloud' to the Florentine commander (the battle was fought on St Peter and St Paul's day, 29 June), and is in general rousing and rhetorical – as the Signoria doubtless hoped Leonardo's fresco would be. A very different account was later written by Machiavelli himself in his *Istorie fiorentine*, where the battle is described as a brief skirmish, during which only one man was killed – and he only by accident, when his horse fell on him.[106] But now, for the painter, here was the propaganda version.

The commission is clear: a stirring scene of Florentine military valour, a giant *trionfo* to bolster the republic's resolve in these days of uncertainty. But from the outset – as one can see from the many preparatory drawings – Leonardo's treatment caught also a powerful sense of the horror and brutality of war.[107] We see in those drawings the snarling mouths of the fighters, the terrified rearing of the horses, the stretched muscles, the hacking weapons. There is in them an element of catharsis: a confrontation of his own complicity in the warmongering of the day. In these drawings are distilled certain grisly scenes he had witnessed during his months with Borgia. And he also knew the kind of things to focus on to catch the lurid drama of the battlefield, for more than a decade earlier in Milan he had penned a long text entitled 'How to represent a battle':

First you must show the smoke of the artillery, mingling in the air with the dust thrown up by the movement of horses and soldiers ... The air must be filled with arrows in every direction, and the cannon-balls must have a train of smoke following their flight ... If you show one who has fallen you must show the place where his body has slithered in the blood-stained dust and mud ... Others must be represented in the agonies of death, grinding their teeth, rolling their eyes, with their fists clenched against their bodies and their legs contorted ... There might be seen a number of men fallen in a heap over a dead horse.[108]

This quality of scrimmage, of formless mêlée, of contortion and commotion, is precisely seen in his preparatory sketches. Thus, between Florentine spin and eyewitness truth, Leonardo gropes towards the composition.

News that Leonardo is at work on a major new project has reached the ears of the ever-hopeful Isabella d'Este in Mantua, but has not deterred her. In a letter dated 14 May 1504 she instructs Angelo del Tovaglia to ask

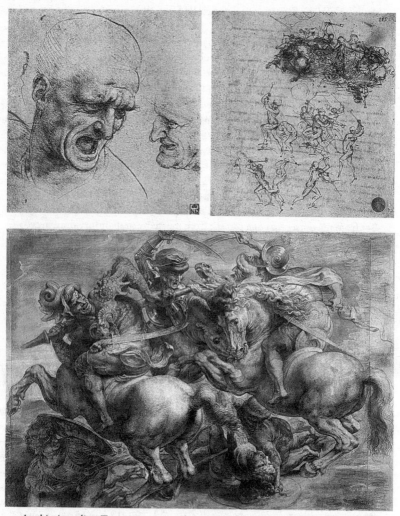

Anghiari *studies.* Top: *preparatory drawing of the heads of two soldiers, and a* *mêlée of horsemen in combat, c.* 1503–4. Bottom: *a copy of Leonardo's lost* Battle of Anghiari, *attributed to Peter Paul Rubens.*

Leonardo to paint her a small religious painting – 'and if he gives an excuse that he has no time, because of the work he has begun for the most excellent Signoria, you can tell him that it will be a recreation and relaxation when the fresco grows wearisome, and that he can paint it whenever it seems pleasant to do so.' On the same date she writes a letter to Leonardo himself, to be delivered by Tovaglia. It reads:

Maestro Leonardo –
Understanding that you are settled in Florence, we are hopeful that we can get from you what we have so much desired, which is to have something from your hand. When you were in these parts, and did my portrait in charcoal, you promised me that sometime you would do one in colour for me. As this is now almost impossible, since it is not convenient for you to travel here, we hope you will want to satisfy the obligations of our agreement by converting our portrait into another figure even more gracious, that of a Youthful Christ, of about twelve years old, at the age when he disputed in the Temple, done with that air of sweetness and comeliness [*suavita*] in which your art so especially excels . . .

She winds up in a tone of steely courtesy: 'In expectation of your devoted reply, we offer you our best wishes . . .'

Tovaglia duly delivered the letter to the artist at Santa Maria Novella, but received the familiar polite brush-off: 'He has promised me he will do it at certain hours, when he can spare the time from the work he has undertaken for the Signoria.' Tovaglia has also been asked to chase up Pietro Perugino, who is supposed to be producing a painting for Isabella's *studiolo*. He concludes wryly:

I will continue to encourage Leonardo in this, and also Perugino in the other. Both of them are full of promises, and seem very desirous to serve Your Ladyship, however I fear there will be a competition in lateness [*gara de tarditate*] between them. Who knows which of them will win this – my money is on Leonardo![109]

Isabella did not give up, and a couple of years later she found a more promising emissary, someone with family connections with Leonardo – Alessandro Amadori, canon of Fiesole, the brother of Leonardo's first stepmother, Albiera. But, as we gather from Amadori's letter to her, this new tack proved equally fruitless.[110]

By the early summer of 1504 Leonardo is ready to synthesize his small sketches and clay models into the single full-scale image of the cartoon, drawn and painted on to the huge patchwork of paper held in a framework in the refectory of Santa Maria Novella. In June a baker named Giovanni di Landino brings '88 lb of sifted flour . . . for coating the cartoon'. From the apothecary come 28 pounds of Alexandrian white lead and 36 pounds of baking soda and 2 pounds of gesso, 'required by Leonardo for painting'. And a blacksmith is paid for iron pins and rings and wheels for 'Leonardo's carriage' – '*il carro di Leonardo*': another platform, this time on wheels, enabling him to move around the large area of the cartoon.

⤜ MICHELANGELO ⤛

Whether or not it was originally in the minds of the Signoria, by the late summer of 1504 the decision was documented: Leonardo's fresco or mural on the wall of the Council Hall was to be matched by one by Michelangelo, illustrating another famous Florentine victory, the Battle of Cascina, on the opposite wall. They thus envisaged the two greatest Florentine artists of the day working opposite one another in the Council Hall, and it is hard to believe they did not conceive this as a sort of competition, or indeed a clash of the Titans, in which the natural rivalry of excellence, spiced (as it seems) with personal antagonism, would spur each man on to greater feats of artistic ingenuity.

When Leonardo left Florence in 1482, Michele Agnolo di Lodovico Buonarroti was a seven-year-old boy living with a stonemason's family at a marble-quarry in Settignano owned by his nobly descended but impecunious father. By the time that Leonardo returned, eighteen years later, Michel-angelo was the charismatic new star, the new blood pumping through the veins of Renaissance sculpture.[111] Having been the apprentice of Domenico Ghirlandaio for three years (1488–91), and the protégé of Lorenzo de' Medici until the latter's death in 1492, he had swiftly established a name for himself with such early Florentine works as the marble *Cupid* and the dramatic bas-relief *The Battle of the Centaurs*, in which the classical influ-ence of Lorenzo's sculpture-garden is already mixed with the straining muscles and contorted limbs of his mature work. In 1496 he was summoned to Rome by Cardinal San Giorgio: there he created the tipsy, subversive *Bacchus*, which has, as Vasari notes, 'the slenderness of a youth combined with the fullness and roundness of a female form', and the beautiful *Pietà* of St Peter's. In late 1500 or 1501 he returned to Florence, and it was probably then that he and Leonardo met for the first time. We might imagine (though only imagine) Michelangelo among the throng packed into the Annunziata to view Leonardo's *St Anne* cartoon in the spring of 1501 – a brash, tousled, powerfully built young man, shabbily dressed, with an aura

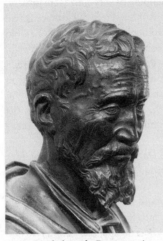

Michelangelo Buonarroti.

of aggressive self-confidence, and already sporting the famous boxer's nose, having had it smashed in a fight with a fellow sculptor, Pietro Torrigiano.

He soon began work on his most characteristic – and characteristically Florentine – work, the monumental *David*, described in contemporary documents as the 'marble giant' or simply 'the giant'. The contract with the Signoria is dated 16 August 1501, with a term of delivery of two years; according to Vasari the fee was 400 florins. Over 16 feet tall and weighing about 9 tons, the *David* is said to have been carved from a spoiled block of marble which had been hanging around in the *fabbriceria* of the Duomo for years; it had been 'botched', according to Vasari, by a sculptor called Simone da Fiesole, presumably meaning Simone Ferrucci; another account names the botcher as Agostino di Duccio. Vasari also says that Gonfalonier Soderini 'had often talked of handing the block over to Leonardo', but gave it to Michelangelo instead. There is no real confirmation of this.[112]

By mid-1503 the great sculpture was taking shape: 'freed' in Michelangelo's famous phrase, 'from the prison of the marble'. A note beneath a rough sketch of David's left arm furnishes a vivid gladiatorial image of the sculptor: '*Davide colla fromba e io coll'arco*' – 'David with his sling and I with my bow', in other words with the bow-shaped marble-drill.[113] Leonardo meanwhile – if we accept the evidence supplied by Vasari – was starting work on his portrait of Lisa del Giocondo: no doubt a good deal less remunerative. These two famous works epitomize the dual mentality of the Renaissance: the one big and breathtakingly confident; the other cool, interior, ungraspable.

On 25 January 1504 the works department of the Duomo convened an extraordinary committee (routine enough administratively, but extraordinary for its concentration of Renaissance artistic talent) to decide on the most 'convenient and congruous' location to display the massive marble giant, which was now 'almost finished'.[114] Thirty men were invited: it is noted in the margin that one of them, Andrea da Monte Sansavino, was absent in Genoa, so it appears that the remaining twenty-nine were present. Besides Leonardo there were Andrea della Robbia, Piero di Cosimo, David Ghirlandaio (younger brother of the late Domenico), Simone del Pollaiuolo (known as Il Cronaca), Filippino Lippi, Cosimo Rosselli, Sandro Botticelli, Giuliano and Antonio da Sangallo, Pietro Perugino and Lorenzo di Credi. Also present were 'Vante *miniatore*', to whom Leonardo had lent money in 1503; 'Giovanni *piffero*', probably the musician Giovanni di Andrea Cellini; and 'El Riccio *orafo*', Curly the goldsmith, who may be the same as the 'Riccio Fiorentino' later named by the Anonimo Gaddiano as one of Leonardo's assistants on the *Anghiari* fresco.

Leonardo's opinion about the placing of *David* is recorded in the minutes of the meeting. 'I say that it should be placed in the Loggia' – the Loggia dei Lanzi, opposite the Palazzo Vecchio – 'as Giuliano has said, behind the low wall where the soldiers line up. It should be put there, with suitable ornaments, in such a way that it does not interfere with the ceremonies of state.' This opinion, shared by Giuliano da Sangallo but counter to the general view, already expresses an antagonism, a deliberate refusal to be impressed. Let this oversized statue be sidelined in a corner where it won't get in the way. The true wish expressed is the sidelining of the sculptor himself: this awkward, intrusive genius. Further nuances of umbrage may have arisen in relation to that earlier Florentine *David*, sculpted by his master Verrocchio, for which the teenage Leonardo is said to have been the model: now, forty years on, this new *David* outmodes that image of his own youthful promise.

His advice was not heeded, and in May the statue was duly placed on the platform outside the main entrance of the Palazzo Vecchio, where it remained for several centuries, and where the nineteenth-century replica now stands. The diary of Luca Landucci gives a vivid account of the transporting of it (and sheds incidental light on the problem of vandalism in Renaissance Florence):

14 May 1504 – The marble giant was taken out of the works department at the 24th hour [8 p.m.], and they had to break down the wall above the door so that it could get through. During the night stones were thrown at the giant to injure it, therefore it was necessary to keep watch over it. It took four days to get it to the Piazza [della Signoria], arriving there on the 18th at the twelfth hour of the morning [8 a.m.]. It was moved along by more than forty men. Beneath it were fourteen greased beams which were changed from hand to hand.[115]

It was finally erected on 8 July, Donatello's *Judith* having been banished to an inner courtyard to make room. Perhaps Leonardo was present at this ceremony or perhaps he was pointedly absent: back at Santa Maria Novella, aloof on his wheeled trolley, attending to certain small adjustments of the *Anghiari* cartoon.

It was perhaps around this time that the rivalry between the two artists erupted in a brief public spat, which is recorded by the Anonimo Gaddiano in a vivid little vignette which leaps out of the generally rather bland pages of his biography of Leonardo. It is preceded by the phrase '*Dal Gav.*', which suggests that the source was the same 'P. da Gavine' whom the account mentions as Leonardo's companion. It is, in other words, an eyewitness account.

Leonardo was walking with P. da Gavine through [Piazza] Santa Trinità, and they passed the Pancaccia degli Spini where there was a gathering of citizens arguing over a passage of Dante; and they called out to the said Leonardo, asking him to explain the passage. At that point, by chance, Michele Agnolo was passing by, and Leonardo answered their request by saying, 'There's Michele Agnolo, he'll explain it for you.' Upon which Michele Agnolo, thinking he had said this to insult him, retorted angrily, 'Explain it yourself – you who designed a horse to cast in bronze, and couldn't cast it, and abandoned it out of shame.' And so saying he turned his back on them and walked off. And Leonardo was left there, his face red because of these words.

The anecdote is precisely located: they are in the Piazza Santa Trinità; the group discussing Dante is lounging around an old loggia in front of the medieval *palazzo* of the Spini family (now Palazzo Ferroni-Spini). This building stands on the southern side of the piazza and runs down to the river-front by the Ponte Santa Trinità. It no longer has a loggia, but one can work out where this was by looking at the frescos by Domenico Ghirlandaio painted in the mid-1480s in the nearby church of Santa Trinità. They depict the life of St Francis but are placed, as is Ghirlandaio's way, in a contemporary Florentine setting. The central fresco, showing the miraculous healing of a child, is precisely set in Piazza Santa Trinità: viewed from a point to the north of the piazza, it shows the church on the right (though without its late-sixteenth-century façade), the receding line of the Ponte Santa Trinità in the middle background, and the Palazzo Spini on the left. There is nothing resembling a loggia on the two walls visible (the northern and western walls), thus confirming what common sense would anyway suggest: that it was on the southern side, looking out over the river.[116] We can thus place this trenchant exchange between Leonardo and Michelangelo precisely on the Lungarno, a little to the east of the bridge, in front of what is now the smart fashion-outlet Salvatore Ferragamo.

It is also closely characterized: the retiring Leonardo, who pleasantly declines the invitation to pontificate about the *passo dantesco*; the touchy, intemperate Michelangelo furiously reacting to this supposed slight (where none can have been intended, as the story is given, unless there was a touch of sarcasm about it, as if to say, 'Here's Michelangelo, who knows everything.'). The latter's abrupt departure – *'voltò i rene'*, literally 'he turned his kidneys' – leaves Leonardo speechless, embarrassed and angry: *'per le dette parole diventò rosso'* – he became red. Leonardo was instinctively courteous, Michelangelo instinctively offensive.

On the following page of the Anonimo's manuscript, after a digression about Michelangelo's skill as an anatomist, there is a further instance of Michelangelo's jeering tone towards Leonardo: 'On another occasion Michele Agnolo, wanting to hurt [*mordere* – literally 'to bite'] Leonardo, said to him, "So those idiot Milanese actually believed in you?"' *'Que' caponi de' Melanesi'* is literally 'those Milanese big heads', but *caponi* carries the sense of stupidity or obstinacy rather than boastfulness. If this too is a genuine report, it shows real sneering antipathy.

There is no hint in the text as to the date of the Santa Trinità episode. It could have occurred between early 1501 (when Michelangelo returned from Rome) and summer 1502 (when Leonardo left Florence to join Borgia), or between March 1503 (Leonardo's return to Florence) and early 1505 (Michelangelo's departure for Rome). Both insults refer to Leonardo's failure with the Sforza Horse, which might suggest the earlier date, but they would be equally appropriate in the context of the *David* committee – Leonardo's sniffy attitude to the statue calling forth this invective about his own failures in the arena of large-scale sculpture. This would place the spat in early 1504 – spring 1504, perhaps, when the weather is warm enough for men to lounge in a loggia discussing Dante. In the text the anecdote is preceded by some comments about the painting of the *Anghiari* fresco, also from 'Gav.' or Gavine.

It is in this context of bitter rivalry that the Signoria hit on the idea of getting Michelangelo to paint another battle-scene in the Council Hall to counterpoint – or compete with – Leonardo's. As Michelangelo himself later phrased it, he 'undertook to do half the Council Hall'.[117] His subject, the Battle of Cascina, was part of an earlier war against Pisa. The first indication of Michelangelo's involvement is a document dated 22 September 1504, in which he is granted (as Leonardo had been the previous year) free use of a large studio space, the *sala grande* at the Ospedale di Sant'Onofrio. This was ratified on 29 October.[118] Here, Vasari relates,

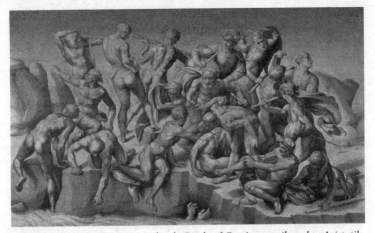

Copy of Michelangelo's cartoon for the Battle of Cascina, *attributed to Aristotile da Sangallo.*

he started work on a vast cartoon which he refused to let anyone see. He filled it with naked men who are shown bathing in the River Arno because of the heat when suddenly the alarm is raised in the camp because of an attack of the enemy. And as the soldiers rush out of the water to dress themselves, Michelangelo's inspired hand depicted them . . . in various unusual attitudes, some upright, some kneeling or leaning forward, or halfway between one position and another, all exhibiting the most difficult foreshortenings.

The following February Michelangelo received payment of 280 lire from the Palazzo della Signoria 'for his labour in painting the cartoon'. This was then the equivalent of about 40 florins: we don't know precisely what time-span this covers, but it seems to compare favourably with Leonardo's stipend of 15 florins a month. Michelangelo's cartoon was probably complete by then. 'When they saw the cartoon,' says Vasari, 'all the other artists were overcome with admiration and astonishment.' Shortly after this Michelangelo departed for Rome, to discuss the ill-fated project of the tomb for Julius II. He seems to have taken no further part in the Council Hall project: there is no evidence that he ever began painting. The cartoon itself is lost, but survives in a fine copy at Holkham Hall, Norfolk, the former seat of the Earls of Leicester and until the 1980s the home of the Leonardo notebook called the Codex Leicester.

How Leonardo viewed this challenge or intrusion is not recorded, but he seems to have left Florence in September or early October 1504, and though

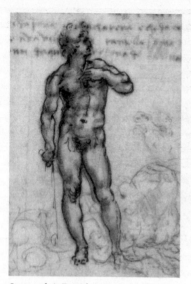

Leonardo's David, c. *1504. A drawing after, but not of, Michelangelo's* David.

there are other reasons for his departure, this coincides precisely with the commissioning of Michelangelo 'to do half the Council Hall', and may in part be a piqued withdrawal from the scene: a walk-out. He had by this stage completed his own cartoon, probably by the end of July, which is the date of his last recorded payment; he did not begin painting in the Palazzo Vecchio until the first weeks of 1505. Confrontation is not in his nature: he avoids or eludes it. Thus begins the great clash of the Renaissance giants: Michelangelo is there at the door, ready to fight – but the room is empty.

Around this time Leonardo writes a brief passage criticizing pictures showing exaggeratedly muscular torsos: 'You should not make all the muscles of the body too conspicuous, unless the limbs to which they belong are engaged in the exertion of great force or labour ... If you do otherwise you will produce a sack of walnuts rather than a human figure.' This may well be a dig at the muscled figures of Michelangelo's *Cascina* cartoon. He repeats the idea in another notebook: the body should not be made to look like a 'bundle of radishes' or a 'sack of walnuts'.[119] He enjoys this phrase. *'Un saco di noce ...'* One imagines him saying it, deadpanning it, making people laugh: his weapon. It is rather better as a put-down than those blunt-edged insults that Michelangelo threw at him that day at the Ponte Santa Trinità.

For all this, it is certain that Leonardo's later anatomical drawings show the influence of Michelangelo. There is also a small sketch at Windsor which looks rather like the *David* – in art parlance it is 'after *David*'.[120] This is the only surviving drawing by him which is demonstrably based on a contemporary art-work. Despite all the needle and resentment, primacy is given to the old artistic imperative: what can I learn from him?

→→ A DEATH AND A JOURNEY ←←

Amid these momentous artistic events – the creation of the *Anghiari* cartoon, the hauling of the marble giant through the streets of Florence, the emerging face of the *Mona Lisa* – life proceeds according to the rhythms and necessities to which even Renaissance geniuses are subject, and by chance there survives a list of Leonardo's household expenses over four days in May 1504, written in the well-formed hand of '*Tommaso mio famiglio*' – 'my servant Tommaso' – otherwise known as Zoroastro. The heading reads, 'On the morning of St Zanobio's Day, 25 May 1504, I had from Lionardo Vinci 15 gold ducats and began to spend them.'[121]

On that first day, a Saturday, Tommaso disbursed nearly 200 soldi (10 lire or 2½ ducats), of which 62 soldi went to a certain 'Mona Margarita', who appears elsewhere in the accounts as associated with horses ('*di cavali mona malgarita*'), and 20 soldi went on 'repairing the ring'. An account was settled at the barber's, a debt was paid at the bank, some velvet was purchased, and the rest was spent on food: eggs, wine, bread, meat, mulberries, mushrooms, salad, fruit, partridge, flour. Saturday was the big-spending day – perhaps for a party of some sort, for on the following three days Tommaso buys only the basics: bread, wine, meat, soup and fruit. The daily expenditure on bread is constant (6 soldi) and that on wine fairly constant (usually 9 soldi). On the basis of this small sample Leonardo was spending about 12 lire a week on food for his household. The fact that meat is bought every day does not show that Leonardo was at this point a meat-eater, only that he did not insist on others in his household abstaining. According to Scipione Ammirato, Tommaso was also vegetarian: 'He would not kill a flea for any reason whatever. He preferred to dress in linen so as not to wear something dead.'

These accounts cover three sides of paper; on the fourth side are notes in Leonardo's hand – 'To make the great canal first make the smaller one and bring the water in by it', and 'This is how piles should be driven in' – and sketches in red chalk preliminary to one of his maps of the Arno. The household business thus inserts itself among his water-moving projects of 1503–4.

Another list of expenses, in Leonardo's hand, belongs to around the same time – a spicy fare of 'peppered bread', eels and apricots, as well as two dozen laces, a sword and a knife, and a little cross from a man called Paolo have been bought. There is another visit to the barber, and also a curious item which has attracted some note: '*per dire la ventura: 6 soldi*'.[122] That a man so axiomatically unimpressed by superstition spent good money for having his 'fortune told' is surprising. What is it that he wishes to know about his destiny?

Further accountings are found on a Codex Atlanticus sheet:[123]

> On the morning of St Peter's Day, 29 June 1504, I took out 10 ducats, of which I gave one to my servant Tommaso to spend . . .
> On Monday morning [1 July] 1 florin to Salai to spend on the house . . .
> On the morning of Friday 19 July I have 7 florins left and 22 in the cashbox . . .
> Friday 9 August 1504 I took 10 ducats out of the cashbox . . .

And on the same page, amid these small disbursements, Leonardo records the death of his father:

> On Wednesday at the 7th hour Ser Piero da Vinci died, on the 9th day of July 1504.

A more extended note is on another sheet: 'On the 9th day of July 1504, Wednesday, at the 7th hour, died Ser Piero da Vinci, notary to the Palazzo del Podesta, my father, at the 7th hour. He was eighty years old, and left ten sons and two daughters.'[124] This has a more formal, obituarizing tone, but one discerns again that jumpy mix of punctiliousness and repetition which is found in the note about Caterina a decade earlier: emotion sublimated into tics of detail. Not just repetition, but error: 9 July 1504 was not a Wednesday but a Tuesday – the days blur. And Ser Piero was not eighty at his death, but seventy-eight, as shown by his birth-date inscribed by Antonio da Vinci in the family record-book, which is unlikely to be wrong.

There are so many unanswered questions about Leonardo's relationship with his father – our questions, because we lack the evidence; his questions, because as often between father and son there was a core of distance which they could not cross. 'He left ten sons and two daughters,' Leonardo writes, including himself in this quota, but he will soon learn that he alone has been left nothing in his father's will: the last rejection.

A solitary fragment of discourse between them survives: the opening sentence of a letter from Leonardo – undated, but from the handwriting apparently written not long before this. 'Dearest father,' it reads: 'On the last day of last month I received the letter you wrote to me, which caused me in a brief space of time both pleasure and sadness: pleasure in that I learned from it you are well, for which I thank God, and displeasure to hear of your troubles . . .'[125] This is not just formal: it reads like a composition, with its neatly balanced clauses, its modicums of pleasure and sadness. This respectful but wooden salutation is written from left to right, the 'normal' way. Leonardo is for a moment the kind of son his father wanted him to be – but the letter is discontinued, and remains among his papers. On the back of the page he draws the wing of a flying-machine.

A coda to this is another letter – again just a fragment – which he wrote to one of his half-brothers, probably Domenico da Vinci, congratulating him on the birth of a son. 'My beloved brother,' he begins, warmly enough, 'I hear you have an heir and are extremely pleased about it.' But he then goes on to wonder why 'you are so pleased about having created a deadly enemy, who with all his heart desires liberty, which he will only get with your death.'[126] It is intended as an avuncular joke, perhaps – Leonardo was more than thirty years older than Domenico – but if so it is a dark one: the son as malcontent subject chafes under the parental yoke; the father's death brings 'liberty' to him.

Accounts and memoranda continue through August. A new apprentice arrives: 'On Saturday morning, 3rd August 1504, Jacopo the German came to live with me in the house, and agreed with me that I should charge him one carlino per day.'[127] Also in August came the news that the proposed diversion of the Arno near Pisa was finally to be put into action. It does not seem that Leonardo was actively involved in this, but it is likely that he was in touch with Machiavelli about the progress of the project. The Signoria finally voted to proceed on 20 August 1504; work began immediately, as mentioned in Landucci's diary on 22 August. As we have seen, the whole enterprise was a disaster which cost the Signoria 7,000 ducats and resulted in eighty deaths, and the project was abandoned in mid-October.

And where was Leonardo as this fiasco was played out on the Pisan flatlands – a fiasco for which he might take a share of the blame? Probably out of town. We know from dated notes that he was in Piombino by mid-October 1504, and it is pretty certain that en route there from Florence he spent some time in Vinci with his uncle Francesco. As noted earlier, his departure coincides with the Signoria's decision to commission Michelangelo to paint alongside him in the Palazzo Vecchio – a decision which becomes visible with the requisitioning of studio space for him at Sant'Onofrio on 22 September.

Shortly before his departure from Florence in September or October 1504 Leonardo drew up the last and most extensive catalogue of his books. There are two lists, written across a double-page spread of Madrid Codex II.[128] The longer one is headed '*Richordo de libri ch'io lasscio serati nel cassone*':

'A record of the books I am leaving locked in the large chest'. The shorter is headed '*In cassa al munistero*': 'In the chest at the monastery' – presumably Santa Maria Novella. The total number of books is 116. Another list splits fifty books into different sizes and types:

25 small books
2 large books
16 very large books
6 books on vellum
1 book bound in green chamois

It seems that this last list refers to bound manuscripts rather than printed books (the word *libro* was used for both) – the '6 books on vellum' must certainly be manuscripts, as vellum (stretched calf- or lamb-skin) was not used for printing. It is just possible that this is an inventory of Leonardo's own manuscripts and notebooks in 1504. Alternatively it is a subdivision of the actual book-list, suggesting that getting on for half of Leonardo's 116 books were handwritten codices. For instance the '*vita civile di matteo palmieri*' is certainly a manuscript: the first printed edition of Palmieri's *Della vita civile* was not published till 1529. Also the '*libro di regole latino*' by Francesco da Urbino, who taught Latin grammar at the Florentine Studio, is not known in a published edition at this date. Some of the items in the list do seem to be Leonardo's own works – for example the '*libro di chavalli scizati per cartone*' is clearly a sketchbook of studies for the horses of the *Anghiari* cartoon, and the '*libro di mia vocaboli*' ('my vocabulary book') is probably the Trivulzio Codex. The '*libro di notomia*' ('book of anatomy') may also be his (compare his memorandum of *c.* 1508: 'Have your books of anatomy bound').

The Madrid book-lists are a trove of insights into Leonardo's interests and influences. Some entries which are not found in the earlier Atlanticus book-list of *c.* 1492 are these:

- *batista alberti in architettura* – Alberti's *De re aedificatoria*, first published in Florence in 1485.
- *isopo illingia francosa* – Aesop's Fables in French, perhaps *Les Fables de Esope* (Lyons, 1484), interestingly implying that Leonardo had learned French, presumably further to his French contacts in Milan in 1499.
- *galea de matti* – Sebastian Brandt's *Ship of Fools*. No Italian edition is known so this too may be manuscript, or it may be one of the French editions published in Paris in 1497–9.
- *sonetti di meser guaspari bisconti* – sonnets by Gasparé Visconti,

courtier-poet at the Sforza court, friend of Bramante, and probably also of Leonardo; the *Rithmi* of 1493 may be the collection referred to.

- *arismetricha di maestro luca* – Pacioli's *Summa arithmetica*, as purchased by Leonardo for 119 soldi in *c*.1494.

- *franco da siena* – certainly a reference to the Sienese architect Francesco di Giorgio Martini, whom Leonardo knew in Milan, and probably to the manuscript copy of his *Trattato di architettura* now in the Laurentian Library in Florence, with marginal annotations by Leonardo.

- *libro danticaglie* – 'book of antiquities', perhaps the mysterious *Antiquarie prospetiche Romane* dedicated to Leonardo in the late 1490s, though it could be his friend Bernardo Rucellai's *De urbe Roma* (1471).

One also notes Leonardo's growing collection of popular literature – books to be read for pleasure and relaxation, such as Luca Pulci's romantic poem *Ciriffo calvaneo* (Venice, 1479); the chivalric romances *Attila flagellum dei*, attributed to Nicola da Casola (Venice, 1491), and *Guerino meschino*, by Andrea da Barberino (Padua, 1473); Masuccio Salernitano's *Il novellino* (Naples, 1476); and the curious and frequently erotic poem *Geta e Birria*, by Ghigo Brunelleschi and Ser Domenico da Prato (Florence, *c.* 1476).

With his books inventoried and boxed up Leonardo heads out of town for Vinci, a natural place for him to be in the aftermath of Ser Piero's death, and particularly so because on 12 August Uncle Francesco had drawn up his own will, in which he left Leonardo certain properties in the Vinci area. This bequest was no doubt a reaction to the exclusion of Leonardo from his father's estate; it was in fact a contravention of an earlier agreement between Ser Piero and Francesco, made in 1492, in which it was promised that 'after the life of Francesco all his goods will go to Ser Piero and his children' (meaning, of course, his legitimate children). Francesco's will has not survived, but we know from later litigation – he died in 1507 – that Leonardo's legacy included a property called Il Botro, a name meaning a ravine. The place may be depicted in a sketch-map at Windsor showing a property situated between two rivers (see page 24). It has two buildings, and some land which 'yields 16 staia of grain'; to the north of it is a *lecceto* – a grove of holm-oaks. The owners of adjoining plots of land are noted; that one of the names is 'ser piero' suggests that the map cannot have been drawn much later than 1504. The local historian Renzo Cianchi has identified the area shown in the map as Forra di Serravalle, about 4 miles east of Vinci.[129]

A small sketch of the Mont'Albano hills probably belongs to this visit,[130] as does that drawing of a Vinci oil-press – *'molino della doccia di Vinci'* – which we looked at earlier. Its adaptation of the olive-press into a 'machine to grind colours' would be related in his mind to the *Battle of Anghiari* fresco which he was soon to begin painting on the wall of the Council Hall, and which would certainly need industrial quantities of paint.

From Vinci he travelled on down towards the coast of Piombino, where he had been two years earlier on Borgia business. The town was now once more under the Florence-friendly lordship of Jacopo d'Appiano. A dated note finds Leonardo 'at the castle' of Piombino on 20 October. Another reads, 'On All Saints' Day [1 November] 1504 I made to the Lord of Piombino this demonstration.' He neglects to say what the 'demonstration' demonstrated: perhaps the 'method for drying the marshland of Piombino' sketched on a sheet of the Codex Atlanticus.[131] On the same day he writes this beautiful note: '1504 at Piombino on All Saints Day, as the sun was setting, I saw the green shadows produced by the ropes, masts and yardarms against the white surface of the wall. This was because the surface of the wall was not tinged by the sunlight but by the colour of the sea opposite it.'[132]

November brought its customary storms and many years later he recalled scenes witnessed on the waterfront at Piombino:

> *De venti di Piombino a Piombino*
> *ritrosi di venti e di pioggia con*
> *rami e alberi misti coll'aria.*
> *Votamenti dell'acqua che piove nelle barche*

[Of the winds of Piombino at Piombino: gusts of wind and rain, with branches and trees blown into the air. The emptying of rainwater from the boats.][133]

These intensely compacted notes are the verbal equivalent of the swift *in situ* sketch. We see him, a solitary rain-soaked figure out on the strand, watching the waves, watching the fishermen baling out their boats, storing the moment.

By the end of November he was back in Florence, where we find him burning the midnight oil, tussling over the old mathematical conundrum of squaring the circle (that is, constructing a circle and a square with identical area – a mathematical impossibility because of the indeterminate nature of π). In a dramatic nocturnal note, the words squeezed in vertically among geometric figures, he writes, 'On St Andrew's night [30 November] I con-cluded the squaring of the circle, and the light was at an end, and the night, and the paper on which I was writing; it was concluded at the end of the hour.'[134] The lamplight gutters, the dawn comes in, but these conclusions will prove as always to be temporary.

→→ THE *ANGHIARI* FRESCO (II) ←←

In December 1504, after a hiatus of about four months, Leonardo begins work on the critical phase of the *Anghiari* fresco – the actual painting of it, from the cartoon, on to the wall of the Council Hall. On 31 December the works department of the Palazzo Vecchio pays suppliers for nails and cloth delivered that month to 'cover the window where Leonardo da Vinci is working', and for wax, sponges and turpentine 'to wax the windows'. On 28 February 1505 there are further payments for iron, trivets and wheels 'to make Leonardo's carriage [*carro*], that is the platform' – another custom-made mobile scaffolding, like the one he used in Santa Maria Novella, which has now been constructed in the Council Hall. The cost of this contraption is nearly 100 lire, as is noted by the parsimonious accountants, who on 14 March order that 'the platform for Leonardo da Vinci's picture, which is now being done in the Hall of the Great Council, and all the planks and panels which have been used to make it, should be returned and restored to the Department of Works when the said picture is completed.' These entries suggest that Leonardo was equipped to begin painting the fresco around the end of February 1505 – precisely the date by which he had previously promised to have the whole thing completed.[135]

On 14 April, a new pupil: '1505 – Tuesday evening, 14 April, Lorenzo came to live with me; he says he is 17 years old.' He is immediately set to work, for on 30 April the accounts include payment to 'Lorenzo di Marco, journeyman, for 3½ sessions in the Council Hall on the picture which Leonardo da Vinci is doing'.[136] He is paid at a basic rate of 9 soldi a day. Also disbursed during this month of intense activity are '5 gold florins to Ferrando Spagnolo, painter, and to Tommaso di Giovanni, who is grinding the colours.' This 'Ferrando the Spaniard' is a shadowy painter to whom various Leonardesco works are attributed, among them the sultry *Madonna and Child with a Lamb* (Brera Gallery, Milan); a free version of the *Madonna of the Yarnwinder* (private collection); and even – according to some – the Uffizi *Leda*. He is probably Fernando (or Hernando) Yañez de la Almedina, who is documented in Spain after 1506; some of his works, such as the *Epiphany* and *Pietà* in Cuenca cathedral, show strong influence of Leonardo and Raphael.[137] The other man mentioned, Tommaso di Giovanni the colour-grinder, is of course Zoroastro. In a later account-entry he is described as Leonardo's '*garzone*', a lowly status which reflects the incomprehension of the accountants.

To Lorenzo, Fernando and Tommaso may be added a certain Rafaello di Biagio, painter, whose work seems to have been less skilled since his rate of pay is only 2 soldi per diem, and another mysterious character who is not mentioned in the accounts but who is named by the Anonimo Gaddiano as one of Leonardo's assistants on the fresco – 'Il Riccio Fiorentino who lives at the Porta della +' (i.e. the Porta alla Croce). He is presumably the same as the 'Riccio, goldsmith' who was on the *David* committee convened in January 1504. Another name missing from the accounts is Salai, whom one would expect to be involved. This is Leonardo's team.

In a dramatic note headed 'On Friday in June, at the 13th hour', Leonardo writes:

On 6 June 1505, on Friday, at the stroke of the 13th hour [about 9.30 a.m.] I began to paint at the Palazzo. At the moment of putting down the paintbrush the weather changed for the worse, and the bell in the law-courts began to toll. The cartoon came loose. The water spilled as the jug which contained it broke. And suddenly the weather worsened, and the rain poured down till nightfall. And it was as dark as night.[138]

This extraordinary, almost apocalyptic memorandum has the usual ambiguities. When he says he 'began to paint' – or more precisely to apply colours (*colorire*) – does he simply mean he began the day's painting at that time, or that this was the day when he first started to colour in the figures? And what quite does he mean by '*il cartone straccò*'? The verb *straccare* means to become tired or stale or worn-out; hence in this context to sag or come loose. How is this connected to the abrupt change of the weather? Is it a case of ominous synchronicity – the storm, the bells, the studio mishap – or has a sudden gust of storm-wind blown in through the veiled and waxed windows of the Council Hall, tearing the cartoon off its frame and knocking over the jug of water?

Time rolls on; the work moves slowly; there are mutterings in the Signoria as the money continues to be doled out. Vasari has a story which sums up the declining momentum of the project:

It is said that when he went to the bank for the salary which he was accustomed to receive from Piero Soderini every month, the cashier wanted to give it to him in piles of *quattrini* [small coins]. He did not want to take them, saying, 'I am no penny painter!' There were complaints about this behaviour, and Piero Soderini was turning against him. So Leonardo got many friends of his to gather up a whole pile of *quattrini*, and he took them to him to return the money: but Piero did not want to accept them.

This explosion of temperament is like the *scandalo* in Milan, when he had stormed out of the Duchess's chambers – another unexpected storm from one who usually kept his emotions well-hidden.

This anecdote remains as the documents dwindle. The last recorded payments are dated 31 October 1505, though the work must have continued, perhaps fitfully, through till the following May, when Leonardo was very grudgingly given permission by the Signoria to leave Florence.

The *Anghiari* fresco is perhaps the most intensely documented of all Leonardo's paintings – more so even than the *Virgin of the Rocks*, since the documentation concerns the actual execution of the painting, rather than just the contractual ramifications of it. We know the amount of paper he used for the cartoon, the price he paid for the paints, the quantity of wood used for the scaffolding, the names of his principal assistants and the rates they were paid, and possibly even the precise day and hour he began to 'colour' the painting on to the wall of the Council Hall.

The only thing we are missing is the work itself. The fresco was never completed, but a large central portion of it was. This has long since vanished from view: in fact it is not even certain which wall of the hall it was painted on – the consensus used to be that it was on the east wall, but now the west wall is favoured. Either way, if anything of it remains, it lies somewhere beneath the enormous fresco-cycle painted in the early 1560s by none other than Giorgio Vasari. It is hard to imagine that Vasari would have painted over an original Leonardo in good condition, so there are two inferences available – the pessimistic and the optimistic: that in Vasari's view nothing remained which was worth saving, or that he took steps to protect what remained before covering it.

Our knowledge of what the fresco – or the fragment of it which was completed – actually looked like rests on various early copies.[139] There is an anonymous copy in oils, painted on a wooden panel; it is called the Tavola Doria, as it was for a long time in the collection of Prince Doria d'Angri in Naples. It shows the dramatic collision of men and horses prefigured in the preparatory drawings; it also has some lacunae – blank gaps – which enhance the idea that it is a direct copy from the fresco. It is not in itself a very good painting, but it may accurately represent the original in an unfinished or deteriorated state. Another important copy is an engraving by Lorenzo

Zacchia, dated 1558. This has more detail than the Tavola Doria, but it is not certain where this detail comes from. It could conceivably be based on the original cartoon, but Zacchia himself describes the work as 'taken from a panel painted by Leonardo' (*ex tabella propria Leonardo Vincii manu picta*). It may in fact be a version of the Tavola Doria, which Zacchia believed (or claimed to believe) was the work of Leonardo himself. If so, the additional details and filled-in lacunae would be his own interpolations rather than an alternative reporting of the original fresco.

Most of the details of the Zacchia engraving are also found in the superb watercolour version in the Louvre, attributed to Rubens (page 374). This is actually done on top of an earlier drawing. Beneath the Rubens additions of *c.* 1603 – the watercolour over-painting, the lead-white heightening, the glued-on extension on the right-hand side of the sheet – there is an Italian drawing datable to the mid sixteenth century, roughly contemporary with the Zacchia engraving. Though Rubens (born in 1577) could not have seen the original fresco, he has brilliantly caught the angry turmoil of the skirmish: seven figures – four on horseback, three on the ground – locked in combat, a pyramidal composition reaching to an apex of two clashing swords. The extraordinary, writhing horseman on the left (who represents Francesco Piccinino, son of the Milanese *condottiere*) has the attributes of Mars on his armour, and becomes in Rubens's imaginative rendering a kind of archetype: a universal soldier.

There is plenty of anecdotal evidence to suggest that, as with the *Last Supper*, there were technical problems in painting the *Anghiari* fresco, which revealed themselves fairly quickly. Antonio Billi, writing sometime around 1520, speaks of it as abandoned:

He did . . . a cartoon of the war of the Florentines, when they defeated Niccolò Piccinino, the captain of the Duke of Milan. He began to work from this in the Sala del Consiglio, using a medium which did not stick [*materia che non serrava*], and so it remained unfinished. It was said that the cause of this was that he was deceived about the linseed oil he used, which was adulterated.

If Billi is right, we might lay the blame for this great artistic loss on a grocer named Francesco Nuti, who was paid on 31 August 1505 for '8 pounds of linseed oil supplied to Leonardo da Vinci for the picture'.[140]

The fresco was still visible on the wall in the 1540s. The Anonimo Gaddiano says of it, '*anchora hoggi si vede, et con vernice*', which seems to mean that the work could still be seen, preserved under an application of varnish; and in 1549 Antonio Francesco Doni advised a friend, 'Go up the stairs of the Sala Grande, and take a close look at a group of horses and men, a battle-study by Leonardo da Vinci, and you will see something miraculous.'[141]

A fresco visible and 'miraculous' in 1549, the optimists say, must surely have still been visible when Vasari began his redecoration of the hall some twelve years later – and may be there still. But to find a lost wall-painting you must first find the wall. Early accounts describe the fresco as being on one side of the tribune – the dais where the Signori and Gonfalonier sat when the council was in session – but the evidence is maddeningly ambiguous as to where the tribune was.[142]

In 1974 an American conservation scientist, H. Travers Newton, used Thermavision ('an infra-red Vidicon system supercooled with liquid nitrogen') to probe the walls.[143] This machine produces a 'thermal map' of materials present beneath the surface (different materials absorb and emit heat at different rates). The first findings were exciting. The east wall revealed only normal architectural elements, but the west wall displayed what Newton described as an 'anomalous layer' beneath Vasari's frescos. This was confirmed by ultrasound, which uses ultrasonic soundings to register variations of density; in 1974 this could 'read' the stratifications of a wall up to a depth of about 4 inches. From these twin probes, the 'anomalous layer' was defined as an area about 75 feet wide by 15 feet high. Next, core samples were removed from both walls. The east wall exhibited the normal sequence of layers one would expect from the Vasari fresco: a top layer of plaster, an underlayer of rendering, and then the supporting wall; some traces of colour were found, suggesting an underdrawing in some areas. The same was found on the west wall above and below the 'anomalous layer', but in that area itself things were different. All the core samples showed a layer of red pigment beneath Vasari's intonaco, and some showed other pigments laid over this red ground. These included two suggestive of Leonardo's practice – a green copper carbonate similar to that used in the Last Supper, for which Leonardo gives a recipe in the Trattato; and blue smalt, as found in the Louvre Virgin of the Rocks. Azurite was also found, which is not suitable for use in true fresco, so it suggests the anomalous area is not a conventional fresco.

This raised exciting possibilities, though Newton's interpretation of the data is not universally accepted. There is currently a stasis. Any further investigation would be invasive, and the idea of damaging Vasari's fresco and finding nothing but a giant blur beneath it is not attractive to the decision-makers: as the Florentine councillor Rosa di Giorgi put it in 2000, 'Vasari may not be Leonardo, but he is still Vasari.'[144] There is talk of adapting the 'geo-radar' system developed by NASA to map sub-surface features on the earth's surface; a version of this is already used by archaeologists to map ruins before uncovering them, but it remains to be proved whether it can detect pigments on a flat surface.

Meanwhile Maurizio Seracini, whose investigations of the *Adoration of the Magi* caused such controversy, points back to the east wall,[145] and to a tiny green flag which forms an apparently insignificant detail in the vast panorama of the Vasari fresco. On it, visible from the ground through binoculars, is a small inscription – two words, perhaps an inch high, written in white paint which Seracini's chemical analysis shows to be contemporary with the rest of the fresco: words put there by Vasari. They read, '*Cerca Trova*' – 'Seek and you shall find.'

⤜ THE SPIRIT OF THE BIRD ⤛

A bird is a machine working according to mathematical laws. It lies within the power of man to reproduce this machine with all its motions, but not with as much power ... Such a machine constructed by man lacks only the spirit of the bird, and this spirit must be counterfeited by the spirit of man.

Codex Atlanticus, fol. 161r-a

In 1505 Leonardo was dreaming once more of the possibilities of human flight, and was filling a small notebook with notes and diagrams and light airy scribbles which comprise his most focused and purposive text on the subject. After a chequered history, in which the kleptomanic Count Libri plays a part, this notebook has come to rest in the Royal Library in Turin, and is known as the Turin Codex. It contains that famous fairground-barker proclamation, found on two separate pages in slightly different phrasing, which announces, 'The big bird will take its first flight above the back of the Great Cecero, filling the universe with amazement, filling all the chronicles with its fame, and bringing eternal glory to the nest where it was born.'[146] The 'big bird' is certainly Leonardo's flying-machine. Neat, highly specific drawings show parts of it (rotating wing-joints on folios 16–17, for example) but no full view – perhaps for reasons of secrecy.

The announcement seems to mean that he was planning a trial flight of the machine from the summit of Monte Ceceri, near Fiesole, just north of Florence. He spells it 'Cecero', which is an old Florentine word for a swan – a conjunction of meanings that would be congenial to Leonardo: a good omen, an emblematic connection. A jotting dated 14 March 1505 finds him sky-gazing on the road to Fiesole: 'the *cortone*, a bird of prey which I saw going to Fiesole, above the place of the Barbiga'.[147] This adds a touch of specificity to the possible flight of the 'big bird', but it is curious that there is no independent record of this momentous event, no letter-writer or diarist who mentions it: either it was a well-kept secret or it never happened.

Girolamo Cardano states in his *De subtilitate* (1550) that Leonardo was an 'extraordinary man' who tried to fly 'but in vain' – *'tentavit et frustra'*. If he – or someone: Zoroastro? – tried to fly from Monte Ceceri in early 1505 we must assume the trial was a failure, in which context one reads with some trepidation the page of the Turin Codex entitled *'Per fugire il pericolo della ruina'* – 'To escape the perils of destruction':

The destruction of such a machine may occur in two ways. The first is that the machine might break up. The second would be if the machine turned on its side, or nearly on its side, because it should always descend at a very oblique angle, and almost exactly balanced on its centre. To prevent breaking up, the machine should be made as strong as possible in whichever part it may tend to turn over ... Its parts must have great resistance so they can safely withstand the fury and impetus of the descent by the means I have mentioned: joints of strong leather treated with alum, the rigging made of cords of the strongest silk. And let no man encumber himself with iron bands, which are very soon broken when twisted.[148]

In these details one has a physical sense of this creature, this mathematical bird-machine: the creaking of the leather, the wind in the rigging, the 'fury' of the descent. One recalls that one of his earliest texts on the possibility of flight – 'A man with wings large enough, and duly attached, might learn to overcome the resistance of the air . . .' – is accompanied by his specifications for a parachute.

More than a study of the flying-machine, the Turin Codex is a study of its primary model: the bird. The pages are full of observations on the aerodynamics and physiology of birds, and of beautiful little sketches, squiggled yet acute, which swoop and soar and turn and flutter across its pages: ornithological pictograms. This notebook is a Leonardo poem on the subject of birds and their flight, and it is indeed around this time that he writes the famous marginal note about the kite, beginning: 'Writing like this so particularly about the kite seems to be my destiny.'

The birds of the Turin Codex, the marginalium about the kite, the trial flight from Swan Mountain – all these seem to merge into the strange elusive talisman of Leonardo's *Leda and the Swan*. It is elusive to the point of non-existence: there is no painting that can be thus described. It is one of those mysteriously notional Leonardo works which exist only before and after – in various preparatory sketches which are certainly in his hand, and in various finished paintings which are certainly not. Some of the paintings are of very high quality and may have been painted under his supervision; close similarities between them suggest they are based on a lost original, though whether this original was an actual painting or a full-size cartoon is uncertain. The Anonimo Gaddiano included 'una Leda' in a list of Leonardo's paintings, but he (or someone else) later crossed the words through. Vasari did not mention the painting at all. G. P. Lomazzo certainly believed there was an authentic Leonardo Leda around – in fact he says that 'la Leda ignuda' ('the nude Leda') was one of the few paintings which Leonardo actually finished – but one can never be quite sure with Lomazzo, and he may in fact be talking about one of the extant studio versions or copies. There was once a Leda attributed to Leonardo in the French royal collection, but it disappears from the inventories in the late seventeenth century. According to tradition it was removed, on the grounds of immorality, by Madame de Maintenon.

The paintings – Leonardo's, if it ever existed, and the copies and studio versions – belong to a later period, but the idea certainly originated at this time. The earliest studies are on a sheet which also contains a drawing of a horse for the Battle of Anghiari and is therefore datable to c. 1504.[149] There is no swan, but the presence of the hatching babies can be discerned among the squiggles. These sketches evolve into two more finished drawings – one in the Duke of Devonshire's collection at Chatsworth, the other in the Boymans Museum in Rotterdam – in which all the mythological elements are in place: the attentive swan, the fleshy innamorata, the hatchling children, the fecund vegetation. The style of the drawings reflects the influence of Michelangelo at this time – especially the Chatsworth drawing, with its strange whorled hatching and the statuesque heftiness of the female figure.

In all these Leda is shown kneeling (the Leda inginocchiata) in a pose reminiscent of classical sculptures of Venus. This is perhaps the earlier conception, though the standing Leda (the Leda stante) who appears so uniformly in the painted versions also dates back to this time. There is no extant drawing of this pose comparable to the Chatsworth and Rotterdam drawings, but there is a small sketch on a sheet in Turin which once again has sketches relating to the Anghiari fresco. A lost cartoon of the standing Leda was copied by Raphael, probably during his Florentine sojourn of 1505–6, when he seems to have had contact with Leonardo and produced

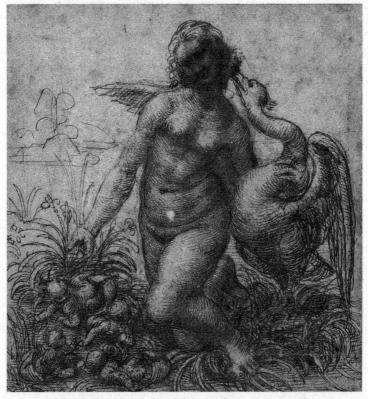

The Chatsworth drawing of Leda and the Swan, c. *1504-6.*

his portrait of Maddalena Doni, which shows familiarity with the *Mona Lisa*. This Leda cartoon was later owned by Pompeo Leoni, as appears from an inventory of his estate, dated 1614, which includes a 'cartoon 2 braccia high' – thus a full-scale cartoon – 'of a Leda standing, and a swan who sports with her, emerging from a marsh with certain cupids in the grass'.[150] Apart from the misinterpreting of the children as cupids, this is a clear sighting of the lost cartoon.

It is not known who, if anyone, commissioned the painting. It is possible the idea flickers into being as a composition for Isabella d'Este's *studiolo*: it inhabits the same sort of classical-mythological world as paintings commissioned by the Marchioness from Mantegna and Perugino. Or it may have had a Florentine patron – the rich banker Antonio Segni, perhaps: a 'friend' (according to Vasari) and a classical enthusiast, for whom Leonardo did a superb drawing of Neptune in his chariot.[151] Also part of Leonardo's classical tendency at this time is a fugitive painting of Bacchus, about which there is an exchange of letters in April 1505 between Alfonso d'Este, Duke of Ferrara – the brother of Isabella – and one of his business agents. The Duke is anxious to purchase the painting, but learns that it has already been promised to Georges d'Amboise, Cardinal of Rouen. The painting is also mentioned in a Latin poem by an anonymous Ferrarese author, possibly Flavio Antonio Giraldi. The references suggest it was an existent work rather than just an idea; I will look later at some possible traces of it.[152]

The classical myth of Jupiter copulating in the guise of a swan with the beautiful princess Leda – one of Jupiter's many divine 'interventions' of this sort – was certainly well known. Among classical sculptures there are some highly erotic renditions, with the swan between her legs in species-defying coitus. Leonardo's painting was perhaps seen as risqué, but its dominant motif is not so much erotic as generative. The myth becomes one of fecundity and fertility. The woman is rounded, full-hipped – both consort and mother. Around her spring phallic reeds and rampant flowers; beside her stands the superphallic swan-god. Everything burgeons.

The Platonists would interpret the legend of Jupiter and Leda as an allegory of the influx of divine spirit into the terrestrial world. This seems to link the painting with Leonardo's comment about human flight, quoted at the top of this chapter, in which he expresses his desire to instil into a man the one thing his aviational technology cannot supply – 'the spirit of the bird'. This text is from around 1505, contemporary with the first drawings on the Leda theme. It was at this time too that he recorded that childhood memory of the kite which 'came' to him in his cradle: that strange transaction of the bird putting its tail in his mouth seems to enact once more, in a more personal arena of recovered or invented memory, this idea of receiving 'the spirit of the bird', the shamanistic secret of flight.

A page of the Turin Codex seems to sum up this intensely personal involvement in the idea of flight. As he writes his notes on the page, accompanied by the typical bird-sketches, the subject of his sentences changes from 'the bird' ('If the bird wishes to turn quickly . . .' etc.) to 'you', and the indeterminate 'you' of Leonardo's notebooks, the imagined auditor of his thoughts and observations, is always essentially Leonardo himself. He is, in his imagination, already up there:

If the north wind is blowing and you are gliding above the wind, and if in your straight ascent upward that wind is threatening to overturn you, then you are free to bend your right or left wing, and with the inside wing lowered you will continue a curving motion . . .

In a text in the margin the two subjects merge almost seamlessly:

The bird that mounts upward always has its wings above the wind, and does not beat them, and moves in a circular motion. And if you want to go westward without beating your wings, and the wind is in the north, make the incident movement straight and below the wind, and the reflex movement above the wind.[153]

These are almost literally 'flights of the mind': in his mind, in his words, he is flying. And on this page of notes, actually staring out from behind the text – that is, already on the page when Leonardo wrote it – is a faint red-chalk drawing of a man's head. It is hard to make out, hard to detach from the lines of handwriting superimposed on it, but it is a strong face, long-nosed, with a familiar hint of long hair falling, and it seems to me very likely that it is a portrait of Leonardo by one of his pupils. It would be our only image of him during these years of greatness – the years of the *Mona Lisa* and *Anghiari* and *Leda*, of Borgia and Machiavelli and Michelangelo. The drawing must be from about 1505 – the two dated notes in the codex are March and April 1505. It would show him at the age of fifty-three, and for the first time he is bearded. It is an elusive image, as ever: a shadowy face half-obscured by a sentence about wings '*suprando la resistentia dellaria*' – 'conquering the resistance of the air'.

This conquest of the air is always seen as the ultimate expression of Leonardo as aspirant Renaissance man, but these flights of which he dreams are not entirely distinct from those more prosaic flights with which the rest of us are familiar: flights of escape, of evasion, of irresolution – flights semantically referrable to fleeing rather than flying. Twenty years earlier, beneath a drawing of a bat, he wrote, 'animal which flees from one element to another'. In his obsession with flight there is a kind of existential restlessness, a desire to float free from his life of tensions and rivalries, from the dictates of warmongers and art-lovers and contract-wavers. He yearns for this great escape, and in failing he feels himself more captive.

PART SEVEN

Return to Milan
1506–1513

The eye as soon as it opens sees all the stars of the hemisphere. The mind in an instant leaps from east to west.

Codex Atlanticus, fol. 204v-a

THE GOVERNOR

In late May 1506 Leonardo received the grudging permission of the Signoria to leave Florence for Milan. In a document notarized on 30 May he undertook to return within three months, on pain of a fine of 150 florins. His guarantor was Leonardo Bonafé, superintendent of the Ospedale di Santa Maria Nuova where his savings were held: Leonardo's bank manager.[1] This is the tone of the times in the Soderini government. In the event Leonardo would not return for fifteen months, and then only because of a family dispute.

The French governor of Milan, Charles d'Amboise, was no doubt keen to attract him north again, but the ostensible reason for Leonardo's departure was the continuing contractual disputes over the *Virgin of the Rocks*. This painting had been troublesome ever since its delivery to the Confraternity of the Immaculate Conception in about 1485, and according to the *supplica* lodged by Leonardo and Ambrogio de Predis in about 1492 it had still not been properly paid for. The original painting (the Louvre version) seems to have left Italy in 1493, having probably been bought by Ludovico Sforza and given by him to Emperor Maximilian, and at some point after this Leonardo and Ambrogio (but mostly Ambrogio) began work on a substitute copy for the Confraternity. This second *Virgin of the Rocks* (the London version) was delivered to the Confraternity perhaps before Leonardo's departure from Milan in 1499, or perhaps by Ambrogio sometime after that. The latest date for the delivery would be 1502, for in March 1503 Ambrogio lodged another *supplica*, addressed to Louis XII of France, now the *de facto* ruler of Milan, complaining once again that he and Leonardo were owed money. The king ordered a judge, one Bernardino de' Busti, to look into it. The case wallowed in the bog of Italian litigation for three years, but in the *arbitrato* handed down in April 1506 the judgement went against the painters. The central panel of the altarpiece was adjudged to be 'unfinished' – that, at least, is the usual meaning of *imperfetto*, though it is possible that it means here 'not good enough', which in turn would probably mean 'too much Ambrogio and not enough Leonardo'. At any rate Leonardo is considered the key to resolving the matter, and the court orders him, *in absentia*, to complete the painting within two years.[2]

It was this situation, presumably communicated to him by Ambrogio de Predis, which precipitated Leonardo's request the following month to be given leave from his duties in the Palazzo Vecchio to travel up to Milan. Contractual language was something that the Florentine authorities could understand. But beneath this runs a deeper theme of restlessness, which is in part the old theme of Leonardo's difficult relationship with Florence. Much had changed in his life since he first left for Milan nearly a quarter of a century previously, but one catches an echo of that earlier departure. In 1482 he left behind him an unfinished masterpiece – the *Adoration* – and a somewhat lurid homosexual reputation. In 1506 he leaves on a note of dispute and distrust over the *Anghiari* fresco, and perhaps with a first inkling of its technical problems; also, probably, the failure of the flight from Monte Ceceri. These echoes are recurrences: soured relations, abandoned projects, irresolution, escape.

Leonardo arrives once more in Lombardy with a sense of relief and release, but different this time in his status: his arrival is eagerly anticipated by the French masters of Milan. He seems to have had an affinity with the French. He had dealt with them amicably enough when they swept into Milan in 1499, and had apparently offered his services to Count Ligny. By 1501 he was painting the *Madonna of the Yarnwinder* for the French courtier Florimond Robertet. Perhaps the affinity was simply that the French appreciated him, far more – he might have felt – than did his Italian patrons, with whom he had a kind of hot–cold relationship which always seemed ready to founder into tensions and impatience. A particular instance of their appreciation was King Louis's desire to remove the *Last Supper* so that he could take it to France; however, as Vasari drily comments, 'its being done on the wall made the king give up his desire, and it remained among the Milanese.'

Leonardo was warmly received by the governor, Charles d'Amboise, Comte de Chaumont – the 'high-spirited' count, as Serge Bramly calls him, for the chroniclers tell us he was 'as fond of Venus as of Bacchus'.[3] D'Amboise was thirty-three years old. The portrait of him by Andrea Solario was painted around this time, and is very Leonardesque with its slight *contrapposto*. It shows an intelligent, concentrated face, with a large nose noticeable even in full face: *un homme sérieux*. He was a tremendous admirer of Leonardo,

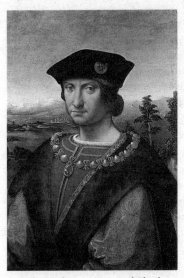

Andrea Solario, portrait of Charles d'Amboise, c. 1508.

and a few months later wrote in exalted terms: 'We loved him before meeting him in person, and now that we have been in his company, and can speak from experience of his varied talents, we see in truth that his name, though already famous for painting, has not received sufficient praise for the many other gifts he possesses, which are of an extraordinary power.'[4]

Leonardo was his honoured guest at the castle, in the rooms of which were many memories of days and nights in the Sforza court. In a later letter he asks about lodgings in the city, 'not wishing to trouble the Governor further',[5] which perhaps also means not wishing to be quite so closely billeted on him – Leonardo always needed space. But for now there is the energy of novelty, and talk of grand new projects – in particular of d'Amboise's plans for a summer villa outside the Porta Venezia. It was planned for a site between two small rivers, the Nirone and the Fontelunga, there to blend pleasingly and pastorally into the natural forms of the landscape. Leonardo's notes and sketches show everything carefully geared to the pleasure and delight of the master of the house – porticos and loggias, and big airy rooms opening on to the sumptuous pleasure-gardens. Even the stairs should not be too 'melancholic' – in other words too steep and dark. Leonardo envisages a wonderful, *Arabian Nights* garden of sweet-smelling orange- and lemon-trees, and a bower covered over with a fine copper net to keep it full of songbirds, and a babbling brook with its grassy banks 'cut frequently so that the clearness of the water may be seen upon its shingly bed' – one thinks of the river-bed in the Verrocchio *Baptism of Christ* – 'and only those plants should be left which serve the fishes for food, like watercress and suchlike'. The fish should not be eels or tench which muddy the water, nor pike which will eat any other fish. A small canal would flow among the tables, with flasks of wine cooling in the water. The pièce de résistance was a little mill powered by water but with sails like a windmill:

With this mill I will generate a breeze at any time during the summer, and I will make water spring up fresh and bubbling . . . The mill will serve to create conduits of water through the house, and fountains in various places, and there will be a certain pathway where the water will leap up from below whenever someone walks there, and so this will be a good spot for anyone who wants to spray water over women . . . With the mill I will create continuous music from various instruments, which will sound for as long as the mill continues to turn.[6]

This last device recalls the musical fountain he saw and heard at Rimini in 1502: 'Let us create a harmony from the waterfall of a fountain by means of a bagpipe which produces many consonances and voices', he wrote then, citing a passage in Vitruvius 'about the sound made by water'.[7] He brings a certain learnedness, a certain gravity, to these pastoral diversions.

Probably connected with the d'Amboise villa are some ideas for a 'temple of Venus' – what in later country-house contexts would be called a 'folly':

You will make steps on four sides, leading up to a naturally formed meadow on the summit of a rock. The rock will be hollowed out and supported at the front with pillars, and beneath it a huge portico where water flows into various basins of granite and porphyry and serpentine, within semicircular recesses; and let the water in these be continually running over. And facing this portico, towards the north, let there be a lake, and in the middle of it a little island with a thick shady wood.[8]

Here is Leonardo visualizing a landscape: the words sketching it in ('let there be a lake'), the mind's eye moving across the water to find the point of focus, the 'little island'. On the verso of the sheet he pens a rather elegant piece about the dangerous allures of the goddess Venus:

To the south of the southern seaboard of Cilicia may be seen the beautiful island of Cyprus, which was the realm of the goddess Venus; and there have been many who, impelled by her loveliness, have had their ships and rigging broken upon the rocks which lie amid the seething waves. Here the beauty of some pleasant hill invites the wandering mariners to take their ease, where all is green and full of flowers, and soft winds continually come and go, filling the island and the surrounding sea with delicious scents. But, alas, how many ships have foundered there!

This very literary piece echoes a passage in Poliziano's *Stanze* of 1476, thus recalling the Venusian imagery of the Medici *giostra*.[9]

Leonardo's envisaging of Charles d'Amboise's villa and gardens survives only in sketches and notes, but is full of exquisite detail and elegance. A sense of sheer pleasure – the wine cooling in the brook, the splashing of girls in their summer dresses, the sound of water 'continually running over' in the Venusian grotto – is only faintly shadowed by the idea that these pleasures, like all others, will inevitably lead to pain. It is hardly an idea original to Leonardo, but it seems to have been often on his mind: it is expressed rather intensely in his 'Oxford allegories' of the mid-1480s, and here again sensual pleasure brings doom and shipwreck, men 'broken upon the rocks' of carnal temptation.

Leonardo had promised to return to Florence, and the unfinished *Battle of Anghiari*, within three months – that is, by the end of August 1506 – but he did not want to go, and his new patron did not want him to go either. On 18 August Charles d'Amboise wrote courteously to the Signoria, asking them to allow Leonardo to stay a bit longer 'so he can supply certain works which he has at our request begun'. This presumably refers to the summer villa. There may be other 'works' – canal engineering, for instance: a constant preoccupation in Milan – or there may be none, the phrasing a mere formula to imply worthwhile industry. The letter was backed up by a more formal missive, signed by the vice-chancellor of the duchy, Geoffroi Carles, requesting a one-month extension of Leonardo's leave of absence, and promising his return to Florence on the due date 'without fail, to satisfy Your Excellencies in all things'. On 28 August the Signoria wrote back granting permission – probably not because they wanted to, but because the French were too powerful an ally to fall out with over such matters.[10] Florence was already mending fences with Pope Julius II, further to disputes between him and Michelangelo. Thus the great Clash of the Titans envisaged three years previously was dribbling off into small acrimonies.

The end of September came and went, and Leonardo did not return. On 9 October Gonfalonier Soderini wrote personally to Charles d'Amboise: a grim letter. He was angry with d'Amboise for 'making excuses', and even angrier with the absconded artist:

Leonardo . . . has not behaved as he should have done towards the republic, because he has taken a large sum of money and only made a small beginning on the great work he was commissioned to carry out, and in his devotion to Your Lordship he has made himself a debtor to us. We do not wish any further requests to be made on this matter, for this great work is for the benefit of all our citizens, and for us to release him from his obligations would be a dereliction of our duty.

The tone of this letter, as much as its statements, shows the gulf of antipathy between Leonardo and Soderini. Leonardo knows that the complaint against him is justified, but everything about the letter is calculated to annoy him – its suggestion of dishonourableness, its description of him as a 'debtor', the invocations of 'duty', the republican cant about the fresco being 'for the benefit of all our citizens'.

From Milan a lofty silence, and then on 16 December Charles d'Amboise wrote to Soderini, promising that he would not stand in the way of Leonardo's return, but taking the opportunity to rebuke the Gonfalonier for his base accusations and his inability to accommodate Leonardo's peculiar genius:

If it is fitting to recommend a man of such rich talent to his fellow citizens we heartily recommend him to you, assuring you that everything you can do to increase either his fortune and well-being, or the honours to which he is entitled, would give us, as well as him, the greatest pleasure, and we should be much obliged to you.

An ironic letter of 'recommendation': that a Frenchman in Milan should have to explain Leonardo's greatness to his own 'fellow citizens' – with the further irony implied that the best way to improve Leonardo's 'fortune and well-being' would be to let him stay away from Florence. In this letter d'Amboise writes that eulogy of Leonardo I quoted earlier ('We loved him before meeting him . . .' etc). None of Leonardo's other patrons has left any comparable show of warmth and admiration.

Scarcely had Soderini digested this barbed lecture when there arrived news from his ambassador in France, Francesco Pandolfini, that King Louis was enchanted by a 'little picture' of Leonardo's he had recently been shown – probably the *Madonna of the Yarnwinder*, painted for his secretary Florimond Robertet – and that he wanted Leonardo to remain in Milan and paint something for him. He might paint, said the King, 'certain little pictures of Our Lady, and other things as they occur to my fantasy, and perhaps I will also get him to paint my own portrait'. This regal whim was formalized in a peremptory letter to the Florentine Signoria on 14 January 1507: 'We have necessary need of Master Leonardo da Vinci, painter of your city of Florence . . . Please write to him that he should not leave the said city [Milan] before our arrival, as I told your ambassador.'

The King's writ proved decisive in this strange tug-of-war, and on 22 January 1507 the Signoria acceded to his 'gracious request' that Leonardo should remain in Milan. It was a victory for Leonardo, though one that left a bitter taste. In the event he would be back in Florence before the summer was out, though it was not Soderini or civic duty that called him back there.

*

Over the next few months Leonardo was busy. In February he was probably with Charles d'Amboise at the taking of Baiedo, north of Milan, where a troublesome baron, Simone Arrigoni, was captured. Leonardo noted the trickery by which Arrigoni was 'betrayed'.[11] Also from this time are some designs for a new church, Santa Maria della Fontana, to be built in the suburbs outside Milan, on the site of a spring to which miraculous powers were attributed. The church still exists – unfinished. And on 20 April, just a few days after his fifty-fifth birthday, he got a present in the form of a letter from Charles d'Amboise to the ducal treasurers, formally restoring to him the ownership of his vineyard, which had been confiscated sometime after the French takeover of 1500.[12]

At the end of this month King Louis arrived in Milan, having snuffed out a rebellion at Genoa en route. The French chronicler Jean d'Auton describes the route from the Duomo to the castle, now Via Dante, festooned with 'triumphal arches of greenery in which the arms of France and Brittany were displayed, and images of Christ and the saints, and a triumphal chariot bearing the cardinal virtues, and the god Mars holding in one hand an arrow in the other a palm' – all of this, and the masques and dances which followed, bearing the imprimatur of the man the King was pleased to call 'our dear and well-beloved Léonard da Vincy'.[13]

Leonardo the entertainer, the pageant-maker, the choreographer of spectacles: a role he had missed in the more strait-laced ethos of republican Florence. The stage-managing of victory parades in an occupied city is not the most laudable of Leonardo's activities, but it is hard to resist his enjoyment, and indeed a certain thoughtlessness is probably what he enjoyed about it.

It was probably at this stage that King Louis granted Leonardo an income in the form of dues paid by users of the Naviglio di San Cristofano, a stretch of the city's canal system. It took a while, and some prompting letters, for the gift to be ratified, but these rights – referred to as 'the twelve ounces of water' – were still owned by Leonardo at his death, and were bequeathed to one of his servants in his will.[14]

Meanwhile there was the *Virgin of the Rocks* to attend to, adjudged 'unfinished' in the *arbitrato* of April 1506. In the same judgement the Confraternity was ordered to pay the painters a *conguaglio*, or adjusted fee, of 200 lire – considerably less than they had asked for, but more than the 100 lire the Confraternity had originally offered. The painting needed work if there was to be any money, but what state it was in, and what was done to it, we don't know. By the summer of 1507 there appears to be some tension between Leonardo and Ambrogio de Predis. In early August they went as far as to nominate an arbitrator – one Giovanni de Pagnanis, a Dominican friar – to resolve their differences. By this point the painting had probably been completed; the quarrel was about the apportioning of the payments. The matter seems to have been resolved, and on 26 August 1507 the Confraternity paid up the first half of the fee due. This was collected by Ambrogio, his 'partner' Leonardo being by this stage back in Florence.[15]

⤖ 'GOOD DAY, MASTER FRANCESCO . . .' ⤌

Sometime before his temporary return to Florence in the summer of 1507 Leonardo met a young Milanese aristocrat named Francesco Melzi. Melzi was perhaps taken on as a pupil – and he was later an excellent draughtsman and painter – but his chief purpose in the entourage soon became scribal rather than artistic. He became Leonardo's secretary or amanuensis – one might even say his intellectual confidant – and, after Leonardo's death, his literary executor: the guardian of the flame. His elegant italic script is found scattered throughout Leonardo's papers – in texts copied for or dictated by Leonardo; in annotations, captions and collation marks – and more than anyone else it is Melzi we must thank for the survival of so many of Leonardo's manuscripts.

Giovanni Francesco Melzi[16] was well bred and well educated, but his family was not rich. His father, Girolamo Melzi, served as a captain in the Milanese militia under Louis XII; much later he was involved as an engineer in the reconstruction and expansion of the city walls (this in the early 1530s, after the restoration of the Sforza) – a country gent with skills: a type Leonardo knew in his bones. The family seat was at Vaprio, a picturesque old villa perched above the Adda river. On a drawing in the Biblioteca Ambrosiana, dated 14 August 1510, Melzi signs himself '*Francescho de Melzo di anni 17*', in which case he was born in 1492 or '93 and was about fourteen when he entered Leonardo's ambit.[17] This drawing, a fine profile in red chalk of an elderly bald man, is the earliest known work by Melzi. He was evidently by then a practising member of Leonardo's studio. (Some discern an influence of Bramantino in his drawing style, and he may have studied under that fine painter before joining Leonardo.) His punctilious skills are shown in some closely worked copies of Leonardo drawings at Windsor. The beautiful red-chalk portrait of Leonardo in profile is almost certainly by Melzi: there are two versions, at Windsor and the Ambrosiana, the former retouched by the master.

Vasari met the aged Melzi during a visit to Milan in 1566, and added the following passage to the 1568 edition of the *Lives*:

Many of Leonardo's manuscripts on human anatomy are in the possession of Messer Francesco Melzi, gentleman of Milan, who in the time of Leonardo was a very beautiful boy, and much loved by him, just as today he is a handsome and courteous old man. He cherishes and preserves these writings as if they were relics, as well as the portrait which is a happy memory of Leonardo.

Vasari's phrasing – that Melzi had been a '*bellissimo fanciullo*', and '*molto amato da*' Leonardo – echoes the language he uses of Salai and carries the same assumption of 'Socratic' love. This did not necessarily mean actively homosexual love, though one suspects that in Leonardo's case Vasari thought that it did mean that. However, Melzi had a notably hetero-sexual life after Leonardo's death, marrying the nobly descended Angiola Landriani, who was said to be one of the most beautiful women in Milan, and fathering eight children. We don't know – but we can guess – what Salai thought of this young interloper, this 'very beautiful boy' whose charming manners and educated hand whispered privilege. Melzi had the class that Salai could never have (though to say that Salai was 'common' is to identify one of the things that Leonardo loved about him). Salai is snazzy, brittle, a bit of a wide boy; he is good with money – usually someone else's.

What the '*bellissimo*' Melzi actually looked like is uncertain – there is no good reason for saying (as Bramly and others do) that a painting in the Ambrosiana showing a round-faced young man in a hat is a portrait of him by Boltraffio. It is likely that Leonardo drew him, but though there are various young men in the later sketchbooks, there is no clue as to which might be Melzi – none of them becomes a regular, indeed habitual, subject as Salai did. It is argued by Pietro Marani that Melzi's own *Portrait of a Young Man with a Parrot*, though probably a late work of the 1550s, is a portrait of himself when young; it has a melancholic, nostalgic air.[18]

The earliest reference to Francesco Melzi in Leonardo's papers is a draft of a letter to him, in Leonardo's hand, written in Florence in early 1508.[19] There are two drafts on the sheet. The first is briefer, and strikes a personal note which Leonardo then thinks better of:

Good day, Master Francesco,
Why in God's name have you not answered a single one of all the letters I've sent you. You just wait till I get there and by God I'll make you write so much you'll be sorry.

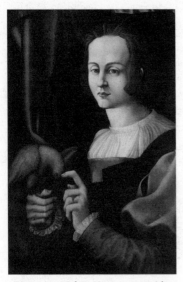

Francesco Melzi's Young man with a
Parrot, *possibly a self-portrait.*

The tone is fond, joshing, but not
perhaps without a genuine hint of
hurt that the young man has not, as
it appears, bothered to reply to him.
There is also a strong suggestion that
Melzi's role as secretary or scribe is
already established ('I'll make you
write so much you'll be sorry') if not
yet formalized.

From this point on Melzi is an
indispensable part of the Leonardo
retinue. He is doubtless the 'Cecho'
and 'Cechino' (diminutives of Francesco) in name-lists of *c.* 1509–10,
in which he appears alongside Salai,
Lorenzo and others.[20] He travels
with Leonardo to Rome in 1513,
and then to France, where he is
more and more essential to the ageing *maestro*, and where he is distinguished in the French accounts as
'Francisque de Melce, the Italian gentleman who is with the said Maistre
Lyenard', and receives a handsome salary of 400 écus a year – as opposed
to Salai, who is merely 'servant to Maistre Lyenard' on 100 écus a year.[21]
He is a happy presence in Leonardo's household: discreet, efficient, talented,
devoted – the perfect amanuensis (or, as we would now say, personal
assistant). He is an intellectual companion for the solitary Leonardo: more
learned and less complex than the troublesome Salai.

→→ BROTHERS AT WAR ←←

What brought Leonardo back down to Florence was the death of his uncle
Francesco in early 1507; or more precisely it was the matter of Uncle
Francesco's will. As we saw, the will had been drawn up in 1504, shortly
after the death of Ser Piero. It named Leonardo as sole heir, almost certainly
in response to his exclusion from his father's will. There had always been
a closeness between Leonardo and Francesco, the easy-going, country-
dwelling young uncle of his childhood. But the bequest contravened an
earlier agreement that Francesco's estate should be inherited by Ser Piero's

legitimate children, and they, led by the inevitable notary of the new generation, Ser Giuliano da Vinci, swiftly moved to challenge the will.[22] Leonardo
probably learned of this in June 1507, for on 5 July one of his *garzoni*,
probably Lorenzo, wrote a letter home to his mother, in which he says he
will be returning soon to Florence, with the *maestro*, but that he won't be
there long because they have to get back to Milan '*subito*'. Meanwhile, he
asks, 'Remember me to Dianira, and give her a hug so she won't say I've
forgotten her' – for a moment we look in on the life of Leonardo's apprentice:
a young man a long way from home.[23]

In the event Leonardo did not leave Milan until at least the middle of
August. In the interim, on 26 July, he secured the first of his trump cards in
the case against the brothers – a letter to the Signoria, signed by the French
king, asking them to intervene in Leonardo's favour. In this letter Leonardo
is called '*nostre peintre et ingeneur ordinaire*' – 'painter and engineer in
ordinary' to the King ('ordinary' in the courtly sense meaning a permanent
official position, as opposed to 'extraordinary' or temporary). This is the
first documentation of his status at the French court. A further letter to the
Signoria, this time from Charles d'Amboise, is dated 15 August. It announces
Leonardo's imminent return to Florence 'to conclude certain differences that
have arisen between him and some of his brothers', and asks the Signoria
to expedite the matter as swiftly as possible.[24] Leonardo's permission to
leave has been granted 'with the greatest reluctance', because he is working
on a 'painting very dear to the King'. This is presumably one of 'the two
Madonnas of different sizes, done for our most Christian king' which
Leonardo mentions in a letter of early 1508 – works apparently lost –
though it is just possible it refers to the equally chimerical *Leda*, which was
later catalogued in the French collection.

From Florence, on 18 September, Leonardo wrote a letter to Cardinal
Ippolito d'Este, brother of Isabella, from which we learn some details of the
case.[25] Leonardo's 'cause is being argued' before a member of the Signoria,
Ser Rafaello Hieronimo, who has been specifically assigned by Gonfalonier
Soderini to adjudicate the case, and 'to decide and conclude it before the
festival of All Saints', i.e. 1 November 1507. Ser Rafaello, it appears, is
known to Ippolito d'Este – he is perhaps one of the numerous d'Este 'agents'
in Florence. Hence the letter, which asks Ippolito 'to write to the said Ser
Rafaello, in that dextrous and persuasive manner which Your Lordship has,
recommending to him Leonardo Vincio, your most devoted servant, as I am
and always will be, and requesting and pressing him not only to do me
justice, but to do it with as little delay as possible'.

This document is in one sense unique: it is the only letter we *know* that

Leonardo sent; all his other letters survive only in draft, among his papers, but this one sits visibly and tangibly in the Estense archives in Modena. Unfortunately neither the text nor the signature – '*Leonardus Vincius pictor*' – is in Leonardo's hand. As in other formal documents (e.g. the letter of introduction to Ludovico Sforza), he has availed himself of someone with better handwriting – in this case Machiavelli's assistant Agostino di Vespucci, who had earlier written up that summary of the Battle of Anghiari. The only physical touch of Leonardo on the paper is on the verso: the wax seal, showing a head in profile, is probably an impression of a signet ring on Leonardo's hand.

Another draft letter reveals the acid relations between Leonardo and his *fratellastri* or half-brothers, who are said to have 'wished the utmost evil' to Francesco during his lifetime, and to have treated Leonardo 'not as a brother but as a complete stranger'. Part of the dispute concerned the property called Il Botro which Francesco had bequeathed him. Leonardo writes, 'You do not wish to repay his heir the money he lent for Il Botro', which implies that he had lent Uncle Francesco money to purchase or improve the property. There is a reference to '*la valuta del botro*' ('the value of Il Botro') in a memo list in the Codex Arundel. In neither case is *botro* capitalized, so it could also be translated as 'ditch' or 'ravine' – perhaps a quarry or lime-pit. Leonardo refers to experiments done at his 'pit' (*bucha*) in the Codex Leicester, which he began around this time.[26]

In his letter to Ippolito d'Este Leonardo spoke of the case being resolved by November 1507, but it was not, and in early 1508 he wrote to Charles d'Amboise, 'I am almost at an end of the litigation with my brothers, and believe I will be with you this Easter.'[27] In 1508 Easter Sunday was 23 April. It is probable that he was back in Milan around then, though whether the lawsuit was wrapped up is another matter, as a further letter on the subject is in Melzi's hand, and was therefore written after Leonardo's return to Milan.

While in Florence, Leonardo and Salai (and probably Lorenzo) stayed in the house of a wealthy intellectual and art patron, Piero di Braccio Martelli. He was a noted mathematician and linguist, and a friend of Bernardo Rucellai, and the uncongenial business of the lawsuit was at least partly counterbalanced by the free-and-easy atmosphere of the Palazzo Martelli.[28] The house stood on Via Larga; it was later swallowed up by the church and convent of San Giovannino, built in the 1550s. Among Leonardo's fellow guests or lodgers there was the sculptor Giovanni Francesco Rustici, of whom he seems to have been fond. Rustici was about thirty, little more than half Leonardo's age. Vasari gives a colourful account of him. As well as

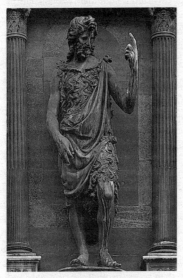

Giovanni Rustici's St John, *at the Baptistery in Florence.*

being a talented sculptor he was an 'amateur alchemist and occasional necromancer', which makes him sound like Zoroastro. Among his associates was the young Andrea del Sarto, a fine painter with a strong tinge of Leonardismo; del Sarto was later Vasari's master, which suggests that Vasari's information on Rustici is likely to be good. He says of Rustici's studio that it 'looked like Noah's ark . . . It contained an eagle, a crow who could speak like a man, snakes and a porcupine trained like a dog which had an annoying habit of pricking people's legs under the table'.[29] I cannot resist an image of Leonardo inclining confidentially towards this crow – a mynah bird? – that 'could speak like a man'. How much he wishes to ask it.

According to Vasari, the tangible product of Leonardo's friendship with Rustici was the sculptural group *St John Preaching to a Levite and a Pharisee*, which stands above the north door of the Baptistery opposite the Duomo. 'All the time he [Rustici] was working on this group he would let no one come near him except Leonardo, right up to the casting stage.' The left-hand figure has been compared to the pensive old man of the *Adoration*; the St John, though executed in the workmanlike style of Rustici, has the trademark hand pointing heavenwards.

Here in the Palazzo Martelli, in the long intermissions of the lawsuit, Leonardo set about organizing his manuscripts, as recorded on the first folio of the Arundel Codex:

Begun at Florence, in the house of Pietro di Braccio Martelli, on 22 March 1508. This will be a collection without order, made up of numerous sheets that I have copied up, hoping later to put them in order, in their proper places, according to the subjects which they treat.

The Codex Arundel is not itself the 'collection': in its present state – probably put together in the 1590s by Pompeo Leoni – it is highly miscellaneous.

Only the first thirty folios belong with this initial statement: consistent in paper, ink, handwriting and subject-matter – mainly physics and mechanics – they were probably written up at precisely this time in spring 1508. But even as he begins, this task of organizing and classifying his manuscripts seems suddenly daunting:

I fear that before I have completed this I shall have repeated the same thing several times, for which do not blame me, reader, because the subjects are many, and the memory cannot retain them and say, This I will not write because I have already written it. And to avoid this it would be necessary, with every passage I wanted to copy, to read through everything I had already done so as not to replicate it.[30]

The sheer unwieldiness of his writings is borne in on him. He has retrieved them from the Ospedale di Santa Maria Nuova, where he had stored them on his departure in 1506; they are piled up on his desk at the Palazzo Martelli; one glimpses what they looked like in Filippino Lippi's beautiful depiction of stacked scholarly manuscripts in the *Vision of St Bernard* (Badia, Florence). A precious resource, but also a chaos. Another note reminds us of their vulnerability to loss and damage: 'Look over all these subjects tomorrow and copy them, and then cross through the originals and leave them in Florence, so that if you lose those you carry with you, the invention will not be lost.'[31]

He feels an impending exhaustion from this great swirl of subjects (or, as he calls them, *casi* – 'cases'), the fruit of more than twenty years' study. But he will not have to tackle them alone: he has a helping hand in this Herculean task of classification and transcription – or at least he will have when he gets back to Milan. And so he tells young Melzi, in that bitter-sweet letter of reproach written at precisely this time, 'by God I'll make you write so much you'll be sorry.'

Also at this time he was compiling the densely written pages of the Codex Leicester (named after its eighteenth-century owner Thomas Coke, Earl of Leicester, and now owned by Microsoft billionaire Bill Gates).[32] It is the most unified of Leonardo's notebooks, and though the outer dates of composition are *c.* 1507–10, it has a look of consistency, even doggedness. The handwriting is small and regular, the drawings are cramped into the margin, but the myopic look of the pages belies the vastness of their scope. The Codex Leicester is concerned with what we today call geophysics: it investigates the fundamental physical structure of the world, anatomizes the macrocosmic body, dismantles the moving parts of the terrestrial machine. This leads into areas of pure physics – gravity, impetus, percussion – and into closely argued discussion of fossils (imperiously countering the orthodox view that they were relics of the biblical deluge). But the particular emphasis is on water: its forms and powers, its tides and currents, and their effects – atmospheric, erosive, geological – on the face of the earth, a preoccupation poetically distilled into that famous landscape in the *Mona Lisa*. This brief synopsis does not include the marvellous pages concerning the sun and moon. Leonardo wonders about the luminescence of the moon – does it mean that the moon is composed of some bright reflective material like crystal or porphyry, or is its surface covered with rippling water? And why, if the phases of the moon are caused by the shadow of the earth, is the rest of the moon sometimes dimly seen during the crescent phase? (In the latter case he correctly deduced that this secondary light is reflected from the earth, pre-dating by several decades the findings of Kepler's teacher Michael Mastlin.)[33]

The Codex Leicester is not a ground-breaking work of modern science: its cosmology is essentially medieval, as is its search for microcosmic correspondences and underlying geometrical symmetries. Its most famous passage is a sustained poetic analogy between the earth and the body of man:

We may say that the earth has a spirit of growth, and that its flesh is the soil, its bones are the successive strata of rock, its cartilage is the tufa, its blood the veins of its waters. The lake of the blood that lies around the heart is the ocean. Its breathing is by the increase and decrease of the blood in its pulses, and even so in the earth is the ebb and flow of the sea.[34]

In these respects the codex is more a philosophical than a scientific text, but the philosophy is under constant scrutiny. There is always that typically Leonardian modulation between the visionary and the practical: a dialogue between them. He tussles with the cosmological theories of the ancients, putting them to the test of 'experience'. He studies the surface tensions of dewdrops on the leaves of a plant so that he can learn more about that 'universal watery sphere' in which, according to Aristotle, the universe is enclosed. He builds a tank with glass sides so he can observe miniature water-flows and earth-deposits. A discussion of atmospheric effects draws on his own observations from the Alpine peaks of Monte Rosa: 'as I myself have seen'.

Some of his experiments can be tied closely to these months in Florence. Two drawings illustrating water-currents are captioned 'at Ponte Rubaconte', another name for the Ponte alle Grazie downriver from the Ponte Vecchio. And in a contemporary passage in the Atlanticus he notes, 'Write of swimming underwater and you will have the flight of a bird through the air. There is a good place at the spot where the mills discharge into the

Arno, by the falls of Ponte Rubaconte.'[35] These 'falls' are the weir: it is shown on the 1472 'Chain Map' of Florence, with boatmen and fishermen, and it is still there today. These vividly place Leonardo's researches on and indeed in the Arno, 'swimming under water' to understand more about the movement of a bird through the invisible currents of the air.

But the codex has also that note of impending dizziness on the subject of organization. He breaks off from a description of ripple-effects, saying:

I will not consider the demonstrations here because I will reserve them for the ordered work. My concern now is to find subjects and inventions, gathering them as they occur to me; later I will put them in order, putting together those of the same kind. So, reader, you need not wonder, nor laugh at me, if here we jump from one subject to another.[36]

And on the following page comes the same disclaimer: 'Here I shall discourse a little more about finding waters even though it seems somewhat out of place; when I come to compile the work I will put everything in order.' The manuscripts are infused with clarity, with what Giorgio Nicodemi has called Leonardo's 'serene and accurate habits of thought',[37] yet they have this literal lack of definition, this unfinished, procrastinated quality. Everything he writes is provisional, a rough draft for that perfect 'ordered work' he would never write.

⤗ DISSECTIONS ⤙

Litigations, transcriptions, cases, letters: Leonardo's life in the early months of 1508 – the last he would spend in Florence, as it turned out – seems oddly scribal, one might even say notarial. The stacks of paper in his *studiolo* on Via Larga threaten to dwarf him as he sits writing. His shoulders are getting rounder; his eyesight is troubling him; his beard is flecked with grey. There is some artistic activity of which we know next to nothing: the mysterious 'two Madonnas of different sizes' for King Louis; the eternally ongoing *Mona Lisa*; the advisory work on Rustici's sculptural group for the Baptistery; and perhaps some last touches to the giant fragment of the *Battle of Anghiari*, though there is no documentation of this, nor of his relations – if any – with the Gonfalonier. Leonardo abandoned relationships as easily as he abandoned pictures – a skill, the psychiatrist might say, which he learned early on from his father.

But perhaps the most significant activity of these last months in Florence – the activity that opens a new chapter of intensely focused investigation –

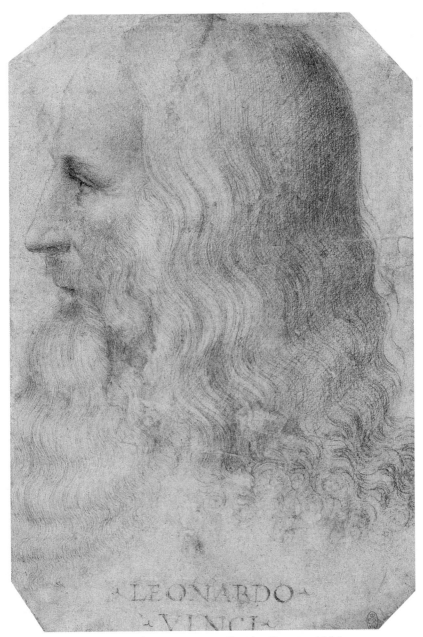

15. Leonardo in late middle age. Portrait attributed to Francesco Melzi, *c.* 1510–12.

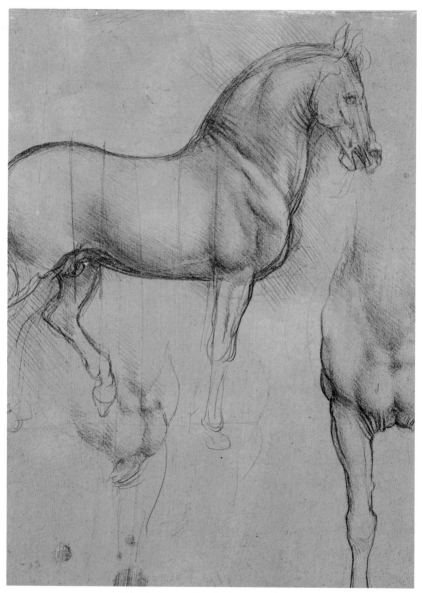

16. Metalpoint studies of a horse, early 1490s.

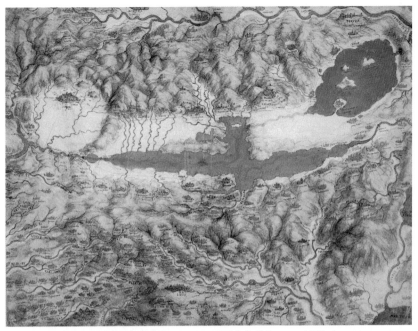

17. Leonardo, Bird's eye map of Val di Chiana, c. 1502–4.

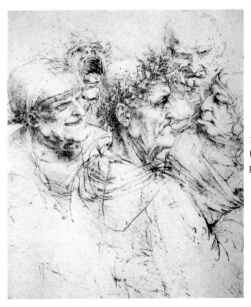

18. Five grotesque heads (possibly a man tricked by gypsies).

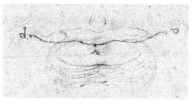

19. The smile. Detail from a sheet of studies of lips and mouths.

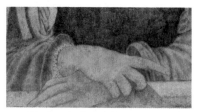

20. The hands. Detail from a sixteenth-century copy of Leonardo's portrait drawing of Isabella d'Este.

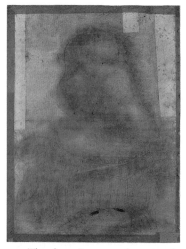

21. The ghost. Image on the verso of Leonardo's portrait of Isabella d'Este.

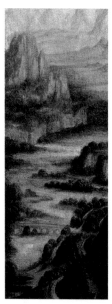

22. The bridge. Detail from the *Madonna of the Yarnwinder* by Leonardo and assistants.

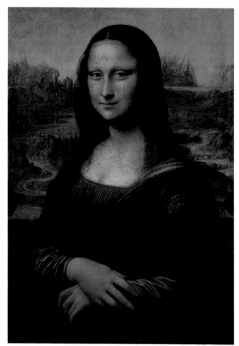

23. *Mona Lisa.*

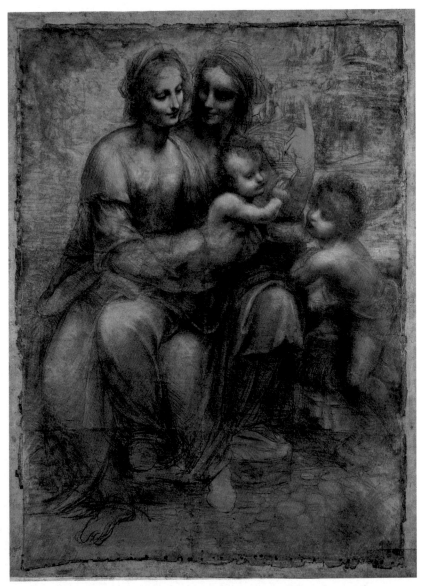

24. Cartoon for a *Virgin and Child with St Anne and the Infant St John*
('Burlington House cartoon').

25. Reversed image of a portrait sketch of Leonardo, *c.* 1510.

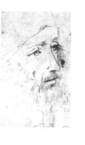

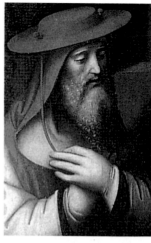

(Right) 26. Detail from Giampietrino's altarpiece at Ospedaletto Lodigiano.

27. One of the late 'Deluge' drawings.

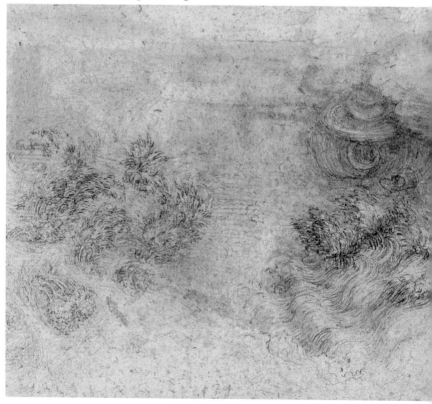

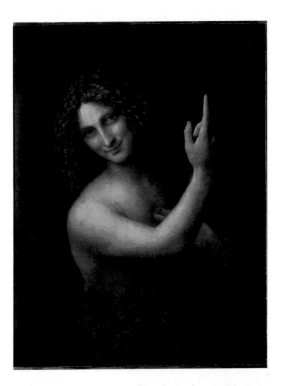

(Above) 28. *St John the Baptist*, possibly Leonardo's last painting.

(Right) 29. *Leda and the Swan*. Version of a lost work of Leonardo's by a pupil or follower (Cesare da Sesto?).

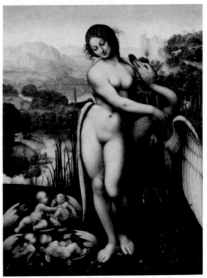

30. The mystery of creation. Detail from a sheet of studies of the foetus in the womb.

finds him with not a pen or a paintbrush in his hand but a scalpel. In a famous memorandum of late 1507 or early 1508 Leonardo records his dissection of the corpse of an old man:

This old man, a few hours before his death, told me he had lived for more than a hundred years, and that he was conscious of no deficiency in his person other than feebleness. And thus, sitting on a bed in the hospital of Santa Maria Nuova in Florence, without any movement or sign of distress, he passed from this life. And I made an anatomy to see the cause of a death so sweet.

He also, at around the same time, dissected the body of a two-year-old child, 'in which I found everything to be the opposite to that of the old man'.[38]

His immediate interest centres on the vascular system. Next to a drawing showing the superficial veins of the arm, he notes the difference between the veins and arteries of the 'old man' and the 'boy'. He suspects that the old man's death was attributable to 'weakness caused by a lack of blood in the artery which feeds the heart and lower members'. He finds the arteries to be 'very dry, thin and withered', and 'in addition to the thickening of their walls, these vessels grow in length and twist themselves in the manner of a snake.' He also notes that the liver, deprived of adequate blood supply, 'becomes desiccated, like congealed bran in colour and substance'; and that the skin of the very old has 'the colour of wood, or dried chestnuts, because the skin is almost completely deprived of nourishment'. Later, in a different ink, he writes a curt reminder: 'Represent the arm of Francesco the miniaturist which exhibits many veins.' On a related sheet he discusses whether the heart or the liver is the key organ of the vascular system, and concludes (with Aristotle, against Galen) that it is the heart, which he likens to the stone of a peach from which the 'tree of the vessels' grows.[39]

This highly practical, textural language – snake, bran, wood, chestnuts, peach-stone – is in marked contrast to the more metaphysical tone of his earlier anatomy of the late 1480s, with its interest in the 'confluence of the senses', and the traffic of 'vital spirits', and other traditional medieval postulates. A similar movement away from the metaphysical is found in his small tract on optics (now Paris MS D), written later in 1508, which stresses the purely receptive nature of the eye and the absence of any invisible or 'spiritual' rays emanating from it. (The traditional model held perception to be proactive in this way.) The eye may be the 'window of the soul', as he is fond of saying, but it is also a miniature machine whose working parts must be disassembled and understood.

Of the same period, c. 1508–9, are beautifully drawn diagrams showing

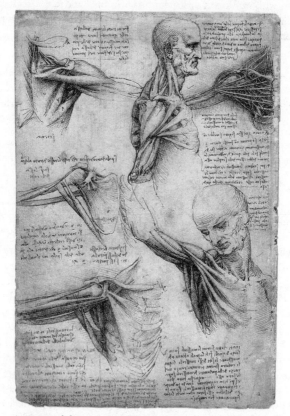

Anatomical dissection of the shoulder and neck, from a
Windsor folio of c. 1508–9.

lungs and abdominal organs, perhaps of a pig, again with botanical analogies.[40] These show Leonardo battling with problems of how to show anatomy – looking for that diagrammatic technique which combines surface detail with transparency. The anecdote in Vasari about him inflating a pig's gut until it filled the room serves as a macabre footnote to this dissection of a pig. He likes to scare and unsettle people: the theatrical side of him.

Also from this time is the famous drawing showing the distended vulva of a woman, the genitalia unrealistically cavernous even if the drawing represents a multiparous or post-partum woman.[41] I am tempted to connect this strange exaggeration with Leonardo's earlier text about the 'cavern',

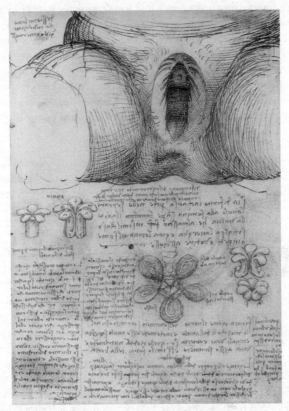

Female genitalia and studies of the anal sphincter, c. 1508-9.

and to suggest that the fear he expressed about looking into that 'threatening dark cave' was in part an unconscious confrontation with the disturbing mysteries of female sexuality. Within that Freudian sort of interpretation, the 'marvellous thing' that might be glimpsed within the cave would be the mystery of generation and birth. Here, however, in his notes below the drawing, Leonardo is content with a more laconic metaphor: 'The wrinkles or ridges in the folds of the vulva have indicated to us the location of the gatekeeper of the castle.' The image of a woman's sex as a defended 'castle' or 'fortress', to be besieged and breached by the insistent male, is a commonplace of amorous poetry.[42]

On a related sheet are views of a standing female showing her uterus in early pregnancy; drawings of male and female genitals; a study of a cow's uterus with a small foetus in it; and a detail of the cow's placenta, whose tissues Leonardo describes as 'interwoven like burrs'.[43] These studies on reproduction seem to link with the generational theme of the *Leda*, on which he was plausibly at work in *c.* 1508–9 – there is a visual echo of Leda in the outline of the pregnant female. On the verso of the sheet is a wonderful page of studies of the mouth and its muscles, among them those ghostly lips which seem to have floated, Cheshire Cat-style, from the face of Mona Lisa.

The notes about the 'old man', written in late 1507 or early 1508, contain the first clear reference to Leonardo himself performing a human dissection, but he had probably done others before this, for on another anatomical page dated *c.* 1508 he claims to have personally dissected – *disfatto*: taken to pieces – 'more than ten human bodies'.[44] He boasts of his finesse with the scalpel. To arrive at 'a true and perfect knowledge' of the body's veins he has removed 'in the most minute particles all the flesh that lies around these veins, without causing any flow of blood save a scarcely perceptible bleeding of the capillary veins'. He also notes the procedural problems in the days before refrigeration: 'As a single body would not last long enough, it was necessary to use several bodies in succession, so as to arrive at a complete knowledge [of the veins]; I repeated this process twice, in order to observe the variations.' And he describes the challenges, indeed horrors, of the task. 'You' – the reader, the would-be anatomist – 'will perhaps be deterred by the rising of your stomach.'

Some of these dissections were doubtless done, as were those of the 'old man' and the 'boy', at the hospital of Santa Maria Nuova. He knew the place well: it served as his bank and on occasions his depository. He must have had some kind of official licence for these – even the 'doctors and scholars' of the Florentine Studio had to seek permission from the magistrates before conducting a public dissection at Santa Croce in 1506.[45] But it seems that not all the dissections Leonardo performed were done there. He speaks feelingly of 'the fear of living at night-time in the company of these dead men, dismembered and flayed and terrible to behold'. He is perhaps playing this up a bit, but the implication is that he has done dissections in his own lodgings or studio, hence the specific fearfulness of spending the night with the corpses, which would not be required if he were dissecting them at Santa Maria Nuova.

Dissection was still controversial. It was permitted, under licence, but it remained a dubious activity around which clustered rumours and superstitions – an implication of the 'black arts', of the fetishes and concoctions of medieval magic. The frequent use of cadavers from the gallows added a further frisson. Leonardo was keen to dissociate himself from such goings-on, which is why the passage describing his dissections also contains a spirited attack on fraudulent magicians:

Nature revenges herself on those who wish to perform miracles . . . for they live always in the direst poverty, as is and forever will be the case with alchemists who seek to create gold and silver, and engineers who wish to create living force out of dead water in perpetual motion, and most idiotic of all, necromancers and sorcerers.

Later, in Rome, Leonardo's researches brought him into conflict with the Church, and he was 'hindered in anatomy' by an ill-wisher who reported his activities to the Pope. Such attitudes hardened with the Counter-Reformation. Half a century later the great Belgian anatomist Andreas Vesalius, author of the *De humanis corporis fabrica* (1543), was condemned to death by the Inquisition for 'body-snatching' and dissection; the sentence was commuted to a pilgrimage to Jerusalem, but he died on the return journey, aged fifty.

When Leonardo talks of spending the night in the company of corpses we get a hint of dissections done behind closed doors, clandestine, tinged with heresy. For Leonardo the imperative of investigation is always stronger than that of personal comfort or doctrinal safety.

↠ BACK IN THE STUDIO ↞

In his letters from Florence to Milan, carried up by Salai in early 1508, Leonardo says he hopes to be back there by Easter – late April – and he probably was. As per the 1506 agreement with the Confraternity, delivery of the reworked *Virgin of the Rocks* was due by 26 April, and perhaps some final touches were applied by the *maestro* before the painting was handed over. This is the beautiful, blue-tinged London version of the *Virgin of the Rocks*, part Ambrogio de Predis and part Leonardo: less shimmery and suggestive than the Louvre version, technically sharper, emotionally cooler. It was certainly in the Confraternity's possession sometime before mid-August, for on 18 August there is another little flurry of legal documentation in the form of an 'acquittance' releasing the Confraternity from its earlier contract with the painters.[46] From this it is clear that the painting was now in 'its place' – in other words above the altar in the Confraternity's chapel at San Francesco Grande – and in fact it remained there until the suppression of the Confraternity in 1781. It was brought to Britain four years later by the Scottish collector Gavin Hamilton.[47]

That the painting was delivered in 1508 did not mean that the painters got paid the final payment for which they had waited so long. The Confraternity was as loath as ever to part with cash, and in the acquittance of 18 August it was agreed that in lieu of payment the painters would make yet another copy of the painting which they could sell. The Confraternity undertook to 'deposit the said painting in a room in the convent of San Francesco for a period of up to four months so that Dominus Leonardus and his assistants can make a copy of it, except that on holy days it is to be restored to its place'. On the same date Ambrogio and Leonardo signed an agreement in which Ambrogio undertook to execute this copy, at his own expense and labour, under instruction from Leonardo. All proceeds from the sale of it were to be divided equally between them 'in good faith and without fraud'. We know nothing of this third version of the *Virgin of the Rocks*, assuming it was ever painted; of known early copies it is more likely to be the version in a Swiss private collection than the inferior version in the Chiesa di Affori in Milan.[48] Leonardo's input is minimal but magisterial. He 'instructs', Ambrogio 'executes'; each receives half the proceeds – the inequality of their labour precisely reflecting the inequality of their status as master and assistant.

As he settles back into Milanese life, Leonardo returns with renewed vigour to the studio. We know from these latest documents that he was living in the parish of Santa Babila, at or near the Porta Orientale, and probably his studio was there. (The house in the vineyard outside Porta Vercellina was still occupied by Salai's father, and anyway could not have accommodated a busy studio, which has a constant requirement of materials and which functions typically in an artisan quarter.) In this studio we can place Salai, by now a thoroughly proficient painter; Francesco Melzi, whose earliest datable drawing is from 1510; young Lorenzo, now once more separated from his little sister Dianira; and also, as we will soon see, one of the best of Leonardo's young Lombard followers, Giovanni Pietro Rizzoli, known as Giampietrino.

And here too we can place the two great paintings of this period, two long-gestated works which now come to some kind of fruition – the *Virgin and Child with St Anne* and the *Leda* – and very probably a third, wrapped in an aura of suspendedness from which she would never quite escape, the *Mona Lisa*. Thus on the easels of Leonardo's studio we find this extraordinary assortment of four women, each of them a superb study in femininity, each painted from a different model, then teased out into the idealized forms of feminine beauty – four meditations, one might say, on motherhood: St Anne the mother of Mary, Mary the mother of Christ, Leda the mother of those bird-children, and Lisa the actual Florentine housewife and mother.

As we saw, Leonardo had worked intensively on the *St Anne* in Florence in 1500–1501, intending it for the altarpiece of Santissima Annunziata, and in 1501 had exhibited a full-sized cartoon, now lost, which caused a sensation in Florentine art-circles. Now, seven years later, he is at work on the theme again, and the result is the superb drawing in the National Gallery in London (Plate 24), known as the Burlington House cartoon because it hung for many years at the Royal Academy's headquarters at Burlington House. It is a huge drawing (55 × 40 inches), though its sense of size is in part due to the drastic foregrounding of the four figures, so that they occupy practically all the picture space; it looks like a blown-up photograph from which the surrounds have been cropped. The foremost figure, Mary, though seated, takes up virtually all the vertical space; in fact the toes of her right foot are lost beneath the bottom of the frame. The ensemble has a sculptural quality – from this sense of size, from the dense modelling of the figures, and even from the colouring, which gives them a dull coppery gleam (though this is in part the action of time on the picture surface). Yet in this sculpted group Leonardo achieves a subtlety of texture that goes beyond the possibilities of sculpture, and the cartoon seems to embody one of his instances of the superiority of painting over sculpture: 'Sculpture cannot represent luminous and transparent bodies, such as veiled figures in which the bare flesh below the veils can be seen.'[49]

The composition of the Burlington House cartoon, like that of the *Virgin of the Rocks*, is broadly pyramidic, but within that enclosing shape the dynamic of the drawing is circular, spiralling. The eye is drawn into a vortex, the chief whorl of which is a line which begins with the face of the Christ-child, moves upwards in a flowing movement around the heads of the two adults, descends down the side of Mary's head and along her arm, but then, instead of completing the circle, shoots off through the signpost finger of St Anne pointing heavenward. Around this central movement, which is also expressed in the lines of the two women's headgear, are the eddies and flows of the drapery, an undulation of knees and a repeated undulation of feet, and then the scattering of little pebbles – the soothing disorder of the river-bed.

As in so many Leonardo compositions, there is a hinted narrative. The day is hot; they sit on a rock beside a stream or shallow pool, cooling their feet in the water as they sit. Behind them is a rugged brown landscape, dry-looking. We are in the foothills, rather than the mountains – rocky, hard, not much vegetation to shade us – but we have a sense (as in the landscape behind the Gioconda) of human activity. There is the hint of a road or track winding down behind Mary's right shoulder, and on the other side of the group are four lines that look like the silhouette of a gate, and a curving shape that could be a simple bridge – a suggestion of the way these people have come to get here. And in the midst of it all is that hand – which amid the swirls and patina and hatching is almost a blank space – which signifies to us that this is not just a family group passing the time together, but a moment of spiritual significance.

Preparatory drawings exist for the cartoon, done in pen and ink over black chalk on a sheet now in the British Museum.[50] The largest of the three is not just a preparatory sketch – it is an actual template for the full-size cartoon. The ensemble has arrived at a point of definition, via the intensive wrestling and probing that remain evident on the page, and the composition is framed and measured, ready to be scaled up to the near-life-size dimensions of the cartoon. The cartoon itself was drawn on to a glued-up assemblage of sheets (the same process recorded in the *Anghiari* documents of 1504). Leonardo used eight sheets of linen-rag paper – four full sheets, and four narrower ones top and bottom – and drew on them in charcoal heightened with white chalk. The media could not be more basic: coal and chalk, as used by cavemen. The effects he achieves belong to another dimension, the tracery of *moti mentali* across the paper.

The fine quality of the linen-based paper has contributed to the drawing's survival through the many vicissitudes which are etched on its surface and which seem also to be part of its identity. There are scars of water damage, of rollings and foldings. A rip has been sealed up on the back with three large patches of paper; unseen behind the top left-hand corner of the cartoon is an old print showing the heads of some Roman emperors. In the seventeenth century the drawing was stuck on to canvas: the fingerprints of the craftsman, left as he frantically tried to counteract the grip of the glue, are visible under a magnifying glass. It arrived in England, in circumstances unknown, sometime in the eighteenth century – it is first listed as part of the Royal Academy collection in 1779. Since then it has endured various invasive restorations. The forger Eric Hebborn claimed he redrew all the white-chalk lines in the 1950s, during a secret restoration after the cartoon was left leaning against a hot radiator in the basement of Burlington House, but his story has not been confirmed.[51] Its transfer to the National Gallery in 1962 did not mark the end of its tribulations. On the evening of 17 July 1987 a man stood in front of the cartoon and fired at it from point-blank range

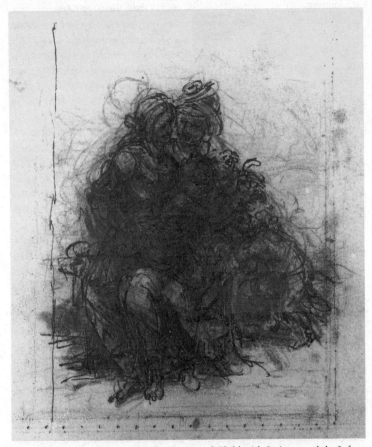

Scaled preparatory drawing for the Virgin and Child with St Anne and the Infant St John *(Burlington House cartoon).*

with a single-barrel 12-bore shotgun. The protective glass prevented any of the pellets reaching the picture surface, but the contusion of the impact was severe – a shallow crater about 6 inches across disfigured the picture. The restoration took over a year, and involved the mapping, storing and replacing of more than 250 fragments of paper, 'some of them no bigger than spores'.[52]

The cartoon was never used for a painting: perhaps Leonardo considered it a final expression of that particular idea. The oil painting of the *Virgin*

427

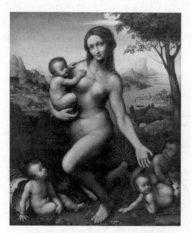

Giampietrino, Kneeling Leda.

and Child with St Anne in the Louvre, inferior in power, shows a different grouping. The lamb, reportedly present in the 1501 cartoon, reappears, though this is not quite a return to that earlier design, as there is no infant St John in the picture. The group swivels, the mood changes, the painting is bathed in a sweetness which to some seems sentimental, and the chief charge of the picture is the tantalizing if spurious motif of the bird, discerned a century ago by the Freudian Pfister, and once seen impossible not to see. The date of the painting is unknown and opinions vary. The most plausible view is that it was composed a little later than the cartoon, perhaps *c.* 1510–11; it was one of the three paintings shown to Cardinal Luigi of Aragon in France in 1517.

Also in the studio at this time, it would seem, is an evolving version of the *Leda*. The various paintings of the standing Leda (Plate 29) are mysterious, and there is no documentation (though many opinions) as to who painted them and when. But as we have seen, there was another Leda motif entirely, found in various preparatory drawings of 1504–5, in which she is shown kneeling. Of this there is only one known painted version, and it can be closely tied to Leonardo's Milanese workshop at this time. The painting, in oils on a panel of alder wood, is by his talented assistant Giampietrino, though when it turned up in Paris in 1756, and was purchased by the Landgrave of Hesse-Kassel, it was described as 'a *Caritas* by Leonardo da Vinci'. A *caritas* – a personification of Charity – was a specific grouping of a mother and three children, and indeed at this stage the fourth child (the one at bottom right) had been painted over. In 1803 Goethe wrote, 'Among the treasures of the Gallery at Kassel is the *Caritas* by Leonardo da Vinci, which more than all others draws the attention of artists and lovers.'[53] At some point the painting's connection with the kneeling-Leda drawings was established, and the fourth child was recovered. The attribution to Leonardo persisted for a while, for the picture is of a very high quality, but Giampietrino's authorship is now undisputed. The facial type and the curvaceous body of the kneeling Leda are echoed, indeed reiterated, in a number of other works by Giampietrino. Leda's face is very similar in all the paintings of her: Leonardo's pen-and-ink studies at Windsor (page 441) are the template for this.[54] (It is possible that we know the name and even the address of the model who provided this definitive 'look' – but that is a matter for a later chapter.)

Recent technical examination of the Giampietrino *Leda* has revealed further close links with the Leonardo workshop.[55] Infra-red reflectographs disclose an underdrawing beneath the paint surface, defined by a clear outline of puncture-marks showing that the painting was produced from a full-sized cartoon. This cartoon would be Leonardo's evolution of the drawings of the kneeling Leda which he had done in *c.* 1504: the pose is closest to, but not identical with, the drawing at Chatsworth. But the painting has further secrets to reveal, for beneath the underdrawing is another substratum, on which can be seen a drawing of part of the *St Anne* ensemble; only a fragment of this composition remains, but where it does it follows precisely the line of the painted version in the Louvre. We thus find beneath Giampietrino's kneeling *Leda* a reminiscence of the lost cartoon for the Louvre *Virgin and Child with St Anne*. There are many variables here, but the likely date for the Louvre painting, *c.* 1510–11, is likely enough for the Giampietrino *Leda* also, though it is possible that the *Leda*'s landscape background was painted later by another artist, Bernardino Marchiselli or Bernazzano, assistant to Cesare da Sesto and a specialist in just this kind of sweeping, autumnally tinged Lombard landscape.[56]

Also on the drawing-board in Leonardo's studio at this time are his designs for the funeral monument of the *condottiere* Giangiacomo Trivulzio, the former enemy of the Sforza who was now Marshal of Milan. In a will drawn up in 1504 Trivulzio set aside 4,000 ducats for a monumental tomb in the basilica of San Nazaro Maggiore. He envisaged a suitably grandiose equestrian statue, and the name of Leonardo cannot have been far from his mind. The possibility of this lucrative project was perhaps another reason for Leonardo's return to Milan in 1506. The ghost of the ruined Sforza Horse stirs in his mind. There are many studies for the monument, which was to feature a bronze horse and rider (the horse being specified by Leonardo as a *corsiere* or charger) on top of an elaborately carved marble arch. The horses are drawn with wonderful realism and empathy. This is his last series of horses: dynamic, precise, learned, the culmination of decades of connoisseurship.[57] The rider is idealized, a youthful warrior – in reality Trivulzio was a burly figure with a face like a prizefighter.

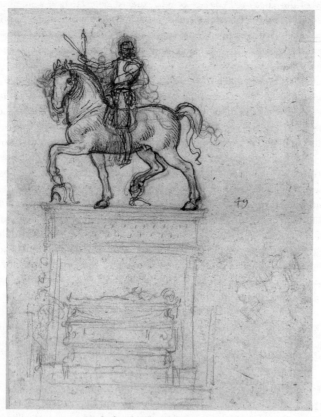

Study for the Trivulzio monument.

In a document headed '*Sepulcro di Messer Giovanni Jacomo da Trevulzo*' Leonardo estimates the costs of the monument:[58]

Cost of the metal for the horse and rider	500 ducats
Cost of casting it, including the ironwork to go inside the model, and the binding of the mould, and the necessaries for the furnace in which it is to be cast	200 ducats
Cost of making the model in clay and then taking a mould of it in wax	432 ducats
Cost of labour for polishing it after it is cast	450 ducats

Thus the statue alone is estimated at 1,582 ducats. For the plinth and the arch some 13 tons of marble were required, adding a further 1,342 ducats for materials and labour. This is his *preventivo* or estimate. Perhaps it is inaccurate, as Italian *preventivi* so often are, but it matters little, for the Trivulzio monument is another of Leonardo's might-have-beens. There is no evidence that the project got beyond the planning stage, and in the event Trivulzio lived on till 1518, when he died at Chartres, a few months before Leonardo.

⤙ THE WORLD AND ITS WATERS ⤚

On 12 September 1508 Leonardo opened up a new notebook with a cover of thin grey card and inscribed it, '*Cominciato a Milano a dì 12 di settembre 1508*'. It is a notebook of 192 pages; at the end of it he writes the date October 1508, so it seems he filled the entire book over a concentrated period of six weeks or so – perhaps less. The compactness and regularity of the handwriting would confirm this. He gave it the title '*Di mondo ed acque*' – 'Of the World and Its Waters' – though it is now known less sonorously as Paris MS F. He instructs himself:

Write first of water, in each of its motions; then describe all of its beds and the substances therein . . . and let the order be good, for otherwise the work will be confused. Describe all the forms that water assumes from its largest to its smallest wave, and their causes.[59]

The pages on water have small, vivid sketches – superb examples of Leonardo's mastery in representing complex volatile structures. He treats of '*retrosi*' (back-currents) and vortices (p. 150). He coins the phrase *aqua panniculata* – creased or crumpled water – to describe agitated surfaces. The fascination with the intricate forms of running water seems to be echoed in the rolling, flowing tresses of the *Leda*, on which Leonardo – or at any rate his assistants – were probably working at this time. The interest in water is also practical. There is a machine 'for excavating earth so as to make the water of the *padule* deeper', which can be linked to canalization projects under way at this time.[60]

The flying-machine is under consideration once more. A curt note reads, 'Anatomize the bat, and keep to this, and base the machine on this.'[61] He had earlier recognized the bat as the physiological model for the wings of the machine, 'because the membranes serve as the framework of the wings', but now – perhaps as a result of the failed trial on Monte Ceceri – he seems to be stressing the bat as a more stable model for flight in general. He later notes that bats 'can follow their prey upside down, and sometimes in a slanting position, and so in various ways, which they could not do without causing their own destruction if their wings were of feathers with gaps in between'.[62]

His passion for geometry is undimmed: we find him delving into the arcana of square- and cube-roots, and tussling with the Delos problem, so called because it is expressed in the classical story of Apollo, who delivered the islanders of Delos from plague and demanded in return that they double the size of their altar to him; as the altar was a perfect cube of marble, they were obliged to work out a cube-root in order to satisfy him.[63]

There are discussions of optics and light which shade into cosmological theory. A powerfully written discourse 'In Praise of the Sun' covers a two-page spread, citing and disputing the opinions of Epicurus and Socrates about the size of the sun, and concluding:

In the whole universe there is nowhere to be seen a body of greater magnitude and power than the sun. Its light gives light to all the celestial bodies which are distributed throughout the universe. From it descend all the vital forces [*anime*], for the heat that is in all living creatures comes from these vital forces, and there is no other heat and no other light in the universe.[64]

There is an echo here of the old Platonic-planetary magic of Ficino, but if one substitutes 'solar system' for 'universe' the passage makes perfect scientific sense. It tends towards an idea of heliocentricity, but does not actually express it. The famous note reading, '*Il sole non si muove*' ('The sun does not move'), found on a Windsor sheet of *c.* 1510, has been taken as an inspired astronomical insight pre-dating Copernicus by thirty years, but this cannot be certain. The idea of heliocentricity – though not the proof – is as old as Pythagoras, and anyway the words appear on their own, with no preamble or explanation, and are as likely to be a jotting connected with a pageant or masque, or perhaps the motto of an emblem illustrating some quality of steadfastness.[65]

He also pursues in MS F his fascination with geological and aetiological cycles, which is such a feature of the contemporary Codex Leicester. He considers the possibility of the earth's emergence from the sea, and foresees, in a prophetic tone, the return of the earth to the 'lap' (*grembo*) or womb of the sea.[66] In this passage we hear the first germs of his apocalyptic Deluge drawings, where the drama of natural cataclysms conveys also an idea of the collapse of categories and distinctions – an engulfing of the intellect by a Nature uncontrollable and in the end unknowable.

Among these big themes there is also that quality of momentariness which is such a pungent aspect of the notebooks. Here are some of the phrases scribbled down on the cover:

inflate the lungs of a pig
Avicenna on fluids
map of Elefan of India which Antonello Merciaio has
enquire at the stationers' for Vitruvius
ask Maestro Mafeo why the Adige rises for seven years and falls for seven years
go every Saturday to the hot baths and you will see naked men.[67]

Broadly contemporary with this notebook is another, Paris MS D, a booklet of twenty pages, neatly and consistently written, and wholly concerned with a single subject – the science of vision. Some of it elaborates previously written notes, particularly drawing on MS A of the early 1490s. It is a further sign of Leonardo's thoughts tending towards compilation, finalization, and hence publication.[68]

The same desire is undoubtedly to be seen in his anatomical sheets of this period, a gathering of eighteen folios on one of which is the note 'In the winter of this year 1510 I expect to complete all this anatomy.' In these the graphic illustrations aligned with short blocks of explanatory text constitute what would now be called the 'layout' for a printed page. A note refers explicitly to a future printed edition: 'As regards this benefit I give to posterity, I show the method of printing it in order, and I beseech you who come after me not to let avarice constrain you to make the prints in [. . .]' The last word is missing owing to paper-loss near the margin, but enough is left to suggest the word *legno*, wood.[69] He wishes, in other words, that his anatomical writings should be illustrated not with woodcuts – cheaper, as he says, but much cruder – but with the more expensive and accurate process of copper engraving. This is confirmed by Paolo Giovio, who had first-hand knowledge of Leonardian anatomy through their shared connection with the anatomist Marcantonio della Torre. Leonardo, he says, 'tabulated with extreme accuracy all the different parts of the body, down to the smallest veins and the composition of the bones, in order that this work on which he had spent so many years should be published from copper engravings for the benefit of art'. As Carlo Pedretti notes, this expectation may explain the slightly lifeless drawing-style in these anatomical folios: 'The calligraphic precision of line, and a shading rendered by a minute, uniform hatching, are characteristics that Leonardo was expecting from copper engravings.'[70]

Another compilation of this period, no doubt also with a printed edition in mind, is the manuscript 'book' on painting which Melzi catalogued (after Leonardo's death) as Libro A. It formed an important part of Melzi's compilation of Leonardo's writings on painting, the Codex Urbinas, which in turn provided the copy-text of the *Trattato della pittura*. The original manuscript is lost, but some of its contents are recoverable from Melzi's text. It also contained some notes on hydraulics which were copied by Leonardo himself into the Codex Leicester.[71] Thus in his studio in Milan the great project of inquiry proceeds, page by page, pen-nib by pen-nib, towards the distant goal of publication. 'In this labour of mine', he promises, men 'will discern the marvellous works of Nature.'

⤙ *FÊTES MILANAISES* ⤚

The French seemed genuinely keen to exploit those talents which Leonardo himself enjoyed, and as in the Sforza years there were masques and entertainments – *feste*, which one might now call fêtes. Among those who witnessed these shows was the young physician Paolo Giovio, who later wrote in his biography of Leonardo, 'He was the marvellous inventor and arbiter of all elegance and of all theatrical delights.'

In the Arundel Codex are rapid sketches of a stage-set featuring a range of rugged, Leonardesque mountains, which opens to reveal a large hemispherical chamber or cavern. A diagram shows the mechanism of pulleys and counterweights that would operate this set behind the scenes. Notes explain the theatrical effect: 'a mountain which opens ... and Pluto is discovered in his residence'. This theatrical cavern is the 'residence' of the king of Hades: a glimpse of hell, furnished with devils and furies, and Cerberus, and 'many naked children weeping'.[72] These are almost certainly designs for a performance of Agnolo Poliziano's operetta *Orfeo*. Leonardo had probably been involved in an earlier production, in Mantua in 1490, starring his protégé Atalante Migliorotti, and now reprises it for the court of Charles d'Amboise. The play retells in sprightly Florentine verse the old story of Orpheus's journey to the underworld to rescue his wife, Eurydice, from the clutches of Pluto, with appropriate musical accompaniment for each – contrabass viols for Orpheus, treble viols for Eurydice, trombones for Pluto, and guitars for Charon, ferryman of the dead. A sheet at Windsor has some costume studies and a profile of a youth with curly hair which may be a portrait of the actor playing Orpheus.[73]

Another relic of this production, probably, is a pen-and-ink sketch showing 'Orpheus being attacked by the Furies'. This surfaced in 1998 among a collection of prints and drawings by Stefano della Bella, but was reported in 2001 as having been damaged during a botched restoration. It is done in a greenish ink, which Leonardo used in other documents and drawings of this time such as the estimate for the Trivulzio monument.[74]

These fugitive fragments are all that remain of Leonardo's Milanese production of *Orfeo*, itself a text with elements of nostalgia – for the Florence of Poliziano, for the beautiful Atalante – and perhaps with certain echoes and undertones reminiscent of his own early text about the 'cavern' and the 'fear and desire' he felt as he looked into it.

Another Leonardo production was the victory pageant of 1 July 1509, staged in honour of Louis XII as he returned to Milan at the head of his troops after the decisive defeat of the Venetians at Agnadello in mid-May. There was an allegoric representation of a battle between a dragon (France) and a lion (Venice) – another of Leonardo's lion themes, though in this allegory the lion was no doubt expediently defeated – while in the Piazza del Castello was exhibited 'a horse of immense size, in relief' with the image of the King on it. We learn of this from a contemporary chronicle, and from G. P. Lomazzo, who gives an account which he seems to have heard at first hand from Francesco Melzi.[75]

A tight-lipped note in the Codex Atlanticus has a rather different angle on these Italian wars and their futile wastage: 'The Venetians have boasted of spending 36 million gold ducats in ten years of war against the Empire, the Church and the kings of Spain and France. This works out at 300,000 ducats a month.'[76]

These spectacles show Leonardo once more in that role of court artist he had assayed in the Sforza years. In a similar vein are some *imprese* or emblems he drew at this time. The heyday of the Renaissance emblem has not yet come: one of its chief exponents would be Leonardo's admirer Paolo Giovio, whose emblem-books were known to Shakespeare via the translation of Samuel Daniel.[77] Andrea Alciato, author of the famous *Emblematum liber* (1531), defined an emblem as an image 'drawn from history or nature' which 'elegantly signifies something'. The true emblem consists of a *corpo* or body, which is its visual pictorial form, and an *anima* or spirit, which is the verbal motto that accompanies it. The motto should not declare the 'sentiment', or meaning, of the emblem too readily: this is for cultivated men and women to contemplate and ponder for themselves.[78] Its effect lay precisely in its poetic suggestiveness, its bodying forth of metaphysical ideas through apparent simplicity and brevity of expression.

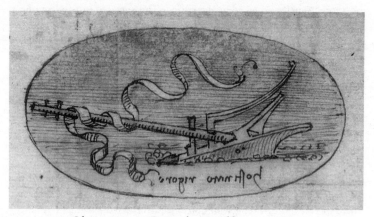

Obstinate rigour. Design for an emblem, c. 1508–9.

Like a Japanese haiku, the Renaissance emblem is a lapidary art-form which blossoms into complex, personally interpreted ideas.

A Windsor sheet has three finished emblems.[79] The first shows a plough, with the motto *hostinato rigore* (obstinate rigour). This motto has been held to sum up a side of Leonardo's character – his rigorously experimental, investigative temper – though in so far as a plough moves in a straight line it is not so characteristic: Leonardo's furrows are tangential, labyrinthine, like the knot-patterns of the *fantasie dei vinci*. The second shows a compass turned by a water-wheel, and a star above, with the motto *destinato rigore* – literally 'destined rigour', but more loosely translated as 'an unwavering course'. A note beside this reads, '*Non a revoluzione chi a tale stella e fisso*' – 'He who is fixed to such a star will not revolve' (hence not be subject to vicissitudes). The presence of tiny fleurs-de-lis within the star shows that it represents the French king.[80] The third emblem shows a lamp with a candle inside it, and winds blowing around it from all points of the compass. There is no motto, but a similar device is found in another notebook, with bellows producing the winds and the motto '*Tal el mal che non mi noce quale il bene che non mi giova*' – 'As the evil which does not harm me so the good which does not profit me.'[81] Inside the lamp the flame is protected both from the strong wind which would put it out and from the gentle wind which would fan it. This protection one would associate once more with the King, the fixed star of the previous emblem, though if so it comes with an idea that royal patronage is double-edged: it shelters the artist from the buffetings of fortune, but also isolates him from the 'good' gentle winds (of experience? of Nature?).

Another series from the same time, though merely rough sketches, shows an emblem featuring a flower (*Iris florentina*) with a scroll enclosed in a circle. Leonardo tries out various mottos – '*Prima morte che stanchezza*', '*Non mi satio di servire*', etc. – on a theme of unswerving service. But a marginal note, like a theatrical 'aside' to the audience, suggests an element of scepticism about such devotion: 'Hands into which the ducats and precious stones fall like snow never grow tired of serving, but such service is only for its usefulness, and is not for one's own benefit.'[82] The verso of the sheet has some vivid sketches, reminiscent of the Pain/Pleasure allegories of the mid-1480s. They show masks held in front of faces, being melted by the sun's rays. The basic key reads:

Truth: the sun
Falsehood: a mask.

Again he tries out different mottos, such as '*Nulla occulta sotto il sole*' – 'Nothing is hidden under the sun.'[83]

Are these emblems Leonardo's own expressions of service to King Louis, or are they done on behalf of someone who wishes to express such sentiments – his old friend Galeazzo Sanseverino, perhaps, the former son-in-law of the Moor, who had adroitly and somewhat cynically switched allegiance to the French and later became superintendent of the King's stables at Blois?

Musical shows, victory parades, courtly emblems: these are some of the more minor accomplishments required of the King's 'painter and engineer in ordinary', to be fitted in among such other duties as painting Madonnas, designing summer villas, and rerouting canals. We have some details of the financial rewards that Leonardo reaped from all this. A list of payments from the royal treasurer shows that he received a total of 390 scudi between July 1508 and April 1509 – a good sum, though there is a faintly ominous downward tendency in the payments: 100, 100, 70, 50, 50, 20.[84] The larger payments of late summer 1508 are perhaps connected with the *Orfeo*. A separate account, written on the inside cover of MS F, reads, 'On the [blank] day of October 1508 I received 30 scudi.' Of this sum, he notes, he lent 13 to Salai 'to make up the dowry of his sister'.[85]

⤜ LA CREMONA ⤛

There is a small and easily overlooked list of six names in the bottom right corner of a large sheet of geometrical designs and anatomical studies at Windsor.[86] Written in Leonardo's smallest and most spidery style, it reads as follows:

loren
loren
salai
cecho
chermonese
fachino

An item below this reads '9 *tessci*' – 'nine skulls' – but it is separated by a space and does not appear to be part of the list. On the basis of its geometrical contents and references the sheet is datable to around 1509.

Four of the six names can be easily interpreted. Salai we know. Cecho or Cecco (a common diminutive of Francesco) is Melzi. One of the two Lorens is the Lorenzo who joined Leonardo's studio in Florence in 1505 and wrote home to his mother in 1507. And the last name on the list is not really a name at all, but simply a porter (*facchino*), suggesting that a journey is imminent, and that this party of six will accompany Leonardo, and look after him, on it. A plausible context would be Leonardo's trip to Pavia in late 1509 or early 1510, to attend the anatomy lectures of Marcantonio della Torre: an extended visit, accompanied by his travelling entourage.

The other two names are mysterious. I have no idea who the second Loren or Lorenzo was, but the one who interests me is 'Chermonese'. There is no doubt that this is Leonardo's spelling of Cremonese, i.e. a native of the northern Italian town of Cremona, already famed as a centre of musical-instrument-making. We find the same spelling in a note of 1499, written in Milan, in which he reminds himself to 'take the works of Leonardo Chermonese', referring to the Cremonese mathematician Leonardo di Antonio Mainardi.[87]

On the evidence of this scribbled list there is a person from Cremona in Leonardo's retinue in 1509. This person belongs in a list of six names, but may well differ from the other five in one respect – she was a woman. We have here, I believe, a sighting of a mysterious woman called Cremona, with whom Leonardo was involved in some undefined way.

*

La Cremona has appeared quite recently in Leonardo's story. Nothing was known of her until 1982, when there appeared a handsome new edition of the writings of the early-nineteenth-century Lombard artist and critic Giuseppe Bossi, edited by Roberto Paolo Ciardi. Bossi was a prodigious admirer of Leonardo who did a full-size copy of the *Last Supper*, as well as some detailed drawings which have served as evidence for later restorers. He had his detractors – among them Stendhal, who nailed him as 'a fat celebrity of the kind that passes here for a great man' – but he is still highly respected among Leonardo scholars for his monograph on the *Last Supper* (1810) and for his early edition of the Codex Leicester, based not on the original, which was by then ensconced in Norfolk, but on a complete copy of it which he tracked down in Naples. His own transcription is now in the Grand-Ducal Library at Weimar; it was purchased on the advice of Goethe, after Bossi's early death in 1815.[88] Ciardi's new edition of Bossi's writings included previously unknown manuscripts among which was the draft of an essay which had never reached print, about the representation of the passions in art. In this Bossi refers often to Leonardo, citing his masterful depiction of passions in the *Last Supper*, and then, developing an idea that in order to represent passions adequately you have to experience them yourself, he writes:

That Leonardo . . . loved the pleasures of life is proved by a note of his concerning a courtesan called Cremona, a note which was communicated to me by an authoritative source. Nor would it have been possible for him to have understood human nature so deeply, in order to represent it, without becoming, through long practice in it, somewhat tinged with human weaknesses.[89]

This is it, *tout court*. Unfortunately Bossi did not name the 'authoritative source' who communicated this 'note' to him. We cannot be sure that his information is accurate, though there is no doubt he was very knowledgeable about Leonardo, and that he had access to manuscripts since lost. It is possible his source was Carlo Amoretti, the Ambrosian librarian, who made copies of many fugitive Leonardo papers. Or perhaps Bossi was shown something in Naples, where he found that copy of the Codex Leicester, and where he also copied from a version of the 'Ambrosian apograph', a seventeenth-century collection of extracts from material in the Ambrosiana.

'Courtesan' was a designation with many shades of meaning, but Bossi essentially means a prostitute. In the Roman census of 1511–18, *cortesane* are classified in descending order of respectability as *cortesane honeste*, *cortesane putane*, *cortesane da candella e da lume*, and *cortesane da minor sorte*. The top-of-the-range 'honest' courtesans were beautiful and accomplished women who were the mistresses of the rich and powerful; the 'whore' (*putane*) courtesans were the city's street-walkers and brothel-dwellers; courtesans 'of the candle' and 'of the light' traditionally lodged in the houses of candle-makers and lantern-sellers, adjuncts to shops that were busy after dark; and beneath them all were the ragged working-girls of 'the lesser sort'. In this census are found two courtesans named Maria Cremonese; as Leonardo was himself in Rome during some of the period of the census, it is not impossible that one of them is La Cremona herself.[90] (Leonardo himself would doubtless have figured in the census records too, but they are incomplete: about half the document is missing.)

It is axiomatic that artists sometimes use prostitutes for models. The Roman courtesan Fillide Melandrone appears frequently in Caravaggio's paintings. Was La Cremona a model? One looks again at those wonderful later studies for the head of Leda at Windsor. They are very different from the first Leda drawings of *c.* 1504 – different in style, but also different because they have a particular face, which now becomes fixed as the face of Leda and is echoed closely in all the surviving paintings. The woman's elaborately braided hair, also found in the paintings, was a style associated with courtesans – see for instance the erotic engravings accompanying Aretino's *I xvi modi* (*The Sixteen Positions*).[91] The conventional date of these later Leda drawings is around 1508–9, which is just about the time that the mysterious Chermonese appears in Leonardo's entourage. The voluptuous full-frontal nudity of the *Leda* may be precisely in Bossi's mind when he speaks of Leonardo enjoying the 'pleasures' of a woman in order to learn about the passions he was depicting.

And it may even be that we have the address where Leonardo found her, for tucked away in the bottom right-hand corner of a large anatomical sheet at Windsor is the following cryptic memorandum: *'femine di messer iacomo alfeo elleda ne fabri.'* The only reasonable interpretation of the non-existent *elleda* is that it is two words run together – *è Leda* – and so, expanding the terseness of the note into a proper sentence, we get, 'Among the women of Messer Giacomo Alfeo at the Fabbri is Leda.' Alfeo is perhaps the same as the 'Messer Iacopo Alfei' who traded invective sonnets with Leonardo's friend Bellincioni – the honorific is that of a knight or a doctor of law: a prosperous society figure. The Fabbri was an area of Milan around the small city gate known as the Pustarla dei Fabbri (the Blacksmiths' Gate).[92] Pedretti suggests that the *femine* referred to were Alfeo's daughters, but the word is equally if not more likely to refer to serving-women or mistresses. This sheet is also dated to *c.* 1508–9. It contains a large anatomi-

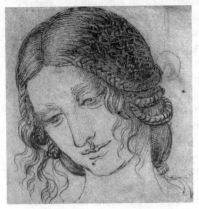

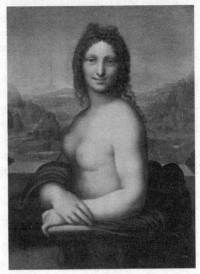

Reflections of Cremona? Study for the head of Leda (left), and the 'Nude Gioconda' at the Hermitage.

cal study of a standing female; the outline is pricked for transfer, and is indeed found transferred on another Windsor sheet – the very one that includes the name Chermonese.

These hints seem to offer a tantalizing fragment of biography for Bossi's 'courtesan called Cremona'. She was a kept woman in the house of Giacomo or Jacopo Alfei in Milan; she was used by Leonardo as the model for Leda; she became part of his entourage, and was listed as such as he prepared to leave for Pavia in 1509. A lesser-known sketch at Windsor, probably by a pupil, shows a young, partially nude woman with one hand cupping her right breast and the other touching or covering her genitals. (At least that is one reading of it: the drawing merges into a separate study of her left leg, so it is hard to be sure what the intention is.) The sheet also has anatomical studies of *c.* 1508–9 and this may possibly be another glimpse of Cremona.[93] We slide here towards that mysterious group of paintings which goes under the generic title of the 'Nude Gioconda', showing a bare-breasted woman in a pose more or less reminiscent of the *Mona Lisa*. None of the surviving examples is by Leonardo, though the best of them, known as the *Mona Vanna* (Hermitage), is plausibly attributed to Salai. It explicitly quotes the *Mona Lisa* – the chair, the loggia, the vistas of mountains beyond – but the woman's face and braided hair are closer to the *Leda*. A version now in the Accademia Carrara in Bergamo was catalogued in Milan in 1664 as a portrait by Leonardo of 'a woman believed to be a prostitute' ('*mulier creditur meretrix*').[94]

Bossi's allusion to La Cremona suggests that Leonardo had a sexual relationship with her – suggests, in fact, that Leonardo said as much in that note which 'proved' that he 'loved the pleasures of life'. It is around this time that Leonardo writes an odd and somewhat opaque sentence about sex: 'The man wants to know if the woman is pliable to the demands of his lust, and perceiving that she is and that she has a desire for him, he makes his request and puts his desire into action; and he cannot find out if he does not confess, and confessing he fucks.'[95]

'*Confessando fotte*' – there is really no other way to translate this phrase. It is the only time in all his manuscripts that he uses *fottere*. It should not be taken as an obscenity, but nor can it quite be explained away as simple vernacular frankness. He chooses the harshly emphatic and physical verb over various blander alternatives that he uses elsewhere (*usare con, fare il coito*, etc.); its sudden physicality is expressive of the overall point of the sentence, which seems to be that sexual desire begins with a vague interrogative curiosity – would she or wouldn't she? – and that merely posing the question, verbally 'confessing' the desire, tends to lead precipitously to the act itself. Is this little meditation in part autobiographical?

On an anatomical sheet of *c.* 1510 is another interesting comment: 'The act of coition and the parts of the body involved in it are of such ugliness that if it were not for the beauty of the faces and the adornments of the lovers, and the reined-in desire, nature would lose the human species.'[96] Again the language is revealing: between them beauty and desire – especially a desire that has been repressed and reined in (*frenata*) – override the inherent '*bruttura*' of heterosexual love. These comments add some credibility to that fugitive note referred to by Bossi.

It is a biographer's job to be sceptical more often than romantic, but I find no inherent difficulty in the idea that Leonardo, at the age of about fifty-seven, had some kind of relationship or entanglement with a beautiful young prostitute whose serene features and curvaceous body served as the model for the *Leda* and perhaps for the lost original of the 'Nude Gioconda'. This could be an entirely new chapter in his sex-life, or it could be that his homosexuality should not be regarded as a dogma. Leonardo had many relationships with women. The majority of his paintings are of women, and they retain a frisson of physical proximity, an atmosphere of the shared moments that went into their making. His relationships with Ginevra de' Benci, or Cecilia Gallerani, or Lisa del Giocondo – and with all the other nameless girls and women who modelled for his Madonnas – are in them.

Whatever his customs and preferences, it seems unlikely that this 'disciple of experience' who made all knowledge his province would have denied himself, at least once in his life, the sexual knowledge of a woman. This is indeed the logic of Bossi's mention of La Cremona, which is as near as we get to Leonardo's mention of her: that she taught him those heterosexual 'pleasures' without which his understanding of life would be incomplete; that he was beneficially 'tinged with human weaknesses' by this unexpected autumnal *coup de foudre*.

⤙ THE 'MEDICAL SCHOOLS' ⤚

On a page of anatomical drawings Leonardo writes, '*In questa vernata del mille 510 credo spedire tutta la notomia*' – 'In this spring of 1510 I expect to complete all the work on anatomy.'[97] This was perhaps written in Pavia, where Leonardo spent some months attending the anatomy lectures of Marcantonio della Torre, a new master in the field. Theirs was described by Vasari as a mutually beneficial partnership: 'each helped and was helped by the other.' Leonardo refers to della Torre as 'messer Marcantonio' in a note concerning a certain '*libro dell'aque*'.[98] This 'book of waters' may be about urine-diagnosis, much used by physicians at this time.

Marcantonio della Torre was in his late twenties, a Veronese. His father, Girolamo, was a celebrated professor at Padua, where Marcantonio began his career. In 1509 he migrated to Pavia, and there – probably towards the end of that year – arrived Leonardo to study with him or under him at the famous old university. Pavia was a city with pleasant memories – he had spent some days there in 1490 with Francesco di Giorgio Martini (dead since 1502), measuring up the cathedral, admiring the prancing horse of the famous *Regisole*, and watching the workmen replacing the embankment along the Ticino river which runs through the city.

We may imagine that Marcantonio gave Leonardo the place of honour in the anatomy theatre. While his assistants carved up the cadaver and he lectured on the various body parts to his students, Leonardo rapidly recorded with drawings. Among della Torre's pupils was the young Paolo Giovio, whose comments on Leonardo's anatomical work are probably based on first-hand knowledge:

He dedicated himself to the inhuman and disgusting work of dissecting the corpses of criminals in the medical schools, so that he might be able to paint the various joints and muscles as they bend and stretch according to the laws of nature. And he made wonderfully skilled scientific drawings of every part of the body, even showing the tiniest veins and the inside of bones.

These dissections done 'in the medical schools' may specifically refer to Leonardo in Pavia. In 1508 Leonardo said he had performed 'more than ten' human dissections; nine years later, in conversation with Cardinal Luigi of Aragon, he put the number at thirty. By this reckoning – his own – he performed about twenty dissections between 1508 and 1517: some of these would have been done in the 'schools' in Pavia, and some in Rome, where he speaks of his work 'at the hospital'.

Much of della Torre's written work has perished, but one piece that survives is a spirited attack on '*abbreviatori*' – in other words those who simply rehashed previous knowledge in digestible form. His particular *bête noire* was the author Mundinus (or Mondino de Liuzzi), whose *Anatomia* had been published in Pavia in 1478 and whom Leonardo himself quotes on a couple of occasions.[99] Della Torre urged a return to the original texts of Galen which Mundinus had merely paraphrased. This may be connected with Leonardo's own diatribes against these same 'abbreviators'. On a sheet of closely written notes about the action of the heart is a marginal comment: 'Make a discourse censuring scholars who are the hinderers of anatomical studies, and the abbreviators thereof.' And on the verso is another: 'Those who abbreviate such works should be called not abbreviators but expungers [*obliatori*, literally those who bring *oblio* or oblivion].' The threatened 'discourse' is probably the long tirade on another anatomical sheet:

The abbreviators of works insult both knowledge and love, seeing that the love of something is the offspring of knowledge of it ... It is true that impatience, the mother of stupidity, praises brevity, as if we did not have a whole lifetime in which to acquire complete knowledge of a single subject, such as the human body.[100]

The page contains two drawings showing a dissected heart opened up like a sliced fruit.

The shallow-brained abbreviators are an affront to Leonardo as he amasses his own painstaking portfolio of notes and drawings, whose purpose by now is clear: to create a masterwork on anatomy, suitable for publication, and offering for the first time a detailed visual description of the workings of the human body. This was Leonardo's great innovation – not only to describe anatomy with the inadequate instrument of language, as in the medieval texts on the subject, but also to display it in sharp visual detail, free of the abstractions, metaphors and general mental clutter to which language, he felt, always tended:

O writer! What words can you find to describe the whole arrangement [of the heart] as perfectly as is done in this drawing? For lack of true knowledge you describe it confusedly and convey little knowledge of the true shapes of things . . . My advice is not to trouble yourself with words unless you are speaking to the blind.[101]

He developed the technique of multiple representation, ranging from the all-round view to transparency, from cross-section to the precise *sfumatura* of the enclosing shape:

True knowledge of the shape of any body is arrived at by seeing it from different aspects. Thus to express the true shape of any limb of a man . . . I will observe the aforesaid rule, making 4 demonstrations for the 4 sides of each limb. And for the bones I will make 5, cutting them in half and showing the hollow of each of them, of which one is full of marrow, and the other spongy or empty or solid.[102]

This plurality of points of view – sometimes up to eight different angles – creates a sequence which has been described as almost cinematographic.

In the 'inhuman and disgusting' business of dissection, with its sawing of bones and its rummaging among guts, and the spurting up of pressurized human fat when the skin is incised, we find Leonardo a long way from the image of the dandified, rosewater-scented artist of his younger days. The anatomical drawings are the product of Leonardo at his most grimly empirical. In them, writes Edward Lucie-Smith, 'he puts his skill at the service of truth rather than of some ideal of beauty . . . The anatomical drawings in this sense are not beautiful at all, but represent the way in which physical beauty must, literally, be sacrificed to the kind of truth which can only be reached through butchery.'[103]

For all this, Leonardo never quite renounced his fascination with analogies – between anatomical structures and geometric forms (as can be seen in his drawings which seek to relate the tricuspid valve of the heart to semicircular 'lunes') and between human and plant organisms (as in the drawing which places a germinating bean seedling next to a study of the human trachea).[104]

Leonardo's intense collaboration with Marcantonio della Torre was abruptly ended by Marcantonio's death in 1511, at the age of twenty-nine. He died on the shores of Lake Garda, a victim of the plague which devastated the Verona region – his homeland – in that year. He was probably infected while ministering to the sick.

⤛ *CHEZ* MELZI ⤜

The death of Marcantonio della Torre in 1511 was an intellectual and perhaps a personal loss, and it was not the only one. On 10 March 1511 Charles d'Amboise died – not yet forty years old – and with him went something of Leonardo's precious security. Charles had been a personal patron, and though his successor as governor, the elegant young *chevalier* Gaston de Foix, continued to favour Leonardo, he was not a Maecenas. Leonardo was still on a stipend, paid from the King's coffers: in 1511 he received 400 lire, the same as in the previous year, but no longer bolstered by other largesses from d'Amboise.[105] He also had his income of canal dues, the 'twelve ounces of water' granted by the King in 1507. What paintings were issuing from his studio we don't know: perhaps some copies and variations of the *Leda* and the *St Anne*; perhaps some decorous Madonnas for French courtiers. The Trivulzio monument continues to occupy his sketchbook, but there is no evidence of any contract or payment. There is a new tenant at his house in the vineyard, but the arrangements are handled by Salai, whose purse opens only one way. These are dribs and drabs: a period of liberality has passed.

For some of the year, Leonardo was out of the city, once more among the rivers and mountains which fed his soul. His precise brief is not clear, but it probably had a military overtone. This was a time of renewed military tension. The bellicose Pope Julius II, having allied with the French in the subjection of Venice, had now turned against them: the foreigner must be chased out of Italy. In Rome he plotted his *Lega Santa* or Holy League: a strengthened bloc of Italian states, allied to Spain and the Habsburg empire. In Innsbruck, at the court of Maximilian, a new generation of Sforza waited in the wings.

During this period Leonardo dedicated himself to a series of fluvial studies found in Paris MS G and the Codex Atlanticus. If initially motivated by military requirements (relief-mapping, fortifications, etc.), they were soon transformed into a wide-ranging study of Lombard water-courses, particularly in the river-basins of the Adda and the Martesana. He produced nothing to match the great bird's-eye maps of Tuscany done for Cesare Borgia, but once again the collection of strategic military data is a spur to other achievements. This is a pattern with Leonardo: the alarming expansion of view from the specific to the panoramic, the mental movement equivalent to soaring.

Judging from his notes and drawings, Leonardo was in the area known as La Brianza, north-east of Milan, in 1511. He remarks on the prodigious timber of the region (I preserve his toponyms, which have the quality of a timbre or tone of voice): 'At Santa Maria a O [Hoe] in the valley of Ranvagnan [Rovagnate] in the mountains of Brigantia [Brianza] there are chestnut poles of 9 braccia and of 14 braccia; you can buy a hundred of 9 braccia for 5 lire.'[106] Rovagnate is in the southern part of the Brianza region, on the old ore-trail known as the Carraia del Ferro. Moody studies of snow-capped mountains done in red chalk on red prepared paper, with highlights in white, are from this time. Some are based on views from the Carraia del Ferro. Above one of them are some vivid notes:

Here the gravel-stones are whiter than the water except when the water foams, and the lustre of water where it is lit tends to the blue of the air, and in the shadows it tends to green, and sometimes to dark blue. The low grass which spreads across the gravel-plains has different colours according to the richness or thinness of the terrain, and so is sometimes brownish, sometimes yellow, and sometimes tending to green or greenish-yellow.[107]

These austere upland colours are found in his late landscapes – in the Louvre *Virgin and Child with St Anne* and in the Bacchic *St John*. In the foothills of Monviso he sees marble 'flawless, as hard as porphyry'.

By the end of 1511 Swiss soldiers in the service of the Holy League were menacing the northern approaches to Milan. On 16 December they fired Desio, less than 10 miles from the city walls. The conflagration was seen and recorded by Leonardo in a dramatic drawing again on brick-red prepared paper. His note is very faded, and was already so in the sixteenth century, when Melzi felt it necessary to copy it out: 'On the 16th day of December, at the fifteenth hour [10.30 a.m.] fires were set. On the 18th day of December 1511 at the fifteenth hour this second fire was set by the Swiss near Milan at the place called Dexe [Desio].'[108]

In the early spring of 1512 came the showdown between the French and the Holy League at Ravenna. In the battle on Easter Day, 11 April, Gaston de Foix, governor of Milan, was killed. The French claimed the victory, but their dominion of Lombardy hung in the balance, and by the end of the year Milan was once more the city of the Sforza. The triumphal re-entry of 29 December 1512 was headed by Massimiliano Sforza, Ludovico's legitimate son, and his half-brother Cesare, son of Cecilia Gallerani. The Moor himself had died four years earlier in his prison at Loches, but his broad powerful features are discernible in these younger scions.

*

Amid these revolutions Leonardo is nowhere to be seen: he has slipped away, as so often. Not a single dated note or record survives from the year 1512. Between the second firing of Desio on 18 December 1511 and a sectional study of an ox's heart dated 9 January 1513 the Leonardo calendar is blank. For much of this time he was holed up at the Villa Melzi, the country-house of Girolamo Melzi, father of Francesco: a handsome four-square villa (though probably pretty basic in its amenities) perched on a bluff above a wide curve of the Adda river near the village of Vaprio d'Adda, or as Leonardo – a great one for vernacular forms – writes it, 'Vavrio'. Here the illustrious house-guest finds peaceful refuge from the upheavals and rivalries and importunate commissions of the city. The villa is only about 20 miles from Milan, so we need not assume he was in complete seclusion, but there is no record of him in the city before March 1513, and it seems that this was indeed a period of rural retreat.

Here with Francesco or Cecco Melzi, now nearly twenty, he embarks on a programme of writing and sketching. There is a series of late anatomical sheets, some of them probably a working-up of notes and drawings done at speed during lectures and dissections at Pavia, and some the product of animal dissections done there at the villa. The structure and activity of the heart is a constant theme. There are water studies on the Adda. A note reads, 'Flux and reflux of water as demonstrated at the mill of Vaprio.'[109] A beautiful drawing of a small ferry-boat can still be identified with a particular stretch of the river between Vaprio and Canonica, though the ferry itself has been replaced by a bridge. The turbulent currents of the water are carefully observed, but the power of the drawing is in its snapshot of particulars: the landing-stage, the little stone bridges, the oxen standing on the deck of the raft-like *traghetto*, and one of them left lowing on the shore.[110]

While at the Villa Melzi Leonardo projected various home-improvements. A rough ground-plan shows parts of the interior and exterior of the villa; notes refer to the 'garden passage', and there are sketches of a terraced garden overlooking the river. Another folio toys with a design proposing cupolas over the corner towers and an arcaded retaining wall on the river frontage.[111] The dated anatomical drawing of 9 January 1513 has also a sketch-plan of the villa, and a note reading *'chamera della Torre da Vaveri'* ('the room in the tower at Vaprio'). Perhaps the room was his studio. On the left-hand side of the page is a sketch of a fortress on the bend of a river, with several artillery positions firing around it. This little drawing turns out to be another piece of reportage, like the fires of Desio. It shows the castle of Trezzo a few miles from Vaprio, which was bombarded by the Venetians

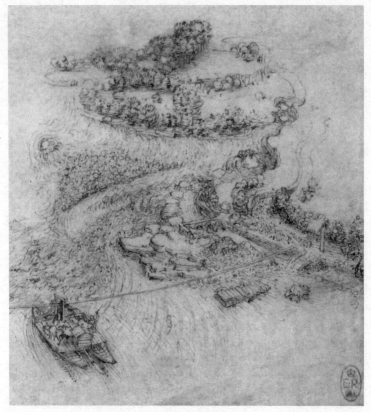

Ferry-boat on the Adda, c. 1512.

on 5 January 1513, just four days before the date at the top of the page.[112] Thus the war laps around Leonardo's country retreat, and thus coolly he notes it down in visual shorthand in a corner of the page.

⤞ PORTRAIT OF THE ARTIST AT SIXTY ⤝

During this period of seclusion on the banks of the Adda, on 15 April 1512, Leonardo reached the age of sixty. A well-known drawing at Windsor dates from around this time, since it has architectural drawings relating to Villa Melzi on the verso.[113] It shows an old bearded man in profile, weary and

449

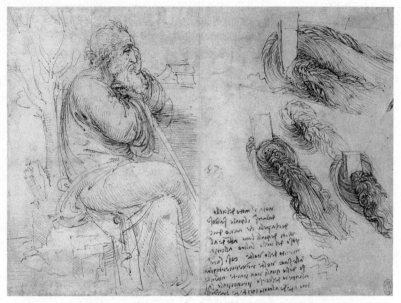

Old man and water studies, probably drawn at Vaprio.

contemplative, sitting on a rock with his legs crossed and his hand resting on a tall walking-stick. Beside him are swirling eddies of water, and for a moment you might think the old man was staring at them. This is an illusion, as there is a well-defined fold in the paper, and it is clear that the portrait of the old man and the study of the water are two distinct works, possibly done on different occasions. None the less, by intention or serendipity, they become a unified composition when the page is unfolded – a teasing, melancholy composition; a riddle or rebus whose answer is old age. What story makes sense of this alignment of old man and trilling water? Is he staring down at the water, or is he seeing it in his mind's eye? The text beneath the water studies makes explicit their visual comparison of water-currents and braided hair – 'Observe the curling motion [*moto del vello*] of the water, how like it is to that of hair' – so the story, if there is one, might be taken to include the old man's wistful reminiscence of some bygone amour. The hair looks like the fantastical tresses of the *Leda* drawings, and so the bewitching Cremonese slips into the frame, but one thinks also of the ringletted hair of the teenage Salai in which Leonardo had 'delighted'.

These are games of interpretation – but not wholly pointless ones, because the chance apposition of images points up certain characteristics which are already there in the old man: an air of nostalgia, of resigned reminiscence. Leonardo enjoyed the imagination's power to construct meanings out of randomness – he wrote of seeing the stains on a wall as beautiful landscapes – so the 'found' picture on the unfolded sheet would surely have been noticed if not intended by him.

It is sometimes said that the old man is a self-portrait, but this is misleading. He is too old to be an accurate depiction of Leonardo at sixty or sixty-one: he is nearer to the iconic image of the Turin self-portrait, which probably dates from the last years of the artist's life, though he has none of the poignant majesty of that image. He is, as Kenneth Clark says, a 'self-caricature' rather than a self-portrait: a rueful depiction of himself as decrepit, disenchanted, marginalized.[114] Leonardo has always had this half-humorous image of himself as an old man – that comic figure with the 'nutcracker' profile, gamely confronting the provocative youth opposite him – and now, suddenly, he is sixty, and feeling it.

There are three portraits which can claim to show us the true image of Leonardo at around the age of sixty, all of them the work of pupils. Two are drawings in the Windsor collection; the third is from a painting, and is here proposed for the first time as an authentic likeness of Leonardo.

The famous and beautiful profile portrait in red chalk (Plate 15), inscribed underneath in elegant contemporary capitals 'Leonardo Vinci', is considered the 'most objective and accurate portrait of the master to survive', and is the prototype of the profile portrait which became the standard image of Leonardo in the mid sixteenth century (in the woodcuts used by Vasari and Giovio, for example).[115] It is plausibly attributed to Francesco Melzi. It is a very accomplished drawing, and almost certainly later than Melzi's earliest dated drawing of mid-1510. The long wavy hair falls with a suggestion of lankness, and is apparently now grey or silvery – one cannot tell, because the chalk is red, but that is the impression given. But it is still profuse and vigorous, as is the bushy beard. The superbly modelled profile shows both refinement and a certain strength; the nose is long, the eye steady, the lips faintly feminine, the moustache neatly combed. It is the profile of a man who was beautiful in youth (as early accounts of Leonardo insist) and who is still strikingly handsome. He is not yet the old man of the Turin self-portrait; indeed, he is noticeably free of wrinkles. I would say this is a portrait of Leonardo at around sixty, done by Melzi at Vaprio d'Adda in 1512 or 1513. Unusually for a drawing in the Windsor collection the sheet has been clipped at the corners for mounting, and the reverse shows signs of

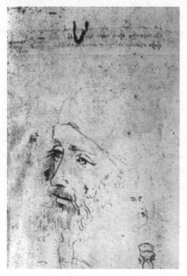

Portrait sketch of Leonardo, c. 1510.

having been attached to a support. It may well have been the portrait seen by Vasari when he visited Melzi at Vaprio in 1566, noting that 'Francesco cherishes and preserves these papers as relics of Leonardo, together with the portrait of that artist of such happy memory.'

Less well known and more elusive is a small pen-and-ink sketch on a sheet containing studies of horses' legs.[116] This is almost certainly a portrait of Leonardo by one of his pupils (the shading is right-handed, so it is not a self-portrait). The face is in three-quarter profile to the left, but the features compare closely to those of the red-chalk profile. The studies of horses' legs may be connected to Leonardo's project for the Trivulzio monument, c. 1508–11; the portrait sketch is the other way up from the horse studies, though which was on the paper first is impossible to say. Leonardo looks a couple of years younger than in the Melzi profile, so a date of about 1510 would be plausible. Interestingly, the sketch shows him wearing some kind of hat, minimally suggested by the wavery line across his forehead and the cross-hatched shadow beyond his right cheek. Most of the sixteenth-century portraits of Leonardo, though undoubtedly derived from the Melzi profile, show him in a hat. In the woodcut portrait in Vasari's *Lives* he wears a *berretta* with ear-flaps, which is perhaps the kind of headgear suggested in the Windsor sketch. This detail of the Leonardo 'image' may derive from lost portrait-drawings of which this Windsor sketch is a vestigial relic.

I certainly suspect the existence of a drawing showing the features of the Windsor sketch in reverse – i.e. in three-quarter profile to the right. It can be reconstructed simply enough by tracing a reproduction of the Windsor sketch through to the other side of the paper (Plate 25). Pupils frequently used reverse tracings and mirror images, thus producing two models from a single drawing; this technique is often found in Leonardo's own drawings.[117] And this reverse version of the Windsor sketch is not quite lost – its features are precisely preserved in the bearded figure of St Jerome in a painting by Leonardo's Milanese pupil Giovanni Pietro Rizzoli or Giampietrino (Plate 26). Apart from the opposite direction of the three-quarter profile, the Jerome resembles the Windsor sketch in every respect – the line of the nose, the moody eyes, the beard, even the line of the hat (the cardinal's hat traditionally worn by St Jerome) and the hood.

The painting is an altarpiece of the *Madonna and Child with St Jerome and St John the Baptist*. Giampietrino painted it in 1515; it was commissioned by the Jeromite order for the church at Ospedaletto Lodigiano, near the Lombard city of Lodi, and it hangs in the church still.[118] It is visibly influenced by Leonardo, as was all Giampietrino's work. The Christ-child playing with a lamb quotes from the Louvre *Virgin and Child with St Anne*, and the face of the Madonna is closely modelled on the London *Virgin of the Rocks*. These are both works from Leonardo's second Milanese period, when Giampietrino was attached to his studio. As we have seen, Giampietrino's own version of the kneeling *Leda* was painted over an underdrawing of part of the *St Anne* group, now visible only by X-ray. The Windsor sketch can be dated to around 1510, which is broadly the time of the Louvre *St Anne* and the versions of *Leda* – the time of Giampietrino's involvement in the workshop. The sketch is not in itself a significant drawing, just a briefly elaborated doodle. It is significant because it is an eyewitness portrait of Leonardo, and because it is mirrored in the *St Jerome* at the Ospedaletto Lodigiano, which is therefore also a refracted portrait of him. The probable link between them is a lost drawing of Leonardo by Giampietrino. It was the source of the Windsor sketch, which is a brief copy of it in reverse, and it was used by Giampietrino as the model or cartoon for the features of St Jerome in the Lodigiano altarpiece – a tribute to his old master, by then down in Rome, but seen in the painting as he would have been seen in Milan, nearing sixty: the beard flecked with silver, the chiselled face, the intensity of the eyes, the fondness for hats.

PART EIGHT

Last Years
1513–1519

Observe the flame of a candle and consider its beauty. Blink your eye and look at it again. What you see now was not there before, and what was there before is not there now. Who is it who rekindles this flame which is always dying?

Paris MS F, fol. 49v.

Leonardo was briefly in Milan in early 1513: a tentative appearance, perhaps, uncertain how the new duke, Massimiliano, would view one who had
collaborated so thoroughly with his father's enemies. On 25 March he is
mentioned, in a register at the Duomo, as living or lodging with one
Prevostino Viola.[1] Around this time he notes down the name of Barbara
Stampa, the daughter of Filippo Stampa and the wife of Carlo Atellani (or
della Tela), both of whom were loyal Sforza servants and now much in
favour. She ran a lively salon at the luxurious Atellani house near the Grazie,
later frescoed by Bernardino Luini. Their back garden shared a boundary
with Leonardo's vineyard: prosperous, cultivated neighbours. Another
family of Sforza loyalists were the Crivelli: 'Ask the wife of Biagino Crivelli
why the capon nurtures and hatches the eggs of the hen if he is made drunk.'[2]
For the disciple of experience no question is too small. But of any activities
in Milan we know nothing, and it is probable he was mostly at Vaprio.

News, meanwhile, filtered up from Florence, where the pendulum of
political fortunes had swung back to the Medici, represented by the new
generation – Giovanni and Giuliano, the two surviving sons of Lorenzo,
and their cousin Giulio. In the summer of 1512, after eighteen years in
exile, they returned to govern Florence: a bloodless coup, though backed
by the presence of troops in Prato. On 1 September, Gonfalonier Soderini
left by one of the city's gates, on his way to exile on the Dalmatian
coast, and Giuliano de' Medici entered by another. He came in on foot,
with no military escort, dressed in the traditional Florentine *lucco* or
gown. He went neither to the Palazzo Vecchio, nor to the Palazzo Medici,
but to the house of one the Medici supporters within the government,
Antonfrancesco degli Albizzi. It was a masterpiece of political understatement: the modest return of a Florentine citizen by the consensus of his fellow

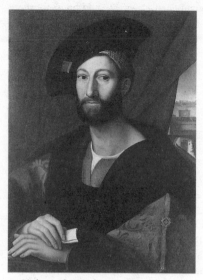

Giuliano de' Medici in a portrait by or after Raphael.

citizens. The arrival of the head of the family, Giuliano's elder brother, the obese, scholarly, politically acute Giovanni, now a powerful cardinal in Rome and already tipped as the next pope, was less modest – he entered the city with a troop of 1,500 soldiers, looking every inch a *magnifico*. But there were no executions, no expropriations; power was transferred with quiet efficiency, like a bill of exchange at the Medici bank.

The demise of Pope Julius II completed the Medici game-plan, and Giovanni hastened back down to Rome, where on 11 March 1513 the conclave of cardinals duly elected him Pope Leo X. Giuliano was left in charge of Florence, but the new Pope, doubting his capricious brother's capacity to deal with the Florentine factions, decided to replace him with their malleable young nephew Lorenzo di Piero. Recalled to Rome, Giuliano was loaded with new titles to assuage any resentment he might feel. He became Prince of Parma, Piacenza and Modena, but declined the dukedom of Urbino, recognizing the legitimacy of Francesco della Rovere, nephew of the late Pope, who had been a friend to him in his exile. He was also named gonfalonier to the papal army (as Cesare Borgia had been during the papacy of Alexander VI), a position which obliged him to be based permanently in Rome.

And now from Giuliano de' Medici in Rome, sometime in the summer of 1513, comes an invitation to Leonardo to join him there, in this new Medicean court in the Eternal City.

On the opening page of a new notebook, Paris MS E, Leonardo writes, 'I left Milan for Rome on 24 September 1513, in the company of Giovan, Francesco de Melzi, Salai, Lorenzo and Il Fanfoia.' The first and last names have caused puzzlement. 'Giovan' could be either Giovanni Antonio Boltraffio or Giampietrino, though there is no evidence that either went to Rome; or he could be an unknown *garzone*; or it could be (since there are no commas in the original) that he is not a separate person at all, and that Leonardo has, unusually, used both of Melzi's forenames, Giovanni Francesco. 'Il Fanfoia', found nowhere else in Leonardo's papers, remains mysterious. There is a known forename, Fanfulla, of which it may be a dialect variation; or perhaps it is a descriptive nickname. 'Fanfoia' is not a word in its own right, but is suggestive of *fanfano*, a babbling; *fanfaro*, a musical march (whence 'fanfare'); and indeed *fanfarone*, a braggart – a group of words connoting noise and showiness. Could it possibly be another nickname of the many-monikered Tommaso Masini, a.k.a. Gallozzolo, Zoroastro, Alabastro, Indovino, et al?

The date, at least, is precise. Leonardo and his entourage left Milan on 24 September 1513, more than seven years after he had arrived from Florence with the intention of staying three months – a statistic which speaks volumes about his deep attachment to the city (and to its seriously wealthy dukes and governors): he spent, in all, more than a third of his life there. The landscapes of his paintings, imprinted with reminiscence of the Tuscan hill-country of his youth, are bathed in the more northerly and subtle light of Lombardy, which at his departure in September is already beginning to soften, as the grapes ripen in his vineyard and the evening comes in a little earlier than expected.

They journeyed south-east down the Via Emilia – through Lodi, Piacenza, Parma, Reggio Emilia, Modena and Bologna, and thence south through the Apennine mountains. He probably did not stay long in Florence. A note of expenses reads, '13 ducats for 500 pounds from here [Milan] to Rome' – this is the carriage fee for his luggage all the way to Rome.[3] This quarter-ton of personal effects would include the *Mona Lisa*, the *Virgin and Child with St Anne* and the *Leda*, the portfolios of drawings and sketches, the majority of the great anatomical folios, all of the notebooks we know and a great many we do not, the 116 books of the Madrid list (minus a few dispersed, plus some acquired since), as well as such pieces of studio equipment, scientific instrumentation, furniture, clothing and personal mementoes that escaped, for reasons of value or sentiment, the injunction to 'sell what you cannot take with you'.

He may have stopped long enough to see a few friends, and to attend to matters listed in a memorandum in the Codex Atlanticus.[4] Among unidentified names – a shoemaker called Francesco, a stationer called Giorgio – is a query: 'whether the priest Alessandro Amadori is still living'. This is an old acquaintance: the brother of Leonardo's first stepmother, Albiera. He is mentioned twice in the list: Leonardo is keen to see him. He must have known him from childhood; they had met again in 1506, when the priest brought him a letter from Isabella d'Este. Albiera was herself only sixteen years older than Leonardo, so Alessandro may have been quite close to him in age. As noted earlier, he may well be the 'uncle' who owned Leonardo's lost cartoon of *Adam and Eve*, an early Florentine work. Vasari, writing in the 1540s, says this uncle had 'not long ago' presented the cartoon to Ottaviano de' Medici. If this is Alessandro, we can be glad to note that the answer to Leonardo's query of 1513 is – yes.

Among those he did not meet in Florence was Niccolò Machiavelli. Too closely associated with the Soderini government, Machiavelli was dismissed from his secretarial posts in November 1512. The following February he was implicated in an anti-Medici plot fomented by Pietro Paolo Boscoli and Agostino Capponi, whom he very nearly followed to the execution block. Imprisoned and tortured in the Bargello, he was exiled to his small estates at Sant'Andrea in Percussina, where he took somewhat reluctantly to the life of an impoverished country squire, and between coppicing woodlands, snaring thrushes and playing backgammon in the local inn, sat down to write his famous study of power-politics, *The Prince* (or, to give it its correct title, *Dei principati – Of Principalities*), first conceived ten years earlier during those fraught missions to the Borgia and now distilled and concentrated by the bitterness of more recent experiences. He intended to dedicate it to Giuliano de' Medici, hoping that the gesture would revive his shipwrecked fortunes – a hope perhaps encouraged by news that his former friend Leonardo da Vinci was now entering Giuliano's service.[5]

Leonardo was probably in Rome by the end of October 1513. If he accomplished all the tasks on the memo-list mentioned above, he arrived with a pair of 'blue spectacles'. I am tempted to say he arrived *wearing* a pair of blue spectacles – a marvellous image: Leonardo in shades – though they were probably more in the nature of goggles, intended for use in the strange metallurgical experiments which are one of the features of the Roman sojourn.

Handsome, feckless, somewhat mystically inclined, Giuliano di Lorenzo de' Medici had inherited his father's personal charms but none of his political dynamism. Born in 1479, he was named after his assassinated uncle. We see him at the age of about five in the beautiful fresco by Domenico Ghirlandaio in Santa Maria Novella: a small brown-haired boy turning to look at the painter, he is standing next to the gaunt and slightly dishevelled figure of Agnolo Poliziano, the poet of *Orfeo*, who was tutor to Lorenzo's children. Behind him is his brother Giovanni, seen in the fresco as a round-faced boy with lank blondish hair, the features already heralding those of the jowly pontiff painted by Raphael some thirty-five years later.

Giuliano was fifteen when the tide turned against the Medici in 1494. In exile he was a guest of the Duke of Urbino and the Marquess of Mantua. As we have seen, it is possible he met Leonardo in Venice in 1500, and possible he admired the unfinished portrait of Isabella d'Este which Leonardo was working on, and possible he asked him to paint a similar portrait of Lisa Gherardini, whom he had known and fancied in Florence. A lot of possibles, but they would explain why Leonardo, standing in front of the *Mona Lisa* in France in 1517, described it as a portrait of a 'certain Florentine lady, done from life at the instigation of the late Magnifico Giuliano de' Medici'. The alternative explanation is that it was 'instigated' by Giuliano when Leonardo was with him in Rome, and that it portrays one of his mistresses of the period, but none of these later pretenders to the seat on the loggia is at all convincing. Nevertheless the painting was physically there in Rome, and has no doubt its Roman phase of retouchings and recoatings as it slowly metamorphoses into the Louvre icon. And it is perhaps at this time, within the ambit of Giuliano's patronage, that the painting's flighty cousin – the so-called 'Nude Gioconda' – makes her appearance in Leonardo's studio.

Giuliano is among the interlocutors in Castiglione's *The Courtier*, nominally based on conversations at a gathering of 'noble and talented persons' at the castle of Urbino in March 1507. The book was written after the death of the Duke, Guidobaldo da Montefeltro, the following year, and was fastidiously polished and redrafted until its publication in 1528, becoming in the process a nostalgic vision of the perfect Renaissance house-party. Also included in the conversations are Pietro Bembo, son of Ginevra de' Benci's courtly lover Bernardo, and Dom Miguel da Silva, the Portuguese prelate who was later one of Zoroastro's patrons in Rome. Castiglione dedicated the book to da Silva, recalling some members of the Urbino circle who had since died, among them Giuliano de' Medici, 'whose goodness, nobility and courtesy the world deserved to enjoy longer'. It is likely that da Silva and Giuliano were friends in the Rome of Leo X, where da Silva was for many years Portuguese ambassador, and it may be through this connection that Zoroastro gained his patronage.

No one has anything worse to say of Giuliano than that he was a bit of a dreamer. As commander of the papal troops he was ineffectual. He was a courtier more than a soldier, and a dilettante scholar more than a courtier. Vasari describes him as 'a great student of natural philosophy, and especially of alchemy' – the latter brings Zoroastro to mind again, and has a bearing on some of Leonardo's experiments undertaken in Rome. Raphael's portrait of him, mentioned by Vasari, was painted around this time; the version in the Metropolitan Museum, New York, is either the original or a contemporary copy of it. A similar image of him is from the workshop – or indeed Medici image-factory – of Agnolo Bronzino, done in the late 1550s. Both works show Giuliano much as he was when Leonardo entered his service in late 1513: a dark, bearded man in his mid-thirties, handsome in a slightly decadent way, a man of scholarly refinement and precarious health, not entirely fitted for the new mantles of power now thrust upon him.

This new or renewed link with Giuliano brings Leonardo back into the Medici fold, healing whatever resentments he might have harboured from his dealings with Lorenzo de' Medici thirty years previously. According to the contemporary testimony of Benedetto Varchi, Giuliano treated Leonardo *'piu tosto da fratello che da compagno'* – 'more like a brother than a friend'.[6]

An emblem of Giuliano's recorded by Paolo Giovio may be a Leonardo invention. It is a version of the *broncone medoceo* or Medici stump, which shows a cut trunk of laurel growing new shoots, but the enigmatic motto – 'GLOVIS' – is not found in other versions. Read backwards it suggests *'si volge'*, meaning one makes a turn, a change of direction, which recalls another Leonardo emblem-motto, 'Thoughts turn towards hope.'[7] An apt motto for the reascendant Medici of 1513, and perhaps for Leonardo in Rome, in a mood of optimism: another fresh start.

⇥ AT THE BELVEDERE ⇤

On 1 December 1513 one of the Pope's architects, Giuliano Leno, listed various building-works to be carried out in the Vatican precincts, among them 'things to be done at Belvedere in the rooms of Messer Lionardo da Vinci'.[8] The Villa Belvedere, built some thirty years previously by Pope Innocent VIII, was essentially the Pope's summer palace, cool and elevated and surrounded by beautiful gardens. Judging from the list of 'things to be done' Leonardo had not yet taken up residence there by 1 December. The work required was not major, and we may perhaps imagine him installed by the end of the year in what is to be, essentially, his last Italian home. The list gives us a glimpse of the layout of Leonardo's Roman apartments. Among the requirements are:

- pinewood partitions, one of which is specified as for the kitchen
- framework for a ceiling to create a loft

- the widening of one window
- paving-tiles
- four dining-tables of poplar, on trestles
- eight stools and three benches
- a chest
- a counter for grinding colours on

The dining arrangements suggest a quite numerous household, and indeed we will find those seats filled by some rather dubious new assistants.

Leonardo had made a couple of brief visits to Rome, but had never lived there before. The city had a population around 50,000, much fewer than Milan's. It was famed both for its antiquities and for its grandiose novelties: chief among the city's architects was Leonardo's old friend Bramante, whose projects demolished whole neighbourhoods – earning him the *soprannome* 'Maestro Ruinante'. It was also notorious for the corruption and venality of the papal court – 'that sewer of iniquity', as Lorenzo de' Medici called it in a famous letter to his son the future pope. The court of Leo X had none of the Caligulan excesses attributed to the Borgia papacy, but the tone of Vatican life remained lascivious. There were some 7,000 prostitutes in the city, many in brothels licensed by the papal authorities; syphilis was epidemic, and Benvenuto Cellini was not being flippant when he described it as 'a kind of illness very common among priests'.[9] Something of this air of corruption seeps into a strange drawing known as the *Angelo incarnato*, of which more later.

But amid all this the Belvedere was a little world apart, and there is a reclusive air to Leonardo in Rome. The palace was quite new, but the gardens in which it stood were huge, ancient and half-wild. Alberti had drawn up plans for a new, classicized garden, with porticoes and curved flights of steps, and grottoes containing fountains and 'laughable statues' ('laughable' because odd or strange, as was suitable for grottoes: hence 'grotesque').[10] But Alberti's plans were not realized, and the gardens remained a dense swathe of woods, orchards, fish-ponds, fountains, statues and hidden pergolas, stretching down the slopes to the valley at the foot of the Belvedere. It is perhaps here, more than in the city or at the court, that we glimpse the gaunt, bearded figure communicating with 'Nature, the mistress of all masters' – or if not with her then at least with one of the gardeners, as appears from an anecdote from Vasari:

When the gardener of the Belvedere found a very odd-looking lizard, Leonardo attached wings to its back with a mixture of quicksilver; they were made from scales stripped from other lizards and they quivered as it walked along. He gave the creature eyes, horns and beard, and then he tamed it, and kept it in a box to show his friends and frighten the life out of them.[11]

Whether or not authentic the story conveys an imagery of strangeness and sorcery which attaches to Leonardo in Rome. In 1520 a similar creature was reported by Miguel da Silva as being in the possession of Zoroastro – 'a serpent with four legs, which we take for a miracle; Zoroastro believes that some gryphon has carried it through the air from Libya.'

A note from the Belvedere on a summer evening in 1514: 'Finished on 7 July at the 23rd hour at Belvedere, in the studio provided for me by the Magnifico.'[12] What was finished was some geometrical equations, an abiding interest. On another sheet Leonardo writes, 'I now begin my book *De ludo geometrico* [*On Geometric Games*], in which I show further ways to infinity.' Long, obsessive-looking sequences of geometrical 'lunes' – variable figures formed by two arcs of circle enclosing space – seem to belong with these infinity-games.[13]

Of his social life, if any, we know nothing. In Rome at this time were many men he had known – Bramante and Michelangelo; Raphael, whose spell in Florence in 1505 had brought him into contact with Leonardo; the courtly author Castiglione; and even his old pupil Atalante Migliorotti, now employed as a superintendent of works at St Peter's.[14] But their names do not trouble the pages of his notebooks, in which one finds the mesmeric dance of the lunes, and experiments in acoustics, and notes of a trip to Monte Mario in search of fossils, and fragmentary accounts expressed in Roman giuli: 'Salai: 20 giuli; for the house: 12 giuli', and 'Lorenzo owes 4 giuli for the hay that was bought for Christmas.'[15]

In the late summer of 1514 Leonardo accompanied Giuliano on a brief trip north. He records his presence in Parma '*alla Campana*' (i.e. at an inn called The Bell) on 25 September, and 'on the banks of the Po near Sant'Angelo' two days later.[16]

Towards the end of the year comes a pleasant note of family reconciliation. There was another da Vinci in Rome in 1514 – Leonardo's half-brother Giuliano, second son of Ser Piero and the one singled out by Leonardo as the leader of the *fratellastri* during the legal battles of 1507–8. Giuliano, now in his mid-thirties – a husband, a father, and of course a notary – was apparently in Rome to pursue some kind of benefice which he felt was owed to him, and doubtless his rapprochement with Leonardo was not without ulterior motive: contacts were everything in this world, and Leonardo had them. A letter from Leonardo to the papal adviser Niccolò Michelozzi recounts his futile efforts on Giuliano's behalf:

My dear Messer Niccolò, whom I honour as an elder brother. Shortly after I took leave of Your Lordship I went to look in the register to see if my brother's name had been entered. The book was not there, and I was sent hither and thither before I found it. Finally I went to His Lordship the Datary and I said to him that I hoped His Lordship might ask tomorrow for the supplication to be read and registered. His Lordship answered that this would be very difficult, and that the supplication required many things which could not easily be done, seeing that the benefice was for such a small sum, and that if it had been something more substantial it would have been registered without such difficulty.[17]

Thus drily Leonardo records the realities of papal bureaucracy: if the benefice had been bigger the matter could have been dealt with, presumably with a percentage to oil the deal. The papal datary (the officer responsible for registering and dating papal bulls) who replied so unhelpfully to Leonardo's enquiries was a Monsignor Baldassare Turini, a fellow Tuscan, from the hill-town of Pescia. He seems to have valued Leonardo's skills, if not the size of his brother's benefices, for according to Vasari he commissioned two small paintings from him.[18]

The eventual outcome of Giuliano da Vinci's supplication is not recorded, but we have a more human document in the form of a letter to him from his wife, Alessandra, in Florence.[19] The letter, dated 14 December 1514, is mostly about her problems with a goldsmith named Bastiano – 'There's a chain he lent you and he's going crazy about it . . . I don't know what chain he is talking about but I think it's the one I'm wearing round my neck' – but she appends a long and rather poignant postscript, which includes a greeting to Leonardo:

Ser Giuliano: La Lessandra your wife is very sick, and is almost dead with the pain. I forgot to ask you to remember me to your brother Lionardo, a most excellent and singular man. Everyone knows that La Lessandra has lost her wits and has become a woman of shadows. And above all else I commend and recommend and completely recommend myself to you, and keep in mind that Florence is just as beautiful as Rome, especially as your wife and your daughter are here.

This is a sweet letter, with its story of the gold chain, and its loneliness, and its salutations to her '*eccellentissimo e singularissimo*' brother-in-law Leonardo. The fact that it remains among Leonardo's papers must surely mean that Giuliano gave it to him, at some meeting between them in Rome in the winter of 1514–15.

Leonardo used the empty space at the bottom of the letter for some notes on geometry, and on the verso he wrote, 'My book is in the hands of Messer Battista dell'Aquila, private steward to the Pope.' Below this are the words '*De Vocie*' – 'On the Voice' – which may be the title of the book which dell'Aquila now has. The phrase recurs in Leonardo's Roman notebook: '*De vocie* – why a swift wind passing through the pipes makes a shrill sound.'[20] There is material on vocal acoustics scattered through the later anatomical notes. Is this treatise or 'book' in dell'Aquila's hands because the papal steward wants the pleasure of reading it, or do we discern a note of official surveillance, perhaps connected with the controversy over Leonardo's anatomical studies in 1515?

On 9 January 1515 Leonardo writes, 'The Magnifico Giuliano left Rome at dawn to go and marry a wife in Savoy; and on the same day occurred the death of the King of France.'[21] In fact Louis XII had died ten days earlier, so this perhaps tells us the day that Leonardo learned of his death. Giuliano de' Medici's bride was Philiberte of Savoy, the aunt of the new king, François I: it was decidedly a marriage of political alliance.

Going into France, Giuliano seems to have taken with him some Leonardian designs, for at Lyon on 12 July 1515, a 'mechanical lion' designed by Leonardo was the pièce de résistance of a pageant in honour of François. This mechanism utilized the same principles as the automata or robots of the 1490s (which in turn embodied ideas already explored in the late 1470s). An account of it is given by G. P. Lomazzo: 'One day, before François I, King of France, he [Leonardo] set in motion a Lion, made with wonderful artifice; it moved from its place in the hall and when it came to a halt its breast opened, and was full of lilies and other flowers.'[22] The lion is an old symbol of Florence; the lilies are the fleurs-de-lis of France. Thus Leonardo's automaton enacts, in a banqueting-hall in Lyon, the political amity between the Medici and the new French king. Leonardo was not there himself, however, as Lomazzo's account might imply.

⤞ THE BAPTIST AND THE BACCHUS ⤝

'The story goes' – says Vasari –

that when the Pope commissioned a work from him, Leonardo immediately set to work distilling oils and plants to make the varnish, at which Pope Leo exclaimed, '*Oimè, costui non e per far nulla, da che comincia a pensare alla fine innanzi il principio dell'opera*' ['Alas this man will never do anything, because he is already thinking of the end before he has even begun the work'].

This expresses well the Pope's prickly relationship with Leonardo (though he was not the first of Leonardo's customers to express such exasperation), and the departure of Giuliano at the beginning of 1515 introduces a note of uncertainty into Leonardo's status at Rome. It will be a troubled year.

It is possible that the work commissioned by this Florentine pope was a painting of Florence's patron saint, St John the Baptist. This is only a guess, but Leonardo's half-length *St John* (Plate 28) is certainly a late painting – quite possibly his last – and it may have begun in this way. If so the Pope's contemptuous comment shows also his limited understanding of Leonardo's art, for it was precisely those subtle distillations of 'oils and plants' which gave the *St John* its lustrous, multi-layered picture surface, its aura of mystery and evanescence. Among the retorts and alembics of the Belvedere studio Leonardo contemplates his 'capricious mixtures' (as Vasari calls them), and contemplates the shape and mood of the painting he will create with them. The patron is impatient – '*Oimè!*' – not perceiving that the master is already at work.

There are actually two late paintings of St John the Baptist by Leonardo, both now in the Louvre. There is the half-length, dark-grounded *St John*, mentioned above, and there is the larger painting of him full length, sitting in a landscape, which it is convenient to call *St John in the Desert*, though by virtue of certain additions to the figure – apparently added long after Leonardo's death – the painting is often referred to as *St John with the Attributes of Bacchus* (page 473). There is not a scrap of documentation for either of these paintings. All we know is that one of them – a '*San Iohanne Baptista giovane*' – was seen by Antonio de Beatis in France in 1517, and that both were in the French royal collection by the seventeenth century. The *St John in the Desert* may be the earlier of the two: the tree in the landscape can be compared to the tree in the Louvre *Virgin and Child with St Anne*. The date-range for these late works is broad, but in its beauty and mystery the half-length *St John* seems more than any of them an enigmatic final statement, or indeed a final question. According to Beatis, Leonardo was no longer painting in France, but one cannot quite imagine a painting he had with him standing or hanging in his studio without an occasional touch here, or another layer of varnish there, from the master or his pupils, and so the period of 'composition' – if the activity is not too attenuated for this word – would extend on into the last years and days of his life.

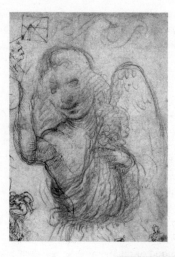

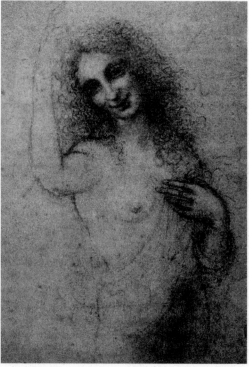

Angelic transformations. Pupil's study of the announcing angel on a sheet of c. 1504–5 (left), and the full-frontal Angelo incarnato of the Roman years.

Like all these late works, the *St John* is the final stage of a long process of definition and redefinition. The earliest recorded stage is a small sketch at Windsor which is on a sheet containing studies for the *Battle of Anghiari* and is therefore datable to *c.* 1504-5.[23] Compositionally the *St John* has its roots in that Florentine period in which other late works like the *Leda* and the *Virgin and Child with St Anne* also germinated. The Windsor sketch actually shows an announcing angel – the angel Gabriel – rather than St John, but the pose is the same, with the right forearm pointing vertically upward, and the left hand pressed against the chest. The sketch is in the hand of a pupil (Salai? Ferrando Spagnolo?), but it is probably Leonardo who has corrected the angle of the right arm. The composition is precisely reflected in a painting now in Basle, by an unknown 'follower' of Leonardo, and in a drawing by Baccio Bandinelli, the Florentine sculptor best known for his public spats with Michelangelo and Cellini, and for his statue of *Hercules and Cacus* outside the Palazzo Vecchio.[24] Both these later versions combine the face of the half-length *St John* with the particular pose of the angel in the Windsor sketch. There are also studies of that left hand: one in the Codex Atlanticus is by a pupil; the other – a superb study in red chalk at the Venice Accademia – is Leonardo's.[25]

The most extraordinary variant of this figure is a small drawing on blue paper, rediscovered in 1991, having been sequestered for years in the private collection of a 'noble German family'.[26] In this the 'angel' – in the same pose, but no longer with a wing to identify it as an angel – is shown with a disturbingly ambiguous face, a pronounced female nipple, and, beneath the gauzy veil of the cloth which he holds in his left hand, a large erection. (An effort was made at some point to erase this last feature, resulting in a grey-brown discoloration around it: this is the original colour of the paper showing through the blue preparation of the surface.) The drawing is datable to *c.* 1513-15 – the Rome years – and is probably contemporary with *St John*.

This troubling image, now generally called the *Angelo incarnato* – the 'Angel made flesh' – caused a sensation when it was first exhibited in New York in 1991, and has since exercised scholars and indeed psychiatrists. André Green writes:

Here one meets all the contradictions, not only between feminine and masculine, but between a certain ecstasy and a sadness tending almost to anguish. The mouth is too sexy and childish, closed and half-open, dumb and about to speak. The curling hair is an attribute which may be of either sex. We feel, in short, uneasy and this is doubtless further provoked by the erection which can be seen behind the veil. There is perhaps something satanic behind this angelic being, but we cannot say if our anxieties of interpretation reflect our own difficulty in finding an overall coherence in the work, or if they stem from the incompatibility of heavenly aspirations and orgasmic pleasures.[27]

The art-therapist Laurie Wilson sees 'the perverse ugliness' of the drawing as arising from 'difficulties in representing or controlling negative feelings' – a product, one might gloss, of sexual guilt.[28] There is a challenge in such ugliness – an invitation to respond to the drawing as a kind of specialist transsexual pornography. The angel has become an unsavoury-looking catamite fished up from the lower reaches of the Roman flesh-market. The angelic salutation is travestied as the prostitute's come-on; the hollows of the face suggest sickness, which in turn suggests syphilis; and there is a needy, pleading look in those unpleasantly large, doll-like eyes. (Curious how the big eyes are already a feature of the pupil's angel-sketch of *c.* 1505: this is a part of the initial conception.)

There is some background to this, because there had always existed a current of imagery – scurrilous or symbolic, according to how it was presented – referring to the Annunciation as a kind of impregnation of the Virgin by the angel Gabriel, who brings the Holy Spirit which 'quickens' her womb. The erotic interpretation of this is found in such risqué works as Pucci's *Queen of the Orient*, which Leonardo knew and quoted from, in which a young man's prodigious member is said to be a gift from the angel Gabriel: 'She said: "My love where did you get that thing?" And he replied: "The Angel Gabriel by the will of God manifested it to me". "No wonder" (said she) "that it's such a beauty if it's come straight down from heaven." '[29] The blasphemous idea of the Annunciation as an erotic encounter is heard in Elizabethan England, where the Earl of Oxford, a louche young aristocrat who had travelled extensively in Italy, liked to scandalize his dinner-guests by saying that 'Joseph was a wittol [i.e. cuckold]', and where Christopher Marlowe, that great Elizabethan exponent of Machiavelli, was reported as saying that 'the angel Gabriel was bawd to the Holy Ghost because he brought the salutation to Mary.'[30]

The 'salutation' to Mary is precisely expressed by the raised right hand in the sketches and drawings of the announcing angel which we find from *c.* 1505, and in the *Angelo incarnato* the gesture is given this tarnishing overtone of prostitution which is part of sixteenth-century atheistic lore.

All this seems to recall that cryptic note which Leonardo wrote, and then crossed out, on a sheet now in the Codex Atlanticus. The sheet is also datable to around 1505, as there is once more a small *Anghiari* horse on the verso. The words Leonardo wrote are 'When I made a Christ-child you put me in prison, and now if I show Him grown up you will do worse to me.' The first part of the sentence has been interpreted as referring to his run-in with the Officers of the Night in 1476, which possibly involved a painting or terracotta featuring Jacopo Saltarelli as the youthful Christ, and the second part to some later proposed work which Leonardo feared would prove even more scandalous. The subtext of this is the troublesome adjacency of homosexuality and spirituality in his depiction of angels and young Christs: the models he used were sexually desirable young men, and a certain homoerotic charge is present in all his angels (the *Annunciation*, the *Virgin of the Rocks*, the San Gennaro terracotta) and is most luridly incarnated in the full-frontal *Angelo incarnato*.

The relationship between this angel and the Louvre *St John* is paralleled in other late works – compositional variations on a theme, as in the different positionings of Leda or the shifting group of the St Anne ensemble – but in the *St John* the variation is a kind of concealment, almost a bowdlerizing. The right arm no longer extends forward, exposing the front of the angel or saint; it crosses over his chest, concealing that budding adolescent breast, and also concealing those graceful fingers of the left hand (though it remains precisely the same left hand in the part that is visible). Further concealment is provided by the cloak of animal fur, and indeed by the positioning of the lower edge of the painting, which cuts the body off above the hips. The hollow-eyed visage of the *Angelo incarnato* has transformed into a lustrous, glowing face framed in rich auburn curls: the androgyny of the figure is expressed without being explicitly specified, as in the drawing. In retreating from the sexually specific, Leonardo creates a more profound and elegant ambivalence. The Louvre painting retains an almost poignant trace of the homosexual come-hither – and the likeness of the face to an idealized image of Salai anchors this to Leonardo's personal life – but it is subsumed into the numinous lustre of the painting. The tone of malady and corruption in the *Angelo incarnato* has been healed by those magical 'oils and plants' distilled at the Belvedere. Slowly, soothingly, repeatedly they are applied to the panel, layer by superfine layer, until the figure we see there – at once sexual and spiritual, masculine and feminine, sinner and saint – seems to resolve all the conflicts of our divided and irresolute lives.

Though figuratively and gesturally linked to the announcing angel, the *Angelo incarnato* contains another reference entirely, and could equally be entitled the *Bacco malato*, or 'Sick Bacchus', a motif well known in the work of Caravaggio.[31] This would suggest a modulation between Christian and pagan iconography of the sort we find in the *Leda*. Leda is a pagan version of the Madonna, an image of miraculous motherhood who has been impregnated not by the Holy Spirit in the form of a dove but by a notoriously randy classical deity disguised as a swan.

Bacchus is the Roman version of Dionysus – the name is a corruption of Iacchus, an epithet given to Dionysus for his rowdiness (from the Greek *iache*, a shout) – and, like Dionysus, he is more than the god of wine and revelry: he is an archaic principle of generative nature, and thus priapic as represented here by Leonardo. He was a son of Jupiter, and was said to have 'sprung from Jupiter's thigh' (because after the death of his mother, Semele, Jupiter sewed him in his thigh to nurture him) – undoubtedly a further coding of him as phallic. The figure of Bacchus is comparable to that of Leda – a symbol of pagan fertility and generation – and it would appear this link was specific, once again, to Leonardo's output around *c.* 1505, for it was at precisely that time that the Duke of Ferrara was writing letters about a certain 'Bacchus by Leonardo', and in so far as the letters refer to someone who owns it, this seems to be a genuine lost work emanating from Leonardo's Florentine studio, at much the same time as the early studies for *Leda*. This lost *Bacchus* may have had certain figurative similarities to the Windsor drawing of the announcing angel, also *c.* 1505.

The sickness of Bacchus, to which the later, Roman, 'angel' alludes, is part of his nature as a vegetation or fertility god: it indicates the post-generative, post-coital withering – he is an autumnal god, a god of decline. In Leonardo's version he is still tumescent while incipiently sick – a dynamic of time or process is woven into the drawing. The party is almost over, but not quite.

This Bacchic theme is also germane to the other Leonardo painting of St John, the full-length *St John in the Desert*, which specifically has the attributes of Bacchus. The painting is first documented in the French royal collection at Fontainebleau in 1625. It is described in early Fontainebleau catalogues as '*St Jean au désert*', but in the 1695 catalogue this title is crossed out and substituted with '*Baccus dans un paysage*'.[32] This has led to the assumption that the Bacchic attributes – the panther-skin, the crown of vine-leaves, the grapes, and the Bacchic staff or thyrsus formed from the Baptist's cross – were added in the late seventeenth century. Technical examination neither confirms nor refutes this hypothesis (X-ray analysis cannot help: the painting was treated with white lead when it was transferred to canvas in the nineteenth century, and this renders it opaque to radiation.) It is equally possible that this modulation between the Baptist and the Bacchus was part of the original conception, and was simply not noticed by

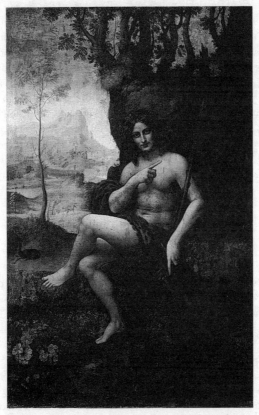

St John in the Desert, *later catalogued as a Bacchus.*

the early cataloguers. The Baptist was traditionally represented wearing a coat of sheepskin, which becomes a panther-skin by the addition of some spots or speckles – panthers were at this time considered synonymous with leopards.[33]

An early variant of the painting, attributed to the Leonardo follower Cesare da Sesto, suggests that this pagan overtone was intrinsic to the Leonardo *St John*. Cesare was himself in Rome in about 1513, and may have had contact with Leonardo there. His Baptist precisely echoes Leonardo's, even down to the splayed big toe of the left foot.[34] He is not a Bacchus – there is no coronet of vine-leaves, no panther-skin, no bunch of grapes – but two things strike me. The first is that the face of Cesare's Baptist has something of the sickly pallor and hollow eyes of the *Angelo incarnato*, and also his gauzy mantle. The second is that the cross he rests in the crook of his left arm is entwined at the tip with a snake, and thus becomes an allusion to the caduceus of Mercury. Mercury, the messenger or herald of the gods, is a parallel to St John the Baptist, who was sent to 'prepare . . . the way of the Lord', and can also be related to that other messenger, the angel Gabriel. So here Cesare too is playing the game of pagan attributes and accoutrements, and this persistent but protean figure from Leonardo's late years takes on another shape – Angel, Baptist, Bacchus, Mercury: messengers of the spirit-world, of new life quickening in the midst of sickness and death. 'Who is it who rekindles this flame which is always dying?'

⤞ THE DELUGE ⤝

And then the thunder spoke . . .
T. S. Eliot, *The Waste Land*

On the verso of the *Angelo incarnato* are three words in Leonardo's hand, originally written in red chalk, then gone over, by him, in the same black chalk or charcoal that he used for the drawing on the other side. They read:

astrapen
bronten
ceraunobolian

This curious list is a transliteration of three Greek words, meaning 'lightning flashes', 'storms', 'thunderbolts'. They have been related to a description by Pliny of the legendary prowess of the Greek painter Apelles, who could 'depict that which cannot be depicted', namely atmospheric phenomena such as these.[35] Leonardo was often compared to Apelles in gratulatory poems, and mentions him admiringly as one who painted 'fictions full of great meanings';[36] now, near the end of his career as a painter, we here find him pondering the magical power of the painter or draughtsman to capture the fugitive, inexpressible effects of Nature in violent agitation – *Sturm und Drang*.

Leonardo had always vibrated to the drama of storms. That early literary fragment about the cave actually begins with a description of a storm – 'a whirling wind racing through a deep sandy valley, its rushing movement driving to its centre everything that obstructs its furious course'. In his painter's notes of the early 1490s there is a passage on 'How to represent a tempest':

You must first show the clouds scattered and torn, and flying with the wind, mixed with clouds of sand blown up from the seashore, and boughs and leaves swept along and scattered with other light objects which are flying around . . . while the wind flings sea-spray around and the stormy air takes on the look of a dense and smothering mist.[37]

In these descriptions there is a sense of huge vectors and currents at work, and of the different materials which move in different ways through them, and act as markers of the storm's invisible potencies. We have glimpsed him on the rainswept strand at Piombino, studying the complex mechanics of crashing breakers. On another occasion, near Florence, he watched with awe the effects of a whirlwind:

The returning eddies of the wind . . . strike upon the waters and scoop them out in a great hollow, and lift them into the air in the shape of a column with the colour of a cloud. I saw this on a sandbank in the Arno. The sand was hollowed out to a depth more than the height of a man, and the sand and gravel were whirled around in a scattered mass over a wide area. It appeared in the air in the form of a great bell-tower, and the top spread out like the branches of a huge pine tree.

Another tornado or gale is recorded in a note of 1508: 'I have seen motions of the air so furious that they have caught up in their course whole roofs of great palaces and carried them away.'[38]

Now in Rome he returns intensively to this 'fury' of whirling movements, and pens a series of writings and drawings on the theme of 'The Deluge'. Put together they add up to a kind of portfolio: they may be part of the ever-intended treatise on painting, or they may represent thoughts for an actual painting of the biblical flood. There are half a dozen texts on the subject, all dating to around 1515. The longest, which fills both sides of a sheet at Windsor, is divided into two sections entitled 'Description of the deluge' and 'How to represent it in painting'; the style is big and rhetorical, as he tends to be with this sort of subject. A note headed 'Divisions' summarizes the ingredients of the Leonardian tempest. It begins with the physical – floods, fires, earthquakes, whirlpools, etc. – then focuses on the human dimensions of the catastrophe:

Broken trees loaded with people. Ships broken in pieces, smashed against rocks. Flocks of sheep; hailstones, thunderbolts, whirlwinds. People on trees which are unable to support them; trees, rocks, towers and hills covered with people; boats, tables, troughs and other means of floating. Hills covered with men, women and animals, and lightning from the clouds illuminating everything.[39]

These mental images of refugees, and makeshift boats, and flocks of sheep in a hailstorm, suggest the mapping-out of a large-scale painting or fresco. So too does another note, titled 'Representing the deluge', which says, 'Neptune will be seen in the midst of the water with his trident, and Aeolus with his winds ruffling the trees.'[40] But if there was a specific project – an apocalyptic *Noah's Flood* to rival Michelangelo's *Last Judgement* on the wall of the Sistine Chapel – it came to nothing.

Or rather it resulted in the 'Deluge drawings' (Plate 27), which are collectively a late masterpiece. There is a series of ten, done in black chalk on uniformly sized sheets of white paper (6 × 8 inches).[41] They are explosive, convulsive; the pen-strokes curl and jab to express churning vortices of energy, centrifugal tunnels of water, bursting scattershots of rock. What exactly is being shown? We could be looking back to some bleak cataclysm in distant astronomical time, or forward to the thunderbolt of nuclear fission, to the mushroom-cloud and the fallout. They are in one sense 'scientific': part of Leonardo's inquiry into the 'marvellous works' of Nature. They are a test he has set himself: to represent accurately – which means also to understand accurately – the mechanics of upheaval, to discern in it some subtle, elastic pattern, like the fractals of modern chaos theory. They are attempts, one might say, to anatomize a storm. Yet they convey also that the attempt may fail. They speak of categories engulfed, of illusory mental constructs swept away in this 'deluge' of destructive power.

The force of the drawings is such that they seem to burst upon the paper. You sense the physical event of their composition – the sudden, intent, strenuous gestures; and you sense something too of the *accidenti mentali*, or mental events, which they express. Leonardo is confronting the raw energy of Nature; the confrontation is harrowing. These whirling banshee-forms seem like an onrush of mental disruption and chaos: a brain-storm. Some of the drawings have an almost hallucinogenic quality, as if he were passing through some kind of interior shamanistic ordeal. But then as you continue to look at them, and into them, you perceive that they contain also a kind of peace. They become mesmeric. Their curvilinear force-fields resolve into mandala-like forms. You regain a sense of the surface of the drawings: marks of black chalk on rough white paper, interweavings, *fantasie* fetched back from the abyss.

→→ SICKNESS, DECEPTION, MIRRORS ←←

The sickly catamite of the *Angelo incarnato*, the catastrophic visions of the Deluge: these do not argue much for Leonardo's health and happiness at this time, and indeed in the summer of 1515, in the queasy Roman heat, Leonardo was ill. We learn this from the draft of a letter to Giuliano de' Medici, then in Florence; the date is July or August 1515. Giuliano had himself been ill with consumption, and Leonardo's letter begins, 'So greatly did I rejoice, most illustrious Lord, at the desired restoration of your health that my own malady almost left me.'[42]

What is this 'malady'? The only external clue we have to the elderly Leonardo's physical condition is that in 1517, according to Antonio de Beatis, his right hand was 'paralysed'. As Beatis goes on to say that this paralysis stopped him from painting, it has been argued that he was mistaken and that it was actually Leonardo's left hand that was affected. This is false logic. We can be fairly sure that some of Leonardo's drawings belong to 1517–18, probably including the great Turin self-portrait; his left hand cannot, therefore, have been paralysed. This means that Beatis was accurate, and may suggest that the paralysis affected rather more than just the hand – was perhaps a general paralysis on the right-hand side: a condition that could well have prevented Leonardo from painting large pictures, though not from drawing. The typical cause of this would be a stroke (or, as they tended to call it then, an 'apoplexy'). This, or some premonition of it, may be the malady he refers to in the summer of 1515.

A rhyme of medical precepts copied out by Leonardo can be dated fairly precisely to this time, and may be related to his illness. It is a doggerel sonnet of sixteen lines. The prescription is as follows:

> If you want to be healthy observe this regime.
> Do not eat when you have no appetite, and dine lightly,
> Chew well, and whatever you take into you
> Should be well cooked and of simple ingredients.
> He who takes medicine is ill advised.
> Beware anger and avoid stuffy air.
> Stay standing a while when you get up from a meal.
> Make sure you do not sleep at midday.
> Let your wine be tempered [i.e. mixed with water], taken a little and often,
> Not between meals, nor on an empty stomach.
> Neither delay nor prolong your visits to the privy.

If you take exercise, let it not be too strenuous.
Do not lie with your belly upward and your head
Downward. Be well covered at night,
And rest your head and keep your mind cheerful.
Avoid wantonness and keep to this diet.[43]

This seems a digest of sound common sense: today the poem would be an article about having a 'healthy lifestyle'. He copies it out because he has not been well; the downplaying of exercise ('let it not be too strenuous') suggests a regime for recuperation. It brings us also an authentic sense of these last years – frugal, simple, pared down. He was certainly by this point vegetarian, and noted for it. In January 1516 a Florentine traveller, Andrea Corsali, writes to Giuliano de' Medici from Cochin, and mentions 'a gentle people called Guzzarati [i.e. Gujarati] who do not feed on anything that has blood, nor will they allow anyone to hurt any living thing, like our Leonardo da Vinci; they live on rice, milk and other inanimate foods'.[44] Such frugality is another aspect of Leonardo's eccentricity in flesh-minded Rome.

A fragment of the sonnet on health is repeated on another folio in the Codex Atlanticus, also *c.* 1515, with architectural sketches probably related to the Vatican.[45] It is this folio which contains the little riddle or pun or aphorism '*li medici mi crearono e distrussono*', in which the subject of the sentence may be either the Medici or the medical profession. The double-meaning would certainly be present in Leonardo's mind, and in this context of illness of 1515 the point may precisely be an oscillation between the two, thus something like 'The Medici created me but my doctors are killing me.' The first part would refer to Giuliano's patronage, rather than to more distant and tenuous relations with Lorenzo back in the early 1480s. 'Created' would carry a specific meaning of 'made me their creature': *creato* is used in precisely this way to mean a dependant or servant. He might ironically describe himself as the 'creature' or *creato* of Giuliano.

As the draft letter to Giuliano also makes clear, Leonardo's nerves were considerably frayed at this time by the behaviour of a German assistant, Giorgio or Georg, whom he describes at one point as an 'ironworker'. (Leonardo spells the name 'Giorzio', a Lombard form.) He tells the story at length – a marvellous little window on to life in the Belvedere, though poignant in its contrast with that other narrative of apprentice misdemeanours, the boy Salai's twenty-five years previously. Here there is no twinkle of fondness, no playful exasperation: Leonardo is angry and a bit shaky about the whole thing, though there are also some touches of wry humour. He writes:

I greatly regret that I have been unable completely to satisfy your Excellency's wishes because of the wickedness of that German deceiver, for whom I have left nothing undone which I thought might give him pleasure. At first I invited him to lodge and board with me, so I could oversee his work and more conveniently correct his errors, and also so he could learn Italian and be able to talk more easily without an interpreter. From the start his allowance was always paid to him in advance, which no doubt he would willingly deny if I did not have the agreement, signed by myself and the interpreter.

(This allowance was itself in dispute – an undated account in the Vatican archives shows that Giorgio received an allowance of 7 ducats a month, but according to Leonardo he 'claimed he had been promised 8'.)[46]

But soon there were suspicions of disloyalty and double-dealing:

First he asked to have some models done in wood, just as they were being finished in iron, saying he wished to take them away to his own country. This I refused, and told him I would give him a design, showing the width, length, height and form of what he had to do. And so we remained at ill will.

The next thing was that in the room where he slept he made himself another workshop, with pincers and tools, and there he worked for others. After work he would go and eat with the soldiers of the Swiss Guard, where there are plenty of good-for-nothings though none to match him. And afterwards he and two or three others would go off together with guns to shoot birds among the ruins, and so they continued until evening. And when I sent Lorenzo to urge him to work, he said he did not want to have so many masters ordering him about, and that he was working for Your Excellency's Wardrobe. And so two months passed, and so it went on, and then one day, meeting Gian Niccolò of the Wardrobe, and asking him if the German had finished his work for the Magnifico, he told me it was not true, and that he had only given him a couple of guns to clean.

As he was only rarely in the workshop, and as he consumed a good deal of food, I sent him word that if he liked we could make a separate bargain on each thing he made, and that I would give him what we agreed to be a good price. But he consulted with his colleague, and gave up his room here, and sold everything.

The skiving, surly apprentice Giorgio is not, however, the villain of the story. Leonardo reserves this distinction for another German, whom he calls Giovanni degli Specchi – John (or Johann) of the Mirrors.[47] He has exerted a malign influence over Giorgio:

That German, Giovanni the mirror-maker, was in the workshop every day, wanting to see and know everything that was being done, and then broadcasting it around, and criticizing whatever he could not understand . . . At last I found that this Maestro Giovanni the mirror-maker was the cause of all this [i.e. of Giorgio's behaviour], for two reasons: the first is that he said my coming here had deprived him of the conversation and favour of Your Lordship, and the other is that he said the rooms of this ironworker [Giorgio] suited him for working on his mirrors, and of this he has given proof, for as well as making him [Giorgio] my enemy, he made him sell all he had and leave his workshop to him [Giovanni], where he now works with a number of assistants making many mirrors to send out to the fairs.

The mirrors that feature in this saga of professional jealousies lead us to an ambitious project now under way in Leonardo's studio. He was pursuing a new theme or dream: solar power – in particular the channelling of solar heat by means of parabolic mirrors:

The rays reflected from a concave mirror have a brilliance equal to the sun in its own place . . . And if you say that the mirror itself is cold and cannot throw out warm rays, I answer that the ray comes from the sun, and must resemble its cause, and that it can pass through any medium one wants it to pass through. When the ray from the concave mirror passes through the windows of the metal-furnaces it does not itself become hotter.[48]

The mention of furnaces shows the industrial application of his experiments. Those 'blue spectacles' he acquired on his way through Florence may be related to this work, for as he notes here, the human eye cannot 'dwell on the radiance of the solar body'; the sun's rays 'strike the eye with such splendour that it cannot bear them'. As in the 'Deluge' drawings, we have a sense of Leonardo confronting the primal forces of Nature, plugging himself into pure but dangerously powerful energy-sources. As he had written many years before, 'He who can drink from the fountain does not go to the well.'[49]

His interest in the harnessing of solar heat goes back at least seven years – there are designs for burning-mirrors in the Codex Arundel: beneath one he writes, 'This is the mirror of fire.'[50] The principle of burning-mirrors was of course ancient: Archimedes famously employed them against the Roman army besieging Syracuse, and on a more mundane level they were used to generate heat for soldering. Perhaps they had been used by Verrocchio, for in his Roman notebook Leonardo writes, 'Remember the solders used for soldering the ball on Santa Maria del Fiore,' recalling that vertiginous day on the lantern of Florence cathedral more than forty years earlier.[51] But in Rome he is working on something larger and more complex, and it may be that Giovanni the mirror-maker's snooping presence is connected with this. In a series of notes scribbled on blue paper Leonardo describes a 'pyramidical' structure which brings 'so much power to a single point' that it makes water boil in 'a heating-tank like they use in a dyer's factory'. (He adds that the device could be used for heating a swimming-pool, which seems an anticlimax but reminds us that he has clients to please.) There is also an astronomical use of these multifaceted mirror-structures: 'To see the real nature of the planets, open the covering and display a single planet on the base, and the movement reflected from the base will describe the properties of that planet.' This seems to anticipate the principle of Newton's reflecting-telescope; the note is accompanied by a diagram which does indeed look like a telescope.[52]

In a laboratory at the Belvedere secret chemical treatments are prepared. There are recipes for a varnish that will prevent the mirror surface from misting or tarnishing, and for a cryptic substance called 'fire of gypsum' (*ignea di gesso*) which is 'composed of Venus and Mercury' (i.e. copper and quicksilver, though 'Mercury' may be an esoteric reference to the 'secret fire' or *ignis innaturalis* of the alchemists).[53] A glimpse of Zoroastro's Roman laboratory a few years later – a fireplace converted into a brick furnace 'where we distil and separate the elements of everything'; a table 'cluttered with pots and flasks of all sorts, and paste and clay and Greek pitch and cinnabar' – helps us to picture the scene at the Belvedere, and to place in it Leonardo the magus or adept (or, as many in Rome must have seen him, the mad inventor), with his long grey beard and his blue goggles and his secret contraption for capturing sunlight.

Amid all this Leonardo continued his anatomical studies and performed the last of his dissections, probably at the famous Roman hospital in Santo Spirito. Here too, it seems, was scope for the malice of Giovanni: he has 'hindered me in anatomy,' complains Leonardo, 'denouncing it before the Pope and also at the Hospital'.

The particular focus of this controversy was probably Leonardo's research on embryology. The famous Windsor study of the foetus in the womb, generally dated to the last Milanese years, has some additional notes and drawings made later in Rome, and these touch on the vexed theological question of the soul of an unborn child. Leonardo writes that the foetus is a 'creature' wholly dependent on its mother's soul, as on her body: 'The same soul governs these two bodies, and shares its desires and fears and sorrows with this creature, as it does with all the other animal parts [of the mother].'[54] When a pregnant woman died, therefore, her unborn child had no soul to save. In the Rome of 1515 this smacked of the heretical Aristotelian position that the soul was materially composed, and died with the body. At just this time the Pope's theologians were entrenching their position

Embryological studies, a possible source of controversy in Rome.

against this and other heresies – the Aristotelian works of Pietro Pomponazzi were burned in 1516[55] – and this may have been the titbit of suspicion brought 'before the Pope' by the mirror-man, thus 'hindering' Leonardo's studies.

An idea of Leonardo as theologically unorthodox came down to Vasari: 'He had a very heretical state of mind. He could not be content with any kind of religion at all, considering himself in all things much more a philosopher than a Christian' – so Vasari wrote in the first edition of 1550, though he removed the passage from the second, perhaps thinking it sounded too critical.

⊰⊱ LAST VISIT TO FLORENCE ⊰⊱

That little joke of the Pope's about Leonardo's working habits has a sombre aftertaste. '*Comincia a pensare alla fine . . .*' He begins to think of the end.

On 8 October 1515 Leonardo enrolled in the Confraternity of St John of the Florentines, which had its headquarters across the Tiber from the Vatican. He may have done so for a number of reasons: a resurgence of his sense of himself as Florentine; a late touch of religiosity; a desire to ensure a decent burial. Burial was one of the roles of these lay associations or confraternities – they were '*confraternità della buona morte*', providing mutual assistance in case of sickness, and arranging funerals in case of death. His election is recorded, with the usual faintly bizarre particularities, in the Confraternity's register:

Novice: Leonardo da Vinci, painter and sculptor, was voted in by the committee by a majority of 3 black beans, and was then voted in by the whole company by a majority of 41 black beans and 2 white beans. He was put forward by Maestro Gaiacqo the doctor, who was his guarantor for the entry fee.

However in a later, undated note in the ledger the governor of the Confraternity proposes to cancel Leonardo's membership – '*mettere nel buondì*': 'to bid him good day' – because he has not paid the entry fee in the appointed time.[56]

It may be that Leonardo's failure to pay his dues was a matter of circumstance rather than a change of heart, for in this month of October 1515 he left Rome as a member of the papal entourage, bound for Florence and Bologna, where a historic meeting was scheduled between the Pope and the new French king, François I (recently victorious over the revived Sforza of Milan at the Battle of Marignano): a meeting of superpowers which should

ensure their alliance and – so it was touted by Pope Leo – a new period of
'peace for Christianity'. The sneering joke, the hindered studies: Leonardo
has an edgy relationship with the sharp-witted, gross-featured Pope, so
different from the quixotic Giuliano. But he is part of the retinue for this
papal visit, and he is glad enough to be out of Rome for a while.

They journeyed first to the old port of Civitavecchia. It was probably on
this occasion that Leonardo made some notes on the ancient harbour there:
'4 braccia long, 2½ braccia wide, 2¼ braccia deep: thus are the stones which
stand in the front parts of the breakwater of the port of Civitavecchia.'[57]
His curiosity is undimmed despite the physical setbacks of this year.

The papal circus arrived in Florence on 30 November, with a triumphal
entry for the Florentine pope. Among those who witnessed the junkets was
the apothecary Luca Landucci: 'All the chief citizens went in procession to
meet him and among others about fifty youths, only the richest and foremost,
dressed in a livery of clothing of purple cloth with fur collars, going on foot,
and each with a type of small, silvered lance in his hands – a most beautiful
thing.'[58] The procession passed through a triumphal four-fronted arch, one
of the architectural ephemera constructed for the occasion. Leonardo did a
drawing of it, and at the top of the sheet are three words in the hand of
Melzi: '*illustrissimo signor magnifico*' – i.e. Giuliano de' Medici, with whom
Leonardo was reunited here.[59]

Among the grandiose schemes planned by the papal spin-doctors was a
convocation of artists and architects to discuss the urban regeneration of
Florence, and particularly the Medici quarter – the surrounds of the old
Palazzo Medici on Via Larga, and the church of San Lorenzo with its Medici
chapels. Painters, architects, sculptors, woodcarvers and decorators had
been informed of the papal intentions. New façades, in the form of full-scale
wooden models, had been erected in front of San Lorenzo and the Duomo.
Leonardo's own ideas for a new façade for San Lorenzo are recorded in a
drawing at the Venice Accademia. Typically, he is not content with just
the façade, but imagines a complete transformation of the surroundings,
enlarging and lengthening the adjacent piazza as a scenographic background
for the renovated church. Another sketch-plan envisages the demolition of
whole blocks of housing in front of the church, and a long piazza extending
to Via Larga, where the side-wall of the Palazzo Medici is transformed
into the façade facing the square.[60] Thus Leonardo sketches out imperious
swathes of destruction through the old streets and quarters of his youth –
purely practical, architectural considerations, but one has the feeling he is
rather enjoying himself as the Medicean modernizer: a 'Maestro Ruinante'
like his friend Bramante.

During the week that the papal court spent in Florence, Leo X presided over a consistory of cardinals in the Council Hall of the Palazzo Vecchio, where the magnificent fragment of Leonardo's *Battle of Anghiari* could still be seen. It is likely that Leonardo was present. Forty years later the Medici grand-duke Cosimo I commissioned Giorgio Vasari to paint the huge cycle of frescos which now covers the walls – controversially so, because of the ghostly presence of the *Anghiari* fresco beneath it – and among the scenes included was a representation of this dynastic moment when a Medici pope sat in state in the political heart of Florence. In the background of the scene Vasari included a group of four men, which he explained thus:

I have painted in life-size, so that they may be recognizable there in the background of the composition, distinct from the ranks of the consistory, Duke Giuliano de' Medici and Duke Lorenzo his nephew, conversing with two of the greatest geniuses of their time: one of them, the old man with that mane of white ringletted hair, is Leonardo da Vinci, the great *maestro* of painting and sculpture, who is shown talking to Duke Lorenzo standing next to him; and the other is Michelangelo Buonarroti.[61]

This little grouping ironically reconciles the two artists, precisely here in the Palazzo Vecchio where their rivalry began, and enshrines them as the twin stars of Medici-fostered art. The portrait of Leonardo is stereotypical – it is based on the Melzi profile, which Vasari had seen at Vaprio[62] – but it retains a kind of folk-memory of Leonardo's last recorded visit to Florence.

On about 7 December 1515 the papal procession wound up towards Bologna. Here the Pope and François I conferred, and here Leonardo met for the first time his last and most devoted patron. The new king was twenty-one years old, immensely tall, charismatic, with his confidence riding high after his routing of the Sforza's Swiss mercenaries at Marignano. He had an enormous nose, and an amorous reputation to match – 'he is lascivious and enjoys entering the gardens of others to drink different waters', as Antonio de Beatis puts it. His motto was '*Nutrisco et extinguo*': 'I feed and I extinguish.' That the King already knew of the great Leonardo is certain – through the paintings so highly prized by his father-in-law, Louis XII; and the *Last Supper*, which he had doubtless seen in reconquered Milan; and that ingenious mechanical lion which had performed for him at the Lyon triumphs of July. And so once more Leonardo is drawn into a French ambit, which for him means a patronage underwritten by a sovereign ruler such as Italy could not boast, and by a cultivated appreciation which he did not always enjoy from his Italian masters. Among the French courtiers in Bologna was one Artus Boissif, and on 14 December Leonardo drew his portrait in red chalk, annotated by Melzi, 'Portrait of M. Artus, chamberlain to King Francesco I, at the meeting with Pope Leo X.'[63]

The Pope left Bologna on 17 December, somewhat rattled by François's high-handed attitude and only partly mollified by the royal grant of a dukedom to Giuliano de' Medici, who became Duke of Nemours. But Giuliano did not enjoy his new title long, for he died of consumption three months later, on 17 March 1516, at the age of about thirty-seven.[64] Leonardo lingered on in Rome for a few months after this, his activities obscure, his life once more in flux. Some measurements for the Basilica of San Paolo Fuori are dated August 1516: they are the last brief record of Leonardo in Italy.[65]

→→ MAISTRE LYENARD ←←

Leonardo's decision to leave for France must surely have been made by the summer of 1516, since he well knew the difficulties of crossing the Alps after autumn. No summons or supplication survives: no diplomatic communiqué; no curlicued laissez-passer. The meeting with the King in Bologna and the death of Giuliano de' Medici are the prelude, and then one day the decision is made, and sometime in August or September, at the age of sixty-four, Leonardo embarks on the longest journey of his life.

He probably stopped at Milan on the way; Salai remained there, attending to the house in the vineyard which had become his province, and which would be formally ceded to him in Leonardo's will.[66] From Milan, escorted perhaps by emissaries from the King, accompanied by Melzi and a Milanese servant named Battista de Vilanis, Leonardo heads north into the mountains. A note in the Codex Atlanticus was probably written along the way: 'River Arna at Ginevra, a quarter of a mile into Savoia where the fair is held.'[67]

By the end of the year he is settled in the Loire valley, by the royal stronghold of Amboise, in the service of the French king, with a handsome pension of 1,000 scudi per annum. An authorization or record of two years' payment is in the Archive Nationale in Paris: 'A Maistre Lyenard de Vince, paintre ytalien, la somme de 2000 écus soleil, pour sa pension di celles deux années.'[68] In the same document Leonardo is formally styled 'paintre du Roy' – 'the King's painter'.

His relationship with François was rich. The young king was awestruck, fascinated and very generous. Many years later the Florentine sculptor Benvenuto Cellini had these recollections from François himself, whom he too served:

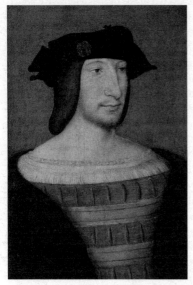

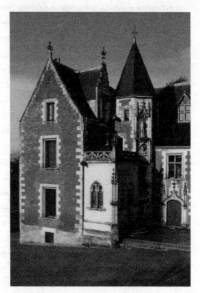

François I of France,   *The manor-house at Cloux*
c. 1515–20.   *(now Clos Lucé).*

Because he was a man of such plentiful and great talents, and had some knowledge of Latin and Greek, King François was completely besotted [*innamorato gagliard-issimamente*] with those great virtues of Leonardo's, and took such pleasure in hearing him discourse that there were few days in the year when he was parted from him, which was one of the reasons why Leonardo did not manage to pursue to the end his miraculous studies, done with such discipline. I cannot resist repeating the words which I heard the King say of him. He said he could never believe there was another man born in this world who knew as much as Leonardo, and not only of sculpture, painting and architecture, and that he was truly a great philosopher.[69]

Perhaps the most important of the King's gifts was not the generous salary but a place to live. Leonardo's last address was the handsome manor-house of Cloux (now Clos Lucé) half a mile south of the great chateau of Amboise. It was then quite new, built in the late fifteenth century by Estienne Leloup, bailiff to King Louis XI. Among those who had lived there was the Count Ligny whom Leonardo had known in Milan in 1499. The house is of red brick and grey tufa. It stands on gently sloping ground, behind a long protective wall in which a watch-tower and a small gun-emplacement remain from its days as a fortified manor-house. On the inside of the defensive wall is a long upper gallery forming a kind of loggia. To the north of the house an L-shaped range of stables and workshops forms a courtyard closed on three sides. On the fourth side, to the west, the land drops away sharply. Here are the kitchen gardens and, lower, a green-mantled pool.

The house was smaller then than it is now – the rooms to the west of the spired central tower are eighteenth century – but the layout of the central part is probably unchanged since Leonardo's day. The main front door, south-facing, leads in next to a little chapel, built for Anne de Bretagne, wife of Charles VIII.[70] Downstairs there is the large hall, where the household ate and visitors were received, and next to it the kitchen, with its terracotta floor, its cooking-range, and iron rings in the cross-beam for hanging meat and game. To the right of the front door is a wide staircase. The top landing gives on to two large rooms. The one above the dining-hall is said to have been Leonardo's studio. The windows face north-west, giving a distant view of the turrets and spires of the chateau, and trees, and a sense of space where the river is – the same view can be seen in a delicate black-chalk drawing at Windsor, probably by Melzi.[71] The upper room above the kitchen is said to have been Leonardo's bedroom, and is probably the room where he died.

The house has a mellow, well-appointed, comfortable feel. It is pleasantly spacious rather than grand and formal. Even its spires have a slightly playful air, mimicking in miniature the chateau down the road. The large fireplaces, the oak beams, the soft Touraine light at the windows, the faint aura of old wood-smoke – one is persuaded that Leonardo felt rested and tranquil in these twilight years. With the house, probably, came the housekeeper or cook Mathurine. In the only reference to her, in Leonardo's will, she is called Maturina: but the will survives in an Italian copy, in which other French names are Italianized, and she is more likely to be local than Italian (unless, of course, La Cremona had become with age La Maturina). In French books about Leonardo – of which there is a long and honourable tradition – she is invariably Mathurine, and the cuisine of Leonardo's last years unimpeachably French.

Here he sets once more to organizing his manuscripts and drawings, and to producing more of each, though Beatis tells us he no longer painted. As ever, there are books he wants – in Melzi's hand: 'Egidius Romanus, *De informatione corporis humani in utero matris* [*On the Formation of the Human Body in the Womb*]', which had been published in Paris in 1515, and 'Rugieri Bacon in a printed edition'[72] – the great English scholiast Roger Bacon, a Leonardian figure of thirteenth-century Oxford, who discoursed on the possibility of human flight. On fine days he can be seen in the town, or down on the river, sketching the courses of the Loire – or, as he writes it, the 'Era' – as it 'passes through Anbosa'.[73] His spellings are unacclimatized. The expatriate, it is said, is a foreigner in two countries: the one he lives in and the one he has left behind.

➤➤ THE CARDINAL CALLS ◄◄

Autumn in the Loire valley, the perfect time to visit, and at Amboise in early October 1517 arrives a party of distinguished Italian sightseers. Cardinal Luigi of Aragon was a grandson of the King of Naples and a cousin of Isabella of Aragon, Leonardo's former neighbour at the Corte Vecchia in Milan. He was a thin-faced man in his early forties: a probable portrait of him by Raphael is in the Prado in Madrid. He had jockeyed for the papacy after the death of Julius II in 1513, and, though defeated in this hope by the election of Leo X, he remained close to Leo – mostly in the encouraged belief that the Pope would create him King of Naples. Leonardo may have met him in Rome, where he was known for his lavish hospitality and his beautiful mistress, the courtesan Giulia Campana, by whom he had a daughter, Tullia.

There hung over him a graver charge: that he had ordered the murder of his brother-in-law Antonio da Bologna, and possibly even that of his sister Giovanna, Duchess of Amalfi, who mysteriously disappeared in early 1513. It is not impossible that Leonardo knew something of this as well, as Antonio da Bologna was in Milan in 1512, and was murdered there the following year. The story is famously recounted in John Webster's Jacobean tragedy *The Duchess of Malfi*, in which Luigi appears ('The Cardinal') in a sinister role; Webster based his play on an English version of a novella by Matteo Bandello, the young boy who had watched Leonardo at work on the *Last Supper*.[74]

The Cardinal was on the homeward leg of a protracted European journey, partly to distance himself from a conspiracy against Pope Leo the previous year, and partly to meet the new King of Spain, Charles V; he did so at Middelburg, on the coast of Holland. English agents there kept a wary eye and reported back to Cardinal Wolsey about Aragon's ostentatious arrival at Charles's court, with his retinue of forty horsemen, and his cloak draped carelessly about his shoulders and his sword strapped to his side: 'Your Grace may conjecture what manner of man he is ... The said Cardinal's profession is rather of a temporal lord than spiritual.'[75] Thereafter the

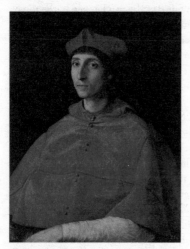

Raphael's Portrait of a Cardinal, *probably a portrait of Luigi of Aragon.*

Cardinal descended south through France. Among his travelling party was his chaplain and secretary, Antonio de Beatis, whose chatty travel diary is the source of what follows.[76]

On 9 October they were at Tours ('Turso'), and from there, after an early lunch, they went on to Amboise, 'a distance of seven leagues'. Beatis finds it 'a small well-kept town in a fine position'; they are put up in the chateau, on its 'little hill'; it is 'not strongly fortified, but the rooms are comfortable, and the view is lovely'. The following day, 10 October, they went to 'one of the suburbs' of the town, 'to see messer Lunardo Vinci the Florentine'. We have a slight sense that Leonardo is another tourist attraction to be 'done' by the Cardinal.

Beatis's brief but vividly specific account of their visit to Clos Lucé is our last snapshot of Leonardo. It begins with an error: Leonardo is described as 'an old man of over seventy', which again might seem faintly touristic – an exaggeration which makes him even more picturesquely venerable – though it can also be taken as an eyewitness statement that Leonardo looked some years old than he really was (sixty-five). The account continues:

He showed His Lordship three pictures, one of a certain Florentine lady, done from life at the instigation of the late Magnifico Giuliano de' Medici, another of the young St John the Baptist, and another of the Madonna and Child placed on the lap of St Anne: all quite perfect [*perfettissimo*, which might also mean 'completely finished']. However, we cannot expect any more great work from him, since he is now somewhat paralysed in his right hand. He has trained up a Milanese pupil who works well. And while Master Leonardo can no longer colour with such sweetness as he used to, he is none the less able to do drawings and to teach others. This gentleman has written a great deal about anatomy, with many illustrations of the parts of the body, such as the muscles, nerves, veins and the coilings of intestines, and this makes it possible to understand the bodies of both men and women in a way that has never been done by anyone before. All this we saw with our own eyes, and he told us he had already dissected more than thirty bodies, both men and women, of all ages. He has also written, as he himself put it, an infinity of volumes on the nature of waters, on various machines, and on other things, all in the vernacular, and if these were to be brought to light they would be both useful and delightful. Besides his expenses and lodgings, he receives from the King of France a pension of 1,000 scudi a year, and his pupil gets three hundred.

One pores over this page, as if with a magnifying-glass, trying to capture its traces of documentary reality, its frissons of presence. Just the other side of this text are these people who are physically there with him – 'All this we saw with our own eyes': *oculatamente*.

After cordialities in the salon downstairs, the refreshments provided by Mathurine, and a brief holy interlude in the little chapel – for these very worldly visitors are men of the cloth – they have been conducted up the stairs to the inner sanctum of Leonardo's studio, where the autumnal light is augmented by candles, and now they are listening to him as he describes and explains, with what one discerns as a mix of innate courtesy and magisterial brusqueness. As they look at the *Mona Lisa* he tells them something, but not a lot. She is a Florentine lady; he painted her at the request – no, the urging: *instantia* – of the late Magnifico Giuliano. They look at the soft-toned *Virgin and Child with St Anne* and the sultry *St John*, and then come out the great folios of anatomical drawings, the pages turned by the indispensable Melzi, and for a moment they feel a shiver at their proximity to this gentle-looking old man whose hands have dismembered corpses and unravelled intestines – 'more than thirty bodies, both men and women, of all ages': a moment of volubility. These feats of anatomy are given special prominence by Beatis as something unique, 'never . . . done by anyone before', and perhaps this is a valuation expressed or anyway implied by Leonardo himself as he spoke to his guests.

There are other books – on water, on machinery. Beatis notes that these are in the 'vernacular', and should be 'brought to light' – by which he presumably means published – but he does not mention the oddest feature about them. This is a curious omission: Leonardo's mirror-writing was not something widely known and therefore not worth mentioning, so one has to wonder if Beatis actually saw any of it.[77] The visitors were probably shown particular sheets and pages: properly worked-up drawings. Leonardo is an old hand: he has received these studio visits a hundred times. He affects a certain nonchalance, but shows people just exactly what he wants them to see, and the rest is a kind of hinterland of wonders, to be indicated with a vague magisterial wave of his good hand: the manuscripts and notebooks, *libri* and *libricini*, heaped around on the desks and shelves of his studio – 'as he himself put it, an infinity of volumes'. One hears the disarming mix of self-pride and self-mockery, the phrase arrived at, savoured for its ironies, almost a punchline, as he contemplates the tonnage of paper and ink he has created, the intractable multiplicity of his investigations, the impossible distances that the mind must fly to encompass it all.

'An *infinity* of volumes . . .'

And young Melzi, whose love of Leonardo will be expressed by a curatorial career stretching on over more than half a century, smiles ruefully at these words.

The visitors take their leave, well pleased, and the punctilious Beatis writes up his journal that evening (or so one assumes: the manuscript that survives is a fair copy or digest, done sometime after the date of the last entry, 31 August 1521). The following day they proceed to another royal castle, Blois ['Bles'], and see 'a portrait in oils of a certain lady of Lombardy, done from life; she is rather beautiful, but in my opinion not as beautiful as Signora Gualanda'. This painting was plausibly Leonardo's portrait of Lucrezia Crivelli, which today hangs in the Louvre; it may well have been removed to Louis XII's chateau at Blois some time after the French takeover of Milan in 1499; it would not yet have acquired its misleading title of *La Belle Ferronnière*. Isabella Gualanda was the noted Neapolitan beauty and friend of the poetess Costanza d'Avalos; she is not the 'true' subject of the *Mona Lisa*, otherwise Beatis would have said so when he saw the painting the previous day.

Of course one wants to shake Antonio by the shoulders to get some more out of him: all that he saw and felt and knew but failed to mention. Was Leonardo tall still, or shrunken? Was his voice – the voice that once sang so beautifully to the tune of a *lira* – sonorous or quavery? One wants to ask why the 'somewhat paralysed' right hand should have meant that the left-handed *maestro* was unlikely to do any more painting. Is there a more general diminution suggested in the next sentence – he cannot 'colour with such sweetness as he used to' – implying a loss of technique more than a physical handicap?

What Beatis fails to mention can in part be supplied by looking once more at the famous self-portrait in red chalk at the Biblioteca Reale in Turin, which must show Leonardo at around this time – a man in his mid-sixties, but looking, just as Beatis says he did, like 'an old man of over seventy'. In the popular imagination it is the definitive self-portrait of Leonardo, and has fixed him in this druidic mode within our minds. There are doubts among some art-historians, who feel that the style and the medium suggest an earlier date. Is it perhaps a portrait of his father, not long before Ser Piero's death in 1504; or some antique god or philosopher from the time of the *Leda* studies; or simply some old man 'of striking appearance', one of those faces which fascinated him and which, according to Vasari, 'he would follow all day long to draw'? Even the Italian inscription below the drawing is controversial, faded to the point of illegibility: does it describe it as a 'portrait of himself in old age' or merely as a drawing 'done by him in old age'? But like many others, I continue to believe in it as a potent and unflinching portrait of himself at the end of his life – the 'conventional' view: like the view that the *Mona Lisa* really does show Mona Lisa. The sheet is unusually long and thin, and the drawing may well have been cropped at the sides, almost losing the shape of the shoulders.[78] In fact they are just visible, in angled horizontal lines at either side of the head, almost at the level of the mouth, and seeing them one realizes that the iconic image of the Turin drawing is not the erect, commanding figure he now seems but an old man hunched and bent beneath the weight of the years: venerable still, but also vulnerable. He has almost become that stooped decrepit figure drawn at the Villa Melzi some five years earlier, sitting on a rock, watching the play of the river as it journeys on past him.

Contemporary with the Turin self-portrait is the haunting black-chalk drawing at Windsor known as the *Pointing Lady* (page 501), sometimes associated with Matelda in Dante's *Purgatorio* – a soft, romantic, windswept figure on a riverbank, surrounded by tall flowers. Martin Kemp calls it an 'emotional pendant to the Deluge drawings', promising 'transition into a world of ineffable tranquillity rather than immersion in a world of physical destruction'.[79] She turns back towards the spectator – turns, in Dante's words, 'like a woman who's dancing' – but her left hand points away from us, into the depths of the picture, signalling something we cannot see.

➤➤ 'NIGHT WAS CHASED AWAY' ◄◄

At the end of 1517 Leonardo attends François at Romorantin, upriver from Amboise, where he is ambitiously planning for the King a vast new palace complex, complete with a connecting network of canals between the Loire and the Saône. Designs for this are found in the Codex Atlanticus, a reprise of those utopian city-scapes sketched out thirty years earlier.[80] The Romorantin project never left the drawing-board, though architectural historians point to the influence of Leonardo's designs on the evolution of

chateau-design in the Loire. He remained there until 16 January 1518: 'On
the eve of St Anthony's I returned from Romorantino to Ambuosa.' An
official requisition of horses from the King's stables – '*pour envoyer à
Maistre Lyonard florentin paintre du Roy pour les affers du dit seigneur*' –
remains among his papers.[81]

With the spring comes the season of masques and pageants and parties,
for which his ardour is quite undimmed. At Amboise on 3 May 1518 there
is a double festivity with a Florentine overtone, celebrating the baptism of
the King's son, the Dauphin Henri, and the marriage of his niece, Madeleine
de la Tour d'Auvergne. Her husband was Lorenzo di Piero de' Medici,
nephew of the Pope, and now Duke of Urbino (the dukedom so courteously
refused by his late uncle Giuliano). Among the attendant Florentines were
probably men who knew Leonardo, and many others who knew of him,
and so the news of him would travel back to Florence. The marriage was
brief: both partners were dead within a year, though not before producing
a daughter, Caterina, who later became Queen of France – the infamous
'Madame la Serpente', Catherine de' Medici.

The show put on by Leonardo is described in newsletters sent to the
Gonzaga in Mantua: the Marchioness was still keeping a distant eye on
Leonardo, the one who got away.[82] In the square standing to the north of
the chateau a triumphal arch was set up. On it stood a nude figure bearing
lilies in one hand and an effigy of a dolphin (for the Dauphin) in the other.
On one side of the arch was a salamander with the King's motto, '*Nutrisco
et extinguo*'; on the other was an ermine with the motto '*Potius mori quam
foedari*' ('Better to die than be besmirched') – an *impresa* of the Duke of
Urbino, and for Leonardo a memory of Milanese days, and the captivating
Cecilia Gallerani. One of the Gonzaga envoys writes of the tremendous
esteem which Leonardo enjoys with King François. The King is anxious to
employ more Italian painters, he reports; the name of Lorenzo Costa, court
artist at Mantua, has been mentioned.

A couple of weeks later, on 15 May, there was another pageant, almost
certainly organized by Leonardo. The siege and capture of a castle were
represented, commemorating the Battle of Marignano three years previously. From its battlements, falconets fired up carnival missiles of rag and
paper, while great booming mortars delighted the crowd by raining down
'inflated balloons which bounce around when they land in the square, to
the great delight of all and with no harm done to anyone: a new invention,
beautifully done'.[83] Leonardo's great skill of surprise, his mastery of the
theatrical moment, never deserted him.

Some fine drawings of costumed masqueraders are among the last of

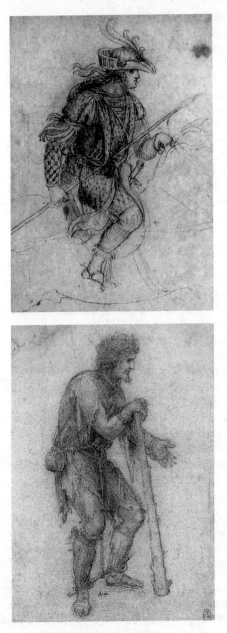

*Masquerader on horseback,
and in the guise of a poor
prisoner.*

Leonardo's works, done in black chalk like the *Pointing Lady* – this is the favoured medium of his late drawings, the line precise and assured, yet tending also to a soft, cloudy gleam. We see a horseman in a raffish broad-brimmed hat; a young man with flowing gauzy sleeves and a hunting-horn at his waist; an elaborately coiffed woman whose muscular legs suggest she is actually a man – ludic figures that seem part Renaissance showbiz and part ethereal magic. The ragged, mendicant prisoner in shackles, with his food-bowl and his wild-man staff, is also an actor in costume rather than an actual prisoner.[84] For a moment one sees – in the curls of the hair, in the face behind the small fluffy beard – a reminiscence of Salai. But how much Salai was part of the French household is uncertain. He is listed in the French accounts, which cover two years, 1517–18, as receiving 100 écus – a decent sum, but only an eighth of what was paid to Melzi; the disparity may well be explained by his absence for some of the time. He was certainly back in Milan in spring 1518: he is recorded there on 13 April, lending a sum of money.[85] There is no mention of him among the witnesses of Leonardo's will a year later.

19 June 1518: a big thank you to the King of France – a party in his honour, put on in Leonardo's gardens at Cloux. All week the workmen have been busy constructing the tall wooden scaffolding. Over this is draped a canopy of blue cloth spangled with stars, creating a kind of pavilion or marquee. It covers an area 30 × 60 braccia (60 × 120 feet). Inside there is a raised dais for the royal guests. The columns of the scaffold are festooned with coloured cloths and wreaths of ivy. The lighting and the music and the scents of the midsummer evening one must imagine.

The show was a reprise of what was, as far as we know, Leonardo's first production, the *Paradiso*, performed at the Castello Sforzesco in 1490 for the doomed young Duke of Milan and his bride, Isabella of Aragon. And by coincidence this last *festa*, almost thirty years later, was seen by another young Milanese, Galeazzo Visconti, and recounted by him in a letter to the news-hungry Gonzaga:

The whole courtyard was canopied in sheets of sky-blue cloth which had stars in gold in the likeness of the heavens, and then there were the principal planets, with the sun on one side and the moon on the other: it was a wonderful sight. Mars, Jupiter and Saturn were there, in their proper order, and the twelve celestial signs . . . and there must have been four hundred torches burning, so that it seemed the night was chased away.[86]

The show finishes, the royal compliments are received, the revellers disperse. The gardens of Cloux are quiet once more. There is a scattering of festive debris, the smell of trampled grass, and what was for a few minutes a vision of paradise is now just a big blue tent which they will take down in the morning. This *festa* is the last identifiable work by Leonardo da Vinci, an ephemeron so fragile that soon no trace of it remained except in the memories of those who were there and saw with their own eyes the night 'chased away'. *'Pareva fusse cacciata la notte . . .'*

A few days later Leonardo wrote the last of those little dated notes: miniature graffiti which say nothing more than here I am, on this day, in this place: 'On the 24th day of June, St John's Day 1518, in Amboise in the palace of Clu.' A flagged moment, perhaps recalling the great St John's Day parades and festivities in Florence. Around this time, in similarly nostalgic vein, he draws a brief sketch-plan and captions it, 'The lion-house in Florence'.[87] It is perhaps intended as an idea for Romorantin, but it remains on the page as the marker of an old man in exile, prey to the random offerings of memory. He remembered the lion he had seen there, stripping the skin off a lamb; perhaps it was the one he used for the lion in his painting of St Jerome. *Leone . . . Leonardo.* He had always been the lion, perhaps since childhood, and indeed it would not be a bad synopsis of the Turin self-portrait to say he looks there like a grizzled old lion, with his mane of grey hair and his fierce eyes: a lonely survivor.

And around this time he is sitting at a table, in his studio at Cloux, working on some geometry – another little theorem, another piece of the jigsaw – when he hears a voice calling him, and he knows he must put down his pen, and put aside his questions, because he must live with the rest of us in this material world of appetites and contingencies, represented at this moment, not at all unpleasantly, by a bowl of Mathurine's hot vegetable soup, which is almost as good (though he would never tell her that 'almost') as a Tuscan minestrone.

So he writes on the page, *'Etcetera, perche la minesstra si fredda'* – the 'etcetera' a mere formulaic squiggle, the glyph of non-completion.

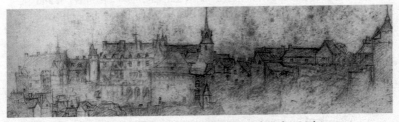

The view from Clos Lucé, in a sketch attributed to Melzi.

⇥ THE GREAT SEA ⇤

When I thought I was learning to live I was also learning to die.

Codex Atlanticus, fol. 252r-a

At Clos Lucé on Saturday 23 April 1519, the day before Easter, Leonardo da Vinci, 'painter to the King', drew up his will in the presence of the royal notary, Guillaume Borian, and seven witnesses: Francesco Melzi, Battista de Vilanis, two French priests and three Franciscan friars.[88] Conspicuously missing from the list of witnesses is Salai. His absence from Amboise is confirmed by other documents, which locate him in Paris on 5 March and again on 16 May. On both occasions he met there with one Giovanni Battista Confalonieri, an agent of Massimiliano Sforza, Duke of Milan. On the second occasion he received a payment of 100 scudi, paid to him on behalf of the Duke, and the promise of a further 500 over the next four years. What sort of services was Salai offering in return? One possibility is that he was being paid to supply political information gleaned from his proximity to King François at Amboise – a last disreputable twist to his long and often ambivalent relationship with Leonardo.[89]

In the will Leonardo gives instructions for his burial in the church of St Florentin at Amboise; for the procession that will accompany his body 'from the said place to the said church'; for the saying of three high masses and thirty low masses in his memory; for the distribution of 40 pounds of wax in thick candles to be placed in the churches where the masses were celebrated; and for the funeral itself, with 'sixty tapers to be carried by sixty poor men who shall be given money for carrying them'.

The bequests of the will are as follows:

- To Messer Francesco da Melzo, gentleman of Milan, each and all of the books the Testator is at present possessed of; and the instruments and portraits appertaining to his art and calling as a painter . . . and the remainder of his pension, and all sums of money which are owing to him from the past until the day of his death; and each and all of his clothes which he now possesses at the said place of Cloux
- To Battista de Vilanis his servant, one half of his garden outside the walls of Milan . . . and the right of water which King Louis XII of pious memory gave to the said da Vinci, being the stream of the Naviglio di Santo Cristoforo; and each and all of the furnishing and utensils of his house at the said place of Cloux

- To Salai his servant, the other half of the same garden, in which garden the same Salai has built and constructed a house which shall be and remain henceforth the property of Salai
- To Maturina his serving woman, a cloak of good black cloth lined with fur, and a length of cloth, and a single payment of two ducats
- To his brothers now living in Florence, the sum of four hundred scudi which he has deposited with the treasurer of Santa Maria Nuova in the city of Florence, with all the interest and usufruct that may have accrued up to the present time

The apportioning is somehow elegant: to Melzi the unparalleled intellectual inheritance of his writings and paintings; to Salai and Battista property; to Mathurine a fur coat; and to the da Vinci brothers cash.[90]

The Florentines called it 'entering the great sea'. Did Leonardo embark on this last journey philosophically, in the equanimity of pious resignation? His writings suggest not.

O slumberer, what is sleep? Sleep is the semblance of death. O why then do you not create such works that after your death will make you seem perfectly alive, instead of sleeping while you are alive and making yourself seem like the sad dead . . .

Every hurt leaves a displeasure in the memory, except for the supreme hurt, which is death, which kills the memory together with life . . .

The soul desires to remain with its body, because without the physical instruments of that body it can do nothing and feel nothing.[91]

Sleeping, forgetting, feeling nothing: these are images of death consonant with the essentially Aristotelian materialism of the Renaissance scientist. Of the resurrection and the life to come we hear nothing. And when Leonardo does write of the divinity of the soul it is still to maintain that it must 'dwell in its works' – the material world, the body – in order to be 'at ease': 'Whatever it is, the soul is a divine thing, therefore leave it to dwell in its works, and be at ease there . . . for it takes its leave of the body very unwillingly, and indeed I believe that its grief and pain are not without cause.' This is from an anatomical folio of c. 1510, where he writes exaltedly of anatomy as 'this labour of mine' wherein are discernible 'the marvellous works of Nature'.[92] Physical life is the soul's habitat, death its eviction; it leaves 'very unwillingly', and does not seem headed for a home on high.

Vasari engineers a deathbed repentance for Leonardo which sounds less than convincing: 'Feeling he was near to death he earnestly resolved to learn the doctrines of the Catholic faith and of the good and holy Catholic religion, and then, lamenting bitterly, he confessed and repented, and though he could not stand up, supported by his friends and servants he received the blessed sacrament from his bed.' It could be true, though this late conversion to the Faith sounds like something wished more by Vasari than by Leonardo. More convincing is Vasari's further comment that Leonardo 'protested that he had offended God and mankind by not working harder at his art, as he should have done'. It was not sin and hellfire he feared, but the dreadful weight of that last 'etcetera', and the empty grey paper beneath it – all that had not been completed.

He died on 2 May 1519, at the age of sixty-seven. According to Vasari, our only source, King François was present, and cradled him in his arms. As the final seizure came – 'a paroxysm, messenger of death' – the King 'held his head up, to help him and bring him comfort'. It is an affecting image – if one detaches it from a pair of thoroughly over-egged French paintings on the subject, done in the early nineteenth century – but it has since been discovered that on 3 May, the day after Leonardo's death, a royal edict was issued at Saint-Germain-en-Laye. As it took two days on horseback to travel there from Amboise, King François could not have been at Leonardo's side on 2 May and at Saint-Germain on the 3rd. The veracity of Vasari's account now hinges on the unresolved question of whether or not this edict – boldly inscribed '*Par le Roy*', but not actually signed by him – required the King's presence in Saint-Germain.[93] Though 'duly considering the certainty of death', as the incipit of his will puts it, Leonardo departs on this characteristic note of uncertainty, and, in the absence of any known last words, the troublesome quirk of the Saint-Germain edict reminds us of his profound conviction that everything must be doubted, and tested, before it is held to be true.

Vasari concludes, 'All those who knew him grieved without measure the loss of Leonardo,' at which point I forget about the King altogether, and see Francesco Melzi by the bedside in tears. It was not until 1 June that Melzi wrote to the half-brothers in Florence with news of the death. 'He was like the best of fathers to me,' he wrote. 'As long as I have breath in my body I shall feel the sadness, for all time. He gave me every day the proofs of his most passionate and ardent affection.'[94] Melzi, this young man of whom we know so little, repaid that affection: as the assiduous guardian and editor of that 'infinity' of writings and drawings which – perhaps even more than the paintings – take us directly into the life of Leonardo, as if they are themselves a kind of memory, cluttered with fragmentary records

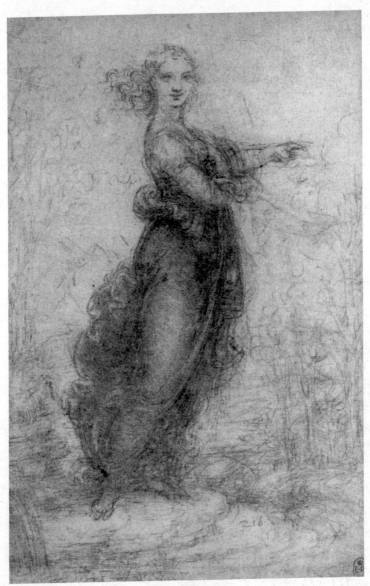

The Pointing Lady.

of the travails of his days, the secrets of his dreams, the flights of his mind.

His bodily remains fared less well than this metaphysical cargo of memories, dreams and reflections. There must have been a provisional interment in May, for the substantial funeral envisaged in the will did not take place for over three months; the burial certificate in the register of the royal collegiate church of St Florentin is dated 12 August 1519. The church suffered during the French Revolution, and in 1802 was deemed to be past saving. It was demolished, and the stones and leads – including those in the graveyard – were used for repairing the chateau. It is said that the gardener of the church, one Goujon, took up all the scattered bones and buried them in a corner of the courtyard, Leonardo's perhaps among them.

In 1863 the poet and Leonardiste Arsène Houssaye excavated the site of St Florentin; among the shards he found fragments of a tomb-slab inscription ('EO [. . .] DUS VINC') and one nearly whole skeleton whose remarkable skull-size immediately convinced him he had found the remains of Leonardo. 'We have never before seen a head so magnificently designed by or for intelligence,' he wrote. 'After three and a half centuries, death had not yet been able to reduce the pride of this majestic head.'[95] These bones now lie buried in the chapel of St Hubert, within the precincts of the chateau, beneath a plaque set up by the Comte de Paris. Their only connection with Leonardo, however, is the dubious phrenological deduction of Houssaye.

It is just possible that the capacious skull interred at St Hubert once housed the mind of Leonardo da Vinci, but one certainty, at least, is that it does so no longer. The cage is empty; the mind has flown.

Notes

Alphabetical references refer to the manuscripts and collections listed in Sources. Author/date references refer to the books and articles listed there.

Introduction

1. Ar 245v, dated by comparison with CA 673r/249r-b, written 24 June 1518; see Pedretti 1975.
2. R 1566. In the surviving transcripts of Leonardo's will, in Italian, she is 'Maturina', but she was almost certainly French, hence Mathurine.
3. K² 50v.
4. Ben Jonson, *Timber, or Discoveries* (London, 1640), in *Complete Poems*, ed. G. Parfitt (Harmondsworth, 1975), 394.
5. Richter's 1939 index of Leonardo manuscripts totals 5,421 pages (taking 'page' to mean one side of a manuscript folio) but omits the following: versos of glued-down fragments in the Codex Atlanticus; notebook covers and inside-covers with manuscript contents; and the two Madrid codices discovered in 1967. These bring the count up to about 7,200 pages. See Richter 1970, 2.400–401; PC 1.92–7. On reported sightings of Libro W (designated thus by Leonardo's secretary Melzi) in Milan in 1866 and 1958: Pedretti 1965, 147–8. See Part V n. 17.
6. Charles Rogers, *A Collection of Prints in Imitation of Drawings* (2 vols., London, 1778), 1.5. On the provenance of the collection (probably brought from Spain by the Earl of Arundel and sold to Charles in *c.* 1641) see Clark and Pedretti 1968, 1.x–xiii.
7. Giambattista Giraldi Cinzio, *Discorsi* (Venice, 1554), 193–6, citing the reminiscence of his father, Cristoforo Giraldi, a Ferrarese diplomat in Milan.
8. L 77r.
9. CA 534v/199v-a.
10. RL 12665r. The lines are added to his 'Description of the Deluge', *c.* 1515, but undoubtedly record earlier observations at Piombino, probably in autumn 1504.
11. K 1r. The page is very faded; the correct reading of the second line was established by infra-red examination in 1979.

12. Ar 1r, written in early 1508, when he was beginning the task of organizing his manuscripts; cf. Leic 2r: 'So, reader, you need not wonder, nor laugh at me, if here we jump from one subject to another.'

13. F 35r; RL 19095v; RL 19070v (cf. 19115r: 'Show the movement of the woodpecker's tongue.').

14. CA 520r/191r-a; PC 2.313. He wrote this *c.* 1490–92, above a drawing of a spiral entitled '*Corpo nato dalla prospettiva*' ('Body born of perspective'): see illustration on p. 58. On the same sheet, now separated (CA 521v/191v-b, R 1368), he wrote, '*M°* [i.e. Maestro] Leonardo fiorentino in Milano.' Other autographs in the notebooks: Fors 3 62v, *c.* 1493, written left to right (see illustration on p. 58); Fors 1¹ 3v, '*principiato da me Leonardo da Vinci*', dated 12 July 1505; CA 1054r/379r-a, '*Io Lionardo*' – 'I, Leonardo'.

15. CU 122r–125v, McM 396–410.

16. Michelangelo 1878, 12.

17. The most comprehensive edition of Vasari's writings remains the nine-volume *Opere*, ed. G. Milanesi (Florence, 1878–85; 2nd edn 1906), in which the annotated Life of Leonardo is 4.57–90. See also *Le vite*, ed. R. Batterani and P. Barocchi (4 vols., Florence, 1966–76). The earliest English translation was a brief selection by William Aglonby, 1685; the most accessible modern translation is by George Bull (Harmondsworth, 1987), in which the Life of Leonardo is 1.255–71. On my selective references to Vasari and other early biographers, see Sources: Early biographies.

18. Biblioteca Nazionale, Florence, Codex Magliabechiano XIII 89 and XXV 636; see Benedettucci 1991.

19. Codex Magliabechiano XVII 17. The account of Leonardo occupies fols. 88r–91v and 121v–122r. See Fabriczy 1893; Ficarra 1968.

20. Giovio's life of Leonardo ('*Leonardi Vincii vita*') was first published by G. Tiraboschi in 1796; a parallel text in Latin and English is in Richter 1970, 1.2–3. Additional material on Leonardo, from another part of the *Dialogi*, is in PC 1.9–11.

21. On the genesis of the *Lives*, see Boase 1971, 43–8.

22. Material on Leonardo is also found in Lomazzo's *Sogni e raggionamenti* ('Dreams and discourses'), a manuscript of the early 1560s containing imagined dialogues (British Library, Add. MS 12196, 50r-224r, especially Raggionamenti 5 and 6, 117v-175r); and in his *Idea del tempio della pittura* (*The Idea of the Temple of Painting*) (Milan, 1590). His writings are collected in *Scritti sulle arti*, ed. R. Ciardi (2 vols., Pisa, 1973).

23. RL 12726. A copy, probably also by Melzi, is in the Biblioteca Ambrosiana, Milan.

PART ONE: Childhood, 1452–1466

1. Uzielli 1872, doc. 1.
2. E. Repetti, *Dizionario geografico della Toscana* (Florence, 1845), 5.789. Cf. Uzielli 1896, 36–42. In the 1940s the house was donated to the Comune of Vinci by its owner, Count Guglielmo Rasini di Castelcampo; it was opened to the public in 1952, the four-hundredth anniversary of Leonardo's birth.
3. Cianchi 1960; Vecce 1998, 23–5.
4. ASF, Notarile anticosimiano 16192, 105v.
5. See Bruschi 1997 on the possibility that Leonardo's baptismal record was still extant in the mid nineteenth century. On 13 October 1857 Gaetano Milanesi wrote to Cesare Guasti, 'If you go to Pistoia, would you please tell Mons. Breschi that I would be very obliged if he would let me have Leonardo da Vinci's baptismal certificate, which he has discovered.' Breschi was dean of the diocese of Pistoia and Prato, to which the parish of Vinci belonged. Nothing seems to have come of Milanesi's enquiry, though the recent discovery of a letter to Breschi from Fr Ferdinando Visconti, then the parish priest of Vinci, has excited interest. It was posted on 17 May 1857 (five months before the date of Milanesi's letter). A sizeable portion of paper, almost exactly square, is missing from the lower part of the second page – was this the fugitive document? If so, what happened to it?
6. Cianchi 1953, 64–9.
7. See J. Temple-Leader, *Sir John Hawkwood* (London, 1992); T. Jones, *Chaucer's Knight: The Portrait of a Mercenary* (London, 1994); Chaucer, 'The Parson's Tale', *Canterbury Tales*, Fragment X, 1 (ed. F. Robinson, Oxford, 1957, 254).
8. Cianchi 1953, 69–70; Vecce 1998, 22.
9. This house, described as 'in the *borgo*', was probably built on the extramural plot of land mentioned in the 1427 *catasto*, and is almost certainly the town-house recorded in more detail in the 1451 *catasto*; Leonardo must have known it well as a child.
10. Viroli 1998, 7–9; this copy was possibly the one later used by Niccolò Machiavelli when writing his *Discourses on Livy* (1513).
11. Ridolfi 1963, 4.
12. On Ser Piero's early career: Cecchi 2003, 122–5; Vecce 1998, 384. The insignia: ASF, Notarile anticosimiano 16826, 1r.
13. Cf. Antonio da Vinci's 1457 declaration (see n. 18 below), which says of Francesco, 'He is in the country and does nothing.' These are formulaic disclaimers.
14. See Eissler 1962, 95–8, for psychoanalytical reflections on Leonardo's 'very live' relationship with Francesco.
15. The manuscript, which has many scribal errors, actually describes Leonardo as the '*legittimo . . . figluolo*' of Ser Piero. The adjective as it stands is redundant, and it is generally assumed that '*illegittimo*' or '*non legittimo*' is meant. The idea that Caterina was 'of good blood' may perhaps imply that she too was illegitimate.

16. Schlossmuseum, Weimar; PC 2.110: a double-sided sheet of anatomical studies originally joined to RL 19052.

17. On Accattabriga and his family: Cianchi 1975, with facsimiles of documents; Vecce 1998, 27–30.

18. ASF, Catasto antico 795, 502–3; Villata 1999, no. 2. This is the first official documentation of Leonardo's existence.

19. In 1427 she is 'Monna Piera donna di Piero [Buti]', aged twenty-five; but she must have died young, as in later *catasti* Piero Buti's wife is Monna Antonia.

20. Of the other children whose lives are traceable, Piera married a Vinci man, Andrea del Bianccho, in 1475, and was a widow by 1487; Lisabetta also married, and produced a daughter, Maddalena, in *c.* 1490 – as far as we know, Caterina's first grandchild.

21. CA 186v/66v-b. The original reads, '*Questo scriversi distintamente del nibio par che sia mio destino, perche nela prima / ricordatione della mia infantia e' mi parea che, essendo io in culla, che un nibbio venissi me / e mi aprissi la bocha chola sua coda, e molte volte mi percuotesse con tal coda dentro alle labra.*'

22. J. Parry-Jones, *Birds of Prey* (Newent, n.d.), 10.

23. Written thus on the inside cover of the notebook, and repeated almost identically on fol. 18v.

24. Tn 18v: 'The *cortone*, a bird of prey which I saw going to Fiesole, above the place of the Barbiga, on 14 March 1505'.

25. The source of the error was the German edition of Dmitry Merezhkovsky's *Romance of Leonardo da Vinci* (1903), which rendered the correct Russian *korshun* (kite) as *Geier*.

26. Freud 2001, 36–7.

27. Ibid., 41, 77. Freud's broader interpretation of the kite fantasy draws on theories of infantile sexuality expounded in 'On the sexual theories of children' (1908). He also identifies a homosexual content ('the situation in the fantasy ... corresponds to an idea of the act of fellatio'), thus finding in the fantasy an unconscious link between early mother-fixation and adult homosexuality.

28. H[1] 5v. This bestiary version suggests to Beck 'that the "dream" of the kite was neither a dream nor a memory but a fantasy based on the reintegration of some literary text familiar to Leonardo' (Beck 1993, 8).

29. The connection between birds and parentage is found elsewhere in the bestiary: 'Although partridges steal one another's eggs, nonetheless the young born of those eggs always return to their true mother' (H[1] 8v); and, in what seems a classically Freudian text, 'Pigeons are a symbol of ingratitude, for when they are old enough not to need feeding any more, they begin to fight with the father, and this struggle does not end until the young one drives the father out, and takes his wife, making her his own' (ibid., 7r).

30. I 64v, CA 1033r/370r-a.

31. CA 393r/145r-a; PC 2.279. The camel: H[1] 10v. '*Usare con*' = to be familiar with, or used to, hence a euphemism for sexual intimacy. The phrase is found in the

'Confessionale' of Leonardo's half-brother Lorenzo di Ser Piero da Vinci, *c.* 1520 (Florence, Biblioteca Riccardiana 1420, 80r), which refers to illegitimate children produced by men 'who have sex just once with a woman [*useranno un tempo con una femmina*] . . . such as a concubine or a serving-girl', a comment which may refer to his father's relations with Caterina. On Lorenzo, see Part II n. 90 below.

32. Pfister, 1913, 147. Freud incorporated this, with some reservations, into his second edition, 1919: see Freud 2001, 70–72.

33. CA 765r/282r-b. According to an unreliable tradition the mill was owned by Leonardo's uncle Francesco. By the later sixteenth century it was owned by the Ridolfi family, and it appears on the 'Guelf map' of Vinci (*c.* 1580) as 'Mulino di Doccia di Ridolfi'.

34. CA 1033r/370r-a. On sixteenth-century oliviculture see P.Vettori, *Trattato dello lodi de gl'ulive* (Florence, 1569); Vezzosi 1990.

35. In 1504–5, the probable date of the note, Leonardo was painting the *Battle of Anghiari* mural in Florence, a large-scale project requiring industrial quantities of paint.

36. CA 18r/4r-b.

37. Ma I 46v–47r, mid-1490s; an earlier horse-driven press ('*strettoio*') is in CA 47r/14r-a. See Vezzosi 1990, 14–17.

38. Dante, *Paradiso*, canto 14, 129, also playing on *vinci* = conquer (line 124); cf. Boethius, *De Consolatione*, Bk 3: '*Felice è quei che spezza il vinco del amor terreno*' – 'Happy is he who breaks the bonds of earthly love.' Leonardo uses the word in C 19v, describing a trick using 'an osier-shoot [*vincho*] and an arrow'.

39. On the academy engravings see below, Part V n. 111; the spelling of the words varies (often 'Achademia'). On the '*fantasia dei vinci*' by Correggio (a patron of Leonardo's friend Antonio Cammelli), see Kemp 1981, 187.

40. CA 888r/324r. A memo list of *c.* 1490 (CA 611r/225r-b) includes the phrase '*gruppi di Bramante*': Richter (R 1448) translates *gruppi* as 'groups', but it is probably a variant of *groppi*, referring to knot-designs by Leonardo's friend Donato Bramante.

41. Lomazzo 1584, 430; PC 2.328.

42. The 'Madrid book-list' of *c.* 1504 (Ma II 2v–3v) contains three copies of Aesop: a '*favole d'isopo*', an '*isopo in versi*', and a French edition, '*isopo illingia francosa*', perhaps *Les Fables de Esope* (Lyons, 1484).

43. Newsletter printed in Florence in 1516, titled *Letter of Andrea Corsali to the Illustrious Duke Giuliano de' Medici which arrived from the Indies in the month of October 1516.* Leonardo was in Giuliano's service in 1513–16. See Vecce 1998, 317, 442.

44. Ammirato 1637, 2.242.

45. Horse shown from behind: RL 12308r. Ox and ass: RL 12362r. Others: Zöllner 2003, nos. 89–93. Also early is the proportional study of a horse, RL 12318, perhaps connected to Verrocchio's project for the equestrian statue of Bartolomeo Colleoni. See Clayton 2002, 34.

46. Zöllner 2003, no. 13, silverpoint on buff-coloured prepared paper. At auction it 'soared past its £3.5m estimate in seconds' (Maeve Kennedy, *Guardian*, 11 July 2001).

47. RL 12653.

48. BM 1895-9-15-447 (Zöllner 2003, no. 157); I 48r. See also RL 12361 – red chalk with right-handed shading, thus probably a Melzi copy – and RL 12714.

49. F 47r, *c.* 1508.

50. See Part III n. 10 below.

51. H 109r.

52. RL 12363.

53. CA 477v/175v-a.

54. See Embolden 1987, 213–15, for a full list of trees and plants mentioned by Leonardo. Leonardo's depiction of the complex organic clusterings of wild plants is seen in his studies of brambles (RL 12419–20, '25–6, '29), probably related to early studies for the *Leda*, *c.* 1504–5, and in his depiction of a woodland copse (RL 12431r) with a single tree (*robinia*) on the verso.

55. CU 12r, McM 42.

56. BN 2038, 27v, formerly part of A, *c.* 1490–92.

57. CA 505v/184v-c, R 493. The word 'philosopher' in the heading appears to be crossed out.

58. Bramly 1992, 86.

59. CU 12r–12v, McM 42.

60. Uffizi GDS 436E; RL 12685.

61. For recent attempts to identify the landscape, see Natali 1999, 137–48, Nanni 1999, 7–17.

62. Tn 6v.

63. Landucci 1927, 35. The Capella di Santa Cecilia in Lucca, which originally housed a miraculous image of the Virgin, was also built outside the walls, though it is now enclosed in the larger arc of the Renaissance walls.

64. Bramly 1992, 84–5; PC 2.314.

65. Pedretti 1992, 163.

66. CA 327v/119v-a: 'Because I am not well-educated I know certain arrogant people think they can justifiably disparage me as an unlettered man.'

67. On the two educational systems of the Italian Renaissance, see Burke 1972.

68. RL 19086.

69. Ghiberti 1998, 46; Alberti, *De re aedificatoria* (1485; also called *De architectura*), 1.3.

70. F 96v. Cf. E 55r: 'My intention is first to record the experience and then by means of reason show why it must be so.'

71. CA 323r/117r-b, one of a series of texts headed 'Proemio' ('Preface'), written *c.* 1490 (PC 1.109). His views are summed up by one of the empiricist mottos of the Royal Society: '*Nullius in verba*' – 'Take no man's word for it.'

72. CA 392r/141r-b, R 660.

73. Ibid. After Giotto, he says, 'this art declined again, because everyone imitated what had been done by him', but was then revived by 'Tommaso the Florentine, called Masaccio', whose 'perfect works' were once more based on a study of Nature.

74. BN 2038, 19r.

75. CA 349v/206v-a.

76. Vezzosi 1998, 20, interpreting geometric patterns on a folio at Christ Church College, Oxford. Cf. Leic 28v and F 48v for rough-sketched designs for potters' lathes.

77. Donatello's *Magdalene*: Museo del Opera del Duomo, Florence. The Vinci *Magdalene*: Museo della Collegiata di Sant'Andrea, Empoli. The *Madonna of the Welcome* has been attributed to Bartolomeo Bellano.

78. King 2000, 113–17. The design of the craft is debated. A near-contemporary illustration by Marciano Taccola depicts it as a fourteen-wheeled wagon converted into a raft – an amphibious vehicle like a modern 'duck' – while other descriptions suggest a boat or barge with paddle-wheels. Its motive was economic: the high price of Carrara marble was partly due to the costs of transporting it from the quarry, in the Apuan Alps 60 miles north-west of Florence.

79. On Leonardo's left-handedness see Bambach 2003a, 31–57; on the evolution of his handwriting see PC 1.100–103. The earliest notice of his mirror-script is by his friend Luca Pacioli: 'He wrote in reverse, left-handed, and it could not be read except with a mirror, or by holding the back of the sheet up against the light' (*De viribus quantitatis* ['Of the Powers of Quantity'], Bologna, Biblioteca Universitaria MS 250, before 1508). An eighteenth-century owner of the Codex Leicester, probably the Roman painter Giuseppe Ghezzi, compared the script to Hebrew ('He wrote according to the custom of the Jews') and thought its motive was secrecy: 'He did this so that all could not read his writings so easily.' Leonardo's left-handed shading and hatching are an important tool for identifying his work, particularly in pen and ink. The lines typically (but not exclusively) course from lower right to upper left, the direction of a line being signalled by a slight indentation at the beginning of the stroke and by a small angular hook at the end where the pen left the paper. Leonardo was able to draw right-handed, and to write in the conventional direction (see illustration), but did not retrain himself to do so, as did Michelangelo, another natural southpaw.

PART TWO: Apprenticeship, 1466–1477

1. Michelangelo was apprenticed by his father to the Ghirlandaio workshop on 1 April 1488, a couple of weeks after his thirteenth birthday. The contract was for three years at a wage averaging 8 florins a year (Vasari 1987, 1.327–8). Botticini was also waged when he entered Neri di Bicci's workshop on 22 October 1449 (GDA, s.v. Botticini). However, both had previous artistic training, and were thus

taken on as assistants (*garzoni*). In the case of an unskilled pupil (*discepolo*) the boy's family paid the *maestro* for tuition and upkeep; this was probably the arrangement between Ser Piero and Verrocchio. That Leonardo began his apprenticeship in *c.* 1466 is argued by Beck 1988, 5–6, and Brown 1998, 76–7. Earlier writers like Clark and Venturier favoured *c.* 1469–70, because Ser Piero's 1469 tax return lists Leonardo among his *bocche* at Vinci; but this is a generalized claim of dependence, and it was anyway rejected by the inspectors, who put a cancelling line next to Leonardo's name. Vasari's statement that Ser Piero was a 'friend' of Verrocchio is strengthened by recently discovered documents which show him acting as Verrocchio's notary in various rental agreements between 1465 and 1471: see Cecchi 2003, 124.

2. *Necrologia Fiorentina*, San Biagio; cited Cianchi 1953, 49.

3. First documented in Ser Piero's tax return of 1469 (ASF, Catasto 1469, Quartiere San Spirito, Gonfalone Drago, filza 909/239, carta 498). The house was demolished when Via delle Prestanze (now Via Gondi) was redeveloped in the 1490s.

4. Cianchi 1953, 74.

5. Benedetto Dei, *Cronica Fiorentina* (1472), in Fanelli 1980, 82–5.

6. Kupferstichkabinett, Berlin. The map is a large woodcut attributed to the workshop of Francesco Rosselli; its name derives from the device of a lock and chain in the top left-hand corner (not visible in the reproduction on pp. 62–3). It shows a composite view of the city from the area between Bellosguardo and Monte Oliveto. See L. Ettlinger, 'A fifteenth century view of Florence', *Burlington Magazine* 581 (June 1952), 162–7.

7. Hibbert 1993, 155.

8. Rubinstein 1995, 72.

9. Bracciolini: *Dialogus contra avaritiam*, ed. G. Germano (Livorno, 1998). Savonarola: Lucas-Dubreton 1960, 46n.

10. Landucci 1927, 48 (20 August 1489); Lucas-Dubreton 1960, 131.

11. Machiavelli, *La Mandragola*, 2.3, 14–15.

12. Accused of promoting worthless supporters to political office, Cosimo retorted, 'A worthy man can be made with two braccia of crimson cloth' (i.e. to make the *lucco* or mantle of the Florentine legislator). Half a century later his great-grandson Pope Leo X espoused the same policy: 'Assure yourself of the *Otto* and the *Balia* [legislative committees], and . . . be sure to elect to the offices of the *Monte* [the city bank] keen-witted, secret and trusty men entirely devoted to you'. See Villari 1892, 2.43, 456. On Cosimo: Kent 2000.

13. Cecchi 2003, 123–4; other religious foundations which regularly used Ser Piero's services were La Badia Fiorentina and Sant'Apollonia.

14. Vecce 1998, 33. Cf. Vasari on the early career of Brunelleschi, also the son of a notary. His father wanted him to take up the profession, and was 'upset' because he showed no aptitude for it. 'Seeing the boy was always investigating ingenious problems of art and mechanics, he made him learn arithmetic and writing, and then apprenticed him to the goldsmith' art with a friend of his so that he might

study design' (Vasari 1987, 1.134). This seems parallel to Leonardo's course fifty years later.

15. G. Calvi, RV 13 (1926), 35–7. The rental agreement is dated 25 October 1468; the premises were owned by La Badia. In 1472 Ser Piero chose the church as the site of the family tomb (Beltrami 1919, no. 6), and he was buried there in 1504.

16. Jardine 1996, 37–44.

17. CA 42v/12v-a, R 1439.

18. Hauser 1962, 2.3–6.

19. Cristoforo Landino, *Comento sopra la Commedia di Dante* (Florence, 1481), iv r; Baxandall 1988, 114–17.

20. These feats are described in the anonymous *Life* of Alberti, in Latin, which survives in an eighteenth-century transcription by Antonio Muratori; though written in the third person, it is almost certainly a precocious – and not very reliable – autobiography, written *c*. 1438. See Grafton 2000, 14–17.

21. Ibid., 18. In one of his *facetiae,* Leonardo wrote of 'a good man who was censured by another for being illegitimate'. He replied, 'Judged by the laws of humanity and nature I am legitimate, while you are a bastard because you have the habits of a beast rather than a man' (Ma II 65r, PC 2.276).

22. Grafton 2000, 9–29; M. Baxandall, 'Alberti's self', *Fenway Court* (1990–91), 31–6.

23. Biblioteca Nazionale, Florence, Codex Magliabechiano XI 121. In 1468 Toscanelli installed a marble gnomon inside the dome of Florence cathedral, by which he could 'determine midday to half a second' (F. Streicher, 'Paolo dal Pozzo Toscanelli', *Catholic Encyclopedia* (New York, 1912), vol. 14).

24. Cited in G. Uzielli, *La vita e i tempi di Paolo dal Pozzo Toscanelli* (Rome, 1894), 20.

25. GDA s.v. Uccello.

26. On the varied output of Verrocchio's studio, see Butterfield 1997, Rubin and Wright 1999. 'Verrocchio & Co.': Clark 1988, 49. Paul Hills remarks on the 'coarsening' of Verrocchio's style through commercialism: 'Between invention and replication something is lost' ('The power of make-believe', *TLS*, 7 January 2000).

27. In 1462 Verrocchio's *bottega* is described as 'at the top' (*a capo*) of Via Ghibellina, but the street did not then begin at the corner of the Bargello, as it does today; this western stretch of the street was then called Via del Palagio. The *bottega* probably stood near the present intersection of Via Ghibellina with Via Giuseppe Verdi. See Brown 2000, 13. This is probably the area referred to by the diarist Landucci as the 'Canto delle Stinche'; he records a murder taking place there in 1500, 'outside the butcher's shop at the corner of Via Ghibellina next to the Stinche' (Landucci 1927, 176).

28. For Verrocchio the area outside the Porta alla Croce had other associations. Here, in August 1452, the teenage Andrea threw a stone during a scuffle with other youths; it hit a fourteen-year-old woolworker called Antonio di Domenico,

who later died of the injury, and Andrea was briefly arrested on a charge of manslaughter. See Vasari 1878, 3.358n; Butterfield 1997, 3.

29. Butterfield 1997, 21–31; on Leonardo as model, Nicodemi 1934, 14–15, Brown 2000, 10.

30. GDA, s.v. Ferrucci; other pages of the sketchbook are in London, New York, Berlin, Dijon, Chantilly and Hamburg. The page with a line of Leonardo hand-writing (Louvre) is reproduced in Pedretti 1998, 22.

31. ASF, Tribunale della Mercanzia 1539, 301r–302v; Covi 1966, 103. The document is part of a legal dispute between Verrocchio's brother Tommaso and his executor Lorenzo di Credi.

32. 'Pistole d'ovidio' in a book-list of the early 1490s (CA 559r/210r-a); 'ovidio metamorfoseos' in the 'Madrid book-list' of c. 1504 (Ma II 2v–3v). Leonardo quotes from the Metamorphoses on a folio of c. 1480, CA 879r/320r-b.

33. The Uffizi portrait is variously credited to Credi, Raphael and Perugino himself; on the pen-and-ink drawing (Uffizi GDS 250E) see Rubin and Wright 1999, 144.

34. Gilbert 1992, 34. On Florentine artistic apprenticeship see also Rubin and Wright 1999, 78ff.; Luchinat 1992.

35. Cennini 1933, 4–5.

36. PC 1.11 (part of the fragmentary supplement to Giovio's Leonardi Vincii vita).

37. Rubin and Wright 1999, no. 29; cf. RL 12515.

38. The drapery study illustrated (Louvre, Cabinet des Dessins RF 2255; Zöllner 2003, no. 183) is similar but not identical to the Virgin's drapery in the Annunciation. It is also close to the drapery of the Madonna in another work from the Verrocchio studio, Lorenzo di Credi's Pistoia altarpiece (c. 1476–85), but it is closest of all to Domenico Ghirlandaio's Madonna Enthroned with Saints, c. 1484 (Uffizi), one of various suggestions of interchange between these two workshops.

39. Vezzosi 1997, 32.

40. Drapery in the Trattato: CU 167r–170v, McM 559–74. 'Thin cloths' etc.: RL 19121r.

41. The Youthful Christ (see illustration, p. 122), about 13 inches (33 cm) high, is in a private collection (Coll. Gallendt, Rome). On its identity with the 'little head' (testicciola) owned by Lomazzo, see M. Kemp, ALV 4 (1991), 171–6; Pedretti 1998b, 15–16.

42. Lomazzo 1584, 159.

43. CA 888r/342r.

44. BM 1895-9-15-474, metalpoint on cream-coloured paper, usually dated c. 1472–5. According to Vasari, Verrocchio's Darius was commissioned by Lorenzo de' Medici to send to Matthias Corvinus, king of Hungary, together with a companion piece showing Alexander the Great; the Darius is echoed in a glazed terracotta profile from the della Robbia workshop, c. 1500, which is very similar to Leonardo's drawing. The profile is a type found elsewhere in Verrocchio's work: in one of the soldiers of his silver relief for the Baptistery, the Beheading of St John, 1477–80; and in his statue of Bartolomeo Colleoni done in Venice in the mid-1480s.

45. He did not get this commission: six Virtues were painted by the Pollaiuolo brothers and one, *Fortitude* (Uffizi), was subcontracted by them to Botticelli (GDA 4.493, s.v. Botticelli).

46. A 1r, R 628.

47. See Dunkerton and Roy 1996 for a technical analysis of Florentine panel paintings of the 1470s and '80s (by Botticelli, Ghirlandaio, Filippino Lippi et al.) in the National Gallery, London. The artists' choice of paint was 'relatively conservative'; they used some oil paint for specific colours, but generally preferred the 'light and brilliant tonality' of egg tempera; 'they seem to have rejected, perhaps quite consciously, the more innovative and experimental technique of the oil medium.'

48. Baxandall 1988, 6.

49. An 'artificial' malachite, a precipitate of copper salts, was also used: it is found in the landscape of Uccello's *Battle of San Romano* (National Gallery, London), dating from the 1430s; see Dunkerton and Roy 1996, 28, 31.

50. CA 704bv/262r-c; cf. a similar recipe in CA 195v/71v-a (R 619), a sheet containing fragments of poetry datable to c. 1480 (see p. 154 above).

51. Villata 1999, no. 17. The Ingesuati, whose monastery stood outside the Porta a Pinti, were another of Ser Piero da Vinci's clients (Cecchi 2003, 123).

52. Dull landscapes: CU 33v, McM 93. Indecorous *Annunciation*: CU 33r, McM 92. Botticelli's *Annunciation* (Uffizi) is not the only candidate for Leonardo's criticism (see, for example, Luca Signorelli's, Johnson Coll., Philadelphia). 'Sandro!': CA 331r/120r-d; the dispute hinted at here may be part of a deeper split between the religiosity of Botticelli in his post-Savonarolan phase and the proudly scientific Leonardo (Argan 1957, 127f.)

53. Baxandall 1988, 111–14. Giovanni Santi or de Santis was court painter to the Duke of Urbino. The ostensible context of the poem is the Duke's visit to Florence in the spring of 1482, but these lines seem to have been written earlier. By 1482 Perugino was about thirty-three and Leonardo thirty, thus hardly 'young men', and neither was still in Florence. The poem also commends Ghirlandaio, Filippino Lippi, Botticelli and Luca Signorelli ('*il cortonese Luca*'). The phrase '*par d'amori*' probably means 'equal in the number of their lovers', i.e. equally admired.

54. On Credi's *Annunciation* (Louvre), see Marani 1999, 67–8; Zöllner 2003, 220.

55. GDA 19.675, s.v. Lorenzo di Credi; Covi 1966.

56. Contracts for Piero della Francesca's *Madonna della Misericordia*, San Sepolcro, 1445, and Filippino's Strozzi-chapel frescos, 1487: Baxandall 1988, 20–21.

57. According to Vasari, the Pollaiuolo *Tobias* (Gall. Sabauda, Turin) was by both brothers in collaboration, and was painted for the guild hall of Orsanmichele (Vasari 1987, 2.74).

58. Brown 2000, 14–19; cf. W. Suida, 'Leonardo's activity as a painter', in Marazza 1954, 315–29.

59. Scalini 1992, 62–3.

60. Landucci 1927, 33, 42. Gostanzo 'won twenty *palii* [in various cities] with his Barbary horse, Draghetto' – the 'Little Dragon'.

61. CA 629av/231v-b, R 707. Architectural designs on the verso are for the summer-house of Charles d'Amboise, *c.* 1508, suggesting that the 'comedy' was for the French in Milan. 'Birds which can fly': Lomazzo 1584, 106.

62. Baxandall 1988, 71–6; Ventrone 1992, 57–9.

63. Martines 2003, 14.

64. Lubkin 1999, app. 4.

65. Machiavelli, *Istorie Fiorentine*, Bk 7, ch. 28 (Machiavelli 1966, 2.729).

66. Coll. Bartolini-Salimbeni, Florence. The painting is sometimes attributed to Giovanni Battista Bertucci (or Utili).

67. Vasari 1987, 1.235–6. The orb we see today is not Verrocchio's, which was dislodged by lightning on the night of 17 January 1600 and was replaced by the present ball, which is larger than Verrocchio's, in March 1602.

68. Landucci 1927, 9, and note citing entries in the *Quaderno di Cassa* of the Opera del Duomo.

69. G 84v.

70. Vasari 1987, 1.146–7. The incident is not found in the earlier biography attributed to Antonio Manetti.

71. On the construction of the dome, see King 2001, 83–107; R. Mainstone, 'Brunelleschi's dome of S. Maria del Fiore', *Transactions of the Newcomen Society* 42 (1969–70), 107–26.

72. Kemp 1989, 219–22, on which this paragraph is based. See also Pedretti 1976, 9–13; Reti 1965. The later date is suggested by details of Brunelleschian mechanisms on a sheet dated 1478 (Uffizi GDS 446E).

73. Reversible hoist or *collo grande* (illustrated): CA, 1083v/391v (Kemp 1989, plate 120). On this device, also called the 'ox hoist', and a drawing of it by Mariano Taccola, see King 2001, 58–61. Revolving crane: CA 965r /349r-a (Kemp 1989, plate 121). Crane on rails: CA 808r/295r-b (Pedretti 1976, plate 7).

74. CA 909v/333v.

75. Milanese domes: B 18v, 21r, 22r, etc.; CA 849v/310v-a. Herring-bone bricks: CA 933v/341v-a.

76. ASF Accademia del Disegno 2, 93v; Villata 1999, no. 5.

77. G. Moreni, *Notizie* (Florence, 1793), 6.161; Ottino della Chiesa 1967, 88; Marani 2000a, 48–52.

78. Brown 1998, 76–9, 194–5.

79. The lectern also quotes from the tomb of Carlo Marsuppini, sculpted in the 1450s by Desiderio di Settignano, and doubtless seen by Leonardo in the church of Santa Croce a few minutes' walk from the *bottega*.

80. Kemp 1981, 54. Errors of perspective: Clark 1988, 53.

81. Baxandall 1988, 49–56.

82. Ibid., 50, citing Roberto Caraccioli, *Sermones de laudibus sanctorum* (Naples, 1489).

83. Clark 1988, 62.

84. Natali 1998, 269–70; Cecchi 2003, 126–7. Simone di Cione was abbot in 1471–3 and 1475–8.

85. CA 225r/83r-a, c. 1513–15; PC 2.351. A meeting between them in Florence in 1506 is recorded in a letter from Amadori to Isabella d'Este (see p. 375). Ottaviano de' Medici (d. 1546) was a younger cousin of Lorenzo, whose grand-daughter Francesca he married.

86. Ottino della Chiesa 1967, 89.

87. CU 6v, McM 24.

88. CU 135r, McM 554, from BN 2038 29r. Dragon drawings: RL 12370; Louvre, Coll. Rothschild 7810.

89. Lomazzo 1584, Bk 2, ch. 20; W. Suida, *Leonardo und sein Kreis* (Munich, 1929), fig. 117.

90. Antonio was the first of twelve legitimate children belatedly fathered by Ser Piero: his second child, Maddalena, died in infancy, but the others survived him. Six were born to his third wife, Margherita di Francesco di Iacopo di Guglielmo (d. 1486), and six to his fourth wife, Lucrezia di Guglielmo Giuliani. The latter was nearly forty years younger than Ser Piero, and twelve years younger than Leonardo, and outlived both of them. Most prominent among Leonardo's half-brothers was the second son, Giuliano (b. 1480), who became notary to the Signoria in 1516 and Florentine *orator* at the Helvetic League in 1518. Lorenzo (b. 1484) was a wool-merchant who penned an edifying religious essay, the 'Confessionale' (see Part I n. 31). Guglielmo (b. 1496) inherited the house at Anchiano, which was sold by his grandson and namesake in 1624. The youngest son, Giovanni (b. 1498), is heard of as 'innkeeper and butcher' at Mercatale, near Vinci, where Accattabriga once had his kilns. The son of Bartolomeo (b. 1497), Pierfrancesco or Pierino da Vinci, became a talented sculptor, but died in his early twenties in 1553.

91. Ottino della Chiesa 1967, 89–90; Walker 1967.

92. On Ginevra and her family see articles in DBI; Fletcher 1989; Cecchi 2003, 129–31. Cecchi notes the notarial presence of Ser Piero, who handled various Benci documents between 1458 and 1465, including the will of Ginevra's grandmother Maddelana in 1460. Leonardo remained friendly with Ginevra's brother Giovanni (1456–1523), and in 1482 left the unfinished *Adoration of the Magi* in his safe keeping. (Vasari says he left it at the 'house of Amerigo de' Benci', which is sometimes misinterpreted as referring to Ginevra's father; it refers to Giovanni's son, who was head of the family when Vasari was writing.) Giovanni is mentioned in Leonardo memoranda of the early 1500s: 'the map of the world which Giovanni Benci has' (CA 358r/130r-a), and 'book of Giovanni Benci's' (L 1v). It is possible that the latter is the book of veterinary science (Jordanus Ruffus, *De medicina veterinaria*) now in the Laurentian Library, Florence, bearing the inscription '*Questo libro è di Giovanni d'Amerigo Benci, 1485*', and further possible that the same book is described in Leonardo's book-list of 1504 as '*libro di medicina di cavalla*' ('book about medicine for horses'): see Solmi 1908, 92; PC 2.361.

NOTES TO PART TWO: APPRENTICESHIP

93. As in all Renaissance texts, *virtus* or *virtù* has a more complex meaning than today's morally tinged 'virtue'. Philosophically it refers to the spiritual essence contained, or imprisoned, inside the material world – the sense still used, with an alchemical overtone, when we talk of the curative 'virtues' of a plant. In an applied sense it refers to personal qualities of intellectual power, excellence, aspiration, talent; Leonardo uses the word frequently in this sort of sense.

94. RL 12558r. A hypothetical reconstruction of the original *Ginevra*, based on the extant portrait, the Windsor hands and the Verrocchio posy, has been generated by the Washington National Gallery's Department of Imaging: Brown 2000, plate 3. The Verrocchio bust was not the only sculpture of Ginevra: an account of works destroyed in the Savonarolan bonfires of 1497–8 includes a sculpted head of 'the beautiful Bencia' (Butterfield 1997, 96).

95. Bembo's copy of *De amore*: Bodleian Library, Oxford, Can. Class. Lat. 156. *Bembicae Peregrinae*: Eton College Library, Cod. 156. See Fletcher 1989, 811. The emblem of the laurel and palm in the *Peregrinae* (111v) was drawn by Bembo's friend Bartolomeo Sanvito; it is very close to Leonardo's version, and may have been a direct source of it. Technical analysis of the *Ginevra* (Zöllner 2003, 219) shows that the motto on the reverse originally read '*Virtus et Honor*', as in the *Peregrinae* emblem. On Bembo see N. Giannetto, *Bernardo Bembo, umanista e politico Veneziano* (Florence, 1985). His son was the famous humanist Pietro Bembo, one of the interlocutors in Castiglione's *The Courtier*.

96. Poliziano, *Stanze per la Giostra* (1476), Bk 1, lines 43–4.

97. Brown 2000, 124–5.

98. On the philosophical context of Botticelli's paintings see Gombrich 1945; G. Ferruolo, 'Botticelli's mythologies, Ficino's *De amore*, Poliziano's *Stanze per la giostra*', *Art Bulletin* 3 (1965).

99. Ficino, *De vita coelitus*, ch. 18, in *Opera omnia* (Basle, 1576), 557; see Yates 1965, 71. On Ficinian magic, see D. P. Walker, *Spiritual and Demonic Magic from Ficino to Campanella* (London, 1959).

100. Yates 1965, 281–2. The '*furor amoris*' ('ecstasy of love') which Ficino associates with Venus becomes a familiar motif in Elizabethan poetry; a sonnet sequence by the Italian occultist Giordano Bruno, *Gli eroici furori* (London, 1586), is a particular link. This train of influence suggests a remote but attractive consanguinity between Leonardo's *Ginevra* and Shakespeare's *Venus and Adonis* (1593).

101. Leonardo probably owned a copy of Ficino's *Theologica Platonica*, completed in 1474 and published in 1482. In his book-list of *c.* 1492 (CA 559r/210r-a) he includes a book or manuscript designated '*de immortalità d'anima*': the subtitle of Ficino's book is '*De animarum immortalitate*'. But the phrase '*Ermete filosofo*' ('Hermes the philosopher'), jotted on the cover of Paris MS M, is not enough to show that Leonardo knew Ficino's translations of the mystical Hermetica, the *Pimander*. To call Leonardo an 'Aristotelian' should not be taken as dogmatic. Bembo himself, Fletcher notes (1989, 814), 'proved resistant to the philosophical

aspects of Ficino's neo-Platonism', having been deeply influenced by Aristotelian and Averroist teachers at Padua university.

102. CA 18/4r-b, v-b (R1553, 1359). On the identity of Bernardo see PC 2.384. Another name on the sheet is 'Franco d'Antonio di Ser Piero', i.e. Uncle Francesco. Bramly (1992, 154) notes that the last three words, written '*di s pero*', also spell out '*dispero*' ('I despair'): it is tempting to hear a punning comment about his relationship with his father, though the name refers in this instance to Leonardo's great-grandfather.

103. ASF, Ufficiali di Notte 18/2, 41v (9 April), 51r (7 June); Villata 1999, nos. 7, 8.

104. Smiraglia Scognamiglio 1896, 313–15. Milanesi's reference: Vasari 1878, 4.22n. Uzielli 1884, 200–201, 441–8.

105. *Sogni* (see Introduction n. 22), 136v–137v. Possibly Lomazzo had confidential first-hand information about Leonardo's private life from Melzi; more likely he is stating something that other biographers knew but did not state. The statement is discreet in that Lomazzo never published the *Sogni*.

106. Ar 44r; Pedretti 2001, 71–4. In anatomical texts Leonardo generally uses *verga* or *membro* for the penis, but see RL 19030r, *c.* 1506–8, where the *cazzo* is said to be 'the minister of the human species'. On 'The Running Cock' (Fors 2 40r), see C. Pedretti, ALV 4 (1991); A. Marinoni, RV 24 (1992), 181–8. Phallic animals: CA 132–133v/48r-a, r-b.

107. Saslow 1986; Rocke 1996; Orto 1989. See also Alan Bray, *Homosexuality in Renaissance England* (London, 1982).

108. Cellini 2002, 301. Though Botticelli was not convicted, an assistant of his was, in 1473. See R. Lightbown, *Sandro Botticelli: Life and work* (London, 2 vols., 1978), 1.152–4.

109. Rocke 1987.

110. Dante, *Inferno*, cantos 14–15. Dante's response is complicated by the presence of his former teacher, Ser Brunetto Latino, among the damned. On hardline attitudes further to the 1484 papal bull 'Summis desiderantes affectibus', see M. Consoli, *Independence Gay* (Viterbo, 2000), ch. 1; T. Herzig, 'Witchcraft and homosexuality in Pico's *Strix*', *Sixteenth-Century Journal* 34/1 (2003), 60–71.

111. Kupferstichkabinett, Berlin, Codex Hamilton 201; Vatican, Biblioteca Apostolica, Reginense Lat. 1896. Between them these contain illustrations for 25 cantos of the *Inferno* (cantos 2–7, 9 and 14 are lost), all 33 cantos of the *Purgatorio*, and 31 cantos of the *Paradiso* (cantos 31 and 33 are missing, possibly never done).

112. Giovanni di Renzo: ASF, Catasto 1427, Indice delle famiglie. Bartolomeo, Antonio, Bernardo: ASF, Catasto 1457, Sommario dei campioni 2 (Santa Croce), C3. One of these three, who are assessed together in 1457, may be the father of Giovanni (thus named after his grandfather) and Jacopo; their actual *portata* (filza 798, carta 78) has so far proved elusive, though Jacopo, who was only seventeen in 1476, would not be on it.

113. DBI s.v. Benci, Antonio (the birth-name of Pollaiuolo, the latter being a

soprannome referring to his father's trade of poulterer; no relationship to Ginevra's family is apparent).

114. CA 680v/252v-a. Dated *c.* 1504–5 by Pedretti (PC 2.311–12) for its similarities to CA 84r/30r-b, which has a sketch related to the *Anghiari* mural. A standing man on RL 12328r, also *c.* 1505, may conceivably be connected to the 'grown up' Christ. Richter (R 1364n) gallantly but implausibly suggests that the debacle over the Christ-child arose from the *Madonna and Child with a Cat* studies of the late 1470s, which 'would have been considered strange and irreverent by the Church authorities'.

115. CA 1094r/394r-b; 32r/9r-b.

116. BN 2037, 10r.

117. Uffizi GDS 446E. Different readings: R 1383; Thiis 1913, 151; PC 2.327–8.

118. It is possibly a studio patronym: 'Fioravanti pupil of Domenico'. The workshops of Domenico Ghirlandaio and Domenico di Michelino (mentioned by Leonardo in a note of *c.* 1480, CA 42v/12v-a) spring to mind, but the name is very common.

119. On the Fortaguerri monument, see Butterfield 1997; GDA 19.675–6.

120. RL 12572. The study of St Donatus (Coll. Wildenstein, New York) is attributed to Verrocchio, but recent analysis reveals left-handed brush-strokes in the shading of the face and throat. It was shown at the exhibition '*Leonardo e dintorni*' (Arezzo, 2001).

121. RL 12685, *c.* 1503–4, marked as 'Sangenaio'. On the church, see G. Lera, *Capannori: vicende di una civiltà contadina* (Lucca, 1996), 88.

122. L. Bertolini and M. Bucci, *Arte sacra dal VI al XIX secolo* (Lucca, 1957), no. 210; Pedretti 1998b, 16–22; local information, 11 June 2003.

123. D 4r.

124. Jean Lemaire, *Plainte du désiré* (1509), in Nicodemi 1934, 8.

125. CA 807r/295r-a.

126. CU 20v, McM 51.

127. Fors 3 83r.

PART THREE: Independence, 1477–1482

1. ASF, Mediceo avanti il principato 37, 49; ALV 5 (1992), 120–22.

2. ASF, Signori e Collegi 94, 5v (10 January 1478), 27r (16 March); Villata 1999, nos. 9, 10.

3. It is also possible that the Anonimo was confused – Filippino did later paint an altarpiece for the Palazzo Vecchio (*c.* 1486), though it was commissioned by the Otto di Pratica (the magistrature) and has no connection with the San Bernardo commission; and he did paint an altarpiece to substitute for an unfinished work by Leonardo (his *Adoration of the Magi* for the monastery of San Donato). The Anonimo's statement may be a garbling of these two paintings.

4. Clark 1933, 136–40; see illustrations on p. 239 above.

5. B. Berenson, *Study and Criticism of Italian Art*, vol. 3 (London, 1916); S. Brandi, *La Fiera litteraria* (Rome, 1967).

6. E. de Liphart, *Starye Gody* (St Petersburg, 1909), in Ottino della Chiesa 1967, 90.

7. Embolden 1987, 120.

8. Uffizi GDS 212F (illustrated), sometimes attributed to Verrocchio; Louvre, Cabinet des Dessin 486 (Zöllner 2003, no. 118); BM 1860–6–16–100r (Zöllner 2003, no. 4).

9. C. Pedretti, 'Il disegno di Oporto', RV 27 (1997), 3–11. Windsor word-lists: RL 12561.

10. Madonna and child with the infant St John: RL 12276; Clark and Pedretti 1968, 1.3–4. Madonna and child with a cat: rapid sketches: BM 1857–1–10–1r, v (verso illustrated), 1860–6–16–98; Musée Bonnat, Bayonne (Zöllner 2003, nos. 110–13); more finished studies: BM 1856–6–26–1r, v; private coll.; Uffizi GDS 421E (Zöllner 2003, nos. 115–17, 119).

11. On the conspiracy, see Martines 2003; Acton 1979; Machiavelli, *Istorie Fiorentine*, Bk 8, chs. 1–9 (Machiavelli 1966, 2.738–46); A. Poliziano, *Conjurationis Pactianae commentario*.

12. Martines 2003, 257ff.

13. Vasari 1987, 1.239–40; G. Milanesi, *Archivio storico* 6 (1862), 5.

14. Landucci 1927, 28, though another contemporary source, Belfredello Alfieri's *Chronichetta*, dates the execution to the 29th (R 664n).

15. Musée Bonnat, Bayonne. Poliziano described Bernardo as a 'desperado' (*uomo perduto*), but the Baroncelli were an established Florentine clan of the Santa Croce quarter; Maddalena Bandini Baroncelli (d. 1460) was Ginevra de' Benci's paternal grandmother. It is not impossible that Leonardo knew the man whose execution he recorded.

16. ASF, Operai Palazzo, Stanziamenti 10, 79v, 80v.

17. See Brescia and Tomio 1999 for recent discoveries, including a seventeenth-century transcript of his funeral monument at Sant'Agata.

18. Ammirato 1637, 2.242. 'Zoroastro', after the Persian magus Zarethustra, is garbled to 'Geroastro' in the anonymous *Antiquarie prospettiche Romane*, IV (see Part V n. 119). Ammirato adds two further variations: 'Alabastro' and 'Chiliabastro'.

19. I² 49v, R 704; cf. I² 47v, showing costumes decorated with shells, beads and cords.

20. H 106v.

21. Benvenuto della Golpaja, 'Libro di macchine' (Venice, Biblioteca Nazionale di San Marco, H IV 41); Pedretti 1957, 26.

22. Ar 148r–v, R 1548–9.

23. ASF, Antica Badia Fiorentina, Familiari XI 322, 146ff; Brescia and Tomio 1999, 69–70. The letter also mentions Tommaso's sister, Maddalena, 'riding furiously through the woods' at Quaracci, looking like an '*amazone*'.

24. CA 950v/346v-a. On the tarantula, see also H 17v: 'The bite of a tarantula fixes a man in his intention, that is, what he was thinking when he was bitten.' Though nowadays referring to hairy spiders of tropical America (genus *Mygale*), the original tarantula was a large spider found in southern Italy (genus *Lycosa*). It was named after the Pugliese town of Taranto. Its bite was supposed to cause 'tarantism', a hysterical malady resembling St Vitus's dance (or Sydenham's chorea), though the cause of these communal hysterias is now thought to be ergot-poisoning.

25. A. Grazzini, *Le Cene*, ed. C. Verzone (Florence, 1890), 140–41.

26. V. Borghini, *Discorsi* (Florence, 1584), 163; Pedretti 1976, plate 13.

27. Vasari 1876, 4.446.

28. Hydraulic devices: CA 1069r/386r-b (illustrated), 1069v/386v-b; 26r/7r-a, 26v/7v-a; 1048r/376r-a (Zöllner 2003, nos. 509, 511–14). Hygrometer: Louvre, Cabinet des Dessins 2022; Zöllner 2003, no. 130. Vasari also says that as a 'young man' Leonardo 'was the first to propose canalizing the Arno river between Pisa and Florence'. This is often dismissed as a confusion with Leonardo's later canalization projects, *c.* 1503–4, but it is perfectly possible that he had earlier thoughts that way. Brunelleschi's aborted project to inundate the plain around Lucca (at war with Florence in the 1420s) would be a precedent.

29. CA 42v/12v-a

30. A 64r, *c.* 1490–92; PC 2.119–20. The treatise (Biblioteca Riccardiana, Cod. 211) may have been written for Toscanelli's friend Brunelleschi.

31. CA 5r/1 bis r-a.

32. On Argyropoulos, see DBI; G. Cammelli, *Giovanni Argiropulo* (Florence, 1941).

33. Alberti, *De re aedificatoria* (1485), Bk 10, ch. 10; Pedretti 1976, 8.

34. Uffizi GDS 447E; Pedretti 1957, 211–16.

35. 'Antonio da Pistoia': CA 18r/4r-b. On Cammelli, see DBI; A. Capelli, 'Notizie di Antonio Cammelli', in Cammelli 1884, xxv-lix. He is also sometimes known as Antonio Vinci, referring to his birthplace, San Piero a Vincio, then a village outside the western gate of Pistoia.

36. Capelli, 'Notizie' (see n. 35), xxxiii, xlii, citing Berni's sonnet, 'Il medico Guazzaletto', and Aretino's *Ragionamenti*.

37. Cammelli 1884, 180.

38. Ibid., 165.

39. CA 80r/28r-b.

40. CA 195r/71r-a; Pedretti 1957, 79–89; Luca Pulci, *Pistole*, 8.130–32.

41. CA 55r/16v-a; PC 2.386. Cf. Cammelli's sonnet against Bellincioni, envisaging him 'crowned with a wreath of stinging nettles' (Cammelli 1884, 53). On Bellincioni see DBI, and Fanfani's introduction to the *Rime* (Bellincioni 1876). Bellincioni praised Leonardo's 'drawings and colours, of which both ancients and moderns are in awe' (Sonnet 77, *c.* 1485–90), and collaborated with Leonardo in Milan in 1490 (see pp. 257–8 above).

42. National Music Museum, South Dakota, no. 4203 (http://*www.usd.edu*/

smm); Winternitz 1982, 25–38; Katherine Powers, 'The lira da braccio in the angel's hands in Renaissance Madonna Enthroned paintings', *Music in Art* 26 (2001).

43. Cellini 2002, 9–11.

44. T. Smollet, *Travels through France and Italy* (London, 1776), letter 27 (28 January 1765).

45. CU 18v, McM 41. On Ficino's orphic hymns, see Yates 1965, 78–80.

46. RL 12697; my thanks to Sasha, who played me this melody. Another version of this riddle is in RL 12699.

47. The 32 inch (85 cm) replica, constructed by Cremonese lutenist Giorgio Scolari and acoustic scientist Andrea Iorio, was exhibited in 2002. The stringed instrument in the shape of a monster's head (BN 2037, fol. C, formerly part of MS B, *c.* 1487–90) is the nearest we get to the 'skull lyre' and may conceivably be the illustration referred to by Amoretti (1804, 32–3). On Leonardo's other musical inventions, see Richter 1970, 1.69f., Winternitz 1982.

48. A 22v.

49. CA 888r/324r. Richter reads it as 'Atalanta' (R 680), though this legendary Greek beauty was usually depicted running rather than raising her face. On Migliorotti, see Vecce 1998, 72–5. There is a fragmentary draft of a letter to him ('Talante') by Leonardo (CA 890r/325r-b).

50. Louvre, Cabinet de Dessins 2022, *c.* 1480; Zöllner 2003, no. 130. The musician is top right; the sheet also contains a design for a hygrometer with notes, and some figure studies suggestive of a Last Supper.

51. RL 12276. The lower half of a sketch of a kneeling angel (BM 1913–6–17–1) is also related to the painting, though not a study for it.

52. Papa 2000, 37.

53. On the similarity to Santa Maria Novella, see Pedretti 1988, 280; Papa 2000, 40. My suggestion that the painting was commissioned by Rucellai is speculative, but no more so than the idea that it was commissioned for the Ferranti chapel at the Badia, and that the later *St Jerome* painted for the chapel by Filippino Lippi (*c.* 1489) was a substitute for it (A. Cecchi, *Uffizi studi e ricerche* 5 (1998), 59–72). On the possibility that Leonardo travelled with Rucellai to Milan in 1482, see p. 177 above. He seems to have taken the painting with him: it is echoed on the title-page of the Milanese poem *Antiquarie prospettiche romane*, addressed to Leonardo *c.* 1495–1500. The 'San Girolamo' recorded among the paintings owned by Leonardo's pupil Salai in 1524 (Shell and Sironi 1991) is unlikely to be the extant painting, but may be a copy of it by Salai. An inventory of paintings in Parma in 1680 includes a St Jerome attributed to Leonardo, but the description and the measurements given do not correspond with the extant painting (Chiesa 1967, 92). According to a well-worn story, the picture was rediscovered in the early nineteenth century by Cardinal Fesch, an uncle of Napoleon, who found half of it in a Roman junk-shop, and the other half many months later in a shoemaker's shop, being used as a bench. The story sounds apocryphal (one happy chance too

many), though it is true that the painting was at one stage sawn in two. In 1845 it was bought from Fesch's estate by Pope Pius IX for the Vatican Gallery, at a cost of 2,500 francs.

54. Landucci 1927, 44, 275. On a late sheet (CA 803r/294r-a, c. 1517–18), Leonardo sketches a ground plan of the Florentine lion-house ('*stanze de lioni di firenze*').

55. RL 19114v. Bestiary: H¹ 11r, R 1232, cf. H¹ 18v.

56. RL 12692r. On Alberti's fables, with a fictional 'letter to Aesop', see Grafton 2000, 213–14. Leonello d'Este also used a lion as his emblem.

57. Ar 155r, R 1339.

58. Ar 224r, 231v.

59. This is not to exclude other possible glosses on the cave, among them a Freudian analogy with bodily orifices. The gaping vulva in an anatomical sheet of c. 1509 (RL 19095v, see illustration on p. 421) might suggest that the 'threatening dark cave' refers at a subconscious level to the disturbing mysteries of female sexuality. The cave as 'residence of Pluto' may also relate to misogynistic imagery of female genitalia as a 'hell', as found in Ghigo Brunelleschi and Ser Domenico da Prato's erotic poem *Geta e Birria* (Florence, c. 1476), where the protagonist plunges his member 'into the measureless depths of hell' ('*senza misura nello 'nferno*'): Leonardo owned a copy of this poem in 1504. In one of Leonardo's fables (CA 188r/67r-b, R 1282), a goblet of wine prepares for the 'death' of being swallowed into the 'foul and fetid caverns of the human body'.

60. Bramly 1992, 156.

61. Vasari 1987, 1.331.

62. Leonardo's memorandum '*Fatiche d'erchole a pier f ginori / L'orto de medici*' ('The Labours of Hercules for Pierfrancesco Ginori. The garden of the Medici'), CA 782v/288v-a, may refer to the San Marco gardens, and to a statue he was intending to copy, but the date of the note is c. 1508, long after Lorenzo was dead.

63. E. Camesasca, *L'Opera completa del Perugino*, Rizzoli Classici dell'Arte 3 (Milan, 1969), 91–2.

64. CA 429r/159r-c, R 1368A; cf. F 96v on physicians as 'destroyers of lives'.

65. RL 12439, formerly CA 902r/329r-b; Pedretti 1957, plate 23.

66. ASF, Corporazioni religiose soppresse 140/3, 74r; Villata 1999, no. 14.

67. ASF, ibid., 75r, 77v, 79r, 81v; Villata 1999, nos. 15–17.

68. On the religious iconography of the painting, see Natali 2001, 40ff.; Zöllner 2003, 56–9.

69. Beck quoted by Catherine Milner, *Daily Telegraph*, 3 June 2001. A letter denouncing the plan as a 'folly' was signed by forty experts including Sir Ernst Gombrich (*Artwatch UK*, June 2001).

70. Conversation with Alfio del Serra, 29 June 2001.

71. Melinda Henneburger, 'The Leonardo cover-up', *New York Times*, 21 April 2002.

72. On Vasari's woodcuts and their accuracy: Boase 1971, 68–72. On Renaissance self-portraiture: Zöllner 1992; Woods-Marsden 1998.

73. The face in a medallion in Mantegna's early fresco *St James Preaching* (Erematani, Padua) was probably also a self-portrait, but the frescos were destroyed by Allied bombing in 1944, and the photographs that remain do not show the face clearly.

74. Pedretti 1998a, 25; Grafton 2000, 127–33.

75. Vecce 1998, 75–6; Pedretti 1957, 34. For a later connection between Rucellai and Leonardo, see Benvenuto della Golpaja, 'Libro di macchine' (see Part III n. 21), 7v, where a drawing of a hydraulic device is said to be 'a copy of an instrument sent by Leonardo da Vinci to Bernardo Rucellai'; the drawing resembles some studies in G 93v–95r, *c.* 1510.

76. Bellincioni, *Rime* (Milan, 1493), 1v; Uzielli 1872, 99.

77. CA 1082r/391r-a. I give the paragraphs in the order indicated by corrections on the original (e.g. paragraph 9, about naval weapons, appears in the original after paragraph 4). The renumbering is obviously later than the text, but probably not much later as it is in the same hand.

78. Mangonel: 'a military engine for casting stones'; caltrop: 'an iron ball with four sharp prongs . . . used to impede cavalry' (*Shorter Oxford Dictionary*).

79. On some drawings related to weaponry described in the prospectus, mostly mid-1480s, see Part IV n. 9. That they only existed on paper is not provable, of course. The light, portable bridge of paragraph 1 is realized in the wooden bridge 'using neither iron nor rope' which Leonardo constructed for Cesare Borgia's troops in 1502 (Luca Pacioli, *De viribus quantitatis*, 2.85); and some machinery for draining trenches (paragraph 2) was designed, and probably used, for the abortive Arno deviation of 1503–4. But of actual weapons produced to his specifications there is no record.

80. Studies for the monument by Antonio del Pollaiuolo: Staatliche Graphische Sammlung, Munich; Metropolitan Museum of Art, New York.

PART FOUR: New Horizons, 1482–1490

1. CA 1113r/400r-b, referring to a journey from Milan to Florence in September 1513.

2. C 19v.

3. Bramly 1992, 198. On Ludovico Sforza, see Lopez 1982; Malaguzzi-Valeri 1913–23; C. Santoro, *Gli Sforza* (Milan, 1929).

4. CA 199v/73v-a, *c.* 1510. Other sketch-maps of the city are in RL 19115 and CA 184v/65v-b. Of early printed maps the fullest is Braun and Hogenberg's (*Civitatis orbis terrarum* (1572), vol. 1, map 42), based on an engraving by Antonio Lafreri, 1560. There do not seem to be any printed maps before the sixteenth-century expansion. The only medieval gate still standing is the elegant triple-arched Porta Nuova (or Porta Orientale), dated 1171.

5. The Porta Romana reliefs are now in the Museo d'Arte Antica at the Castello

Sforzesco, as is the relief of a woman making an obscene gesture (sometimes said to show the wife of Barbarossa) from the Porta Tosa, removed in the sixteenth century on the orders of St Carlo Borromeo.

6. Codex Magliabechiano II 4, 195; PC 2.31.

7. Ma I, note on inside cover.

8. Bramly 1992, 200.

9. Scattershot cannon: RL 12652. Armoured car (illustrated): BM 1860-6-16-99. See Kemp 1989, 138-9, 230-32.

10. Artillery-yard: RL 12647.

11. CA 611r/225r-b, R 1448. A painting in the Portinari family chapel in Sant'Egidio, described by Vasari, is now identified with *The Passions of Christ*, c. 1470, by the Flemish master Hans Memling (Galleria Sabauda, Turin). Its dramatic rendition of the Last Supper may have influenced Leonardo's treatment of the subject: see R. Papa, 'Giuda, disordine e la grazia', in Pedretti 1999.

12. On Dei, see DBI; L. Courtney, *The Trumpet of Truth* (Monash, Australia, 1992); and his *Cronica*, ed. R. Barducci (Florence, 1984). '*In principio era buio*': Pulci, *Morgante maggiore* (1482), canto 28, 42; P. Orvieto, *Annali d'italianistica* 1 (1983), 19-33.

13. See n. 50 below.

14. Landucci 1927, 33 and note.

15. On Bramante, see DBI; A. Bruschi, *Bramante* (London, 1977); Malaguzzi-Valeri, 1913-23, vol. 2: *Bramante e Leonardo*.

16. On Ambrogio and his family, see Shell 2000, 123-30.

17. Beltrami 1919, docs. 23-4. On the complex history of this painting, see Davies 1947; Sironi 1981; Marani 2003; Zöllner, *Burlington Magazine* 143 (2001), 35-7; Zöllner 2003, 223-4.

18. Clark 1988, 90-91. One of the difficulties of this argument is that the painting was to fit a frame constructed in 1482 (Maino was paid for it on 7 August 1482). A study for the Christ-child (BM 253a) is on blue prepared paper of a type that Leonardo used in Florence, but other sheets of the same kind of paper (CA 1094r/394r-b; RL 12652r) have drawings probably done in the early years in Milan. See PC 2.312.

19. ASM, Autografi dei pittori 102/34, 10; Glasser 1977, 345-6. A document apparently showing the payment of 730 lire to Leonardo and the de Predis on 28 December 1484 may give the date of completion of the Louvre painting (Shell and Sironi 2000), but Marani questions the reading of the date, which he thinks is 1489 (Marani 2003, 7).

20. For some of the links in this speculative chain, see Ottino della Chiesa 1967, 93-5; Marani 2001, 140-42; Gould 1975. On Ambrogio's presence in Innsbruck, see Shell 1998a, 124; Malaguzzi-Valeri 1913-23, 3.7-8.

21. RL 12519. Cf. Clark and Pedretti 1968, 1.92; Clayton 2002, 55.

22. On the setting, see R. Papa, 'Il misterio dell'origine', *Art e dossier* 159 (2000).

23. Embolden 1987, 125-32.

24. Triv 6v, (R 891) with diagram.

25. CA 184v/65r-b, R 1203, *c.* 1493

26. CA 950v/346v-a. 'Spirits of wine' = aqua vitae. Cf. B 3v: 'Note how spirit collects in itself all the colours and scents of wild flowers.'

27. B 15v–16r (illustrated), 36r–39r, etc. The lavatory: 53r. A painting of the 'ideal city' in the *studiolo* of Federico da Montefeltro in Urbino is attributed to Francesco di Giorgio Martini, whom Leonardo knew in Milan. In a later phase of urban planning (n. 25 above) Leonardo envisaged a scheme for dividing Milan into ten satellite towns, each with 5,000 dwellings. Cf. Fors 3 64v, which studies an area between the Porta Romana and the Porta Tosa, representing one of these tenths.

28. CA 1059v/381v-b, *c.* 1485.

29. *Daily Telegraph*, 17 March 2000 (preparation) and 27 June 2000 (jump); *Sunday Times*, 2 July 2000. The 'coated linen' (*pannolino intasato*, literally 'blocked-up linen') of Leonardo's specification probably means starched.

30. Inventory nos. JBS 17r, v (both illustrated), 18r, v. One of the allegories (18r), featuring snakes, foxes and an eagle, is clearly political, though its exact message is obscure: see Kemp 1989, 156–7.

31. Triv 96r, 98r; G. Perro, *Archivio storico Lombardo* 8, Pt 4 (1881); R 676n.

32. RL 19097, *c.* 1493.

33. Kunsthalle, Hamburg; Zöllner 2003, no. 396.

34. Popham 1946, 58.

35. On the handwriting of MS B, see Marinoni's introduction to the facsimile edition, 1990; Calvi 1925, 45; Pedretti 1995, 22.

36. According to notes by Gulielmo Libri, one of the lost pages of MS B (fol. 3) bore the date 1482. See PC 2.401. The fragmentary but unmistakable outline of the standing Leda on fol. 94r (now BN 2037, fol. D) is mysterious: no studies of Leda are known before *c.* 1504. It was possibly a chance imprint from a later sheet.

37. B 39v.

38. B 33r.

39. Kemp 1989, 236–9; M. Cianchi 1984, 45–55. These designs are similar to the ornithopter of CA 824v/302v-a, also *c.* 1487. The design on B 74v (illustrated) was the chief source for the full-size model constructed by James Wink (Tetra Associates for the Hayward Gallery, London, 1989). The model had a wing-span of over 35 feet and was about 10 feet long. Built from materials specified by, or available to, Leonardo – beech-wood, iron and brass, hemp rope, tarred marline, leather, tallow – it weighed in at 650 pounds, illustrating the primary problem of Leonardian aviation: a lack of sufficiently light materials to achieve the power-to-weight ratio necessary for flight.

40. B 89r.

41. Kemp 1989, 236. On the evolution of Leonardo's flying-machines, see Giacomelli 1936.

42. B 88v.

43. B83v. Cf. Pedretti 1957, 125–9; Giacomelli 1936, 78ff.

44. 'Maestro Lodovicho' is not, given his title, Ludovico Sforza, but may be the Milanese engineer Giovan Lodovico de Raufi (Calvi 1925, 87).

45. Fors 1^2, 14 folios, 5.5 × 4 inches (13.5 × 10 cm), is the second of the two notebooks bound together as Forster Codex 1 (the first is later, *c.* 1505). The Forster codices were owned by John Forster, friend and biographer of Dickens.

46. Triv 2r. The Trivulzio Codex, 55 folios, 7.5 × 5 inches (19.5 × 13.5 cm), is midway in size between B and Fors 1^2. It was donated to the Castello Sforzesco in 1935.

47. Belt 1949. On Bisticci: Jardine 1996, 137, 188–94.

48. It might be an edition of Albertus Magnus's work on minerals, e.g. *Mineralium libri v* (Rome, 1476). The '*lapidario*' of the Madrid list is thought to be *Speculum Lapidum* (*The Mirror of Stones*) by Camillo Leonardi di Pesaro, published in 1502 with a dedication to Cesare Borgia; Leonardo may have known the author. This book is too late for the Trivulzian reference.

49. CA 559r/210r-a; notes on the verso reappear on A 52r.

50. CA 852r/311r-a; 265v/96v-b; R 1354. A similar feigned letter of *c.* 1500 is addressed to the 'Diodario [i.e. probably *Defterdar*, or local governor] of Syria' (CA 393v/145v-b, R 1336).

51. Anon., *Il Manganello*, Cvr; Pedretti 2001, 49–50.

52. I^2 139r; Antonio Pucci, *Reina d'Oriente* (Bologna, 1862), 81. Overleaf (I^2 139v) is a literary pun: '*Delle taccole e stornelli*', which means both 'jackdaws and starlings' and 'tricks and satirical poems'.

53. RL 12692r, v. See Marinoni 1954, 1960.

54. RL 12693–6, 12699; CA 207v, 76v-a; Fors 1 41r, 2 63r.

55. CA 1033r/370r-a. The prophecies are later, mostly *c.* 1497–1500; there are about 175 in all, the bulk of them concentrated on two folios of the Atlanticus (CA 1033/370a, 393/145a) and in I^2 63–7.

56. All from CA 1033r/370r-a.

57. I^2 63v, 65r, Fors 1^1 9v, CA 393r/145r-a.

58. The majority of the fables belong to the early 1490s. Those on CA 323/117b and 327/119a are related to the short essays called '*Proemi*' ('Prefaces') which appear on the same sheets, and are datable to *c.* 1490. Those on CA 188/67b ('The Ant and the Grain of Millet', 'The Spider in the Grapes', 'The Ass Who Fell Asleep', 'The Falcon and the Duck', 'The Spider and the Hornet', 'The Eagle and the Owl', etc.) are on a sheet previously joined to CA 207/76a, which is dated 23 April 1490. A few appear in the pocketbook MS H, and are therefore from *c.* 1493–4.

59. CA 187r/67r-a, 188r/67r-b, 207r/76r-a.

60. CA 188v/67v-b (first two); CA 327r/119r-a (also found on a torn folio, CA 994v/358v-a, with the title '*Risposta faceta*' – 'A Witty Retort'); Triv 1v.

61. Beltrami 1919, docs. 31–3.

62. B 27r; Richter 1939, plate C5.

63. CA 730r/270r-c, R 1347A. Cf. Antonio Averlino (known as Filarete): 'I will show you that buildings are just like living men, and . . . they get sick and die, and often they can be healed through the offices of a good doctor' (*Trattato d'architettura*, Bk 1, 15). The medical theories underlying the analogy are found in standard texts like Galen's *De constitutione artis medicae*.

64. Leonardo's model was returned to him in May 1490, so he could repair it, but he does not seem to have bothered: as late as 1494 (Beltrami 1919, doc. 54) the Duomo was expecting him to repay 12 lire he had received. Among others who tendered for the *tiburio* project were the ducal engineer Pietro da Gorgonzola, the Florentine architect Luca Fancelli, and Francesco di Giorgio Martini. There is a review by Bramante of the short-listed models ('Opinio supra domicilium seu templum magnum'), *Archivio storico Lombardo* 5 (1878), 547.

65. BN 2037 5v (illustrated), B 17v, 22r, 25v, 39v, 56v, etc.; Richter 1939, plates 89–93. A similar temple in CA 717r/265v-a, also *c.* 1487, is reminiscent of the apse of Florence cathedral.

66. Alberti, *De re aedificatoria*, Bk 9, ch. 6. On the 'theta progression' and the Renaissance theory of 'incommensurate proportions' to which it belongs, see PC 2.34. Bramante was 'profoundly influenced by Leonardo's vision, though his mastery of volume and interval avoids the rather cluttered effects of Leonardo's unrelievedly dense designs' (Kemp 1989, 206). His *tempietto* ('little temple') of San Pietro in Montorio, Rome, *c.* 1502, is similar to the Leonardo drawings of MS B.

67. CA 1111v/399v-b, *c.* 1490–93. Cf. Ma I 11v, *c.* 1497: 'axles within axles, as at Chiaravalle'.

68. B 11v–12r. Pedretti adduces paleographic evidence that the drawings were done in or before the spring of 1489. The spread of MS B in which they occur contains writing of three distinct kinds; the latest addition is in handwriting very close to that of RL 19059, dated 2 April 1489. A contract to supply Leonardo with stone for the pavilion, dated 28 March 1490, is a later forgery (G. Calvi, RV 14, 344–5).

69. The lost folio (B 3): A. Houssaye, *Histoire de Léonard de Vinci* (Paris, 1869), 84. Plumbing notes: I 28v, 34r ('for heating the water in the Duchess's stove'). See Beltrami 1894, ch. 12.

70. Lubkin 1999, 122.

71. On Cecilia and her family, see DBI; Rzepińska 1990; F. Calvi, *Famiglie notabili Milanesi* (Milan, 1874), vol. 3.

72. P. Ghinzoni, 'Lettera inedita di Bernardo Bellincioni', *Archivio storico Lombardo* 16 (1889), 417f.

73. Sonnet, '*Sopra il retracto de Madona Cicilia qual fece maestro Leonardo*', in *Rime* (Milan, 1493), C6v-C7r.

74. CU 13v, McM 33. The story may anyway be a fiction. Leonardo also claims that a painting can frighten a dog and make it bark, and that he has personal experience of this (CU 5v, McM 31), but in fact dogs cannot interpret painted

surfaces as representations of reality. Another fiction, probably, is that Leonardo addressed Cecilia as 'magnificent Cecilia, most beloved goddess': the words appear on a much later sheet (CA 816r/297v-a, *c.* 1515) and are not in Leonardo's hand.

75. H 12r. Another version, differently worded, appears on the same page, headed 'Temperance reins in all vices'.

76. Bellincioni, *Rime*, sonnet 128; C. Pedretti, '*La Dama con l'Ermellino* come allegoria politica', in S. Ghilardo and F. Barcia, eds., *Studi politici in onore di Luigi Firpo* (Milan, 1990), 164ff. Leonardo's tiny circular drawing (diameter 9 cm) showing a grim-faced hunter about to kill a stoat (Fitzwilliam Museum, Cambridge; Zöllner 2003, no. 401) is doubtless related to the ermine folklore, and may be specifically related to Ludovico's investiture. The ermine was also the emblem of Anne de Bretagne, wife of Charles VIII, and of the dukes of Urbino; Carpaccio's knight (Coll. Thyssen, Lugarno) is often identified as Francesco Maria della Rovere, Duke of Urbino.

77. Aristotele Fioravanti to Galeazzo Maria Sforza, 1476, in M. Gualandi, *Aristotele Fioravanti, meccanico ed ingegnere* (Bologna, 1870), 10.

78. The letters (Beltrami 1919, doc. 51) were first published by A. Luzio, *Archivio storico dell'arte* 1 (1888), 45, 181.

79. Amoretti 1804, 155–8; cf. Rzepińska 1990, on which my account of the painting's later history is based.

80. Pietro Novellara to Isabella d'Este, 3 April 1501 (see Part VI n. 20). On Leonardo's Milanese studio, see Marani 1998, Shell 1995.

81. BN 2038 25r (formerly MS A).

82. On Boltraffio see DBI; Fiorio 1998; M. Davies, *The Earlier Italian Schools*, National Gallery catalogue (London, 1961). On Marco d'Oggiono, see GDA; Shell 1998b; D. Sedoni, *Marco d'Oggiono* (Rome, 1989).

83. G. Casio, *Cronica* (Bologna, 1525), in Pedretti 1998a, 27. In this epitaph on Boltraffio (d. 1516) Casio praises him as a portraitist who 'with stylus and brush made every man more beautiful than Nature made him'.

84. C 15v.

85. Interestingly, the prototypes are earlier Florentine works. Francesco's Sebastian is close to Leonardo's drawing of the Baptist (RL 12572), which is dated by its connection with Credi's Pistoia altarpiece to the mid-1470s; and the pose of Francesco's Baptist echoes Leonardo's *St Jerome*.

86. J. Shell and G. Sironi, 'Some documents for Francesco Galli "dictus Neapolus"', RV 23 (1989), 155–66.

87. H 106v.

88. CA 886r/315v-a (R 1344). Cf. CA 914r/335v-a (R 1345) with similar fragments of the same date, referring to 'two *maestri* continuously in my pay for two years'.

89. Galeazzo (enrolled March 1494): H 41r. The others: CA 189r/68r-a, 713r/264r-b, both *c.* 1497, possibly recording an expanded personnel for painting the *Last Supper*.

90. Lomazzo 1973, 87.

91. On the *Musician* (oil and tempera, 45 × 32 cm), see Ottino della Chiesa 1967, no. 25; Marani 2000a, 160–66.

92. RL 19115r. On Gaffurio, see DBI; C. Sartori, 'Franchino Gaffurio', *Storia di Milano* (Milan, 1961), 9.740–48.

93. Marani 2000a, 165. Other contenders are Josquin des Prez, a French singer who performed often in Milan cathedral, and lutenist Francesco da Milano.

94. Leonardo's portrait of Lucrezia was celebrated by an anonymous court poet in three Latin epigrams (CA 456v/167v-c, R 1560). The first says, 'Vincius might have shown her soul, as he has portrayed everything else. He did not, and this makes the image truer still, for the truth is that her soul belongs to her lover Maurus [i.e. Il Moro].' The *Belle Ferronnière* (oil on wood, 62 × 44 cm) may be the portrait of a 'lady of Lombardy' seen by Antonio de Beatis at Blois in 1517 (see p. 492 above), and is certainly the 'lady of Mantua by Leonardo' in a 1642 catalogue of the French royal collection. It has recently been argued that the *Ferronnière* and the portrait of Cecilia were painted on panels from the same walnut-tree; if so, the former would probably be *c.* 1488–90, and therefore unlikely to show Lucrezia: see B. Fabjan and P. Marani, eds., *La Dama con l'ermellino* (exhibition catalogue, Rome, 1998). However, earlier technical analysis by the Louvre identified the panel as oak (Ottino della Chiesa 1967, no. 28).

95. Clark's argument that the *Litta Madonna* was the 'almost finished' Madonna in profile listed by Leonardo in *c.* 1482 (see Part III n. 4) is challenged by David A. Brown. Brown identifies three preparatory drawings for the painting as the work of Milanese pupils. One showing the Madonna's face in full profile (Metropolitan Museum, New York) is clearly superseded by Leonardo's own study in the Louvre (illustrated), which shows her in the slightly turned profile of the finished painting. By this argument the Louvre study was done in Milan and not, as in Clark's hypothesis, in Florence. Brown sees the painting as part of a Lombard tradition of breast-feeding Madonnas (examples by Foppa and Bergognone). See Brown 1990. Berenson has some tart comments about the sickly tendencies of the Leonardeschi: *North Italian Painting of the Renaissance* (London, 1907), 114.

96. The young man is sometimes identified as Francesco Archinto; the elaborate monogram signature reads 'APMF' – i.e. 'Ambrosius Predis Mediolanus fecit.'

97. R. Wittkower, 'Inigo Jones: Puritanissimo fiero', *Burlington Magazine* 90 (1948), 50–51. Jones's is one of the earliest extant references to Leonardo in England. The earliest, I believe, is in Sir John Harington's 1591 translation of Ariosto's *Orlando furioso*, though this is no more than a name-check ('Leonard') in a list of Italian painters. The original (canto 33, verse 2) first appeared in the 1532 edition of *Orlando furioso*. The most extensive early references to Leonardo in English are in the translation of Lomazzo's *Trattato* by Richard Haydocke, 'student in physic' at Oxford, published in 1598.

98. J. Shell and G. Sironi, 'Giovanni Antonio Boltraffio and Marco d'Oggiono: La resurrezione di Cristo', RV 23 (1989), 119–54.

99. The fee for the *Virgin of the Rocks* was 800 lire, which at current exchange rates was worth about 200 ducats.

100. Colluccio Salutati, *Tractatus de nobilitate legum et medicinae* (c. 1399), in White 2000, 50. Hindered in anatomy: CA 671r/247v-b.

101. RL 19021v.

102. On the *Battle*, engraved by Antonio del Pollaiuolo and widely circulated as a template for depicting muscles, see Mayor 1984, 50.

103. RL 19059v, 19037v, the latter a prospectus headed 'The order of the book'. Both sheets have additions written nearly twenty years later, when Leonardo returned to anatomy with renewed enthusiasm: most of the anatomical folios at Windsor date from the later period, c. 1507–15. Another early sheet is the full-length figure showing the arterial system (RL 12597r), which relates to the intention in the prospectus to 'describe how bodies are composed of veins'. The 'gidone' of the Atlanticus book-list (c. 1492) may be the surgeon's manual *Cyrurgia* by Guido da Cauliaco, a useful book for the trainee anatomist.

104. RL 19057r (illustrated), 19058r-v, 19059r. A slightly later study (RL 12603) records the layers of the skull ('hair, scalp, lacterous flesh, pericranium, cranium, pia mater, dura mater, brain') and draws a section of an onion in comparison.

105. RL 12603. The basic theory, which Leonardo modifies, is found in Aristotle's *De anima*.

106. RL 12613v.

107. Many at Windsor (RL 12601, 12606–7, 19132, 19134–40, etc.), conveniently gathered and elegantly analysed in Clayton 2002; see also Biblioteca Reale, Turin, inv. no. 15574DC, and Accademia, Venice, inv. no. 236r, v (Zöllner 2003, 226, 229–30).

108. Accademia, Venice, inv. no. 228.

109. Villata 1999, no. 44.

110. For Lorenzo's reply, dated 8 August 1489, see L. Fusco and G. Corti, 'Lorenzo de' Medici on the Sforza monument', ALV 10 (1997), 35.

111. C 15v. Payment from Stanga: B 4r.

112. RL 12318r, c. 1479; it is interesting to compare the drawing style with the more robust and detailed proportional analysis on blue paper (RL 12319r) for the Sforza monument.

113. RL 12358; Clark and Pedretti 1968, 1.41.

114. RL 12357. The prostrate foe also features in Pollaiuolo's study for the monument in Munich.

115. CA 399r/147r-b. The trotting horse was later excised from the sheet and is now RL 12345.

116. RL 12319 (R 716), '*il ginetto grosso di Messer Galeazzo*'; RL 12294 (R 717), '*Siciliano* ["The Sicilian"] *di Messer Galeazzo*'.

117. Pietro Aretino to Vasari, 7 June 1536, in *Lettere* (Venice, 1538), 101v; PC 2.11.

118. Noyes 1908, 254.

119. Fors 3 49v, R 1512. The ground-plan among the rebuses (RL 12692) is hard to see in reproduction, as only part of the metalpoint has been inked in; it is repeated, in the same scale, in CA 217r/80r-a.

120. Baldassare Taccone, *Coronazione e sposalitio de la serenissima regina Maria Bianca* (Milan, 1493), 99.

121. Matteo Bandello, *Novelle* (Lucca, 1554), 1.58, in *Opere*, ed. F. Flora (Milan, 1996), 1.646–7.

122. CA 1006v/361v-b; PC 2.221.

123. Girolamo Cardano (Jerome Cardan), *De subtilitate libri xxi* (Basle, 1611), 816.

124. Leic 9v, R 989.

125. H³ 137v, *c.* 1493–4.

126. CA 207r/76r-a, R 1143; CU 20v, McM 51 (part of the *paragone*, or comparison, between painting and other arts.)

PART FIVE: At Court, 1490–1499

1. On the festivities, see Malaguzzi-Valeri 1913–23, 1.530; E. Solmi, *Archivio storico Lombardo* 31 (1904); Lopez 1982, 58–65. The couple had been married by proxy in 1488, but Isabella's arrival in Lombardy was overshadowed by a quarrel between the Moor's secretary Stefano da Cremona and the King of Naples's secretary Giovanni Pontano (see the splenetic sonnet by Bellincioni, 'Contra il Pontano') and by the death of her mother. Leonardo may have been involved in entertainments at the welcoming banquet at Tortona in January 1489, which featured a series of mythological interludes: that of Orpheus playing the lyre, surrounded by a 'troupe of pretty boys' (*stuolo di amorini*), sounds like his work, and may be a first outing for Atalante Migliorotti's performance in the role a year later, for Isabella d'Este. Another entertainment was a life-size automaton of a soldier on horseback set up in the piazza. The rider had a black face and a white tunic, representing the Moor in the ermine livery bestowed on him by Isabella's grandfather the King of Naples. This 'automaton' – essentially a pantomine horse with a man inside working the mechanism – sounds oddly like an early version of the Sforza Horse. It is hard to think of anyone in Milan more likely to have created this than Leonardo, but there seems to be no evidence that he did.

2. Bellincioni, *Rime*, 149v; Beltrami 1919, doc. 41.

3. Biblioteca Estense, Modena, Cod. Ital. 521a; Villata 1999, no. 49.

4. B 4r, Ar 227r.

5. Castiglione 1967, 66.

6. C 15v.

7. Tristano Calco, *Nuptiae Mediolanensium et Estensium principum* (Milan, 1634), 94–5; G. Calvi, *Archivio storico Lombardo* 43 (1916), 479ff; Vecce 1998,

132–4. The imagery of the *uomo selvatico* is associated with native Americans in Amerigo di Vespucci's *De novo mondo* (Florence, 1505). From *selvatico* (literally 'forest-dwelling') derives 'savage' (the Elizabethan 'salvage' is transitional; the word is used of Caliban in Shakespeare's *Tempest*). A later patron of Leonardo, Charles d'Amboise, had 'an impresa showing a wild man with a greenwood club in hand', with the motto '*Mitem animum agresti sub tegmine servo*' – 'Beneath my rough exterior I have a gentle soul' (Clark and Pedretti 1968, 1.116).

8. CU 5r, 6v, McM 35, 24. Cf. RL 12371, a devil with horns and hanging goitres (*c.* 1508).

9. RL 12585r; Winternitz 1974, 129. Popham (1946, 60) notes the similarity, probably coincidental, with Dürer's drawing of a man on horseback playing bagpipes (V & A, London).

10. RL 12367.

11. RL 12492. For a range of these grotesques see Clayton 2002, 73–99; cf. Clark and Pedretti 1968, vol. 1, app. B; Gombrich 1954. On Hollar's versions see R. Pennington, *A Descriptive Catalogue of the Etched Work of Wenceslaus Hollar* (Cambridge, 1982), in which the 'dame' (christened the 'Queen of Tunis' by Hollar) is no. 1603.

12. RL 12495. Two of the figures appear in Massys's *Martyrdom of St John the Evangelist* (Koninklijk, Antwerp), *c.* 1508–11, and three of them in the *Grotesque Betrothal* (São Paolo), discussed in the next paragraph.

13. Richter 1939, 2.260. A fragmentary and partly illegible text on the verso of the drawing (R 1355, further deciphered in PC 2.309) may conceivably have clues to its meaning to Leonardo: 'If there is any man who is trustworthy and kind he will be treated badly by other men, just as I am . . . I have known this man well, against my will: he is a receptacle of villainy, and a warning to us of rank ingratitude mixed with every kind of vice.' The press of malevolent faces round the old man might relate to Leonardo being 'treated badly by other men', but the text has much else with no discernible relevance to the drawing.

14. Clayton 2002, 96–9.

15. CA 877v/319v-b, R 1534.

16. Lomazzo, 1584, 106–7; PC 2.259. Giraldi: see Introduction n. 7.

17. A curiosity of Paris MS C is that the leather binding (which dates from 1603) was made for a much larger volume. Pedretti shows that the missing portion was another treatise on light and shade, used by Melzi when compiling the Codex Urbinas, and designated 'Libro W'. This seems to have been Leonardo's later reworking (*c.* 1508) of material in MS C. It was probably removed from the binding in or before 1609, when the volume entered the Biblioteca Ambrosiana; early catalogues describe it as it is today. In 1866 it was reported that a certain Dr Ortori had discovered an unknown Leonardo manuscript of 112 pages 'treating of phenomena of light as they relate to painting' (*Gazzetta di Milano*, 30 March 1866). This sounds remarkably like 'Libro W', but nothing further was heard of it, nor of a rumour in the late 1950s that a similar document had been seen in one

of the libraries of the Princes Borromeo in Milan. See Pedretti 1965, 147–8; Pedretti and Cianchi 1995, 24–5.

18. CA 676r/250r-a, R 111. Similarities of paper-type and stitch indentations suggest that this sheet was also once bound together with MS C.

19. BN 2038 (ex MS A), 14v, 29r.

20. Triv 11v, R 177. The medieval scholiast Roger Bacon, whose work interested Leonardo (Ar 71v), says that 'spiritual' in Aristotle 'is not taken from the spirit, nor is the word used in its proper sense ... for it is taken in the sense of imperceptible' (*Optical Science*, ch. 4, in PC 1.167).

21. CU 208v, 196r, McM 844, 840.

22. BN 2038 14v. Cf. CU 41v, McM 132: 'shadows appear smoky, that is indeterminate'; and RL 19076r: shadows with 'smoky edges'.

23. CU 49r–v, McM 218.

24. Thirty-three of the purloined folios, purchased by Lord Ashburnham and returned by him to Paris, now comprise BN 2038.

25. BN 2038 20v, R 520.

26. BN 2038 22v, R 508.

27. CU 33v–34r, McM 93. Explored by C. Pedretti in '*Le macchie di Leonardo*' (*Lettura Vinciana* 54, 17 April 2004: to be published in 2005).

28. Pacioli 1509, 1r; Lomazzo 1584, 158; PC 1.76–82.

29. *Trattato di architettura civile e militare* (Biblioteca Laurenziana, Codice Ashburnham 361): the MS is *c.* 1484 or earlier, but Leonardo's marginal notes and doodles probably date from *c.* 1504 (Vezzosi 1997, 96–7). On Francesco's influence on Leonardo's technical drawings, see Zwijnenberg 1999.

30. Beltrami 1919, docs. 48–50. According to Richter, a ground-plan captioned '*sagrestia*' (B 52r) is a design for the sacristies of Pavia cathedral, which were built in 1492. See Richter 1970, 2.41, 80.

31. B 66r.

32. B 58r, R 1023 (chimneys), R 1506 (Witelo); CA 609r/225r-a. A Witelo MS 'on optics' mentioned by Pacioli, and a '*prospettiva di Vitelleone*' mentioned by Lomazzo, may be the same document (PC 2.187).

33. C 15v.

34. On Salai see DBI, s.v. Caprotti; Shell and Sironi 1992. A rental agreement between Leonardo and Salai's father (July 1501, Villata 1999, no. 153) describes the latter as 'Pietro di Messer Giovanni da Oppreno', again suggesting the grandfather's status.

35. First mention of 'Salai': H[2] 16v. The name may also contain a studio pun: *salare* (to salt or season) had a slang meaning, 'to shirk'; *salai* is therefore an existent word meaning 'I bunked off', and might be applied to a lazy young apprentice. A document of 1510 (Shell and Sironi 1992, doc. 26) refers to 'Giovanni Giacomo known as Salibeni', probably a clerk's garbling. The non-existent 'Andrea Salaino' is one of the supporting figures on the nineteenth-century statue of Leonardo in the Piazza della Scala in Milan.

36. RL 12276v, 12432r.

37. Louvre, Dépt des Arts Graphiques 2251; Bambach 2003, fig. 203. Two profiles of Salai are found on anatomical folios: RL 19093r and Kunsthalle, Hamburg (Pedretti 2001, 63).

38. 'Salaino expenses': L 94r. Rose-coloured stockings: Ar 229v. Sister's dowry: F, inside cover.

39. Salai is first named in a document relating to the property on 6 March 1510 (Shell and Simon 1992, doc. 26). He leased it to one Antonio Meda in September 1513 (ibid., doc. 27) – perhaps on Leonardo's behalf, though this is not stated in any of the documents.

40. CA 663v/234v-a, c. 1508.

41. A brief memorandum in Leic 26v – '*parla co genovese del mare*' ('talk of the sea with the man from Genoa') – has been improbably canvassed as an allusion to Columbus, who was indeed born in Genoa but who was probably dead (d. 1506) when the note was written. Leonardo may well have known the Florentine seafarer Amerigo di Vespucci, after whom 'America' was named. Vasari claimed to own a charcoal sketch by Leonardo showing Amerigo as 'a very handsome old man'; if so, it would have been drawn in or before 1505 (after which Vespucci was continuously in Spain till his death in 1512), and would show him only in his early fifties. It is not impossible that it was an early work showing Vespucci's grandfather, also Amerigo (d. 1471). The 'Vespuccio' mentioned in a list of *c.* 1503 (Ar 132v, R 1452) is probably Machiavelli's secretary Agostino di Vespucci.

42. Mountain range: RL 12410, 12413–14, compared to photographs of the Grigne in Conato 1986, 119–204. Storm over a town: RL 12409. Depiction of rains: CU 25r, McM 55.

43. Written both sides of CA 573b/214e (R 1031–2).

44. Photographs in Conato 1986, 201.

45. Ibid., 206.

46. Leic 11v, R 1029.

47. Head of a bear: private collection (formerly Colville Collection). Bear walking: Metropolitan Museum of Art, New York, 1975. 1.369 (Zöllner 2003, nos. 158–9). The latter has a faint underdrawing of a pregnant woman.

48. RL 12372–5, Clark and Pedretti 1968, 1.52.

49. Leic 4r; A. Recalcati, 'Le Prealpi Lombarde ritratte da Leonardo' (ALV 10, 1997, 125–31). Monte Bo (height 8,385 feet), south-west of Monte Rosa, would fit linguistically, but does not fit Leonardo's description topographically.

50. Paracelsus (i.e. Theophrastus Bombastus von Hohenheim), *Sieben defensiones*, ch. 4, in *Opera*, ed. Johann Huser (Strasbourg, 1603), 1.159.

51. Discovery of Madrid MSS: *New York Times*, 14, 15, 17 (etc.) February 1967; Reti 1968. The provenance of the codices can be broadly tracked. They were probably among the Leonardo manuscripts brought to Spain by Pompeo Leoni, and inherited in 1608 by his nephew Polidoro Calchi; and they were probably the 'two books drawn and written by the hand of the great Leonardo da Vinci, of

great learning and curiosity' seen by Vincencio Carducho in the library of Juan de Espina in the early 1620s. These Espina 'would at no price sell to the Prince of Wales [the future Charles I] . . . considering himself the only worthy owner until our Lord the King should inherit them at his death' (Reti 1968, pt 1, 10). Espina kept his promise, despite the efforts of Lord Arundel to 'change his foolish humour', and on his death in 1642 he left his collection to King Philip IV; the codices were probably part of this bequest. They were transferred from the Escorial to the Biblioteca Nacional sometime before 1800, when they were listed in an inventory prepared by the librarian, Antonio Gonzalez; this was later noticed by Tammaro de Marinis, but he found that the shelf-marks given them in the inventory led to other books and eventually gave up the search (RV 2 (1906), 89ff.).

52. Ma II 157v, 151v.

53. On Renaissance 'lost-wax' casting techniques: Cole 1983, 124–5. On Leonardo's modifications of the technique: CA 976r/352r-c, PC 2.12; Kemp 1981, 205–7.

54. RL 12346.

55. RL 12349. This sheet can be dated to c. 1492; it contains a brief text about the inconveniences of studying what does not interest you, which is repeated almost verbatim in BN 2038 34r (formerly MS A), dated 10 July 1492. The pulleys and cog-wheels on the Windsor sheet are comparable to those on A 62r, which also has two horses' heads squared for proportion.

56. Ma II 140r (illustrated).

57. Vasari 1878–85, 4.276; Vecce 1998, 138–9. Sangallo's design for a *palazzo* for Il Moro is in the Vatican, Codex Barberiniano Latino 4424, 15v.

58. The height of 12 braccia (Ma II 151v) is confirmed by Luca Pacioli (*Divina proportione*, preface); see R. Cianchi, RV 20 (1964), 277–97, for other contemporary statistics and estimates. In 1977 an American pilot and art-collector, Charles Dent, conceived the idea of recreating the Horse from Leonardo's notes and drawings: the end product (23 feet high, 13 tons), sculpted by Nina Akumu, was unveiled at San Siro racecourse, Milan, in 1999 (Neil Ascherson, *Observer*, 25 July 1999). A smaller replica of it stands in the main piazza of Vinci. The cost of the sculpture was about $6 million.

59. Taccone: see Part IV n. 120. Lancino Curzio, *Epigrammaton et sylvarum libri* (Milan, 1521), 1.7r, 49r. The Horse is often said to have been exhibited in the piazza in front of the castle, but Beatrice Sforza, writing to her sister Isabella d'Este, 29 December 1493, speaks of the equestrian 'effigy' of Francesco Sforza being set up under a triumphal arch in the cathedral (Archivio di Stato, Mantua, Vigevano E49/2; Vecce 1998, 145).

60. Ma II 151v.

61. The treatise on 'mechanical elements' is referred to in a note of 1502 about efficient wheel-sizes on a cart, 'as I showed in the first of the 5th [chapter] of the Elements' (L 72r), and in later sheets: RL 19009r, c. 1510, and CA 10r/2r-a, c. 1515. The 'book on physics' is a lost work contemporary with Fors 2^2, c. 1495–

7, which also covers physics (or '*de ponderibus*' – 'the science of weights'), gravity, percussion, etc. See Pedretti 1995, 35.

62. Ma I 12v.

63. Ma I 100v; Reti 1968, pt 1, 16–17: the formula given by Leonardo is 'a hard tin–copper compound ($SnCu_3$) embedded in a softer tin–copper alloy'.

64. Ma I 4r, 16r, Fors 22, 65r, v; Rosheim 2001.

65. CA 812r/296v-a. *Repubblica*, 24 April 2004: the reconstruction consisted of an exhibition model (170 × 150 cm), a working model (50 × 60 cm) and interactive digital designs (http://www.imss.fi.it). On Verrocchio's clock, see Vasari 1987, 1.240: the putto's 'arms are raised to sound the hours with a hammer held in his hands', which 'was considered very attractive and novel at the time'.

66. Rosheim 2001, 23.

67. Lomazzo 1973, 1.299, 2.96.

68. Arrival of Caterina: Fors 3 88r. Payments to her (two of 10 soldi each), 29 January 1494: H^3 64v. Funeral expenses: Fors 2 64v.

69. Freud 2001, 75–6. Cf. Eissler 1962, app. C; Fumagalli 1952, 56. A list of names on Fors 3 88v (i.e. overleaf from the note of Caterina's arrival) reads, 'Antonio, Bartolomeo, Lucia, Piero, Lionardo', which Vecce interprets as referring to Leonardo's grandparents Antonio and Lucia and his father Piero: a brusque family-tree, emotionally connected to the recent arrival of his mother (Vecce 1998, 142). But Bartolomeo cannot be Leonardo's half-brother, as Vecce suggests: he was not born till 1497. A fragmentary note (CA 195r/71r-a, PC 2.310), '*essapimi dire sella chaterina vuole fare*' ('and let me know if La Caterina wants to do it'), probably refers to his mother, but this is much earlier, c. 1480.

70. Fors 3 14r, 17v, 20v, 43v, 44v, 47v.

71. H 16v, 33v.

72. H 64v, 65v, 41r, 38r, 109r, 124v. A visit to Cremona (H 62v) may also have been made at this time: see Part VII n. 92.

73. H 40r. On the political background of these emblems, see Solmi 1912, Reti 1959. The sketched head of a young black boy (H 103v) is probably an allusion to the Moor; there are descriptions (PC 2.214) of an allegorical painting at the Castello Sforzesco showing a black servant (Ludovico) brushing the dress of a lady (Italy).

74. H 130v.

75. The caption (H 288v) is separate from the drawing (Musée Bonnat, Bayonne, 656; Popham 1946, no. 109b), but obviously refers to it.

76. $I^1$138v; cf. related drawing in RL 12497. Leonardo introduces Poverty with the word '*ancora*' in the narrative sense of 'then' ('Then the frightening figure of Poverty comes running' etc.), which suggests he is thinking of a dramatic representation rather than a pictorial image.

77. CA866r/315v-a. On Bascapè: PC 2.296. Bellincioni addressed a fulsome sonnet to him asking him to seek the Moor's permission to publish his poems (R 1344n).

78. H 31v.

79. H 105r.

80. Noyes 1908, 173–5.

81. Vecce 1998, 149–51; M. Sanudo, *La spedizione di Carlo VIII* (Venice, 1873), 118–19.

82. CA 914r/335v–a.

83. Bandello: see Part IV n. 121.

84. In a letter to Prior Vincenzo Bandello, 4 December 1497 (*Archivio storico Lombardo* 1 (1874), 33–4), Ludovico lists what he has commissioned and paid for at the Grazie (tribune, sacristy, dormitories, etc.). The 'paintings' he mentions probably refer exclusively to Leonardo's work: Montorfano's fresco was commissioned by the prior himself. As well as the *Last Supper*, Leonardo painted two lost works in the Grazie: a *Redentore* (Christ the Redeemer), above the door between the monastery and the church; and an *Assunta* (Virgin of the Assumption) in the lunette over the main entrance of the church, destroyed when the door was enlarged in 1603. The former may be related to the *Head of Christ* in the Brera, Milan, which is possibly a Leonardo with later repainting. Small oil portraits of Ludovico, Beatrice and their children in the corners of Montorfano's fresco, now almost indecipherable, are also by Leonardo.

85. RL 12542. A geometrical note and drawing on the lower part of the sheet may be related to Luca Pacioli's *Summa arithmetica* (Venice, 1494), a copy of which Leonardo owned. If so, the publication of the latter (10 November 1494) gives an approximate *terminus a quo* for the compositional study.

86. Accademia, Venice, no. 254; Popham 1946, no. 162. The retouching has distorted Leonardo's intentions, but the drawing and the handwriting are both his.

87. Louvre, Cabinet des Dessins 2022 (Zöllner 2003, no. 130).

88. Judas: RL 12547r (illustrated). Peter: Albertina, Vienna, inv. no. 17614. St James: RL 12552r (illustrated). St Philip: RL 12551r. Hands: RL 12543r. Sleeve: RL 12546r.

89. Fors 2¹6r, Fors 3 1v; Fors 2¹ 3r,v. A 'Cristoforo Castiglione' appears in a Milanese document of 1486 (Calvi 1925, 59); he may be connected to the author Baldassare Castiglione, who was in Milan in the 1490s. Richter translates 'Giovan conte' as 'Count Giovanni', but the way Leonardo writes it, and the fact that the man is 'with' (i.e. in the service of) the Cardinal, makes me think Conte is a name rather than a rank. Luigi of Aragon's comment: Beatis 1979, 182.

90. Fors 2 1v–2r; Clark 1988, 152.

91. On the profound originality of Leonardo's conception of the *Last Supper*, see Kemp 1981, 189ff.; Laurenza 1999; Steinberg 1973, 2002. Among earlier critics see Guiseppe Bossi's monograph, *Il Cenacolo* (Milan, 1810), and Goethe's 'Abendmahl von Leonardo da Vinci', in *Kunst und Altertum* (1818). Max Marmor (ALV 5 (1992), 114–16) gives a translation of Jacob Burckhardt's first essay on the painting, from *Der Wanderer in der Schweiz* 5 ('Bilder aus Italien'), 1839.

92. Marani 2000a, 13–14.

93. Pacioli 1509, preface. The 'dramatic moment' here described is the subject of Steinberg's searching analyses. He advances the 'sacramental' interpretation: that the painting contains a range of images referring to the Eucharist, thus implying a narrative within the composition from Christ's announcement to the taking of the first communion. The hands of Thaddeus (second from right), for instance, can be read as one hand about to slap against the other, as if to say 'What did I tell you?' (broadly Goethe's interpretation), but also as a cupping of the hands as if to take the Eucharistic bread.

94. For Giraldi, see Introduction n. 7.

95. Technical data in Barcelon and Marani 2001, 408ff., on which this paragraph is based.

96. CA 189r/68r-a (written from right to left), CA 713r/264r-b. The former is echoed in I 53v, 'benedetto 17 October', which is doubtless contemporary with the shopping-list dated 17 October 1497 a few pages earlier (I 49v). However, this may mark the end of Benedetto's first year.

97. Barcelon and Marani 2001, 413–14.

98. Beltrami 1919, doc. 70; PC 2.296.

99. CA 866r/315v-a, R 1344.

100. G. Bugatti, *Historia universale* (Venice, 1570) 6.689.

101. Vecce 1998, 165.

102. Vasari 1987, 1.215.

103. Work on the window: Ottino della Chiesa 1967, 96; the entry survives in an eighteenth-century transcription. Ludovico to Stanga: ASM Registro Ducale, s.n., carta 16.

104. Beatis 1979, 182; Vasari 1878–85, 5.424; Barcelon and Marani 2001, 21–35.

105. Clark 1988, 147. Kemp notes that recovered details from recent restorations 'confirm Clark's intuition that the expression of the heads had been deadened by earlier restorations' (ibid., Introduction, 31). There were a dozen copies done within Leonardo's lifetime: the earliest were oil paintings by Bramantino (1503) and Marco d'Oggiono (1506), both lost, though a later copy by Marco (*c.* 1520) is at the Brera, Milan. Two fresco copies by Antonio da Gessate (*c.* 1506) and Andrea Solario (before 1514) were destroyed by Allied bombing in 1943. Giampietrino's superb copy, *c.* 1515–20, formerly in the Certosa, Pavia, now in the Royal Academy collection, is held at Magdalen College, Oxford.

106. Barcelon and Marani 2001, 328.

107. Purchase of the *Summa*: CA 228r/104r-a. On the influence of Pacioli: Marinoni 1982.

108. Pacioli 1509, 28v. The presentation MSS of 1498 are in Milan (Biblioteca Ambrosiana, MS A 170 sup.) and Geneva (Bib. Publique et Universitaire, MS Langues Etrangères 210); an illustration from the Ambrosiana codex is in Vezzosi 1997, 81.

109. RL 19084r: 'He who does not know the supreme certainty of mathematics is wallowing in confusion.' Cf. G 96v.

110. CA 331r/120r-d. The geometry of Pacioli's *Summa* is squarely based on Euclid's *Elements*, though it also borrows from Boethius, Sacrobosco, Leonardo Fibonacci (Leonardo da Pisa) and his old master Piero della Francesca. The first European edition of the *Elements*, translated from Arabic into Latin, had appeared as recently as 1482.

111. Six exemplars are in the Biblioteca Ambrosia, inv. nos. 09595, 09596A–E. See Alberici 1984, 21–2; C. Bambach, ALV 4 (1991), 72–98. A Dürer copy, based on 09596D, is in Pedretti 1992, 25. In a letter from Venice (13 October 1506) Dürer spoke of his studies in the 'art of secret perspective', and of his intention to visit someone in Bologna who would instruct him in it: this may be Pacioli, whose influence is discernible in Dürer's engraving *Melancholia I*.

112. G. Borsieri, *Supplimento della nobiltà* (Milan, 1619), 57–8; PC 2.395.

113. CA 611r/225r-b (cf. Part I n. 40). Lomazzo 1584, 430.

114. Noyes 1908, 161–3. His views on Bramante are contested in sonnets by Bellincioni. A manuscript copy of Visconti's poem 'Paulo e Daria' (Kupferstich-kabinett, Berlin) has pro-Ludovico miniatures somewhat parallel to Leonardo's political emblems of *c.* 1493–4. Visconti is probably the 'Bissconte' whose son was killed by the French in 1500, as recorded by Leonardo (L, inside cover).

115. Vecce 1998, 173.

116. CA 243v/89v-b, 1037v/372v-a, PC 2.236.

117. CA 609r/225r-a, Fors 3 37v, Fors 2¹43v. The 'Messer Fazio' in the third item is Fazio Cardano, father of the mathematician Girolamo Cardano (or Jerome Cardan).

118. Metropolitan Museum of Art, New York, R 705A; Malaguzzi-Valeri 1913–23, 1.534; RV 11 (1920), 226f.

119. Villata 1999, no. 111. A useful edition of this rare pamphlet is at http://*www.liberliber.it*, with an introduction by Rosanna Scippacercola. On the candidates for authorship, see D. Brown, 'The Apollo Belvedere at the garden of Guiliano della Rovere', *Journal of the Warburg and Courtauld Institutes* 49 (1986), 235–7; E. Guidoni, *Ricerche su Giorgione e sulla pittura del Rinascimento* (Rome, 1998). The latter dates the poem to 1497 and attributes it to Bramantino. The dedication to Leonardo is in the form of two *sonneti caudati* (sonnets with a 'tail') as found frequently in the Burchiellesci.

120. On the case for Ambrogio's authorship, see Vecce 1998, 163, 401. On a comparable acronymic signature by him, see Part IV n. 96.

121. P. Marani, *La pittura a Milano al tempo di Bramante* (Milan, 1995).

122. Gottardo Panigarola, Ludovico's chancellor from 1481, might be thought a likely commissioner of the frescos, but the Panigarola family did not own the house till 1548 (G. Mulazzani, *Bramante pittore*, Milan, 1978, 85–6).

123. Ficino, *Divini Platonis omnia opera* (Basle 1561), 637; Pedretti 1977, n.12.

124. Vincenzo de' Pagave, 'Dialogo fra un forestiere ed un pittore' (Milan, Sforza Castle MS C.VI.28), xv–xvi; Pedretti 1977, 123, 129.

125. Bramante had a fondness for painting philosophers: his earliest known work,

a fresco cycle in the Palazzo del Podestà in Bergamo (c. 1478), also features 'seated figures of philosophers' (GDA). Leonardo's estimate for decoration work at Vigevano, c. 1494, included '24 philosophers' (H 124v).

126. CU 127r–v, McM 420. The face of Heraclitus seems to be echoed in a portrait drawing (BM 1895-9-15-481) showing a curly-haired man screwing up his eyes: it is attributed to the Leonardesco artist Giovanni Agostino da Lodi (d. c. 1502). The wrinkling round the eyes and the curling of the hair are similar to the Bramante portrait; both heads are slightly turned from full face, but in opposite directions.

127. Beltrami 1919, doc. 90.

128. Beltrami 1920; cf. G. Biscaro, *Archivio storico Lombardo* 36 (1909).

129. Shell and Sironi 1992, doc. 27. At some point, probably as he prepared to leave Milan in 1499, Leonardo leased the property to Salai's father, Pietro. In an *'istrumento'* of 29 July 1501, drawn up in Florence (Villata 1999, no. 153), Leonardo states that he has received rent due from him. Officially, however, it seems the property was confiscated during the French occupation (hard otherwise to interpret its restoration to him by the French in 1507: see p. 409). Later documents show Salai almost exclusively in charge of it. In his will (R 1539), Leonardo bequeathed half of the land to Salai, and half to his servant Battista de Vilanis.

130. I 50r, 51r, 58r, 59r, 118v (R 1405–6); L 91r; CA 422r/156r-a. Pedretti warns that the calculations should be read with caution: other computations by Leonardo suggest that 1 pertica = 1,862 square braccia. See Pedretti 1972, 290–91.

131. CA 1050v/377v-a; Pedretti 1972, 22, 291–2.

132. CA 484r/177v-b, 1079r/389r-b.

133. Pedretti 1972, 16; Vasari 1987, 1.193 (Life of Piero della Francesca).

134. The figurehead of the Atellani salon was Carlo Attelani's wife, Barbara, whom Leonardo mentions by her maiden name, Barbara Stampa (CA 2r/1r-c). See p. 457 above.

135. I 118r–119v.

136. CA 426/158a (Embolden 1987, fig. 27) has ground-plans, calculations and notes in the hand of the client on the verso and Leonardo's own notes on the recto. CA 1090r/393r-a (Embolden 1987, fig. 28) may show his plans for the Guiscardi garden, with a central path and a circular area at the top, probably a pond or nymphaeum.

137. B 12v.

138. Ottino della Chiesa 1967, 99–100.

139. Kemp 1981, 181–8.

140. Museo d'Arte Antica, Castello Sforzesco: itinerary, rm VII.

141. CA 187r/67r-a.

142. CA 773r/284r, R 1468. Arrigo is later referred to in CA 570v/214r-b, c. 1506–8, PC 2.353.

143. Ma I 61r.

144. CA 289r/104r-b; I 28v, 34r.

145. B. Corio, *L'historia di Milano* (Venice, 1554), 49v.

146. CA 669/247a, R 1379; cf. G. Calvi, RV 3 (1907).

147. CA 628r/230v-c; Vecce 1998, 208.

148. Beltrami 1919, doc. 101. The cash was deposited in Florence on 7 and 15 January 1500.

PART SIX: On the Move, 1500–1506

1. M. Brown, ' "*Lo insaciabile desiderio nostro de cose antique*": new documents for Isabella d'Este's collection of antiquities', in Clough 1976, 324–53. See also Daniela Pizzagalli, *La Signora del Rinascimento: vita e splendore di Isabella d'Este alla Corte di Mantova* (Milan, 2002); Jardine 1996, 408–16.

2. Jardine 1996, 410–11.

3. Archivio del Stato, Mantua, Gonzaga 1439, 55; Beltrami 1919, doc. 103. The painting's relationship to the Louvre drawing is uncertain. A Leonardo drawing of Isabella remained in Mantua, for a year later she was hoping he would send her 'another sketch of our portrait' because her husband had given away 'the one which he [Leonardo] left here' (letter to Fra Pietro Novellara, 29 March 1501: see n. 20). This may or may not have been the Louvre drawing. Isabella's wording assumes the existence of at least one other 'sketch' of her, and there may have been various studies in various poses.

4. CA 638dv/234v-c, PC 2.196–8. Deliberations of the Senate: Vecce 1998, 191.

5. CA 215r/79r-c, *c.* 1515.

6. Ar 270v, *c.* 1517.

7. CU 3r, McM 18.

8. Sabba Castiglione, *Ricordi* (Venice, 1555), 51v. The first edition was published in Bologna in 1546. Vasari says the clay Horse ws 'smashed to pieces' when the French first entered Milan (Vasari 1987, 1.264), but it seems it was still intact in September 1501, when the Duke of Ferrara wrote to Milan about the possibility of acquiring it (Villata 1999, no. 155).

9. Beltrami 1919, doc. 101. The account contained the savings Leonardo had transferred from Milan in December 1499. There is no documentation of him visiting Florence during his eighteen years in Milan, though it is sometimes said he made a short trip back in *c.* 1495. This derives from Vasari's comment (added to the second edition of the *Lives*) that the building of the Council Hall in the Palazzo Vecchio by Simone del Pollaiuolo and Giuliano da Sangallo was 'done according to his judgement and advice' (see Vasari 1987, 1.267, though the phrase is lost in Bull's translation of the passage). This work was begun in 1495.

10. Pietro da Novellara to Isabella d'Este, 3 April 1501: see n. 20.

11. Ser Piero is first recorded as notary to the Servites on 20 August 1466 (Uzielli 1872, 148; Cecchi 2003, 123–4).

12. Vecce 1998, 199. The later fortunes of the Annunziata altarpiece are recounted in Vasari's *Life* of Perugino (Vasari 1987, 2.98).

13. See n. 20.

14. Some believe Leonardo was already working on the *Virgin and St Anne* group before he left Milan, e.g. Popham, who dates the Venice sketch and another at the Louvre to 'about 1498–99' (Popham 1946, 73, 152). The eighteenth-century collector Fra Sebastiano Resta states that Louis XII commissioned a cartoon of Saint Anne from Leonardo in Milan in 1499, and that Leonardo 'made a preliminary sketch which is now in the collection of the Counts Arconati in Milan' (*Lettere pittoriche* (Milan, 1759), 3.326; Ottino della Chiesa 1967, 102). However, Resta is not thought to be reliable: he was keen to establish a provenance for a 'more finished' cartoon on the same subject which he owned. This was not, as he claimed, an original Leonardo, but a copy of the Louvre *Virgin and St Anne* painting (or its cartoon) from the Esterhazy collection in Budapest. A sonnet by the Bolognese poet Girolamo Casio, patron of Leonardo's former assistant Boltraffio, is also advanced as evidence for the early date of the composition. It is entitled, 'For St Anna, whom L. Vinci painted holding in her arms the M[adonna] who does not wish the son to reach down to a lamb'. Boltraffio was with Casio in Bologna in 1500, and Leonardo may have visited them en route from Venice to Florence in April of that year, but there is no indication that the sonnet was written then; the title says Leonardo had 'painted [*dipinse*]' St Anne, which seems to refer to the Louvre painting, probably done in Milan in c. 1509–11. The poem, undated, was first published in Casio's *Cronica* (Bologna, 1525).

15. The drawing, 'done with Leonardo Vinci's own hand', was sent to the Marquis by Francesco Malatesta. In the covering letter (Villata 1999, no. 146) he adds, 'Leonardo says that to make it [the replica of the villa] perfect you would need to transport its setting to the place where you want to build it': an ironic comment, surely, though retailed by Malatesta with apparent seriousness.

16. RL 12689, possibly by Salai; Ar 77r.

17. ASF, Carte Strozziane II 51/1, 454r–v; ALV 4 (1991), 158–70. A note in H¹30v mentions objections by 'the millers of San Niccolò, who do not want their water-course obstructed'.

18. CA 618v/227v-a. (The note is dated Florentine style, '1500 a di 10 marzo', i.e. 1501).

19. G. Mongeri, ed., *Le rovine di Roma* (Milan, 1875), 57r. The album of drawings, of which this is a lithographic facsimile, is in the Biblioteca Ambrosiana, Milan; it is attributed to an artist in the circle of Bramantino (Vecce 1998, 200, 406).

20. Isabella to Novellara, 29 March: Archivio di Stato, Mantua, Gonzaga F II 9, busta 2993, copialettere 12/80; Villata 1999, no. 149. Novellara to Isabella, 3 April: Archivio di Stato, Mantua, Gonzaga E XXVIII 3, busta 1103; Villata 1999, no. 150. Novellara to Isabella, 14 April (illustrated; ibid., no. 151): formerly in Archivio di San Fedele, Milan (G. L. Calvi, *Notizie dei principali professori di belle arti in Milano* (Milan, 1869), 3.97), by the early 1980s in a private collection

in Geneva, and from 1995 in a private collection in New York (see C. Pedretti, ALV 5 (1992), 170–75). Girolamo Casio says of Novellara that his sermons were 'hated [i.e. envied] by St Paul' ('*in pulpito era per San Paolo odito*') and that he 'died young and was buried in Mantua' (*Cronica* (1525), 12r).

21. Florimond Robertet, Baron d'Aluye, Bury et Brou, then in his early forties, was secretary and treasurer successively to Charles VIII, Louis XII and François I. A medallion portrait of him dated 1512 (Bibliothèque Nationale, Paris, Cabinet des medailles no. 4003) is in Starnazzi 2000, plates 7, 8.

22. News reports, 28 August 2003 (the theft occurred on the 27th at about 11 a.m.); an estimated value of the painting is £30 million. A detailed comparative analysis of the two versions is in Kemp 1992. A third version (also privately owned), attributed to Cesare del Sesto, was exhibited at Camaiore in 1998 (Pedretti 1998b, cat. no. 10). A free version attributed to Fernando Yañez de la Almedina (probably the 'Ferrando Spagnolo' of the *Anghiari* accounts: see p. 389) is in the National Gallery of Scotland, Edinburgh. A contemporary copy of the latter, until recently in the Paoletti Chelini collection in Lucca (V. Bernardi, 'Una versione lucchese della *Madonna dell'Aspo*', *Notiziario filatelico* 134, August 1972) seems also to have disappeared.

23. C. Pedretti, 'The missing basket', in Starnazzi 2000, 49–50.

24. Starnazzi 2000, plates 23–25.

25. Villata 1999, no. 154. Manfredo styles himself 'ducal orator'.

26. Beltrami 1919, doc. 113.

27. Villata 1999, no. 159, in response to Isabella's letter of 3 May (ibid., no. 158).

28. F. Guicciardini in E. R. Chamberlain, *The Fall of the House of Borgia* (London, 1989). On the Borgia family, see Michael Mallett, *Borgias: The Rise and Fall of a Renaissance Dynasty* (London, 1969); Ivan Cloulas, *Les Borgias* (Paris, 1987); Russell Aiuto, *The Borgias* (Dark Horse Multimedia, 1999, at http://www.crime library.com); Marion Johnson, *The Borgias* (London, 2002). Hard to find, but worth the search, is Frederick Rolfe (a.k.a. Baron Corvo), *Chronicles of the House of Borgia* (London, 1901), the background to which is entertainingly investigated in A. J. A. Symons, *The Quest for Corvo* (London, 1934), 93ff.

29. Andrea Boccaccio, *c.* 1492, in Aiuto (see n. 28). On Cesare, see DBI; Bradford 1976. His mother, Vanozza, ran a hotel for tourists and pilgrims, La Vacca, which is still in business in the Campo dei Fiori, Rome.

30. Villari 1892, 1.291–3. The full text is in Niccolò Machiavelli, *Legazioni e commisssarie*, ed. S. Bertelli (Milan, 1964), 1.267–8. Cf. Vickie Sullivan, 'Patricide and the plot of *The Prince*: Cesare Borgia and Machiavelli's Italy', *Journal of Medieval and Renaissance Studies* 21 (1993), 83–102.

31. Masters 1999, 79–80.

32. L iv, R 1416; Ar 202v, R 1420. The date of the latter list is uncertain: the item 'boxes in the customs house' has been thought to date the list to 1503, after Leonardo's return from the Borgia adventure, but the boxes might equally have been brought from Milan in 1500, and still be at the customs two years later;

compare the slow passage of 'one bundle of clothes transported from Rome', on which he paid 18 lire customs duty in April 1505 (Beltrami 1919, doc. 165). Another item in the list, '*falleri*', refers to a book, the *Epistole de Phalari* (1472), which is also mentioned in a note of *c.* 1499 (CA 638b/234r-b).

33. Piombino: L 6v. Populonia: L 82v–83r.

34. Starnazzi 1995, 1996, 2000, the latter with photographs of the Balze in relation to Leonardo landscapes (plates 26–30).

35. L 19v, 40r, 8r.

36. L 2r. Another reference to the 'Archimedes of the Bishop of Padua' is on L 94v. Solmi suggests that 'Borges' was Antoine Boyer, Archbishop of Bourges, who was then a cardinal in Rome (Solmi 1908, 96), but in a much later note (CA 968b/349v-f, *c.* 1515) Leonardo refers to a 'complete Archimedes' which was 'formerly in the library of the Duke of Urbino, and was taken from there in the time of Duke Valentino': it seems likely that this is the manuscript he was hoping to get off Borgia in 1502. He may have known of the other manuscript from Pacioli, who was a native of Borgo San Sepolcro.

37. L 8r, cover, 78r, 46v, 36v. He has further thoughts on the musical fountain in Ma II 55r – 'Let us create a harmony from the waterfall of a fountain by means of a bagpipe' – and resolves to 'ask Messer Marcello about the sound made by water as described by Vitruvius'. A jotting on the cover of L, 'Marcello lives at the house of Giacomo da Mengardino', probably refers to the same man: he may be Marcello Virgilio Berti, a scholarly colleague of Machaivelli who lectured at the Florentine Studio.

38. L 47r, 77r.

39. K¹ 2r.

40. L 72r.

41. The original is conserved at Villa Melzi, Vaprio d'Adda (Archivio Melzi d'Eril). The document is in the hand of one of Borgia's secretaries. An autograph letter by Borgia to the Florentine Signoria (Forlì, 6 April 1501) was recently sold at Sotheby's (Books and Manuscripts Sale, 25 May 2000, lot 162). A single page written in a 'particularly elegant italic or cancelleresca hand', with a red wax armorial seal featuring two crested helmets, it sold for over £7,500.

42. L 65v–66r.

43. Pacioli, *De viribus quantitatis* 2.85 (Biblioteca Universitaria, Bologna, MS 250, 193v–194r).

44. CU 59v, McM 266, describing the contorted bodies of soldiers in action, 'who take part in such discord or, one might say, in this most brutal kind of madness [*pazzia bestialissima*]'.

45. L 29r; cf. CA 133r/48r-b.

46. He recalls conversing at Nantes with the King's foreign minister: 'When the Cardinal of Rouen said to me that the Italians do not understand war, I replied to him that the French do not understand the State, because if they understood it they would not have let the Church come to such greatness' (Machiavelli 1961,

43–4; 1966, 1.67). In other words, they had unwisely aggrandized the Pope by supporting Cesare Borgia – a prescient comment in November 1500.

47. Dispatch of 7 October 1502, in *Legazioni* (see n. 30), 1.341; Villari 1892, 1.310.

48. CA 121v/43 v-b.

49. Masters 1999, 85–7.

50. Map: RL 12284. Rough sheet: RL 12686. Similar sketches and data on Urbino and Cesena are found in MS L, and may have resulted in similar maps.

51. RL 12278. On Leonardo's maps of 1502–4, see Clayton 1996, 89ff.

52. Rough sheets and notes: RL 12682, CA 336r/122r-a.

53. RL 12277; Clayton 1996, 94–5. The scale is about 1:570,000. On Leonardo's use of the map at Urbino, see Susan Kish, 'The cartography of Leonardo da Vinci', in *Imago et mensura mundi: Atti del XI⁰ congresso internazionale di storia della cartografia*, ed. Carla Clivia Marzoli, 3 vols., Florence, 1985.

54. Villari 1892, 1.314–15.

55. Ibid., 1.320–22; Viroli 2000, 62–5. Machiavelli later wrote up these events in a report drily entitled 'Description of the method used by Duke Valentino to murder Vitellozzo Vitelli' (Machiavelli 1966, 2.785–91). Cf. Richard Cavendish, 'Cesare Borgia at Senigallia', *History Today*, 12 January 2002.

56. L 33v; cf. another reference to Siena, L 19v.

57. Machiavelli 1961, 60–61; 1966, 1.77.

58. He withdraw money from his Florentine bank on 4 March: see n. 64.

59. Topkapi Museum, Istanbul, E 6184; first published by E. Babingher, *Nachrichten der Akademie der Wissenschaften in Göttingen* 52 (1952), 1ff. A reproduction of part of the document is in Vecce 1998, plate 38.

60. L 66r, R 1109.

61. Vasari 1987, 1.346–7; Condivi 1976, ch. 33.

62. PC 2.214. Topographical notes: CA 910r/334r. The bridge was designed by Andrea Gurrieri da Imola.

63. See 'The Leonardo project', http://www.vebjorn-sand.com; *Guardian*, 1 November 2001.

64. The bank's records (Beltrami 1919, doc. 123) date the transaction to 4 March, though Leonardo's own note of it reads, 'Saturday 5 March I withdrew 50 gold ducats from Santa Maria Nuova, leaving 450' (CA 211r/77r-b). The bank is probably right: the first Saturday of March 1503 was the 4th. On the verso of Leonardo's note is '*in africo addì 5 di marzo* 1503', probably written by the river Affrico outside the city walls.

65. Ar 229v. The 'rose pink' (*rosato*) favoured by Leonardo and Salai seems to have had a particular connotation of dressiness: Cosimo de' Medici, seeking to smarten up the scruffy Donatello, sent him a 'pink cloak' to wear on feast days (Lucas-Dubreton 1960, 217). I translate '*pitocco*' as 'tunic'. The word, now obsolete, is defined in elderly dictionaries as a 'short garment [*veste corte*] comparable to the *cotta* worn by soldiers'; the latter is a tabard (a 'loose upper garment

without sleeves': *Shorter Oxford Dictionary*) or surcoat. The *pitocco*'s shortness is contrasted with the toga-like *lucco* worn by respectable Florentines. In Machiavelli's *Mandrake* (1516), an amorous young blade dons a '*pitocchino*' before serenading his girlfriend with lute songs. Leonardo has some scathing comments on the 'mad inventions' of fashion – garments at one time worn so long 'that men continually had their arms laden with clothes so as not to tread on them', and then, at the opposite extreme, 'going only as far as their hips and elbows, and so tight that they suffered great torment' (CU 170r–v, McM 574).

66. Beltrami 1919, doc. 125; CA 98r/35v-a.

67. From the contemporary report on the Pisa diversion by Biagio Buonaccorso (see n. 73). An excellent account of this project is in Masters 1999, 96–133.

68. Villata 1999, no. 178. Sketches of La Verruca are in Ma II 4r and 7v– 8r, the latter showing its setting in the Pisan hills.

69. Sketch of the Arno: Ma II 1r. Guiducci's dispatch: Villata 1999, no. 180.

70. Ibid., no. 181. Giovanni di Andrea Piffero recurs in documents relating to the *Anghiari* mural: an intermediary between Leonardo and the Signoria. On Giovanni Cellini as *piffero*, see Cellini 2002, 10–16.

71. CA 562r/210r-b, Masters 1999, 123–7. The route of the intended diversion is shown on various rough sketch-maps: RL 12279, Ma II 22v–23r, 52v–53r.

72. Mechanical digger: CA 4r/1v-b, Zöllner 2003, no. 544. Shovel-loads and barrow-loads: Ma II 22v.

73. Biblioteca Nazionale, Florence, MS Machiavelli C 6.78; PC 2.175–7. Part of this report, with a diagram showing the path of the diversion, is reproduced in Masters 1999, fig. 7.4 (printed back to front, however). Cf. Landucci 1927, 216 (22 August 1504).

74. CA 127r/46r-b, R 1001; cf. CA 1107r/398r-a.

75. RL 12279, R 1006. Cf. RL 12678, 12683. The system of locks and sluices for the canal is studied in RL 12680.

76. Sassoon 2002.

77. Today the *Mona Lisa* and *La Gioconda* refer interchangeably to the same painting, but that inveterate dealer of Leonardian wild-cards G. P. Lomazzo clearly refers to them as two separate paintings: 'the portrait of the *Gioconda* and that of *Monna Lisa*, in which he has marvellously caught, among other things, the mouth in the act of laughing' (Lomazzo 1584, 434). The relative pronoun is plural ('*quali*') so he definitely means two paintings. The explanation of this may be the so-called 'Nude Giocondas', a group of paintings probably based on a lost Leonardo original, showing a bare-breasted woman in the *Mona Lisa* pose, the most famous of which, attributed to Salai, is in the Hermitage (see p. 441). It is possible that Lomazzo is distinguishing between the original portrait (the *Mona Lisa*) and the later sauced-up version (the *Gioconda*). Elsewhere he speaks of a '*Monna Lisa Napoletana*' (Lomazzo 1590, 6), which might also mean the 'Nude Gioconda' (i.e. as distinct from the 'Florentine' *Mona Lisa*), except that he says it is in the French royal collection at Fontainebleau, which none of the 'Nude Gioconda'

paintings ever was. The earliest documentary reference to a painting called *La Gioconda* (or '*La Joconda*') is in 1525 (Shell and Sironi 1991; Jestaz 1999).

78. The phrasing suggests that Vasari wrote this passage sometime before the death of François in March 1547.

79. Cassiano dal Pozzo, whose account of the painting (Biblioteca Barberini, Rome, LX/64, 192v–194v) is the first actual record of its presence in the French royal collection.

80. J. Atkinson and D. Sices, eds., *Machiavelli and his Friends: Their Personal Correspondence* (De Kalb, Ill., 1996), 87. The only other portrait Leonardo is known to have painted in Florence, the *Ginevra*, is unlikely to be in Ugolini's mind: it had been done a quarter of a century before, and was probably taken to Venice (Vasari had certainly never seen it). Ugolini may, of course, be referring to portrait drawings by Leonardo.

81. RL 12514; a derivative drawing, perhaps by Cesare da Sesto, is in Venice (Accademia, no. 141; Starnazzi 2000, plate 10). The pose shown in the unfinished portrait of Isabella is unknown (see n. 3 above). In her letter to Leonardo of 14 May 1504 (see p. 375) Isabella suggests that, if he cannot travel to Mantua, he might 'satisfy the obligations of our agreement by converting our portrait into another figure even more gracious, that of a Youthful Christ of about 12 years old'. If by 'converting' her portrait she means changing its features, this makes it unlikely that the portrait was in full profile: this pose would be highly unusual for a representation of Christ.

82. RL 19055v (Anat MS B 38v). A text on the same subject (RL 19046r, Anat MS B 29r) is datable to c. 1508; see PC 1.345–8.

83. Biographical material on Lisa was first compiled by Giovanni Poggi (*Il Marzocco*, 21 December 1913; Poggi 1919, 35). The fullest account of her is in Zöllner 1993, on which my account is based.

84. Maddalena married Agnolo Doni in early 1504; Raphael's portraits of them (Palazzo Pitti, Florence) are dated c. 1505–6. The affinities with the *Mona Lisa* are particularly strong in the preparatory drawing (Louvre), which features the framing columns that are vestigially present in Leonardo's painting. These also appear in Raphael's *Woman with a Unicorn* of the same period (Galleria Borghese, Rome), whose pose is also reminiscent of the *Mona Lisa*. It seems that Raphael saw the portrait, or its cartoon, during his sojourn in Florence in c. 1504–6. His *Madonna and Child with Saints* at San Florenzo, Perugia, which has the date 'MDV' or 'MDVI' (1505 or 1506) on the hem of the Virgin's mantle, was possibly painted in Florence; the Baptist on the left echoes the Leonardo prototype seen in RL 12572 and in Credi's Pistoia altarpiece (see p. 124).

85. Zöllner 1993, 126; Maestro Valerio died in January 1521.

86. Beatis 1979, 132.

87. On Pacifica Brandano, see Pedretti 1957, 138–9; Ammirato 1637, 3.134–5. Pacifica and Giuliano's illegitimate son, Ippolito, was created a cardinal by Pope Clement VII. On Isabella Gualanda, see Vecce 1990. Her friend Costanza d'Avalos,

Duchess of Francavilla, has also been canvassed, initially by Adolfo Venturi in *Storia dell'arte in Italia* (Milan, 1925), 9.37–42: a poem by Enea Irpino (*Canzoniere*, MS *c.* 1520) seems to allude to a portrait of her by Leonardo showing her wearing a black veil ('*sotto il bel velo negro*'), though proponents of La Gualanda claim the poem refers to her. More recently Caterina Sforza, illegitimate daughter of Duke Galeazzo Maria, has been proposed, on the basis of a supposed likeness of the *Mona Lisa* to an earlier portrait of Caterina by Lorenzo di Credi. For Freud the famous half-smile was a recovered memory of Leonardo's mother; for others the painting is an idealized portrait representing no one in particular, or it is a depiction of Chastity. In the face of these uncertaintries Kemp laconically captioned the painting *Portrait of a Lady on a Balcony* (Kemp 1981), though even this will not satisfy those who believe that she is really a man, and perhaps even Leonardo himself in drag.

88. Beatis 1979, 133–4.

89. Shell and Sironi 1991.

90. A small documentary curiosity is that in the original *imbreviatura* listing Salai's goods the painting is referred to not as '*La Joconda*', but as '*La Honda*'. Discarding the supernumerary Latin *h*, one arrives at the curious idea that the clerk who wrote this list thought the painting was called *La Onda* – '*The Wave*': in a strictly chronological sense this is the painting's first known title.

91. Zöllner 1993, 118. Zöllner further wonders if Piero del Giocondo was Vasari's source on the painting; but Vasari might have had an even better source – Lisa herself. She was certainly alive in 1539, when she transferred ownership of a property in Chianti to her daughter Ludovica (document discovered by Giuseppe Pallanti: *Sunday Telegraph*, 1 August 2004), and she was probably still living in 1551. That she was alive when Vasari wrote about the painting tends to strengthen his account of it: this is the kind of simple human factor which tends to be overlooked by the ingenious proponents of alternative sitters.

92. Sassoon 2001, 113–15, citing Gautier's review of Paul Foucher's play *La Joconde* (1855), and his *Les dieux et les demi-dieux de la peinture* (Paris, 1865). Gautier was the dedicatee of Baudelaire's *Les Fleurs du mal* (Paris, 1857), which includes a fine poem mentioning Leonardo, '*Les phares*' ('Beacons'): '*Léonard de Vinci, miroir profond et sombre . . .*' – 'Leonardo da Vinci, deep dark mirror'.

93. Sassoon 2001, 128, 98, citing the journals of Jules Michelet (ed. C. Digeon, Paris, 1976, 3.83) and Edmond and Jules de Goncourt (Paris, 1956, 1.719).

94. See Yeats's introduction to *The Oxford Book of Modern Verse* (Oxford, 1936), viii. Pater's influential essay on Leonardo originally appeared in *Fortnightly Review*, November 1869. Sassoon discerns echoes of it in Joyce's *Portrait of the Artist as a Young Man* (1916): see Sassoon 2002, 157–8. On the nineteenth-century 'cult' of Leonardo see also Severi 1992.

95. Oscar Wilde, 'The Critic as Artist' (1890), in *Complete Works* (London, 1969), 1028–9. See also his short story 'The Sphinx without a Secret'.

96. E. M. Forster, *A Room with a View* (1907; repr. Harmondsworth 1955), 95.

97. Somerset Maugham, *Christmas Holiday* (1939), 213; Berenson 1916, 1–4; T. S. Eliot, 'Hamlet and his Problems', in *The Sacred Wood* (1920, repr. 1960), 99.

98. Full and entertaining accounts of the theft and its aftermath are in Sassoon 2002, 173–210; McMullen 1975, 197–215. See also A. Manson, *Le roman vrai de la IIIe République* (Paris, 1957), vol. 3: '*Le vol de la Joconde*'. For some cultural ramifications of the theft, see Leader 2002.

99. Alfredo Geri, in McMullen 1975, 209.

100. See Johannes Wilde, 'The hall of the Great Council of Florence', *Journal of the Warburg and Courtauld Institutes* 8 (1944), 65–81.

101. Villata 1999, no. 183.

102. ASF, Signori e collegi 106, 40v–41r (Villata 1999, no. 189). Cf. the later *deliberazione* authorizing payment of 45 florins for three months, April–June 1504 (ASF, Operai del Palazzo, Stanziamenti 10, 64v; Villata 1999, no. 194).

103. ASF, Signori e collegi 106, 36r; Villata 1999, no. 187. For the activities of February in the next paragraph: ibid., no. 188.

104. CA 1109r/398v-c, PC 2.382.

105. CA 202a/74r-b, v-c, R 669. On Leonardo Dati see Pedretti 1972, 417–25.

106. *Istorie fiorentine*, Bk 5, ch. 33, in Machiavelli 1966, 2.656–7.

107. Numerous preparatory sketches, including battle studies (Accademia, Venice, nos. 214–16; RL 12338–9), individual horsemen (RL 12340r; K 14v), horses in extremis (RL 12326r), and the superb figure studies and head studies at Budapest (Szépművészeti Muzeum, inv. nos. 1174, 1175). See Zöllner 2003, nos. 42–55.

108. A 30v–31r, '*Modo di figurare una battaglia*'.

109. Villata 1999, nos. 190–92. Leonardo had done drawings of Tovaglia's country house in 1500. Salai hoped to take advantage of Leonardo's resistance to Isabella's requests: 'A pupil of Leonardo Vinci called Salai, a young man but very proficient for his age . . . is very desirous to do something fine [*galante*] for Your Excellency' (Luigi Ciocca to Isabella, 24 January 1505: ibid., no. 210).

110. Amadori to Isabella, 3 May 1506: ibid., no. 227.

111. For Michelangelo's biography see DBI, s.v. Buonarroti; Bull 1996; Paul Barolsky, *Michelangelo's Nose: A Myth and its Maker* (University Park, Pa., 1991). On the contemporary *Life* by Ascanio Condivi (1553), heavily influenced by Michelangelo himself, see Michelangelo 1987. On the rivalry with Leonardo, see Goffen 2002.

112. Vasari 1987, 1.337–8; Goldscheider 1940, 9–10. A double-sided sheet of drawings by Leonardo which recently emerged in France (auctioned at Sotheby's, 5 July 2000, reportedly purchased by a Swiss collector for £1.3 million) features a fine chalk-and-ink drawing of Hercules with a club. Pedretti suggests this may be related to Leonardo's supposed efforts with the *David* block (*Guardian*, 18 September 2000), but the monumental style is probably an echo of *David* rather than an idea for the block in its pre-*David* state. It may be related to Leonardo's memo about a sculpture of the 'Labours of Hercules' for Pierfrancesco Ginori, *c.* 1508 (see Part III n. 62).

113. Anthony Burgess, 'Michelangelo: the artist as miracle worker', *Sunday Times*, 2 February 1975.

114. Archivio dell'Opera del Duomo, Deliberazioni 1496–1507, 186; Villata 1999, no. 186.

115. Landucci 1927, 213–14.

116. A much later painting of Piazza Santa Trinità, by Giuseppe Zocchi (1711–67), shows the northern and western walls of the *palazzo* still loggia-free, and a small knot of people at the south-western corner, near the bridge, where the river-front loggia would begin. See the reproduction in Hibbert 1994, 209.

117. Michelangelo to Giovanni Francesco Fattucci, 1523, in P. Barocchi and R. Ristori, eds., *Il carteggio di Michelangelo* (Florence, 1965–79), 3.7–9.

118. Vasari 1987, 1.341–2. Documents in the Fondazione Herbert Horne, Florence, confirm Vasari's statement about Michelangelo's tenancy of Sant'Onofrio. See L. Morozzi, 'La *Battaglia di Cascina* di Michelangelo: nuova ipotesi sulla data di commisssione', *Prospettiva* 53 (1988–9), 320–24.

119. Ma II 128r, PC 1.327; L 79r. Cf. E 19v–20r, a passage beginning 'O anatomical painter', warning against an over-emphasis on 'bones, sinews and muscles' making a painting 'wooden'.

120. RL 12591r.

121. Ar 148r–v, 149v.

122. CA 877r/319r-b, partially transcribed R 1534, addenda in PC 2.378.

123. CA 196r/ 71v-b, R 1526.

124. Ar 272r, R 1372; cf. Eissler 1962, app. C.

125. CA 178r/62v-a, R 1373A. Pedretti thinks the script, though written left to right, is 'the type of handwriting found in the studies for the Arno canal', i.e. 1503–4 (PC 2.319). The mechanical wing on the recto is reproduced in RV 17 (1954), fig. 6.

126. CA 541v/202v-a.

127. Ar 271v. 'Jacopo Tedesco', charged at 1 carlino per day for board and lodging, paid 15 grossini on 9 August and 1 florin on 12 August.

128. Ma II 2v–3r. See Reti 1968, pt 2; Maccagni 1974.

129. RL 12676r. On Il Botro see Part VII n. 26.

130. CA 765v/282 v-b.

131. At the castle: Ma II 24v, with a note beside it, 'The ditch which I am straightening'. Demonstration: Ma II 25r (he actually writes 'on the last day of November, All Saint's Day': another calendar mistake). Drying the marshland: CA 381r/139r-a. These draining and ditching projects seem to echo the recently aborted Arno diversion: expertise is not wasted.

132. Ma II 125r, PC 2.189.

133. RL 12665r; see Introduction n. 10.

134. Ma II 112r.

135. Villata 1999, nos. 211–12.

136. Tn 18r; Villata 1999, no. 218. Cf. Ma II 2r, 'Saturday morning, 1 florin to

Lorenzo'. In a memorandum of *c*. 1504–5 (CA 331r/120r-d, R1444) Leonardo writes, '*Garzone che mi faccia il modello*' ('An assistant who could be a model for me'). Villata suggests this is Lorenzo, and that he was the model for the announcing angel on RL 12328r and the Louvre St John (p. 469 above). See Villata 1999, 184 n. 1, and RV 27 (1997).

137. GDA 19.516–7, s.v. Llanos and Yañez. The identification of 'Ferrando Spagnolo' with Fernando Yañez is rendered less certain by the existence of a colleague confusingly called Fernando Llanos. They are recorded as working together in Valencia, *c*. 1506–10. Llanos is not documented after 1516; Yañez lived on until 1531. That both trained in Italy 'seems likely', says Isabel Mateo Gomez in GDA, 'in the light of the innovations they brought to Renaissance Valencian painting'; Yañez was the more gifted, his work 'more classical and serene, painted with greater clarity and breadth of composition than that of his colleague'. The 'Ferando' mentioned in H 94r–v may be him, in which case he was in Milan by the mid-1490s; the name appears alongside that of the architect Giacomo Andrea. For another reference to a 'Ferrando' painting in Milan in 1494 see Vecce 1998, 152. It is possible he was part of Leonardo's Milanese *bottega*, though these references do not in themselves show this.

138. Ma II 2r.

139. Tavola Doria (private coll., Munich): Zöllner 2003, 242–3. Zacchia engraving: Vecce 1998, plate 40. On the Rubens engraving see Zöllner 1991; there are copies of it in the Royal Collection at The Hague and the Armand Hammer collection in Los Angeles, and an engraving of it by Gerard Edelink (British Museum).

140. Villata 1999, no. 221.

141. Letter to Alberto Lollio, 17 August 1549, in A. F. Doni, *Disegno* (Venice, 1549), 47v–48r.

142. On the layout of the Council Hall, and difficulties of interpreting the evidence, see Rubinstein 1995, 73–5; Johannes Wilde (see n. 100), 75ff.

143. Newton and Spencer 1982.

144. *Daily Telegraph*, 17 July 2000.

145. Melinda Henneburger, 'The Leonardo cover-up', *New York Times*, 21 April 2002.

146. Tn inside cover, 18r

147. Tn 18v. It has been suggested that the date of this entry (and hence of the 'trial flight') should be read as Florentine reckoning, i.e. March 1506 modern style. But the same page contains a note dated 14 April 1505, referring to the arrival of the apprentice Lorenzo (a date confirmed by the *Anghiari* records), and the notes are unlikely to have been written eleven months apart.

148. Tn 13v.

149. RL 12337.

150. Raphael's copy: RL 12759. Leoni's cartoon: ASF, Archivio Mediceo de principiato, Miscellanea 109/54, 228; discovered by Renzo Cianchi ('Un acquisto

mancato', *La Nazione*, 24 November 1967). The items in this inventory, then in the possession of Leoni's son Giambattista, were being offered for sale to Cosimo II de Medici, Grand Duke of Tuscany. Among them was 'a book of about 400 folios, and the folios are more than a braccio long'; the compiler thinks the Duke could have it for 100 scudi. This is an early sighting of the Codex Atlanticus.

151. RL 12570r. On Antonio Segni, see Cecchi 2003, 131–3.

152. Alfonso d'Este to G. Seregno, 1 April 1505 (Beltrami 1919, doc. 162); Vecce 1998, 295, 419.

153. Tn 10v.

PART SEVEN: Return to Milan, 1506–1513

1. Beltrami 1919, doc. 176. According to the Anonimo he left '*desegni . . . con altre masseritie*' ('drawings and other goods') at the Ospedale when he left for Milan.

2. *Supplica* of 1503: Beltrami 1919, doc. 120. *Arbitrato* of 1506: ibid., doc. 170. Cf. docs. 121–2, 167–9, for further paperwork.

3. Bramly 1992, 354.

4. D'Amboise to Gonfalonier Soderini, 16 December 1506, Beltrami 1919, doc. 180.

5. Draft letter to Charles d'Amboise, early 1508, CA 872r/317r-b.

6. Notes and sketches on CA 732bv/271v-a, 629b/231r-b, v-a. Cf. PC 2.28–31; RV 18 (1960), 65–96.

7. Ma II 55r, referring back to the Rimini fountain noted in L 78r; Vitruvius, *De architectura*, Bk 10, ch. 8.

8. RL 12951r, R 1104.

9. A long description of the 'garden of Venus' in Francesco Colonna's strange *Hypnerotomachia Poliphili* (Venice, 1499) may also be a source.

10. Villata 1999, nos. 233–5. The two subsequent letters between d'Amboise and the Signoria (October–December 1506), and the three further to Louis XII's intervention (January 1507): ibid., nos. 236–7, 240–43.

11. CA 117r/41v-b.

12. Uzielli 1872, no. 13. The decree of restitution was issued on 27 April: the owner of the property before this was one Leonino Bilia (Vecce 1998, 269). Salai's father was renting it in 1501, and is again referred to as its tenant in 1510 (Shell and Sironi 1992, no. 26); he probably resided there throughout these changes of ownership.

13. Jean d'Auton, *Chroniques de Louis XII*, in Bramly 1992, 462.

14. Leonardo refers to this grant in letters to Geoffroi Carles and Charles d'Amboise, early 1508, of which drafts remain (CA 872r/317r-b, 1037r/372r-a). He had not then enjoyed any revenues from it due to a dearth of water, 'partly because of the great drought and partly because the sluices have not been regulated'. San Cristofano is presumably the stretch of the Naviglio around San Cristoforo Barona,

south-west of the city. A note of 3 May 1509 (CA 1097r/395r-a) records his presence there. A later draft letter (CA 254r/93r-a, R 1350A) suggests that the revenue (*entrata*) for 'taking this water at San Cristofano' was worth about 72 ducats per annum. In his will (R 1566) the grant is referred to as 'the right of water which King Louis XII of pious memory gave [him]'.

15. Sironi 1981, 21–3; Beltrami 1919, doc. 192.

16. His full name is inscribed (*'Joannes Franciscus Meltius hic scripsit'*) on a manuscript in the Biblioteca Trivulziana, Milan, and is possibly used by Leonardo in a note of 1513 (E IV, see pp. 458–9). On Melzi, see Marani 1998a; Shell 1995; F. Calvi, *Famiglie notabili milanesi* (Milan, 1879), s.v. Melzi.

17. Biblioteca Ambrosiana, Milan, F274 inf. 8; see Marinoni 1982, 136. However, another marginal note, also apparently in Melzi's hand but in a different ink, reads *'anno 19 fr. melzo'*: this perhaps dates some retouching of the drawing.

18. The painting is in a private collection in Milan: see Marani 1998a, 382–3.

19. CA 1037v/372 v-a, R 1350.

20. RL 12280r, CA 65v/20v-b.

21. Shell and Sironi 1992, no. 38.

22. On Uncle Francesco's lost will, see Cianchi 1953, 77–8, 98–100; Cianchi 1984. Properties registered as Francesco's in the 1498 *catasto* included a small house *'nel castello'* (i.e. within the walls of Vinci), a house and vineyard at La Colombaia, a grain-field at Mercatale, and a farm with olive-grove at Croce a Tignano (Smiraglia 1900, doc. 21; Vecce 1998, 251). These may have formed the disputed bequest. A draft letter, in the hand of Melzi (CA 939v/342v-a), refers specifically to the dispute as 'the matter pending between myself and my brother Ser Giuliano, the head of the other brothers'.

23. CA 364r/132 r-a.

24. Villata 1999, nos. 247, 249. The King's letter is countersigned by Florimond Robertet, commissioner of the *Madonna of the Yarnwinder*.

25. Archivio di Stato, Modena, Cancellaria Estense B4. Ippolito was Archbishop of Milan from 1497; in October 1498 he ratified the transfer of property to Mariolo de' Guiscardi, probably the house and garden which Leonardo redesigned (see Part V n. 136). The connection Leonardo is exploiting is thus Milanese rather than Estense.

26. CA 571av/214v-a. The reading *'botro'* is Pedretti's (PC 2.298–9); previous transcribers saw *'vostro'* (i.e. 'your [sc. property]') as does Vecce 1998, 271. Value of Il Botro: Ar 190v–191r. The pit: 'Test at your pit what is the course taken by the object', Leic 9v.

27. CA 872r/317 r-b.

28. Piero Martelli (1468–1525), a member of a 'perpetually pro-Medici family', was later a prominent member of Rucellai's Platonic salon, the Orti Oricellari (Cecchi 2003, 133).

29. Vasari 1878–85, 6.604. We also hear of the 'Company of the Cauldron', a mock confraternity frequented by Rustici, del Sarto, Aristotile da Sangallo et al.,

where the painters created fantastical portraits and figures out of food, anticipating the Mannerist master of culinary portraits Arcimboldo.

30. Ar 1r.

31. CA 571ar/214r-d, PC 1.103, a sheet with notes on water and flight.

32. The codex consists of eighteen sheets of linen paper, folded to make 36 folios. By the late seventeenth century it was in the hands of the Roman painter Giuseppe Ghezzi. He claimed to have found it, in Rome, in a chest of manuscripts and drawings formerly belonging to the Lombard sculptor Guglielmo della Porta. The latter (d. 1577) can be linked almost back to Leonardo himself, for in his youth Guglielmo had been a pupil of his uncle, Giovanni della Porta, a sculptor and architect who was working in Milan cathedral in the 1520s; and this older della Porta had in turn been a pupil of the architect Cristoforo Solario, whom Leonardo knew personally in Milan (Beltrami 1919, doc. 205). Purchased from Ghezzi by Thomas Coke sometime between 1713 and 1717, the codex resided at the family seat, Holkham Hall in Norfolk, in the library created by Coke's ancestor, the Elizabethan lawyer Sir Edward Coke. It was sold at auction in 1980 to the oil-magnate Armand Hammer, and was for a while known as the Codex Hammer. Bill Gates bought it in 1994 for $30 million; it is housed in his mansion at Seattle – the furthest flung of all Leonardo's works. He has modestly declined to rechristen it the Codex Gates, so it is now once again the Codex Leicester.

33. Leic 1r–v, cf. Pedretti 2000, 11. On a blank outer leaf Ghezzi gave the codex the following title: '*Libro originale / Della Natura peso e moto delle Acque / Composto scritto e figurato di proprio / Carattere alla mancina /Dell' Insigne / Pittore e Geometra / Leonardo da Vinci*' ('Original manuscript concerning the nature, force and motion of waters, composed, written and illustrated in the genuine left-handed writing of the renowned painter and geometrician Leonardo da Vinci'), but an earlier hand (perhaps one of the della Porta) gave a better summary of its contents: 'Book written by Leonardo Vincio which treats of the sun, the moon, the course of waters, of bridges and motions'.

34. Leic 34r; cf. A 54v–56r.

35. Leic 13r, 16v; CA 571ar/214r-d.

36. Leic 2r.

37. Georgio Nicodemi, 'Life and Works of Leonardo', in *Leonardo da Vinci* (New York, 1938), cited White 2000, 6–7.

38. RL 19027r, v.

39. RL 19028.

40. RL 19054v.

41. RL 19095.

42. See, for example, Antonio Cammelli's sonnet 'Quando di Vener fu l'alma superba' (*Lubrici* no. 4; Cammelli 1884, 200), where the 'proud captain' breaks through the 'stockade' (*steccata*) after a 'bitter battle'.

43. RL 19055, formerly bound next to RL 19095. The embryological interest foreshadows the famous studies of the human foetus, RL 19101–2, etc.

44. RL 19070v, R 796.

45. Landucci 1927, 217: 'On 24 January [1506] a young man was condemned and hanged, and the doctors and scholars of the Studio, all learned and upstanding men, sought permission from the Otto to anatomize him.' The dissection was performed over a week, with two sessions a day, and had the status of a theatrical event: 'My Master Antonio went every day to watch.' Perhaps Leonardo did too.

46. Sironi 1981, 23–6.

47. Ottino della Chiesa 1967, 94. Hamilton purchased it in July 1785 from Count Cicogna, administrative director of Santa Caterina alla Ruota, which owned the goods and titles of the suppressed Confraternity; he paid 1582 lire. From Hamilton's descendants it passed to Lord Lansdowne, and then to the Duke of Suffolk, who sold it to the National Gallery in 1880 for 9,000 guineas.

48. The Swiss *Virgin of the Rocks* was exhibited at the Palazzo Reale, Milan, in 2000. See F. Caroli, *Il Cinquecento Lombardo: Da Leonardo a Caravaggio* (Milan 2000), cat. no. II.2.

49. Cu 25v, McM 57.

50. BM 1875-6-12-17r; Zöllner 2003, no. 27; Pedretti 1968, 27–8.

51. *Daily Telegraph*, 16 January 1996.

52. J. McEwen, 'Leonardo restored', *Independent Magazine*, 20 May 1989, 53–7.

53. Dalli Regoli 2001, 116–19. It is the only known painted version of the kneeling Leda. Four paintings of the standing Leda, generally ascribed to *c.* 1509–10 or later, are in the Uffizi (called the 'Spirodon Leda', after its former owner Ludovico Spirodon; attributed to Fernando Yañez by Marani, and to the studio of Lorenzo di Credi by Natali: see Dalli Regoli 2001, 140); in the Galleria Borghese, Rome, attributed to Il Sodoma; at Wilton House, Salisbury (see plate 29), attributed to Cesare da Sesto; and in the Johnson Collection, Philadelphia. The Spirodon Leda was briefly owned by Hermann Goering, to whom the Contessa Gallotti Spirodon sold it in 1941.

54. Leda's face: RL 12515–8. Her features are closely echoed in Giampietrino's *Nymph Hegeria* (Coll. Brivio Sforza, Milan), *Venus and Cupid* (Coll. Nembini, Milan) and *Cleopatra* (Louvre), and to a lesser extent in his *Dido* (Coll. Borromeo, Isola Bella) and *Salome* (National Gallery, London). The stance of his Venus is demonstrably based on the standing Leda. Cf. L. Keith and A. Roy, 'Giampietrino, Boltraffio and the influence of Leonardo', *National Gallery Technical Bulletin* 17 (1996), 4–19.

55. Technical report by Hans Brammer (Kassell, 1990), summarized by Jürgen Lehrmann in Dalli Regoli 2001, 116–18. A further connection of Giampietrino with Leonardo's studio in *c.* 1509 is the polyhedron painted on the back of his *Madonna and Child* (Poldi Pezzoli, Milan), which derives from one of Leonardo's illustrations for Pacioli's *Divina proportione* (Venice, 1509); a copy of the painting by Giovan Battista Belmonte bears the date 1509.

56. On Bernazzano, see J. Shell and G. Sironi, 'Bernardinus dictus Bernazanus de

Marchixelis', *Arte Cristiana* 78 (1990), 363ff. The record of a debt of 30 scudi owed to him by Francesco Melzi's father and uncle (Shell and Sironi 1992, 116) gives a hint of complex human interweavings within Leonardo's 'circle' of which we are mostly ignorant. He was a native of Inzago, near Milan: on his possible connection with a Last Supper fresco at Inzago, see n. 115.

57. RL 12343r, 12354r, 12355r, 12356r (illustrated), 12360r, etc.; Zöllner 2003, nos. 74–86. These were first systematically distinguished from Sforza Horse studies by Clark: see Clark and Pedretti 1968, 1.xxvi–xli.

58. CA 492r/179v-a, R 725.

59. F 87r.

60. F 15r; Pedretti 1995, 26. Cf. notes on the canalization of the Adda, *c.* 1508, CA 949r/345r-b.

61. F 41v, R1123A; cf. two sketches of bats in flight on F 48v.

62. Membranes of the bat's wings: Tn 16r. Bats fly upside down: G 63v, *c.* 1510–11.

63. F 59r, R 1148C.

64. F 4v.

65. RL 12689r, PC 2.127–8. Cf. F 41r, *c.* 1508: 'The earth is not the centre of the sun's orbit, nor the centre of the universe,' which is relativist but not specifically Copernican.

66. F 12r.

67. The lungs of a pig: cf. RL 19054v. Avicenna: i.e. the eleventh-century Arab scientist Ibn Sina. 'Map of Elefan': possibly referring to the Siva temple at Elephanta, cf. the description of a temple in CA 775v/285r-c. 'Maestro Mafeo': perhaps Rafaello Maffei, whose encyclopaediac *Anthropologia* (1506) mentions the *Last Supper*, or the Veronese anatomist Girolamo Maffei, probably known to Leonardo via Marcantonio della Torre, also from Verona. The rising of the Adige: cf. Leic 20r, 23r.

68. MS D is a 'meditated version' of earlier notes and a testing by '*isperienza*', or experiment, of established authorities (Avicenna, Alhazen) on the subject (Pedretti and Cianchi 1995, 25).

69. RL 19007v.

70. Pedretti 1965, 140.

71. See Pedretti 1965 for a detailed reconstruction of Libro A.

72. Ar 224r, 231v; Pedretti 1957, 90–98. A folio formerly in the Codex Atlanticus (fol. 50), now in a private collection in Switzerland, has further details of the *mise-en-scène* and the backstage machinery (C. Pedretti, RV 28 (1999), 186–97). Pedretti compares the system of counterweights to those of excavation machines in MS F. On the verso of the sheet is a brief note on water which can be related to material in Leic 18r–19v and Ar 136r–137v (the latter in draft, crossed through when incorporated into Codex Leicester). The same Arundel folios have musical instruments and figure studies in black chalk (the latter by a pupil) which may also be connected with *Orfeo*.

73. RL 12282r; the profile is similar to one on Ar 137r.

74. *Corriere della sera*, 13 September 2001; *Guardian*, 14 September 2001: 'When restorers treated the work with alcohol and water to loosen it from its backing, the ink began to disappear.' As well as in the Trivulzio estimate (see n. 58), the yellow-green ink is found in a study for the monument (RL 12356r), and in plans for the d'Amboise summer villa (see n. 6). A page with a sketch of the Trivulzio horse (CA 786v/290v-b) has some heads gone over in the same ink by a pupil. See PC 2.15–17.

75. *Archivio storico italiano* 3 (1842), 207; Lomazzo 1973, 2.156.

76. CA 584r /218r-a.

77. S. Daniel, *The Worthy Tract of Paulus Jovius* (London, 1585), translated from Giovio's *Dialogo dell'imprese* (written shortly before his death in Florence in 1552, and published in 1555); devices based on this and other works appear in Shakespeare's *Pericles* (*c*. 1608) 2.ii. See H. Green, *Shakespeare and the Emblem Writers* (London, 1885).

78. On Renaissance emblems, see M. Corbett and R. Lightbown, *The Comely Frontispece* (London, 1979), 9–34; F. Yates, 'The emblematic conceit in Giordano Bruno's *De gli eroici furori*', *Journal of the Warburg and Courtauld Institutes* 6 (1943), 180–209. Other important collections are Gabriello Symeoni, *Imprese eroiche e morali* (Lyons, 1559), Scipione Ammirato, *Il Roto* (Naples, 1562) and Girolamo Ruscelli, *Le imprese illustri* (Venice, 1566).

79. RL 12701, cf. rough sketches on RL 12282. Reti attempts to relate them to Leonardo's service of Cesare Borgia in 1502 (Reti 1959), but they are almost certainly *c*. 1508–9.

80. Clark notes that the word '*tale*' is missing from the motto in the earlier sketch on RL 12282: in other words the final form refers to a specific protector ('such a star'), presumably King Louis. See Clark and Pedretti 1968, 1.179.

81. M 4r. Cf. the purely scientific observation in CA728r/270r-a, *c*. 1510: 'The strong wind kills the flame, the temperate wind feeds it.' A similar emblem in G. Ruscelli, *Emblemata* (1583), bears the motto '*Frustra*' ('Frustration' or 'Delay').

82. RL 12700. Another aside is, '"*Non mi stanco nel giovare*" ["I am not tired of being useful"] is a motto for carnival.' The iris (Embolden 1987, 126) also appears on Ar 251v, of about the same date.

83. A side-note reads, 'The fire destroys all sophistication, which is deceit; it only maintains truth, which is gold.' The terminology is chemical, or alchemical: 'sophistication' = adulteration or impurity.

84. CA 522r/192r-a. There follows another payment of '200 francs at 48 soldi per franc' (= approx. 500 lire or 125 scudi). These payments were effected by treasury official Etienne Grolier (father of the author Jean Grolier), whose death in September 1509 is noted on the same folio, in the hand of a pupil, probably Lorenzo.

85. F, inside cover. The marrying sister was either Lorenziola (married Tommaso da Mapello; widowed by 1536) or Angelina (married Battista da Bergamo; widowed in 1524).

86. RL 12280. The recto which contains the list has geometric studies; the verso

has a large anatomical drawing transferred from RL 12281. On the date of these sheets, see Clark and Pedretti 1968, 1.78.

87. CA 669/247a.

88. On Bossi, see DBI; Bossi 1982. Advice of Goethe: Pedretti 1998c, 122 n.6.

89. Biblioteca Ambrosiana, Milan, SP6/13E/B1.f.100, 196.

90. M. Armellini, *Un censimento della città di Roma sotto il pontificato di Leone X* (Rome, 1887), 79, 90; Pedretti 1998c, 128.

91. A note beside the head on RL 12515 ('This can be removed without damaging it') suggests that the braiding worn by the model was a hairpiece.

92. RL 12281. On the Fabbri gate, see L. Beltrami, *La pusterla dei Fabbri* (Milan, 1900); it is marked (as 'fabbri') on Leonardo's sketch-map of Milan, RL 19115v. On Alfei and Bellincioni, see Bellincioni 1876, 241–2. A Cremonese woman mentioned by Leonardo in H 62v, *c.* 1493–4 ('A nun lives at La Colomba in Cremona, who does good work with straw plait'), seems unlikely to be La Cremona.

93. RL 12609.

94. Paolo Maria Terzago, *Museum Septalianum* (Tortona, 1664), no. 33. In the Bergamo painting the bare-breasted woman is surrounded by flowers. McMullen (1975, 156–7) calls her a 'cousin' of the *Flora* or *Columbine*: the latter, also at the Hermitage, is attributed to Melzi, though she is not in the Mona Lisa pose. Another well-known 'Nude Gioconda' is the frizzy-haired siren at Chantilly, done in black chalk and pricked for transfer (McMullen 1975, 66–7). In his guide to the paintings at Fontainebleau (Paris, 1642), perhaps with these racy variations in mind, Père Dan defended Mona Lisa as 'a virtuous Italian lady and not a courtesan as some believe'.

95. Ar 205v, PC 2.248–9.

96. RL 19009r.

97. RL 19016.

98. K 48v.

99. RL 19017r, R 1494 (text concerning muscles of the feet, beginning 'Mondino says that . . .') and RL 12281.

100. RL 19063, R 1210.

101. RL 19071r.

102. RL 19000v, PC 2.114.

103. Edward Lucie Smith, 'Leonardo's anatomical drawings', *Illustrated London News*, November 1979, 94–5.

104. Kemp 1981, 270–77; RL 19099v; Embolden 1987, 93–4.

105. Beltrami 1919, doc. 206.

106. G 1r. Further observations on the Brianza lakes: CA 740r/275r-a.

107. Mountains on red paper: RL 12410–16. 'Gravel stones are whiter than the water': RL 12412.

108. RL 12416.

109. RL 19092v, R 1436.

110. RL 12400. Kemp (1989, 73) has a photograph of the same stretch of the Adda today.

111. CA 173r/61r-b; Embolden 1987, fig. 36. Cupolas: CA 414b/153r-e; Embolden 1987, fig. 37. See also RL 19107v, with architectural studies of Villa Melzi, and a bird's wing related to flight studies in MS E. An engraving of Villa Melzi by Telemaco Signorini, c. 1885, is in Nanni and Testaferrata 2004, fig. 38.

112. RL 19077v. On the siege of Trezzo, see Clark and Pedretti 1968, 3.32; L. Beltrami, *Miscellanea Vinciana* 1 (Milan, 1923).

113. RL 12579.

114. Clark 1988, 237–8; see also Clayton 2002, 68–71, on two other portraits of aged men (RL 12499, 12500): 'An old bearded man drawing an old bearded man cannot have been oblivious to an element of self-portraiture.'

115. RL 12726; Clayton 2002, 110. On the copy at the Biblioteca Ambrosiana, Milan, see L. Beltrami, 'Il volto di Leonardo', *Emporium* 49 (1919), 5. As well as the woodcut portraits in Vasari's *Lives* (1568 edn) and Giovio's *Imagines clarorum virorum* (1589), there are painted portraits in the Museo Giovio, Como (1536); in the Uffizi (late sixteenth century: see Ottino della Chiesa 1967, 85); and in a private collection (triple portrait showing Dürer, Leonardo and Titian, attributed to the workshop of Angelo Bronzino, c. 1560–65; see Vezzosi 1997, 128.) A fresco of the Last Supper at San Rocco, Inzago, was widely publicized after its restoration as being by Leonardo in c. 1500, and as containing a self-portrait in a bearded disciple (*Times*, 24 April 2000). These claims are self-cancelling: the disciple in question is too old to be a self-portrait of c. 1500, when Leonardo was forty-eight (and when he looked, as I have argued, like Bramante's Heraclitus in the Casa Panigarola fresco). However, the disciple has some similarities with the bearded, elderly portraits of Leonardo; if the fresco could be re-dated to c. 1512 or after, the disciple might conceivably be a portrait of him, though not a very good one. This dating would also raise the possibility that the fresco was painted by the Leonardesco artist Bernazzano, who was a native of Inzago (b. 1492).

116. RL 12300v, tentatively accepted as a portrait of Leonardo by Clark (Clark and Pedretti 1.17) and more enthusiastically by Clayton (2002, 110–12).

117. See, for example, reverse images found on the versos of one of the Madonna and Child with a Cat drawings (BM 1826-6-21-1v); of a sketch for the Trivulzio monument (RL 12356v); of the template for the Burlington House cartoon (BM 1875-6-12-17v); and many others.

118. Church of San Pietro e San Paolo (including the former abbey of the Gerolamini or Jeromites), Ospedaletto Lodigiano. The village lies 13 miles south of Lodi. The abbey was constructed in the fifteenth century, under the patronage of the Balbi family of Milan; the site was formerly a piligrims' hospice, the Ospedale di Senna, from which comes the name of the village. It is briefly described by Antonio de Beatis, who spent the night of 1 January 1518 there (Beatis 1979, 184–5). Giampietrino's contacts with the Jeromites of Ospedaletto date from August 1515 (C. Geddo, 'La Madonna di Castel Vitoni', ALV 7 (1994), 67–8; Marani 1998c,

282–3). The altarpiece (a polyptych, now dismembered but all parts *in situ*) was restored in 1996. St Jerome, revered by the Jeromites, is fittingly given the features of Leonardo, revered by Giampietrino.

PART EIGHT: Last Years, 1513–1519

1. Beltrami 1919, doc. 215. The name is probably a misreading of Prevostino Piola or Piora, to whom Piattino Piatti dedicated an epigram (*Elegiae*, 1508, viir); his sister was the stepmother of the Sforza chronicler Bernardino Corio (Villata 1999, no. 285 n. 2).

2. Barbara Stampa: CA 2r/1r-c; Vecce 1998, 301. Mrs Crivelli and the capon: RL 19101r. The query appears, curiously enclosed in a frame that makes it look like an inscription, above a picture of female genitalia. The sheet, which the Crivelli reference dates to 1513 or earlier, contains the beautiful drawing of a foetus (see Plate 30).

3. Stages of the journey: CA 260v/95r-f. Carriage fee to Rome: CA 1113r/400r-b. The latter sheet has a note of distances: 'Milan–Florence, 180 miles; Florence–Rome, 120 miles'. The date of his arrival in Florence is not certain. Beltrami transcribed a document from Santa Maria Nuova as showing that Leonardo deposited 300 florins there on 10 October 1513, but Laurenza (2004, 21–2) shows that this is a misreading.

4. CA 225r/83r-a, PC 2.351. The list is sometimes dated 1515 (when Leonardo was once again in Florence).

5. Letter to Francesco Vettori, 10 December 1513 (Machiavelli 1961, 19): 'It should be welcome to a prince, especially a new prince, and so I dedicate it to his Magnificence Giuliano.' In the event the book was dedicated to Giuliano's nephew Lorenzo di Piero de' Medici, Duke of Urbino.

6. C. Pedretti, ALV 6 (1993), 182.

7. 'GLOVIS': Vecce 1998, 309. 'Thoughts turn to hope': CA 190v/68v-b, with a sketch of a bird in a cage, probably a *calandrino* or meadow-lark, popularly supposed (as explained in Leonardo's bestiary, H 5r) to offer a prognosis to the sick – hopeful unless the bird refused to look at you, in which case you were going to die.

8. Beltrami 1919, doc. 218. Giuliano's Roman residence was the Palazzo degli Orsini (today Palazzo Taverna) at Montegiordano, near the Castel Sant'Angelo; perhaps Leonardo was accommodated there while his studio and living quarters were made ready at the Belvedere.

9. 'Sewer of iniquity': letter to Giovanni de' Medici (Hibbert 1979, 204–5), written in early 1492, when Giovanni was elected cardinal. Syphilis among priests: Cellini 2002, 44, calling it the 'French disease'. The word 'syphilis' was not yet in use: it derives from a poem by Girolamo Fracastoro, *Syphilis* (1530), whose protagonist is a shepherd punished by Apollo with a dose of the pox.

10. Embolden 1987, 57–62.

11. See Part III n. 23.

12. CA 244v/90v-a.

13. *De Ludo geometrico*: CA 124v/45v-a. Geometric lunes or *lunulae*: CA 266r/97r-a, 272v/99v-b, 316/114r-b, v-b. Cf. Pedretti 1965, 161–2.

14. Raphael, who painted Giuliano de' Medici's portrait (see illustration on p. 458), is possibly the 'Rafaello da Urbino' named in two rosters of Giuliano's household employees, April 1515 (ASF, Carte Strozziane I/10, 178–9; Laurenza 2004, app. 3). But his appearance among tailors and gatekeepers seems odd, and this may be an unknown namesake. On an artistic echo of Leonardo in Raphael's Roman work, see n. 23. Castiglione probably met Leonardo in Milan in the 1490s; he was then a student at the university, and had contacts at the Sforza court (cf. Part V n. 89). Passages in *The Courtier*, which he was working on in Rome, suggest his familiarity with Leonardo's *paragone* or comparison between painting and sculpture, presented to Ludovico before 1498 (Castiglione 1967, 96–102). He names Leonardo (with Mantegna, Raphael, Giorgione and Michelangelo) as one of the '*eccellentissimi*' painters of the day (ibid., 82), and is doubtless referring to him when he writes, 'One of the world's finest painters despises the art for which he has so rare a talent, and has set himself to study philosophy; and in this he has strange notions and fanciful revelations that, if he tried to paint them, for all his skill he couldn't' (ibid., 149). Atalante: a fragment of a letter addressed to 'Talante' (CA 890r/325r-b) probably dates from this time.

15. Fossils on Monte Mario: CA 253v/92v-c ('Get them to show you where the shells are on Monte Mario'), a fragmentary page containing geometrical lunes. Monte Mario lies to the north of the Vatican City. Accounts: CA 109b/39r-b, 259r/94r-b. The giulio (minted by Pope Julius II) was worth about a lira.

16. E 80r, 96r.

17. CA 819r/299r-a, in the hand of Melzi. It seems Ser Giuliano had artistic pretensions: a notarial book preserved in ASF has some doodled sketches which Pedretti calls 'Leonardesque' (PC 1.400). According to Milanesi (Vasari 1878–85, 6.25), he was commissioned to design allegorical figures for the Florence carnival in 1516, and later that year he was in Bologna on a diplomatic mission for the Signoria (ASF, Signore Responsive 35, 214).

18. Vasari apparently saw these paintings (one a Madonna and Child, the other of a 'little boy') at the house of Turini's son Giulio in Pescia, but nothing else is known of them.

19. CA 780v/287v-a, PC 2.388–90.

20. E 4v. Other notes on vocal acoustics, with detailed studies on the internal structure of the mouth, throat and trachea, are in RL 19002, 19044–5, 19050, 19055, 19068 etc.

21. G, cover. On the same date the Pope ratified a gift to Giuliano of a large tract of the unsalubrious Paludi Pontine, or Pontine Marshes, south of Rome. Leonardo's coloured map RL 12684 is probably the result of a survey of the area he undertook in the spring or early summer of 1515.

22. Lomazzo cited in Rosheim 2000, 6–7. Michelangelo Buonarroti the younger (Michelangelo's nephew) describes Leonardo's device as 'set to work for the Florentine nation': *Descrizione delle nozze di Maria Medici* (Florence, 1600), 10. See C. Pedretti, 'Leonardo at Lyon', RV 19 (1962).

23. RL 12328r. For arguments about the dating of the half-length *St John*, see Zöllner 2003, 248, Laurenza 2004, 33–4, and sources given there. An angel which appears in two Raphael drawings of *c.* 1514 (Musée Bonnat, Bayonne, 1707; Ashmolean Museum, Oxford, 538) has strong similarities to Leonardo's *St John*, which may strengthen the Roman date for the painting, but which could also refer back to this earlier Florentine prototype of the announcing angel.

24. Öffentliche Kunstsammlung, Basle; Clark 1988, plate 118, dated by him *c.* 1505–7. Bandinelli drawing: current whereabouts unknown, see photograph in Pedretti 2001, 44. The former may be the painting owned by Duke Cosimo de' Medici, as described by Vasari: 'a head of an angel who lifts one arm in the air, foreshortened from the shoulder to the elbow, coming forwards [*venendo innanzi*, i.e. towards the viewer], and the other arm touching his chest with one hand' (Ottino della Chiesa 1967, 110).

25. CA 395ar/146r-b; Accademia, Venice, no. 138.

26. There is a theory that it was stolen from Windsor in the nineteenth century. According to Brian Sewell (*Sunday Telegraph*, 5 April 1992), 'It was well known that the Royal Collection had once contained a number of pornographic drawings by Leonardo. I remember being fascinated by the story when I worked for a while in the Royal Library. The whole episode had passed into the mythology of the place. According to the version I heard, a large man in a Sherlock Holmes cape had arrived one day to have a look at the drawings. He was reputed to be a very eminent German scholar. It was not until some time later that the drawings were found to be stolen ... There is no doubt that the drawings were a considerable embarrassment, and I think everyone was very relieved to find that they'd gone.' Sewell adds that both Kenneth Clark and Anthony Blunt deliberately chose not to mention this in their studies of the Queen's collections.

27. A. Green, 'Angel or demon?' (1996), in Pedretti 2001, 91–4.

28. From the concluding address by Dr Laurie Wilson at 'Renaissance and Antiquity: Vision and Revision: A Psychoanalytical Perspective', New York, 23 March 1991: the congress at which the *Angelo* was first exhibited.

29. A. Pucci, *La reina d'oriente* (Bologna, 1862), canto 3, 42. On Leonardo's knowledge of this poem, see Part IV n. 52.

30. British Library, Cotton MS Titus C6, 7; Harley MS 6848, 185–6. See C. Nicholl, *The Reckoning* (London, 2nd edn, 2002), 321–7, 389.

31. On Caravaggio's *Sick Bacchus* (Galleria Borghese, Rome, *c.* 1593) and other Bacchus paintings, see Maurizio Calvesi, 'Caravaggio, o la recerca della salvazione', in José Frèches, *Caravaggio: pittore e 'assassino'*, trans. Claudia Matthiae (Milan, 1995), 148–51.

32. First described by Cassiano dal Pozzo (Vatican, Barberiniano Latino 5688),

with the comment 'It is a very delicate work but it does not greatly please because it does not encourage devotion, nor does it have decorum.' It is '*St Jean au desert*' in the Fontainebleau catalogues of Père Dan (1642) and Le Brun (1683), and '*Baccus*' in that of Paillet (1695). '*Desert*' merely means a deserted place or wilderness. See Marani 2000a, no. 25; Zöllner 2003, 249.

33. See H 22v, R 1252: 'The panther is all white and spotted with black marks like rosettes.' Cf. Dante, *Inferno*, canto 1, 32: 'a panther [*lonza*], light and nimble and covered with a speckled skin'. The name is now generally applied to American cats (pumas, jaguars, cougars, etc.) which are unspotted. Leonardo also says, 'The panther in Africa has the form of a lioness,' following a traditional notion that panthers were female and leopards male.

34. Private collection, Ottino della Chiesa 1967, 109. Clark thought it possible that Cesare had painted the Louvre *St John in the Desert* as well, from a Leonardo drawing (Clark 1988, 251); the soft, poetic landscape is reminiscent of Bernazzano, who supplied landscapes for some of Cesare's paintings. A red-chalk study, formerly at the Museo del Sacro Monte, Varese, but now lost, may be a copy of an original Leonardo cartoon (ibid., plate 119).

35. The three Greek words are transliterated in Pliny the Elder's *Historia naturalis* (Bk 36, ch. 29), a book mentioned in all Leonardo's book-lists.

36. BN 2038 19v, R 654.

37. BN 2038 21r, R 606.

38. Leic 22v, cf. 30v; F 37v, from a text headed 'Book 43: Of the movement of the air shut in beneath water'.

39. RL 12665 (R 608–9). Cf. CA 215r/79r-c, 419r/155r-a (R 610–11), 302r/108v-b, all of *c.* 1515.

40. G 6v.

41. RL 12377–86 (Zöllner 2003, nos. 451–60) are a unified series; two others, RL 12376 (which relates to the note on G 6v) and RL 12387, are probably earlier. Popham calls the series an 'experiment in abstract design hardly repeated in Europe till modern times . . . The scientist has in these drawings been totally submerged: it is some inner rhythmic sense which dictates to Leonardo the abstract forms of these vision' (Popham 1946, 95–6).

42. CA 671r/247v-b. The drafts of this letter are scattered among various folios, sometimes repetitious: see also CA 768r/283r-a, 500r/182v-c, 252r/92r-b, 1079v/389v-d (R 1351–1353A).

43. CA 213v/78v-b, R 855.

44. See Part I n. 43.

45. CA 429r/159r-c, R 1368A.

46. ASF, Carte Strozziane I/10, 160r; Laurenza 2004, app. 2. This is a schedule of monthly payments ('*provisione*') to Giuliano's retainers, datable to April–July 1515, not as previously thought a payment connected with the papal progress to Bologna at the end of the year. Leonardo receives 40 ducats, of which 33 are for his own *provisione* and 7 for 'Giorgio Tedesco'. Gian Niccolò 'of the wardrobe',

mentioned in Leonardo's letter, receives 11 ducats; Giuliano's secretary, Piero Ardingerli, 6.

47. Giovanni was not an assistant, as is often said: the letter makes it clear he is an independent master with a separate studio in the Belvedere; no documentation of him has yet been found.

48. G 34r, R 885.

49. CA 534v/199v-a. This beautiful catchphrase is part of a polemic against imitators; the passage begins with the recommendation to study and sketch 'in the streets, and in the piazza, and in the fields' quoted on pp. 5–6.

50. Ar 88r. Cf. Ar 73, 78, 84ff., all dated by Pedretti *c.* 1506–8.

51. G 84v (see p. 95), in the context of parabolic mirrors for solar power. Calculations of the power produced are on the following page (G 85r).

52. Pyramidical power-point: CA 1036av/371v-a; cf. CA 750r/277r-a, which gives dimensions of the pyramid (base with sides of 4 braccia = 8 feet or 2.4 metres). Astronomical use: Ar 279v, PC 2.135.

53. G 75v: '*ignea*' written backwards. A similar tic of secrecy is in Ar 279–80, where material on the solar mirrors is misleadingly headed '*perspectiva*'. These relate to the alleged snooping activities of Giovanni degli Specchi.

54. RL 19102r, cf. 19101v, 19128r, etc.; on the later date of the notes see Laurenza 2004, 12–14. 'The' hospital (CA 671r/247r-b) suggests Santo Spirito, but an alternative possibility for the location of his Roman dissections is Santa Maria della Consolazione, on the Campidoglio.

55. The papal bull *Apostolici regiminis*, promulgated in December 1513, condemned those who questioned the immortality of the soul as 'detestable and abominable heretics'. Pomponazzi's suppressed work was *De immortalitate animae* (Rome, 1516). See G. di Napoli, *L'immortalità dell'anima nel Rinascimento* (Turin, 1963).

56. C. Frommel, 'Leonardo fratello della Confraternità della Pietà dei Fiorentini a Roma', RV 20 (1964), 369–73.

57. CA 179v/63v-a, R 769A.

58. Landucci 1927, 205.

59. CA 15r/3r-b.

60. CA 865r/315r-b. Another folio (CA 264v/96v-a) has plans for 'the Magnifico's stables'. Unlike the others, this was a project which became a reality: work began on the Medici stables the following year.

61. Vasari 1878–85, 8.159.

62. Vasari saw the Melzi portrait-drawing in Milan in 1566; he was then still at work on the Palazzo Vecchio frescos (completed January 1572). He may also have known the portrait of Leonardo owned by Paolo Giovio (Museo Giovio, Como), also derived from the Melzi drawing: see Part VII n. 115.

63. Pedretti 1953, 117–20. Leonardo's presence in Bologna on 14 December 1515 adds to doubts about the genuineness of a letter, now lost, purportedly written by him from Milan on 9 December. The letter (Uzielli 1872, no. 23; PC 2.304) is

addressed to 'Zanobi Boni, *mio castaldo* [i.e. my steward or major domo]', and
reproves him for the poor quality of 'the last four flagons of wine', which had
disappointed him because 'the vines of Fiesole, if they were better managed, should
produce the best wine in our part of Italy.' There is no other evidence of this Zanobi,
nor of any vineyards in Fiesole owned by Leonardo (though some might argue
this strengthens the letter's claims, as forgers tend to exploit known connections
rather than invent unknown ones). In 1822 the letter was owned by a collector
named Bourdillon, who had purchased it from 'a lady residing near Florence'. It
has some interesting viticultural advice, but it seems unlikely that the advice is
Leonardo's.

64. Vecce 1998, 329. There is an epitaph in two *canzoni* by Ariosto.

65. CA 471r/172r-a, v-b. Partly illegible, but enough remains to read '*fatto alli*
[. . .]*sto 1516*'.

66. Though his brother-in-law Tommaso Mapello acted as his agent in Milan,
and collected rent on his behalf, Salai probably stayed to deal with a legal dispute
over the building work done in the vineyard the previous year. On 27 October
1516 (Shell and Sironi 1992, doc. 37), two engineers of the Comune were called
on to arbitrate the claims. Salai was certainly in France with Leonardo, and is
mentioned in the royal accounts (see n. 68), but he was not there continuously.

67. CA 237v/87v-b. On CA 1024v/367v-c is a list of French and Flemish cities
where fairs were held (Perpignan, Paris, Rouen, Anvers, Ghent, Bruges). It also
has a list of names, all members of Florentine merchant families (Portinari,
Tovaglia, Ridolfi, etc.), probably commercial contacts in France.

68. Archive Nationale, Paris, KK 289; Shell and Sironi 1992, no. 38.

69. B. Cellini, *Discorso dell'architettura*, in *Opere*, ed. B. Maier (Milan, 1968),
858–60.

70. Frescos in the chapel, probably later sixteenth century, include a Madonna
standing on a shining crescent, identified as '*Virgo lucis*' ('Virgin of light'): this
may be the origin of the name Clos Lucé. In Leonardo's time it was simply Cloux,
or as he writes it 'Clu'. These paragraphs are based on my own visit to Clos
Lucé in December 2002, and on information from J. Saint-Bris, *Le Château du
Clos-Lucé* (Amboise, n.d.).

71. RL 12727. The shading is right-handed. Clark attributes the drawing to Melzi,
though finding it 'unusually sensitive' in its handling; he earlier thought it might
be by Andrea del Sarto, who was in Amboise in 1518 (Clark and Pedretti 1968
1.185–6).

72. CA 476v/174r-b; Ar 71v.

73. Ar 269r. The same spelling is in CA 284r/103r-b: '*dí dell'Asensione in Anbosa
1517 di Maggio nel Clu*', the earliest dated note (21 May 1517) of Leonardo in
Amboise.

74. On the interweavings of fact and imagination in Webster's play see Banks
2002, xvii–xxii.

75. Thomas Spinelly to Cardinal Wolsey, July 1517, in Banks 2002, 186–7.

76. Beatis 1979, 131–4. The original of his journal is in the Biblioteca Nazionale, Naples, X.F.28.

77. Pacioli's comments about Leonardo's mirror-writing (see Part I n. 79) are certainly earlier than 1517, but had not been published. There would obviously have been some knowledge of this Leonardian quirk in Rome, where the Cardinal lived, but Beatis's silence on the matter is surprising.

78. The inscription, probably sixteenth century, is in imitation of Leonardo's hand: see Richter 1970, 2.343n, Popham 1946, 154. The line of the shoulders: Pedretti 1992, 36.

79. RL 12581. Kemp 1989, 153; Dante, *Purgatorio*, Canto 28, 52ff.

80. CA 582r; 583r/217v-c, v-b; 209r/76v-b.

81. Romorantin to Amboise: CA 920r/336v-b. Requisition of horses: CA 476r/174r-b, v-c.

82. Letters of Stazio Gadio and Luigi Gonzaga, May 1518, Beltrami 1919, docs. 240, 242.

83. Solmi 1976, 621–6; Vecce 1998, 338.

84. Rider: RL 12574 (illustrated). Hunter: RL 12575. Man in drag: RL 12577. Prisoner: RL 12573 (illustrated). On Leonardo's late mastery of black chalk, see Ames-Lewis 2002.

85. Shell and Sironi 1992, doc. 39. The sum he lent was nearly 500 lire: a sizeable amount of disposable cash. His recorded annual income (French accounts plus rent on the vineyard house) was about 320 lire per annum. He may well have been doing good business as a painter.

86. Galeazzo Visconti to the Gonzaga, Beltrami 1919, doc. 240.

87. CA 673r/249r-b; 803r/294r-a.

88. R 1566. The original will was in the Vinci family in the eighteenth century: it was published by Amoretti (1804, 121) from a transcript made in the 1770s by Vincenzio de Pagave.

89. Shell and Sironi 1992, 114 and doc. 41. Further mysterious dealings are revealed in a document which apparently shows that 'Messire Salay' received over 6,000 lire for certain *'tables de paintures'* supplied to King François (Jestaz 1999, 69). The inference is that these were Leonardo's paintings, commandeered in some way by Salai despite being bequeathed by Leonardo to Melzi. After Leonardo's death Salai lived in Milan, in the house in the vineyard. On 14 June 1523 he married Bianca Caldiroli, who brought a handsome dowry of 1,700 lire, but he died six months later, on 15 January 1524, *'ex sclopeto'* (i.e. of wounds): a violent death at the age of forty-four.

90. The Anonimo Gaddiano, writing in the early 1540s, gives some details of the bequests. His source was probably one of Leonardo's half-brothers, since he adds, 'He left 400 ducats to his brothers, which he had deposited at the Spedale di Santa Maria Nuova, but after his death they found only 300 ducats there.' In fact the sums they drew out of the account in 1520–21 (Uzielli 1872, nos. 28–31) add up to 325 florins.

91. 'O slumberer': CA 207v/76v-a, folio dated 23 April 1490. 'Every hurt': H², 33v, R 1164. 'The soul desires': CA 166r/59r-b, R 1142.

92. RL 19001r (Anatomical MS A, 2r).

93. In his *Rime* (Milan, 1587), 93, Lomazzo implies the absence of the King from the bedside: '*Pianse mesto Francesco re di Franza / quando il Melzi che morto era gli dissi / Il Vinci*' ('His Majesty François, King of France, wept when Melzi told him that Vinci was dead'). This would be strong evidence, given that Lomazzo knew Melzi personally, but in other accounts in the *Sogni* and the *Idea del Tempio* (Lomazzo 1973, 1.109, 293) he follows the Vasarian version of the story.

94. Uzielli 1872, no. 26. Like the will, the original of Melzi's letter was seen and transcribed at Vinci in the eighteenth century, but has since disappeared.

95. A. Houssaye, *Histoire de Léonard de Vinci* (Paris, 1869), 312–19.

Sources

LEONARDO'S MANUSCRIPTS

Miscellanies

Ar Codex Arundel. British Library, London (Arundel MS 263). 283 folios, with a typical format of 210 × 150 mm.
Facsimile edition: *Il Codice Arundel 263*, ed. Carlo Pedretti and Carlo Vecce (Florence, 1998), with chronological re-ordering of folios.

CA Codex Atlanticus. Biblioteca Ambrosiana, Milan. Miscellaneous collection of drawings and writings, formerly of 401 folios in large format, 645 × 435 mm, compiled by Pompeo Leoni in the sixteenth century, recently reorganized (1962–1970) into 12 volumes with a total of 1,119 folios. The discrepancy is because many of the folios of the original compilation had smaller pieces glued or mounted on them; in the new arrangement these smaller items have been separated. As is conventional, I give both the new and the old folio references: e.g. CA 520r/191r-a refers to the recto of new folio 520, which was formerly item 'a' on the recto of old folio 191.
Facsimile edition: *Il Codice Atlantico*, ed. Augusto Marinoni (24 vols., Florence, 1973–80).

RL Royal Library, Windsor. A collection of 655 drawings and manuscripts, catalogued as folios 12275–12727 (general) and 19000–19152 (anatomical). The anatomical folios were previously bound into three volumes: Anatomical MS A (= RL 19000–19017), B (= RL 19018–59) and C, divided into six *'quaderni di anatomia'*, or anatomical notebooks, numbered I–VI (= RL 19060–19152).
Facsimile edition: *The Drawings of Leonardo da Vinci in the Collection of Her Majesty the Queen*, ed. Kenneth Clark and Carlo Pedretti (3 vols., London, 1968).

Paris manuscripts

A   Paris MS A. Institut de France, Paris (MS 2172). 64 folios, 212 × 147 mm. See also BN 2038.

B   Paris MS B. Institut de France, Paris (MS 2173). 84 folios, 231 × 167 mm. See also BN 2037.

C   Paris MS C. Institut de France, Paris (MS 2174). 42 folios, 310 × 222 mm.

D   Paris MS D. Institut de France, Paris (MS 2175). 10 folios, 158 × 220 mm.

E   Paris MS E. Institut de France, Paris (MS 2176). 96 folios, 150 × 105 mm.

F   Paris MS F. Institut de France, Paris (MS 2177). 96 folios, 145 × 100 mm.

G   Paris MS G. Institut de France, Paris (MS 2178). 93 folios, (originally 96), 139 × 97 mm.

H   Paris MS H. Institut de France, Paris (MS 2179). 142 folios, 128 × 90 mm, consisting of three pocket-books bound together: H^1(fols. 1–48), H^2 (fols. 49–94) and H^3 (fols. 95–142).

I   Paris MS I. Institut de France, Paris (MS 2180). 139 folios, 100 × 75 mm, consisting of two pocket-books bound together: I^1 (fols. 1–48) and I^2(fols. 49–139).

K   Paris MS K. Institut de France, Paris (MS 2181). 128 folios, 96 × 65 mm, consisting of three pocket-books bound together: K^1 (fols. 1–48), K^2 (fols. 49–80) and K^3(fols. 81–128).

L   Paris MS L. Institut de France, Paris (MS 2182). 94 folios, 109 × 72 mm.

M   Paris MS M. Institut de France, Paris (MS 2183). 94 folios, 96 × 67 mm.

BN 2037   Institut de France, Paris (MS 2184). 13 folios, 231 × 167 mm. Formerly part of MS B, stolen by G. Libri in *c*. 1840, and returned by Lord Ashburnham (hence also known as Ashburnham 1875/1); thereafter at the Bibliothèque Nationale, Paris. Though now at the Institut de France, the BN collocation is generally used.

BN 2038   Institut de France, Paris (MS 2185). 33 folios, 212 × 147 mm. Formerly part of MS A (subsequent history as for BN 2037). Also known as MS Ashburnham 1875/2.

Facsimile edition: *I manuscritti dell' Institut de France*, ed. Augusto Marinoni (12 vols., Florence, 1986–90).

Other notebooks and manuscripts

Fors   Forster Codices. Victoria & Albert Museum, London. Three volumes containing five notebooks. Fors 1^1, 40 folios; Fors 1^2, 14 folios, 135 × 103 mm. Fors 2^1, 63 folios; Fors 2^2, 96 folios, 95 × 70 mm. Fors 3, 88 folios, 94 × 65 mm.
Facsimile edition: *I Codici Forster*, ed. Augusto Marinoni (3 vols., Florence, 1992).

Leic   Codex Leicester. Bill Gates Collection, Seattle. 88 folios, 94 × 65 mm. Previously known as the Codex Hammer.

Facsimile edition: *The Codex Hammer*, ed. Carlo Pedretti (Florence, 1987).

Ma   Madrid Codices. Biblioteca Nacional, Madrid (MSS 8936, 8937). Ma I, 184 folios, 149 × 212 mm. Ma II, 157 folios, mostly 148 × 212 mm.

Facsimile edition: *The Madrid Codices* , ed. Ladislaus Reti (New York, 1974).

Tn   Codex on the Flight of Birds. Biblioteca Reale, Turin. 13 folios, 213 × 153 mm.

Facsimile edition: *Il Codice sul volo degli uccelli*, ed. Augusto Marinoni (Florence, 1976).

Triv   Trivulzian Codex. Castello Sforzesco, Milan, Biblioteca Trivulziana MS N2162. 55 folios, 195 × 135 mm.

Facsimile edition: *Il Codice nella Biblioteca Trivulziana*, ed. A. Brizio (Florence, 1980).

Selections and Commentaries

CU   Vatican Library, Codex Urbinus Latinus 1270. Selections from various notebooks and manuscripts made *c.* 1530 by Francesco Melzi; abbreviated edition published as *Trattato della pittura* (Paris, 1651).

McM   A. Philip McMahon, *The Treatise on Painting by Leonardo da Vinci* (2 vols., Princeton, NJ, 1956). Translation (vol. 1) and facsimile (vol. 2) of CU; cited by numbered section (McM 1–1008).

R   Jean-Paul Richter, *The Literary Works of Leonardo da Vinci* (2 vols., London, 1st edn 1883, 2nd edn 1939, repr. 1970). Cited by numbered extract (R 1–1566).

PC   Carlo Pedretti, *Commentary on the Literary Works of Leonardo da Vinci compiled by Jean Paul Richter* (2 vols., Berkeley, Cal., 1977).

FREQUENTLY CITED SOURCES

ALV   *Achademia Leonardo Vinci: Yearbook of the Armand Hammer Center for Leonardo Studies at UCLA* (Florence, 1988–)

ASF   Archivio di Stato, Florence

ASM   Archivio di Stato, Milan

BM   British Museum, London

DBI   *Dizionario biografico degli Italiani* (currently up to 'G') (Rome, 1960–)

GDA   *Grove Dictionary of Art*, ed. Jane Turner (34 vols., London, 1996)

GDS   Gabinetto dei Disegni e delle Stampe (Department of Drawings and Prints), Uffizi, Florence

RV   *Raccolta Vinciana* (Milan, 1905–)

Early biographies

For reasons of space I do not give individual page references for my very frequent citations from the four main early biographical sources on Leonardo (Antonio Billi, Anonimo Gaddiano, Paolo Giovio, Giorgio Vasari). The 'biographies' by Billi, the Anonimo and Giovio are a couple of pages long; the *Life* of Leonardo in Vasari's *Lives of the Artists* is longer, but the interested reader can easily locate the quotation in George Bull's translation (see Vasari 1987), where the *Life* is pp. 255–71, and can pursue it further by consulting Milanesi's annotated edition (see Vasari 1878–85). For details of these sources, see Introduction nn. 17–20, and 'Books and articles' below.

BOOKS AND ARTICLES

Acton, Harold. 1972. *The Pazzi Conspiracy*. London

Alberici, Clelia. 1984. *Leonardo e l'incisione: Stampe derivate da Leonardo e Bramante dal xv al xix secolo* (exhibition catalogue). Milan

Ames-Lewis, Francis. 2002. 'La matita nera nella pratica di disegno di Leonardo da Vinci'. *Lettura Vinciana* 41. Florence

Ammirato, Scipione. 1637. *Opusculi*. 3 vols. Florence

Amoretti, Carlo. 1804. *Memorie storiche su la vita, gli studi e le opere di Leonardo da Vinci*. Milan

Argan, Giulio Carlo. 1957. *Botticelli*. New York

Bambach, Carmen. 2003a. 'Leonardo, left handed draftsman and writer'. In Bambach 2003b, 31–57

— 2003b. (ed.). *Leonardo: Master Draftsman* (exhibition catalogue). New York

Banks Amendola, Barbara. 2002. *The Mystery of the Duchess of Malfi*. Stroud

Barcelon, Pinin Brambilla, and Marani, Pietro. 2001. *Leonardo: The Last Supper*. Trans. H. Tighe (original edn 1999). Chicago

Baxandall, Michael. 1988. *Painting and Experience in Fifteenth Century Italy*. Oxford

Beatis, Antonio de. 1979. *The Travel Journal*, ed. John Hale (Hakluyt Society, 2nd series, 150). London

Beck, James. 1988. 'Leonardo's rapport with his father', *Antichità viva* 27, nos. 5–6

— 1993. 'I sogni di Leonardo'. *Lettura Vinciana* 32. Florence

Bellincioni, Bernardo. 1876. *Le rime*, ed. P. Fanfani. Bologna

Belt, Elmer. 1949. 'Leonardo da Vinci's library'. *Quarterly Newsletter of the Book Club of California*, autumn 1949

Beltrami, Luca. 1894. *Il castello di Milano sotto il dominio dei Visconti e degli Sforza*. Milan

— 1919. *Documenti e memorie riguardanti la vita e le opere di Leonardo da Vinci*. Milan

— 1920. *La vigna di Leonardo*. Milan

Benedettucci, F. (ed.). 1991. *Il libro di Antonio Billi*. Anzio

Berenson, Bernard. 1903. *The Drawings of the Florentine Painters*. 2 vols. London

Boase, T. S. R. 1979. *Giorgio Vasari: The Man and His Book*. Princeton

Bossi, Giuseppe. 1982. *Scritti sulle arti*, ed. Roberto Paolo Ciardi. 2 vols. Florence

Bracciolini, Poggio. 1913. *Facezie*, ed. D. Ciampoli. Rome

Bradford, Sarah. 1976. *Cesare Borgia: His Life and Times*. London

Bramly, Serge. 1992. *Leonardo*. Trans. Sîan Reynolds (original edn 1988). Harmondsworth

Brescia, Licia, and Tomio, Luca. 1999. 'Tomasso di Giovanni Masini da Peretola, detto Zoroastro'. RV 28, 63–77

Brown, David A. 1983. 'Leonardo and the idealized portrait in Milan'. *Arte Lombardo* 67, 102–16

— 1990. 'Madonna Litta'. *Lettura Vinciana* 29. Florence

— 1998. *Leonardo: Origins of a Genius*. New Haven and London

— 2000. 'Leonardo apprendista'. *Lettura Vinciana* 39. Florence

Brucker, Gene. 1977. *The Civic World of Early Renaissance Florence*. Princeton

Bruschi, Mario. 1997. 'La fede battesimale di Leonardo: Ricerche in corso e altri documenti'. ALV 10 (supplement)

Bull, George. 1996. *Michelangelo: A Biography*. Harmondsworth

Burckhardt, Jacob. 1878. *The Civilization of the Renaissace in Italy*. Trans. S. G. C. Middlemore. London

Burke, Peter. 1972. *Culture and Society in the Italian Renaissance*. New York

Butterfield, Andrew. 1997. *The Sculptures of Andrea del Verrocchio*. New Haven and London

Calvi, Gerolamo. 1925. *I manoscritti di Leonardo*. Bologna

Cammelli, Antonio. 1884. *Rime edite e inedite*, ed. A. Capelli and S. Ferrari. Livorno

Cecchi, Alessandro. 2003. 'New light on Leonardo's Florentine patrons'. In Bambach 2003b, 121–39

Cellini, Benvenuto. 2002. *My Life*. Trans. Julia Conaway Bondanella and Peter Bondanella. Oxford

Cennini, Cennino. 1933. *The Craftsman's Handbook*. Trans. Daniel V. Thompson. New York

Cianchi, Mario. 1984. *The Machines of Leonardo*. Florence

Cianchi, Renzo. 1953. *Vinci, Leonardo e la sua famiglia*. Milan

— 1960. 'La casa natale di Leonardo'. *Università popolare* 9–10 (September–October 1960)

— 1975. *Ricerche e documenti sulla madre di Leonardo*. Florence

— 1984. 'Sul testamento di Francesco da Vinci'. *Nouvelles de la république de lettres* 1, 97–104

Clark, Kenneth. 1933. 'The Madonna in profile'. *Burlington Magazine* 12, 136–40

— 1969. 'Leonardo and the antique'. In O'Malley 1969, 1–34

— 1973. 'Mona Lisa'. *Burlington Magazine* 115, 144–50

— 1988. *Leonardo*. Rev. edn, with introduction and notes by Martin Kemp (original edn 1939). Harmondsworth

Clark, Kenneth, and Pedretti, Carlo. 1968. *The Drawings of Leonardo da Vinci in the Collection of Her Majesty the Queen*. 3 vols. London

Clayton, Martin. 1996. *Leonardo da Vinci: A Curious Vision* (exhibition catalogue). London

— 2002. *Leonardo da Vinci: The Divine and the Grotesque* (exhibition catalogue). London

Clough, C. (ed.). 1976. *Cultural aspects of the Italian Renaissance*. Manchester

Cole, Bruce. 1983. *The Renaissance Artist at Work*. London

Conato, Luigi Giuseppe, 1986. 'Elementi del paesaggio lecchese e Leonardo'. In *Studi Vinciani* (q.v.), 195–210

Condivi, Ascanio. 1976. *The Life of Michelangelo*, ed. H. Wohl (original edn 1553). Oxford

Covi, Dario. 1966. 'Four new documents concerning Andrea del Verrocchio'. *Art Bulletin* 48 (1), 97–103

Dalli Regoli, Gigetta (ed.). 2001. *Leonardo e il mito di Leda* (exhibition catalogue). Florence

Davies, Martin. 1947. *Documents concerning the Virgin of the Rocks in the National Gallery*. London

Dunkerton, Jill, and Roy, Ashok. 1996. 'The materials of a group of late fifteenth-century Florentine panel paintings'. *National Gallery Technical Bulletin* xvii, 20–31

Eissler, Kurt. 1962. *Leonardo da Vinci: Psychoanalytic Notes on the Enigma*. London

Embolden, William. 1987. *Leonardo da Vinci on Plants and Gardens*. Bromley

Fabriczy, Cornelius von. 1891. 'Il libro di Antonio Billi e le sue copie nella Biblioteca Nazionale di Firenze'. *Archivio storico italiano* 7, 299–368

— 1893. 'Il codice dell'Anonimo Gaddiano nella Biblioteca Nazionale di Firenze'. *Archivio storico italiano* 12 (3, 4), 15ff.

Fara, Amelio (ed.). 1999. *Leonardo a Piombino e l'idea di città moderna tra Quattro e Cinquecento*. Florence

Ficarra, A. (ed.). 1968. *L'Anonimo Magliabechiano*. Naples

Fiorio, Maria Teresa. 1998. 'Giovanni Antonio Boltraffio'. In *The Legacy of Leonardo* (q.v.), 131–62

Fletcher, Jennifer. 1989. 'Bernardo Bembo and Leonardo's portrait of Ginevra de' Benci'. *Burlington Magazine* 131, 811–16

Franck, Jacques. 1995. 'The *Mona Lisa*: should a myth be restored?' ALV 7, 232–6

Freud, Sigmund. 2001. *Leonardo da Vinci. A Memory of His Childhood*. Trans. Alan Dyson (original edn 1910). London

Fumagalli, Giuseppina. 1952. *Eros e Leonardo*. Milan

— 1960. 'Gli "omini salvatichi" di Leonardo'. RV 18, 129–57

Galluzzi, P. (ed.). 1974. *Leonardo da Vinci letto e commentato* (various authors, *Letture Vinciane* 1–12 (1960–72)). Florence

Gerard, Kent, and Hekma, Gert (eds.). 1989. *The Pursuit of Sodomy: Male Homosexuality in Renaissance and Enlightenment Europe*. New York and London

Ghiberti, Lorenzo. 1998. *I commentarii*, ed. L. Bartoli. Florence

Giacomelli, R. 1936. *Gli scritti di Leonardo sul volo*. Rome

Gilbert, Creighton E. (ed.). 1992. *Italian Art 1400–1500: Sources and Documents*. Evanston, Ill

Glasser, H. 1977. *Artists' contracts of the Early Renaissance*. New York

Goffen, Rita. 2002. *Renaissance Rivals: Michelangelo, Leonardo. Raphael, Titian*. New Haven and London

Goldscheider, Ludwig. 1940. *The Sculptures of Michelangelo*. With photographs by J. Schneider-Lengyel. London

Goldthwaite, Richard. 1980. *The Building of Renaissance Florence*. Baltimore

Gombrich, Ernst. 1945. 'Botticelli's mythologies: a study in the Neoplatonic symbolism of his circle'. *Journal of the Warburg and Courtauld Institutes* 7

— 1950. *The Story of Art*. London

— 1954. 'Leonardo's grotesque heads: prologomena to their study'. In Marazza 1954, 199f.

Gould, Cecil. 1954. 'Leonardo's great battle-piece: a conjectural reconstruction'. *Art Bulletin* 36, 111–28

— 1975. *Leonardo the Artist and Non-Artist*. London

Grafton. Anthony. 2000. *Leon Battista Alberti: Master Builder of the Italian Renaissance*. London

Gregori, M. (ed.). 1992. *Maestri e botteghe*. Florence

Hale, John. 1994. *The Civilization of Europe in the Renaissance*. London

Hauser, Arnold. 1962. *The Social History of Art*. (original edn 1951). 4 vols. London

Hibbert, Christopher. 1979. *The Rise and Fall of the Medici*. Harmondsworth

— 1993. *Florence: Biography of a City*. Harmondsworth

Hollingsworth, Mary. 2004. *The Cardinal's Hat: Money, Ambition and House-keeping in a Renaissance Court*. London

Jardine, Lisa. 1996. *Worldly Goods*. London

Jestaz, Bertrand. 1999. 'François I, Salai et les tableaux de Léonard'. *Revue de l'art* 126 (4), 68–72

Kemp, Martin. 1981. *The Marvellous Works of Nature and Man*. London and Cambridge, Mass

— 1986. 'Analogy and observation in the Codex Hamner'. In *Studi Vinciani* (q.v.), 103–34

— 1989. *Leonardo da Vinci* (exhibition catalogue). London

— 1992. *The Mystery of the* Madonna of the Yarnwinder (exhibition catalogue). Edinburgh

Kemp, Martin, and Walker, Margaret (eds.). 1989. *Leonardo on Painting*. New Haven and London

Kent, Dale. 2000. *Cosimo de' Medici and the Florentine Renaissance*. New Haven and London

King, Ross. 2001. *Brunelleschi's Dome* (original edn 2000). Harmondsworth

Laurenza, Domenico. 1999. 'Il teatro delle passioni'. In Pedretti 1999

— 2001. *De figure umana: Fisiognomia, anatomia ed arte in Leonardo*. Florence

— 2004. 'Leonardo nella Roma di Leone X: Gli studi anatomici, la vita, l'arte'. *Lettura Vinciana* 53. Florence

Leader, Darian. 2002. *Stealing the Mona Lisa: What Art Stops Us from Seeing*. London

The Legacy of Leonardo. 1998. Trans. I. Coward, A. Curtiss and A. Ellis. London

Lomazzo, Giovanni Paolo. 1584. *Trattato dell'arte della pittura*. Milan

— 1590. *Idea del tempio della pittura*. Milan

— 1973. *Scritti sulle arti*, ed. Roberto Carlo Ciardi. 2 vols. Pisa

Lopez, Guido. 1982. *Leonardo e Ludovico Il Moro: La roba e la libertà*. Milan

Lubkin, Gregory. 1999. *A Renaissance Court: Milan under Galeazzo Maria Sforza*. Berkeley

Lucas-Dubreton, Jean. *Daily Life in Florence*. 1960. Trans. A. Lytton Sells. London

Luchinat, Cristina Acidini. 1992. 'Arts in the workshop during the Laurentian age'. In Gregori 1992

Maccagni, Carlo. 1974. 'Riconsiderando il problema delle fonti di Leonardo: L'elenco di libri nel codice 8936 di Madrid'. *Lettura Vinciana* 10 (1970). In Galluzzi 1974

MacCurdy, Edward. 1938. *The Notebooks of Leonardo da Vinci*. 2 vols. London

Machiavelli. Niccolò. 1961. *The Prince*. Trans. George Bull. Harmondsworth

— 1966. *Opere*, ed. Ezio Raimondi, 2 vols. Milan

McMullen, Roy. 1975. Mona Lisa: *The Picture and the Myth*. Boston

Malaguzzi-Valeri, Francesco. 1913–23. *La corte di Lodivico Il Moro*. 4 vols. Milan

Marani, Pietro. 1998a. 'Francesco Melzi'. In *The Legacy of Leonardo* (q.v.)

— 1998b.'The question of Leonardo's bottega: practice and transmission of Leonardo's ideas on art'. In *The Legacy of Leonardo* (q.v.)

— 1998c. 'Giampietrino'. In *The Legacy of Leonardo* (q.v.).

— 1999. *Il Cenacolo: Guide to the Refectory*. Trans. Margaret Kunzle and Felicity Lutz. Milan

— 2000a. *Leonardo da Vinci: The Complete Paintings*. London

— 2000b. (ed.). *'Hostinato rigore': Leonardiana in memoria di Augusto Marinoni*. Milan

— 2003. 'La *Vergine delle Rocce* della National Gallery di Londra: Maestro e bottega di fronte al modello'. *Lettura Vinciana* 42. Florence

Marazza, Achille (ed.). 1954. *Leonardo: Saggi e ricerche*. Rome

Marinoni, Augusto. 1954. *I rebus di Leonardo raccolti e interpretati*. Florence

— 1960. 'Rebus'. RV 18, 117–28

— 1974. (ed.). *Leonardo da Vinci: Scritti letterari*. Milan

— 1982. *La matematica di Leonardo da Vinci*. Milan

— 1982. (ed.). *Leonardo all'Ambrosiana*. Milan

Martines, Lauro. 1963. *The Social World of the Florentine Humanists*. Princeton

— 2003. *April Blood: Florence and the Plot against the Medici*. London

Masters, Roger. 1999. *Fortune is a River: Leonardo da Vinci and Niccolò Machiavelli's Magnificent Dream to Change the Course of Florentine History* (original edn 1998). New York

Mayor, Hyatt. 1984. *Artists and Anatomists* (exhibition catalogue). New York

Michelangelo. 1878. *The Sonnets of Michael Angelo Buonarroti*. Trans. J. A. Symonds. London

— 1987. *Michelangelo: Life, Letters and Poetry*. Trans. George Bull and Peter Porter. Oxford

Michelet, Jules. 1976. *Histoire de la France au seizième siècle: Renaissance et reforme* (*Œuvres complètes*, 7). Paris

Nanni, Romano. 1999. 'Osservazione, convenzione, ricomposizione nel paesaggio Leonardiano del 1473'. RV 28, 3–37

— 2001. 'Leonardo nella tradizione di Leda'. In Dalli Regoli 2001, 23–45

Nanni, Romano and Testaferrata, Elena (eds.). 2004. *Vinci di Leonardo: Storia e memoria*. Vinci

Natali, Antonio. 1985. 'Re, cavalieri e barbari'. *Uffizi studi e ricerche* 2

— 1998. 'Lo sguardo degli angeli: Tragitto indiziario per il *Battesimo di Cristo* di Verrocchio e Leonardo'. *Mittelungen der Kunsthistorischen Institutes in Florence* 42, 252–73

— 1999. 'La natura artefatta'. In Fara 1999, 137–48

— 2001. 'Le pose di Leda'. In Dalli Regoli 2001, 46–64

Newton, H. Travers, and Spenser, J. R. 1982. 'On the location of Leonardo's *Battle of Anghiari*'. *Art Bulletin*, March 1982, 45–52

Nicodemi, Giorgio. 1934. 'I "ritratti" di Leonardo da Vinci'. RV 15, 1–21

Noyes, Ella. 1908. *The Story of Milan*. London

Nuland, Sherwin B. 2000. *Leonardo da Vinci*. New York

O'Malley, C. D. (ed.). 1969. *Leonardo's Legacy*. Berkeley

Origo, Iris. 1992. *The Merchant of Prato* (original edn 1957). Harmondsworth

Orto, Giovanni dall'. 1989. ' "Socratic love" as a disguise for same-sex love in the Italian Renaissance'. In Gerard and Hekma 1989

Ottino della Chiesa, Angela. 1967. *Leonardo pittore*, Rizzoli Classici dell'Arte 12. Milan

Papa, Rodolfo. 1999. 'Giuda, il disordine e la grazia', in Pedretti 1999

— 2000. 'Lo spazio dell'ascesi: Il San Gerolamo di Leonardo'. *Art e dossier* 159, 33–8

Park, K. 1994. 'The criminal and the saintly body: autopsy and dissection in Renaissance Italy'. *Renaissance Quarterly*, 1–33

Pater, Walter. 1986. *The Renaissance*, ed. Adam Phillips (original edn 1873). Oxford

Pedretti, Carlo. 1953. *Documenti e memorie riguardanti Leonardo da Vinci a Bologna e in Emilia*. Bologna

— 1957a. *Leonardo da Vinci: Fragments at Windsor Castle from the Codex Atlanticus*. London

— 1957b. *Studi Vinciani*. Geneva

— 1965. *Leonardo da Vinci on Painting: A Lost Book*. London

— 1968. 'The Burlington House cartoon'. *Burlington Magazine* 100, no. 778

— 1972. *Leonardo da Vinci: The Royal Palace at Romorantin*. Cambridge, Mass

— 1973. *Leonardo da Vinci: A Study in Chronology and Style*. London

— 1975. 'Perche la minesstra si fredda'. *Lettura Vinciana* 14. Florence

— 1976. *Il primo Leonardo a Firenze*. Florence

— 1977. 'The Sforza Mausoleum'. *Gazette des beaux-arts* 89, 121–31

— 1986. 'Postille all'onomastica Vinciana di Nando de Toni'. In *Studi Vinciani* (q.v.), 93–101

— 1988. *Leonardo architetto*. Milan

— 1992. 'Il "bello spettacolo"'. ALV 5, 163–5

— 1998a. 'Leonardo: Il ritratto'. *Art e dossier* 138 (supplement)

— 1998b. (ed.). *Leonardo e la Pulzella di Camaiore* (exhibition catalogue). Camaiore

— 1998c. 'Quella puttana di Leonardo'. ALV 11, 121–39

— 1999. (ed.). 'Leonardo: *Il Cenacolo*'. *Art e dossier* 146 (supplement)

— 2000. (ed.). *Codex Leicester: Notebook of a Genius*. Sydney

— 2001. (ed.). L'Angelo incarnato *tra archeologia e leggenda* (exhibition catalogue). Florence

Pedretti, Carlo, and Cianchi, Marco. 1995. 'Leonardo: I codici'. *Art e dossier* 100 (supplement)

Pfister, Oskar. 1913. 'Kryptolalie'. *Jahrbuch für psychoanalytische und psychopathologische Forschungen* 5, 117–56

Poggi, Giovanni. 1919. *Leonardo da Vinci: La* Vita *di Giorgio Vasari nuovamente commentata*. Florence

Popham, A. E. 1946. *The Drawings of Leonardo da Vinci*. London

Reti, Ladislaus. 1959. ' "Non si volta chi a stella è fisso": Le imprese di Leonardo da Vinci'. *Bibliothèque d'humanisme et renaissance* 21, 7–54

— 1965. 'Tracce dei progetti perduti di Filippo Brunelleschi nel Codice Atlantico'. *Lettura Vinciana* 4. Florence

— 1968. 'The two unpublished manuscripts of Leonardo da Vinci in the Biblioteca Nacional of Madrid'. *Burlington Magazine* 110, nos. 778, 799

— 1974. (ed.). *The Unknown Leonardo*. Maidenhead

Richter, Jean Paul (ed.). 1970. *The Literary Works of Leonardo da Vinci*, 2 vols. London

Ridolfi, Roberto. 1963. *The Life of Niccolò Machiavelli*. Trans. Cecil Grayson (original edn 1954). London

Roberts, Jane, and Pedretti, Carlo. 1977. 'Drawings by Leonardo da Vinci at Windsor newly revealed by ultra violet light'. *Burlington Magazine* 119, no. 891, 396–408

Rocke, Michael J. 1987. 'Il controllo dell'omosessualità a Firenze nel XV secolo: Gli Ufficiali di Notte. *Quaderni storici* 22 (3), 701–23

— 1996. *Forbidden Friendships: Homosexuality and Male Culture in Renaissance Florence*. Oxford

Rosheim, Mark Elling. 2001. 'L'automata programmabile di Leonardo'. *Lettura Vinciana* 40. Florence

Ross, James, and McLaughlin, Mary (eds.). 1981. *The Portable Renaissance Reader*. Harmondsworth

Rubin, Patricia Lee, and Wright, Alison. 1999. *Renaissance Florence: The Art of the 1470s* (exhibition catalogue). London

Rubinstein, Nicolai. 1995. *The Palazzo Vecchio, 1298–1532*. Oxford

Rzepińska, Maria. 1990. *Lady with an Ermine*. Trans. Mary Filippi (original edn 1977). Cracow

Saslow, James. 1986. *Ganymede in the Renaissance: Homosexuality in Art and Society*. London

Sassoon, Donald. 2001. *Mona Lisa: The History of the World's Most Famous Painting*. London

Scalini, Mario. 1992. 'The chivalric "ludus" in Quattrocento Florence'. In Gregori 1992, 61–3

Schapiro, Meyer. 1956. 'Leonardo and Freud: an art-historical study'. *Journal of the History of Ideas* 17, 287–32

Scritti vari in onore di Rodolfo Renier. 1912. Turin

Severi, Rita. 1992. 'The myth of Leonardo in English decadent writers'. ALV 5, 96–103

Shell, Janice. 1995. *Pittori in bottega: Rinascimento a Milano*. Milan

— 1998a. 'Ambrogio de Predis'. In *The Legacy of Leonardo* (q.v.), 123–30

— 1998b. 'Marco d'Oggiono'. In *The Legacy of Leonardo* (q.v.), 163–78

Shell, Janice, and Sironi, Grazioso. 1991. 'Salai and Leonardo's legacy'. *Burlington Magazine* 133, 95–108

— 1992. 'Salai and the inventory of his estate'. RV 24, 109–53

— 1993. 'Some documents for Giovanni Pietro Rizzoli: Il Giampietrino' RV 25, 121–46

— 2000. 'Un nuovo documento di pagamento per *La Vergine della Rocce* di Leonardo'. In Marani 2000b, 27–31

Sironi, Grazioso. 1981. *Nuovi documenti riguardante* La Vergine delle Rocce *di Leonardo*. Florence

Smiraglia Scognamiglio, Nino. 1896. 'Nuovi documenti su Leonardo da Vinci'. *Archivio storico dell'arte* 2, 313–15

— 1900. *Ricerche e documenti sulla giovanezza di Leonardo da Vinci*. Naples

Solmi, Edmondo. 1908. *Le fonti dei manoscritti di Leonardo da Vinci*. Turin

— 1912. 'La politica di Ludovico il Moro nei simboli di Leonardo da Vinci'. In *Scritti vari* (q.v.)

— 1976. *Scritti Vinciani*. Florence

Starnazzi, Carlo. 1995. 'Leonardo in terra di Arezzo'. *Studi per l'ecologia del Quaternario* 17

— 1996. 'La *Gioconda* nella Valle dell'Arno'. *Archeologia viva* 58

— 2000. *La Madonna dei Fusi di Leonardo da Vinci e il paesaggio del Valdarno Superiore*. (exibition catalogue). Arezzo

Steinberg Leo. 1973. 'Leonardo's *Last Supper*'. *Art Quarterly* 36 (4), 297–410

— 2002. *Leonardo's Incessant Last Supper*. New York

Stites, R. S. 1970. *The Sublimations of Leonardo da Vinci*. Washington, DC

Studi Vinciani in memoria di Nando de Toni. 1986. Brescia

Thiis, Jens. 1913. *Leonardo: The Florentine Years*. London

Toni, Nando de. 1934. 'Saggio di onomastica Vinciana'. RV 14, 54–117

Uzielli, Gustavo. 1872. *Ricerche intorno a Leonardo da Vinci* (1st series). Florence

— 1884. *Ricerche intorno a Leonardo da Vinci* (2nd series). Rome

— 1896. *Ricerche intorno a Leonardo da Vinci* (rev. and enlarged edn of 1st series). Turin

Vasari, Giorgio. 1878–85. *Le opere*, ed. Gaetano Milanesi. 9 vols. Florence

— 1987. *Lives of the Artists*. Trans. George Bull. 2 vols. Harmondsworth

Vecce, Carlo. 1990. 'La Gualanda'. ALV 3, 51–72

— 1998. *Leonardo*. Rome

Ventrone, Paola. 1992. 'Entertainment in Laurentian Florence'. In Gregori 1992, 57–9

Vezzosi, Alessandro. 1984. *Toscana di Leonardo*. Florence

— 1990. *Il rinascimento dell'olivo: Leonardo e Botticelli*. Florence

— 1997. *Leonardo da Vinci: Renaissance Man*. Trans. Alexandra Bonfante-Warren. London

Villari, Pasquale. 1892. *The Life and Times of Niccolò Machiavelli*. Trans. Linda Vallari (original edn 1878). 2 vols. London

Villata, Edoardo. 1999. *Leonardo da Vinci: I documenti e le testimonianze contemporanee*. Milan

Viroli, Maurizio. 2000. *Niccolò's Smile*. Trans. A. Shugaar (original edn 1998). New York

Walker, J. 1967. 'Ginevra de' Benci by Leonardo da Vinci', *National Gallery of Art Report and Studies on the History of Art*, Washington, DC

Wasserman, Jack. 1975. *Leonardo*. New York

— 1989. 'A Florentine *Last Supper* sketch: a question of gesture'. ALV 2, 110–13

White, Michael. 2000. *Leonardo: The First Scientist*. London

Winner, M. (ed.). 1992. *Der Künstler über sich in seinem Werk*. Hamburg

Winternitz, Emanuel. 1974. 'Leonardo and music'. In Reti 1974, 110–34

— 1982. *Leonardo da Vinci as a Musician.* New Haven and London

Woods-Marsden, Joanna. 1998. *Renaissance Self-Portraiture: The Visual Construction of Identity and the Social Status of the Artist.* New Haven and London

Yates, Frances. 1965. *Giordano Bruno and the Hermetic Tradition.* London

— 1983. 'The Italian academies' (lecture, 1949). In *Collected Essays* vol. 2, 6–29. London

Zöllner, Frank. 1991. 'Rubens reworks Leonardo: the "Fight for the standard" '. ALV 4, 177–90

— 1992. ' "Ogni pittore dipinge sé": Leonardo da Vinci and auto-mimesis'. In Winner 1992, 137–60

— 1993. 'Leonardo's portrait of Mona Lisa del Giocondo'. *Gazette des beaux-arts* 121, 115–31

— 2003. *Leonardo da Vinci: The Complete Paintings and Drawings.* London

Zwijnenberg, Robert. 1999. *The Writings and Drawings of Leonardo da Vinci: Order and Chaos in Early Modern Thought.* Trans. C. van Eck. Cambridge

Illustrations

29. Follower of Leonardo (Cesare da Sesto?) *Leda and the Swan*, c. 1505–15 (?) (Collection of the Earl of Pembroke, Wilton House Trust, Salisbury. Photo: Bridgeman Art Library)

30. Leonardo, *Studies of the Foetus in the Womb and of the Structure and Size of Female Genitalia* (detail), c. 1510–12 (The Royal Library, Windsor Castle (RL 19101r). The Royal Collection © 2004, Her Majesty Queen Elizabeth II)

BLACK-AND-WHITE ILLUSTRATIONS
(NUMBERS REFER TO PAGE NUMBERS)

6. Leonardo, pages from Paris MS B showing a test for the wing of a flying-machine (Bibliothèque de l'Institut de France, Paris (MS B (MS 2173), 88v–89r). Photo: © RMN – R. J. Ojeda)

8. Leonardo, *Sheet of Studies of Geometric Figures and the Bust of an Old Man in Profile* (detail), c. 1490 (The Royal Library, Windsor Castle (RL 12283r). The Royal Collection © 2004, Her Majesty Queen Elizabeth II)

12. Leonardo, *Head of a Bearded Man (Self-Portrait)*, c. 1512–18 (?) (Biblioteca Reale, Turin. Photo: © Scala, Florence)

18 (top). Contemporary photograph of Vinci, Tuscany (Photo: © Corbis/David Lees)

18 (bottom). Photograph, c. 1900, of the alleged birthplace of Leonardo in Anchiano, in its pre-restored appearance

24. Leonardo, *Map of a River Bed* (detail), c. 1506–7 (The Royal Library, Windsor Castle (RL 12676r). The Royal Collection © 2004, Her Majesty Queen Elizabeth II)

32. Leonardo, drawings of birds in flight from *On the Flight of Birds* (Biblioteca Reale, Turin. Photo: © Scala, Florence)

36. Follower of Leonardo, after a design by Leonardo, *Leda and the Swan* (detail), 1505–15 (?) (Galleria degli Uffizi, Florence. Photo: Alinari Archive, Florence)

37. Leonardo, *The Virgin and Child with St Anne*, c. 1502–13 (?), marked to show Oskar Pfister's 'hidden bird' (Musée du Louvre, Paris. © Photo RMN)

39 (top). Leonardo, *Study of Figures Working*, c. 1506–8 (The Royal Library, Windsor Castle (RL 12644r). The Royal Collection © 2004, Her Majesty Queen Elizabeth II)

39 (bottom). Leonardo, *Design for a Colour-Grinding Machine*, c. 1504–5 (Codex Atlanticus (CA 765r). Biblioteca Ambrosiana, Milan)

41 (top). Engraving after Leonardo, design for an emblem inscribed '*Academia Leonardi Vinci*', c. 1500 (?) (Biblioteca Ambrosiana, Milan (9596B))

41 (bottom). Leonardo, *Study for the Head of Leda* (detail), c. 1506–9 (The Royal Library, Windsor Castle (RL 12516r). The Royal Collection © 2004, Her Majesty Queen Elizabeth II)

45 (top left). Leonardo, *Sheet of Studies of an Ox, a Donkey and other Figures*,

c. 1478–80 (The Royal Library, Windsor Castle (RL 12362r). The Royal Collection © 2004, Her Majesty Queen Elizabeth II)

45 (top right). Leonardo, *Study of a Horse and Rider for The Adoration of the Magi, c.* 1481 (Private collection. Photo: Bridgeman Art Library)

45 (bottom left). Leonardo, *Study of a Dog and Cat, c.* 1480 (© Copyright the Trustees of The British Museum, London (inv. 1895-9-15-477))

45 (bottom right). Leonardo, *Study of the Proportions of a Dog's Head*, 1497–9 (Bibliothèque de l'Institut de France, Paris (MS I (MS 2180), 48r). Photo: © RMN – Le Mage)

48 (top left). Leonardo, *View towards Monsummano, 5 August 1473* (detail), 1473 (Gabinetto dei Disegni e delle Stampe, Galleria degli Uffizi, Florence. Photo: © Scala, Florence)

48 (top centre). Leonardo, detail of Monsummano from *Map of the Arno Valley Showing Proposed Canal Route, c.* 1503–4 (The Royal Library, Windsor Castle (RL 12685r). The Royal Collection © 2004, Her Majesty Queen Elizabeth II)

48 (top right). Contemporary photograph of the tump at Monsummano (Photo: Author)

52. Leonardo, *The Annunciation* (detail) 1472 (Galleria degli Uffizi, Florence. Photo: © Scala, Florence – courtesy of the Ministero Beni e Att. Culturali)

58 (top). Leonardo, Extract from notebook entry featuring his signature, *c.* 1490 (Codex Atlanticus (CA 520r). Biblioteca Ambrosiana, Milan)

58 (bottom). Leonardo, Extract from notebook entry featuring his signature, *c.* 1493 (Codex Forster (III, 141, 62v). Victoria & Albert Museum, London. Photo: © Victoria & Albert Museum Picture Library)

62–3. Anon, The 'Chain map' of Florence (Carta della Catena), *c.* 1470–72 (Museo di Firenze Com'era, Florence. Photo: © Scala, Florence)

75 (left). Andrea del Verrocchio, *David, c.* 1466–70 (Museo Nazionale del Bargello, Florence. Photo: Alinari Archive, Florence)

75 (right). Anonymous artist in the circle of Verrocchio and Lorenzo di Credi, study of a naked man in the pose of David, from a sketchbook attributed to Francesco di Simone Ferrucci, early 1480s (?) (Cabinet des Dessins, Musée du Louvre, Paris (RF 451r) © Photo RMN)

79. Leonardo, *Drapery Study for a Seated Figure, c.* 1475–80 (?) (Cabinet des Dessins, Musée du Louvre, Paris (RF 2255). © Photo RMN – J. G. Berizzi)

81. Leonardo, *Drawing of a Warrior in Profile, c.* 1472 (© Copyright the Trustees of The British Museum, London (inv. 1895-9-15-474))

86 (top left). School of Verrocchio, *Portrait of a Man (Portrait of Verrocchio?)*, 1470s (Gabinetto dei Disegni e delle Stampe, Galleria degli Uffizi, Florence (250Er). Photo: Alinari Archive, Florence)

86 (top right). Sandro Botticelli, *The Adoration of the Magi* (detail), *c.* 1478 (Galleria degli Uffizi, Florence. Photo: © Scala, Florence – courtesy of the Ministero Beni e Att. Culturali)

86 (bottom left). Pietro Perugino, *Self-Portrait*, 1500 (Palazzo dei Priori, Collegio del Cambio, Perugia. Photo: © Scala, Florence)

86 (bottom right). Lorenzo di Credi, *Self-Portrait*, 1488 (Widener Collection. Image © Board of Trustees, National Gallery of Art, Washington, DC)

89. Studio of Verrocchio (and Leonardo?), *Tobias and the Angel*, c. 1470–72 (?) (© The National Gallery, London)

90. Andrea del Verrocchio, *Portrait Bust of Lorenzo de' Medici*, c. 1480 (Palazzo Medici-Riccardi, Florence. Photo: Alinari Archive, Florence)

97 (top). Filippo Brunelleschi, The dome of the cathedral (Santa Maria del Fiore), Florence, 1420–46 (Photo: Alinari Archive, Florence)

97 (bottom). Leonardo, *Design for a Reversible Hoist*, 1478 (Codex Atlanticus (CA 391v). Biblioteca Ambrosiana, Milan)

102. Leonardo, *Madonna of the Carnation*, c. 1472–8 (?) (Bayerische Staatsgemäldesammlungen, Alte Pinakothek, Munich. Photo: © Scala, Florence)

109 (left). Andrea del Verrocchio, *La Dama del Mazzolino (Woman with a Bunch of Flowers)*, c. 1476 (Museo Nazionale del Bargello, Florence. Photo: © Scala, Florence – courtesy of the Ministero Beni e Att. Culturali)

109 (right). Leonardo, *Study of Hands (Study for Ginevra de' Benci?)*, c. 1476–8 (The Royal Library, Windsor Castle (RL 12558r). Photo: Alinari Archive, Florence)

119. Sandro Botticelli, *Inferno XVI* (detail), illustration for Dante's *Divine Comedy*, mid-1490s (facsimile of original drawing in the Biblioteca Apostolica Vaticana, Rome, reproduced in F. Lippmann, *Drawings by Botticelli for Dante's Divina Commedia* (London, 1896))

122. Attributed to Leonardo in Verrocchio's workshop, *Head of the Youthful Christ*, 1470s? (Collection Aglietti-Gallendt, Rome)

123. Circle of Verrocchio, *Head of a Young Man*, c. 1475 (Pierpont Morgan Library, New York. Photo: © Scala, Florence)

137 (top left). Attributed to Leonardo, *Study of a Child's Head or Putto (Preparatory Sketch for the Benois Madonna)*, c. 1478–80 (Galleria degli Uffizi, Florence. Photo: Alinari Archive, Florence)

137 (top right). Leonardo, *Young Woman Bathing an Infant (Il Bagnetto)*, c. 1480–83 (Faculdade de Belas Artes, Universidade do Porto, Porto (inv. 99.1.1174))

137 (bottom left). Leonardo, Sketches of a Child with a Cat, c. 1478–80 (British Museum, London (inv. 1857-1-10-1v). Photo: Alinari Archive, Florence)

137 (bottom right). Leonardo, Study for a Madonna and Child with a Cat, c. 1478–80 (British Museum, London (inv. 1856-6-21-1r). Photo: Alinari Archive, Florence)

140. Leonardo, *Sketch of Hanged Man (Bernardo di Bandino Baroncelli)*, 1479 (Musée Bonnat, Bayonne. © Photo RMN – R. G. Ojeda)

147 (top). Leonardo, *Design for a Device for Unhinging a Prison Door from the Inside* (detail), c. 1480–82 (Codex Atlanticus (CA 34r). Biblioteca Ambrosiana, Milan)

147 (bottom). Leonardo, *Hydraulic Devices (Archimedean Screw) and other*

192. Leonardo, *Study for a Hoist and for a Cannon in an Ordnance Foundry*, *c.* 1487 (The Royal Library, Windsor Castle (RL 12647r). The Royal Collection © 2004, Her Majesty Queen Elizabeth II)

200 (left). Leonardo and Ambrogio de Predis, *The Virgin of the Rocks (The Virgin with the Infant Saint John Adoring the Infant Christ Accompanied by an Angel)* (detail), *c.* 1495–9 and 1506–8 (© The National Gallery, London)

200 (right). Leonardo, *Head and Shoulders Drawing of a Naked Infant in Profile*, *c.* 1495–7 (The Royal Library, Windsor Castle (RL 12519r). The Royal Collection © 2004, Her Majesty Queen Elizabeth II)

203. Leonardo, *Notes and Drawings for an Ideal City*, *c.* 1487–8 (Bibliothèque de l'Institut de France, Paris (MS B (Ashburnham), 15v–16r) © Photo RMN – R. G. Ojeda)

204. Leonardo, *Sketches and Notes on Flying-Machines and Parachutes* (detail), *c.* 1485 (Codex Atlanticus (CA 1058v). Biblioteca Ambrosiana, Milan)

205. Leonardo, *Allegory of Pleasure and Pain*, *c.* 1484–6 (Governing Body of Christ Church, Oxford (inv. JBS 17v). Photo: Alinari Archive, Florence)

208. Leonardo, *Allegory of Envy Riding on Death*, *c.* 1484–6 (Governing Body of Christ Church, Oxford (inv. JBS 17r). Photo: Alinari Archive, Florence)

211 (top). Leonardo, *Study for a Flying-Machine*, *c.* 1487–90 (Bibliothèque de l'Institut de France, Paris (MS B (MS 2173), 74). © Photo RMN – Bulloz)

211 (bottom). Leonardo, *Design for a Vertically Standing Flying-Machine*, *c.* 1487–90 (Bibliothèque de l'Institut de France, Paris (MS B (MS 2173), 80r). © Photo RMN – Bulloz)

219. Leonardo, *Large Sheet of Puzzle-Writing, Chiefly in the Form of Pictograms Featuring a Pun on the Name 'Leonardo'* (detail), *c.* 1487–90 (The Royal Library, Windsor Castle (RL 12692v). The Royal Collection © 2004, Her Majesty Queen Elizabeth II)

225. Leonardo, *Plan for a Centralized Church*, 1487–90 (Bibliothèque de l'Institut de France, Paris (MS 2184 – Ashburnham, formerly MS B), 5v). © Photo RMN – Bulloz)

239 (top left). Leonardo, *Study for the Head of a Woman (Study for the Litta Madonna)*, *c.* 1488–90 (Cabinet des Dessins, Musée du Louvre, Paris. © Photo RMN – M. Bellot)

239 (top right). Leonardo, *Litta Madonna*, *c.* 1488–90 (State Hermitage Museum, St Petersburg. Photo: © Scala, Florence)

239 (bottom left). Ambrogio de Predis, *Lady with a Pearl Necklace (Portrait of Beatrice d'Este)*, *c.* 1490 (?) (Pinacoteca Ambrosiana, Milan. Photo: © Scala, Florence)

239 (bottom right). Giovanni Boltraffio, *Madonna and Child*, *c.* 1495 (Collection of G. G. Poldi Pezzoli. Museo Poldi Pezzoli, Milan)

243. Leonardo, *Anatomical Study of the Human Skull in Sagittal Section, Seen from the Side*, 1489 (The Royal Library, Windsor Castle (RL 19057r). The Royal Collection © 2004, Her Majesty Queen Elizabeth II)

246. Leonardo, *Vitruvian Man (The Proportions of the Human Figure, after Vitruvius)*, c. 1490 (Galleria dell'Accademia, Venice. Photo: © Scala, Florence – courtesy of the Ministero Beni e Att. Culturali)

258. Giovanni Boltraffio, *Portrait of a Young Woman (Isabella of Aragon?)*, 1490s (Pinacoteca Ambrosiana, Milan. Photo: Alinari Archive, Florence)

261 (top). Leonardo, *Study of Two Masks of Monsters*, 1493–5 (The Royal Library, Windsor Castle (RL 12367r). The Royal Collection © 2004, Her Majesty Queen Elizabeth II)

261 (bottom). After Leonardo (Francesco Melzi?), *Grotesque Portrait of an Old Woman*, c. 1490–91 (RL 12492r) (The Royal Library, Windsor Castle. The Royal Collection © 2004, Her Majesty Queen Elizabeth II)

268. Leonardo, sketch showing the penumbra of a shadow made by man at an arched window, c. 1490–92 (Bibliothèque de l'Institut de France, Paris (MS A (MS 2172), 1r) © Photo RMN – G. Blot)

274 (top). Leonardo, *Profile Drawing of a Young Man (Possibly Salai)*, c. 1508–10 (The Royal Library, Windsor Castle (RL 12557r). The Royal Collection © 2004, Her Majesty Queen Elizabeth II)

274 (bottom). Giovanni Boltraffio (or after Boltraffio), *Narcissus*, c. 1500 (?) (Galleria degli Uffizi, Florence. Photo: Alinari Archive, Florence)

275. Leonardo, *Double Portrait of a Young Man and an Old Man*, late 1490s (Galleria degli Uffizi, Florence. Photo: Alinari Archive, Florence)

281. Leonardo, *Device for Securing the Piece-Mould of a Horse's Head for Casting*, c. 1491–3 (Biblioteca Nacional, Madrid (Codex II (MS 8936), 156v–157r). Photo: © Scala, Florence)

282. Leonardo, *Study of the Diminishing Power of an Unwinding Spring*, 1493–7 (Biblioteca Nacional, Madrid (Codex I (MS 8937), 16r))

294 (top). Leonardo, *Preliminary Sketch for The Last Supper*, c. 1494–5 (The Royal Library, Windsor Castle (RL 12542r). The Royal Collection © 2004, Her Majesty Queen Elizabeth II)

294 (bottom left). Leonardo, *Study for The Last Supper (Judas)*, c. 1495 (The Royal Library, Windsor Castle (RL 12547r). The Royal Collection © 2004, Her Majesty Queen Elizabeth II)

294 (bottom right). Leonardo, *Study of St James the Elder for The Last Supper*, c. 1495 (The Royal Library, Windsor Castle (RL 12552). The Royal Collection © 2004, Her Majesty Queen Elizabeth II)

304. Jacopo de' Barbari, *Portrait of Fra Luca Pacioli*, c. 1495 (Museo di Capodimonte, Naples. Photo: © Scala, Florence – courtesy of the Ministero Beni e Att. Culturali)

305. Leonardo, Dodecahedron, Plate XXVI in *De divina proportione* by Fra Luca Pacioli (Venice, 1509) (Bibliothèque Nationale, Paris. Photo: Bridgeman Art Library)

312 (left). Donato Bramante, *Heraclitus and Democritus* (detail), c. 1490–97

(Pinacoteca di Brera, Milan, formerly Casa Panigarola. Photo: Alinari Archive, Florence)

312 (right). Leonardo, *Vitruvian Man (The Proportions of the Human Figure, after Vitruvius)* (detail), *c.* 1490 (Galleria dell'Accademia, Venice. Photo: © Scala, Florence – courtesy of the Ministero Beni e Att. Culturali)

317. Leonardo, Detail of the decoration for the Sala delle Asse, 1498 (Castello Sforzesco, Milan. Photo: Bridgeman Art Library/Alinari)

318. Detail showing the area of Leonardo's vineyard, from *Map of Milan*, engraving by Josef Hoefnagel from *Civitates Orbis Terrarum*, ed. Georg Braun and Frans Hogenburg, *c.* 1572 (The Stapleton Collection. Photo: Bridgeman Art Library)

327. Leonardo, *Portrait of Isabella d'Este*, 1500 (Musée du Louvre, Paris. Photo: © Scala, Florence)

338. Leonardo and assistants, *Madonna of the Yarnwinder (Reford version)*, *c.* 1501–4 (?) (Private collection)

340. Letter from Fra Pietro Novellara to Isabella d'Este, dated 14 April 1501 (Private collection, formerly Archivio Gonzaga, Mantua)

346 (left). Leonardo, *Portrait Drawings of a Bearded Man (Cesare Borgia?)* (detail), *c.* 1502–3 (Biblioteca Reale, Turin (inv. 15573). Photo: Alinari Archive, Florence)

346 (right). Santi di Tito, *Portrait of Nicolò Machiavelli*, after 1560 (Palazzo Vecchio, Florence. Photo: © Scala, Florence)

351. Leonardo, *Map of Imola*, *c.* 1502–3 (The Royal Library, Windsor Castle (RL 12284). The Royal Collection © 2004, Her Majesty Queen Elizabeth II)

355 (top). Leonardo, *Design for a Bridge over the Golden Horn from Pera to Constantinople*, *c.* 1502 (Bibliothèque de l'Institut de France (MS L (MS 2182), 66r) © Photo RMN – G. Blot)

355 (bottom). Bridge built by Norwegian artist Vebjørn Sand, at Aas, Norway, based on Leonardo's design for a bridge to span the Golden Horn inlet. (© Vebjørn Sand, reproduced by courtesy of Brickfish Creative Services, international project liaison for the Global Leonardo Project. www.vebjornsand. com. Photo: Terje Sten Johansen/Studio S)

374 (top left). Leonardo, *Study of the Heads of Two Soldiers for The Battle of Anghiari*, *c.* 1503–4 (facsimile) (Gabinetto dei Disegni e delle Stampe, Galleria degli Uffizi, Florence. Photo: © Scala, Florence)

374 (top right). Leonardo, *Study of Horses and Foot Soldiers, Sketch for The Battle of Anghiari*, *c.* 1503–4 (Galleria dell'Accademia, Venice. Photo: © Scala, Florence – courtesy of the Ministero Beni e Att. Culturali)

374 (bottom). Attr. Peter Paul Rubens after an original by Leonardo, *The Battle of Anghiari*, before 1550 and *c.* 1603 (Musée du Louvre, Paris. © Photo RMN – M. Bellot)

377. Daniele da Volterra, *Portrait Bust of Michelangelo*, after 1564 (Casa Buonarroti, Florence. Photo: Alinari Archive, Florence)

Library, Windsor Castle (RL 12579r). The Royal Collection © 2004, Her Majesty Queen Elizabeth II)

452. Studio of Leonardo, Detail of a sketch of a man's face, from *Sheet of Studies of Horses' Legs*, c. 1510 (?) (The Royal Library, Windsor Castle (RL 12300v). The Royal Collection © 2004, Her Majesty Queen Elizabeth II)

458. Copy after Raphael, *Portrait of Giuliano de' Medici, Duke of Nemours*, sixteenth century (The Jules Bach Collection (1949 (49.7.12)). All rights reserved, The Metropolitan Museum of Art, New York)

468 (top). Leonardo and pupil, *Sheet of Sketches of an Announcing Angel and Various Studies of Machines, Horses and Riders* (detail), c. 1504–6 (The Royal Library, Windsor Castle (RL 12328r). The Royal Collection © 2004, Her Majesty Queen Elizabeth II)

468 (bottom). Leonardo (with redrawing by a pupil?), *Angelo incarnato*, c. 1513–15 (Private collection)

473. Workshop of Leonardo (?), *St John the Baptist (with the Attributes of Bacchus)* (or *St John in the Desert*), c. 1513–19 (Musée du Louvre, Paris. © Photo RMN – C. Jean)

482. Leonardo, *Sheet of Embryological Studies*, c. 1510 (The Royal Library, Windsor Castle (RL 19102r). The Royal Collection © 2004, Her Majesty Queen Elizabeth II)

487 (left). French School, *Portrait of François I, King of France*, c. 1515–20 (Musée Condé, Chantilly. Photo: Bridgeman Art Library)

487 (right). The manor-house at Cloux (now Clos Lucé) (Photo: Author)

490. Raphael, *Portrait of a Cardinal (Cardinal Luigi of Aragon?)*, sixteenth century (Museo del Prado, Madrid. Photo: Bridgeman Art Library)

495 (top). Leonardo, *Drawing of a Young Man in Costume on Horseback*, c. 1513–17 (The Royal Library, Windsor Castle (RL 12574r). The Royal Collection © 2004, Her Majesty Queen Elizabeth II)

495 (bottom). Leonardo, *Drawing of a Man Disguised as a Beggar (or Prisoner)*, c. 1513–17 (The Royal Library, Windsor Castle (RL 12573r). The Royal Collection © 2004, Her Majesty Queen Elizabeth II)

497. Circle of Leonardo in France (Cristoforo Solario or Francesco Melzi?), *The Château d'Amboise seen from Clos Lucé*, c. 1516–19 (The Royal Library, Windsor Castle (RL 12727). The Royal Collection © 2004, Her Majesty Queen Elizabeth II)

501. Leonardo, *Pointing Lady in a Landscape (Matelda?)*, c. 1515–17 (The Royal Library, Windsor Castle (RL 12581). The Royal Collection © 2004, Her Majesty Queen Elizabeth II)

INDEX

Pages including relevant illustrations are shown in italic.

PENGUIN ART HISTORY

REMBRANDT'S EYES
SIMON SCHAMA

'A capacious, generous book full of new ideas and information about not only Rembrandt but also his life, his times and his contemporaries. With Schama you look at a picture and see it as you hadn't before' Doris Lessing, *Daily Telegraph* Books of the Year

Rembrandt's Eyes shows us why Rembrandt is such a thrilling painter, so revolutionary in his art, so penetrating of the hearts of those who have looked for three hundred years at his pictures. More than anything else, Schama's understanding of Rembrandt's mind, and of the dynamic of his life, allows him to re-create Rembrandt's story on the page. Through a combination of scholarship and literary skill, he enables us to see the life through Rembrandt's own eyes. Despite the paucity of conventional historical evidence, it is as intelligently true a biography of Rembrandt as we are ever likely to have, and the most dazzling achievement of this most poetic, most unpredictable and most engaging of contemporary historians.

'A profound and captivating study ... its skill at reconstructing the artist and his age suggests that we no longer need look only towards novelists and poets for "creative" writing. The music of history and biography can be equally powerful' Peter Ackroyd, *The Times*

'[A] supreme contribution to art history' Anita Brookner, *Spectator* Books of the Year

'Sumptuous ... Impassioned and learned, expansive and discursive, *Rembrandt's Eyes* not only leaves us with a fierce appreciation of the artist's work but also immerses us inexorably in his world' Michiko Katutani, *The New York Times*

PENGUIN HISTORY

REFORMATION: EUROPE'S HOUSE DIVIDED
DIARMAID MacCULLOCH

Winner of the Wolfson History Prize and the British Academy Book Prize

'Magisterial and eloquent' David Starkey

'Monumental ... *Reformation* is set to become a landmark' Lisa Jardine, *Observer*

'A triumph of human sympathy' Blair Worden, *Sunday Telegraph*

'From politics to witchcraft, from the liturgy to sex; the sweep of European history covered here is breathtakingly panoramic. This is a model work of history' Noel Malcolm, *Sunday Telegraph*, Books of the Year

At a time when men and women were prepared to kill – and be killed – for their faith, the reformation tore the western world apart. Acclaimed as the definitive account of these epochal events, Diarmaid MacCulloch's history brilliantly re-creates the religious battles of priests, monarchs, scholars and politicians, from the zealous Luther to the radical Loyola, from the tortured Cranmer to the ambitious Philip II.

Weaving together the many strands of reformation and counter-reformation, ranging widely across Europe and even to the New World, MacCulloch also reveals as never before how these upheavals affected everyday lives – overturning ideas of love, sex, death and the supernatural, and shaping the modern age.

'A masterpiece of readable scholarship ... In its field it is the best book ever written' David L. Edwards, *Guardian*

'A historical *tour de force*... breathtaking' Daniel Johnson, *Daily Telegraph*